RITALIN
Theory and Patient Management

Laurence L. Greenhill, M.D.
Betty B. Osman, Ph.D.
Editors

Mary Ann Liebert, Inc. publishers

Printed in the United States of America
10 9 8 7 6 5 4 3 2

Table of Contents

Section 8
MECHANISMS OF ACTION

Preface

This book is designed to be a key reference and guide for professionals involved in research or in the clinical use and management of Ritalin (methylphenidate). Chief among these are child psychiatrists, pediatricians, family physicians, and pediatric neurologists who prescribe, administer, and monitor Ritalin therapy in their practices.

Based on data from the IMS-NDTI Drug Data National Prescription Auditing Service, it is estimated that approximately 750,000 individuals in the United States are being treated with Ritalin (as of 1990). Approximately 70 percent of that number are children.

Physicians—pediatricians in particular—are increasingly called upon to prescribe Ritalin, and to answer questions about the effects of the drug, dosage, and titration, and case management. Although the body of research on methylphenidate has expanded significantly in the past decade, the practicing physician may have neither the time nor the resources to locate and review all the current information.

Other healthcare professionals as well, including nurses, and psychologists, as well as social workers and educators, are confronted with requests for information about the appropriate use of Ritalin, risks and side effects, as well as about the administration of and dosage schedules for the drug. They may also be in a position to help monitor and evaluate the treatment, particularly for children, the primary consumers of Ritalin in the United States today.

Ritalin: Theory and Patient Management is predicated on the idea that the drug merits different approaches because of its multiplicity of roles: as treatment modality for hyperactivity and other behavior disorders of childhood, residual attentional deficits disorders in adults (ADHD–Residual State), AIDS-related problems, head injuries, narcolepsy, and adult schizophrenia.

Although research studies and clinical practice have clearly documented the efficacy of methylphenidate treatment, and dispelled myths and misconceptions about the drug, there has not been a single volume to date on the subject of Ritalin. This text will fill that gap and provide a comprehensive resource for those interested in reviewing current theories and clinical work.

This book would not have been written without the inspiration and encouragement of our publisher, Mary Ann Liebert, Inc., who recognized the need for the book and supported the endeavor. Special thanks, too, to the contributors to this volume who so generously gave of their time, their expertise, and experience to help produce a rich and timely compendium of knowledge.

Thanks to our families and all those who have assisted in the preparation of this book: Elizabeth Field, Roberta Gallagher, Susan Greenhill, and Cathy Johnson.

Betty B. Osman, Ph.D.
Laurence L. Greenhill, M.D.

Introduction

An initial reaction to the publication of a volume on the use of methylphenidate (MPH Ritalin) might well be "Is there really a need for a book on this subject?" One need only look at the table of contents—and the list of distinguished investigators and clinicians assembled as contributors, to be impressed and convinced that such a book is indeed justified, substantive, timely, and does serve a need. What are some of the elements of that need?

First, there is a need for an authoritative and seasoned source of scientific and clinical information. In the past few years, antimedical and antipsychiatric groups have vigorously agitated against the use of Ritalin as a dangerous and mind-altering drug given to normally rambunctious children. One or two of these groups in particular, have been able to generate much publicity, create controversy, and arouse fears which never were supported by any study or by any scientific data, but which were attractive to the media, to the producers and hosts of television talk shows, and to some litigation lawyers.

Second, indications for the use of Ritalin and if you will, the epidemiology (prevalence) of its use are still incompletely known and deserving of continuing scientific study, conservative clinical usage, and innovative clinical trials. As to the first of these issues the core condition for which Ritalin is prescribed is now designated as attention deficit hyperactivity disorder (ADHD); and the topic is addressed in detail in several of the following chapters, including the important chapter by Wender on ADHD and Ritalin usage in adults. Other chapters address the innovative use of Ritalin in such diverse and challenging circumstances as head injury, AIDS dementia, mental retardation, and learning disabilities. These discussions represent a real contribution to the literature and a real service to clinicians with diverse practices.

The issue of the prevalence of its use refers to often asked questions and conflicting studies about whether Ritalin is prescribed excessively and/or inappropriately. These issues are addressed in chapters on patient management and epidemiology of usage. These chapters then, taken together, provide the reader with a very detailed and comprehensive survey of the universe, as we now know it, of the pharmacology, mechanism of action, indications, effects, and clinical usage of the drug. Additional areas of question—large areas where the universe is not yet mapped—are clearly addressed. What more could we ask for?

Third, Ritalin is not a drug prescribed only or even primarily by psychiatrists trained to work with children and adolescents. Pediatricians, family practitioners, neurologists, and general psychiatrists all prescribe Ritalin for both similar and different disorders; this volume recognizes this reality and provides chapters relating specifically to the use of Ritalin in pediatrics and by pediatric nurse practitioners and clinicians, and provides needed information on indications, contraindications, mechanisms of action, and side effects.

The generic form of this drug, methylphenidate was first synthesized in 1955 as a hopefully nonhabitu-ating alternative to Dexedrine as the drug of choice for the treatment of hyperactivity and inattention in a heterogeneous population of behavior-disordered children. Gradually it became the drug of choice for use in children diagnosed as hyperactive, and a better understanding of its clinical use was accompanied by increasing definition and studies of the clinical disorder(s) now called ADHD. It is by far the most frequently prescribed and most intensively studied drug in the field of child psychiatry and childhood psychiatric disorder. This text admirably presents and summarizes what we have learned over these years of study, which represents an impressive body of scientific data and clinical experience. Drs. Greenhill and Osman have presented this material to us as co-editors and they should be congratulated for doing us all this service.

Jerry M. Wiener, M.D.

List of Contributors

Howard Abikoff, Ph.D.
Associate Professor, Department of Child and Adolescent Psychiatry, Schneider Children's Hospital, Albert Einstein College of Medicine, Bronx, New York

Andrea Bergman, Ph.D.
Department of Psychiatry, Elmhurst Hospital Center, Elmhurst, and Department of Psychology, Mt. Sinai School of Medicine, New York, New York

Caryn L. Carlson, Ph.D.
Assistant Professor, Department of Psychology, University of Texas at Austin, Austin, Texas

Barbara Cornblatt, Ph.D.
Professor, Department of Psychology, Mt. Sinai School of Medicine and Director, Department of Psychology, Elmhurst Hospital Center, Elmhurst, New York

Howard B. Demb, M.D.
Associate Professor, Department of Pediatrics, Assistant Professor, Department of Psychiatry, Rose F. Kennedy Medical Center, Albert Einstein College of Medicine, Bronx, New York

Robert M. Diener, M.D.
Senior Advisor, Licensing and Safety Evaluation, Ciba-Geigy, Summit, New Jersey

Josephine Elia, M.D.
Senior Staff Fellow, Psychiatry Branch, National Institutes of Mental Health, Bethesda, Maryland

Francisco Fernandez, M.D.
Associate Professor, Department of Psychiatry and Behavioral Sciences, Baylor College of Medicine, Houston, Texas

Jane E. Fried, M.D.
Assistant Clinical Professor, Division of Child and Adolescent Psychiatry, Columbia College of Physicians and Surgeons, and New York State Psychiatric Institute, New York, New York

Barry Garfinkel, M.D., F.R.C.P. (C)
Director of Child and Adolescent Psychiatry, University of Minnesota Medical School, Minneapolis, Minnesota

Laurence L. Greenhill, M.D.
Associate Professor, Division of Child and Adolescent Psychiatry, Department of Psychiatry, Columbia College of Physicians and Surgeons, and New York State Psychiatric Institute, New York, New York

Susan Walton Greenhill, R.N., M.S.
Nurse Clinician, Children's Evaluation and Rehabilitation Center, Rose F. Kennedy Medical Center, Albert Einstein College of Medicine, Bronx, New York

C. Thomas Gualtieri, M.D.
Medical Director, North Carolina Neuropsychiatry and REBOUND, Inc., Chapel Hill, North Carolina

Jeffrey M. Halperin, Ph.D.
Associate Professor, Department of Psychology, Queens College of the City University of New York, Flushing, New York

Margaret E. Hertzig, M.D.
Associate Professor, Department of Psychiatry, Cornell University Medical College, New York, New York

Mark Hughes, M.D.
Child Psychiatry Fellow, Department of Psychiatry, Vanderbilt University Medical School, Nashville, Tennessee

Robert D. Hunt, M.D.
Associate Professor, Department of Psychiatry, Vanderbilt University Medical School, Nashville, Tennessee

Darlene Jody, M.D.
Sandoz Research Institute, East Hanover, New Jersey

Samuel S. Kupietz, Ph.D.
Clinical Assistant Professor, Department of Psychiatry, New York University Medical Center, New York, New York; and Research Scientist V, Nathan S. Klein Institute for Psychiatric Research, Orangeburg, New York

Benjamin B. Lahey, Ph.D.
University of Miami, School of Medicine, Miami, Florida

Serena Lau
Student, Department of Psychiatry, Vanderbilt University Medical School, Nashville, Tennessee

Jeffrey A. Lieberman, M.D.
Hillside Hospital, Glen Oaks, New York

Lee Mandl
Student, Department of Psychiatry, Vanderbilt University Medical School, Nashville, Tennessee

Keith McBurnett, Ph.D.
Assistant Professor, Department of Pediatrics, Assistant Director, Child Development Center, University of California, Irvine, and California State Developmental Research Institutes, Costa Mesa, California

Richard Milich, Ph.D.
University of Kentucky, Department of Psychology, Lexington, Kentucky

Jeffrey H. Newcorn, M.D.
Assistant Professor, Department of Psychiatry, Mt. Sinai School of Medicine, New York, New York

Betty B. Osman, Ph.D.
Psychologist, Child and Adolescent Service, Department of Psychiatry, White Plains Hospital Medical Center, White Plains, New York

William E. Pelham, Ph.D.
Associate Professor, Department of Psychiatry, and Western Psychiatric Institute and Clinic, University of Pittsburgh School of Medicine, Pittsburgh, Pennsylvania

Judith L. Rapoport, M.D.
Chief of Child Psychiatry Branch, National Institutes of Mental Health, Bethesda, Maryland

Christine A. Redman, M.A.
Senior Staff Psychiatrist, Clinical Brain Imaging Section, Laboratory of Cerebral Metabolism, National Institute of Mental Health, Bethesda, Maryland

Elizabeth Reeve, M.D.
Resident, Department of Child and Adolescent Psychiatry, University of Minnesota Medical School, Minneapolis, Minnesota

Fred W. Reimherr, M.D.
Professor, Department of Psychiatry, University of Utah College of Medicine, Salt Lake City, Utah

Delbert Robinson, M.D.
Hillside Hospital, Glen Oaks, New York

Jeff Ryu
Premedical student, Vanderbilt University, Nashville, Tennessee

Joseph Sergeant, Ph.D.
Professor, Department of Clinical Psychology, University of Amsterdam, Amsterdam, The Netherlands

Vanshdeep Sharma, M.D.
Mt. Sinai School of Medicine, New York, New York

Bennett A. Shaywitz, M.D.
Professor, Department of Neurology, Yale University School of Medicine, New Haven, Connecticut

Sally E. Shaywitz, M.D.
Professor, Department of Pediatrics, Yale University School of Medicine, New Haven, Connecticut

Miriam Sherman, M.D.
Associate Professor, Department of Psychiatry and Behavioral Science, SUNY at Stony Brook, Stony Brook, New York

Mary V. Solanto, Ph.D.
Senior Psychologist, Division of Child and Adolescent Psychiatry, Schneider Children's Hospital, Long Island Jewish Medical Center, New Hyde Park, NY and Associate Professor, Department of Pediatrics, Albert Einstein College of Medicine, Bronx, New York

James M. Swanson, Ph.D.
Professor of Pediatrics, Psychiatry, and Social Sciences, Director, Child Development Center, University of California, Irvine, and California State Development Research Institutes, Costa Mesa, California

Marcus L. Thomeer, Ph.D.
Department of Psychology, University of Texas at Austin, Austin, Texas

Jaap J. van der Meere, Ph.D.
Laboratory of Experimental Clinical Psychology, University of Amsterdam, Amsterdam, The Netherlands

Paul H. Wender, M.D.
Professor, Department of Psychiatry, University of Utah College of Medicine, Salt Lake City, Utah

Jerry M. Wiener, M.D.
Professor, Department of Psychiatry, George Washington University, Washington, D.C.

Lynn Winters, Ph.D.
Department of Medical Genetics, New York State Psychiatric Institute, New York, New York

David R. Wood, M.D.
Professor, Department of Psychiatry, University of Utah College of Medicine, Salt Lake City, Utah

Alan J. Zametkin, M.D.
Senior Staff Psychiatrist, Clinical Brain Imaging Section, Laboratory of Cerebral Metabolism, National Institute of Mental Health, Bethesda, Maryland

Ritalin Effects and Information Processing in Hyperactivity

JOSEPH SERGEANT and JAAP J. VAN DER MEERE

INTRODUCTION

It is obvious that when a clinician makes a diagnosis he or she will want to treat the person. Less obvious is that the word diagnosis means that one will treat on the basis of knowledge which will help to choose between the alternatives. In childhood hyperactivity, the basic symptoms and problematic nature of the disorder has been known for sometime (Rutter, 1989). Since the pioneering work more than fifty years ago of Bradley (1937), it has been known that stimulants (dextro-amphetamine) produce remarkably ameliorative effects in childhood hyperactivity. This has been replicated in a vast number of studies (Barkley, 1977). If we know how to diagnose the disorder and there is a treatment available, why should one be concerned with fundamental knowledge on the relationship between medication and the mechanisms of the disorder? Is this not an example of academic, irrelevant self-indulgence? The reason for wanting to know the action of amphetamine upon fundamental processes thought to be associated with the disorder of hyperactivity is not just academic. There is growing evidence that the long-term follow-up of children treated with the most common amphetamine, Ritalin, is not providing the favorable outcome that one would wish to see from an effective therapy (Mannuzza et al., 1988). This has raised, among other things, the issue of what does Ritalin actually do to the disturbed processes associated with hyperactivity? One such process which has been thought to be disturbed is attention. In this chapter, we address some of the definitions of the term attention. This is followed by a description of general model of human information processing referred to as the cognitive–energetic model (Sanders, 1983). We review selective reports which can be linked to this model and which have employed Ritalin. We suggest that the locus of the effect of Ritalin may be associated with both output motor factors as well as with the activation of the subject.

ATTENTION DEFICITS IN HYPERACTIVITY

Nearly 30 years ago Clements and Peters (1962) described the deficit of children with minimal brain dysfunction (the current term at that time for childhood hyperactivity) as "an impairment in their capacity to hold, scan and reflectively screen out stimuli in sequential order." Clements (1966) specifically listed attention as a defect of these children. This led, in the 1970s, to laboratory research studies of the nature of the attention deficit in hyperactivity. This involved the Montreal group (Sykes et al., 1971), the Toronto group (Kinsbourne and Swanson, 1979), the Champaign group (Sprague et al., 1970), and other American groups (Dykman et al., 1970; Spring et al., 1973) to mention but a few. Characteristic of the work at that time was the fact that attention as a term was poorly defined and differed in its operationalization between the groups. For example, span of attention was operationalized as the frequency of switching behaviors (Rapoport and Benoit, 1975), length of sustained watching of TV (Anderson and Levin, 1976), increased errors on the Continuous Performance Task (CPT) developed by Rosvold, Mirsky, Sarancon, Bransom, and

Department of Clinical Psychology, University of Amsterdam, Amsterdam, The Netherlands
Laboratory of Experimental Clinical Psychology, Groningen, The Netherlands

Beck (1956) and used by Sykes et al. (1973) with hyperactive children and later by Kupietz and Richardson (1978). Others considered slow reaction time as a measure of attention (Sprague et al., 1970; Spring et al., 1973; Stevens et al., 1967). Clearly such a diversity in the operationalization of attention makes one wonder if the researchers were measuring the same concept (Sergeant, 1981) and ponder whether there was any task specificity of the action of pharmacology (Swanson et al., 1979). In order to be specific about the term attention and its operationalization, we consider these two points in the context of the additive factor method.

THE ADDITIVE FACTOR METHOD AND ATTENTION

The stage model of Sternberg (1969), known more generally as the additive factor method (AFM), will be used as the primary methodology in this chapter. This model has been reviewed by us with respect to clinical research in general (Sergeant and Van der Meere, 1990a) and with respect to the diagnostic issue of hyperactivity (Sergeant and Van der Meere, 1990b). We will, only briefly, outline the logic here.

Sternberg proposed that, when two task variables were found to have independent effects on the dependent variable, reaction time, it would be said that the two task variables were localized in independent stages in the information chain. However, when two task variables besides being main effects were also found to interact significantly, it would be said that the two variables operated upon a common stage. This was the basis of his proposal for the discovery of the stages of information processing. A taxonomy of task variables was established, which were found to be either independent or interactive with one another (Sternberg, 1975). In that review, it was clear that there was a considerable body of evidence to support the notion of stages of information processing. Basically, the model is a four-stage model: encoding of input, central processing with decision making, and a motor output system.

The encoding stage of the model was operationalized in the most elementary level of encoding, namely, the physical code level. Sternberg showed that when a stimulus was physically degraded such that it was difficult, but just possible to recognize, it took longer to process this information than when the stimulus was intact. Sternberg showed that the time required to process a degraded stimulus was independent of any time required to process task variables assumed in the model to be associated with the other three remaining stages of processing. Degradation did not result, for example, in a change in processing time for memory search, decision, and motor organization.

The second stage of processing is memory search. The paradigm which Sternberg used was a simple comparison between targets, which were retained in short-term memory and stimuli which were subsequently presented for comparison. The subject was required to indicate whether the presented stimuli were considered targets or nontargets. The number of targets to be processed led to a linear increase in reaction time. There are two reaction time slopes in this paradigm: the target response set and the nontarget response set. These two slopes were observed to sometimes increase in parallel but sometimes diverge from one another. In the latter case, target responses led to a shallower slope and the nontarget slope to a steeper slope. This slope divergence was termed *terminated* search. It was suggested that memory search was terminated when the target was determined, whereas all items in memory were required to be scanned before concluding that the target was absent. Parallel slopes were interpreted to mean that the time required to search for target and nontarget stimuli was equal. This was termed *exhaustive* search. All the members of the target set were searched both in positive and negative cases.

The difference at the intercept between target-detected and target-absent responses was defined as the time required to reach a decision that the target was absent. The difference between intercepts was the operationalization for the third stage of the model: decision making.

The final stage of the model was shown to be influenced by such task variables as the difficulty with which the motor response could be executed. Typical variables for this purpose were: muscular exertion and whether the pattern of response isomorphically mapped the presented stimuli: left stimulus–left response, right stimulus–right response compared with reversal: stimulus left–right response.

The theoretical link between the AFM and the definition of attention was made when it was shown that the central stages of search and decision of Sternberg's model were crucial to selective attention (Schneider and Shiffrin, 1977; Shiffrin and Schneider, 1977). Shiffrin and Schneider defined attention as a limitation in the rate at which information could be processed within working memory. Working memory is the active memory store in which current task demands are processed (Baddeley, 1976). Shiffrin and Schneider noted that there are two general modes of information processing: controlled and automatic. Controlled information processing requires that a task be performed slowly, serially, and usually with some effort. Hence, attention demands are characterized by slowing down the rate at which the system can meet such demands. Automatic processing is characterized by fast, parallel, and effortless processing. In this sense, attentional demands are cost free. Shiffrin and Schneider showed that the primary variable which determined whether the system was required to operate in the controlled or the automatic mode of processing was variation versus consistency of task demands. Varying the target set from one trial to another requires that the system always devote control to the processing of the incoming stimuli. When task demands are held constant, through presenting the same stimuli as targets, the system can learn and make predictions on what stimuli require processing. With a consistent relation between targets and nontargets, the time required to process such information will lessen to such a degree that, after many thousands of trials with consistent target demands, the time required to process such information is virtually negligible. This is termed automatic processing, since the slope time is negligible.

This operationalization of attention as controlled processing led Schneider and Shiffrin to identify two general deficits of attention. The first is the divided attention deficit. When cognitive load increases, the number of elements which require processing of attention can only be met by dividing the attention pool over the elements. This can occur only through slowing down the processing, since in the controlled mode, information must be processed in series. The second deficit of selective attention is the focused attention deficit. The subject by directing attention to a particular point or object is hindered in processing when the target is present at an invalid location. By limiting the veridical processing to specific input locations, stimuli which are the usual targets and appear on invalid position make it difficult for subjects to ignore the invalid input. This is called a focused attention deficit.

The third type of attention deficit which concerns research in ADDH is the sustained attention deficit. This refers to maintaining attention over time. This definition is empirical and not a theoretical one. Fisk and Schneider (1981) argued and demonstrated that sustained attention means the maintenance of controlled processing over time. The reader is referred to Van der Meere and Sergeant (1988a) and Sergeant and Van der Meere (1990b) for a full discussion of sustained attention and the CPT.

It should be noted that performance decrements in speed of processing can be compensated for by trading accuracy for speed. This is referred to as a strategy effect and not a process effect of attention.

SPEED-ACCURACY TRADE-OFF

Human performance may be measured by both the accuracy and speed of processing. This is referred to as the strategic factor of information processing. The accuracy and speed of processing in a task can be independent or correlated (Lachman et al., 1979). In the case of a positive correlation, both dependent variables are said to reflect attentional demands. A negative correlation is said to reflect the trade-off of one dependent variable for the other (Pachella, 1974). This relationship in trading speed for accuracy or the reverse is termed the speed–accuracy trade-off (Pachella, 1974). If one defines and operationalizes attention in terms of the rate of human information processing, reaction time will be the measure of operationalizing attention. When the assumptions of controlled processing are met, reaction time may be considered to monitor the rate of the subject's processing. However, matters change when the subject either sacrifices accuracy for speed or, alternatively adopts a slow processing strategy and sacrifices speed of processing. In both cases, a negative correlation between speed and accuracy of performance will be observed. This means that the dependent variable reaction time is confounded by the accuracy variable of performance. Inspection of the literature on attentional performance in hyperactivity shows that either speed or accuracy is reported. On the basis of this information, it is not possible to decide whether the available publications which fail to report the correlation between speed and accuracy are reporting a dependent variable which accurately monitors a process or are reflecting the operation of the strategy of the subject (Meyer et al., 1988; Swanson and Briggs, 1969). Hence, interpretation of a process deficit is contingent upon the demonstration that strategy factors cannot account for the observed finding.

3

The cognitive energetic model

Another aspect of attention is its energetic character. This is often defined in terms of the effort required to perform a task (Kahneman, 1973), the arousal or activation of a task. This has led performance theorists to refer to the allocation of energy or resources as a task.

The concept of energy and allocation of energy can be placed within the logic of the AFM, if one uses a process–energy model such as that proposed by Sanders (1983). Such a model is necessary in order to integrate available results with other important issues in hyperactivity, such as the arousal, activation, and effort (motivation) applied to tasks. In the cognitive energetic model, the encoding stage is linked to arousal and the motor system to activation. Both energetic pools are linked to a third pool called effort. These energetic pools are defined following Pribram and McGuiness (1975). Arousal is said to be a phasic reaction locked to incoming stimuli. Task variables associated with this pool are stimulus intensity and degradation. Activation is defined as a tonic readiness to respond. Task variables associated with this pool are foreperiod, event rate, and muscle tension. Effort is defined as the energy required to modulate these two pools. A task variable associated with effort is stimulus–response compatibility. Thus the cognitive energetic model has two distinctive features: a lower system which is the stage model of Sternberg and an upper system which involves concepts derived from physiological and psychophysiological research. This enhanced model is important in considering the effect of energizing substances such as amphetamines in human performance.

Measuring drug effects with cognitive tasks

The basic logic of using drugs with cognitive tasks is to show the specificity of the drug effect. Obviously, models which have discrete cognitive processes and predict how to interpret effects are to be preferred over models which lack specificity and have little predictive power. The cognitive energetic model has the advantage that task variables are well-defined and the locus of their effect reasonably robust. Hence, use of a drug with such task variables follows the basic logic of the AFM. Namely, that when a drug and a task variable have acted as two main effects without interaction, it will be said that the drug acts on a stage other than the task variable. When the drug and the task variable are significant main effects and have a significant interaction, then it will be said that the drug and the task variable act on the same stage. This will enable the locus of the drug in the information processing chain to be located. To illustrate the fact that this logic has not been observed and, hence, that it cannot be concluded what the locus of effects are, we briefly turn to literature on the CPT.

It has been reported with consistency that hyperactive children commit more errors than controls in a CPT (Anderson et al., 1973; Horn et al., 1989; Klee and Garfinkel, 1983; Klorman et al., 1979; Levy and Hobbes, 1981; Loiselle et al., 1980; Michael et al., 1981; Nuechterlein, 1983; O'Dougherty et al., 1984; Schachar et al., 1988; Sostek et al., 1980; Sykes et al., 1973; Zentall and Meyer, 1987) or variants thereof (Firestone and Douglas, 1975; Hoy et al., 1978; Prior et al., 1985). Reports of studies using methylphenidate (Ritalin) and the CPT in hyperactive children suggest that attentional defects of such children could be successfully overcome with this treatment. Rapoport et al. (1980) compared the effect of D-amphetamine on hyperactives, control children, and college students using the CPT. They found a comparable time decrement effect and improvement in performance by this drug in hyperactives and controls. Klorman et al. (1979) showed that methylphenidate reduced significantly false positives and speeded reaction times in the X version of the CPT. Klorman et al. (1988) found, that in both a CPT X and a double CPT, methylphenidate improved the accuracy and the speed of performance to an equal degree in hyperactive children with and without aggressive features. Using both the X and the double version of the CPT, Michael and colleagues (1981) observed an extremely high error rate, produced mainly by the younger hyperactive children for both versions of the CPT. Methylphenidate improved both omission and commission error rates. Further, practice was independent of the effect of methylphenidate in this study. Methylphenidate increased the amplitude of the electrocortical potential P300, which was smaller in the ADDH children than controls. This effect was restricted to the simpler X version of the CPT. Coons et al. (1981) used both the X and double CPT with normal young adults. In their first study, there was no effect of methylphenidate on CPT performance or

4

P300. Their second study replicated this finding for the simple X version. The double version was prolonged and methylphenidate decreased omissions and increased P300 amplitude. A later study of adolescents diagnosed earlier as ADDH children replicated the effect of methylphenidate upon improving perceptual sensitivity and found that the P300 amplitude increased with methylphenidate administration (Coons et al., 1987). When Strauss et al. (1984) used the CPT double with an uninterrupted vigil of 45 minutes, a time decrement was observed for omissions as well as d' in the placebo condition. An interaction between drug and placebo with time-on-task was significant and indicated that methylphenidate reduced the time decrement effect. In accordance with the habituation hypothesis, P300 amplitude interacted with drug and time-on-task. Amplitude did not decline in the methylphenidate condition, but did so in the placebo condition. Methylphenidate in this long, double CPT had the additional effect that the latency of P300 remained relatively constant, whereas in the placebo condition latency increased. This suggests that methylphenidate in a double CPT with clear evidence of a time decrement prevents both habituation effects and increases the duration of stimulus evaluation.

These results are encouraging, but hardly specific. It should be observed that differences in CPT performance is not a condition specific to hyperactive children. For instance, children at risk for schizophrenia have also been differential from controls with the CPT. More important for the present discussion is that one cannot define where and on which process Ritalin is operating from these studies. It may be relevant, therefore, to consider what is known about amphetamine in studies which have used task variables which are interpretable within the cognitive-energetic model.

We now discuss the information processing deficit in the hyperactive child in terms of the cognitive models as discussed earlier and the influence that Ritalin has on this deficit. We start with the Sternberg and the Shiffrin and Schneider paradigm.

Encoding

Using undrugged subjects Sergeant and Scholten (1985b) found that encoding did not differentiate hyperactives from controls, although there was some evidence that attention deficit children without hyperactivity did have an encoding defect. It was suggested that this group might have exhibited a strategy difference from controls rather than a true processing deficit. Weingartner et al. (1980) used free recall from word lists and suggested that a possible higher-order encoding deficit was ameliorated by administration of amphetamine. However, the same group recently reported that neither methylphenidate nor dextro-amphetamine at either a high or a low dose interacted with encoding (Borcherding et al., 1988). Using a Posner physical and name identity task in a double-blind crossover design with methylphenidate, Ballinger et al. (1984) found an effect for the drug which failed to interact with level of encoding.

Four studies of hyperactives and normals have further confirmed that encoding is unlikely to be the locus of the ADHD deficit or of the remedial effect of methylphenidate/amphetamine. Using a depth of processing task, Reid and Borkowski (1984) found no interaction between depth of processing and drug–placebo condition. Benezra and Douglas (1988) have reported that hyperactives are comparable with controls in their encoding speed and patterns of spontaneous decay of verbal traces. A second study (Peeke et al., 1984) using the depth of processing model (Posner and Boies, 1971) has shown that methylphenidate has independent effects on depth of processing. This has been replicated by another study (Malone et al., 1988). On both grounds of comparisons between hyperactives and controls using the various encoding task variables, and on grounds of interactions with D-amphetamine and methylphenidate, the available evidence seems to rule out encoding as either the site of the ADHD deficit or the locus of the effect of the remedial effects of these drugs.

Central processes

There is strong evidence that hyperactive children do not have a central processing deficit during automatic processing (Van der Meere and Sergeant, 1988b) or during controlled processing with focused attention (Van der Meere and Sergeant, 1988a) or with divided attention demands (Sergeant and Scholten, 1983; 1985b; Van der Meere and Sergeant, 1987; Van der Meere et al., 1989). Adolescents diagnosed previously as childhood hyperactives (Coons et al., 1987) cannot be differentiated from ADDH, anxiety-disordered children, conduct-disordered children with ADDH, and controls when using these central stages (Werry et al., 1987). Coons et al. (1987) reported that methylphenidate did not influence the rate of search and decision in their sample of adolescents. Confirmation that methylphenidate does not operate on search and decision was provided by early studies with hyperactives (Sprague et al., 1970; Werry and Aman, 1975) and by Callaway (1983) using normals and by Klorman et al. (1988). It should be noted, however, that in the latter study the effect of methylphenidate on reaction time was confined only to normal young adults. These studies suggest that the effect of methylphenidate is located at a stage subsequent to the central stages of search and decision.

Motor organization

The stage subsequent to the central stages is motor organization. Since the research by Frowein (1981), this last block has been subdivided into four separate stages: response selection, motor programming, motor initiation, and motor adjustment. The first stage, response selection, is manipulated by stimulus–response compatibility. Frowein used normal adult subjects to demonstrate that a stimulant (phentermine HCl) did not interact with stimulus degradation; hence encoding was not influenced by this D-amphetamine. It did interact with stimulus–response compatibility and in particular with movement time. It was concluded that this drug had its locus on the output side of the system. A further interaction with time uncertainty, suggested that D-amphetamine affects the motor decision and output of the system. Thus, these results suggested that the locus of the effect of phentermine was not at the input but at the output. Using load and stimulus-response compatibility and five response mappings Fitzpatrick et al. (1988) found that load and compatibility interacted. In their study the assumption of stage independence was broken slightly. Nevertheless, using reaction time Fitzpatrick et al. (1988) were able to replicate that methylphenidate administered to students did not influence search but did speed-up decision and response selection. These studies suggest that the locus of the methylphenidate effect is at the output side of the information processing chain.

Following the Sanders model, the Sternberg-like output processes are linked with the energetic activation system. Hence, the output dysfunction in the hyperactive child may be caused by an activation dysfunction. Activation may be manipulated by differences in event rate (Sanders, 1983). Therefore, evidence concerning the energetic part of the system will be restricted to event rate studies.

It has been known for sometime that the speed at which stimuli are presented in a task generally improves performance, whereas slow presentations lead to poorer performance (Broadbent, 1971). Dalby and colleagues (1977) reported that in a paired-associate learning task, the faster the event rate the better the hyperactive child learns per unit time. The importance of pacing a task has been noted by Van der Meere et al. (1990b). In that study, a fast event rate led to a similar performance level in both hyperactive, learning-disabled, and control children. The relation between event rate, output variables, and methylphenidate has been investigated recently by Tannock et al. (1989). This group found that methylphenidate interacted with length of the mean response time: the longer the delay the greater its effect. Further, there was evidence that the greater the dosage of methylphenidate, the steeper was the inhibition function. These studies suggest that methylphenidate may have properties which interact with motor control and selection.

A task relevant to inhibitory functioning is the differential reinforcement of low rates of responding (DRL) task. Kinsbourne (1990) has shown this task to be both sensitive to differentiating hyperactives from nonhyperactives. This task is sensitive to dosage level of methylphenidate and has been suggested as a behavioral measure of frontal functioning (Gorenstein and Newman, 1980). The role of frontal functioning will be addressed further in the next section.

PSYCHOPHYSIOLOGICAL STUDIES AND MOTOR FUNCTIONING

We now report converging evidence concerning the locus of the deficit in hyperactivity and some research which has used Ritalin. This review is necessarily restrictive in view of the fact that the majority of studies have not used task variables which can be placed within the AFM. A few of the terms used in this section will be briefly defined at this point. One measure to be used is the P300. The event-related potential has a latency in the range 290 to 700 msec after the presentation of a stimulus. It peaks in the vertex and parietal areas and was first reported by Sutton et al. (1965). Since then it has been investigated widely and has been shown to increase in latency but decrease in amplitude when the memory load or cognitive load of a task increases (for review, see Klorman et al., 1988). Complementary to event-related potential research is the use of Brain Electrical Activity Map (BEAM) first described by Duffy et al. (1979). This procedure is an imagining technique which enables the electrophysiological data gathered from a large number of electrodes to be represented pictorially. Another imaging technique, but based on scanning of the brain, is positron emission tomography (PET). A special form of this is single photon emission tomography (SPECT). In the latter a single photon emission dose is administered using the inhalation of Xenon-133 for determination of three-dimensional regional cerebral blood flow (rCBF). These techniques are new and do not necessarily indicate anatomical locus, but probably can be better interpreted to indicate locus of function.

The majority of findings using a standard memory scanning paradigm and the P300 have found that the effect of search and decision is to prolong the latency of P300. This effect is independent of effects of amphetamines and methylphenidate (Brumaghim et al., Study 1, 1987; Callaway, 1983, 1984; Coons et al., 1987; Klorman et al., 1988; Peloquin and Klorman, 1986). This finding has been found in a variety of samples: adults, adolescents previously diagnosed as hyperactives, and normal children. In view of the additive effects of these stimulants on stimulus evaluation and a reduction in reaction time, it was concluded that stimulants effected postevaluation processes. This picture became less clear following two reports from Klorman's laboratory. The first by Brumaghim et al. Study 2 (1987) found that methylphenidate interacted with search and decision such that the negative slope became slower and the positive slope became faster. In terms of Shiffrin and Schneider's model of controlled processing, methylphenidate produced greater controlled processing (negative slope greater than positive slope). The second report by Fitzpatrick et al. (1988) found that with larger levels of load than had been used previously, thus requiring more controlled processing, load increased the latency of P300 to targets and speeded-up nontargets. However, methylphenidate had no effect upon latency of P300. This fails to replicate the Brumaghim et al. (1987) effect of methylphenidate upon latency P300. In the Fitzpatrick et al. study, stimulus–response compatibility factor interacted with load (incompatibility increased P300 latency in low levels of load). There was no interaction with methylphenidate. Thus P300 research suggests that the hyperactivity deficit occurs beyond the central stages. Further, the evidence available suggests that the locus of the effect of methylphenidate is also at some stage beyond the central stages. This evidence converges with that reported by Van der Meere et al. (1989) that the response choice stage (which follows the central stages) interacts with hyperactivity.

Interest in frontal functioning of hyperactives was stimulated by Mattes (1980) who reviewed research using the contingent negative variation and suggested that hyperactive children had a dysfunction associated with motor and frontal processing (Grünewald-Zuberbier, et al., 1975, 1978). However, using the bereitschaftspotential (also an electrophysiological measure of motor functioning) Rothenberger (1984) found that frontal differences between hyperactives and controls were not specific, since children with tics also showed such differences. Using BEAM methodology and an event-related potential: processing negativity (for review, see Näätanen and Picton, 1987), Satterfield et al. (1988) reported that the processing negativity (Nd) measured at the frontal lobe differs between hyperactive and control boys. This finding has had two sources of support. The first is the study by Zametkin et al. (1990) using PET. This study reports that in adults who were formerly hyperactive, the metabolic functions tracked by the PET suggest a deficit of information processing which is functionally located in the frontal lobes. Similarly, Lou (1990) using the SPECT in a study with six hyperactive boys observed that, in comparison to controls, the primary sensory and sensorimotor regions were very active in hyperactives. However, it should be noted that the effects of methylphenidate in this blood flow study were not confined to any specific brain region, since the drug tended to decrease activity also in the occipital, temporal, and parietal lobes. Additional caution needs to be exercised in hypothesizing the location of the hyperactivity disorder solely to frontal lobe functioning. Bylsma and Pivik (1989) used smooth pursuit eye movement methodology in hyperactive children to demonstrate and that there is at least a partial involvement in subcortical structures.

DISCUSSION

Taylor (1984) critically examined the relation between drug response and diagnostic validation. Of Taylor's several points of criticism concerning the evaluation of medication, three issues will be discussed here: (1) the poor measurement of attention/impulsivity, (2) the use of responders only, and (3) the acute-chronic drug responder distinction. To these issues may be added the issue of fatigue and the process strategy distinction.

It is clear from a review of the literature that many investigators employ a task, such as the CPT, with little theoretical knowledge of what the task is measuring (Sergeant and Van der Meere, 1990b). It is necessary for the advancement of research in child psychopathology to employ tasks that have a well-defined theoretical framework in order to identify the locus of the effect of medication. We have reviewed research using the AFM in hyperactivity and, where possible, the locus of the effect of methylphenidate upon attentional performance. Our conclusion is that, in terms of the AFM, methylphenidate has its effect on the output side of the information processing system, but also involves energetic systems such as activation and effort. Within the theoretical framework used here, it has been possible to link diverse sources of study: cognitive and electrophysiological. The research reviewed here is internally consistent and on the basis of this work more specific research can be expected in the future.

The AFM model deals primarily with single-task demands. Sanders (1983) showed that the AFM can also be related to dual tasks. Little work has been published until now concerning the performance of hyperactives on dual tasks. In such tasks management of attentional resources, rather than attentional processes are the object of interest. Whether and how methylphenidate is able to influence dual-task processing and its specificity is a question in need of research. One disadvantage of the dual-task methodology is that it lacks the specificity that the AFM offers. Some combination of both would seem necessary, if research using dual-task methodology is not to suffer from the criticism made by Taylor.

The research cited here uses the acute administration of methylphenidate to examine for drug effects on tasks. Chronic administration research with the AFM or other well-defined attentional tasks is currently absent. Although this distinction is not new, study of children with chronic administration is needed in order to examine if only changes in information processing system are temporary or whether there are long-term benefits/costs in administration.

Similarly, Taylor's criticism of using and reporting responders is still relevant to current research. A taxonomy of the sensitivity and the specificity of levels of methylphenidate to tasks has not yet been constructed. This endangers attempts such as we have made here to localize the effects. It is a fair argument that, since the effects appear to be stronger in the responder group, this does not take into account the proportion of nonresponders, which could be as large or larger than the responder numbers. This, coupled with the uncertainty concerning the duration and specificity of methylphenidate in information processing enables the reader to evaluate how bold our conclusions really are! While not always addressed in research, little research has examined the clinical (group) specificity of methylphenidate. This too is needed in greater detail for adequate evaluation and theoretical definition of the action of methylphenidate.

Tasks are performed over time and at various rates and with different instruction sets. Fatigue, event rate, and speed–accuracy instructions are seldom taken into proper account when reporting attentional studies and the role of methylphenidate. While a sustained attention deficit hypothesis of hyperactivity is becoming more difficult to maintain (Van der Meere and Sergeant, 1989; Van der Meere et al., 1991), effects of time-on-task need to be examined more carefully than hitherto. Practice effects and fatigue require examination of data by blocks. Few studies report this information. Manipulation of the rate at which signal demands are presented is needed to evaluate whether one is dealing with a pure process deficit or an energetic pool dysfunction which is linked to a stage of processing. Speed-accuracy instructions have been shown to have significant effects on hyperactive performance (Sergeant and Scholten, 1985a). Despite this, few researchers report in detail their instructions and, even fewer examine both the speed and the accuracy of performance. For example, methylphenidate has been shown to influence the speed but not the accuracy of performance on the Matching Familiar Figures Test in hyperactives (Tannock et al., 1989). This could mean that methylphenidate only influences speed of processing. Clearly, in view of the well-established effects methylphenidate has on the accuracy of the CPT (for review, see Sergeant and Van der Meere, 1990b), this effect may be task specific or reflect some interaction with instructions. Future research will be needed to clarify this point.

REFERENCES

Anderson, D.R. & Levin, S.R. (1976), Young children's attention to "Sesame Street." *Child Dev.* 47:806–811.

Anderson, R.P., Holcomb, C.G. & Doyle, R.B. (1973), The measurement of attentional deficits. *Except. Child.,* 39:534–540.

Baddeley, A.D. (1976), *The Psychology of Memory.* London: Harper & Row.

Ballinger, C.T., Varley, C.K. & Nolen, P.A. (1984), Effects of methylphenidate on reading in children with attention deficit disorder. *Am. J. Psychiatry,* 141:1590–1593.

Barkley, R.A. (1977), The effects of methylphenidate on various types of activity level and attention in hyperkinetic children. *J. Abnormal Child Psychol.,* 5:351–369.

Benezra, E. & Douglas, V.I. (1988), Short-term serial recall in ADDH, normal, and reading disabled boys. *J. Abnorm. Child Psychol.,* 16:511–526.

Borcherding, B., Thompson, K., Kruesi, M., Bartko, J., Rapoport, J.L. & Weingartner, H. (1988), Automatic and effortful processing in attention deficit hyperactivity disorder. *J. Abnorm. Child Psychol.,* 16:333–346.

Bradley, C. (1937), The behavior of children receiving Benzedrine. *Am. J. Psychiatry,* 94:577–585.

Broadbent, D.E. (1971), *Decision and Stress.* London: Academic Press.

Brumaghim, J.J., Klorman, R., Strauss, J., Lewine, J.D. & Goldstein, M.G. (1987), What aspects of information processing are affected by methylphenidate? Findings on performance and P36 latency from two studies. *Psychophysiology,* 24:361–373.

Bylsma, F.W. & Pivik, R.T. (1989), The effects of background illumination and stimulant medication on smooth pursuit eye movements of hyperactive children. *J. Abnorm. Child Psychol.,* 17:73–90.

Callaway, E. (1983), The pharmacology of human information processing. *Psychophysiology,* 20:359–370.

———— (1984), Human information processing: Some effects of methylphenidate, age and dopamine. *Biol. Psychiatry,* 19:649–662.

Clements, S.D. (1966), Task force one: *Minimal Brain Dysfunction in Children.* National Institute of Neurological Diseases and Blindness, monograph no. 3, Washington, DC: DHEW, p. 9.

———— Peters, J. (1962), Minimal brain dysfunction in the schoolaged child. *Arch. Gen. Psychiatry,* 6:185–197.

Coons, H.W., Peloquin, L.J., Klorman, R., Bauer, L.O., Ryan, R.M., Perlmutter, R.A. & Salzman, L.F. (1981), Effect of methylphenidate on young adults vigilance and event-related potentials. *Electroencephal. Clin. Neurophysiol.,* 51:373–387.

————, Klorman, R. & Borgstedt, A.D. (1987), Effects of methylphenidate on adolescents with a childhood history of attention deficit disorder: 2. *J. Am. Acad. Child Psychiatry,* 26:368–374.

Dalby, J.I., Kinsbourne, M., Swanson, J.M. & Sobol, M.P. (1977), Hyperactive children's underuse of learning time: Correction by stimulant treatment. *Child Dev.,* 48:1448–1453.

Duffy, F.H., Burchfiel, J.L. & Lombroso, C.T. (1979), Brain electrical activity mapping (BEAM): A new method for extending the clinical utility of EEG and evoked potential data. *Ann. Neurol.,* 5:309–321.

Dykman, R.A., Walls, R.C., Suzuki, T., Ackerman, P.T. & Peters, J.E. (1970), Children with learning disabilities: Conditioning, differentiation and the effect of distraction. *Am. J. Orthopsychiatry,* 40:766–782.

Firestone, P. & Douglas, V.I. (1975), The effects of reward and punishment on reaction times and autonomic activity in hyperactive and normal children. *J. Abnorm. Child Psychol.,* 3:201–215.

Fisk, A.D. & Schneider, W. (1981), Control and automatic processing during tasks requiring sustained attention: A new approach to vigilance. *Human Factors,* 23:737–750.

Fitzpatrick, P., Klorman, R., Brumaghim, J.T. & Keefover, R.W. (1988), Effects of methylphenidate on stimulus evaluation and response processes: Evidence from performance and event-related potentials. *Psychophysiology,* 25:292–304.

Frowein, H.W. (1981), Selective drug effects on information processing. *Thesis.* Enschede: Sneldruk Boulevard.

Gorenstein, E.E. & Newman, J.P. (1980), Disinhibitory psychopathology: A new perspective and a model for research. *Pscyhol. Rev.,* 87:301–315.

Grünewald-Zuberbier, E., Grünewald, G. & Rasche, A. (1975), Hyperactive behavior and EEG arousal reactions in children. *Electroencephal. Clin. Neurophysiol.,* 38:149–159.

———— & Netz, J. (1978), Contingent negative variation and alpha attentuation responses in children with different abilities to concentrate. *Electroencephal. Clin. Neurophysiol.,* 44:37–47.

Horn, W.F., Wagner, A.E. & Ialongo, N. (1989), Sex differences in school-aged children with pervasive attention deficit hyperactivity disorder. *J. of Abnorm. Child Psychol.,* 17:109–125.

Hoy, E., Weiss, G., Minde, K. & Cohen, N. (1978), The hyperactive child at adolescence: Cognitive, emotional, and social functioning. *J. Abnormal Child Psychol.,* 67:311–324.

Kahneman, D. (1973), *Attention and Effort.* Englewood Cliffs, NJ: Prentice Hall.

Kinsbourne, M. & Swanson, J.M. (1979), Models of hyperactivity: Implications for diagnosis and treatment. In: *Hyperactivity in Children. Etiology, Measurement and Treatment Implications.* ed. R.L. Trites. Baltimore: University Park Press, pp. 1–20.

———— (1990), Testing models for attention deficit hyperactivity disorder in the behavioral laboratory. In *Attention Deficit Hyperactivity Disorder,* eds. K. Conners & M. Kinsbourne. München: MMV Medizin Verlag.

Klee, S.H. & Garfinkel, B.D. (1983), The computized CPT: A new measure for inattention. *J. Abnorm. Child Psychol.,* 11:487–493.

Klorman, R. Salzman, L.F., Pass, H.L., Borgstedt, A.D. & Dainer, K.B. (1979), Effects of methylphenidate on hyperactive children's evoked responses during passive and active attention. *Psychophysiology,* 16:23–29.

———— Brumaghim, J.T., Coons, H.W., Peloquin, L.J., Strauss, J., Lewine, J.D., Borgstedt, A.D. & Goldstein, M.G. (1988), The contributions of event-related potentials to understanding the effects of stimulants on information processing in attention deficit disorder. In: *Attention Deficit Disorder,* Vol. 5, eds. L.F. Bloomingdale & J.A. Sergeant. Oxford: Pergamon Press.

Kupietz, S.S. & Richardson, E. (1978), Children's vigilance performance and inattentiveness in the classroom. *J. Child Psychol. Psychiatry,* 19:145–154.

Lachman, R., Lachman, J.L. & Butterfield, E.C. (1979), *Cognitive Psychology and Information Processing: An Introduction.* Hillsdale, NJ: Lawrence Erlbaum Associates.

Levy, F. & Hobbes, G. (1981), The diagnosis of attention deficit disorder (hyperkinesis) in children. *J. Am. Acad. Child Psychiatry,* 20:376–384.

Loiselle, D.L., Stamm, J.S., Matinsky, S. & Whipple, S. Evoked potential and behavioural signs of attentive dysfunctions in hyperactive boys. *Psychophysiology,* 17:193–201.

Lou, H.C. (1990), Methylphenidate reversible hypoperfusion of striatal regions in ADHD. In: *Attention Deficit Hyperactivity Disorder,* eds. K. Conners & M. Kinsbourne. München: MMV Medizin Verlag, pp. 137–148.

Malone, M.A., Kershner, J.R. & Siegel, L. (1988), The effects of methylphenidate on levels of processing and laterality in children with attention deficit disorder. *J. Abnorm. Child Psychol.,* 16:379–396.

Mannuzza, S., Gittelman Klein, R., Bonagura, N., Horowitz Konig, P. & Shenker, R. (1988), Hyperactive boys almost grown up. *Arch. Gen. Psychiatry,* 45:13–18.

Mattes, J.A. (1980), The role of frontal lobe dysfunction in childhood hyperkinesis. *Comprehen. Psychol.,* 21:358–368.

Meyer, D., Irwin, D.E., Oman, A.M. & Kounios, J. (1988), The dynamics of cognition and action: Mental processes inferred from speed-accuracy decomposition. *Psychol. Rev.,* 95:183–236.

Michael, B.M., Klorman, R., Salzman, L.F., Borgstedt, A.D. & Dainer, K.B. (1981), Normalizing effects of methylphenidate on hyperactive children's performance and evoked potentials. *Psychophysiology,* 18:665–677.

Näätanen, R. & Picton, T.W. (1987), The N1 wave of the human electric and magnetic response to sound: A review and an analysis of the component structure. *Psychophysiology,* 24:375–425.

Nuechterlein, K.H. (1983), Signal detection in vigilance tasks and behavioral attributes among offspring of schizophrenic mothers and among hyperactive children. *J. Abnormal Psychol.,* 92:4–28.

O'Dougherty, M., Nuechterlein, K.H. & Drew, B. (1984), Hyperactive and hypoxic children: Signal detection, sustained attention, and behavior. *J. Abnormal Psychol.,* 93:178–191.

Pachella, R.G. (1974), The interpretation of reaction time in information processing research. In: *Human Information Processing: Tutorial in Performance and Recognition,* ed. B. Kantowitz. New York: Lawrence Erlbaum Associates, pp. 41–82.

Peeke, S., Halliday, R., Callaway, E., Prael, R. & Reks, V. (1984), Effects of two doses of methylphenidate on verbal information processing in hyperactive children. *J. Clin. Psychopharmacol.,* 4:82–88.

Peloquin, L.J. & Klorman, R. (1986), Effects of methylphenidate on normal children's mood, event-related potentials, and performance in memory scanning and vigilance. *J. Abnormal Psychol.,* 95:88–98.

Posner, M.I. & Boies, S.J. (1971), Components of attention. *Psychol. Rev.,* 78:391–408.

Pribram, K.H. & McGuiness, D. (1975), Arousal, activation and effort in the control of attention. *Psychol. Rev.,* 82:116–149.

Prior, A., Sanson, A., Freethy, L. & Geffen, G. (1985), Auditory attentional abilities in hyperactive children. *J. Child Psychol. Psychiatry,* 26:289–304.

Rapoport, J.L. & Benoit, M. (1975). The relation of direct home observations to the clinic evaluation of school-age boys. *J. Child Psychol. Psychiatry,* 16:141–147.

———— Buchsbaum, M.S., Weingartner, H., Zahn, T.P., Ludow, C. & Mikkelsen, E.J. (1980), Dextroamphetamine—Its cognitive and behavioral effects in normal and hyperactive boys and normal men. *Arch. Gen. Psychiatry,* 37:933–943.

———— Stoner, G., DuPaul, G.J., Birmingham, B.K. & Tucker, S. (1985), Methylphenidate in hyperactive children: Differential effects of dose in academic, learning, and social behavior. *J. Abnorm. Child Psychol.,* 13:227–244.

Reid, M.K. & Borkowski, J.G. (1984), Effects of methylphenidate (Ritalin) on information processing in hyperactive children. *J. Abnorm. Child Psychol.,* 12:169–186.

Rosvold, H.E., Mirsky, A.F., Sarason, I. (1956), A continuous performance test of brain damage. *J. Consult. Psychol.,* 20:343–350.

Rothenberger, A. (1984), Bewegungsbezogene Veränderungen der elektrischen Hirnaktivität bei Kinder mit multiplen Tics und Gilles de la Tourette-syndrom. *Thesis.* University of HE.

Rutter, M. (1989), Attention deficit disorder/hyperkinetic syndrome: Conceptual and research issues regarding diagnosis and classification. In: *Attention Deficit Disorder,* eds. T. Sagvolden & T. Archer. Hillsdale, NJ: Lawrence Erlbaum Associates, pp. 1–24.

Sanders, A.F. (1983), Towards a model of stress and human performance. *Acta Psychologica,* 53:61–97.

Satterfield, J.H., Schell, A.M., Nicholas, T. & Backs, R.W. (1988), Topographic study of auditory event-related potentials in normal boys and boys with attention deficit disorder with hyperactivity. *Psychophysiology,* 25:591–606.

Schachar, R., Logan, G., Wachsmuth, R. & Chajzyk, D. (1988), Attaining and maintaining preparation: A comparison of attention in hyperactive, normal, and disturbed control children. *J. Abnorm. Child Psychol.,* 16:361–370.

Schneider, W. & Shiffrin, R.M. (1977). Controlled and automatic human information processing: 1. Detection, search & attention. *Psychol. Rev.,* 84:1–66.

Sergeant, J.A. (1981), *Attention Studies in Hyperactivity.* Doctoral dissertation. Groningen: Veenstra Visser.

———— Scholten, C.A. (1983), A stages-of-information approach to hyperactivity. *J. Child Psychol. Psychiatry,* 24:49–60.

—— —— (1985a), On resource strategy limitations in hyperactivity: Cognitive impulsivity reconsidered. *J. Child Psychol. Psychiatry,* 26:97–109.

—— —— (1985b), On data limitations in hyperactivity. *J. Child Psychology Psychiatry,* 26:111–124.

—— Van der Meere, J.J. (1990a), Additive factor method applied to psychopathology with special reference to childhood hyperactivity. *Acta Psychologica,* 74:277–295.

—— —— (1990b), Convergence of approaches in localizing the hyperactivity deficit. *Adv. Clin. Child Psychol.,* 13:207–241.

Shiffrin, R.M. & Schneider, W. (1977), Controlled and automatic human information processing: 1. Detection, search and attention. *Psychol. Rev.,* 84:979–987.

Sostek, A.J., Buchsbaum, M.S. & Rapoport, J.L. (1980), Effects of amphetamine on vigilance performance in normal and hyperactive children. *J. Abnorm. Child Psychol.,* 8, 491–500.

Sprague, R.L., Barnes, K.R. & Werry, J.S. (1970), Methylphenidate and thioridazine: Learning, reaction time, and classroom behavior in disturbed children. *Am. J. Orthopsychiatry,* 40:615–628.

—— Sleator, E.K. (1975), What is the proper dose of stimulant drugs in children? *Int. J. Mental Health,* 4:75–118.

—— —— (1977), Methylphenidate in hyperkinetic children: Differences in dose effects on learning and social behavior. *Science,* 198:1274–1276.

Spring, C., Greenberg, L., Scott, J. & Hopwood, J. (1973), Reaction time and effect of Ritalin on children with learning problems. *Percept. Motor Skills,* 36:75–82.

Sternberg, S. (1969), Discovery of processing stages: Extensions of Donder's method. In: *Attention and Performance,* vol. 2, ed. W. G. Koster. Amsterdam: Noord-Holland.

—— (1975). Memory scanning: New findings and current controversies. *Q. J. Exp. Psychol.,* 27:1–32.

Stevens, D.A., Boydstun, J.A., Dykman, R.A., Peters, J.E., & Sinton, D.W. (1967), Presumed minimal brain dysfunction in children: Relationship to performance and selected behavioral tests. *Arch. Gen. Psychiatry,* 16:281–285.

Strauss, J., Lewis, J.L., Klorman, R., Peloquin, L.J., Perlmutter, R.A. & Salzman, L.F. (1984), Effects of methylphenidate on young adults' performance and event-related potentials in a vigilance and a paired-associates learning test. *Psychophysiology,* 21:609–621.

Sutton, S., Braren, M., Zubin, J. & John, E. R. (1965), Evoked potential correlates of stimulus uncertainty. *Science,* 150:1187–1188.

Swanson, J.M. & Briggs, G.E. (1969), Information processing as a function of speed versus accuracy. *J. Exp. Psychol.,* 81:223–239.

—— Barlow, A. & Kinsbourne, M. (1979), Task specificity of responses to stimulant drugs in laboratory tests. *Int. J. Mental Health* 8:67–82.

Sykes, D.H., Douglas, V.I., Weiss, G. & Minde, K.K. (1971), Attention in hyperactive children and the effect of methylphenidate (Ritalin). *J. Child Psychol. Psychiatry,* 12:129–139.

—— —— Morgenstern, G. (1973). Sustained attention in hyperactive children. *J. Child Psychol. Psychiatry,* 14:213–220.

Tannock, R., Schachar, R.J., Carr, R.P., Chajczyk, D. & Logan, G.D. (1989), Effects of methylphenidate on inhibitory control in hyperactive children. *J. Abnorm. Child Psychology,* 17:473–491.

Taylor, E. (1984), Drug response and diagnostic validation. In: *Developmental Psychiatry,* ed. M. Rutter. New York: Guilford Press, pp. 280–329.

Van der Meere, J.J. & Sergeant, J.A. (1987), A divided attention experiment with pervasively hyperactive children. *J. Abnorm. Psychology,* 15:279–392.

—— —— (1988a), Controlled processing and vigilance in hyperactivity: Time will tell. *J. Abnorm. Child Psychology,* 16:641–655.

—— —— Sergeant, J.A. (1988b), Acquisition of attentional skill in pervasively hyperactive children. *J. Child Psychology and Psychiatry,* 29:301–310.

———— van Baal, M. & Sergeant, J.A. (1989), The additive factor method: A differential diagnostic tool in hyperactivity and learning disability. *J. Abnorm. Child Psychology*, 17:409–422.

———— ———— ———— (1990a), The additive factor method: A differential diagnostic tool in hyperactivity and learning disablement. *J. Abnorm. Child Psychology*, 17:409–422.

———— Wekking, E. & Sergeant, J.A. (1990c), Sustained attention in pervasively hyperactive children. *J. Child Psychol. Psychiatry*, 32:275–284.

Weingartner, H., Rapoport, J.L., Buchsbaum, M.S., Bunney, W.E., Ebert, M.H., Mikkelsen, E.J. & Caine, E.D. (1980), Cognitive processes in normal and hyperactive children and their response to amphetamine treatment. *J. Abnorm. Child Psychology*, 89:25–37.

Werry, J.S. & Aman, M.G. (1975), Methylphenidate and Haloperidol in children: Effects on attention, memory and activity. *Arch. Gen. Psychiatry*, 32:790–795.

———— Sprague, R. (1974), Methylphenidate in children—effect of dosage. *Austral. NZ J. Psychiatry*, 8:9–19.

———— Elkind, G.S. & Reeves, J.C. (1987), Attention deficit, conduct, oppositional, and anxiety disorders in children: III. Laboratory differences. *J. Abnorm. Child Psychology*, 15:409–427.

Zametkin, A. (1990), Personal communication. Cited in J.H. Satterfield: BEAM studies in ADD boys. In: *Attention Deficit Hyperactivity Disorder*, eds. K. Conners & M. Kinsbourne ADDH, München: MMV Medizin Verlag, pp. 127–136.

———— Nordahl, F.E., Gross, M., King, A.L., Semdle, W.E., Rumsey, J., Hamburger, S. & Cohen, R.M. (1990), Cerebral glucose metabolism in adults with hyperactivity of childhood onset. *New England J. Medicine*, 323:1361–1366.

Zentall, S.S. & Meyer, M.J. (1987), Self-regulation of stimulation for ADDH children during reading and vigilance task performance. *J. Abnorm. Child Psychology*, 15:519–536.

Ritalin: Diagnostic Comorbidity
and Attentional Measures

JEFFREY M. HALPERIN,[1,2] JEFFREY H. NEWCORN,[2] and VANSHDEEP SHARMA[2]

DIAGNOSTIC COMORBIDITY: ADHD, DISORDERS OF CONDUCT, AND COGNITIVE PROBLEMS

In past decades children with behavior disorders and/or poor academic achievement received a variety of nonspecific diagnoses such as minimal brain dysfunction, hyperkinetic disorder, and learning disabilities. With the advent of *DSM-III* (American Psychiatric Association, 1980) and *DSM-III-R* (American Psychiatric Association, 1987), specific, operationally defined, symptom clusters were introduced in an attempt to define more discrete diagnostic entities, and the use of multiple diagnoses within the same individual was encouraged when these symptom clusters overlapped. The earlier categories have been replaced in *DSM-III-R* with attention deficit hyperactivity disorder (ADHD), oppositional-defiant disorder (ODD), conduct disorder (CD), and a wide range of Axis II specific developmental disorders (SDD). ADHD is characterized by symptoms of inattention, impulsivity, and motor overactivity; ODD is characterized by negativistic, hostile, and defiant behavior; and CD is characterized by a persistent pattern of behavior in which the basic rights of others and major age-appropriate societal rules are violated. The SDD are characterized by poor academic, linguistic, speech or motor skills that are not due to demonstrable neurological disorders, pervasive developmental disorder, mental retardation, or lack of educational opportunities.

Although there is minimal research with the *DSM-III-R* revisions of these diagnostic categories, a sizeable literature has described the interrelationships among their *DSM-III* predecessors. Among children diagnosed as having attention deficit disorder with hyperactivity (ADD/H), 36 to 50% have been found to also fulfill criteria for CD (Munir et al., 1987; Szatmari et al., 1989), 59% meet criteria for ODD (Munir et al., 1987), and at least 25% have comorbid specific developmental disorders (Holborow and Berry, 1986). Moreover, a substantial proportion meet criteria for anxiety and depressive disorders (Anderson et al., 1987; Biederman et al., 1987). The overlap may even be greater with *DSM-III-R*'s ADHD, which appears to identify a larger group of children than its predecessor (Newcorn et al., 1989). Thus, with our current diagnostic nomenclature, a heterogenous group of children receive the diagnosis of ADHD, the majority of whom have at least one other comorbid diagnosis.

Attempts to validate the syndrome of ADHD (or one of its predecessors) have been fraught with difficulties. Several measures significantly distinguish between ADHD children and normal controls, but few consistently distinguish between ADHD children and those with other psychiatric disorders (Koriath et al., 1985; Werry et al., 1987). Furthermore, ADHD children vary considerably in their presenting symptoms (American Psychiatric Association, 1987), response to treatment (Barkley, 1977; Halperin et al., 1986) and long-term outcome (Gittelman et al., 1985; Weiss et al., 1985). Therefore, several investigators have raised doubts as to the validity of the ADHD syndrome (Prior and Sanson, 1986). One approach to

[1]Queens College of the City University of New York, Flushing, New York
[2]The Mount Sinai School of Medicine, New York, New York

unraveling the confusion and attempting to more clearly identify the defining characteristics of distinct subgroups of ADHD children has been to study patterns of comorbidity.

Diagnostic comorbidity is defined by the presence of more than one diagnosis in a single patient and suggests that the child has symptom patterns characteristic of both (or all) of his/her comorbid diagnoses. Thus, children in whom two syndromes occur comorbidly should have the defining symptoms of both syndromes and should resemble both diagnostic groups in terms of correlates of the disorder. However, other possibilities exist. It is conceivable that children with comorbid diagnoses have particular aspects of each syndrome, which, when they co-occur, cause the children to appear consistently different from those with "pure" syndromes. This latter possibility would suggest that children in the comorbid group may represent a distinct subgroup with a slightly different disorder. Alternatively, it is possible that the defining characteristics of the two disorders are overlapping so that comorbidity is virtually guaranteed. In this case, comorbidity would not truly describe two separate disorders, but rather, would represent an artifact of a poorly constructed diagnostic system.

In order to clarify the nature of comorbid diagnoses in children and to determine which of the above possibilities exists, it is necessary to closely examine the specific symptoms believed to comprise the distinct syndromes. A comprehensive review (Hinshaw, 1987) of the relationship between inattention/hyperactivity and aggression in children indicates that while these symptom dimensions often overlap in the same child, they have distinct correlates, suggesting their validity as independent and clinically meaningful symptom dimensions. Inattention/hyperactivity is associated with greater learning and cognitive problems, while aggressive behavior is associated with social disadvantage, family conflict, parental sociopathy, and poorer long-term outcome. Yet, if these dimensions are truly independent, it is difficult to understand why they coexist with such frequency.

One could hypothesize a unitary etiology which simultaneously affects multiple symptom dimensions in a single child. Alternatively, the presence of one disorder could serve as a predisposing factor in the development of a second disorder, making them interrelated, but without a unitary etiology. A third possibility is that the high rate of comorbidity is an artifact of the measures used. Establishing diagnoses in disruptive children requires the collection of data from several sources since the disorder is frequently not visible in the clinician's office. Critical information must be obtained from parents and teachers. The most commonly used assessment tools have been behavior rating scales and clinical interviews.

Behavior rating scales permit the systematic acquisition of information from parents and teachers, and have been a mainstay in the clinical assessment of ADHD children for more than 20 years. Yet, due to halo effects, children with behavior disorders oftentimes are erroneously rated as impaired across symptom domains. Children who are disruptive and defiant are frequently rated by teachers as inattentive and overactive even if they are not (Schachar et al., 1986). Rating scales are likely to indicate the presence of multiple symptoms for most behaviorally disturbed children, regardless of whether these symptoms are truly present. As a result, rating scales are unable to adequately discriminate among distinct, but related psychiatric disorders, and children with disruptive behavior disorders tend to be rated as inattentive, overactive, aggressive, and cognitively impaired, although the coexistence of all of these symptoms in a single child might be infrequent.

The extent to which difficulties similar to those affecting rating scales are present in parent interviews is unclear. However, parent's subjective impressions may be no better for discriminating among these behaviors than teachers. While no studies document the presence of halo effects in clinical interviews, parent reports in the assessment of ADHD have been found to have poor reliability (Rapoport et al., 1986). Consequently, the possibility that selective symptom identification in clinical interview data is inaccurate must be considered. If this were true it might contribute to an artificially inflated rate of comorbid diagnoses within the disruptive behavior disorder domain.

NEUROPSYCHOLOGICAL ASSESSMENT OF ATTENTION

Another approach to identifying symptoms in children is through the use of neuropsychological assessment. This approach provides a more objective assessment of attentional and learning abilities and is far less likely to be susceptible to rater bias and halo effects. Neuropsychological assessments generally include tests of intelligence (e.g., WISC-R), academic achievement, and more specific aspects of linguistic, perceptual/motor, and attentional functioning. Many clinicians and investigators have turned to neuropsychological tests to elicit data which can be helpful in diagnosing ADHD. However, while neuropsychological test data frequently are useful for planning treatment and should not be overlooked as an important source of information, they rarely yield data which help to discriminate ADHD from other related disorders.

The WISC-R is a test of overall intellectual functioning which is an integral part of most child neuropsychological assessments. Factor analytic studies have found that the WISC-R subtests generate orthogonal Verbal, Perceptual Organization, and Freedom from Distractibility factors (Kaufman, 1979). Poor performance on this latter factor, which is comprised of the Arithmetic, Digit Span, and Coding subtests, has frequently been used as an indicator of ADHD. However, the validity of this interpretation is questionable. Several studies have demonstrated that children with learning disabilities perform worse than controls on the Freedom from Distractibility factor, but no study has found this measure to selectively distinguish ADHD children from normal controls (Greenblatt et al., 1991; Rusel, 1974). ADHD children, as a group, score lower than controls on the WISC-R (Halperin and Gittelman, 1982), but no consistent pattern of subtest scores has been found to distinguish them from non-ADHD children. It is unclear whether this factor does not assess attention or whether ADHD children do not uniformly have attentional problems. However, it is of little value for diagnosing ADHD.

Paper and pencil target cancellation tests are also frequently used in the assessment of attention. These tests, which come in a variety of forms, typically require the child to scan a page with letters, numbers, or geometric figures, and cross off as many of the designated targets as possible. Thus, these tests require vigilance, perceptual-motor speed, visual search, and selection. Dependent measures include speed, accuracy, or both. Some data suggest that cancellation test performance may distinguish ADHD children from controls (Aman and Turbott, 1986). Yet, these tests have more consistently been found to distinguish children with learning problems (Rudel et al., 1978). A factor analytic study (Wolf et al., 1987) examining the relationships between various measures of cognitive and attentional functioning suggests that at least some aspects of performance on cancellation tests are more related to performance on perceptual, rather than other attentional measures. Furthermore, preliminary data from our laboratory suggest that cancellation scores are more associated with scores on academic achievement tests than teacher ratings of hyperactivity.

The Matching Familiar Figures Test (MFF) has also been used to distinguish ADHD children from controls. This test of Impulsivity–Reflectivity requires children to perform a matching-to-sample task in which latency to respond and number of errors are measured. Presumably, impulsive children respond quickly, with a high number of errors, while reflective children respond slowly with few errors. The MFF has been shown to distinguish ADHD children from controls, but the data have been inconsistent with regard to which measure appears deviant (for review, see Douglas, 1983). Some studies have found ADHD children to have a shorter response latency while others have found a greater number of errors. Relatively few studies have found ADHD children to differ on both measures, which would suggest greater impulsivity. Furthermore, differences between ADHD children and controls are not specific. A variety of other patient groups, including those with learning problems and conduct disorders have been shown to differ from normal controls on the MFF.

Recently, the continuous performance test (CPT) has been widely used as an objective measure of sustained attention. This test requires the subject to monitor a lengthy series of stimuli and to respond manually whenever a previously designated target stimulus appears. However, the construct validity and diagnostic value of the CPT have remained controversial. Most investigators agree that CPT omission errors reflect deficits in attention, but there is less agreement regarding the meaning of commission errors. Some investigators propose that CPT commission errors reflect impulsivity, but others remain skeptical. Resolution of this issue is important since errors of commission are more prevalent than omission errors in children.

Similar to other purported measures of attention, the CPT has been shown to discriminate several patient populations from normal controls (for review, see Werry et al., 1987). However, its ability to distinguish among distinct patient groups has not been clearly demonstrated. Throughout the past several years, we have done extensive work with the CPT in an attempt to (a) refine the measures generated by the CPT; (b) provide preliminary evidence of construct validity for the measures; and (c) determine the utility of the CPT for defining symptom dimensions which may be used to identify subgroups of ADHD based on patterns of comorbidity.

DIFFERENTIAL ASSESSMENT OF ATTENTION AND IMPULSIVITY

Our experience using the *A-X* CPT, patterned after Rosvold et al. (1956), suggested to us that while many commission errors do indicate impulsive behavior, other psychological processes may be operative. Unlike omission errors, which all occur under similar conditions, commission errors can occur in several different contexts. Specifically, there are four different situations under which a commission error can occur within the *A-X* paradigm: a child may erroneously respond to (1) letters other than *X* following an *A* (A-Not-X error); (2) the letter *A* prior to the onset of the next letter (A-Only error); (3) *X* not preceded by *A* (X-Only error); or (4) letter sequences containing neither *A* nor *X* (Random error).

We hypothesized that CPT commission errors do not comprise a unitary measure that is indicative of a single deficit (e.g., impulsivity), but rather that the different subtypes of commission errors reflect deficits in different psychological processes. Furthermore, we predicted that these differences in underlying psychological processes would be reflected by different reaction times (RT) for the distinct error subtypes. Our hypotheses for the four commission error subtypes were:

1. A-Not-X errors are indicative of impulsivity. Presumably, the subject is primed by the "A" and then responds quickly upon the presentation of the next letter without allowing sufficient time to process its attributes. One would therefore expect these errors to be characterized by relatively fast RTs.

2. A-Only errors also reflect impulsivity or deficits in behavioral inhibition. Again, it is assumed that the subject is primed by the appearance of an "A" and is unable to withhold his response until the next letter appears. This can be considered an extreme form of an A-Not-X error, in which the subject "jumps the gun" and responds prior to the presentation of the next stimulus. It was predicted that this type of error would be characterized by a long RT following the "A," because it reflects some capacity to withhold the response. Although it may be counterintuitive to consider an impulsive error as being slow, we did not believe that this type of error would be due to the child confusing the target stimulus, and thus responding to the "A" instead of the "X." Instead, we believed that despite an effort, the child was not quite able to delay his response until the next letter appeared, thus reflecting impulsivity.

3. X-Only errors reflect inattention to the letter preceding the "X," rather than an impulsive response. This should be reflected by a relatively long RT during which the child is trying to determine whether the preceding letter was an "A."

4. No specific hypothesis was made regarding Random errors because it is less apparent what they indicate. Although the term "Random" is used to classify this error subtype, the statistical concept of randomness is not intended.

CPT commission error subtypes were studied in a heterogeneous sample of child psychiatric patients using a CPT that was programmed to run on a Commodore 64 computer. Twelve letters were presented on a video monitor in a quasirandom sequence for a duration of 200 ms and an interstimulus interval of 1.5 s. The entire task lasted approximately 12 minutes. The number of omission errors, and each of the four types of commission errors, along with RT, were computed. All of the different subtypes of commission errors occurred and were characterized by significantly different RTs as predicted.

Subsequently (Halperin et al., 1988), in a larger sample of nonreferred school children, the error subtype RT findings were replicated. Furthermore, the CPT error subtypes were differentially associated with teacher ratings such that misses and X-Only errors were selectively correlated with ratings of inattention, whereas A-Not-X errors were correlated with ratings of impulsivity, hyperactivity, and conduct problems. A-Only and Random errors were unrelated to teacher ratings of behavior. Thus, the dimensions of inattention and impulsivity could be distinctly assessed using this objective measure.

DISORDERS OF ATTENTION: DISTINCTION BETWEEN DISRUPTIVE DISORDER SUBTYPES

Using these newly developed CPT measures of inattention and impulsivity, along with measures of academic achievement, we attempted to explore the distinctions between behaviorally disturbed subgroups of children based upon patterns of comorbidity (Halperin et al., 1990a). A sample of 85 nonreferred school children, the majority of whom were from the previous study evaluating the error subtypes, was divided into four groups using the Inattention/Overactivity (I/O) and Aggression (A) scales of the IOWA Conners Teacher Rating Scale (Loney and Milich, 1982). The "Pure ADHD" group consisted of children with high I/O and low A ratings; the "Pure CD" group consisted of children with high A and low I/O ratings; the "Mixed ADHD/CD" group was comprised of children with high scores on both scales; and controls had low ratings on both scales.

The pure ADHD group was found to be significantly more inattentive than all other groups and the ADHD/CD group was found to be significantly more impulsive than the CD and Control groups. The CD group did not differ from controls on any CPT measure. Although there were no significant group differences on either measure of academic achievement, there was a trend for the ADHD group to have lower reading scores.

These data indicate that many children who receive high scores on teacher rating scales, consistent with ADHD, are not inattentive as measured by the CPT. Furthermore, they suggest a dissociation between inattention and aggressive (or disruptive) behavior in children, and raise the possibility that children can receive ratings consistent with ADHD by being *either* inattentive *or* disruptive, while relatively few children are *both* inattentive *and* disruptive.

To further explore the relationship of objectively assessed inattention to ADHD, a new sample of 72 nonreferred children was divided into two groups based on teacher's ratings of *DSM-III-R* symptoms for ADHD (Halperin et al., 1990b). Children with at least 8 of the 14 ADHD symptoms were entered into the ADHD group. Those with 4 or fewer symptoms were placed in the control group. Children rated as having 5–7 ADHD symptoms were eliminated from the study in order to achieve separation of ADHD and control groups. Children were further divided into objectively assessed inattentive and noninattentive groups on the basis of their CPT performance. Additionally, each child was rated using the Conners Teacher (CTQ) and Parent (CPQ) Questionnaires (Goyette et al., 1978) and tested using the WISC-R.

Among the ADHD group, 47.4% were inattentive according to the CPT, as compared with 13.6% of the controls (Chi Square = 6.57, $p = .01$). Thus, significantly more ADHD children than controls were objectively assessed as inattentive, but about half of the ADHD children were not found to be inattentive.

Two-way (ADHD X CPT-Inattention) analyses of variance were conducted examining the relationships of ADHD and objectively assessed inattention to behavioral and cognitive functioning. As expected, the ADHD children were rated significantly higher than controls on all factors of the CTQ, and on the Conduct Problems, Impulsivity/Hyperactivity, and Learning Problems factors of the CPQ. However, in addition to these main effects, significant ADHD X Inattention interactions were found selectively for the Conduct Problems factors of both the CTQ and CPQ. On the CTQ, the noninattentive ADHD group was rated significantly higher than the inattentive ADHD group, and on the CPQ, only noninattentive ADHD children were rated as having more conduct problems than controls. With regard to cognitive functioning, there was a trend ($p < .10$) for an ADHD X Inattention interaction such that the inattentive ADHD group had a lower WISC-R FSIQ than the three other groups.

These data are consistent with recent findings of August and Garfinkel (1989), and suggest that ADHD children do not constitute a homogeneous group with regard to attentional dysfunction. Furthermore, comorbid groups of ADHD + CD/ODD may not have the same presenting features as children with "pure" ADHD; the comorbid group may not be inattentive. Thus, there appears to be distinct subgroups of inattentive/cognitively impaired and impulsive/aggressive ADHD children. Objectively determined inattentive ADHD children were found to have low IQ scores, while noninattentive ADHD children were rated as aggressive. These findings were specific for the role of objectively assessed inattention among ADHD children; inattentive and noninattentive control children did not differ on measures of cognitive or behavioral functioning.

These findings were derived from teacher-rated samples; consequently, their applicability to clinically diagnosed ADHD children remains to be demonstrated. Furthermore, the question of whether motor overactivity selectively contributes to elevated ratings of disruptive behavior in noninattentive ADHD children cannot be answered at this time.

ADHD WITH AND WITHOUT COMORBID DISORDERS OF CONDUCT: POSSIBLE NEUROBIOLOGICAL DISTINCTIONS AND IMPLICATIONS FOR METHYLPHENIDATE TREATMENT

The data presented thus far provide preliminary evidence to suggest that ADHD children with and without disruptive behavior problems may comprise distinct inattentive/cognitively impaired (IN/CI) and impulsive/ aggressive (IMP/AGG) subgroups, and challenge the conventional definition of comorbidity in these children. Emerging literature suggesting that IN/CI children have noradrenergic (NE) dysfunction, whereas IMP/AGG children have a disorder mediated by serotonin [5-hydroxytryptamine (5-HT)], lend further credence to the neuropsychologically determined subgroups.

Support for the broader NE hypothesis of ADHD, in varying degrees, is obtained from three lines of research; animal models of inattention, clinical psychopharmacological data, and studies examining the metabolites of NE. Yet, a closer examination of those data raise the possibility that only a subgroup of ADHD children, those with significant inattention, may have NE deficits.

The strongest support for the NE hypothesis of ADHD comes from pharmacologic data which indicate that virtually all medications that are efficacious in ADHD children affect NE transmission and metabolism. The most commonly used medications, methylphenidate and dextroamphetamine, both have primary effects upon central NE mechanisms. Similarly, the NE-mediated tricyclic antidepressants, imipramine and desipramine, and the NE-enhancing monoamine oxidase (MAO) inhibitors, clorgyline and tranylcypromine, significantly improve attention and behavior in ADHD children. However, deprenyl, a selective MAO-B inhibitor, which has little effect on central NE, appears to have little therapeutic effect (for review, see Zametkin and Rapoport, 1987).

Despite the fact that a large literature has consistently demonstrated that 70 to 80% of ADHD children have a positive response to stimulant medication, the magnitude of response is quite variable. In a sample of 38 ADHD children treated with methylphenidate, 78% showed significantly improved behavior ratings. However, only 53% improved sufficiently to no longer meet diagnostic criteria for the study at the conclusion of treatment (Halperin et al., 1986). Thus, a large proportion of ADHD children improve with stimulant therapy, but only about half have a true remission of symptoms. This raises the question as to whether some ADHD children respond to stimulant medication in a nonspecific manner, similar to normals (Rapoport et al., 1980), while others have substantially greater improvement. Furthermore, a large proportion of ADHD children have a poor long-term outcome despite apparent "successful" treatment during childhood (Gittelman et al., 1985).

Similarly, studies examining NE metabolites provide only minimal support for a unitary NE hypothesis of ADHD, but may support the distinction of two ADHD subtypes. Data comparing urinary 3-methoxy-4-hydroxyphenethyleneglycol (MHPG), the major metabolite of NE, in ADHD and normal children have yielded inconsistent results (for review, see Zametkin and Rapoport, 1987); some studies report decreased MHPG, some report no difference, and one study found increased MHPG in ADHD children. These inconsistent findings may be due to either methodological difficulties or the heterogeneity of the ADHD group.

A shortcoming in the methodology involves the use of a short washout period. Stimulant treatment in ADHD children decreases urinary MHPG excretion for at least two weeks after medication is discontinued (Zametkin et al., 1985). Yet, in most of these studies, children received a washout period of two weeks or less. Therefore, reductions (or lack of a difference) in MHPG may have been due to prior drug use. It is notable that the only study (Khan and Dekirmenjian, 1981) to find increased MHPG in ADHD children used a longer, three-week washout period.

The lack of consistent findings may also be due to heterogeneity among samples of ADHD children. Those studies (Khan and Dekirmenjian, 1981; Shekim et al., 1979) that present individual MHPG data highlight the distinctions among ADHD children. In each, about half of the ADHD children had MHPG levels substantially higher than controls, while half had substantially lower levels. These data suggest the presence of two distinct ADHD subgroups with regard to NE function.

Although studies examining the relationship between central NE systems and ADHD have yielded conflicting findings, data associating central NE to inattention have been more consistent. Several animal models of inattention have been developed through the use of hindbrain lesions, which selectively deplete forebrain NE (Aston-Jones, 1985). Furthermore, among adults with Parkinson's disease, elevated CSF MHPG levels are associated with CPT-measured inattention (Stern et al., 1984), and among ADHD children, those with the greatest cognitive deficits have been found to have higher MHPG levels (Shekim et al., 1987). Finally, in ADHD children, the magnitude of clinical improvement following treatment with some noradrenergically mediated drugs is correlated with the magnitude of MHPG reduction (for review, see Shekim et al., 1979; Zametkin and Rapoport, 1987). Therefore, it appears as though high MHPG may be associated with inattention, but not necessarily the diagnosis of ADHD, and that reductions in MHPG may be predictive of clinical response.

In contrast, central 5-HT mechanisms have been associated with physical aggression and impulsiveness in adults (Brown et al., 1982; Coccaro et al., 1989), and animal data strongly suggest that diminished 5-HT activity is related to aggressive behavior (Soubrie, 1986). The role of central 5-HT mechanisms in child behavior disorders has been less extensively studied. In ADHD children, some studies have reported decreased blood levels of 5-HT (Bhagauan et al., 1975; Coleman, 1971), but others have been unable to replicate these findings (Irwin et al., 1981). Furthermore, several studies have failed to find differences in urinary 5-hydroxyindoleacetic acid (5-HIAA) between ADHD children and controls. However, decreased CSF 5-HIAA was associated with aggression in a sample of boys with disruptive disorders (Rapoport et al., 1990) and was found in a sample of aggressive impulsive adults, all of whom had CD in childhood (Brown et al., 1982). Additionally, reduced [^{3}H]imipramine binding sites, a putative index of presynaptic 5-HT activity, was found in a sample of children all of whom had mixed CD + ADHD diagnoses (Stoff et al., 1987), but not in "pure" ADHD children (Weizman et al., 1988). Finally, among ADHD children, there was a trend for those who were most aggressive to have a decreased prolactin response to treatment with fenfluramine, which appears to be an index of overall central 5-HT function (Donnelly et al., 1989). Therefore, central 5-HT dysfunction may be specific to a subgroup of ADHD children characterized by aggressive behavior.

Overall, these findings suggest a dissociation such that central 5-HT mechanisms are more related to childhood and adult aggressive behaviors, while NE dysregulation may be more associated with inattention. Since children rated as having ADHD and conduct problems appear to be aggressive but not inattentive, and "pure" ADHD children appear inattentive but not aggressive, it is possible that pure ADHD children would have a greater response to NE-mediated drugs, whereas the comorbid group may be more responsive to serotonergically mediated medications.

This dissociation of pharmacological effects has not yet been thoroughly investigated. While ADHD children have variable response to methylphenidate, the predictors of positive response are unclear. Aggressive and nonaggressive ADHD children do not appear to differ in their response to methylphenidate (Barkley et al., 1989; Korman et al., 1988). However, Ritalin affects both NE and 5-HT mechanisms. Fenfluramine, a potent serotonergic agonist, has been found to have little effect in ADHD children (Donnelly et al., 1989). Yet, this finding does not refute the serotonergic hypothesis since chronic treatment with fenfluramine decreases stores and turnover of 5-HT, thus resulting in a net reduction, rather than facilitation of 5-HT function.

TOWARD A RECONCEPTUALIZATION OF THE ADHD DIAGNOSIS

In summary, we have described ongoing research which uses the CPT to further our understanding of the relationship between the objectively measured symptom of inattention and the diagnostic entity of ADHD. The data indicate that the CPT can be used to delineate symptoms of inattention and impulsivity in children, which can then be used as a means of syndrome definition and, potentially, as a means of assessing the differential effects of various treatment interventions in distinct diagnostic groups. Taken together, our findings challenge the notion that ADHD children comprise a unitary group whose central deficit may be inattention. Furthermore, they suggest that there may be two meaningful subgroups of ADHD children. One group appears to be characterized primarily by inattention and cognitive problems, while the other is characterized more by aggression or conduct problems, in the absence of significant inattention or cognitive dysfunction. We are conducting further research both with the CPT and other neuropsychological and neurobiological measures to determine whether these two groups truly comprise distinct and divergently valid diagnostic entities.

REFERENCES

Aman, M.G. & Turbott, S.H. (1986), Incidental learning, distraction and sustained attention in hyperactive and control subjects. *J. Abnorm. Child Psychol.*, 14:441–455.

American Psychiatric Association (1980), *Diagnostic and Statistical Manual of Mental Disorders*, 3rd Ed. Washington, DC: American Psychiatric Association.

——— (1987), *Diagnostic and Statistical Manual of Mental Disorders* 3rd Ed. Rev. Washington, DC: American Psychiatric Association.

Anderson, J., Williams, S., McGee, R. & Silva, P. (1987), DSM-III disorders in pre-adolescent children. *Arch. Gen. Psychiatry*, 44:69–76.

Aston-Jones, G. (1985), Behavioral functions of the locus coeruleus derived from cellular attributes. *Physiol. Psychol.*, 13:118–126.

August, G.J. & Garfinkel, B.D. (1989), Behavioral and cognitive subtypes of ADHD. *J. Am. Acad. Child Adolesc. Psychiatry*, 28:739–748.

Barkley, R.A. (1977), A review of stimulant drug research with hyperactive children. *J. Child Psychol. Psychiatry*, 18:137–165.

———McMurray, M.B., Edelbrock, C.S. & Robbins, K. (1989), The response of aggressive and nonaggressive ADHD children to two doses of methylphenidate. *J. Am. Acad. Child Adolesc. Psychiatry*, 28:873–881.

Bhagauan, H.N., Coleman, M. & Coursina, D.B. (1975), The effect of pyridoxine hydrochloride on blood serotonin and pyridoxal phosphate contents in hyperactive children. *Pediatrics*, 55:437–441.

Biederman, J., Munir, K., Knee, D. et al. (1987), High rate of affective disorders in probands with attention deficit disorder and in their relatives: a controlled family study. *Am. J. Psychiatry*, 144:330–333.

Brown, G.L., Ebert, M.H., Goyer, P.F. et al. (1982), Aggression, suicide, and serotonin: relationships to CSF amine metabolites. *Am. J. Psychiatry*, 139:741–746.

Coccaro, E.F., Siever, L.J., Klar, H. et al. (1989), Serotonergic studies of personality disorder: Correlates with behavioral aggression and impulsivity. *Arch. Gen. Psychiatry*, 46:587–599.

Coleman, M. (1971), Serotonin concentrations in whole blood of hyperactive children. *J. Pediatr.*, 78:985–990.

Donnelly, M, Rapoport, J.L, Potter, W. et al. (1989), Fenfluramine and dextroamphetamine treatment of childhood hyperactivity. *Arch. Gen. Psychiatry*, 46:205–212.

Douglas, V.I. (1983), Attentional and cognitive problems. In: *Developmental Neuropsychiatry*, ed. M. Rutter. New York: Guilford Press, pp. 280–329.

Gittelman, R., Mannuzza, S., Shenker, R. et al. (1985), Hyperactive boys almost grown up I. Psychiatric status. *Arch. Gen. Psychiatry*, 42:937–947.

Goyette, C.H., Conners, C.K. and Ulrich, R.F. (1978), Normative data on revised Conners parent and teacher rating scales. *J. Abnorm. Child Psychol.*, 6:221–236.

Greenblatt, E., Mattis, S. & Trad, P.V. (in press), The ACID pattern and the freedom from distractibility factor in a child psychiatric population. *Dev. Neuropsychol.*

Halperin, J.M. & Gittelman, R. (1982), Do hyperactive children and their siblings differ in IQ and academic achievement? *Psychiatr. Res.*, 6:253–258.

———— ———— Katz, S. & Struve, F.A. (1986), Relationship between stimulant effect, electroencephalogram, and clinical neurological findings in hyperactive children. *J. Am. Acad. Child Psychiatry,* 25:820–825.

———— Wolf, L.E., Pascualvaca, D.M. et al. (1988), Differential assessment of attention and impulsivity in children. *J. Am. Acad. Child Adolesc. Psychiatry,* 27:326–329.

———— O'Brien, J.D., Newcorn, J.H. et al. (1990a), Validation of hyperactive, aggressive, and mixed hyperactive/aggressive childhood disorders. *J. Child Psychol. Psychiatry,* 31:455–459.

————Newcorn, J.H., Sharma, V. et al. (1990b), Inattentive and non-inattentive ADHD children: Do they comprise a unitary group? *J. Abnorm. Child Psychol.,* 18:437–449.

Hinshaw, S.P. (1987), On the distinction between attention deficits/hyperactivity and conduct problems/aggression in child psychopathology. *Psychol. Bull.,* 101:443–463.

Holborow, P.L. & Berry, P.S. (1986), Hyperactivity and learning disabilities. *J. Learn. Disabil.,* 19:426–431.

Irwin, M., Bedendink, K., McCloskay, K. & Freedman, D.X. (1981), Tryptophan metabolism with attention deficit disorder. *Am. J. Psychiatry,* 138:1082–1085.

Kaufman, A. (1979), *Intelligent Testing With the WISC-R.* New York: Wiley.

Khan, A. U. and DeKirmenjian, H. (1981), Urinary excretion of catecholamine metabolites in hyperkinetic child syndrome. *Am. J. Psychiatry,* 138:108–12.

Klorman, R., Brumaghim, J.T., Salzman, L.F. et al. (1988), Effects of methylphenidate on attention-deficit disorder with and without aggressive/noncompliant features. *J. Abnorm. Psychol.,* 97:413–422.

Koriath, U., Gualtieri, C.T., Van Bourgondien, M.E. et al. (1985), Construct validity of clinical diagnosis in pediatric psychiatry: Relationship among measures. *J. Am. Acad. Child Adolesc. Psychiatry,* 24:429–436.

Loney, J. & Milich, R. (1982), Hyperactivity, inattention, and aggression in clinical practice. *Adv. Dev. Behav. Pediatr.,* 3:113–147.

Munir, K., Biederman, J. & Knee, D. (1987), Psychiatric comorbidity in patients with attention deficit disorder: A controlled study. *J. Am. Acad. Child Adolesc. Psychiatry,* 6:844–848.

Newcorn, J., Halperin, J.M., Healey, J.M. et al. (1989), Are attention deficit disorder with hyperactivity and attention-deficit hyperactivity disorder the same or different? *J. Am. Acad. Child Adolesc. Psychiatry,* 28:734–738.

Prior, M. & Sanson, A. (1986), Attention deficit disorder with hyperactivity: a critique. *J. Child Psychol. Psychiatry* 27:307–319.

Rapoport, J.L., Buchsbaum, M.S., Weingartner, H. et al. (1980), Dextroamphetamine: Cognitive and behavioral effects in normal and hyperactive boys and normal men. *Arch. Gen. Psychiatry,* 37:933–943.

———— Donnelly, M., Zametkin, A. & Carrougher, J. (1986), Situational hyperactivity in a U.S. clinical setting. *J. Child Psychol. Psychiatry,* 27:639–646.

———— Hamburger, S., Hibbs, E. et al. (1990), Cerebrospinal fluid monoamine metabolites, aggression, and impulsivity in disruptive behavior disorders of children and adolescents. *Arch. Gen. Psychiatry,* 47:419–426.

Rosvold, H.E., Mirsky, A.F., Sarason, I. et al. (1956), A continuous performance test of brain damage. *J. Consult. Psychol.,* 20:343–350.

Rudel, R.G., Denckla, M.B. & Broman, M. (1978). Rapid silent response to repeated target symbols by dyslexic and nondyslexic children. *Brain Language,* 6:52–62.

Rugel, R.P. (1974), WISC subtest scores of disabled readers: A review with respect to Bannatyne's recategorization. *J. Learn. Diabil.,* 7:48–55.

Schachar, R., Sandberg, S. & Rutter, M. (1986), Agreement between teacher ratings and observations of hyperactivity, inattentiveness, and defiance. *J. Abnorm. Child Psychol.,* 14:331–345.

Shekim, W.O., Dekirmenjian, H. & Chapel, J.L. (1979), Urinary MHPG in minimal brain dysfunction and its modification by d-amphetamine. *Am. J. Psychiatry,* 136:667–671.

———— Sinclair, E., Glaser, R. et al. (1987), Norepinephrine and dopamine metabolites and educational variables in boys with attention deficit disorder and hyperactivity. *J. Child Neurol.*, 2, 50–56.

Soubrie, P. (1986), Reconciling the role of central serotonin neurons in human and animal behavior. *Behav. Brain Sci.*, 9:319–364.

Stern, Y., Mayeux, R. & Cote, L. (1984), Reaction time and vigilance in parkinson's disease: possible role of altered norepinephrine metabolism. *Arch. Neurol.*, 41:1086–1089.

Stoff, D.M., Pollack, L., & Vitiello, B. et al. (1987), Reduction of ^{3}H-imipramine binding sites on platelets of conduct disordered children. *Neuropsychopharmacology*, 1:55–62.

Szatmari, P., Offord, D.R. & Boyle, M.H. (1989), Ontario child health study: Prevalence of attention deficit disorder with hyperactivity. *J. Child Psychol. Psychiatry*, 30:219–230.

Weiss, G., Hechtman, L., Milroy, T. & Perlman, T. (1985), Psychiatric status of hyperactives as adults: A controlled prospective 15 year follow-up of 63 hyperactive children. *J. Am. Acad. Child Adolesc. Psychiatry*, 24:211–220.

Weizman, A., Bernhout, E., Weitz, R. et al. (1988), Imipramine binding to platelets of children with attention deficit disorder with hyperactivity. *Biol. Psychiatry*, 23:491–496.

Werry, J.S., Reeves, J.C. & Elkind, G.S. (1987), Attention deficit, conduct, oppositional and anxiety disorders in children: I. A review of research on differentiating characteristics. *J. Am. Acad. Child Adolesc. Psychiatry*, 26:133–143.

Wolf, L.E. & Halperin, J.M. (1987), Assessment of attention in psychiatrically disturbed children: What are we really measuring? *J. Clin. Exp. Neuropsychol.*, 9:61.

Zametkin, A.J. & Rapoport, J.L. (1987), Noradrenergic hypothesis of attention deficit disorder with hyperactivity: A critical review. In: *Psychopharmacology: The Third Generation of Progress*, ed. H.Y. Meltzer., New York: Raven Press, pp. 837–842.

———— ———— Murphy, D.L. et al. (1985), Treatment of hyperactive children with monoamine oxidase inhibitors. *Arch. Gen. Psychiatry*, 42:969–973.

Pharmacological Treatment of Attention Deficit Disorder, Residual Type (ADD-RT) in Adults

PAUL H. WENDER, DAVID R. WOOD, and FRED W. REIMHERR

INTRODUCTION

The theme of this book is to provide a broad overview of the use of methylphenidate in psychiatric disorders. This chapter deals not with this topic but with the use of methylphenidate and other drugs in the treatment of attention deficit disorder, residual type (attention deficit hyperactivity disorder in adulthood). Until fairly recently it was believed that the "hyperactive child syndrome" or minimal brain dysfunction" was outgrown by adolescence. A number of studies employing different methodologies have clearly demonstrated that not only may ADHD persist, but that it may do so to an appreciable degree in perhaps one-third to two-thirds of instances.

The quest for an ideal drug for the treatment of attention deficit disorder (ADD), namely, one which is relatively long-acting and nonabusable, has led the present investigators over the past 9 years to conduct a number of placebo-controlled and open trials of amino acid precursors, stimulants, and monoamine oxidase inhibitors (MAOI) in adults (over 21, mean age approximately 30 years) with attention deficit disorder, residual type (ADD-RT). (The amino acid trials were administered as pharmacological probes to investigate the "biochemical" lesion in ADD-RT and will not be discussed here.) Although these drug trials have been conducted on adults only, they are potentially relevant to the other two types of ADD subjects, namely, children and adolescents: first, because the ethical problems of testing experimental drugs on children and adolescents necessitate pretesting on consenting adults; and, second, because one issue in the drug treatment of adolescents with ADD has been whether or not they respond differently—particularly to the stimulant drugs—from younger, preadolescent, children. Clearly, if the adult response is similar to that seen in children, it may be inferred that adolescents (i.e., an intermediate age group) will respond similarly.

DIAGNOSTIC CRITERIA

Before any testing could be undertaken, it was imperative to determine if the potential subject would have qualified for a diagnosis of ADD in childhood; that is, whether or not he/she had been a "hyperactive" child. Since virtually no subject had been so diagnosed, it was necessary to establish a retrospective diagnosis. If the adult in question had a good memory and adequate "outsight," it was possible to ask about the specific signs and symptoms listed in the *Diagnostic and Statistical Manual–3rd Ed.* (*DSM-III*). If not—as in many cases—the "broad" criteria listed in Part I of the Utah Criteria (Appendix A) were used, along with two specific questionnaires, designated the Wender Utah Rating Instrument. (It may be useful to note that the diagnostic criteria and techniques described above may be applicable to the previously unevaluated adolescent as well as to adults.)

University of Utah College of Medicine, Salt Lake City, Utah
Some of the relevant studies are referred in Wender (1981) and Wender (1985) and a review by Cantwell (1985). This chapter was originally published in the *Psychopharmacology Bulletin* (Vol. 21, No. 2, pp. 222–231, 1985). Bibliographies are from this chapter and from that of Cantwell's (Vol. 21, No. 2, 251–257, 1985), the latter provides a review of studies documenting the persistence of ADHD from childhood.

The first of these two questionnaires is the Parents' Rating Scale (PRS) (Appendix B) which is, in fact, the Conners' Abbreviated Teachers' Rating Scale, a standard brief instrument which has been widely used in epidemiological studies and drug studies in children (Conners, 1969, 1972). In the present studies, the adult subject's mother (rather than his teacher) was asked to complete the questionnaire regarding her offspring's behavior between the ages of 6 and 10. Normative data were obtained on a population of ostensibly normal mothers and fathers—the parents of normal school children—by requesting the grandparents of those children to fill out the same instrument describing the parents as they had been between the ages of 6 and 10. There are 10 items on the PRS, each scored from 0 to 3, so that a minimum summed score is 0 and a maximum score is 30. In our ostensibly normal population a score of 12 or greater places an individual in the 95th or higher percentile of childhood "hyperactivity." Obviously, the PRS requires the presence of a cooperative mother and, since cooperative mothers are not always available, a self-rating instrument was devised: the Adult Questionnaire Childhood Characteristics, in which the propsective subject describes him- or herself as a child. Normative data have also been obtained for this questionnaire and an item analysis is in progress, so that means for the normative and patient groups should soon be available. Although the questionnaire does have face validity and can be used clinically to see if an individual perceives himself as having been an ADD child, in our recent drug studies the presence of an able and willing mother to fill out the PRS has been required, for it has been found that this instrument—as will be discussed presently—is of some predictive value in drug trials. In addition to these techniques for retrospectively diagnosing ADD in childhood, we have modified the *DSM-III* criteria for ADD-RT: *DSM-III* states that in ADD-RT "signs of hyperactivity are no longer present, but other signs of the illness have persisted . . . as evidenced by signs of both attentional deficit and impulsivity." The Utah Criteria, on the other hand, require the presence of both attentional deficits and hyperactivity and two of the following signs or symptoms: affective lability, impulsivity (also required by *DSM-III,* as noted above), hot temper (as opposed to the brooding anger seen in some major depressives and borderline personality disorders—among others), disorganization, and sensitivity to stress. The Utah Criteria's additional signs and symptoms ensure a more certain diagnosis. A fuller description of these characteristics is found in Appendix A.

DRUG TRIALS

Stimulants

The first study was an open (15 patients) and a placebo-controlled pilot study of methylphenidate in 11 patients with ADD-RT (Wood et al., 1976) (see Table 1). Methylphenidate produced a statistically significant therapeutic effect on the target symptoms of "nervousness, poor concentration, fatigue, and hot temper. At followup of up to 10 months, the 10 of the 15 responders who showed a moderate-to-good response continued to do so. In other words, there was no development of tolerance to stimulants, which is analogous to the response of children with ADD, and different from that of stimulant abusers. A possible critical interpretation of the study was immediately apparent: To wit, it could be charged that a heterogeneous group of unhappy people–patients with psychological nonspecifitis—had been given a euphoria-producing drug

TABLE 1. PILOT STUDY (METHYLPHENIDATE):
TREATMENT OUTCOME (90 DAYS OR LONGER
ON STIMULANT)

Physicians' Global Rating	N
+3	8
+2	2
+1	4
≤0	1

TABLE 2. PEMOLINE STUDY TREATMENT
OUTCOME (N = 48)

	Physicians' Global Rating	
	Pemoline (N = 26)	Placebo (N = 22)
+3	6	4
+2	4	3
+1	7	3
≤0	9	12

and that it could be predicted that any euphorogenic agent might have elicited the same positive results. In other words, the possibility existed that the beneficial effect of methylphenidate was nonselective for ADD-RT.

In order to obviate such strictures, the next study was designed to test pemoline (Cylert), a stimulant drug reported to be equal in efficacy to the standard therapeutic medications D-amphetamine and methylphenidate) for "hyperactive" children, which, however, has the advantage of being noneuphorogenic. Forty-eight subjects participated in this study, which was a random assignment, parallel, double-blind, placebo-controlled trial of pemoline (Wender et al., 1981). The trial lasted 6 weeks and, although patients were assessed by a number of measures, it will suffice here simply to report the doctors' global judgments. These were scored on a +3 to −3 scale with 3 representing a marked change, 2 a moderate change, and 1 a slight change. The overall results, shown in Table 2, were negative. There were no statistical differences between patients receiving placebo and those receiving pemoline when the PRS was not taken into account. When the patients were dichotomized into those with a PRS score greater than or equal to 12 (which placed them in the 95th or higher percentile of childhood "hyperactivity") and those with PRS scores less than 12, responses to medication appeared. The outcome for the 21 subjects with PRS scores less than 12 is shown in Table 3. There were no significant differences in outcome between those patients receiving placebo. The same was not the case for the subjects rated as hyperactives by the PRS (Table 4). Of the 27 subjects with a PRS greater than or equal to 12, 18 received pemoline and 8 of these (44%) manifested a moderate to marked therapeutic response, as opposed to 1 of the 8 (12%) receiving placebo. For the subjects with PRS scores greater than or equal to 12, pemoline was statistically significantly more effective than placebo (t test), $p < .025$). The data obtained suggested that a beneficial response is not dependent upon euphorogenic drug activity and that the PRS is a reliable tool for the identification of "hyperactive" adults who respond favorably to stimulant medication.

There are some clinical aspects of treatment with pemoline that should be considered. The mean dose was 65 mg/day, but in many subjects treatment had to be initiated at a very low dose—one half of the smallest available tablet (18.75 mg)—because, even in low doses, the drug produced agitation (likened by some

TABLE 3. PEMOLINE STUDY: TREATMENT OUTCOME
NOT "HYPERACTIVE" IN CHILDHOOD
(PRS < 12)

	Physicians' Global Rating	
	Pemoline (N = 8)	Placebo (N = 13)
+3	1	4
+2	1	2
+1	4	3
≤0	2	4

TABLE 4. PEMOLINE STUDY: TREATMENT OUTCOME
"TRUE HYPERACTIVES" (PRS $\geq$ 12)

	Physicians' Global Rating	
	Pemoline (N = 18)	Placebo (N = 9)
+3	5	0
+2	3	1
+1	3	0
$\leq$0	7	8

subjects to hypercaffeination), headaches, stomachaches, and insomnia. Over a period of time, some patients developed a tolerance to these side effects and the dose could then gradually be increased. A number of these patients then began to show a therapeutic response.

Although sometimes a period of a few weeks was required, it was impossible to determine whether the delayed response was a true latency—as seen with the tricyclic antidepressants—or whether it was simply a function of the time required to build the dose up to the therapeutic level. The two variables were not susceptible to clarification. Because of the time lapse and the drug's unpleasant side effects, it was difficult to work with pemoline. Another difficulty was the necessity of submitting the patient to periodic laboratory tests. Of those patients treated with pemoline, 2 to 3% are reported to develop abnormalities of liver enzymes, so that frequent checks are mandatory. This requirement contrasts sharply with the few precautions necessary with the "standard" stimulant drugs, D-amphetamine and methylphenidate, which are remarkably free of serious toxic reactions. Indeed, in the course of the above study, one subject receiving pemoline experienced a large dip in the number of his polymorphonuclear leukocytes, a condition which took 6 months to reverse itself.

Because of the problems associated with the use of pemoline, the drug is of limited value in the treatment of ADD-RT; therefore, the next study was designed to subject methylphenidate to a more rigorous clinical evaluation than was the earlier pilot study. For this purpose, a double-blind, random assignment crossover trial of methylphenidate and placebo was undertaken (Wender et al., 1985). The efficacy was similar to that of pemoline; 57% of subjects manifested a moderate to marked therapeutic response on methylphenidate, and 11% on placebo, a difference that was statistically significant (t test, $p < .005$) (Table 5). From a clinical standpoint, when the correct dose was reached, the therapeutic response was immediate. Dosage levels and side effects were similar to those seen in children. The average daily amount of methylphenidate was approximately 40 mg/day, which most subjects required in three divided doses (tid). Several of the subjects felt that tid administration was inadequate because they found the duration of action to be on the order of 1.5 to 2 h. Too high a dose of methylphenidate produced irritability in some subjects and excessive sedation in others, which may be similar to the effect seen in those children receiving too much methylphenidate who are reported to be "zombies." Again, side effects were similar to those seen in children and included irritability, anxiety, and insomnia. Although methylphenidate was a much easier drug to work

TABLE 5. SECOND METHYLPHENIDATE STUDY:
TREATMENT OUTCOME

	Methylphenidate	Placebo
+3	14	4
+2	6	1
+1	4	7
0	9	16
$\leq$-1	4	9

with than was pemoline, its major disadvantage was its short duration of action and the need for multiple doses. Whether or not this handicap can be overcome by the use of the slow-release form remains to be determined.

No controlled trials of D-amphetamine have been conducted, but it has been tried on several pemoline- or methylphenidate-responsive subjects. In the doses employed (not over 30 mg/day) it was found that the drug does not produce euphoria. One advantage over methylphenidate is amphetamine's longer duration of action. Additionally, D-amphetamine is produced in a slow-release form which, when effective, allows patients to take just one dose a day. Some patients, however, cannot tolerate this form: In some, it appears that a large bolus of medication is released initially and causes the side effects of too much D-amphetamine; others find that its longer duration of action (over 12 h) produces insomnia.

Monoamine oxidase inhibitors

Both theoretical and practical reasons entered into the decision to try to MAOIs in the treatment of ADD-RT. The practical reason is that the stimulant drugs are shortlived and abusable. Medication that works 24 hours a day is much to be desired. Many ADD-RT subjects have hair-trigger tempers and have engaged in physical fights or self-damaging impulsive acts after their evening dose has worn off and prior to their morning dose. Additionally, a drug that is not abusable either in the ADD-RT population or among others would be ideal; moreover, the sale of prescribed stimulants by our subjects is a potential hazard.

The theoretical reason for drug trials with MAOIs is that, in some respects, ADD resembles a dopamine or phenethylamine (PEA) deficiency disease (i.e., a functional underactivity of dopaminergic and/or PEAergic systems). A response to certain MAOIs would support this hypothesis. [The rationale for this hypothesis has been explained elsewhere (Wender, 1978).] Monoamine oxidase (MAO) occurs in at least two forms, MAO-A and MAO-B. Norepinephrine and serotonin are the preferred substrates of MAO-A while MAO-B is specific to dopamine and PEA. If the dopaminergic and/or PEAergic hypothesis is correct, a MAO-B inhibitor should prove therapeutically useful. All but one of the marketed MAOIs are mixed, that is, they inhibit both MAO-A and MAO-B. The one exception is pargyline (Eutonyl), developed as an antidepressant and marketed as an antihypertensive. In low doses pargyline appears to be a specific MAO-B inhibitor. In an open trial of pargyline (Wender et al., 1983) it was found that the dosage used had to be considerably lower than that recommended for the treatment of hypertension (75 to 150 mg/day). Our subjects often needed and could tolerate doses of only 20 to 30 mg/day. If the dose was increased too rapidly, even 30 mg/day might produce unpleasant orthostatic hypotension. The latency to therapeutic responsiveness with pargyline in patients with ADD-RT was similar to that described with other MAOIs in patients with depression. It took 2 to 4 weeks for a therapeutic effect to appear and, in responding subjects, continued improvement was seen for several weeks after that time. The initial effects included stimulation (which was not therapeutic) and insomnia. Times of administration had to be adjusted to allow patients to be awake and asleep when they wanted to be. Of the 22 subjects entered in the study, 6 dropped out because of side effects. The median dose was 30 mg/day with a range of 10 to 50 mg/day. The outcome is shown in Table 6. Among the 16 completers, 68% manifested a moderate to marked therapeutic response. All subjects were informed of the "cheese" effect and given a list of prescribed foods. Hypertension was not a problem. Other side effects were: orthostatic hypotension and lightheadedness, 9 (severe in 3); headache, 8; sleep disruption, 7; loss of

TABLE 6. PARGYLINE STUDY: TREATMENT
OUTCOME (N = 16)

Physicians' Global Rating	N
+3	4
+2	7
+1	2
≤0	3

libido, 5; agitation and restlessness, 5; appetite loss, 4 (with a weight loss of 14 pounds in 1 patient); difficulty with urination, 3; anorgasmia, 3; ejaculatory difficulty, 2; confusion, tremor, irritability, fatigue, gastric distress, myoclonic spasms, daytime sleepiness, and skin rash, 1. Of the 6 noncompleters, 3 dropped out because of hypotension, 2 because of impotence, and 1 because of a skin rash (diffuse dermatitis).

Finally, we report on an open study of another MAO-B inhibitor, L-deprenyl, now marketed in the U.S. for one treatment of Parkinson's syndrome. In low doses this drug is not associated with the "cheese" effect and does not produce serious hypotension. With the exception of the latter effect, it was similar to pargyline in our experience; however, it usually was therapeutic only in larger doses (30 mg/day)—which are associated with a "cheese" effect—so that its particular benefit would be the apparent absence of hypotension. Of 11 patients, one dropped out after two weeks because of a lack of therapeutic effect and another because of the reappearance of migraine headaches which he had not experienced in five years (and which reappeared again following discontinuation and challenge with deprenyl). Of the 9 completers, 6 manifested a moderate to marked therapeutic response after 2 or more weeks of therapy (Table 7). As with pargyline, there seemed to be a stimulantlike effect which was relatively brief (4–6 h) as well as a longer-lasting "typical" MAO effect. Most of the patients found the shorter duration drug effect useful and elected to take the drug in two divided doses. Side effects were as follows: lightheadedness, 5; sleep disruption, early morning wakening, 4; sleepiness, 3 fatigue, 3; irritability, 3; dry mouth, 2; headache, 2; loss of desire to smoke, 2; increased appetite, 1; strange dreams, 1; deeper sleep, 1; slow reflexes, 1; nausea, 1 heart palpitations, 1; distorted vision, 1; lassitude, 1. Initially, it appeared that L-deprenyl might constitute an ideal drug for the treatment of ADD-RT: long-acting, nonabusable, and without dietary restrictions; however, all 11 patients were given a trial of stimulants and only one preferred L-deprenyl to them.

CONCLUSION

In the present studies of the pharmacological treatment of adults with ADD-RT, about 60% manifested a moderate to marked therapeutic response to the agents tested. For two reasons it has seemed preferable to begin treatment with the stimulants and, of those, either methylphenidate or D-amphetamine: First, methylphenidate and D-amphetamine appear to be effective in a greater fraction of individuals than pemoline; and, second, no laboratory tests are needed to monitor the first two drugs. An issue of practical, and possibly of theoretical, importance relates to tolerance to stimulants. Although it does not develop in most patients, in some, as with children, dose requirement may increase slowly. In the patients in our studies, cross-tolerance has not been a problem. For example, one patient's initial requirement was 10 mg/day of D-amphetamine, but over a period of a year the dose he required increased to 20 mg/day. He was then switched to methylphenidate, to which he initially manifested a good response but to which he slowly became tolerant over a period of about one year. At that time he was again responsive to his initial dose of D-amphetamine. The cycle has been repeated three times with this patient. On the other hand, the MAOIs provide 24-hour-a-day benefit for patients who can tolerate them and they are not generally abusable (although a few instances of their abuse have been reported); however, hypotension is a problem, and the possibility of an impulsive person taking his/her MAOI with a chunk of Stilton washed down with a goblet of Sandeman's remains a concern. Clearly, the ideal drug is yet to be developed. It would have to be an agent with low toxicity, 24-hour-a-day activity, and no potential for abuse. The problem of the abuse potential of the stimulants requires special attention. Our subjects have not abused stimulants and it *appears* that larger

TABLE 7. DEPRENYL STUDY:
TREATMENT OUTCOME (N = 16)

Physicians' Global Rating	N
+2 to +3	6
0 or +1	2
<0	1

than prescribed doses do not produce euphoria; nonetheless, while the patients themselves may not abuse stimulants, individuals may falsify symptoms of ADD in order to obtain medication, and truly ADD adolescent or adult subjects may sell their medication on the illicit market; therefore, there is a need for an effective nonabusable substance.

Finally, there are a variety of psychological problems associated with drug treatment of adults with ADD-RT which are similar to those reported in adolescents with ADD-RT. These patients are considerably lacking in "outsight": They are unaware of how their symptoms impact on other people and are often non-perceptive to changes in symptoms that are produced by medication. Accordingly, they underestimate the effect of medication and frequently discontinue it despite the fact that they may manifest a considerable therapeutic response. Therefore, a major therapeutic thrust must be directed at enabling the patient—whether adult or adolescent—to become aware of his/her problems, their impact on other people, and their changes with medication. This problem is psychological rather than pharmacological, but unless it is resolved, subtleties of pharmacological intervention will be irrelevant.

APPENDIX A

Utah Criteria for ADHD in Adults

I. CHILDHOOD CHARACTERISTICS: Childhood history consistent with ADD of childhood. Obtaining reliable historical data usually requires input from the individual's parents or older sibling. The following are the diagnostic criteria for ADD in childhood:
   A. NARROW CRITERIA (DSM-III)
      That the individual met DSM-III-R criteria for ADHD in childhood.
   B. BROAD CRITERIA: Both characteristics #1 and #2, and one characteristic of #3 through #6.
      1. More active than other children, unable to sit still, fidgetiness, restlessness, always on the go, talking excessively
      2. Attention deficits, sometimes described as "short attention span," distractibility, inability to finish school work
      3. Behavior problems in school
      4. Impulsivity
      5. Over-excitability
      6. Temper outbursts

II. ADULT CHARACTERISTICS
   A. Presence in adulthood of both characteristics #1 and #2—which the patient observes or says others observe about him—together with two of characteristics #2 through #7.
      1. PERSISTENT MOTOR HYPERACTIVITY as manifested by restlessness, inability to relax, "nervousness" (meaning inability to settle down—not anticipatory anxiety), inability to persist in sedentary activities (e.g., watching movies or TV, reading newspaper), being always on the go, dysphoric when inactive.
      2. ATTENTION DEFICITS as manifested by: Inability to keep mind on conversations, distractibility (being aware of other stimuli when attempts are made to filter them out); inability to keep mind on reading materials; difficulty keeping mind on job; frequent "forgetfulness"; often losing or misplacing things, forgetting plans, etc.; "mind frequently somewhere else."
      3. AFFECTIVE LABILITY: Usually described as antedating adolescence and in some instances beginning as far back as the patient can remember. Manifested by definite shifts form a normal mood to depression or mild euphoria or excitement; depression described as being "down", "bored", or "discontented"; mood shifts usually last hours to at most a few days and are present without significant physiological concomitants; mood shifts may occur spontaneously or be reactive.
      4. INABILITY TO COMPLETE TASKS: The subject reports lack of organization in job, running household or performing school work; tasks frequently not completed; subject switches from one

task to another in haphazard fashion; disorganization in activities, problem solving, organizing time.

5. HOT TEMPER, explosive short-lived outbursts. Subject reports he may have transient loss of control and be frightened by his own behavior. Easily provoked or constant irritability. Temper problems interfere with personal relationships.

6. IMPULSIVITY: Minor manifestations include: talking before thinking things through; interrupting other conversations, impatience (e.g., while driving); impulse buying. Major manifestations may be similar to those seen in mania and antisocial personality disorder and include: poor occupational performance; abrupt initiation or termination of relationships (e.g., multiple marriages, separations, divorces); antisocial behavior such as joy-riding, shoplifting; excessive involvement in pleasurable activities without recognizing risks of painful consequences, e.g., buying sprees, foolish business investments, reckless driving. Subject makes decisions quickly and easily without reflection, often on the basis of insufficient information to his own disadvantage; inability to delay acting without experiencing discomfort.

7. STRESS INTOLERANCE. Subject cannot take ordinary stresses in stride and reacts excessively or inappropriately with depression, confusion, uncertainty, anxiety or anger. Emotional responses interfere with appropriate problem solving. Subject experiences repeated crises in dealing with routine life stresses.

B. Absence of the following disorders:
  1. Antisocial Personality Disorder
  2. Major Affective Disorder
C. Absence of signs and symptoms of the following disorders:
  1. Schizophrenia
  2. Schizo-affective Disorder
D. Absence of schizotypal or borderline personality disorders or traits
E. Associated Features: Marital instability; academic and vocational success less than expected on the basis of intelligence and education; alcohol or drug abuse; atypical responses to psychoactive medications; familial history of similar characteristics; family histories of ADD in childhood, alcoholism, drug abuse, antisocial personality and Briquet's Syndrome.
F. Child Temperament Questionnaire (Connor's Abbreviated Rating Scale): Although not necessary for diagnosis, a score of 12 or greater as rated by the patient's mother is helpful for diagnostic purposes and may be predictive of treatment response.

APPENDIX B

Parents' Rating Scale

Patient's name_____#_____Date_____Physician

To be filled out by the mother of the subject (or father only if mother is unavailable).

Instructions: Listed below are items concerning children's behavior and the problems they sometimes have. Read each item carefully and decide how much you think your child was bothered by these problems when he/she was between six and ten years old. Rate the amount of the problem by putting a check in the column that describes your child at that time.

	NOT AT ALL	JUST A LITTLE	PRETTY MUCH	YES/ MUCH
1. RESTLESS (OVERACTIVE)				
2. EXCITABLE, IMPULSIVE				
3. DISTURBS OTHER CHILDREN				
4. FAILS TO FINISH THINGS STARTED (SHORT ATTENTION SPAN)				
5. FIDGETING				
6. INATTENTIVE, DISTRACTIBLE				
7. DEMANDS MUST BE MET IMMEDIATELY; GETS FRUSTRATED				
8. CRIES				
9. MOOD CHANGES QUICKLY				
10. TEMPER OUTBURSTS (EXPLOSIVE AND UNPREDICTABLE BEHAVIOR)				

REFERENCES

Conners, C. (1972), Symposium: Behavior modification by drugs. II. Psychological effects of stimulant drugs in children with minimal brain dysfunction. *Pediatrics,* 49:702–708.

——— (1969), A teacher rating scale for use in drug studies with children. *Am. J. Psychiatry,* 126:884–888.

Wender, P.H. (1978), Minimal brain dysfunction: An overview. In: *Psychopharmacology. A Generation of Progress,* eds. M.A. Lipton, A. DiMascio, & K.F. Killam. New York: Raven Press, pp. 1429–1435.

———, Reimherr, F.W. & Wood, D.R. (1981), Attention deficit disorder ("minimal brain dysfunction") in adults: A replication study of diagnosis and drug treatment. *Arch. Gen Psychiatry,* 38:449–456.

——— Wood, D.R., Reimherr, F.W. & Ward, M. (1983), An open trial of pargyline in the treatment of attention deficit disorder, residual type. *Psychiatry Res.,* 9:329–336.

———, Reimherr, F.W., Wood, D.R. & Ward, M. (1985), A controlled study of methylphenidate in the treatment of attention deficit disorder, residual type (ADD,RT or "minimal brain dysfunction" in adults). *Am. J. Psychiatry.*

Wood, D.R., Reimherr, F.W. & Wender, P.H. (1976), Diagnosis and treatment of minimal brain dysfunction in adults. *Arch. Gen. Psychiatry,* 33:1453–1461.

Toxicology of Ritalin

ROBERT M. DIENER

INTRODUCTION

This chapter outlines and characterizes the toxicity of methylphenidate, the active ingredient of Ritalin. However, before such an objective can be achieved, a few key words and concepts must be defined so that the reader who is unfamiliar with the pharmaceutical research and development process can gain some basic understanding of medicinal toxicity and how to interpret the available data.

First and foremost, there must be a clear understanding as to the definition and use of the term "toxicity." In the context of a pharmaceutical agent, toxicity refers to the quality of being poisonous or having an adverse effect on the individual exposed to the product. The apparent contradiction that a beneficial medicine may also be a poison is not a new concept. Paracelsus in the sixteenth century stated it well when he wrote, "All substances are poisons; there is none which is not a poison. The right dose differentiates a poison and a remedy" (Klassen et al., 1986). Therefore, when one reads that a certain agent produces adverse effects such as convulsions, specific organ damage, or even death, a comparison should always be made to the therapeutic dose so that toxicity will be viewed in its proper perspective. Technically such a ratio of toxic to therapeutic effect is called a therapeutic index, a tool widely used in toxicological assessment.

Having established the fact that safety is relative rather than absolute, it becomes important to be aware of the extensive scientific and regulatory hurdles which have to be overcome before a pharmaceutical product can be marketed in the United States. Under present law (Federal Food, Drug, and Cosmetic Act of 1938, as amended in 1951–1984), all prescription drugs must be proven safe and efficacious for their intended indications. Thus potential medications must undergo an orderly progression of an extensive series of chemical and animal tests, as well as human clinical trials, before gaining marketing approval from the Food and Drug Administration (FDA). The approval process is lengthy, and the necessary testing procedures and evaluations are documented initially in an Investigational New Drug application (IND) and subsequently in a New Drug Application (NDA). FDA approval of the NDA constitutes marketing approval.

Over the years testing requirements have become ever more stringent; however, the concept that the safety of food and new drugs must first be established in animals before humans are exposed has remained a cornerstone since FDA first published safety-testing guidelines and procedures in 1949 (Diener, 1983).

In general, appraisal of safety for pharmaceutical agents progresses from initial physical and chemical characterization through an ever more complex series of animal toxicity studies. The results of these studies which document the relative safety of methylphenidate are summarized in the following sections. It should be noted that most of the animal toxicology data reported in this chapter have not been published previously because much of it is incorporated in the NDA, which is proprietory in nature, while the data from the NTP subchronic mouse and rat studies and the bioassay on amphetamine sulfate are presently still in a draft stage and awaiting completion of review procedures.

Ciba-Geigy, Summit, New Jersey

CHEMICAL AND PHARMACOLOGICAL CHARACTERIZATION

Ritalin (methylphenidate hydrochloride USP) is a white, odorless, crystalline powder. It is freely soluble in water and methanol, soluble in alcohol, and slightly soluble in chloroform and acetone. Its molecular weight is 269.77 (*Physician's Desk Reference*, 1990).

Methylphenidate is a piperidine derivative that is structurally related to amphetamine; however, it is classified pharmacologically as a mild central nervous system (CNS) stimulant with more prominent effects on mental than on motor activities (Franz, 1985).

TOXICOLOGICAL PROFILE

Acute (single dose) toxicity studies

Acute intravenous and oral toxicity studies have been conducted in rats, mice, and rabbits (Ciba Pharmaceuticals, 1955; Sax and Lewis, 1989; Spector, 1956). In the rat (Wistar rats, 10 animals/dose), the median lethal dose (LD_{50}) was 48.3 mg/kg by the intravenous and 367 mg/kg by the oral route. Intravenously, 10 mg/kg produced signs of hyperexcitability, 25 mg/kg caused clonic muscle spasms and hyperpnea, 40–60 mg/kg led to convulsions and death. By the oral route, there were no convulsions, but prolonged hyperactivity was present. All mortality occurred at least 12 hours after medication and only in those animals where the oral dose exceeded 100 mg/kg.

Amphetamine, which was tested in the same manner because of its chemical structural relationship to methylphenidate, produced similar toxicity although it was more severe and prolonged. Comparative results in rats, mice, and rabbits are presented in Table 1.

Methylphenidate was also studied in acclimated mongrel dogs (Ciba, 1955). Compound was administered in single oral doses via tablets or in aqueous solution by gavage. The form of the medication did not significantly change the results of the treatment. Doses of 10 mg/kg produced no observable effects; 20–75 mg/kg produced hyperactivity, mydriasis, muscle twitches, and various degrees of hyperpnea and salivation that usually started 1–2 hours postmedication and lasted for approximately 5 hours; 100 mg/kg caused ataxia, clonic and tonic convulsions, and emesis. Complete recovery occurred within 24 hours after treatment in every case, and lethal doses were not achieved. Gross lesions were not evident in dogs examined at the end of the 48-hour observation periods.

It is rarely possible to extrapolate from acute animal toxicity studies the representative lethal dose in humans, and the various pitfalls for such calculations have been ably discussed by Zbinden and Flury-Roversi (1981). Nevertheless, the data cited above does indicate that at least a 100:1 margin of safety exists between a single dose which represents the approximate human clinical dose and one which produces lethality in at least two animal species.

TABLE 1. COMPARISON OF ACUTE TOXICITY LD_{50}
METHYLPHENIDATE HCL (MPD) VS. DL AMPHETAMINE SULFATE (AMPA) (MG/KG)

Route	Rats		Mice		Rabbits	
	MPD	AMPA	MPD	AMPA	MPD	AMPA
Oral	367[a]	55[b]	190[b]	24[b]	900[c]	85[b]
Intravenous	48[a]	32[a]	41[b]	15[a]	30[c]	25[c]

[a] *Source:* Ciba, 1955.
[b] *Source:* Sax and Lewis, 1989.
[c] *Source:* Spector, 1956.

Subchronic toxicity studies

The term "subchronic" indicates that the material being tested has been administered to animals repeatedly, usually on a daily basis for a prolonged period of time. The exact length of a subchronic study however may vary, although the most common durations of medication are 1, 3, or 6 months. The studies are really very comprehensive toxicity investigations that are usually performed in two species of animals. These particular investigations are the very core of the pharmaceutical nonclinical safety testing program and often determine whether the potential product being tested can be used in humans. Two or three dose levels are used in each study and the doses are designed to represent multiples of the proposed human therapeutic dose. Effects produced in the animals on the various dose levels are compared with results obtained in nonmedicated control animals. Growth, food consumption, body weights, behavior, and hematological and biochemical functions are evaluated at periodic intervals. Gross and histological examination of tissues from all major organs are performed at the conclusion of the study.

The toxicity profile of methylphenidate has been well characterized in a number of subchronic animal studies involving mice (Hazleton Laboratories, 1984), rats (Ciba, 1955; OSTEP, 1985), and dogs (Ciba, 1955). In each instance, preliminary range-finding investigations were conducted to determine the optimal doses that were to be used in the definitive study.

The 90-day mouse toxicity study was conducted in B6C3F1 mice (six groups of 10 males and 10 females) to explore the effects of a wide range of methylphenidate doses and to determine the maximum tolerated dose prior to conducting a carcinogenicity assay in mice (Hazleton Laboratories, 1984). Methylphenidate was incoporated in the diet at concentrations of 125, 250, 500, 1000, or 2000 ppm (approximately 20, 40, 80, 160, and 320 mg methylphenidate/kg body weight/day). A control group was fed unmedicated feed. At the conclusion of the study, all tissues (approximately 48 tissues from all major organs) from control animals, high-dose animals, animals that died on test, as well as livers and kidneys from all animals, were subjected to histological examination. Sperm and vaginal cytology evaluations were performed at the end of the study. Liver sections were obtained for electron microscopy from a few animals in each dose group.

Dose-related decreases in body weight gains were observed in all treatment groups. These decreases ranged from -16% to -54% of control values. Mean absolute liver weight, liver to terminal body weight ratios, and liver to brain weight ratios tended to be increased in the treated animals, although statistical significance was achieved only at the two highest dose levels. Heart weights also tended to be lower in males and were significantly lower at the highest dose level, probably due to the severe body weight losses. The adverse body weight changes were probably also the cause of altered reproductive parameters which included decreases in sperm motility and increases in sperm concentration in the males and alterations in frequency of the various estrous stages in females.

The only treatment-related histological changes occurred in the livers of mice from the three highest dose groups. The changes included the presence of enlarged, but otherwise normal appearing hepatocytes in the central region of liver lobules, and their occurrences correlated well with increased liver weights. Increased incidences of foci of mild hepatocyte degeneration also occurred in males receiving 80 mg/kg or more of medication, while small foci of hepatocellular necrosis were prominent in the males fed 320 mg/kg. Results of electron microscopy of the liver (if any) are not presently available.

In summary, the data from the 90-day mouse toxicity study indicate that all five dose levels used in the study exceeded the maximum tolerated dose (MTD) of the animals on test because they induced excessive decreases in body weight gain over the testing period. Although the exact definition of an MTD is controversial (OSTEP, 1985), it is generally conceded that decrements of more than 10% in body weight gains over a prolonged period of time can adversely affect a number of physiological systems which may in turn produce spurious toxic manifestations. Thus it should not be entirely surprising to find that daily doses of methylphenidate, which ranged from 20 to 320 times the intended human dose, produced some perturbations in reproductive parameters and morphologic evidence of metabolic overload in the liver. It is surprising however that even with doses of this magnitude, methylphenidate produced no drug-related mortality, adverse clinical signs or behavior, or decreases in appetite or food consumption.

Two definitive subchronic toxicity studies in rats have also been conducted. Wistar rats were used in the original study (Ciba, 1955) in which daily doses of 5 or 10 mg/kg of methylphenidate were administered by stomach tube, five days per week, to two groups of rats (5 males, 5 females/group) for three months. The aqueous vehicle was administered to a group of control animals. Feed consumption and body weights were measured and clinical signs observed. Hematology parameters were determined before the initiation of medication and at termination of the study. Tissues of major organs from high-dose animals were examined histologically.

Body weights and feed consumption were not affected by the medication. Hyperactivity was observed in both treatment groups for several hours following intubation. All hematological parameters remained within normal limits and were comparable between control and treatment groups. There were no gross lesions observed at the conclusion of the study. Examination of histological sections of organs from the high-dose animals did not reveal the presence of any drug-related pathology.

Fisher 344 rats were used in a second subchronic toxicity study (Hazleton Laboratories, 1984) in which five groups of animals (10 males, 10 females/group) received methylphenidate in the diet at concentrations of 125, 250, 500, 1000, or 2000 ppm (approximately 7, 15, 30, 60, or 120 mg/kg/day) for a period of 90 days. A control group was maintained on nonmedicated diet. Feed consumption, body weight gains, and clinical signs were monitored during the study. Additionally crown–rump length of the animals, femur length, and bone density determinations were measured at the end of the study in an attempt to evaluate growth. Pretest and monthly blood samples were collected from all animals for radioimmunoassays of growth hormone. Sperm morphology and vaginal cytology were examined in all animals from three of the five dose groups. Complete necropsies were performed and histopathology examinations were conducted on approximately 50 tissues. Liver, thymus, left testis, right kidney, heart, brain, and lungs were weighed and organ/body weight ratios and organ/brain weight ratios calculated. Samples of liver tissue were collected for electron microscopy from a few animals in each dose group.

Results from this extensive investigation essentially confirmed the findings from the initial rat study. Five animals (two males and three females) died during the study, but these deaths were attributed to anesthesia complications during blood collection procedures and were not drug related. There were no consistent differences in feed consumption between control and treated male rats; however, feed consumption values for females in the two highest dose groups were slightly increased over controls during most of the study. Consistent drug-related clinical signs included general hyperactivity, hypersensitivity and vocalization during handling; the effects were noted only in females on the two highest dose levels. Body weight gains were reduced in all groups of treated females and in the males of the two highest dose levels. Most of the reductions were not statistically significant.

Growth, based on nose-to-rump body length, femur length, and bone density measurements, was not altered by medication. Growth hormone values varied greatly among individual animals; there were no statistically significant differences between control and treatment groups.

Sperm counts and sperm motility apparently remained unaffected by medication, but the sperm concentration/gram cauda was greater in treated groups of males, a finding attributed to decreased body weight gains. In the treated females, alterations in the relative frequency of the various estrous stages were observed, as it was in mice.

Liver weights (absolute and relative) were increased in the animals on the two highest dose levels; however, the results were statistically significant only in the highest dose group. There were no treatment-related lesions observed at necropsy. Hypertrophy of liver cells was the only histological manifestation related to treatment. The changes in cell size were generally mild and relegated to males on the two highest dose levels and females in the high-dose group.

An analytical review of the data from the two rat studies indicates that methylphenidate was well tolerated by two different strains of rats. Slight to moderate decreases in body weight gain were manifested which, in part, may be caused by mild hyperactivity. Growth and bone development were not affected by medication; therefore, the data from this study in laboratory rats do not confirm the findings from a report in the literature that growth in height and weight of children was reduced by the prolonged administration of methylphenidate (Mattes and Gittelman, 1983). No gross lesions were evident at necropsy after 90 days of treatment. Histological tissue changes were limited to the livers (hepatocyte hypertrophy) of animals from the two highest dose levels and correlated with increased liver weights. As previously noted in the discussion of the mouse subchronic study, a combination of increased liver weight and hepatocyte hypertrophy is suggestive of hepatic metabolic overload induced by chronic administration of excessive dosages of medication. Such changes are not relevant to humans on normal therapeutic levels of medication.

Two groups of three beagle dogs were administered methylphenidate in doses of 5 or 10 mg/kg body weight per day for a period of four months (Ciba, 1955). The dosage was divided into two treatments given daily except for Saturdays and Sundays. A control group received placebo capsules. Prior to the initiation of medication, all dogs were subjected to routine hematological evaluation and laparotomy to obtain liver biopsy specimens for histological evaluation. The five male dogs were also injected with phenolsulfonphthalein to determine kidney function. Clinical signs, appetite, body weights, and hematologic parameters were monitored during the study.

All premedication clinical laboratory parameters and liver tissue specimens were within normal limits. During the first two weeks of medication some mydriasis and slight hyperactivity were the only signs of treatment noted in either dose group. The effects were observed to start within approximately 20 minutes postmedication. Starting in the third week, the hyperactivity and hyperexcitability of the dogs in both dose groups became progressively more intense and prolonged. Near the end of the study extreme stimulation was common in most of the animals and hyperexcitability was present even in the mornings following a weekend of nonmedication. Nevertheless, convulsions or epileptic seizures did not occur during the study. Appetite remained good throughout the investigation; consistent decreases in body weights were not observed, although slight fluctuations were present. Hematological parameters (erythrocytes, leukocytes, hemoglobin/ hematocrit determinations, and differential counts), evaluated after approximately two months of treatment and again prior to the end of the study, revealed no significant trends and remained within normal limits.

At termination of the investigation all animals were in good health, and except for some focal hemorrhages of undetermined origin observed in the abdominal cavity of one low-dose dog, no gross lesions were observed during necropsy procedures. Histological examination of tissues from high-dose dogs did not reveal any abnormalities. No hepatocyte hyperplasia was noted in the livers.

Analysis of the data from the subchronic dog study indicates that methylphenidate was well tolerated in dogs when given for a prolonged period of time and at doses which produced consistent clinical signs of overdosage and reflected multiples of approximately five and ten times the daily human therapeutic dose. There was no evidence of any effect on hematological parameters. There were no indications of organ toxicity or histopathologic changes. Absence of liver effects in dogs tends to confirm the premise that the hypertrophic changes noted in that organ in rats and mice is predominantly a rodent phenomenon induced by inordinately high doses of drug.

Reproductive and developmental toxicity studies in rats

Before a prescription pharmaceutical preparation can be marketed and recommended for use in childbearing women or during pregnancy, a number of very specific animal studies must be performed which will assess the effect of the medication on the reproductive capacity of the male and female, the pregnant mother, the nursing female, the unborn or nursing offspring, and the adolescent animal. These investigations, presently designated as Segment I, II, or III reproductive studies, are conducted in rodents and/or rabbits, and because of their general utility for assessing developmental and reproductive toxicity, most pharmaceutical products, regardless of their indications, undergo this type of testing procedure. General reproductive performance (effects on conception and the entire reproduction process) is assessed in the Segment I study. Animals are medicated prior to mating, as well as during the mating process, gestation, parturition, and lactation. In the Segment II study, medication is restricted to the period of organogenesis in the pregnant female so that developmental toxicity (effects on gestation, embryo, and fetus) can be assessed. Medication is administered to dams in the last trimester of pregnancy and during parturition and lactation in the Segment III study in order to evaluate potential effects on birth, the lactating dam, the growing fetus, and suckling pup.

All studies of methylphenidate were conducted using modifications of the guidelines suggested by the FDA in 1966 for use in developing study designs. Specific requirements vary internationally and are continually modified (Christian and Hoberman, 1989). Although protocols differ, the critical point is that one or more of the endpoints of reproductive performance (mating, fertility, parturition, lactation, and maternal/pump interaction) and development of the offspring (viability, gender, morphology, and growth) are evaluated in each study, and that in combination the studies address the full complement of endpoints.

A modified Segment I study was carried out in Wistar rats (Ciba, 1966). A group of ten males received daily doses of methylphenidate 2 mg/kg body weight (in the diet) for 60 days prior to mating and during the mating period. A group of five control males received nonmedicated diet. A group of 20 female animals ingested daily doses of methylphenidate 5 mg/kg body weight for 14 days prior to mating with the treated males, during the mating period and for the first 14 days of pregnancy. Ten control females received nonmedicated feed and were mated with the control males. Higher doses of medication were not used because some intermittent excitation had been observed with 10 mg/kg in subchronic studies. At the end of the first two weeks of gestation, females were sacrificed with an overdose of anesthesia and the contents of the uteri were examined.

Methylphenidate under the above circumstances had no effect on conception rate, number of live embryos per dam, number of implantation sites, or number of resorption sites. It was concluded that, methylphenidate at doses representing 2–5 times the daily human therapeutic dose, had no adverse effects on mating, fertilization, conception, or the viability of the embryo.

The effects of methylphenidate on gestation, embryo, and fetus were determined in a modified Segment II study using two groups of 20 mated female Wistar rats fed daily doses of methylphenidate 1.6 or 4.5 mg/kg body weight in the diet during the first 14 days of gestation (Ciba, 1966). An identical group of control females received nonmedicated diet. Half of the animals in all three groups were sacrificed with an overdose of anesthesia on the 20th day of gestation (two days prior to parturition) in order to examine the uterine contents. The remaining animals were allowed to give birth and nurse their offspring until weaning (three weeks postpartum).

Results of the study indicated that methylphenidate had no adverse effects on the behavior or body weight gains of the dams when administered to the mated females during the first two weeks of gestation in doses which approximated two or five times the daily human therapeutic dose. Litter size, size, weight, and viability of fetuses, and numbers of uterine resorption sites were essentially identical in control and treatment groups. The survival rates of sucklings to 24 hours postpartum and to weaning were also very similar in the treated and control groups.

Gross examination of the 20-day fetuses and the weanlings from the medicated dams failed to reveal any abnormalities which could be attributed to medication. Hearts from 48 weanling rats in the high- and low-dose groups were minutely examined under a dissecting microscope for anatomical defects. No evidence of septal defects, transposition of vessels, persistent ductus arteriosus, or other anomalies was revealed.

In a modified Segment III study (Ciba, 1966), methylphenidate was administered in the feed at a dose of 2.2 mg/kg to a group of 10 Wistar rats for three weeks postpartum (from parturition until weaning of the young). A similar group of control rats received basal diet. All litters were restricted to eight pups to simplify comparisons. Treated dams consumed slightly more feed and consequently gained more weight during lactation than did control animals. At 24 hours, and one, two, or three weeks postpartum, there were no differences in mean body weights or mean survival rates of suckling pups from control or medicated groups of animals. It was concluded that methylphenidate, when administered to lactating rats at a dose approximating 2–3 times the human therapeutic dose, did not produce any untoward effects on the lactating dam or suckling offspring.

A reproduction and fertility assessment was also recently performed in Swiss CD-1 mice administered doses of 120, 500, and 1000 ppm (approximately 20, 80, or 160 mg methylphenidate HCl/kg body weight) in the diet. Both male and female mice (20 pairs per treatment group, 40 pairs of control animals) were continuously exposed for a 7-day precohabitation and a 98-day cohabitation period. At weaning the F_1 generation received the same treatment as their parents and were cohabited for one week at sexual maturity. Only the F_1 mice from the control and the highest dose groups were evaluated. Methylphenidate treatment at up to 160 mg/kg, or roughly 200 times the recommended human therapeutic dose, had no apparent effect on fertility or reproduction in either the parental or F_1 generation (Gulati et al., 1989).

Based on the data submitted in the Ritalin NDA from rodent reproduction and developmental toxicity studies, it is concluded that at approximately 2–5 times the human therapeutic dose, methylphenidate does not produce any adverse effects on male or female reproductive performance (mating, fertility, litter size, pup sex ratios or pup viability, morphology, or growth during lactation) or on the viability, morphology, or growth of the offspring in two species of animals. This conclusion is substantiated by the fact that (1) drug-related histological changes of the reproductive organs and morphological changes of sperm were not observed in the NTP subchronic studies and (2) there were no adverse effects on male or female reproductive performance or pup viability, growth, or reproductive performance in the mouse study cited in the previous paragraph. In all three of these studies extremely high oral doses of methylphenidate had been used.

Carcinogenicity studies

Carcinogenicity assessments have been conducted on many pharmaceutical products presently on the market and such procedures now are generally required by the Food and Drug Administration before marketing approval is granted. The testing procedures are standardized and generally conform to those published by NCI in 1976 (National Cancer Institute, 1976) in which rats and mice are administered the test substance daily for a period of two years. Body weights, feed consumption, mortality rates, and tumor incidences are calculated during the study. At the end of the two-year period, which for all intents and purposes constitutes lifetime exposure of the animals to large multiples of the human dose, the animals are sacrificed and the tissues of all major organs are examined histologically for lesions and the presence of tumors. A determination is then made as to whether a significant increase in tumor rate occurred in the groups administered the test compound when compared with the control group.

Methylphenidate currently is being evaluated under the National Toxicology Program (NTP). The two-year rat and mouse studies included in the standard bioassay were initiated in the fall of 1986 after preliminary range-finding studies had been conducted to determine appropriate doses. Data from the bioassays are now undergoing histopathology review, statistical evaluation, and peer review. A published report of the findings are expected in 1992 (Guthrie, 1990).

At the present time, there are no indications that methylphenidate has any carcinogenic potential. Communications with personnel at NTP (Boorman, 1990; Dunnick, 1989) have not indicated that any particular problems have been encountered during the studies. Furthermore, a draft report of a bioassay on DL-amphetamine sulfate has indicated that DL-amphetamine, a more toxic but structurally related stimulant, was not found to have any carcinogenic potential (NIH, 1989). The conclusions of the draft report state, "Under the conditions of these 2-year feed studies, there was no evidence of carcinogenic activity of DL-amphetamine sulfate for male or female F344/n rats or male or female B6C3F1 mice fed diets containing 20 or 100 ppm." These dosages translate into the following: approximately 1 and 5 mg/kg/day in rats (3 and 16 times the recommended human therapeutic dose in children) and 3 and 19–32 mg/kg day in mice (10 and 83 times the human therapeutic dose in children). Because there was no evidence for increased tumorigenicity due to amphetamine in the two rodent species, it is anticipated that corresponding doses of methylphenidate will behave similarly in the studies presently under review.

PHARMACOKINETICS

Pharmacokinetics can be loosely defined as what the body does to a drug. Many studies elucidating the absorption, disposition, metabolism, and excretion of methylphenidate in humans and animals have been conducted and published. Results from a number of these studies show that the drug is well absorbed and extensively metabolized in humans and animals (Egger et al., 1981). The mouse, rat, dog, and monkey have been used to characterize various pharmacokinetic aspects and make comparisons to humans.

The distribution of methylphenidate was studied by whole body autoradiography in the mouse (Schmid, 1971). The ^{14}C-labeled material (the label was incorporated in the carboxyl group) was injected intravenously into mice at a dose of 10 mg/kg. Pairs of mice were then sacrificed 1, 5, and 30 minutes, as well as 2, 6, and 24 hours postmedication. Examination of whole body sections revealed that methylphenidate is rapidly and widely distributed throughout the whole body. After one minute, high activity was observed in the lungs, kidneys, brain, salivary glands, and intestinal tract. Low concentrations of radioactivity were present in the liver, heart, muscle, thymus, and testes. Five minutes after administration, high levels of radioactivity were seen in the central nervous system and excretory organs. After 30 minutes, radioactivity

DIENER

no longer predominated in the extravascular system while significant concentrations remained in the excretory organs. Radioactivity was almost completely eliminated by 24 hours, attesting to the rapid elimination of drug by both the biliary and renal routes.

The metabolism of methylphenidate in the rat and dog was investigated by Egger and colleagues (1981). Methylphenidate was absorbed rapidly and completely from the gastrointestinal tract of both species. Excretion of radioactivity by the dog and rat was rapid and essentially complete within 48 hours. Approximately 86% and 63% of the ^{14}C-labeled methylphenidate was recovered in the urine of the dog and rat, respectively. Metabolite patterns of the drug in urine from both species are complex and involved oxidation, hydrolysis, and conjugation processes. Thirteen metabolites were detected in the dog urine, of which three were major ones. The rat presented a more complicated metabolite pattern than the dog; over 20 metabolites were observed during the workup.

In humans ritalinic acid (α-phenyl-2-piperidineacetic acid) and the lactam acid account for approximately 90% of the urinary excretion products from methylphenidate. In dogs, however, these two metabolites account for only about 50%. Lactam acid, the principal metabolite in the dog, accounted for only 7–10% of the radioactivity in rat urine. In all three species the amount of renally excreted unchanged drug is low (less than 1% in humans and rat; less than 2% in dog).

The pharmacokinetics of methylphenidate were studied by Wargin et al. (1983) in normal adults, children with hyperactivity, rats, and monkeys. Maximal methylphenidate plasma levels (3.5 and 7.8 ng/ml after 0.15 or 0.3 mg/kg, respectively) were found to occur 2.2 hours after the administration of either 0.15 or 0.3 mg/kg to adults. The half life was calculated to be 2.05–2.14 h. In hyperactive children, peak plasma levels (10.8 ng/ml) were achieved 1.5 h after a dose of 0.3 mg/kg; the half life was 2.43 h. Considerable intersubject variability occurred in the study. Comparable data in rats and monkeys were not furnished; however, the absolute bioavailability of methylphenidate was found to be 0.19 in the rat and 0.22 in the monkey, suggesting substantial presystemic elimination of methylphenidate.

ADVERSE EFFECTS AND OVERDOSAGE IN HUMANS

Over a period of more than 30 years of worldwide clinical experience with methylphenidate, remarkably few reports of adverse reactions or serious toxicity have been recorded and/or published in the medical literature. Even reports of adverse effects due to intentional overdosage or drug abuse are relatively rare. A few references are cited by Baselt (1982) about the related hazard of intravenous methylphenidate abuse and the development of talc granulomatosis resulting from the attempted solubilizing and injection of the contents from tablets intended for oral use.

Adverse reactions which may be seen under normal therapeutic regimens but which commonly can be attributed to mild overdosage include nervousness and insomnia (most common), hypersensitivity, anorexia, nausea, dizziness, palpitations, headache, dyskinesia, drowsiness, blood pressure and pulse changes (both up and down), tachycardia, angina, cardiac arrhythmia, abdominal pain, and weight loss during prolonged therapy. In children loss of appetite, abdominal pain, weight loss during prolonged therapy, insomnia, and tachycardia are the most common adverse reactions reported (*Physician's Desk Reference*, 1990).

Toxic psychosis and rare reports of Tourette's syndrome also have been reported. A definite causal relationship has not been established in a few isolated cases of leukopenia and/or anemia and scalp hair loss (*Physician's Desk Reference*, 1990).

REFERENCES

Baselt, R.C. (1982), *Disposition of Toxic Drugs and Chemicals in Man,* 2nd Ed. Davis, CA: Biomedical Publications, p. 525.

Boorman, G. (1990), Personal communication. Research Triangle Park, NC: National Institutes of Health, NIEHS.

Christian, M.S. & Hoberman, A.M. (1989), Current in vivo reproductive toxicity and developmental toxicity (teratology) test methods. In: *A Guide to General Toxicology*, 2nd Ed. eds. J. Marquis and W. Hayes. Basel, Switzerland: S. Karger Publishers, pp. 91–100.

CIBA Pharmaceuticals, Division of CIBA-GEIGY Corp. (1955), New Drug Application (NDA 10-187): Ritalin. Summit, NJ: Ciba.

———— (1966), Supplemental Data to New Drug Application (NDA 10-187): Ritalin. Summit, NJ: Ciba.

Diener, R.M. (1983), Design of carcinogenicity studies: a backward glance. *Toxicol. Path.*, 11(1):37–40.

Dunnick, J.K. (1989), Personal communication. Research Triangle Park, NC: National Institutes of Health, NIEHS.

Egger, H., Bartlett, F., Dreyfuss, R. & Karliner, J. (1981), Metabolism of methylphenidate in dog and rat. *Drug Metab. Dispos.*, 9(5):415–423.

Franz, D.N. (1985), Central nervous system stimulants. In: *The Pharmacological Basis of Therapeutics*, 7th Ed. eds. A. Gilman, L. Goodman, T. Rall & F. Murad. New York: Macmillan, pp. 586–587.

Gulati, D.K., Hope, E., Mounce, R.C. & Russell, S. (1989), Methylphenidate HCl reproduction and fertility assessment in Swiss CD-1 mice when administered via feed. National Toxicology Program Report NTP-89-107; Order No. PB89-178057. Research Triangle Park, NC:

Guthrie, J. (1990), Personal communication. Research Triangle Park, NC: National Institutes of Health, NIEHS.

Hazleton Laboratories America, Inc. (1984), Ninety-day subchronic toxicity study with methylphenidate hydrochloride in rats. Report prepared as draft for National Toxicology Program. Bethesda: NIEHS.

Klassen, C.D., Amdur, M.O. & Doull, J. (eds.) (1986), *Casarett & Doull's Toxicology*, 3rd Ed. New York: Macmillan, p. 12.

Mattes, J.A. & Gittelman, R. (1983), Growth of hyperactive children on maintenance regimen of methylphenidate. *Arch. Gen. Psychiatry*, 40(3):317–321.

National Cancer Institute (NCI). (1976), Guidelines for carcinogenicity bioassay in small rodents. NCI Technical Report No. 1. Bethesda: U.S. Department of Health, Education and Welfare, Public Health Service, NIH.

National Institutes of Health (NIH). (1989), Toxicology and carcinogenesis studies of DL-amphetamine sulfate in F344/n rats and B6C3F1 mice. NTP Technical Report 387 (draft). Research Triangle Park, NC: National Toxicology Program.

OSTEP. (1985), Chemical carcinogens: a review of the science and associated principles. Office of Science and Technology Policy. *Fed. Reg.*, 50:10372.

Physician's Desk Reference (PDR). (1990), Oradell, NJ: Medical Economics Co., pp. 866–867.

Sax, N.I. & Lewis, R.J. (eds.). (1989), *Dangerous Properties of Industrial Materials* 7th Ed. New York: Van Nostrand Reinhold, pp. 248, 2369.

Schmid, K. (1971), Whole body autoradiography and distribution in the mouse. Biology Discussion (internal report). Basel, Switzerland: CIBA-GEIGY LTD.

Spector, W.S. (1956), *Handbook of Toxicology*, Vol. I, *Acute Toxicities of Solids, Liquids and Gases to Laboratory Animals*. Philadelphia: WB Saunders Co., p. 40.

Wargin, W., Patrick, K., Kilts, C., Gualtieri, C.T., Ellington, K., Mueller, R.A., Kraemer, G. & Breese, G.R. (1983), Pharmacokinetics of Methylphenidate in man, rat and monkey. *J. Pharmacol. Exp. Therap.*, 226(2):382–386.

Zbinden, G. & Flury-Roversi, M. (1981), Significance of the LD_{50} test for the toxicological evaluation of chemical substances. *Arch. Toxicol.*, 47:77–99.

Attention Deficit Disorder: Diagnosis and Role of Ritalin in Management

SALLY E. SHAYWITZ and BENNETT A. SHAYWITZ

Attention deficit disorder (ADD)* is now recognized as the most common neurobehavioral disorder of childhood, affecting children from their earliest infancy through their school years and into adult life. Estimates suggest that ADD affects 10–20% of the school-age population (Shaywitz and Shaywitz, 1988b) and it is not uncommon for child neurologists and behavioral pediatricians to indicate that referrals for ADD now comprise perhaps 50 to 75% of their practice. Furthermore, based on studies examining the prevalence of stimulant medication usage in children, it appears that the disorder is being diagnosed more frequently now than a decade ago (Safer and Krager, 1988). Recognizing that optimal management is contingent on a reliable and accurate diagnosis, and that without diagnosis there can be no treatment, we begin our discussion by providing both an historical perspective on the evolution of the construct of ADD and an overview of current concepts of the disorder, particularly those relating to diagnosis. Comprehensive reviews covering other issues in ADD, are readily available (Barkley, 1988; Garfinkel and Wender, 1989; Shaywitz and Shaywitz, 1988a; 1989; Whalen, 1989) and the interested reader may want to refer to these.

ISSUES IN DIAGNOSIS

Historical perspective

Historically the antecedents of our current conceptualizations of ADD can be traced to the late nineteenth and early twentieth century. In a remarkably prescient report, Still (1902) described children with what he termed "morbid defects in moral control." In that same era other physicians were linking the description of similar behaviors to disorders causing brain damage: traumatic brain injury (Goldstein, 1936; Meyer, 1904); the sequelae of von Economo's encephalitis (Hohman, 1922) or a variety of other childhood central nervous system infections (Bender, 1942). In a series of influential reports, Strauss and his associates (Strauss and Lehtinen, 1947; Werner and Strauss, 1941) extrapolated the notion of brain damage to include children with behaviors similar to those observed after known brain injuries. According to Strauss, the conceptual entity of the "brain-injured [damaged] child" depended only on the child's behavior; a history consistent with brain damage was not necessary for diagnosis.

By the 1950s, investigators had become disillusioned by these notions and the concept of brain "dysfunction" rather than brain "damage" began to emerge. According to Laufer and Denhoff (1957), the hyperkinetic behavior disorder was caused by an underlying "injury to or dysfunction of the diencephalon." Even more influential, however, was Clements and Peters (1962) elaboration of the notion of minimal brain dysfunction (MBD). In their view, minimal brain dysfunctions could be inferred from the presence of a

Yale University School of Medicine, New Haven, Connecticut
*What had been termed attention deficit disorder with hyperactivity (ADDH) in *DSM-III* is now referred to as attention deficit hyperactivity disorder (ADHD) in *DSM-III-R*, and what *DSM-III* labeled attention deficit disorder without hyperactivity (ADD without H) is included in a *DSM-III-R* category referred to as undifferentiated attention deficit disorder. Throughout this chapter when we refer to attention disorders (or ADD) we include both ADHD (or ADDH in *DSM-III*) and undifferentiated ADD (ADD without H in *DSM-III*).

cluster of symptoms including specific learning deficits, hyperkinesis, impulsivity, and short attention span and confirmed by findings on examination of "equivocal" neurological signs and a borderline abnormal or a definitely abnormal EEG.

At the time, the notion of MBD was viewed as a real advance in incorporating the diverse manifestations thought to reflect the syndrome while not emphasizing a particular interpretation of the nature of the brain insult. However, this loose conglomeration of behavioral and learning symptomatology created confusion as well. Almost immediately, there developed a schism in the way the medical and the educational communities viewed the disorder. The medical literature accepted the term minimal brain dysfunction and incorporated the entity into a medical model. In contrast, the educational literature focused more on the findings of a learning difficulty and preferred to describe affected children as having a specific learning disability (LD). Despite attempts at operationalization of MBD (Bax and McKeith, 1963; Clements and Peters, 1962), two decades of research have led to the recognition that MBD is meaningless and the term has been abandoned by most investigators. However, its legacy lives on in the current confusion between ADD and LD which can be traced directly to the confounding of learning difficulties and behavioral disturbances in MBD.

Publication of *DSM-III* in 1980 marked a watershed in the evolution of ADD and in diagnosticians' ability to distinguish ADD from LD and from conduct disorder and oppositional disorder. For the first time, specific exclusion and inclusion criteria were established for ADD; LD was not considered a specific criteria though school failure was noted as a common complication. Despite clear criteria for ADD, in retrospect the seeds of some of the current difficulties in differentiating ADD and LD could be discerned in *DSM-III* which differentiated two subtypes of ADD based on the presence or absence of symptoms of hyperactivity: attention deficit disorder with hyperactivity (ADDH) and attention deficit disorder without hyperactivity (ADD without H). *DSM-III* was unclear whether "they are two forms of a single disorder or represent two distinct disorders" (APA, 1980, p. 41). Publication of *DSM-III-R* in 1987 represented a distinct change and unfortunately added considerable confusion to the differentiation of LD and ADD. In contrast to *DSM-III*, *DSM-III-R* blurred the distinction between attention disorder with and without hyperactivity by focusing primarily on ADDH, now termed attention deficit hyperactivity disorder (ADHD), and relegating ADD without hyperactivity to a category now termed undifferentiated attention disorder (U-ADD). The reasons for the decision to demote ADD without H are described by Barkley, Costello, and Spitzer (in press) and related primarily to the belief by some of the committee members that ADD without H might actually ". . . represent a type of inattention believed to accompany the non-verbal learning disabilities (Rourke, 1989) and so might be a new subtype of the existing category of Specific Developmental Disorders." In the opinion of many investigators and thoughtful clinicians, this decision was, indeed, a retrogressive step, again confounding ADD with LD, rather than attempting to disentangle the two.

Current concepts

At the present time, the diagnosis of ADD is established on the basis of a history of symptoms representing the cardinal constructs of ADD: inattention, impulsivity, and, at times, hyperactivity. ADD is a low visibility but high prevalence disorder that can permeate every dimension of a child's life. In a sense, the term low visibility is a misnomer; referring to the "normal" appearance of ADD children, not to the impact that the disorder may have on the child, his family, his classmates, and his community. The three basic features of the disorder may interfere with the child's adjustment in every phase of his existence, both through time and across situations and experiences. The intrusion of the child's symptomatology into every sphere of his existence, his failure to get on with family members, his failures at school and with peers represent a source of frustration and disappointment to both the child and his parents.

Symptom variability

In addition to specific symptoms of the disorder, certain overall trends or characteristics are also evident. Symptoms diagnostic of ADHD manifest a developmental trend; that is, up until age three activity levels increase but then continue a downward trend so that by adolescence gross motor hyperactivity is no longer present. However, attentional deficits persist. Awareness of this developmental pattern is particularly important because it is, at times, mistakenly assumed that since the child is no longer hyperactive, he is free of problems and no longer needy of, for example, special education services. It is critically important that parents and professionals, particularly educators appreciate the differential ontogeny of the activity and attentional components of the syndrome.

Not only do the symptoms of ADD vary over time, they also exhibit situational variability. Both the environmental context and the task demands placed on the child will influence his or her symptomatic expression at any particular time. The variability not only extends to different settings and situations but also refers to the often lack of predictability of the child's behavior from minute to minute or day to day, even in similar situations. Most North American investigators would diagnose ADD on the basis of a history obtained from the parents, reflecting behavior in a particular situation (situational ADD). In contrast, some British investigators (Taylor, 1986) would insist that the symptoms be noted as well by the child's teachers, that is, the symptoms should be observed in many situations (pervasive ADD). This controversy over situational versus symptomatology clearly reflects fundamental differences in the conceptualization of ADD in North America compared with Great Britain. Though this controversy has not been resolved to everyone's satisfaction, the major American diagnostic formulations, *Diagnostic and Statistical Manual of Mental Disorders* (third edition) (*DSM-III*), *Diagnostic and Statistical Manual for Mental Disorders* (third edition-revised) (*DSM-III-R*), and *Diagnostic and Statistical Manual of Mental Disorders* (fourth edition) (*DSM-IV*, in preparation), indicate that a history of symptoms of ADD obtained from the parents are sufficient for the diagnosis of ADD. If the teacher or other observers note the same symptoms, the diagnostician may feel more secure in the diagnosis but observation in several settings is not necessary for the diagnosis.

ADD in young children

A number of research issues have yet to be resolved, and not surprisingly they relate particularly to definition and diagnosis. An especially problematic area is that of the diagnosis of ADD in younger children and in turn the prognostic significance of specific behaviors found in so-called "difficult" young children. Since there may be more natural variability in symptoms and wider latitude in what is considered developmentally appropriate in young children, it has been very difficult to determine which symptoms may be transient and which may presage more enduring problems. Additionally, the more global symptom patterns at earlier ages make it difficult to determine if these symptoms reflect a final common pathway for a myriad of influences, that is a rather nonspecific response of the young organism to a range of stressors or a specific expression of an inherent vulnerability of ADD children. It is unclear whether these symptoms should be considered the earliest manifestations of ADD or if they represent symptoms of other, more severe emotional disorders or in some cases are a transient phenomenon. There is a great need for a better understanding of these early manifestations including their natural course, correlates, and implications. Measures are necessary to be able to better tease apart these global presentations so that, for example, hyperactivity and aggressive components can be clarified and monitored over time. It is equally important to expand our investigations to include a more representative range of young ADD children rather than the often most severely impaired who present to mental health clinics for early assessment.

Subtypes of ADD

Increasing evidence indicates that children who exhibit ADD without evidence of hyperactivity (ADD without H in *DSM-III* or Undifferentiated ADD in *DSM-III-R*) comprise a significant subset of those diagnosed as attention deficit disordered. Thus, Anderson et al. (1987) administered structured clinical interviews to 11 year olds and questionnaires to their parents, the subjects representing a subset of a sample of New Zealand school children followed since age 3 years. Forty five children were identified as attention deficit disorder with hyperactivity and 8 as attention deficit disorder without hyperactivity. Costello et al. (1988) administered structured interviews to 300 children and their parents seen in a general pediatric clinic of a large health maintenance organization. They found 11 cases of attention deficit disorder with hyperactivity and 2 with attention deficit disorder without hyperactivity.

Good evidence supports this differentiation between subtypes of attention disorder, demonstrating that while ADHD and ADD without H do not differ on independent measures of attention (Edelbrock et al., 1984; King and Young, 1982; Lahey et al., 1987; in press), ADDH and ADD without H children demonstrate significantly different behavioral, academic and social patterns (Edelbrock et al., 1984). Of particular interest, Lahey et al. (1987) indicate that ADD without H boys are rated by their teachers as manifesting a poorer school performance than ADDH boys, a finding supported by the high rate of retention (71.5%), high even in relation to ADHD boys (16.7%). More recently, Lahey et al. (1988) investigated a clinic sample of 41 ADHD and 22 ADD nonhyperactive children as well as a large school sample. They found that symptoms clustered into two domains: inattention-disorganized (ADD without H) and hyperactive-impulsive (ADHD), and provide still further support for the construct of ADD without hyperactivity.

Studies indicating that children manifesting inattention but not hyperactivity may represent a high-risk group for school failure mandate that the occurrence of such an attentional subtype be investigated and if validated, definitional rules for its diagnosis provided. This takes on a particular urgency in view of findings of a strong correlation between externalizing behaviors and identification for special education services (Sandoval and Lambert, 1984–85). These data, and those of Berry et al. (1985), indicating that girls with ADD are less likely to be hyperactive and also less likely to receive special education services although they demonstrate significant attentional, cognitive, and language deficits, suggests that current school identification procedures rely heavily on the presence of hyperactivity or other externalizing behaviors. The implication is that children, particularly girls, who may be inattentive and experiencing academic difficulties but who are not hyperactive may not be identified, and as a consequence may not receive appropriate treatment; behavioral, pharmacologic, or educational. Thus ADD children without hyperactivity may represent an underidentified and as a consequence, underserved group of children who are at significant risk for long-term academic, social, and emotional difficulties (Shaywitz et al., 1990).

TREATMENT

Management of ADD represents a complex and intricate balance of a variety of treatment strategies encompassing educational, cognitive-behavioral, and pharmacological interventions. Establishing the diagnosis comprises the initial focus of management and once this has been accomplished, the diagnosis and its implications must then be interpreted to the child, his parents, and critical school personnel. Management of ADD encompasses two general domains: (a) nonpharmacologic (educational and cognitive-behavioral and other psychological and psychiatric approaches); (b) pharmacologic therapies.

Educational management of nonpharmacological therapies

Interrelationships between ADD and LD

Basic to the development of an appropriate educational plan for children with ADD is consideration of the possible relationships between ADD and learning difficulties. Evidence from a number of investigative groups suggests a substantial overlap between attention disorder and learning disabilities (LD). The prevalence of LD in ADD children is estimated to be 9–10% in hyperactive boys (Halperin et al., 1984) and 11% in an epidemiologic sample of 8-year-old Connecticut school children (Shaywitz, 1986). Conversely, the prevalence of hyperactivity in learning-disabled populations has varied from 41% (Holborow and Berry, 1986) to 80% (Safer and Allen, 1976), with a prevalence of 33% reported in an epidemiological sample (Shaywitz, 1986). Studies examining the academic achievement of hyperactive compared with control children support the notion that significantly more ADDH children experience academic achievement problems. They are more likely to perform below expectations in reading and arithmetic and, compared with controls, are behind both in their academic subjects and in more subjects (Cantwell, 1978). Holborow and

Berry (1986) found seven times as many children rated as hyperactive were described as experiencing "very much" difficulty in all academic areas compared with their nonhyperactive classmates.

Nature of association between ADD and LD

Given the substantial overlap between ADD and LD, it is not surprising that investigators have begun to explore the mechanisms underlying this association. Utilizing factor analytic studies, Lahey et al. (1978, 1988) have identified separate LD and hyperactivity factors. Other investigators have employed what Share and Schwartz (1988) refer to as a "multiple comparison" approach. Felton et al. (1987) examined children with ADD alone compared with children with reading disability. Reading-disabled children exhibited difficulty with tasks involving confrontation naming and rapid automatized naming; children with ADD had most trouble with word-list learning and recall. Though these findings have generated considerable controversy (see contrasting views by Share and Schwartz, 1988 and Wood et al., 1988), they suggest that naming and linguistic fluency deficits reflect reading disability while verbal learning and memory deficits are linked to attention disorder. More recently, August and Garfinkel (1989) examined 50 students with ADHD, 11 of whom also exhibited reading disability defined as a discrepancy between ability and reading achievement (referred to as cognitive). Children in this group exhibited deficits in lexical decoding and rapid word naming. Such findings support a language-based deficit for reading disability in these ADD children.

In contrast, other studies (Ackerman et al., 1986; Halperin et al., 1984) comparing hyperactive and mixed hyperactive–reading-disabled groups found very few measures on which the two groups differed, results contrary to the notion that the two are discrete subgroups. A recent report by McGee et al. (1989) compared groups of 13 year olds selected from their ongoing study of New Zealand school children. A battery of tasks including copying, delayed recall, pegboard, mazes, Wisconsin card sort, and word association was administered to four subject groups: (1) ADD without reading disability; (2) ADD with reading disability; (3) reading disability without ADD; and (4) control group without ADD or reading disability. No specific cognitive deficit was demonstrated for ADD alone, though ADD with reading disability and reading disability alone both exhibited verbal deficits. The authors conclude that their findings fail to support "a unique set of cognitive impairments" in ADD. However, criteria for selection of the reading-disabled group were far different from that used in most studies, indexing as reading disabled all children whose reading performance was below the median of reading in the ADD group. Most investigators employ an ability–achievement discrepancy or reading achievement below the 25th percentile. McGee et al.'s (1989) use of less impaired readers may have biased the findings of their study, producing results inconsistent with those of Felton et al. (1987).

Most recently van der Meere et al. (1989) proposed a novel strategy to differentiate the slow and inaccurate task performance, primarily prolonged reaction time, of children with ADD and LD. By combining the additive factor method of Sternberg (1969, 1975) and the selective attention model of Schneider and Shiffrin (1977) they found LD children to be impaired in memory search and decision processes while children with ADD exhibited deficits in motor decision processes. Though the selection criteria for ADD and LD are problematic, the authors' strategy and novel approach to a difficult issue represent a real conceptual advance.

While interesting, these approaches emphasize the relative paucity of research studies utilizing well defined, nonsystem-identified learning-disabled children where both the diagnosis of ADD and LD were made on the basis of rigorous criteria. Studies now in progress should provide a clearer understanding of: (a) the prevalence of the co-occurrence of ADD and LD; and (b) their mechanisms of interaction including the expression and course of one on the other. The ultimate aim, of course, is to provide rational approaches to intervention in children with both disorders.

Rational educational management must recognize the difficulties in differentiating the deficits due to learning disabilities from those primarily related to ADD, as well as the frequent co-occurrence of both disorders (LD and ADD) in the same child. Most cases of LD represent difficulties in reading, and the terms LD and reading disability (or dyslexia) are frequently used interchangeably. Within the last two decades the work of Isabelle Liberman and her colleagues (Liberman and Shankweiler, 1985; Mann et al., 1989) and Frank Vellutino and his associates (Vellutino, 1978, 1979; Vellutino and Scanlon, 1987), as well as other investigators supports the belief that reading disability represents difficulties with language and words—

their use, significance, meaning, pronunciation, and spelling and the problems generated by this lexical difficulty. Thus, children with speech and language difficulties are far more likely to exhibit deficits in reading than children without early language problems. Furthermore, poor readers consistently perform less well than good readers on tasks involving language. Both observations support the position which emphasizes the centrality of language in the genesis of reading disability. Not surprisingly, educational approaches to reading disability are directed toward this deficit in language (for review, see Clark, 1988). Therefore, it is critical to determine if a child diagnosed as ADD also has an accompanying learning or reading disability and, if so, to provide specific intervention for the reading problem.

Educational management children with ADD must not only recognize the frequently associated learning disability but, must recognize and deal effectively with academic issues related to the inattention and impulsivity. Such approaches have been reviewed previously (Atkins and Pelham, 1991; Anastopoulos et al., 1991; Shaywitz and Shaywitz, 1984) and include such measures as: minimizing distracting stimuli by preferential seating, in carrels or in a self-contained classroom; providing a 1:1 tutorial by increasing teacher availability through the use of aides or in a resource room; assuring structure and predictable routines; monitoring and, if necessary, modifying nonacademic structured times such as in the lunchroom, recess or physical education; teaching organizational and work–study skills, such as organizing materials and time.

Cognitive-behavioral therapies (CBT)

Cognitive-behavioral therapy (CBT), a term representing a host of cognitive components and behavioral strategies including operant techniques (positive and negative reinforcement) and parent counseling has come to represent the most widely employed alternative to pharmacotherapy. Cognitive strategies encourage the active participation of the child in the learning and monitoring process; training addresses such issues as: problem definition, problem approach, focusing of attention, choosing an answer, and self-enforcement and coping (Kendall and Braswell, 1985). As noted by Whalen et al. (1985), this enthusiasm for CBT comes both from the recognition that while stimulant medications are often effective, their actions are often circum-scribed and both physiological and psychologic toxicity may occur. Thus, in addition to side effects observed, medications may alter the way the child with ADD views himself and the way that parents perceive their child, effects which Whalen and Henker (1984) refer to as emanative effects of pharmacotherapy of ADD. Furthermore, medications are effective in at most 70% of children, and many others may either refuse medication or discontinue it shortly after initiation (Firestone, 1982). With its focus on self-guidance and problem solving, CBT offers an attractive long-term coping strategy for the child with ADD that is both durable and generalizable. Intuitively, one would expect synergy between both types of therapies; unfortunately, both short- and long-term gains with CBT have been quite limited, and a number of investigators have questioned whether CBT combined with pharmacotherapy offers any advantages to pharmacotherapy alone (Abikoff, 1991; Abikoff and Gittelman, 1985; Brown et al., 1985, 1986). However, formidable methodologic difficulties plague such studies and may obscure the effects of combined CBT and pharmacotherapy. Firestone et al. (1986) noted the importance of considering all subjects, including those who drop out of a study. Thus, in their investigation comparing stimulant medications and parent training in ADD, medications were superior, but when the data were reanalyzed, taking into consideration those who dropped out of the study, no differences were noted between the two treatment regimens. Furthermore, recent studies suggest that CBT may, in fact, be a useful adjunct to pharmacotherapy (Hinshaw et al., 1984; Pelham et al., 1986; Schell et al., 1986).

Psychotherapy

Individual psychotherapy may be a helpful component of therapy in some children who have serious psychiatric problems or are unable to cope with their disability. While the exclusive use of psychotherapy is rarely recommended in ADD, what Satterfield et al. (1980; 1982) term "multimodality" therapy has been demonstrated to be quite effective indeed. As employed by his group, multimodality therapy includes: (a) individual and group psychotherapy for the child; (b) individual education therapy for the child; (c) individual and group psychotherapy for the parents; (d) family psychotherapy; (e) medication. Satterfield et al. (1981) compared outcome after three years in children receiving multimodality therapy for 34 months with those receiving similar therapy for only 9 months. Those receiving less therapy were more antisocial and more inattentive than the group receiving longer duration therapy, suggesting a benefit from treatment. These issues are discussed in more detail by others in this volume and by Cohen and his associates (Hansen and Cohen, 1984, Hunt and Cohen, 1984).

Pharmacotherapy

Scope and prevalence of use

Medication, either used alone or in combination with CBT or psychiatric or psychologic therapy, is the most widely utilized modality employed in the management of ADD. Estimates suggest that drug treatment prevalence rates range from 0.75% to 2.6%, depending upon location and age group surveyed (Gadow and Kalachnik, 1981). A recent study by Safer and Krager (1988) suggests an increase in drug use for the treatment of ADD in recent years. These investigators used data from biannual surveys of school nurses that listed all students receiving medication for "hyperactivity." Over the 16-year period, stimulants (primarily methylphenidate) came to be used almost exclusively. Stimulant use increased steadily in elementary, middle, and high school. In recent years relatively more girls, older students and children from lower income families were receiving stimulants, and many were receiving the medication because of "inattentiveness" rather than "hyperactivity." As noted in an accompanying editorial (Shaywitz and Shaywitz, 1988b), "The data presented can only serve to inform us that the use of stimulants is increasing; it does not tell us about the practices and reasons underlying the increase." This increased use of stimulants might ". . . reflect a regressive step in which all behavioral and learning disorders are indiscriminately lumped together and treated in the same way. Conversely, the increased use of stimulant medication in newly recognized population of affected children, including those with inattention and particularly girls, may reflect an increased awareness of newer concepts of behavioral and attention disorders in which the central role of inattention in the genesis of school problems is recognized."

In the remainder of this chapter we review the effects of stimulants (amphetamine, methylphenidate, pemoline), generally regarded as the most effective, and not surprisingly then, the most widely utilized agents in the management of ADD. We review their mechanism of action, clinical effects, pharmacokinetics and indicate a reasonable and practical clinical approach to their use. Potential toxicity and side effects are, of course, discussed as well. While our focus is on stimulants, it should be recognized that tricyclic agents are assuming increasing importance in the therapeutic armamentarium (Biederman et al., 1989).

Stimulants

Effects on activity and attention

Evidence from several lines of investigation have converged to suggest a role for central monoaminergic mechanisms in the genesis of ADD (see Shaywitz and Shaywitz, 1988a for review). In no small measure, much of this evidence relates to the commonality of the mechanism of action of the stimulants and their therapeutic effects in children with ADD. Thus, investigations in animals (Kuczenski, 1983) demonstrate that amphetamine and methylphenidate act via central monoaminergic systems to: (1) increase release of amine, (2) inhibit reuptake, and (3) to some extent inhibit monoamine oxidase (MAO) activity, all actions that serve to increase the concentration of catecholamine (both dopamine and norepinephrine) at the synaptic cleft. The actions of pemoline are not nearly as well studied, though it is now clear that the early suggestion that pemoline preferentially stimulates dopamine synthesis is not supported by more recent studies. These indicate that pemoline reduces catecholamine turnover and may inhibit catecholamine uptake (Fuller et al., 1978; Molina and Orsingher, 1981).

Historically, a stimulant, D-amphetamine, was the first agent found to be effective in the treatment of hyperactivity (Bradley, 1937) and since that initial report abundant evidence from many investigative groups supports the belief that stimulants (amphetamine, methylphenidate, pemoline) are effective in reducing activity levels and improving attention in 60–70% of children with ADD (Anastopoulos et al., 1991; Barkley, 1977a, 1977b; Conners and Werry, 1979; Gadow, 1983; Kavale, 1982; Ottenbacher and Cooper, 1983; Rosenthal and Allen, 1978; Weiss and Hechtman, 1979; Whalen, 1989; Whalen and Henker, 1976). Investigations employing continuous monitoring of truncal activity recorded automatically for 24 hours per day, for seven days (Porrino et al., 1983) indicate that this reduction in activity levels occurs during academic studies in structured on-task activities; activity during less structured periods such as physical education was actually increased. Furthermore, the reduction in activity appears to be related to a reduction in perceived intensity of activity, rather than the amount of the activity per se (Henker et al., 1986; Whalen et al., 1979, 1981).

Effects on cognition

In contrast to the plethora of studies documenting the salutary effects of stimulants on attention and activity in children with ADD, their effects on cognitive function remain controversial. One reasonable strategy to assess such effects is to compare the effects of the stimulant in children with ADD with children referred primarily for learning disability. Some investigators have failed to note any positive effects of stimulants in primarily learning-disabled children (Gittelman, 1980; Gittelman-Klein and Klein, 1976; Huddleston et al., 1961). However, others (Ackerman et al., 1982) found that while hyperactive subjects demonstrated a more marked clinical response to methylphenidate than a group of primarily learning-disabled children without hyperactivity, all subject groups exhibited "substantial improvement" on the tests of attentiveness. Such findings suggest not only that attentional problems are a significant component in the children selected primarily for reading disability but that stimulants may be effective in those children with reading difficulty regardless of the presence of hyperactivity. Such findings are generally consonant with those of Gittelman et al. (1983) and suggest that methylphenidate may provide some benefit in the treatment of reading-disabled children, although such results still remain somewhat tenuous.

Clearly the examination of drug effects on academic achievement in children with ADD provides an even more direct strategy to examine the effects of stimulants on cognitive processes. Despite some early studies suggesting a positive effect of stimulants on learning or academic achievement (Conners, 1972; Weiss et al., 1971), other investigations reported no significant drug effects on academic achievement (reviewed by Barkley, 1981; Rie et al., 1976a, 1976b). Employing meta-analysis of 61 studies of the effects of drugs on hyperactivity, Ottenbacher and Cooper (1983) indicate that those measures classified as tapping "IQ achievement" were improved by stimulants, although to a considerably lesser degree than were such qualities as "behavioral social," "perceptual motor," and "impulse attention." In contrast, Kavale (1982), employing similar meta-analytic techniques suggests that "cognitive outcomes" are affected almost as much by stimulants as are behavioral outcomes.

As noted by Pelham (1983) and Douglas et al. (1986), explanations for these apparent discrepancies may be found in such methodological issues as: (a) insufficient items on an achievement test to detect short-term changes; (b) failure to control for order effects; (c) testing performed in a relatively artificial laboratory setting. Utilizing an experimental design which minimized such problems, Douglas et al. (1986) noted methylphenidate to induce improvement on mathematical computations and word discovery. In classroom tasks, children on methylphenidate attempted and completed more work, indicating a more efficient performance. Other investigators have now added to the evidence suggesting that stimulant administration to children with ADD results in improvement in academic performance in reading, arithmetic and spelling (Ballinger et al., 1984; Pelham, 1986; Pelham et al., 1986; Rapport et al., 1986; Sebrechts et al., 1986; Stephens et al., 1984).

Most recently, Richardson et al. (1988) examined a clinic referred sample of ADHD children participating in a 28-week long protocol. ADHD was defined by *DSM-III* criteria and reading disability was defined by achievement ≤ 75% normal using a reading grade level determined by an average of three reading tests: Gates-McGinity, Peabody Individual Achievement Test and the Decoding Skills Test. The children received reading instruction throughout the study period. Their findings were most consistent with the hypothesis that methylphenidate improved behavior, which then improved academic learning, with the effects strongest in the early phases of treatment. Methylphenidate appeared to improve verbal retrieval mechanisms leading to an improved ability to learn more difficult words.

Tannock et al. (1989) examined a small clinic referred sample of ADHD (*DSM-III*) children enrolled in a 6-week protocol. Eight of the 12 also exhibited learning disabilities as defined by scores of below the 25th percentile on the Wide Range Achievement Test–Revised. In contrast to Richardson's study, all testing was performed in a laboratory rather than classroom setting. Their results indicated that methylphenidate improved performance on both arithmetic and letter search tasks. These issues have been critically reviewed most recently by Rapport and Kelly (1991) and Swanson et al. (1991).

Effects on conduct and social behavior

Despite the half-century of experience with stimulants in children, their effects on aggressive kinds of behaviors is still not clear. Aggressive behavior, as determined by 5 minute observation periods during relatively short-term amphetamine administration is, indeed, reduced (Amery et al., 1984). As reviewed by Pelham and Murphy (1986), it is likely that combined pharmaco- and behavioral therapy is more effective than either alone in children with both conduct disorder (and/or oppositional disorder) and ADD. To date, however, our inability to more precisely define conduct disorder makes it impossible to determine with certainty those target populations employed in such investigations and the degree to which conduct disorder and ADD are confounded. These issues are discussed more fully elsewhere (Barkley et al., 1989; Shaywitz and Shaywitz, 1991).

Social interactions, are significantly affected by stimulants. Thus, methylphenidate is effective in improving the compliance of ADD children to their mothers' commands (Barkley et al., 1985), though sociability may be decreased (Barkley and Cunningham, 1979). Peer relationships may be affected as well, though it may be difficult to discern if the measures and the setting are not well-suited for such observations. Thus, a number of investigators (Cunningham et al., 1985; Pelham and Bender, 1982; Riddle and Rapoport, 1976) have not been able to document that stimulant medications affect peer interactions. However, such studies employed either relatively insensitive observational methods or simulated classroom settings.

More recent studies suggest that MPH may, indeed, positively influence aggression and anger. Utilizing a naturalistic setting and more sensitive observational methods, Whalen and her associates (1979, 1981) noted that methylphenidate reduced both the intensity and positive affect of boys with ADD. In a more recent study, Whalen et al. (1989) demonstrated that MPH reduces aggression in both the classroom and on the playground. Hinshaw et al. (1989) studied the effects of MPH in 24 boys with ADDH and oppositional disorder enrolled in a summer program for anger control. MPH (0.6 mg/kg) enhanced self-control, decreased physical retaliation tendency, and increased coping strategies in this group. Taken together with what Whalen and Henker (1984) term "emanative effects," such studies support the belief that stimulants exert significant influences on a variety of social interactions.

Ontogeny of stimulant effects

While the effects of stimulants in ADD have been described, for the most part, in school-age children, an emerging literature has begun to document the effects of stimulants in both younger (preschool) and older (adolescent) children as well as in adults. Clinical lore suggests that stimulants are not effective in the preschool child, a notion supported by studies such as that of Schliefer et al. (1975) which failed to document improvement in nursery school behavior after methylphenidate therapy. Clearly, more studies are needed at this age, but until diagnostic criteria for ADD in the preschool child are formulated, such studies will be difficult to conduct. Those issues relating to diagnosis are discussed above (see Evaluation) and reviewed by Campbell (1985, 1989).

In contrast, studies of stimulant effects in adolescents suggest that these pharmacological agents are as effective here as in the school-age child (Garfinkel et al., 1986; Varley and Trupin, 1983). This is not surprising, given the by now well-established phenomenological information core that documents a reduction of activity with maturation but a persistence of inattention and impulsivity.

Despite the initial optimism that ADD in adults might respond to stimulants, this has not been fully realized. In a recent study, Mattes et al. (1984) examined the effects of stimulant therapy in adult psychiatric patients with and without a childhood history of ADD. Methylphenidate appeared to benefit 25% of the subjects, regardless of their history of childhood ADD. However, even in those who responded, the effects were not as pronounced as those observed in childhood ADD. Again, as in the preschool ADD, diagnostic criteria for adult ADD have not been well established and it is not at all clear whether the term, when applied to adults, is describing a particular syndrome or is confounded by the large number of character disorders identified in adult psychiatric practice.

Practical considerations

To a great extent, the decision to initiate pharmacotherapy is based upon a number of diverse and difficult to define general factors such as the physician's clinical judgment, his understanding of the child, the family, and the school environment, and his knowledge of educational practices within his community. However, two very specific considerations are:

1. *Proper class placement*. This represents, perhaps the most critical factor in the success of pharmacotherapy since stimulant therapy will almost certainly be ineffective unless the child's educational placement is satisfactory. Thus, it is vital for the physician to do everything to insure that the school system has properly evaluated the child, and that the most appropriate school placement has been effected.
2. *Focus on target symptoms*. Before beginning a medication regimen, the physician must determine which particular symptoms are the targets of the treatment, and decide at which times these symptoms are most troublesome. Contrary to popular notions, hyperactivity alone is seldom a sufficient reason for initiation of pharmacotherapy. In fact, hyperactivity tends to abate with increasing age, no matter what treatment is employed.

In general, stimulants are more effective in the amelioratins attentional difficulties in school than on improving the child's behavior or performance at home. In part, this dichotomy between satisfactory improvement at school with relatively less improvement at home correlates with the biological availability of the stimulant. It also reflects the fact that those characteristics of attentional deficit that are most amenable to the effects of stimulants, for example, being able to follow a complicated set of directions amid the distractions caused by 25 other children, are put to the test in school. It is rare for the child to be placed in a similar stressful situation at home.

Not surprisingly, prediction of clinical response to stimulants does not appear to depend on either an abnormal neurological examination or abnormal electroencephalogram (Halperin et al., 1986). Some investigators have suggested that such predictions can be reliably determined using double-blind, placebo-controlled methodology to assess the child's performance on specific tests conducted in a laboratory setting (Swanson et al., 1978). While such procedures may be advantageous in particular situations, they are generally too complex, and most experienced clinicians would consider the administration of medication in the child's real-life setting as the only valid therapeutic trial. Parenthetically, it should be noted that a positive response to stimulants may be observed in nonhyperactive children (Rapoport et al., 1980; Werry, 1982), and thus improvement in symptoms with therapy should not be construed as implying that the diagnosis of ADD was, indeed, correct.

Children with ADD characteristically are extremely sensitive to alterations in their environment, and need more time to adjust to new situations. Thus, we recommend initiation of pharmacotherapy only if the child has had an opportunity to adjust to any environmental alteration. This means that, in most cases, medication should not be initiated simultaneously with the beginning a new school year or with the child's entrance into a different or altered classroom setting, such as transfer to special education. Such a practice not only allows the physician to determine the child's baseline functioning without medication, but more importantly, gives the child an opportunity to adjust to his new environment prior to beginning stimulant therapy. However, if past experience suggests that pharmacotherapy has made such a difference in the child's behavior that entry into a new class without medication would probably result in the child being viewed by his new teachers in a negative fashion, it would seem most reasonable to consider beginning medication prior to entry into the new environment. In practice, such a situation is most likely to arise when the child enters, for example, a middle or a junior high school setting and must contend with the additional stresses of a new setting, departmentalized programs, and older peers.

Administration and Dosage. In contrast to previous recommendations that MPH must only be given 30 minutes before breakfast when the stomach is empty to insure absorption, recent studies (Chan et al., 1983; Swanson et al., 1983) have demonstrated that both the pharmacokinetics and the behavioral effects of the drug are indistinguishable whether it is given with breakfast or 30 minutes before breakfast. A reasonable approach is to begin with an initial dosage of 0.3 mg/kg given in the morning immediately before the child leaves for school. Thus, by the time the child reaches school absorption should be complete, and peak levels attained within 2–3 hours. The school should be encouraged to place the child in academic subjects during these morning hours so that the effects of the drug on attentional processes will be maximal at times when the child needs the most help. Thus, by lunchtime, and in afternoon classes, (ideally, nonacademic subjects), the medication effect will be waning but the need for the drug is not as great. Clinical response is monitored by obtaining weekly feedback from the parents and, most importantly, from the school. This may be accomplished most efficiently via weekly rating scales (e.g., Conners, 1972; Yale MIT, Shaywitz, 1986) filled out by the child's primary academic teacher(s). If the child is not responding satisfactorily after two weeks of treatment, MPH dosage should be increased to 0.6–0.8 mg/kg. If response is nil after two weeks at this dose, the physician should consider switching to another medication and possibly reassessing the patient.

Determining the most effective dose of medication is further complicated because an optimum dosage for one target symptom may not be optimum for a different symptom. Thus, Sprague and Sleator (1977) suggest that while high doses of MPH (1.0 mg/kg) may produce improvement in global measures of activity, scores on memory tasks and performance on attentional tests may be poorer at a higher than at a low dose (0.3 mg/kg). However, other investigators have found that within a range of 0.3–0.8 mg/kg, performance on both behavioral and cognitive tasks improves in a dose-related fashion (Charles et al., 1981; Cunningham et al., 1985; Rapport et al., 1985; Sebrechts et al., 1986; Shaywitz et al., 1982). A more recent review (Swanson et al., 1991) suggests that depending on the cognitive task, the relationship of dose to performance may either follow a quadratic (U-shaped) function or a linear function.

At least one study documents what many clinicians know only too well: poor compliance in taking stimulant medications may be a significant problem in children with ADD. Thus Kaufman et al. (1981) studied medication compliance over an 18-week period in 12 school-age boys with ADD assigned to either methylphenidate, amphetamine, or placebo. The percent of children compliant for a given week ranged between 25 and 83%. Furthermore, they found 5 of 12 children taking methylphenidate when they were supposed to be taking placebo. Poor compliance in taking medications may explain some of the variability and conflicting results of various studies of the effects of stimulants.

On many occasions the child will do well in the morning at the 0.3 mg/kg dose but the effects appear to wear off by early afternoon. In this situation, it is reasonable to add another 0.3 mg/kg dose in the morning (for a total morning dose of 0.6 mg/kg). If afternoon function is still problematic, a second 0.3 mg/kg dose may be given three hours later. Experience has shown that "piggy-backing" a second dose in this manner before the initial dose has worn off eliminates the problems seen with decreasing availability of the medication. Another option would be to employ a stimulant with a longer duration of action, such as amphetamine, or pemoline. However, although D-amphetamine has an apparent biological half-life of 6.6 hours for tablets and 8.4 hours for sustained release preparation, the behavioral effects last no longer than 4 hours with either preparation (Brown et al., 1979).

Still another possibility is to consider the use of the sustained-release preparation of MPH (SR-20). An early study claiming that SR-20 was equivalent to regular MPH failed to incorporate such standard methodology as placebo controls, diagnostic criteria of the cohort, and equivalent mg/kg dosages

(Whitehouse et al., 1980). Most recently Pelham et al. (1987) compared the behavioral effects of SR-20 to 10 mg MPH administered at breakfast and 4 hours later. The standard preparation was found to be more effective than SR-20 in 7 of 10 children who responded to MPH. Greenhill (see this volume) also noted that the positive effects of MPH appeared to wane when the sustained-release preparation was used for six months. Such findings suggest that at the present time, standard MPH is the preparation of choice, and we would not recommend the use of the SR-20 form of the drug in the treatment of ADD.

Pemoline will also provide a longer duration of action. Though not as widely used as methylphenidate and amphetamine, the improvement rate in ADD following pemoline is similar to that observed with the other stimulants. Furthermore, its action may be continued even after treatment is stopped (Conners and Taylor, 1980). It is supplied in capsules of 18.75, 37.5, and 75 mg. Dosage varies between .5 and 3.0 mg/kg (Zametkin et al., 1986), with a starting dose of 18.75 mg/day and a dosage range of 37.5–112.5 mg/day. However, pemoline may adversely affect liver function and periodic monitoring of liver function tests is required when the drug is used. This necessity for frequent blood sampling has limited the clinical usefulness of the agent.

Another important issue to be considered is whether medication should be administered daily, or only on school days, with drug holidays when the child is away from school. Administration solely during school hours offers the advantage of limiting potential toxicity while maximizing the effect of MPH when it is most needed, namely, during the school day. Our routine is to prescribe MPH each school day, but omit the drug on weekends, school holidays, during the summer, and for the first 4–6 weeks of the new school year. Discontinuing therapy at the end of one school year enables us to evaluate how the child will do off medications and offers a regular opportunity to discontinue medications permanently. Thus, if it appears that the child is doing well without medication during the initial portion of the new school year we do not resume pharmacotherapy. However, careful followup is critical since, as the school year continues and academic pressures increase, initial sanguine assumptions about the lack of a need for medication may prove to be overly optimistic.

Clearly such a procedure may need to be modified in particular situations. Thus, on occasions when a particular child's impulsivity and activity are preventing optimum peer and family interaction, we have continued MPH on weekends. Furthermore, if the physician believes that the child's response to medication has been so dramatic and that starting a new school year without medication would be detrimental to the best interests of the child, he may decide that medication should be initiated as soon as school begins.

Pharmacokinetics

The development of a gas chromatographic assay for MPH (Hungand et al., 1978; Shaywitz et al., 1982) facilitated the determination of blood levels and permitted studies designed to explore a number of clinically relevant issues including the pharmacokinetics of MPH and the relationship between MPH concentrations and behavioral response.

Several investigative groups have examined the pharmacokinetics of oral MPH (Gualtieri et al., 1984; Sebrechts et al., 1986; Shaywitz et al., 1982; Winsberg et al., 1982). After a lag phase of about 0.5–1 hour, MPH reaches a peak plasma concentration 2.5 hours after administration. Two and three hour concentrations are, on the average, within 80 and 90% of the observed peak with maximal concentrations averaging 11.2 ng/ml at a dose of .34 mg/kg and 20.2 ng/ml at a dose of .65 mg/kg. Single point specimens obtained 2 hours after administration in children taking medication chronically approximate those found at the same time period after a single acute dose (Shaywitz et al., 1982). Elimination half-life averages 2.5 hours (Shaywitz et al., 1982). Swanson et al. (1978) have reported a "behavioral half-life" between 2 and 4 hours, which is quite consistent with the biological half-life observed for MPH. This effect contrasts with that observed after D-amphetamine, which demonstrates a much higher peak concentration (65.9 ng/ml after 0.45 mg/kg dose) and a longer half life (about 7 hours). In contrast to MPH, the behavioral effects observed after D-amphetamine were reported not to correlate with peak drug levels (Brown et al., 1979).

More recently several investigative groups have examined the pharmacokinetics of pemoline. A wide individual variation was observed with maximum plasma concentrations occurring approximately 3 hours after administration and peak concentrations averaging 4.3 mg/L. In contrast to previously reported studies in adults where elimination half-life averaged 11–13 hours, pemoline half-life in children averaged 7–8.5 hours (Collier et al., 1985; Sallee et al., 1985).

Physicians have come to rely on blood levels of a number of pharmacological agents (e.g., anticonvulsants) and the development of an assay for MPH suggested initially that blood levels of the drug might be helpful in the management of ADD. Although we (Sebrechts et al., 1986) and others (Winsberg et al., 1982) have found a significant positive correlation between blood levels and response on tests of attention, blood levels are so well correlated with oral dosage that there does not appear to be any real advantage of plasma levels over simply adjusting dose. Thus, except in unusual circumstances, we do not find MPH blood levels of practical utility in the pharmacotherapy of ADD.

Side effects

Insomnia or sleep disturbances and decreased appetite represent the most frequently observed side effects of stimulants, with weight loss, irritability, and abdominal pains almost as common. These and a host of other less frequent side effects (e.g., headaches, nausea, dizziness, dry mouth, constipation) usually disappear as the child becomes tolerant to the medication, or resolve if the dosage is reduced (Golinko, 1984). Although significant cardiac arrhythmias have been reported in young adults following intravenous methylphenidate (Lucas et al., 1986), cardiovascular function in ADD children receiving oral stimulants is reassuringly normal (Brown et al., 1984). Whether stimulants affect growth remains an important question. Mattes and Gittelman (1983) noted a significant decrease in height percentile after 2, 3, and 4 years of MPH therapy. Furthermore, they emphasized that the reduction in height was related to the total yearly dose of MPH. This latter study supports conclusions reached by an FDA subcommittee, and suggests that the effects of MPH appear to be dose related, with higher doses administered for prolonged duration producing the greatest decrement in height. This problem may be minimized if the drug is discontinued for a time to allow catch-up growth to occur. In practice, this suggests that if the medication could be omitted for long periods (e.g., summer vacations, holidays, weekends), the total yearly dose would be reduced and presumably the detrimental effects on stature lessened. Similar effects on growth have been reported with pemoline as well (Friedmann et al., 1981).

In contrast to the other side effects which are either transient or are reversed by a reduction in drug dosage, the emergence of Gilles de la Tourette's syndrome (TS) is of more concern, and instances of TS appearing in association with the administration of MPH have been reported (Lowe et al., 1982). Because MPH acts via central catecholaminergic mechanisms, and TS may result from stimulation of supersensitive dopaminergic or noradrenergic neurons, it is reasonable to believe that the onset of the tics after MPH was more than simply coincidental. Good evidence suggests that TS occurs more frequently in the offspring of parents with TS and in the siblings of affected individuals. Thus, in those children with ADD whose parents or siblings have a history of tics, caution must be used in the administration of stimulants (Cohen et al., 1984). Tics have also been a reported consequence of combinations of stimulants plus other neuroleptics (amphetamine + haloperidol; methylphenidate, imipramine, thioridazine) in two children with ADD (Gualtieri and Patterson, 1986). In light of the well-established relationship between TS and obsessive–compulsive disorders, a recent report (Koizumi, 1985) of the emergence of obsessive-compulsive symptoms in three children, two following D-amphetamine and one following methylphenidate therapy, add further support for a possible relationship between ADD and TS. Despite these caveats, stimulants remain the most effective pharmacotherapy for ADD, including ADD occurring in association with TS. Clinical indications may warrant the administration of stimulants to such children, always accompanied by warnings to the parents that the symptoms of TS may be exacerbated by the medication.

Nontraditional, controversial, and idiosyncratic therapies definition

This category encompasses a wide range of therapies which Golden (1984) defined operationally as sharing the following characteristics:

1. Their theoretical justification is not consistent with modern scientific knowledge.

2. The effectiveness of therapy is claimed for a broad range of problems that usually are not rigorously defined.

3. The possibility of adverse effects are minimized since the treatment usually relies on the use of "natural" substances (vitamins, special diets) exercises, or simple manipulations of the body.

4. Their initial presentation is often in media other than peer-reviewed scientific journals.

5. Controlled studies that do not support the therapy are discounted as being improperly performed or biased because of the unwillingness of the medical and scientific establishment to accept "novel" ideas.

6. Support for the therapy is provided by the emergence of lay organizations which proselytize new members, and attempt to develop special interest legislation and regulations.

Golden notes that investigations suggest that the orientation of groups advocating such therapies may reflect as much a social movement as a medically oriented one (Vissing and Petersen, 1981). Characteristics include testimonials, antiprofessionalism, and an often expressed view that there is a conspiracy between the government and the medical establishment to withhold the therapy.

These so-called therapies can be categorized as (a) dietary and (b) what Silver (1986) terms neurophysiologic retraining. Details have been reviewed by us previously (Shaywitz & Shaywitz, 1988b) and the reader is referred to that publication for details.

Adverse effects

Such therapies are clearly quite appealing, not only to parents but to professionals as well, and although not helpful, at least seemingly innocuous. However, even brief reflection provides good evidence of real harm from such approaches. Perhaps the greatest harm results from the parents' investing inordinate energy in nonproductive treatments, leaving little time and energy for well-documented effective management methods. Thus, the parent whose energies are bound up in an idiosyncratic management regimen may not have the energy to insure that the child's classroom is optimal and the teacher is providing the most effective school environment. It may be that parents omit pharmacotherapies that have proved effective, even, as noted by Golden (1984) to the point of omitting the use of anticonvulsants in a child who has a seizure disorder.

Given the poor self-image characterizing many children with ADD, and recognizing food to be a very important component of the child's interaction with society, there is a real danger that some of the dietary therapies may serve to further isolate the child from his peers and others in his environment.

The effects of dietary therapy are obvious, not only on the child, who is the particular target of the therapy, but on other children and adults in the family constellation. Thus, the preparation and implementation of a special diet for one child in the family often means that the other children not only must also eat the same meals, but that they are denied the time and attention necessary for their well-being. Thus, the time and energy necessary for the preparation of special diets might be more productively spent on other family activities. Still another negative effect is the expense involved in many of these unproved treatment modalities. Thus, special diets are indeed expensive, and may foster additional resentment of the parents and siblings toward the child with ADD.

Evaluation of the safety of such idiosyncratic therapies must also take into consideration the possibility that, while seemingly innocuous now, they may be shown later to have significant and permanent side effects. As noted by Golden, the use of oxygen to treat respiratory problems in premature infants was initially believed to be not only effective but to have no side effects. We all know now that oxygen therapy may result in retrolental fibroplasia and blindness, but who would have predicted that the use of such a "natural" substance could produce such severe side effects. One has only to reflect on the history of such treatments as lobotomy or the use of DES (see Valenstein, 1986) to recognize how difficult it is to accurately predict the long-term safety of any therapy.

SUMMARY

We have reviewed the diagnosis and management of attention deficit disorder, focusing particularly on the role of stimulant therapy in ADD. Historical review suggest that ADD has roots which extend back almost 90 years. ADD is defined on the basis of inclusion and exclusion criteria which are established by history and reflect behavioral concerns. ADD is a chronic disorder affecting the child's home, school, and community life. The primary symptoms of the disorder manifest a developmental pattern, activity diminishes while attentional deficits persist. Major sources of concern are the secondary and often more resistent problems of learning difficulties, behavioral problems, lack of peer acceptance, and low self-esteem. An often frustrating and perplexing characteristic of the disorder is its marked variability; over time, across situations, and within the same child and similar situations.

Educational management represents an important priority and often forms the cornerstone of all other therapies, nonpharmacologic or pharmacologic. Cognitive behavioral therapies represent the most widely employed alternative to pharmacotherapy. Although the effects of CBT alone are disappointing, recent studies suggest that such therapies may provide a useful adjunct to pharmacotherapy and may be helpful when children are tapered off medication. Psychotherapy, or a combination of psychotherapy and medication (multimodality therapy) may also be useful.

Pharmacotherapy for ADD originated 50 years ago, and at this time the ameliorative effects of medications in ADD are well established. Despite concerns in the early 1970s that medication, primarily stimulants, were being prescribed too frequently, recent data and the experience of most clinicians indicate this probably is not the case. The general skepticism of experienced clinicians, coupled with a climate where parents are reluctant to medicate children serves to limit their use except where indicated. While the effects of stimulants on attention and activity seem well established, effects on cognition, conduct, and social behavior are more controversial. Within recent years, a great deal has been learned about the pharmacokinetics of stimulants in children with ADD, providing a rational basis for administration. It is also clear that side effects are minimal, the most serious being the possibility of the emergence of tics. While stimulants are clearly the most effective agents, tricyclic antidepressants and monoamine oxidase inhibitors may also be effective.

Nontraditional, controversial, and idiosyncratic therapies continue to be used in ADD, both by professionals and laypersons alike. To date, there is no indication that such approaches as a food additive-free diet, elimination of sugar, megavitamin therapy, patterning, or treatment of alleged vestibular dysfunction have any benefit above their placebo effects. Though appealing for their simplicity, their adverse effects are not often recognized. Thus, they may divert parents' energies from more effective management strategies, are often expensive, and may have long-term side effects not immediately apparent.

ACKNOWLEDGMENTS

Supported by grants from the National Institute of Child Health and Human Development (PO1 HD 21888 and P50 HD25802), the United States Office of Education (GOO-8535118) and the Connecticut State Department of Education. We thank Carmel Lepore for her invaluable assistance in the preparation of this chapter.

REFERENCES

Abikoff, H. (1991), Cognitive training in ADHD children: Less to it than meets the eye. *J. of Learn. Disabil.*, 24:205–209.

———— Gittelman, R. (1985), Hyperactive children treated with stimulants. Is cognitive training a useful adjunct? *Arch. Gen. Psychiatry,* 42:953–961.

Ackerman, P.T., Dykman, R.A., Holcomb, P.J. & McCray, D.S. (1982), Methylphenidate effects on cognitive style and reaction time in four groups of children. *Psychiatry Res.*, 7:199–213.

———Anhald, J.M., Dykman, R.A. & Holcomb, P.J. (1986), Effortful processing in children with reading and/or attention disorders. *Brain Cogn.*, 5:22–40.

American Psychiatric Association (1980), *Diagnostic and Statistical Manual of Mental Disorders*, 3rd Ed. (DSM III). Washington, DC: American Psychiatric Association.

——— (1987), *Diagnostic and Statistical Manual of Mental Disorders*, 3rd Ed., rev. (DSM III-R). Washington, DC: American Psychiatric Association.

American Psychiatric Association (Ed.). (in preparation), *Diagnostic and Statistical Manual of Mental Disorders*, 4th Ed. (DSM IV). Washington, DC: American Psychiatric Association.

Amery, B., Minichello, M.D. & Brown, G.L. (1984), Aggression in hyperactive boys: Response to d-amphetamine. *J. Am Acad. Child Psychiatry*, 23:291–294.

Anastopoulos, A.D., DuPaul, G.J. & Barkley, R.A. (1991), Stimulant medication and parent training therapies for attention deficit-disorder. *J. Learn. Disabil.* 24(4):210–218.

Anderson, J.C., Williams, S., McGee, R. & Silva, P.A. (1987), DSM-III disorders in preadolescent children. *Arch. Gen. Psychiatry*, 44:69–76.

Atkins, M.Ṡ. & Pelham, W.E. (1991), School-based assessment of attention deficit-hyperactivity disorder. *J. of Learn. Disabil.*, 24(4):197–204.

——— ——— & Licht, M.H. (1989), The differential validity of teacher ratings of inattention/overactivity and aggression. *J. Abnorm. Child Psychol.*, 17:423–435.

August, G.J. & Garfinkel, B.D. (1989), Behavioral and cognitive subtypes of ADHD. *J. Am. Acad. Child Adolesc. Psychiatry*, 28:739–748.

Ballinger, C.T., Varley, C.K. & Nolen, P.A. (1984), Effects of methylphenidate on reading in children with attention deficit disorder. *Am. J. Psychiatry*, 141:1590–1593.

Barkley, R.A. (1977a), The effects of methylphenidate on various types of activity level and attention in hyperkinetic children. *J. Abnorm. Child Psychology*, 5:351–369.

——— (1977b), A review of stimulant drug research with hyperactive children. *J. Child Psychol. Psychiatry*, 18:137–165.

——— (ed.) (1981), *Hyperactive Children*. New York: Guilford Press.

——— (1988), The effects of methylphenidate on the interactions of preschool ADHD children with their mothers. *J. Am. Acad. Child Adolesc. Psychiatry*, 27:336–341.

——— Cunningham, C.E. (1979), The effects of methylphenidate on the mother-child interactions of hyperactive children. *Arch. Gen. Psychiatry*, 36:201–208.

——— Karlsson, J. & Pollard, S. (1985), Effects of age on the mother-child interactions of ADD-H and normal boys. *J. Abnorm. Child Psychol.*, 13:631–637.

——— McMurray, M.B., Edelbrock, C.S. & Robbins, K. (1989), The response of aggressive and nonaggressive ADHD children to two doses of methylphenidate. *J. Am. Acad. Child Adolesc. Psychiatry*, 6:873–881.

——— Costello, A. & Spitzer, R. (in press). The development of the DSM-III-R criteria for disruptive behavior disorders.

——— Gittelman, R. (1985), Hyperactive children treated with stimulants. Is cognitive training a useful adjunct? *Arch. Gen. Psychiatry*, 42:953–961.

Bax, U. & MacKeith, R.C. (1963), "Minimal brain damage"—a concept dysfunction. In: *Minimal Cerebral Dysfunction*, eds. R.C. MacKeith & M. Bax London: SIMP with Wm. Heinemann.

Bender, L. (1942), Post encephalitic behavior disorders in childhood. In: ed. L. Bender *Encephalitis: A Clinical Study*. New York: Grune & Stratton.

Berry, C.A., Shaywitz, S.E. & Shaywitz, B.A. (1985), Girls with attention deficit disorder: A silent minority? A report on behavioral and cognitive characteristics. *Pediatrics*, 76:801–809.

Biederman, J., Baldessarini, R.J., Wright, V., Knee, D. & Harmatz, J.S. (1989). A double-blind placebo controlled study of desipramine in the treatment of ADD: I. Efficacy. *J. Am. Acad. Child Adolesc. Psychiatry,* 28:777–784.

Bradley, C. (1937), The behavior of children receiving benzedrine. *Am. J. Psychiatry,* 94:577–585.

Brown, G.L., Hunt, R.D., Ebert, M.H., Bunney, W.E. & Kopin, I.J. (1979), Plasma levels of d-amphetamine in hyperactive children. *Psychopharmacology,* 62:133–140.

Brown, R.T., Wynne, M.E. & Medenis, R. (1985), Methylphenidate and cognitive therapy: A comparison of treatment approaches with hyperactive boys. *J. Abnorm. Child Psychol.,* 13:69–87.

―――― ―――― & Slimmer, L.W. (1984), Attention deficit disorder and the effect of methylphenidate on attention, behavioral, and cardiovascular functioning. *J. Clinical Psychiatry,* 45:473–476.

―――― ―――― Borden, K.A., Clingerman, S.R., Geniesse, R. & Spunt, A.L. (1986), Methylphenidate and cognitive therapy in children with attention deficit disorder: A double-blind trial. *Devel. Behav. Pediatr.,* 7:163–170.

Campbell, S.B. (1985), Hyperactivity in preschoolers: Correlates and prognostic implications. *Clin. Psychol. Rev.,* 5:405–428.

―――― (ed.). (1990), *Behavior Problems in Preschool Children: Clinical and Developmental Issues.* New York: Guilford Press.

Cantwell, D.P. (1978), Hyperactivity and antisocial behavior. *Am. Acad. Child Psychiatry,* 17:252–262.

Chan, Y.M., Swanson, J.M., Soldin, S.S., Thiessen, J.J., MacLeod, S.M. & Logan, W. (1983), Methylphenidate hydrochloride given with or before breakfast: II. Effects on plasma concentration of methylphenidate and ritalinic acid. *Pediatrics,* 72:56–59.

Charles, L., Schain, R.J. & Zelniker, T. (1981), Optimal dosages of methylphenidate for improving the learning and behavior of hyperactive children. *Behav. Pediatr.,* 2:78–81.

Clark, D.B. (1988), *Dyslexia: Theory & Practice of Remedial Instruction.* Parkton, MD: York Press.

Clements, S.D. & Peters, J.E. (1962), Minimal brain dysfunctions in the school-aged child. *Arch. Gen. Psychiatry,* 6:185–187.

Cohen, D.J., Riddle, M.A., Leckman, J., Ort, S. & Shaywitz, B.A. (1984), Tourette's syndrome. In: *Neuropsychiatric Movement Disorders,* eds. D.V. Jeste & R.J. Wyatt Washington, DC: American Psychiatric Press, (pp. 19–52).

Collier, C.P., Soldin, S.J., Swanson, J.M., MacLeod, S.M., Weinberg, F. & Rochefort, J.G. (1985), Pemoline pharmacokinetics and long term therapy in children with attention deficit disorder and hyperactivity. *Clin. Pharmacokin.,* 10:269–278.

Conners, C.K. (1972), Symposium: Behavior modification by drugs. II. Psychological effects of stimulant drugs in children with minimal brain dysfunction. *Pediatrics,* 49:702–708.

―――― & Taylor, E. (1980). Pemoline, methylphenidate, and placebo in children with minimal brain dysfunction. *Arch. Gen. Psychiatry,* 37:922–930.

―――― & Werry, J.S. (1979), Pharmacotherapy. In: *Psychopathological Disorders of Childhood,* eds. H.C. Quay & J.S. Werry. New York: Wiley.

Costello, E.J., Costello, A.J., Edelbrock, C., Burns, B.J., Dulcan, M.K., Brent, D. & Janiszewski, S. (1988), Psychiatric disorders in pediatric primary care. *Arch. Gen. Psychiatry,* 45:1107–1116.

Cunningham, C.E., Siegel, L.S. & Offord, D.R. (1985), A developmental dose-response analysis of the effects of methylphenidate on the peer interactions of attention deficit disordered boys. *J. Child Psychol. Psychiatry,* 26:955–971.

Douglas, V.I., Barr, R.G., O'Neill, M.E. & Britton, B.G. (1986), Short term effects of methylphenidate on the cognitive, learning and academic performance of children with attention deficit disorder in the laboratory and the classroom. *J. Child Psychol. Psychiatry,* 27:191–211.

Edelbrock, C., Costello, A.J. & Kessler, M.D. (1984), Empirical corroboration of attention deficit disorder. *J. Am. Acad. Child Psychiatry,* 23:285–290.

Felton, R.H., Wood, F.B., Brown, I.S., Campbell, S.K. & Harter, M.R. (1987), Separate verbal memory and naming deficits in attention deficit disorder and reading disability. *Brain Language*, 31: 171–184.

Firestone, P. (1982), Factors associated with children's adherence to stimulant medication. *Am. J. Orthopsychiatry*, 52:447–457.

———— Crowe, D., Goodman, J.T. & McGrath, P. (1986), Vicissitudes of follow-up studies: Differential effects of parent training and stimulant medication with hyperactives. *Am. J. Orthopsychiatry*, 56:184–194.

Friedmann, N., Thomas, J., Carr, R., Elders, J., Ingdahl, I. & Roche, A. (1981), Effect on growth in pemoline-treated children with attention deficit disorder. *Am. J. Disturb. Child.*, 135:329–332.

Fuller, R.W., Perry, K.W., Bymaster, F.P. & Wong, D.T. (1978), Comparative effects of pemoline, amfoelic acid, and amphetamine on dopamine uptake and release in vitro on brain 3,4-dihydroxy-phenylacetic acid concentration on spiperone-treated rats. *J. Pharm. Pharmacol.*, 30:197–198.

Gadow, K.D. (1983), Effects of stimulant drugs on academic performance in hyperactive and learning disabled children. *J. Learn. Disabil.*, 16:290–299.

———— & Kalachnik, J. (1981), Prevalence and pattern of drug treatment for behavior and seizure disorders of TMR students. *Am. J. Mental Defic.*, 85:588–595.

Garfinkel, B.D. & Wender, P. (1989), Attention deficit hyperactivity disorder. In: *Comprehensive Textbook of Psychiatry*, eds. H. Kaplin & B. Sadock, Baltimore: William Wilkins, (pp. 1828–1837.)

———— Brown, W., Klee, S.H., Braden, W., Beauchesne, H. & Shapiro, S.K. (1986), Neuroendocrine and cognitive responses to amphetamine in adolescents with a history of attention deficit disorder. *J. Am. Acad. Child Psychiatry*, 25:503–508.

Gittelman, R. (1980), Indications for the use of stimulant treatment in learning disorders. *J. Am. Acad. Child Psychiatry*, 19:623–636.

———— Klein, D.F. & Feingold, I. (1983), Children with reading disorders-II. Effects of methylphenidate in combination with reading remediation. *J. Child Psychol. Psychiatry*, 24:193–212.

Gittelman-Klein, R. & Klein, D.F. (1976), Methylphenidate effects in learning disabilities. *Arch. Gen. Psychiatry*, 33:654–655.

Golden, G.S. (1984), Controversial therapies. *Pediatr. Clin. North Am.*, 31:459–469.

Goldstein, K. (1936), Modification of behavior consequent to cerebral lesion. *Psychiatric Q.*, 10:539–610.

Golinko, B.E. (1984), Side effects of dextroamphetamine and methylphenidate in hyperactive children—a brief review. *Neuropsychopharmacol. Biol. Psychiatry*, 8:1–8.

Gualtieri, C.T. & Patterson, D.R. (1986), Neuroleptic-induced tics in two hyperactive children. *Am. J Psychiatry*, 143:1176–1177.

———— Hicks, R.E., Patrick, K., Schroeder, S.R. & Breese, G.R. (1984), Clinical correlates of methylphenidate blood levels. *Thera. Drug Mon.*, 6:379–392.

Halperin, J.M., Gittelman, R., Klein, D.F. & Ruddel, R.G. (1984), Reading disabled hyperactive children: A distinct subgroup of attention deficit disorder with hyperactivity? *J. Abnorm. Child Psychol.*, 12:1–14.

Hansen, C.R. & Cohen, D.J. (1984), Multimodality approaches in the treatment of attention deficit disorders. *Pediatr. Clin. North Am.*, 31:499–513.

Henker, B., Astor-Dubin, L. & Varni, J.W. (1986), Psychostimulant medication and perceived intensity in hyperactive children. *J. Abnorm. Child Psychology*, 14:105–114.

Hinshaw, S.P., Henker, B. & Whalen, C.K. (1984), Cognitive-behavioral and pharmacologic interventions in hyperactive boys; comparative and combined effects. *J. Consult. Clin. Psychology*, 52:739–749.

———— Buhrmester, D. & Heller, T. (1989), Anger control in response to verbal provocation: Effects of stimulant medication for boys with ADHD. *J. Abnorm. Child Psychol.*, 17:393–407.

Hohman, L.B. (1922), Post encephalitic behavior disorders in children. *Johns Hopkins Hosp. Bull.*, 380:372–375.

Holborow, P.L. & Berry, P.S. (1986), Hyperactivity and learning difficulties. *J. Learn. Disabil.*, 19:426–431.

Huddleston, W., Staiger, R.C., Frye, R., Musgrove, R.S. & Stritch, T. (1961), Deanol as aid in overcoming reading retardation. *Clin. Med.*, 8:1340–1342.

Hungund, B.L., Henna, M. & Winsberg, B.G. (1978), A sensitive gas chromatographic method for the determination of methylphenidate (Ritalin) and its major metabolite a-phenyl-2-piperidine acetic acid (ritalinic acid) in plasma using a nitrogen-phosphorous detector. *Psychopharmacol. Commu.*, 2:203.

Hunt, R.D. & Cohen, D.J. (1984), Psychiatric aspects of learning difficulties. *Pediatr. Clin. North Am.*, 31:471–497.

Kaufman, R.E., Smith-Wright, D., Reese, C.A., Simpson, R. & Jones, F. (1981), Medication compliance in hyperactive children. *Pediatr. Pharmacol.*, 1:231–237.

Kavale, K. (1982), The efficiency of stimulant drug treatment for hyperactivity: A meta-analysis. *J. Learn. Disabil.*, 15:280–289.

Kendall, P.C. & Braswell, L. (1985), *Cognitive-Behavior Therapy for Impulsive Children*. New York: Guilford Press.

King, C. & Young, R.D. (1982), Attentional deficits with and without hyperactivity: Teacher and peer perceptions. *J. Abnorm. Child Psychol.*, 10:483–495.

Koizumi, H.M. (1985), Obsessive-compulsive symptoms following stimulants. *Biol. Psychiatry*, 20:1332–1333.

Kuczenski, R. (1983), Biochemical actions of amphetamines and other stimulants. In: *Stimulants: Neurochemical, Behavior, and Clinical*, ed. I. Crease. New York: Raven Press, pp. 31–63.

Lahey, B.B. & Carlson, K. (1991), Validity of a diagnostic category of attention deficit disorder without hyperactivity: A review of the literature. *J. of Learn. Disabil.*, 24(2):110–120.

——— Schaughency, E.A., Hynd, G.W., Carlson, C.L. & Nieves, N. (1987), Attention deficit disorder with and without hyperactivity: Comparison of behavioral characteristics of clinic-referred children. *J. Am. Acad. Child Adolesc. Psychiatry*, 26:718–723.

——— Stempniak, M., Robinson, E.J. & Tyroler, M.J. (1978), Hyperactivity and learning disabilities as independent dimensions of child behavior problems. *J. Abnorm. Psychol.*, 87:333–340.

——— Pelham, W.E., Schaughency, E.A., Atkins, M.S., Murphy, H.A., Hynd, G., Russo, M. & Hartdagen, S. (1988), Dimensions and types of attention deficit disorder. *J. Am. Acad. Child Adolesc. Psychiatry*, 27:330–335.

Laufer, M. & Denhoff, E. (1957), Hyperkinetic behavior syndrome in children. *J. Pediatr.*, 50:463–474.

Liberman, I.Y. & Shankweiler, D. (1985), Phonology and the problems of learning to read and write. *Remed. Spec. Educ.*, 6:8–17.

Lowe, T.L., Cohen, D.J., Detlor, J., Kremenitzer, M.W. & Shaywitz, B.A. (1982), Stimulant medications precipitate Tourette's syndrome. *J. Am. Med. Assoc.*, 247:1729–1731.

Lucas, P.B., Gardner, D.L., Wolkowitz, O.M., Tucker, E.E. & Cowdry, R.W. (1986), Methylphenidate-induced cardiac arrhythmias. *N. Engl. J. Med.*, 315:1485.

Mann, V.A., Cowin, E. & Schoenheimer, J. (1989), Phonological processing, language comprehension, and reading ability. *J. Learn. Disabil.*, 22:76–89.

Mattes, J.A. & Gittelman, R. (1983), Growth of hyperactive children on maintenance regimen of methylphenidate. *Arch. Gen. Psychiatry*, 40:317–321.

——— Boswell, L. & Oliver, H. (1984), Methylphenidate effects on symptoms of attention deficit disorder in adults. *Arch. Gen. Psychiatry*, 41:1059–1063.

McGee, R., Williams, S., Moffitt, T. & Anderson, J. (1989), A comparison of 13-year-old boys with attention deficit and/or reading disorder on neuropsychological measures. *J. Abnorm. Child Psychol.*, 17:37–53.

Meyer, A. (1904), The anatomical facts and clinical varieties of traumatic insanity. *Am. J. Insanity*, 60:373–441.

Molina, V.A. & Orsingher, O.A. (1981), Effects of Mg-pencoline on the central catecholaminergic system. *Arch. Intern. Pharmacodyn.*, 251:66–79.

Ottenbacher, K.J. & Cooper, M.M. (1983), Drug treatment of hyperactivity in children. *Devel. Med. Child Neurol.*, 25:358–366.

Pelham, W.E. (1983), The effects of psychostimulants on academic achievement in hyperactive and learning-disabled children. *Thalamus: (Intern. Acad. Res. Learn. Disabil.)*, 3:1–47.

——— (1986), The effects of psychostimulant drugs on learning and academic achievement in children with attention deficit disorders and learning disabilities. In: *Psychological and Educational Perspectives on Learning Disabilities,* eds. J. Torgeser & B. Wong New York: Academic Press pp. 259–295.

——— (1990), Behavior therapy, behavioral assessment, and psychostimulant medication in treatment of attention deficit disorders: An interactive approach. In: *Attention Deficit Disorders V: Current Concepts and Emerging Trends in the Treatment of Attention and Behavior Problems in Children,* eds. J. Swanson & L. Bloomingdale. London: Pergamon, pp. 169–195.

——— & Bender, M.E. (1982), Peer relationships in hyperactive children: Description and treatment. In: *Advances in Learning and Behavioral Disabilities,* eds. K. Gadow & E. Biale. New York: JAI Press, pp. 365–436.

——— ——— (1986), Attention deficit and conduct disorders. In: *Pharmacological and Behavioral Treatments: An Integrative Approach,* ed. M. Hersen. New York: Wiley, pp. 108–148.

——— & Murphy, G.A. (1990), Hyperactivity/attention deficit disorders. In: *International Perspectives in Behavioral Medicine,* Vol. 3, eds. D. Byrne & G. Caddy. Norwood, NJ: Ablex.

——— Walker, J.L. & Milich, R. (1986), Effects of continuous and partial reinforcement and methylphenidate on learning in children with attention deficit disorder. *J. Abnorm. Psychol.,* 95:001–006.

——— Sturges, J., Hoza, J., Schmidt, C., Bjilsma, J.J., Milich, R. & Moorer, S. (1987), Sustained release in standard methylphenidate effects on cognitive and social behavior in children with attention deficit disorder. *Pediatrics,* 80:491–501.

Porrino, L.J., Rapoport, J.L., Behar, D., Sceery, W., Ismond, D.R. & Bunney, W.E., Jr. (1983), A naturalistic assessment of the motor activity of hyperactive boys I. Comparison with normal controls. *Arch. Gen. Psychiatry,* 40:681–693.

Rapoport, J., Weingartner, H., Zahn, T.P., Ludlow, C. & Mikkelsen, E.J. (1980), Dextroamphetamine: Its cognitive and behavioral effects in normal and hyperactive boys and normal adult males. *Arch. Gen. Psychiatry,* 37:933–946.

Rapport, M.D., & Kelly, K.L. (1991), Psychostimulant effects on learning and cognitive function: Findings and implications for children with attention deficit hyperactivity disorder. *Clinical Psychology Review,* 11:61–92.

——— DuPaul, G.J., Stoner, G., Birmingham, B.K. & Masse, G. (1985), Attention deficit disorder with hyperactivity: Differential effects of methylphenidate on impulsivity. *Pediatrics,* 76:938–943.

——— ——— ——— & Jones, J.T. (1986), Comparing classroom and clinic measurements of attention deficit disorder: Differential, idiosyncratic, and dose-response effects of methylphenidate. *J. Consult. Clin. Psychol.,* 54:334–341.

Richardson, E., Kupietz, S.S., Winsbedrg, B.G., Maitinsky, S. & Mendell, N. (1988), Effects of methylphenidate dosage in hyperactive reading-disabled children: II. Reading achievement. *J. Am. Acad. Child Adolesc. Psychiatry,* 27:78–87.

Riddle, K.D. & Rapoport, J.L. (1976), A 2 year followup of 72 hyperactive boys. *J. Nerv. Mental Dis.,* 162:126–134.

Rie, H., Rie, E., Stewart, S. & Ambuel, J. (1976a), Effects of methylphenidate on underachieving children. *J. Consult. Clin. Psychol.,* 44:250–260.

——— ——— ——— ——— (1976b), Effects of ritalin on underachieving children: A replication. *Am. J. Orthopsychiatry,* 46:311–313.

Rosenthal, R.H. & Allen, T.W. (1978), An examination of attention, arousal, and learning dysfunctions of hyperkinetic children. *Psychol. Bull.*, 85:689–715.

Rourke, B.P. (1989), *Nonverbal Learning Disabilities: The Syndrome and the Model.* New York: Guilford.

Safer, D.J. & Allen, R.D. (1976), *Hyperactive Children: Diagnosis and Management.* Baltimore: University Park Press.

——— & Krager, J. M. (1988), A survey of medication treatment for hyperactive/inattentive students. *J. Am. Med. Assoc.*, 260:2256–2258.

Sallee, F., Stiller, R., Perel, J. & Bates, T. (1985), Oral pemoline kinetics in hyperactive children. *Clin. Pharmacol. Ther.*, 37:606–609.

Sandoval, J. & Lambert, N.M. (1984–85), Hyperactive and learning disabled children: Who gets help? *J. Spec. Educ.*, 18:495–503.

Satterfield, J., Satterfield, B.T. & Cantwell, D.P. (1980), Multimodality treatment: A two-year evaluation of 61 hyperactive boys. *Arch. of Gen. Psychiatry*, 37:915–918.

——— ——— ——— (1981), Three year multimodality treatment study of 100 hyperactive boys. *J. of Pediatr.*, 98:650–655.

——— Hoppe, C. & Schell, A. (1982), A prospective study of delinquency in 110 adolescent boys with attention deficit disorder and 88 normal adolescent boys. *Am. J. Psychiatry*, 139:795–798.

Schell, R.M., Pelham, W.E., Bender, M.E., Andree, J.A., Law, T. & Robbins, F.R. (1986), The concurrent assessment of behavioral and psychostimulant interventions: A controlled case study. *Behav. Assess.*, 8:373–384.

Schleifer, M., Weiss, G., Cohen, N.J., Elman, M., Cvejic, H. & Kruger, E. (1975), Hyperactivity in preschoolers and the effect of methylphenidate. *Am. J. Orthopsychiatry*, 45:38–50.

Schneider, W. & Shiffrin, R.M. (1977), Controlled and automatic human information process: I. Detection, search and attention. *Psycholog. Rev.*, 84:1–66.

Sebrechts, M.M., Shaywitz, S.E., Shaywitz, B.A., Jatlow, P., Anderson, G.M. & Cohen, D.J. (1986), Components of attention, methylphenidate dosage, and blood levels in children with attention deficit disorder. *Pediatrics*, 77:222–228.

Share, D.L. & Schwartz, S. (1988), A note on the distinction between attention deficit disorder and reading disability: Are there group-specific cognitive deficits? *Brain Language*, 34:350–352.

Shaywitz, B.A. & Shaywitz, S.E. (1989), Learning disabilities and attention disorders. In *Pediatric Neurology* Vol. II, ed. K. F. Swaiman St. Louis: C.V. Mosby, pp. 857–894.

——— ——— (1991 Supplement). Comorbidity; A critical issue in attention deficit disorder. *The Journal of Child Neurology*, 6:S13–S22.

Shaywitz, S.E. (1986), Early recognition of vulnerability-EREV. Technical report to Connecticut State Department of Education.

——— Shaywitz, B.A. (1984), Evaluation and treatment of children with attention deficit disorders. *Pediatr. Rev.*, 6:99–109.

——— ——— (1988a), Increased medication use in attention-deficit hyperactivity disorder: Regressive or appropriate? *J. Am. Med. Assoc.*, 260:2270–2272.

——— ——— (1988b). Attention deficit disorder: Current perspectives. In: *Learning Disabilities: Proceedings of the National Conference*, (eds.) J.F. Kavanaugh & T.J. Truss, Jr. Parkton, MD: York Press, pp. 369–367.

——— Hunt, R.D., Jatlow, P., Cohen, D.J., Young, J.G., Pierce, R.N., Anderson, G.M. & Shaywitz, B.A. (1982), Psychopharmacology of attention deficit disorder: Pharmacokinetic, neuroendocrine, and behavioral measures following acute and chronic treatment with methylphenidate. *Pediatrics*, 69:688–694.

——— Shaywitz, B.A., Fletcher, J.M. & Escobar, M.D. (1990), Prevalence of reading disability in boys and girls: Results of the Connecticut Longitudinal Study. *J. Am. Med. Assoc.*, 264:998–1002.

Silver L.B. (1986), Controversial approaches to treating learning disabilities and attention disorder. *American Journal of Diseases of Children,* 140:1045–1052.

Sprague, R.L. & Sleator, E.K. (1977), Methylphenidate in hyperkinetic children: Differences in dose effects on learning and social behavior. *Science,* 198:1274–1276.

Stephens, R.S., Pelham, W.E. & Skinner, R. (1984), State-dependent and main effects of methylphenidate and pemoline on paired-associate learning and spelling in hyperactive children. *J. Consult. Clin. Psychol.,* 52:104–113.

Sternberg, S. (1969), Discovery of processing stages: Extensions of Donders' method. In: *Attention and Performance* (Vol. 2), ed. W. G. Koster Amsterdam: North-Holland, pp. 276–315.

—— (1975), Memory scanning: New findings and current controversies. *Q. J. Exp. Psychol.,* 27:1–32.

Still, G.F. (1902), The Coulstonian lectures on some abnormal physical conditions in children. *Lancet,* 1:1008–12, 1077–82, 1163–68.

Strauss, A.A. & Lehtinen, L.E. (1947), *Psychopathology and Education in the Brain-Injured Child.* New York: Grune & Stratton.

Swanson, J., Kinsbourne, M., Roberts, W. & Zucker, M.A. (1978), Time–response analysis of the effect of stimulant medication of the learning disability of children referred for hyperactivity. *Pediatrics,* 61:21–29.

—— Sandman, C.A., Deutsch, C. & Baren, M. (1983), Methylphenidate hydrochloride given with or before breakfast: I. Behavioral, cognitive, and electrophysiologic effects. *Pediatrics,* 72:49–55.

—— Cantwell, D., Lerner, M., McBurnett, K. & Hanna, G. (1991), Effects of stimulant medication on learning in children with ADHD. *J. of Learn. Disabil.,* 24:219–230.

Tannock, R., Schachar, R.J., Carr, R.P. & Logan, G.D. (1989), Dose–response effects of methylphenidate on academic performance and overt behavior in hyperactive children. *Pediatrics,* 84:648–657.

Taylor, E.A. (1986), Attention deficit. In: *The Overactive Child,* ed. E. A. Taylor. Philadelphia: JB Lippincott Co., pp. 73–106.

Valenstein, E.S. (1986), *Great and Desperate Cures.* New York: Basic Books.

van der Meere, J., van Baal, M. & Sergeant, J. (1989), The additive factor method: A differential diagnostic tool in hyperactivity and learning diasability. *J. Abnorm. Child Psychol.,* 17:409–422.

Varley, C.K., & Trupin, E.W. (1983), Double-blind assessment of stimulant medication for attention deficit disorder: A model for clinical application. *Am. J. Orthopsychiatry,* 53:542–547.

Vellutino, F.R. (1978), Toward an understanding of dyslexia: Psychological factors in specific reading disability. In: *Dyslexia, an Appraisal of Current Knowledge,* eds. A.L. Benton & D. Pearl. New York: Oxford University Press, pp. 61–111.

—— (1979), *Dyslexia: Theory and Research.* Cambridge, MA: MIT Press.

Vellutino, F.R. & Scanlon, D. (1987), Phonological coding, phonological awareness, and reading ability: Evidence from a longitudinal and experimental study. *Merrill-Palmer Q.,* 33:321–363.

Vissing, Y.M. & Petersen, J.C. (1981), Taking laetrile: Conversion to medical deviance. *CA: A Cancer Journal for Clinicians,* 31:365–369.

—— & Hechtman, L. (1979), The hyperactive child syndrome. *Science,* 205:1348–1354.

Weiss, G., Minde, K., Douglas, V. & Nemeth, E. (1971), Studies on the hyperactive child. *Arch. Gen. Psychiatry,* 24:409–414.

Werner, H. & Strauss, A.A. (1941), Pathology of the figure-background relation in the child. *J. Abnorm. Soc. Psychol.,* 36:236–248.

Werry, J.S. (1982), An overview of pediatric psychopharmacology. *J. Am. Acad. Child Psychiatry,* 21:3–9.

Whalen, C.K. (1989), Attention deficit and hyperactivity disorders. In: *Handbook of Child Psychopathology* (Second edition), eds. T.H. Ollendick & H. Hersen. New York: Plenum Press.

—— Henker, B. (1976), Psychostimulants and children: A review and analysis. *Psychol. Bull.,* 83:1113–1130.

————— ————— (1984), Hyperactivity and the attention deficit disorders: Expanding frontiers. *Pediatr. Clin. North Am.*, 31:397–427.

————— ————— Collins, B.E., McAuliffe, S. & Vaux, A. (1979), Peer interaction in a structured communication task: Comparisons of normal and hyperactive boys and of methylphenidate (ritalin) and placebo effects. *Child Devel.*, 50:388–401.

————— ————— Dotemoto, S., Vaux, A. & McAuliffe, S. (1981), Hyperactivity and methylphenidate: Peer interaction styles. In: *Psychosocial Aspects of Drug Treatment for Hyperactivity,* eds. K.D. Gadow & J. Loney. Boulder, CO: Westview Press, pp. 381–415.

————— ————— & Hinshaw, S.P. (1985), Cognitive-behavioral therapies for hyperactive children: Premises, problems and prospects. *J. Abnorm. Child Psychol.*, 13:391–410.

————— ————— Buhrmester, D., Hinshaw, S.P., Huber, A. & Laski, K. (1989), Does stimulant medication improve the peer status of hyperactive children? *J. of Consulting Clinical Psychology,* 57:545–549.

Whitehouse, D., Shah, U. & Palmer, F.B. (1980), Comparison of sustained-release and standard methylphenidate in the treatment of minimal brain dysfunction. *J. Clin. Psychiatry,* 41:282–285.

Winsberg, B.G., Kupietz, S.S. & Sverd, J. (1982), Methylphenidate oral dose plasma concentrations and behavioral response in children. *Psychopharmacology,* 70:329–332.

Wood, F.B., Felton, R.H. & Brown, I.S. (1988), The dissociation of attention deficit disorder from reading disability: A reply to Share and Schwartz. *Brain Language,* 34:353–358.

Zametkin, A.J., Linnoila, M., Karoum, F. & Sallee, R. (1986), Pemoline and urinary excretion of catecholamines and indoleamines in children with attention deficit disorder. *Am. J. Psychiatry,* 143:359–362.

Ritalin Versus Dextroamphetamine in ADHD: Both Should Be Tried

JOSEPHINE ELIA and JUDITH L. RAPOPORT

INTRODUCTION

Dextroamphetamine and methylphenidate remain the drugs of choice for attention deficit hyperactivity disorder (ADHD) and response rates to these agents from 70 to 85% are reported (Barkley, 1977). Although a variety of other medications have been tried in ADHD, none of the alternatives have proved as useful as these two stimulants (Wiener, 1985; Zametkin et al., 1985).

While both drugs are Class II (controlled) substances, methylphenidate is designated the drug of choice in most psychopharmacology texts. The reasons for this are unclear. In 1971, in some states, medical assistance programs removed dextroamphetamine from the approved prescription list, making methylphenidate the only drug available to certain populations (Arnold and Knopp, 1973), which undoubtedly furthered the relative increased use of methylphenidate.

"Nonresponse" to the stimulants has been defined in different ways, and at least some nonresponders are always reported. Charles Bradley (1950), in a summary of his work of a decade with several hundred children with behavior disorders treated with benzedrine (a racemic mixture of D and L amphetamine) and dextroamphetamine, reported that 60 to 75% were improved, 15 to 25% showed no change, and 10 to 15% showed unfavorable effects. Dosage ranges for benzedrine consisted of 10–40 mg given in a single daily dose, with most children responding to 20 mg. Dosages of dextroamphetamine used were in the range 5–30 mg. This is one of the few reports to distinguish between behavioral nonresponse and adverse effects.

Millichap and Fowler (1967, 1968) summarized clinical trials in which a total of 337 patients (total of six studies) received methylphenidate with 84% benefitting from therapy. Of 415 patients (total of nine studies) treated with amphetamine, 69% showed improvement. Side effects, including anorexia, irritability, insomnia, and stomachache occurred in 12 to 14% of patients treated with either of these stimulants. The slightly more favorable response rate for methylphenidate, arrived at by combining patients from different trials (which had different designs, used different dosages and improvement criteria) may have further influenced the prescription bias (Millichap, 1968). Barkley (1977) reviewed 15 studies using amphetamines and 14 studies using methylphenidate, finding a mean of 75% of subjects who improved for both drugs, but the author cites difficulties with defining improvement.

Pelham and Hoza (1987) dispute the use of single measures of drug response in predicting a child's overall response and function in a natural environment. He found that neither a learning task, an attention task (continuous performance test, CPT), or behavioral rating (ACTRS), alone or in combination, could predict direct observations and other ratings of multiple behaviors gathered in multiple settings.

Intraindividual variability, state contingent effects, differential symptom response variability, as well as side effects, have made the definition of response and (nonresponse) very difficult. For example, Conners (1973b) reports different patterns or stimulant drug "improvement" in six subgroups he identified in a sample of 262 children originally diagnosed as "minimal brain dysfunction."

Direct clinical comparison of the two drugs are few. Between group studies (Conners, 1971, 1972) as well as some within subject studies (Arnold et al., 1978; Huestis et al., 1975; Vyborová et al., 1984; Winsberg

National Institutes of Mental Health, Bethesda, Maryland

et al., 1974) have as mentioned, shown similar overall clinical efficacy for the two drugs. However, in those studies, behavioral nonresponse and adverse effects were not distinguished.

Huestis et al. (1975) found an overall high response rate (89%) according to psychiatric, parent, and teacher ratings, when both medications were tried in a group of 12 boys and 6 girls with disruptive behaviors. Dosage ranges were 5–25 mg for dextroamphetamine and 30–60 mg for methylphenidate. While both drugs were effective, some children responded better to one than the other as evidenced by the choice of discharge medications (10 children on D-amphetamine, 6 on methylphenidate).

Methylphenidate and dextroamphetamine were found to be significantly better than placebo, but not different from each other in a double-blind crossover study in 29 children with "minimal brain dysfunction" (Arnold et al., 1978). Eighty-nine percent of the subjects improved sufficiently on at least one drug to warrant continuation of treatment. Six children responded only to dextroamphetamine, while another six responded only to methylphenidate. Optimal mean single doses were reported, consisting of 0.8 mg/kg for MPH and 0.4 mg/kg for D-amphetamine given twice per day. Psychiatric, parent, and teacher ratings were used to determine response rates.

Vyborova (1984) studied 30 hyperactive children on methylphenidate and dextroamphetamine, using a single-blind crossover design. Both drugs significantly reduced motor restlessness. Improvement in behavior (as rated by the modified Cerny's scale for children) was noted in 63% of the children after dextroamphetamine and in 53% after methylphenidate. Dextroamphetamine was more effective in decreasing "social maladaptability" but caused more side effects. However, since the same dosage (0.45 mg/kg/day) was used for both drugs these results may have been skewed by the relative potency of dextroamphetamine and/or the particular rating scale employed.

Winsberg et al. (1974) compared the two stimulant drugs in a group of 18 children hospitalized for "incorrigible school and home behavior." Sixty percent of their sample responded (decreased scores on Conners 39-item teacher rating) to both methylphenidate (maximum dose 30 mg bid) and dextroamphetamine (maximum dose 20 mg bid). All methylphenidate responders were also dextroamphetamine responders, while three subjects responded only to dextroamphetamine, suggesting that a small number of children may respond selectively to one stimulant.

In a recent study (Borcherding et al., 1990; Elia et al., 1991) the clinical effects of dextroamphetamine and methylphenidate were compared within a single, large clinical sample of 48 boys, ages 6–12, with attention deficit, hyperactivity disorder. A wide range of doses (up to 1.5 mg/kg/day of dextroamphetamine and up to 3.0 mg/kg/day of methylphenidate) were administered. A day hospital setting assured compliance, permitted direct observations of behavioral change, and evaluation of side effects so that behavioral improvement could be better differentiated from adverse drug effects. While both stimulants produced striking clinical improvement to both drugs on individual and global behavioral ratings, several clinical group as well as individual differences were found. Methylphenidate was found to produce a greater decrease in motor activity than dextroamphetamine (Borcherding et al., 1989).

Dextroamphetamine tended to produce more compulsive behaviors which were also more likely to resemble clinical obsessive compulsive disorder than did methylphenidate while abnormal movements and compulsive behaviors tended to co-occur on methylphenidate only (Borcherding et al., 1999). Adverse effects such as sleep and appetite disturbances were found to be common with both drugs while ratings of "increased sadness" and "nervous habits and mannerisms" were significantly increased with methylphenidate but not dextroamphetamine (Elia et al., 1991).

While the differences were not statistically significant, parent ratings usually favored dextroamphetamine treatment. This might, in principle be due to the longer half life of that drug, enabling parents to witness more drug effect in the home.

INDIVIDUAL DIFFERENCES IN RESPONSE TO THE TWO STIMULANTS

Considerable individual variability in clinical response was also found, with 14 subjects being "nonresponders" to at least one drug. More specifically, response rates to dextroamphetamine and methylphenidate were 88% and 79%, respectively, consistant with previous studies of each drug alone. Six boys were rated nonresponders to dextroamphetamine, ten to methylphenidate, with only two subjects overlapping. Therefore, with 46 of 48 subjects responding to at least one medication, a "true" response rate after both stimulants and a range of doses were considered was 96%.

While there was general agreement for "response" between the Hyperactivity factor of the Teacher Conners and the global improvement factor of the Clinical Global Impression Scale (NIMH, 1985), there were several instances in which the severity of adverse effects negated the behavioral improvement.

Discharge medication choice, based on physician-rated overall improvement, did not favor one drug over the other (22 were discharged on methylphenidate, 25 were discharged on dextroamphetamine). Of the 20 subjects who were taking methylphenidate at the time of screening, 11 were discharged on dextroamphetamine, and the two who were taking dextroamphetamine at the time of screening were discharged on methylphenidate, indicating the clinical importance of trying both stimulants because of individual variability in response. These results are not due to bias in the sample, since an almost equal number of children who had never been treated in the past with stimulants were discharged on each drug.

The very small number of behavioral nonresponders supports the findings of Rapoport et al. (1978) that stimulant drug response is nonspecific and almost universal. A similar proportion (almost all) of a group of normal boys and of hyperactive boys showed improved attention and decreased motor activity following dextroamphetamine.

Most of the children referred as nonresponders to one stimulant responded to the other drug, or to a higher dosage of the same drug. One child however, responded at a lower dose than he had been prescribed, suggesting that tolerance had developed and response was re-established after he had been off medication for several weeks. We are impressed therefore, with the phenomenon of short-term tolerance to the stimulant drugs, a subject needing study in its own right and often confused with nonresponse. Here, drug holidays and/or a switch to another stimulant may be helpful.

Limitations of stimulant drug treatment, from a broader perspective, are shown by the Children's Global Assessment Scale (C-GAS) (Shaffer et al., 1983), with values ranging from 1 (the most functionally impaired) to 100 (the healthiest), and a score of 70 or above indicating normal functioning. Even though the restless and inattentive behavior improved significantly on both drugs, the highest mean C-GAS score for subjects was 56.8 for methylphenidate and 55.8 for dextroamphetamine, indicating major components of overall functioning which are not affected by either drug. Thus, children who display improved behavior in the classroom (less hyperactive, more attentive, less impulsive) may still be depressed and have impaired social functioning. Additionally, long-term study with this measure might be necessary to truly assess social changes which may alter slowly following behavioral improvement. Since for both the behavioral changes and the adverse effects, the results were surprisingly constant across all weeks of drug therapy, and absent during all weeks on placebo, it is unlikely that the present differential results are attributable to factors other than drug effects.

CLINICIAN GUIDELINES

An important message for clinicians is that both drugs need to be tried because the overlap of defining who is a nonresponder by any definition (e.g., unimproved behavior or presence of adverse effects) is not great. Unfortunately, there are no predictors of differential drug response, thus necessitating a trial of both. Since there are no factors noted to predict a better response to one stimulant than the other, the decision to start with methylphenidate or dextroamphetamine may be arbitrary.

Doses for methylphenidate may be started at 5 mg bid and increased weekly (maximum total daily dose 2.5 mg/kg/day). Teacher, parent, and patient feedback should be recorded prospectively, using various rating scales. Dose should be increased by 5 or 10 mg weekly, and maintained at a constant level for at least one week at a time in order to obtain ratings of behavior over a sufficient period of time.

Even if behavioral improvement is noted on methylphenidate and side effects are well tolerated, a trial of dextroamphetamine should follow. The usual initiating dose of dextroamphetamine is 5 mg qd or bid, which again should be increased every week (maximum total daily dose 1.5 mg/kg/day).

The prospectively gathered ratings and subjective reports of parents and patients should be reviewed at the end of the week and dosage increased if behavior is not optimal and adverse effects are tolerable.

At the completion of the two trials, all the information is reviewed and the period of highest functioning (behavioral, academic, social), and minimal adverse effects can be identified. The patient should then be maintained on that medication. Follow-up continues to be essential for monitoring efficacy as well as adverse effects.

Clinical instruments

1. Teacher feedback including behavioral as well as academic achievement is important. The shortened version of Conners Teacher Rating Scale (Conners, 1973) can be used to rate behavior. A weekly log indicating completion of homework, test grades, and/or other projects can be used to reflect academic achievement (Fig. 1).
2. Parental feedback concerning behavior at home and social functioning is essential. Parents may also use Conners Teacher Rating Scale, omitting items 2 and 4 if not applicable.
3. Feedback from the child concerning behavioral, social, and academic functioning, is also essential.
4. Records of adverse effects observed by parents, teachers, and patients using the Subject's Treatment Emergent Symptom Scale (STESS) (Guy, 1976). (Fig. 2). Additionally, overfocused (unable to terminate activity), or repetitive (overerasing, rewriting) behaviors as well as tics should be recorded.

In conclusion, patients should be given a trial of both medications, and information regarding their efficacy and adverse effects should be gathered systematically and prospectively in order to determine the most effective maintenance medication and dosage.

TEACHER'S QUESTIONNAIRE

Name of the Child _____ Grade _____

Date of Evaluation _____

Please answer all questions. Beside each item indicate the degree of the problem by a check mark (√).

	Score 0	1	2	3
	Not at all	Just a little	Pretty much	Very much
1. Restless in the "squirmy" sense.				
2. Demands must be met immediately.				
3. Distractibility or attention span a problem.				
4. Disturbs other children.				
5. Restless, always "up and on the go."				
6. Excitable, impulsive.				
7. Fails to finish things that he starts.				
8. Childish and immature.				
9. Easily frustrated in efforts.				
10. Difficulty in learning.				

Possible range: 0 to 30
Cut-off point: 15

FIG. 1. Conners Teacher Rating Scale. Note: Parents may use same scale, omitting items 2 and 4.

RITALIN VS. DEXTROAMPHETAMINE IN ADHD

STESS-R   Revised-DAW011687

NAME: FOR OFFICE USE ONLY

AGE: PROTOCOL: ☐☐☐☐☐☐☐☐
                           PATIENT ID (34-41)
RATING PERIOD:

RATER _____   ☐☐☐☐☐☐ ☐☐☐☐
                           MON DAY YR   CODE PHASE
TODAY'S DATE _____   BIRTHDATE (42-47) (48-49) (50-51)

DIRECTIONS: Has child had trouble with any of the following items? Check appropriate box for each item if problem was observed or child reported the problem within the specified rating period. ***SPECIAL NOTE*** Please rate this checklist for BOTH day AND night problems.

0 = NOT AT ALL
1 = JUST A LITTLE
2 = PRETTY MUCH
3 = VERY MUCH

0 = NOT AT ALL
1 = JUST A LITTLE
2 = PRETTY MUCH
3 = VERY MUCH

Item	0	1	2	3	#
Eating	0	1	2	3	1
Drinking	0	1	2	3	2
Dry mouth/lips	0	1	2	3	3
Wetness in mouth	0	1	2	3	4
Constipation	0	1	2	3	5
Diarrhea	0	1	2	3	6
Stomach cramps	0	1	2	3	7
Muscle cramps	0	1	2	3	8
Sick to stomach	0	1	2	3	9
Wetting the bed	0	1	2	3	10
Urinating	0	1	2	3	11
Itchy or scratchy skin	0	1	2	3	12
Rashes	0	1	2	3	13
Colds or sniffles	0	1	2	3	14
Headache	0	1	2	3	15
Dizziness	0	1	2	3	16
Playing sports	0	1	2	3	17
Shakiness	0	1	2	3	18
Pronouncing words	0	1	2	3	19
Doing things with hands	0	1	2	3	20
Sitting still	0	1	2	3	21
Tiredness	0	1	2	3	22

Item	0	1	2	3	#
Feeling sleepy	0	1	2	3	23
Trouble falling asleep	0	1	2	3	24
Bad dreams	0	1	2	3	25
Getting along w/ parents	0	1	2	3	26
Getting along w/ kids	0	1	2	3	27
Crying	0	1	2	3	28
Getting mad	0	1	2	3	29
Not being happy	0	1	2	3	30
Being sad	0	1	2	3	31
Paying attention	0	1	2	3	32
Jerks/twitches or unusual movements	0	1	2	3	33
Behavior worsens in evening	0	1	2	3	34
Does things over and over a certain number of times before they seem quite right	0	1	2	3	35
Has trouble making up his mind	0	1	2	3	36
Overly neat and clean	0	1	2	3	37
Meticulous; pays close attention to detail	0	1	2	3	38

FIG. 2.

REFERENCES

Arnold, E., Christopher, J., Huestis, R. & Smeltzer, D.J. (1978), Methylphenidate vs dextroamphetamine vs caffeine in minimal brain dysfunction. *Arch. Gen. Psychiatry,* 35:463–473.

Arnold, L.E. & Knopp, W. (1973), The making of a myth. *J. Am. Med. Assoc.,* 223:1273–1274.

Barkley, R.A. (1977), A review of stimulant drug research with hyperactive children. *J. Child Psychol. Psychiatry,* 18:137–165.

Borcherding, B.G., Keysor, C.S., Cooper, T.B. & Rapoport, J.L. (1989), Differential effects of methylphenidate and dextroamphetamine on the motor activity level of hyperactive children. *Neuropsychopharmacology*, 2:253–263.

—— —— Rapoport, J.L., Elia, J., Amass, J. (1990), Motor/vocal tics and compulsive behaviors on stimulant drugs: Is there a common vulnerability? *Psychiatry Res.*, 33:83–94.

Bradley, C. (1950), Benzedrine and dexedrine in the treatment of children's behavior disorders. *Pediatrics* 5:24–36.

Conners, C.K. (1971), The effect of stimulant drugs on human figure drawings in children with minimal brain dysfunction. *Psychopharmacologi (Berl.)*, 19:329–333.

—— (1972), Psychological effects of stimulant drugs in children with minimal brain dysfunction. *Pediatrics*, 49:702–708.

—— (1973a), Rating scales for use in drug studies with children. *Psychopharmacol Bull.* (Special issue, *Psychopharmacotherapy in Children*), 24–48.

—— (1973b), Psychological assessment of children with minimal brain dysfunction. *Ann. NY. Acad. Sci.*, 283–302.

Elia, J., Borcherding B.G., Rapoport, J.L. & Keysor, C.S. (1991), Methylphenidate and dextroamphetamine treatments of hyperactivity. Are there true non-responders? *Psychiatry Res.*, 36:141–155

Guy, W. (1976), Subject's treatment emergent symptom scale. *ECDEU Assessment Manual for Psychopharmacology*. DHEW ADAMH/NIMH Publication No. 76-338: Washington, DC: DHEW, pp. 347–350.

Huestis, L.R., Arnold, L.E. & Smeltzer, D.J. (1975), Caffeine versus methylphenidate and d-amphetamine in minimal brain dysfunction: A double-blind comparison. *Am. J. Psychiatry*, 132:868–870.

Millichap, J.G. & Fowler, G.W. (1967), Treatment of "minimal brain dysfunction" syndromes. *Pediatr. Clin. North Am.*, 14:767–777.

Millichap, J.G. (1968), Drugs in management of hyperkinetic and perceptually handicapped children. *J. Am. Med. Assoc.*, 206:1527–1530.

NIMH (1985), Clinical Global Impression Scale (CGI). *Psychopharmacol. Bull.*, 21:839–843.

Pelham, W.E. & Hoza, J. (1987b), Behavioral assessment of psychostimulant effects on ADD children in a summer day treatment program. In: *Advances in Behavioral Assessment of Children and Families*, ed. R. J. Prinz. Vol. 3, pp. 3–33. Greenwich, CT: JAI Press.

Rapoport, J.L., Bucshbaum, M.S., Zahn, T.P., Weingartner, H., Ludlow, C. & Mikkelsen, E.J. (1978), Dextroamphetamine: Cognitive and behavioral effects in normal prepubertal boys. *Science*, 199:560–563.

—— Conners, C.K. & Reatig, N. (eds.) (1985), Rating scales and assessment instruments for use in pediatric psychopharmacology research. *Psychopharmacol. Bull.*, 21:713–1111.

Shaffer, D., Gould, M.S., Brasic, J., Ambrosini, P., Fisher, P., Bird, H. & Aluwahlia, S. (1983), A children's global assessment scale (CGAS). *Arch. Gen. Psychiatry*, 40:1228–1231.

Vyborova, L., Nahunek, K., Drtilkova, I., Balastikova, B. & Misurec, J. (1984), Intraindividual comparison of twenty one day application of amphetaminil and methylphenidate in hyperkinetic children. *Activ. Nerv. Sup. (Praha)*, 26:268.

Wiener, J.M. (ed.) (1985), *Diagnosis and Psychopharmacology of Childhood and Adolescent Disorders*. New York: Wiley.

Winsberg, B.G., Press, M., Bialer, I. & Kupietz, S. (1974), Dextroamphetamine and methylphenidate in the treatment of hyperactive/aggressive children. *Pediatrics*, 53:236–241.

Zametkin, A.J., Rapoport, J.L., Murphy, D.L., Linnoila, M. & Ismond, D. (1985), Treatment of hyperactive children with monoamine oxidase inhibitors. *Arch. Gen. Psychiatry*, 42:962–996.

Alternative Therapies for ADHD

ROBERT D. HUNT, SERENA LAU, and JEFF RYU

The recognition in the 1970s that imipramine was effective in the treatment of attention deficit disorder with hyperactivity (ADHD) raised fundamental questions about medication and diagnostic specificity. While phenomenological diagnosis became more empirically precise through greater definition of symptomology, pharmacological treatment suggested that a few basic neurophysiological symptoms must underline a broad spectrum of disorders. The recent addition of serotonergic antidepressants and clonidine to the possible repertory of psychopharmacological treatment of ADHD provides an opportunity for a better understanding of how different facets of ADHD may be meditated by intersecting brain mechanisms. As evident by this book, much has been learned about the effectiveness of methylphenidate (MPH, or Ritalin) for various components of attention, activity, aggression, and socialization in ADHD. The link between psychopharmacological response and neurochemical actions is in forming our understanding of basic brain mechanisms in ADHD.

The need for alternative medications in the treatment of ADHD is evidenced by the diversity of patients who present with core symptoms of overactivity, inattention, impulsivity, and by the limitations of their response to the psychostimulants alone. There is virtually no disorder in which there is a direct correspondence between diagnosis and treatment. Especially early in development, patients present with symptoms that are less clearly differentiated. Within the spectrum of ADHD important pharmacological distinctions may be guided by the relative preponderance of hyperactivity versus distractability, and the presence of comorbid diagnosis such as learning disabilities, depression, anxiety disorder, intermittent explosive disorder, or suggestions of underlying disorganization or thought disorder. The patient's age may affect the distribution of these symptoms and the selection and dose of medication. Young children with severe hyperactivity are often extremely aroused and have a brittle response to methylphenidate. Adolescents may respond better to antidepressants that pose less risk for abuse. Although prepubertal children with externalizing symptoms are rather rarely depressed or anxious, the coexistence of these symptoms may respond better to an antidepressant than a psychostimulant. Patients with Tourette's disorder often present a complex clustering of symptoms in which distractability and tics respond to Ritalin like the opposite ends of a seesaw. Similarly, some patterns of aggression, thought disorder, or hypomania may become activated during treatment with psychostimulants. Ritalin may not be the optimal medication for children at these developmental stages or with these comorbid disorders.

An additional need for alternative medications is presented by the pharmacokinetics and side effects of the psychostimulants themselves. The short duration of action of Ritalin can produce a roller-coaster-like effect. Several times per day the ADHD child may swing from being out of control, to being well controlled, even excessively inhibited. Insomnia limits the use of medication in the evenings, often resulting in a loss of control or even a rebound hyperactivity in which the child was calm at school, but becomes frenetic at home in the evening. Appetite suppression limits the use of Ritalin in some children who are thin and may lose weight.

The basal brain activating effects of Ritalin, evident by insomnia, anorexia, and a slight increase in pulse, can lead to a breakthrough or activation of severe aggression or thought disorder in some children. The combination of basal brain activation and cortical inhibition produces a state of heightened arousal coupled with increased cortical suppression, somewhat similar to placing a lid on a pressure cooker. Some ADHD

Vanderbilt University School of Medicine, Nashville, Tennessee children appear to be overinhibited, unspontaneous, and overcontrolled on doses of psychostimulants needed to control their hyperactivity. These side effects may limit compliance with Ritalin in spite of its effectiveness (Brown et al. 1987).

There is a complex relationship between the dose–response evident for control of attention and control of behavior. Sprague and Sleater (1977) suggested that optimal performance of a pattern-matching task occurred at a lower dose, while control of hyperactivity required a higher dose of psychostimulant. While most subsequent studies have not found this dissociation of dose-response effect, different components of cognition may be variously affected by Ritalin. Most attentional studies have utilized stimulus-bound tasks—tasks in which the subject must respond directly to a stimulus on the screen—by reacting to it, matching it, or memorizing it. These tasks do not correlate well with classroom learning. Furthermore, they do not assess the role of attention in the more complex components of cognition: reasoning, problem solving, and abstraction. Perhaps Ritalin narrows the attentional field and increases the strength of the "signal" being processed. It is less clear whether Ritalin enhances processing competencies required to abstract or reason, processes that often require ignoring external stimuli in preference to inner contemplation. This component of contemplation and reasoning may correlate more highly with classroom learning in later grades. Other medications that strengthen frustration tolerance may facilitate this form of classroom learning and effortful problem solving.

ANTIDEPRESSANT DRUG THERAPY AND ADHD

Recent studies have evaluated the use of antidepressant drug therapy in the treatment of ADHD, in the search for an effective and safe alternative to stimulant drugs. Possible advantages of antidepressants over stimulants include:

1. A longer duration of action, for once-daily dosing without symptoms of rebound or insomnia
2. Greater flexibility in dosage
3. The readily available option of monitoring plasma drug levels
4. Minimal risk of abuse or dependence (Biederman et al., 1989)

Medications studied in the recent literature include imipramine (IMI), desipramine (DMI), nortriptyline, bupropion, and monoamine oxidase inhibitors (MAOIs). Of these antidepressants, DMI may be the most effective.

Tricyclic antidepressants (TCAs)

The tricyclics have been used in ADHD since initial studies by Rapoport et al. (1974) documented their usefulness. More recent studies have focused on the desmethylated metabolite, desipramine, that appears to have fewer side effects. The behavioral effects may be more pronounced than the cognitive effects, although this may reflect the limitations in the type of cognitive tasks employed (Swanson, 1985). The most effective tricyclic antidepressants for ADHD may be those that affect the noradrenergic system. Antidepressants have a longer duration of action than Ritalin, and may concurrently improve mood. However, they require monitoring of blood level and EEG for cardiovascular safety.

Imipramine

Imipramine, a long-acting antidepressant, was recognized to be an active treatment for ADHD in the mid-1970s. Several controlled studies found it to improve symptoms of hyperactivity, but there remains reservation in suggesting it for widespread use due to the high frequency of side effects (Werry, 1980).

Many studies were conducted in the 1970s on imipramine (Gittleman-Klein, 1974; Greenberg et al., 1975; Gross, 1973; Huessy and Wright, 1970). Early studies also included a comparison of amitriptyline and MPH and found both to be effective (Yepes et al., 1977). A study by Rapoport et al. (1974), compared imipramine (80 mg/day), methylphenidate (20 mg/day), and placebo in 76 hyperactive boys. Both active medications were found to be superior to placebo. Side effects were more pronounced with IMI than with methylphenidate. They included decreased appetite, sedation, and increase in diastolic blood pressure. The increase in BP necessitated the withdrawal of three children from imipramine. No ECG or liver function abnormalities were noted.

While both stimulants were rated superior to placebo by all examiners, methylphenidate was clearly favored over imipramine. The authors suggest that this was possibly due to the relatively low dose of imipramine used in this study.

Quinn and Rapoport (1975) next compared baseline and outcome measures in a one-year prospective followup study of the same 76 hyperactive boys: This study found that those who maintained treatment demonstrated similar and significant improvements in their classroom behavior ratings at the end of one year, regardless of the drug being used. It is notable, however, that while there was improved behavior over baseline, classroom ratings of the two groups were still high in comparison to norms. The chief reason for discontinuing medication was adverse side effects.

In a study by Waizer et al. (1974), involving 19 hyperactive boys with serious classroom behavioral problems, imipramine therapy (137 mg/day) was found to be effective in improving hyperactivity as well as defiance, inattentiveness, and sociability. The most prominent side effect produced by imipramine therapy was weight loss (seen in 78% of the subjects). The average amount lost over the eight weeks was 0.9 kg. Recovery was quickly achieved on placebo, with an average increase of 1.3 kg in four weeks. Other symptoms noted in the group included mild anorexia, insomnia, and mild drowsiness. Imipramine therapy proved to be effective in improving overall classroom behavior in this population of hyperkinetic children. Although this change deteriorated during placebo treatment, there is some evidence of sustained improvement over baseline, possibly attributable to the long-acting property of imipramine. In a study of ten ADHD children known to be unresponsive to MPH, imipramine ($X = 3.7$ mg/kg) was ineffective in improving behavior.

While it is frequently hoped that stimulant nonresponders will improve on imipramine or another tricyclic, this study suggests that many patients may respond or nonrespond identically to both medications. Most studies suggest that both psychostimulants and imipramine are more effective than placebo. Generally, a slight therapeutic advantage has been attributed to the psychostimulants and they generally remain the medication of first choice. However, behavioral response to imipramine is nearly equivalent to that seen with stimulant use. One advantage of imipramine is that it is long-acting and therefore does not have to be given at school. Imipramine may be helpful in those ADHD patients with concurrent mood disturbance. Cardiac side effects must be monitored and may constitute an important limitation in the use of imipramine.

Desipramine

Several recent studies have focused on desipramine (DMI), the desmethyl metabolite of IMI that has more specific effect than a noradrenergic presynaptic uptake blocker, and is often less sedating than IMI (Garfinkel et al., 1983; Gastfriend et al., 1984).

In a double-blind study of 29 ADHD boys, desipramine 100 mg 9 A.M. ($x = 3.38$ mg/kg/day), was found to be more effective than placebo in improving behavior (Donnelly et al., 1986). Behavioral hyperactivity was significantly improved on day 3 and 14 ($p = 0.003$) during treatment with DMI while placebo produced no behavioral change. However, there was no facilitation on the cognitive tasks. There was no correlation between medication level and behavioral response. Neurochemical changes constituted an important correlate of behavioral change. On the 3rd and 14th treatment day urinary 3-methoxy-5-hydroxy phenethyl glycol (MHPG), vanillylmandelic acid (VMA), and norepinephrine (NE) all decreased in the responsive patients. Standing plasma NE and MHPG also decreased during treatment. Side effects showed no significant change in STESS; however, DMI prompted an increase in heart rate and an increase in diabetic blood pressure. DMI elicited behavioral but not cognitive improvement in ADHD.

In this study behavioral change occurred by the Day 3, more quickly than the usual affective response to antidepressants. There was no improvement on the continuous performance task (CPT) measure of attention. A therapeutic blood level appeared essential to clinical improvement. In this small group, treatment response factored with change in norepinephrine metabolism, but did not correlate with blood level of medication.

Treatment of children with ADD using desipramine (X = 4.7 mg/kg/day) has been evaluated in several studies by Biederman et al. (1986, 1988, 1989). The effectiveness of DMI was compared with placebo in a group of 60 ADHD males (Biederman et al., 1989). The results of this study showed an overall response rate of 68% (DMI daily dose 4.6 mg/kg) over a 10% response rate of the placebo control group. Of those treated with DMI, 68% were 'much' or 'very much' improved, while only 10% of the placebo group improved ($p = 0.001$). However, on the cognitive tests, there was no significant change. Mood showed a nonsignificant trend toward improvement in depression ratings ($p = 0.05$), even though these subjects were not initially clinically depressed. The major side effects consisted of dry mouth (32%); decreased appetite or headaches (29%); abdominal discomfort or tiredness (26%); dizziness or insomnia (23%). This study produced several significant findings: DMI was clearly more effective than placebo in the treatment of ADHD. Behavioral improvement appeared more prominent than cognitive effects. Side effects were primarily anticholinergic and generally well tolerated.

The cardiovascular side effects of DMI were examined in a separate report from the same study in which 31 DMI-treated subjects were compared with 27 placebo-unresponsive subjects. Cardiovascular side effects consisted of a clinically unimportant, but statistically significant increase in diastolic blood pressure (BP), heart rate (HR), and EKG conduction. DMI-treated patients showed higher incidence of sinus tachycardia and intraventricular conduction defects consisting of the right bundle-branch block.

Treatment with doses 3–5 mg/kg may be necessary in some cases of childhood ADHD, and careful monitoring of serum drug levels and EKG should be used in pediatric populations. Since cardiac side effects from antidepressants do not correlate closely with blood level, EKG monitoring is necessary to identify emergent intraventricular conduction defects. DMI treatment has been associated with cardiac deaths (Riddle et al., 1991; Popper and Elliot, 1990).

Desipramine in ADHD Associated with Tics: Several clinical problems present special cases for the use of antidepressants, for example, children with concurrent tics and ADHD. The effect of DMI treatment (50–100 mg/day) in ADHD associated with tics was studied in seven boys (Riddle et al., 1988). Beneficial treatment response was noted in 71% who were rated as moderately or markedly improved on the CGI. The main side effects included tachycardia, which developed in 4 patients. One patient experienced increased diastolic blood pressure; one had increased sedation. No patient had an increase in the incidence of tics.

Although this study is limited by its small size and uncontrolled design, the authors note that DMI appears to be safe and effective in children with ADHD associated with tics. While the results of the DMI study were similar to prior studies with IMI, DMI's precursor, there was significantly fewer adverse effects due to the greater selectivity of DMI.

Tricyclic antidepressants (TCAs) act predominantly by enhancing functional availability of catecholamines and indoleamines to block presynaptic uptake. Antidepressants vary significantly in their relative effect on norepinephrine, dopamine, serotonin, and other neurotransmitters. DMI is the TCAs with the most selective effects on norepinephrine reuptake and activity at $alpha_1$-adrenergic receptors. It has relatively low affinity at muscarinic and histaminergic receptors and only moderate affinity at $alpha_1$-adrenergic receptors; it is very weak agonist of $alpha-_2$, beta-adrenergic, and dopaminergic receptors. DMI is associated with fewer risks of adverse effects than amitriptyline, clomipramine, doxepin, and IMI (Biederman et al., 1989). These studies suggest that DMI is a reasonable alternative in cases where psychostimulants have failed, or when ADHD is associated with depression or anxiety, or tics.

DMI appears to be effective in treating ADHD. Because of its more specific action on norepinephrine, it may have some advantage over other neurotransmitters in treatment of highly active children. However, direct comparative studies between antidepressants have not been performed. Most studies have been relatively brief, and the long-term effectiveness requires further confirmation. The lack of change on cognitive tests suggest that DMI's effects may not occur at the level of these concrete tasks. But DMI may improve task performance by modulating affect and frustration. Multimodal studies that monitor the effect on classroom grades and learning would be helpful.

Nortriptyline

Nortriptyline is a potent, activating antidepressant, thought to act by inhibiting the activity of serotonin and acetylcholine, and increasing the pressor effect of norepinephrine.

Nortriptyline was found to have positive effects in 60 ADHD adolescents treated with stimulants who previously responded poorly or had substantial side effects and were switched to nortriptyline. Initial dosage was 10 mg at night for two weeks, followed by 25 mg bid for two weeks. Of the 60 patients, 54 improved in symptoms of attention deficit as shown by home and school evaluation forms. Teacher reports documented improvement in attitude, increase in attention span, and most significantly, a decrease in impulsivity (Saul, 1985).

Summary

The tricyclic antidepressants have well-established effectiveness in ADHD, but do not yet have definitive indications. They may be most useful in ADHD patients with concurrent depression or anxiety (Pliszka, 1987; Zametkin and Rapaport, 1983). Antidepressants are frequently utilized in adolescents to minimize the exposure to psychostimulants that may have potential for abuse. It is not clear that their effect on cognition is as potent as their effect on behavior. They may affect cognition indirectly through modulating excessive affective-arousal mechanisms.

Desipramine has become the most frequently used tricyclic antidepressant for ADHD patients due to its lower sedative and side effect profile. Recent reports of sudden death underscore the need for careful monitoring of cardiovascular response.

Monoamine oxidase inhibitors

In one study comparing two forms of monoamine oxidase inhibitors (MAOIs) to D-amphetamine and placebo, in 14 prepubertal children, clorgyline and tranylcypromine appeared clinically effective (Rapoport, 1986; Zametkin et al., 1985). Both MAOIs appeared as efficacious as D-amphetamine and were safe when dietary and multidrug restrictions were followed. The main side effect from MAOIs was mild sedation that persisted into the third to fourth week.

MAOIs appear to be clinically effective in this single, small study of ADHD. Given the risks inherent in dietary control, these medications should be used with extreme caution in impulsive children. Under well-controlled conditions, they may have value in otherwise refractory patients. The multineurotransmitter mechanisms of action of MAOIs suggest that effective medications work because they act upon a number of different neurotransmitters.

New antidepressants

Bupropion

Bupropion is a recently approved antidepressant. It weakly blocks the neuronal uptake of serotonin and norepinephrine, and possibly is a weak dopamine agonist. Data from animal studies indicate that bupropion is not associated with the alteration of CNS receptors often implicated in the action of other antidepressant drugs. In two published studies, bupropion appears promising for some symptoms of ADHD.

In an outpatient study of 30 prepubertal children, a modest beneficial response to bupropion 6 mg/kg/day) was noted by clinicians and teachers (Casat et al., 1989). Clinicians rated 18 of 20 children improved. There was significant reduction of classroom hyperactivity as reported by teachers ($p = 0.016$), but no difference was noted between active drug and placebo groups on CPQ Hyperactivity ratings, CPQ, or CTQ Conduct ratings. Parents noted no behavioral change from bupropion, and no improvement was detected in measures of cognitive performance. The main side effects consisted of a skin rash and periodic edema that occurred in one child. In this short-term placebo comparison of bupropion DHD clinicians rated a significant improvement, while teachers showed only a modest positive trend. Cognitive testing demonstrated no improvement. Bupropion appears to be safe, but not very effective. It may reduce hyperactivity in the classroom but have less effect at home.

An uncontrolled, single-blind study assessed effectiveness of bupropion, 150 mg/day, in 17 preadolescent males, and reported significant behavioral improvement in 12 patients (Simeon et al., 1986). The major side effects were mild nausea, stomach discomfort, increased appetite, and nausea and vomiting. Although this was an uncontrolled trial, the results suggest that bupropion may be effective and safe for treatment of hyperactivity, especially if associated with conduct disorder.

Collectively, these two studies are inconclusive. In the larger, better controlled study by Casat, clinical improvement was marginal. In the smaller, less controlled study, there was a more significant effect and the suggestion that bupropion may have concurrent antiaggressive and antidepressant effects.

COMMENTS ON USE OF ANTIDEPRESSANTS

The overall findings of clinical research support the utility of antidepressants in ADHD. Studies have not adequately defined which clinical subtypes would preferentially respond to antidepressants compared with psychostimulants. Psychostimulants still remain the medication of first choice. Failure to respond to psychostimulants may be a negative predictor of response to antidepressants.

The relationship of clinical response to dose and blood level of antidepressants suggests a similar treatment profile to that used for depression. While antidepressants are generally well-tolerated and can be administered twice daily, routine monitoring of cardiovascular side effects is essential. Further research may also validate the duration of treatment effectiveness and the stability of dose and blood levels over time.

Patients with concurrent depression or anxiety and ADHD may be the specific subgroup most likely to benefit from antidepressants. However, further research in such a comorbid population is necessary to validate this presumption. Additionally, patients with ADHD and tics may respond to antidepressants. While clinical use has favored antidepressants in adolescents, further studies should compare psychostimulants and antidepressants in ADHD children of different ages.

The cognitive effects of antidepressants require further exploration. Several studies suggest that antidepressants have much weaker effects than stimulants on classical measures of stimulus-bound attention (e.g., CPT). Since these laboratory tests do not correlate closely with classroom learning or grades, there may be significant improvement from antidepressants in applied learning that is not reflected in these concrete measures of attention.

CLONIDINE IN ADHD

Clonidine is an imidazoline derivative, used for over two decades as an antihypertensive agent. In the 1980s clonidine has been used in child psychiatry to reduce the activation or arousal component of attention deficit hyperactivity disorder, Tourette's syndrome, and aggression. Clonidine is not specific for all the symptoms of any diagnosis (Cohen et al., 1980). Preliminary studies suggest that clonidine effectively reduces arousal in very hyperactive children. It appears useful in patients with aggression associated with highly aroused ADHD. For patients with combined hyperarousal and distractibility, clonidine given concurrently with Ritalin may be optimal. When administered transdermally (skin patch), clonidine is the first psychotropic medication for children that maintains a constant and effective blood level for about 5 days. This form is preferred by many children, since no "pills" are required.

Clinical indications (see guidelines for using clonidine in ADHD)

Preliminary studies and clinical experience suggest that clonidine may be useful in *ADHD children* with the following associated conditions:

- Very highly aroused, Overactive ADHD
- ADHD with oppositional, aggressive/Conduct disorder
- Motor tics
- Growth impairment
- Poor response to psychostimulants

Clonidine is *not* useful for treatment of distractibility in ADD *without* hyperactivity.

Therapeutic efficacy

Initial studies assessed the effectiveness of clonidine in ADHD through comparison with placebo, and then in relation to methylphenidate in samples of 10 children each. Clonidine was found to be significantly better than placebo in effects on behavior as rated by parents, teachers, and clinicians in a double-blind study (Hunt et al., 1985). Ten boys, ages 8–13 years (X = 11.6 ± 0.54 year) met *DSM-III* diagnostic criteria for ADHD. Their behavior at baseline was evaluated using the CBCL and the Conners questionnaires completed by parents and teachers. Subjects were >1.5 SD above normal on the Hyperactivity Index as rated by both parents and teachers. The diagnosis was confirmed using the DICA interview of both parents and children. Baseline ratings were obtained during a two-week drug-free period.

Coded placebo was administered for two weeks prior to and following active clonidine. Clonidine dose was gradually increased over 10 days to a therapeutic level of about 4.5 μg/kg/day, constituting an average daily dose of 0.23 mg/day usually administered as 0.05 mg qid. Active treatment was continued for two months, and then tapered with return to placebo. Behavioral response was monitored by parent, teacher, and clinician ratings every two weeks. Parents and teachers completed the Conners 48-item and 28-item behavior rating scales, respectively. Clinicians rated the children utilizing a quantitative adaptation of the *DSM-III* diagnostic criteria for ADHD and also made global assessments of improvement during treatment. Neuromaturational assessment of visual–motor coordination was conducted monthly.

Clonidine was found to be significantly more effective than placebo as rated by teachers, parents, and clinicians. Teachers noted significant improvement in overall behavior ratings ($p = 0.001$), hyperactivity index ($p = 0.001$), conduct ($p = 0.4$), and inattention ratings ($p = 0.5$); parents also reported improvements in overall ratings ($p = 0.003$), hyperactivity index ($p = 0.004$), conduct problems ($p = 0.01$), and learning problems ($p = 0.007$). Clinicians noted overall improvements in the treated group on total score of cardinal *DSM-III* symptoms of ADHD, with 3 subjects having >25% improvement, and in areas of inattention, impulsivity, and hyperactivity. Based on the criteria of >50% improvement in at least two settings, 70% of ADHD children were improved. Upon tapering of clonidine and return to placebo, behavioral control quickly deteriorated to pretreatment levels. The major side effect was sedation, occurring about 1 hour after administration of clonidine and lasting about 30–60 minutes. This sedation decreased to minimal levels or disappeared within three weeks in all but one child. There was no evidence of psychomotor retardation on the behavioral ratings, athletic participation, or the visual-motor components of neuromaturational assessments. Blood pressure was reduced by about 10%, and was clinically nonsignificant. One child with prior symptoms of depression became more depressed on clonidine; children who had no prior symptoms of depressive disorder did not exhibit emergent symptoms on treatment.

Even in this small sample size, using a well-controlled, double-blind study, very significant improvement was evident from clonidine in contrast to pre- and posttreatment placebo. The medication was well-tolerated and often preferred by parents and children in subjects previously treated with Ritalin.

The next problem was to compare clonidine with methylphenidate. A separate population of 10 ADHD children was treated with clonidine, methylphenidate and placebo using a crossover design. Clonidine and methylphenidate were equally effective and significantly better than placebo as rated by parents and teachers (Hunt, 1987).

In a fashion similar to that above, 10 boys, ages 8–13 years (X = 11.6 ± 0.56 years) were selected who met *DSM-III* diagnostic criteria for ADHD. Subjects were >1.5 SD above normal on the Hyperactivity Index as rated by both parents and teachers. The diagnosis was confirmed using the DICA interview of both parents and children. Patients were rated by teachers, parents, and clinicians at baseline and every other week. Treatment included clonidine (gradually increased to 5 μg/kg/day), low-dose (0.3 mg/kg) and high-dose (0.6 mg/kg) methylphenidate (given in divided doses, 2/3 rd in AM), and placebo (qid). Teachers did not know the treatment condition. Clonidine was administered for 8 weeks while each dose of MPH was administered for one week in random sequence separated by a two-week placebo washout. Patients demonstrated significant response to both clonidine ($p = 0.005$) and methylphenidate ($p = 0.05$ and $p = 0.01$ for low-dose and high-dose, respectively) when compared with baseline and washout placebo ratings. Teachers expressed a slight preference for methylphenidate, perhaps reflecting its preferential effect on distractibility. Parents rated a nonsignificant preference for clonidine, indicating that it improved hyperactivity, impulsivity, cooperation, and oppositionality on weekends and in the evenings.

This study and our subsequent clinical experience in large numbers of patients has substantiated the therapeutic benefit of clonidine. It is slightly less effective than methylphenidate. However, clonidine is often preferred by parents for its stabilizing effect, lack of evening and weekend withdrawal, and its absence of anorectic or insomniac effects. Teachers showed slight preference for the effects of methylphenidate (MPH). A similar pattern and incidence of side effects has been noted.

Transdermal clonidine

Clonidine is unique among pediatric psychotherapeutic medications in being available in transdermal vehicle of administration. This form has significant potential advantages in a disorder in which taking medication can create significant embarrassment and the relatively short behavioral half-life of clonidine and psychostimulants requires multiple doses producing a roller-coaster pattern of behavioral control. Transdermal clonidine was compared with oral using an open design in subjects who previously demonstrated good therapeutic response to oral clonidine (Hunt, 1987, 1988).

In the prior group of 10 ADHD patients, those who responded to oral clonidine ($n = 8$) were subsequently shifted to an open trial of transdermal clonidine, administered at an equivalent dose. This open design was selected in order to control for the effectiveness of transdermal clonidine separate from the effectiveness of clonidine alone. After determining the optimal dose of clonidine for each subject (X = 5.0 μg/kg; 0.23 mg/day) for each patient (X age = 11.4 ± 0.6 years) all subjects were shifted to transdermal clonidine and monitored for at least one month. Parent, teacher, and clinician behavioral ratings were obtained every 2 weeks. Results showed no significant difference in overall therapeutic response between transdermal and oral clonidine. The important difference was in tolerance and side effects. When the clonidine patches were comfortable, they were universally preferred by patients and parents. The children appreciated the privacy and consistency bestowed by the transdermal clonidine. The duration of clinical effect was 5 rather than 7 days. The main side effect of transdermal administration was local contact dermatitis, with associated pruritis and erythema. This occurred in about 40% of the patients treated.

Transdermal clonidine is often a preferred route of administration due to its consistency of effect and privacy. Subsequent clinical and research experience has supported these preliminary observations (Chen and Vidt, 1989; Hunt, et al., 1990). Adherence of the patch is reduced during periods of heat and humidity. Further research is needed to clarify blood-level comparability of the oral and transdermal vehicles.

Differential effects of clonidine and methylphenidate

The next issue was to attempt to differentiate the clinical response and the type of patients that optimally respond to clonidine vs MPH. Our recent research has addressed differences in clinical effects of clonidine and methylphenidate. Clonidine is more effective in reducing high levels of activity and arousal that indirectly impede learning and may prompt aggressive behavior. Psychostimulants appear to have more direct effects on distractibility. Hence, these medications appear useful for distinct groups of ADHD children.

Methylphenidate narrows the attentional field and focuses attention, analogous to using a zoom lens. It is clearly superior for mild to moderately hyperactive children with primary attentional difficulties. Clonidine may be preferable for severely overactive, aggressive ADHD children, with generally intact cognitive functioning. The high level of arousal in the overactive group indirectly impairs attention, probably via cognitive flooding. In a highly aroused state, many routine or trivial stimuli are imbued with significance, and require excessive processing—leading to an overloading of functionally intact cognitive processes that impairs selective and sustained attention. The major effect of clonidine is to reduce excessive arousal in highly overactive ADHD children. The most responsive ADHD children appear to have an early onset, to be extremely energetic, and often exhibit associated oppositional or conduct disorder. In this group, clonidine improves frustration tolerance—often leading to an increase of task-oriented behavior, enhanced learning and effort, and improved compliance and cooperativeness. Clonidine has no direct effect on distractibility.

Combined clonidine and methylphenidate

Clonidine has been effectively utilized in conjunction *with* MPH in ADHD children who are *both* highly aroused and very distractible. Used concurrently, the dose of MPH was able to be reduced by about 40% and the net beneficial effects were increased. The response was smoother, less fluctuant or brittle, and the side effects of both medications appeared reduced (Hunt et al., 1989; submitted).

Sixty-three ADHD patients were treated in random sequence with clonidine or MPH alone, and in combination for 4–6 weeks in each medication condition. The average age = 10.3 ± 1.8 years range 6–15 years. The mean school grade = 4.5 ± 1.1. The dose of MPH was initially increased to 0.5 mg/kg/day and then individually titrated using behavioral ratings, clinical interviews, and side effects. The dose of clonidine was elevated to a level of 4–5 µg/kg (about 0.2 mg/day). After three weeks, the final dose was clinically optimized based on clinical response. Dependent behavioral measures obtained during treatment included weekly parent ratings [Parent Questionnaire, Iowa Scale for ADHD and Aggression, and R-CBCL (Quay)]. Teacher behavioral ratings were also obtained weekly. The final therapeutic dose of clonidine was 0.23 ± 0.025 mg/day. When administered alone, the mean MPH dose was 27.3 mg (± 3.1 mg). When administered concurrently with clonidine, the dose of MPH required to produce optimal clinical response was significantly reduced by 40% (27.3 to 16.4 mg/day), with $p < 0.05$. The Parent Questionnaire has provided the initial data for comparison of the effects of clonidine and MPH. The changes in percent improvement on behavioral factors are similar for both drugs when utilized alone. However, given in combination, a significant improvement in the factor of Conduct Problems occurred (56% reduction, $p < 0.05$).

Patients who may benefit from the combined medication are those ADHD subjects who continue to have significant motor hyperactivity while on methylphenidate, or who have brittle clinical symptoms or severe withdrawal in the evening. We have also used clonidine and MPH in some patients who did not tolerate Ritalin alone due to aggression, irritability, weight loss, insomnia, or delayed growth. Clonidine-responsive subjects who remain distractible may respond to combined medication achieved by a gradual titration of MPH added to a stable dose of clonidine.

Neurobehavioral mechanisms of action

The effect of clonidine in reducing the intensity of a variety of behavioral expressions of excessive arousal may provide an index of the role of locus coeruleus-based noradrenergic influence on behavior. The principal mechanism of action of clonidine is as an alpha$_2$ noradrenergic agonist. The the doses generally used in child psychiatry, clonidine reduces the endogenous release of norepinephrine (NE) by activating autoinhibitory effects of the presynaptic receptor. However, the behavioral patterns of many diagnoses reflect a continuum of multiple neurotransmitter effects. Norepinephrine may affect the responsivity of many behavioral systems and the sensitivity of other neurotransmitter systems. Clonidine may indirectly modify the expression of other neurotransmitters, such as dopamine, which may mediate the focus and breadth of attention in ADHD, or the control of movements in Tourette's. Serotonin may mediate the capacity to inhibit thoughts or aggressive behaviors. Thus, the use of clonidine in child psychiatry may be helpful in defining the relative contribution of components of neurochemical systems in child psychopathology (Bunney and DeRiemer, 1982; Hunt et al., 1990).

Since the direct effects of clonidine appear to be limited to reducing the noradrenergic contribution to arousal-based symptoms, clonidine is frequently used as an adjunctive agent in those disorders in which other neurochemical systems are involved. For example, in ADHD, clonidine may be utilized concurrently with the dopaminergic-releasing psychostimulants, such as methylphenidate or D-amphetamine, to increase attentional focus. In Tourette's disorder, clonidine may be paired with dopamine-blocking agents such as pimozide or haloperidol to reduce motor tics. In conjunction with these other agents, clonidine has a potentiating effect—probably by reducing the augmenting or amplifying role of NE in neurophysiology.

Much of clonidine's effect on specific behaviors or symptoms may be indirect benefits from reducing excessive arousal (Halliday et al., 1989). For example, in ADHD, clonidine has no direct effect on distractibility, though it reduces activity and improves frustration tolerance and thereby has powerful effects on task orientation—the ability to approach and complete demanding tasks. Similarly, in Tourette's syndrome, clonidine probably has little direct effect on dopaminergically mediated motor tics (Cohen et al., 1988; Goetz et al., 1987; Leckman et al., 1988). However, clonidine can reduce the anxiety and arousal experienced by many ADHD children that potentiates and exacerbates tics. As an antiaggressive agent, clonidine appears to be effective in reducing aggression related to hyperactivity, but is unlikely to be effective in controlling impulsive or premeditated aggression in nonaroused patients (Jouvent et al., 1988).

Neurochemical mechanisms of action

Methylphenidate and clonidine have very different neurochemical mechanisms of action, probably reflecting differences in neurotransmitter and brain regional effects. MPH releases presynaptically stored dopamine (DA) and norepinephrine (NE), producing an *increase* in basal brain arousal, evident by increase in BP and pulse, and decrease in appetite and sleep. However, MPH also facilitates improved behavioral inhibition and cognitive selective attention—probably by activation of cortical dopaminergically mediated inhibition systems.

Clonidine is an alpha$_2$-noradrenergic agonist that acts somewhat like exogenous norepinephrine (NE) (Hunt et al., 1988). In the doses prescribed for children, clonidine's preferential presynaptic effect reduces the firing of the locus coeruleus and inhibits the release of endogenous NE, leading to a decrease in plasma and urinary NE, and its metabolite, 3-hydroxy-4-methoxyphenethylene glycol (MHPG) (Hunt et al., 1984; Martin et al., 1984). Alpha$_2$ NE receptors located on the platelet appear to be down-regulated after 2 to 3 weeks of clonidine treatment, leading to a buffering of response to activating stimuli. Clonidine inhibits NE release partially through presynaptic inhibition of locus coeruleous firing—thereby *reducing* basal brain arousal. Reduced arousal can diminish the background "noise" and reduce the amount of stimuli that must be processed (improved signal:noise ratio).

Pharmacokinetics: dosage and blood levels

Oral Clonidine: The usual dose of clonidine is 0.15–0.3 mg/day which is about equivalent to 3–6 μg/kg/day. This dose level is reached gradually. Clonidine may be begun at night to facilitate sleep and enable tolerance to the sedative effects, and then increased at a rate of 0.05 mg (1/2 tablet) every third day. The median dose for an 8–12-year-old ADHD patient is about 0.25 to 0.3 mg per day. A maximal dose would be about 0.4–0.5 mg/day, approximately 8 μg/kg. Oral clonidine is commonly given 3 to 4 times a day, with meals and at bedtime (Hunt, 1988).

Pharmacokinetics: Clonidine is rapidly absorbed from the gut, achieving peak plasma level at 90–150 minutes. The excretion half-life in children is approximately 8 to 12 hours, with considerable cross-subject variability. The behavioral effects of clonidine last about 3 to 5 hours. Patients notice the most side effects (usually sedation) within 30 to 90 minutes after a dose, and may experience a loss of behavioral effect after 4 to 6 hours, depending on dose and severity of symptoms. Some clinical effect is longer lasting and may reflect gradual receptor down-regulation (Lowenthal et al., 1988).

Transdermal Clonidine: The transdermal or skin patch preparation of clonidine can be worn for about 5 days. It is available in doses labeled: "TTS" (Transdermal Therapeutic System) '1,' '2,' and '3' that correspond approximately to 0.1, 0.2, or 0.3 mg/day, respectively. These doses can be further refined by cutting the patch to achieve intermediate dose levels. Children are usually begun on oral clonidine to verify response, and then shifted to transdermal, since absorption from the transdermal appears somewhat more variable. The patches adhere quite well, except during the summer in humid climates. Select a relatively hairless and inaccessible area, such as the lower back. Prepare the skin by washing the area with soap and water, then dry. Remove the plastic backing and attach like a band aid, placing the surface that was adhered to plastic against the skin. A protective white adhesive covering about the size of a silver dollar can be worn optionally. We usually do not begin using this protective cover routinely, since it may increase the frequency of local dermatitis—erythema and itching. A topical steroid cream may reduce problems with local irritation. Although development of localized contact sensitization to transdermal clonidine may predispose to development of a generalized skin rash on subsequent return to oral clonidine administration, we have not seen this difficulty in our 50 patients who resumed transdermal clonidine.

Therapeutic Blood Levels: Therapeutic blood level parameters have not yet been established for clonidine.

Clinical management of clonidine in ADHD

Duration of Treatment: It usually takes about two weeks to see a specific response other than sedation, and about one month to see a significant clinical improvement. The sedation and tiredness often clear within the first month. Maximal effect may not be achieved for 2 to 3 months, since children seem to demonstrate a gradual maturation as their frustration tolerance is improved.

Long-Term Effects: ADHD children have been maintained on clonidine for up to five years without loss of effect nor significant change in dose. However, a few children do lose response or require a slightly higher dose during the first month. Occasionally, the dose must be increased after several months of treatment, but we have only seen this in about 20% of patients. We often continue children on clonidine during the summer, albeit at a reduced (2/3–1/2) dose. We discontinue all medications in virtually every child annually for a placebo-controlled trial to verify continued need for medication.

Adult ADHD: Clonidine has not been sufficiently studied in adult ADHD to allow for adequate assessment of its efficacy. However, since arousal tends to diminish with age, but distractibility may persist, clonidine may be less effective in adult ADHD than methylphenidate.

Side effects and toxicity

Sedation: The most frequent and troublesome side effect is sedation, usually experienced as sleepiness. This is usually most pronounced during the first 2–4 weeks and commonly decreases thereafter. On qid doses, the most common time of sleepiness is 1–2:30 P.M. Sedation is more severe in less highly active or aroused ADHD children. In about 15% of cases, this tiredness persisted at oral doses clinically required to decrease activity and enhance frustration tolerance.

After establishing a therapeutic oral dose the clinician may shift to the transdermal route of clonidine administration, that produces less of a pulse of plasma level, and hence is often less sedating. The tiredness may also decrease with combined treatment with MPH. For a few children (about 10%), oral clonidine was discontinued due to tiredness.

Cardiovascular Effects: As an antihypertensive agent, clonidine may produce hypotension. While this is common in adults, hypotension in children is very rarely significant. In over 100 children systematically monitored for this, we observed about a 10% decrease in systolic pressure; this rarely produces clinical symptoms or discomfort. Acutely, clonidine mildly diminishes cardiac output (10–20%) and decreases peripheral vascular resistance. However, during long-term treatment, cardiac output returns to baseline, while peripheral resistance and pulse remains decreased. The frequency of symptoms suggestive of orthostatic hypotension is less than 5%. Clonidine does not alter renal blood flow nor glomerular filtration rate. Plasma renin and aldosterone excretion may decrease. Cardiac dysrhythmia with the use of clonidine has been reviewed by Dawson et al. (1989).

Other Effects: Clonidine can induce depression. This has been observed in about 5% of our patients. All cases have been children with some definite depressive symptoms before treatment or who had a prior history

CLINICAL GUIDELINES FOR USING CLONIDINE IN ADHD:

1. **ADMINISTRATION:** START AND STOP __GRADUALLY__
2. **OPTIMAL DOSE:** CLONIDINE 3 − 5 μg/kg/day
3. **SCHEDULE:**   2 − 4 × / day
4. **MONITOR:**
   __*BEHAVIOR:__   HYPERACTIVITY, INATTENTION, MOOD,
   __*PHYSIOLOGY:__ DROWSINESS, BLOOD PRESSURE, WEIGHT,

STARTING CLONIDINE:
SCHEDULE FOR INCREASING DOSE: 1/2 TAB q. 3 rd day.

DAY	1	2	3	4	5	6	7	8	9	10	11	12
DATE	——	——	——	——	——	——	——	——	——	——	——	——
DAY	——	——	——	——	——	——	——	——	——	——	——	——
AM	- - -	- - -	- - -	X	x	x	x	x	x	x	x	x
NOON	- - -	- - -	- - -	- - -	- - -	- - -	X	x	x	x	x	x
PM	- - -	- - -	- - -	- - -	- - -	- - -	- - -	- - -	- - -	X	x	x
NIGHT x	X	x	x	x	x	x	x	x	x	x	x	x

__X = HALF TABLET__

OPTIMAL DOSE: CLONIDINE 3-5 μg/kg/day

SCHEDULE: 2 − 4 × / day

PROPOSED RELATIONSHIP BETWEEN SYMPTOMS, NEUROCHEMISTRY, AND TREATMENT

Clinical	Neurochemical	Treatment
Overaroused, Normal Inhibited Hyperactive, Distractible, Explosive	Excessive Norepinephrine	Clonidine
Normal Aroused, UnderInhibited Psychostimulants Less Hyperactive, Distractible	Diminished Dopamine	
OverAroused, UnderInhibited Hyperactive, Inattentive, Disorganized Often Explosive, Aggressive	↑ Norepinephrine ↓ Dopamine	Both

MECHANISM OF ACTION OF MEDICATION

	CLONIDINE:		RITALIN:	
Acute Neurochemical				
NE	Decr. Release		Increase Release	
DA	No Acute Effect		Increase Release, Direct	
Other	—		Increase Serotonin	
Physiological				
BP	Decrease		Slight Increase	
P	Slight Decrease		Increase	
Appetite			Mild Increase	Decrease
Weight	? Increase		Decrease	
Growth	? Increase		Decrease	
Sleep	Increase		Decrease	

of depression themselves or in the family history. Clonidine enhances sleep and appetite and may increase weight, which is often welcome if a child has been anorectic on psychostimulants. Clonidine is a potent releaser of growth hormone and may even facilitate growth. High-dose, long-term clonidine has been noted to produce retinal degeneration in animals, due to concentration of medication in the choroid. Thus, most of the side effects of clonidine are opposite those of MPH. When combined with MPH clonidine is usually well tolerated.

Tolerance: Tolerance has been noted in antihypertensive effect in adults. Clonidine should be withdrawn gradually. Sudden withdrawal from chronic, high-dose clonidine can produce nervousness, agitation, headache, and hypertension associated with increased catecholamine release.

Overdose: Acute overdose may produce hypotension, sedation, and somnolence. Treatment with gastric lavage and/or tolazoline 10 mg i.v. every 30 minutes can reverse these effects.

Drug Interactions: Clonidine has been safely utilized in conjunction with other antihypertensive or diuretic agents in adults. Concurrent use of antidepressants may reduce the effect of clonidine, and create a risk of corneal damage secondary to dryness of the eye. Clonidine may enhance the sedative effects of alcohol, barbiturates, or other sedatives or potentiate mucus dryness of anticholinergic agents. However, anticholinergic effects (dryness, constipation, urinary retention) are much less serious in children than in adults. Initially, some headache, dizziness, and nausea may occur; glucose may be increased chronically.

Medical Workup and Followup: In the baseline evaluation, the physician should consider: BP and pulse; CBC and U/A; electrolytes, thyroid indices, fasting blood sugar; liver function tests: alkaline phosphatase, SGOT, SGPT, bilirubin; EKG.

Summary

Clonidine acts primarily to reduce arousal in severely hyperactive ADHD children. The mechanism of action of clonidine is to reduce norepinephrine release and basal-brain activation. Research to date suggests that it may be helpful in treating very active ADHD patients, especially those with early onset and arousal-dependent aggression. The calming effect of clonidine appears helpful in increasing on-task behavior, school performance, and reducing oppositionality. It may be helpful in patients with associated tics or growth impairment.

Administered in oral form, clonidine can be given throughout the day. It produces some initial sedation, facilitates sleep and may slightly stimulate appetite and growth. Clonidine may be administered in a transdermal vehicle (skin patch) that can enable a steady therapeutic effect. Combined with methylphenidate, clonidine may reduce the dose of Ritalin required and minimize side effects. Both medications concurrently may be helpful in ADHD children who are active, aggressive, oppositional, and distractible. The main side effects are initial sedation and mild hypotension; depression occasionally occurs in individuals with a personal or family history. Slow initiation and withdrawal of dose diminishes side effects.

Additional multicenter research with behavioral, cognitive, and neurochemical monitoring is needed to validate these preliminary findings.

NEUROLEPTICS

In some cases of ADHD that are refractory to methylphenidate and other stimulants, neuroleptic drugs such as haloperidol and thioridazine have been useful alternatives, or additions to stimulant treatment. While there is some empirical observation of improvement in behavioral ratings of some ADHD patients, theoretical debate related to conflicting mechanisms of action has added to the practical concern about these drugs, especially regarding the risk for developing tardive dyskinesia.

Clinical efficacy

Several studies of neuroleptics in severely disturbed children suggest that they are effective. However, many of these children are more disturbed than typical ADHD children, and may be excluded from the diagnosis because they have a pervasive developmental disorder or atypical personality disorder.

In the 1970s, clinical studies by Werry and Aman (1975) with haloperidol and Gittelman-Klein et al. (1976) with thioridazine found no changes in cognitive performance, but some improvement was noted in behavior as rated by teachers, parents, and physicians. Campbell et al. (1983) noted that haloperidol and lithium were equivalently effective in decreasing the severe hyperactivity and aggression of hospitalized children, but the neuroleptics had greater sedative effects. However, compared with placebo, low-dose neuroleptics improved social behavior and cognitive organization in children who where cognitively disorganized. Zahn et al. (1975) found that neuroleptics had a cognitive blunting effect compared with placebo or D-amphetamine.

A recent study by Levy and Hobbes (1988) investigated the effect of adding haloperidol treatment in ADHD boys already receiving methylphenidate. They found that haloperidol alone had a negative impact on cognitive performance, as measured by vigilance tasks, when compared with placebo. Pretreatment with haloperidol two hours before methylphenidate administration resulted in blockage of improvement on vigilance performance usually seen with methylphenidate alone. Since the haloperidol pretreatment seemed to block the effects of methylphenidate, the authors suggest that dopaminergic actions are important in the beneficial cognitive effects seen with stimulant treatment in ADHD children. These observations suggest that while the cognitive focusing effects of MPH are mediated by dopamine, the behavioral effects may reflect multiple neurotransmitter systems. Unfortunately, this study did not address the subgroup of patients with ADHD refractory to stimulant treatment, in whom empirical observations of success have been noted after addition of neuroleptics.

Other reports have focused on the use of stimulant–neuroleptic combinations to control the attentional problems seen in adolescent schizophrenics. While these studies are not directly relevant to ADHD, many children who initially present as ADHD may have more severe disturbances.

In a case report, Rogeness and Macedo (1983) described an 11-year-old boy with schizophrenia whose behavior problems had been refractory to many drugs, including MPH, thiothixene, and haloperidol. A combination of MPH and chlorpromazine resulted in improved attention, appropriate behaviors, and allowed for outpatient treatment to begin. Similarly, in a study of adolescent schizophrenic patients, Erickson et al. (1984) observed the effects of neuroleptics on performance of the CPT. Thiodiazine or thiothixene did not enhance performance on the CPT, and produced sedation.

Side effects

In addition to sedation, the risks of developing extrapyramidal effects or tardive dyskinesia from neuroleptics remains high. These concerns have sparked much debate, including the concerns raised by Gualtieri and Hicks (1985) who question whether or not neuroleptics provide any relief from ADHD symptoms.

Mechanism of action

The use of neuroleptics in combination with stimulants hinges on the theory that beneficial effects of stimulants are due to central changes in multiple neurotransmitters rather than a single transmitter. The dopamine-blocking effect of the major tranquilizers would seem to counteract positive stimulant effects on dopaminergic activity, if that were the only mechanism of pharmacological action. In a recent review article, Zametkin and Borcherding (1989) discussed the role of dopamine and noradrenaline in the disorder and suggest that a network of neurochemical systems interact to produce the behavioral and cognitive changes in ADHD patients. Well-controlled studies of neuroleptic effects on ADHD alone and in combination with stimulants would seem warranted to determine why positive changes are seen in the subgroup of patients described above.

Summary

Neuroleptics have a limited role in ADHD. The patients most likely to benefit are probably those with underlying thought disorder or personality disorganization. Although these individuals may have a broader-based disturbance than ADHD, they often present initially with symptoms of hyperactivity and distractibility. The decision to treat with neuroleptics must reflect consideration on the possible risk for tardive dyskinesia and conservatism in dose selection and monitoring.

DIETARY INTERVENTION

Since Feingold introduced the concept that food dyes, preservatives, and colorizations may increase hyperactivity, many parents have utilized dietary restriction in their ADHD children. In spite of considerable testimonal evidence that this restriction decreases hyperactivity, initial well-controlled studies have failed to find a consistently robust effect. This lack of response to dietary challenges occurred even in children whose parents presented dietary diary histories of negative effects of these foods.

In a comprehensive review of various Feingold diet studies, Wender (1986) found that of approximately 240 children evaluated in numerous diet studies, only 1% demonstrated any consistent behavioral change in the desired direction. More than 90% of the subjects showed no significant change when challenged with food colorings. An early trial of the Feingold diet on 15 hyperkinetic children concluded that the diet reduced hyperkinetic symptoms, but the authors stressed that this conclusion was put forth with significant reservations (Conners et al., 1976). This trial of the Feingold diet suggests that a diet low in natural salicylates, artificial colors, and artificial flavors could lower the hyperactivity of some children. However, the authors expressed apprehension in accepting these conclusions too readily. They cited the small sample size of their study and the lack of complete consistency throughout their results (possibly due to the subjective measures of change) as reasons for their doubt. Behavioral effect of major dietary intervention was considered a factor as well.

Another test of the Feingold diet placed 36 hyperactive boys on experimental and control diets. No support for the Feingold diet was observed (Harley et al., 1978). The subjects were 36 boys, age 6–13 years ($X =$ 9.5), who met at least two of the following criteria: (1) scored 15 or above on the Conners P-TQ, (2) a score of 15 or more as rated by the child's teacher, and (3) a primary diagnosis of hyperkinetic reaction given by the child's physician. All medications were terminated for two weeks prior to a two-week baseline period. Subjects were then assigned in double-blind fashion to the experimental (Feingold) or control diet. The diets were designed to be indistinguishable in appearance, taste, nutritional value, and variety. Subjects were maintained on the diets for three weeks in the spring and again for four weeks in the fall of one year. Extensive procedures were undertaken to ensure dietary compliance. Neuropsychological data and laboratory observation were completed at baseline and at the completion of each diet period. An average of three classroom observations per week made by a team of trained students was obtained throughout the study. Conners P-TQ were completed weekly by the child's parents and teacher. No significant neuropsychological effects of the diet were found. Classroom observation yielded no significant change in classroom hyperactivity or disruptive behavior attributable to the diet or diet order. P-TQ ratings by parents and teachers were rarely in agreement, with only four of the 36 children consistently rated as improved on the experimental diet. Analysis of variance of mean P-TQ scores indicate improved behavior as rated by parents, but not for teacher ratings.

Results of this study show that while some positive diet effects were judged to be present by parents, they became greatly reduced in teacher ratings, and basically disappeared in objective observational data. One should keep in mind that parents' ratings usually have been found to be less reliable than teacher ratings.

Another challenge of the Feingold hypothesis was performed in 26 hyperactive children who were given Ritalin and placebo medication in combination with challenge and control cookies (with and without artificial food colors and additives, respectively). Stimulant medications were found to be substantially more effective than diet in reducing hyperactive behavior (Williams et al., 1978).

The subjects of this study ranged from 5 to 12 years old, had been clinically diagnosed as hyperactive, and had been receiving stimulant medication to which they were responsive for at least three months. The children were placed on a modified Feingold diet and then randomly assigned in double-blind, crossover style to one of 24 possible orderings of treatment involving active drug (average daily dose 10 to 25 mg MPH), placebo drug, challenge cookies, and control cookies. Behavior was assessed several times a week by parents and teachers using Conners 11-item, 40-item, and 96-item checklists. Daily diet diaries were kept by the parents to check for compliance with the Feingold diet. Contrasting effects of diet were noted between parent and teacher ratings. There were, however, consistent results showing reduced hyperactive behavior while receiving stimulants than while receiving placebo, regardless of dietary status. Both parent and teacher ratings showed that there was some decrease in hyperactive behavior in response to the Feingold diet ($p = 0.1$ (NS); $p = 0.025$, respectively); this reduction was greatest when the children were not taking medication.

This study gives clear evidence to suggest that stimulant medication is more effective in treating hyperactivity than the Feingold diet. It also suggests, however, that in a subset of hyperactive children a modified version of the Feingold diet seems to be effective, particularly in the absence of psychostimulant medication.

In a more recent study of the Feingold diet in 39 young adolescents with learning disabilities (half with concurrent ADHD), again no clinical benefit was observed from this intervention (Gross et al., 1987).

The effect of dietary control compared with placebo on the behavior of hyperactive children was evaluated in 39 children, ages 11–17 years. While all subjects had learning disabilities, 18 exhibited hyperkinetic syndrome as rated by school psychologists. Seven had been previously treated with MPH; 5 with other psychostimulants; and 5 with neuroleptics or anticonvulsants. They were placed on the Feingold diet, which is low in salicylates and tartrazine and avoids preservatives, artificial flavors, or colors. These outpatients were monitored on video tape for motor restlessness and disruptive behavior. The authors' impression was that the Feingold diet appears to be distasteful for typical children. There seems to be no clinical advantage provided by these diets for most hyperkinetic children.

In contrast, two recent studies suggest some therapeutic benefit from dietary control. In a study of 76 hyperactive children, many exhibited behavioral improvement while on a restricted diet. This improvement subsequently deteriorated when they were later challenged with a diet containing multiple additives (Egger et al., 1985).

The hyperactive children were treated with an oligoantigenic diet (one containing only a few variety of foods). In those children who responded, the investigators identified the provoking foods by reintroducing them sequentially. These same foods were then reintroduced in a randomized, double-blinded, crossover, placebo-controlled manner to determine their effect on the development of overactivity. Overall, 62 (86%) of the children showed improvement on the oligoantigenic diet as evidenced by increased managability at home and school; with 21 (29%) of them achieving a normal range of behavior. Of those who completed the crossover, placebo-controlled trial ($n = 28$), symptoms returned or were exacerbated much more often when the patients were on active food than on placebo.

In this study, 48 foods were identified to provoke overactivity, with artificial colorants and preservatives being the most common. Notably, no child was sensitive to these two alone.

Another study reported modest results from eliminating not only food colorings and additives, but any food felt to be provocative of undesirable behavior (Kaplan et al., 1989). The subjects of this 10-week study were 24 hyperactive preschool age boys with existing sleep problems or physical signs and/or symptoms (e.g., stuffy nose, stomachache). They were placed on a diet that eliminated not only artificial colors and flavors but also chocolate, monosodium glutamate, preservatives, caffeine, and any other substance that the families thought might be affecting their child. Approximately 10 subjects (42%) exhibited about 50% improvement in behavior. Another 4 (16%) exhibited a 12% improvement with no placebo effect. The remaining 10 children (42%) were unresponsive to dietary intervention.

Summary

Dietary intervention was initially enthusiastically pursued by parents following Feingold's initiatives. However, most well-controlled studies fail to find objective benefit from restrictive diets nor discontrol following dietary challenges with additives, preservatives, or food coloring. Several recent studies suggest there may be therapeutic benefit from restriction from multiple food "antigens" in some subjects.

Further research is needed to define which patients and what food restrictions may be useful. The underlying mechanism of action of food responses and its putative relationship to allergic processes also requires further clarification.

AMINO ACID SUPPLEMENTATION

Since activity of catecholamines and indolamines has been implicated in the neuropathology of ADHD, the clinical effect of precursors to these agents has been studied. Disturbances in the release or uptake of the neurotransmitters serotonin (5-HT), norepinephrine (NE), and dopamine (DA) play a possible role in the pathophysiology of ADHD. As precursors to these neurotransmitters, phenylalanine (Phe), tryptophan (Trp), and tyrosine (Tyr) in increased amounts could lead to increased levels of neurotransmitters. This suggests that Phe, Trp, and Tyr could theoretically be used as alternative treatments for increasing CNS catacholamine levels.

A trial was conducted using DL-phenylalanine in adults (21–45 years) with residual ADD (Wood et al., 1985). Thirteen subjects (5 male, 8 female) completed a two-week placebo crossover trial. The dose of phenylalanine was gradually increased from 50 mg tid to a maximum of 400 mg tid. Improvement was noted in symptoms of mood (depression and lability), but not in symptoms of distractibility or hyperactivity. Furthermore, patients who continued on the precursor supplementation after the two-week trial became refractory.

Amino acid supplementation has also been studied in prepubertal children (Nemzer et al., 1986). The subjects were 14 children (X age = 9.3 years) who met *DSM-III* criteria for ADHD and scored above 15 on the Conners Parent and ≥40 on the Conners' Teacher's Questionnaire. They were treated with tryptophan (100 mg/kg/day), tyrosine (140 mg/kg/day), D-amphetamine (5 mg/day if <32 kg or 10 mg/day if >32 kg), or placebo. During treatment, blood levels of both tryptophan and tyrosine were measured weekly. Tryptophan was better than D-amphetamine in 5/14 subjects, as rated by parents; tyrosine was not better than amphetamine. The main side effect of tryptophan was daytime sleepiness, which was problematic in one subject. The authors suggested that tryptophan might be useful during stimulant medication weekend holidays.

Summary

Dietary supplementation, although interacting has not been universally helpful. Tryptophan has shown to be beneficial in some patients, but has been withdrawn from the market because it induces a serious medical condition (Nemzer et al., 1986). Negative report of DL-phenylalanine and tyrosine suggests they are not useful.

CONCLUSION

Attention deficit hyperactivity disorder is a multifaceted disorder with several component features. The differential distribution of symptoms may reflect primary disturbances in selective neurotransmitter and neurofunctional systems. Although Ritalin remains the primary medication of choice for most patients, other medications may have a significant role in treatment of specific patients. These medications may have their primary effect on affective or arousal components of the disorder in selected individuals.

Antidepressants have demonstrated utility in treatment of ADHD. Desipramine is frequently the most useful due to its profile of modest anticholinergic side effects. Other medications that have been found effective in some studies include imipramine, amitriptyline, nortriptyline, and MAOIs. However, their utility may be limited by side effects. Bupropion and other new generation antidepressants may also contribute to the treatment of selected ADHD patients. While these medications generally have the advantage of more stable administration and effect, their specific indications are not yet determined. Although antidepressants appear effective in ADHD patients who are not depressed, they may have special value in ADHD patients with comorbid affective disorder.

Clonidine appears useful in ADHD patients who are highly aroused, very hyperactive and prone to secondary aggression, oppositionality, or tics. Clonidine may be used in conjunction with Ritalin for patients with concurrent distractibility.

Dietary restriction and use of amino acid precursors have not usually been found effective. While there may be select cases that respond, reliable predictors of response are not yet available. The effectiveness of noradrenergic antidepressants and of clonidine suggest a role for noradrenalin systems in ADHD, in addition to the importance of dopaminergic effects on breadth of attention.

These studies suggest that important therapeutic alternatives exist for treatment of ADHD children who do not respond well to Ritalin, or whose treatment is limited by side effects. Further research may better define selected patient populations or symptoms clusters that optimally respond to each medication.

ACKNOWLEDGMENTS

Funding for this research and paper was provided through the March of Dimes.

We extend appreciation to Andrew Ragland, William Cooper, Richard LoCicero, and Lee Mandl for contributions to this article.

REFERENCES

Biederman, J., Baldessarini, R.J., Wright, V., Knee, D. & Harmatz, J.S., (1989), A double-blind placebo controlled study of desipramine in the treatment of ADD. *J. Am. Acad. Child Adolesc. Psychiatry,* 28(5):777–784.

Biederman, J., Gastfriend, D.R., Jellinek, M.S. et al. (1986), Desipramine in the treatment of children with attention deficit disorder. *J. Clin. Psychopharmacol.,* 6:359–363.

Biederman, J., Gonzalez, E., Bronstein, B. et al. (1988), Desipramine and cutaneous reactions in pediatric outpatients. *J. Clin. Psychiatry,* 49:178–183.

Bunney, B.S. & DeRiemer, S.A. (1982), Effects of clonidine on nigral dopamine cell activity: Possible mediation by noradrenergic regulation of serotonergic raphe system. In: *Gilles de la Tourette Syndrome,* eds. A.J. Friedhoff & T.N. Chase. New York: Raven.

Campbell, M., Anderson, L.T. & Green, W.H. (1983), Behavior-disordered and aggressive children: New advances in pharmacotherapy. *Devel. Behav. Pediatr.*, 4(4):265–271.

Casat, C.D., Pleasants, D.Z., Schroeder, D.H. & Parler, D.W. (1989), Bupropion in children with attention deficit disorder. *Psychopharmacol Bull.*, 25(2):198–201.

Chen, S.W. & Vidt, D.G. (1989), Patient acceptance of transdermal clonidine. A retrospective review of 25 patients. *Cleve. Clin. J. Med.*, 56(1):21–26.

Cohen, D.J., Bruun, R.D. & Leckman, J.F. (eds.) (1980), *Tourette's Syndrome and Tic Disorders: Clinical Understanding and Treatment*. New York: John Wiley & Sons.

Cohen, D.J., Detlor, J., Young, J.G. & Shaywitz, B.A. (1988), Clonidine ameliorates Gilles de la Tourette syndrome. *Arch. Gen. Psychiatry*, 37:1350–1357.

Conners, C.K., Goyette, C.H., Southwick, D.A., Lees, J.M. & Andrulonis, P.A. (1976), Food additives and hyperkinesis: A controlled double-blind experiment. *Pediatrics*, 58(2):154–166.

Dawson, P.M., Vander-Zanden, J.A., Werkman, S.L., Washington, R.L. & Tyma, T.A., (1989), Cardiac dysrhythmia with the use of clonidine in explosive disorder. *DICP*, 23(6):465–466.

Donnelly, M., Zametkin, A.J., Rapoport, J.E. (1986), Treatment of childhood hyperactivity with desipramine: Plasma drug concentration, cardiovascular effects, plasma and urinary catecholamine levels, and clinical response. *Clin. Pharmacol. Ther.*, 39:72–81.

Egger, J., Carter, C.M., Graham, P.J., Gumley, D. & Soothill, J.F. (1985), Controlled trial of oligoantigenic treatment in the hyperkinetic syndrome. *Lancet*, 540–545.

Erickson, W.D., Yellin, A.M., Hopwood, J.H., Realmuto, G.M. & Greenburg, L.M. (1984), The Effects of neuroleptics on attention in adolescent schizophrenics. *Biol. Psychiatry*, 19(5):745–752.

Garfinkel, B.D., Wender, P.H. & Sloman, L., (1983), Tricyclic antidepressants and methylphenidate treatment of attention deficit disorder in children. *J. Am. Acad. Child Psychiatry*, 2:343–348.

Gastfriend, D.R., Biederman, J., Jellinek, M.S. (1984), Desipramine in the treatment of adolescents with attention deficit disorder. *Am. J. Psychiatry*, 141:906–908.

Gittelman-Klein, R. (1974), Pilot clinical trial of imipramine in hyperkinetic children. In: *Clinical Uses of Stimulant Drugs in Children*, ed. C. K. Conners. The Hague, Netherlands: Excerpta Medica Foundation, pp. 192–201.

Gittelman-Klein, R., Klein, F.D., Katz, F., Kesore, F, Pollack, E. (1976), Comparative effects of methylphenidate and thioridazine in hyperkinetic children. *Arch. Gen. Psychiatry*, 33:1217–1231.

Goetz, C.G., Tanner, C.M., Wilson, R.S., Carroll, V.S., Como, P.G., Shannon, K.M. (1987), Clonidine and Gilles de la Tourette syndrome: Double-blind study using objective rating methods. *Ann. Neurol.*, 21:307–310.

Greenberg, L., Yellin, A., Spring, C. et al. (1975), Clinical effects of imipramine and methylphenidate in hyperactive children. *Int. J. Mental Health*, 4:144–156.

Gross, M.D. (1973), Imipramine in the treatment of minimal brain dysfunction in children. *Psychosomatics*, 14:283–285.

Gross, M.D., Tofanelli, R.A., Butzirus, S.M. & Snodgrass, E.W. (1987), The Effects of diets rich in and free from additives on the behavior of children with hyperkinetic and learning disorders. *J. Am. Acad. Child Adolesc. Psychiatry*, 26(1):53–55.

Gualtieri, C.T. & Hicks, R.E. (1985), Stimulants and neuroleptics in hyperactive children [letter]. *J. Am. Acad. Child Adolesc. Psychiatry*, 24(3):363–364.

Halliday, R., Callaway, E. & Lannon, R. (1989), The effects of clonidine and yohimbine on human information processing. *Psychopharmacology (Berl.)*, 99(4):563–566.

Harley, J.P., Ray, R.S., Tomasi, L. et al. (1978), Hyperkinesis and food additives: Testing the Feingold hypothesis. *Pediatrics*, 61(6):818–828.

Huessy, H.R. & Wright, A.L. (1970), The use of imipramine in children's behavior disorders. *Acta Paedopsychiatrie*, 37:194–199.

Hunt, R.D. (1987), Treatment effects of oral and transdermal clonidine in relation to methylphenidate—an open pilot study in ADDH. *Psychopharmacol. Bull.,* 23(1):111–114.

Hunt, R.D. (1988), Treatment of ADHD with clonidine: guidelines for physicians. *Psychiatric Times.*

Hunt, R.D., Clapper, L. & Ebert, M.H. (1989), Clonidine and methylphenidate: Combined use in treatment of selected ADHD children. Presentation: American Academy of Child and Adolescent Psychiatry.

Hunt, R.D., Cohen, D.J., Anderson, G. & Minderaa, R. (1988), Noradrenergic Mechanisms in ADDH. In *Attention Deficit Disorder: New Research In Attention, Treatment, and Psychopharmacology,* ed. L.M. Bloomingdale. New York: Pergamon Press.

Hunt, R.D., Capper, L. & O'Connell, P. (1990), Clonidine in child and adolescent psychiatry. *J. Child Adolesc. Psychopharmacol.,* 1(1):87–102.

Hunt, R.D., Cohen, D.J., Anderson, G.M. & Clark, L. (1984), Possible change in noradrenergic receptor sensitivity with attention deficit disorder and hyperactivity: Response to chronic methylphenidate treatment. *Life Sci.,* 35:885–897.

Hunt, R.D., Minderaa, R.B. & Cohen, D.J. (1985), Clonidine benefits children with attention deficit disorder and hyperactivity: Report of a double-blind placebo-controlled crossover study. *J. Am. Acad. Child Psychiatry,* 24(5):617–629.

Hunt, R.D., Minderaa, R.B. & Cohen, D.J. (1986), The therapeutic effect of clonidine in attention deficit disorder with hyperactivity: A comparison with placebo. *Psychopharmacol. Bull.,* 22(1):229–236.

Jouvent, R., Lecrubier, Y., Hardy, M.C. & Widlocher, D. (1988), Clonidine and neuroleptic-resistant mania [letter]. *Br. J. Psychiatry,* 152:293–294.

Kaplan, B.J., McNicol, J., Conte, R.A. & Moghadam, H.K. (1989), Dietary replacement in preschool-aged hyperactive boys. *Pediatrics,* 83(1):7–17.

Leckman, J.F., Walkup, J.T. & Cohen, D.J. (1988), Clonidine treatment of Tourette's syndrome. In: *Tourette's Syndrome and Tic Disorders: Clinical Understanding and Treatment,* eds. D.J. Cohen, R.D. Bruun, & J.F. Leckman. New York: John Wiley & Sons.

Levy, F. & Hobbes, G. (1988), The action of stimulant medication in attention deficit disorder with hyperactivity: dopaminergic, noradrenergic, or both? *J. Am. Acad. Child Psychiatry,* 27:802–805.

Lowenthal, D.T., Matzek, K. M. & MacGregor, T.R. (1988), Clinical pharmacokinetics of clonidine. *Clin. Pharmacokinet.,* 14(5):287–310.

Martin, P.R., Ebert, M.H., Gordon, E.K., Linnoila, M. & Kopin, I.J. (1984), Effects of clonidine on central and peripheral catecholamine metabolism. *Clin. Pharmacol. Therap.,* 35(3):322–327.

Nemzer, E.D., Arnold, L.E., Votolato, N.A. & McConnell, H. (1986), Amino acid supplementation as therapy for attention deficit disorder. *J. Am. Acad. Child Adolesc. Psychiatry,* 25(4):509–513.

Pliszka, R. (1987), Tricyclic antidepressants in the treatment of children with attention deficit disorder. *J. Am. Acad. Child Psychiatry,* 26:127–132.

Popper, C.W. & Elliott, G.R., (1990), Sudden death and tricyclic antidepressants: Clinical considerations for children. *J. Child Adol. Psychopharm.,* 2(1):125–132.

Quinn, P.O. & Rapoport, J.L. (1975), One-year follow up of hyperactive boys treated with imipramine or methylphenidate. *Am. J. Psychiatry,* 10:387–390.

Rapoport, J.L. (1986), Antidepressants in childhood attention deficit disorder and obsessive-compulsive disorder. *Psychosomatics,* 27(11):30–36.

Rapoport, J.L., Quinn, P., Bradbard, G. et al. (1974), Imipramine and methylphenidate treatment of hyperactive boys: A double-blind comparison. *Arch. Gen. Psychiatry,* 30:789–793.

Riddle, M.A., Hardin, M.T., Cho, S.C., Woolston, J.L. & Leckman, J.F. (1988), Desipramine treatment of boys with attention deficit hyperactivity disorder and tics: preliminary clinical experience. *J. Am. Acad. Child Adolesc. Psychiatry,* 27(6):811–814.

Rogeness, G.A. & Macedo, C.A. (1983), Therapeutic response of a schizophrenic boy to a methylphenidate-chlorpromazine combination. *Am. J. Psychiatry,* 140(7):932–933.

Saul, R.C. (1985), Nortriptyline in attention deficit disorder [letter]. *Clin. Neuropharmacol.,* 8(4):382–383.

Simeon, J.G., Ferguson, H.B. & Van Wyck Fleet, J., (1986), Bupropion effects in attention deficit and conduct disorders. *Can. J. Psychiatry,* 31:581–585.

Sprague, R. & Sleater, E. (1977), Methylphenidate in hyperkinetic children: Differences in dose effects on learning and social behavior. *Science,* 198:1274–1276.

Swanson, J.M. (1985), Measures of cognitive functioning appropriate for use in pediatric psychopharmacology research studies. *Psychopharmacol. Bull.,* 21:887–890.

Waizer, J., Hoffman, S.P., Polizos, P. et al. (1974), Outpatient treatment of hyperactive school children with imipramine. *Am. J. Psychiatry,* 131:587–591.

Wender, E.H. (1986), The food additive-free diet in the treatment of behavior disorders: A review. *Dev. Behav. Pediatr.,* 7(1):35–42.

Werry, J. & Aman, M. (1975), Methylphenidate and haloperidol in children. Effects on memory and activity. *Arch. Gen. Psychiatry,* 32:790–795.

Werry, J. (1980), Imipramine and methylphenidate in hyperactive children. *J. Child Psychol. Psychiatry,* 21:27–35.

Williams, J.I., Cram, D.M., Tausig, F.T. & Webster, E. (1978), Relative effects of drugs and diet on hyperactive behaviors: An experimental study. *Pediatrics,* 61(6):811–817.

Wood, D.R., Reimherr, F.W. & Wender, P.H. (1985), Treatment of attention deficit disorder with dl-phenylalanine. *Psychiatry Res.,* 16:21–26.

Yepes, L.E., Balka, E.B., Winsberg, B.G. et al. (1977), Amitriptyline and methylphenidate treatment of behaviorally disordered children. *J. Child Psychol. Psychiatry,* 18:39–52.

Zahn, T.P., Abate, F., Little, B. & Wender, P.H. (1975), Minimal brain dysfunction, stimulant drugs, and autonomic nervous system activity. *Arch. Gen. Psychiat.,* 32:381–387.

Zametkin, A. & Rapoport, J.L. (1983), Tricyclic antidepressants and children. In: *Drugs In Psychiatry,* Vol. I, *Antidepressants,* eds. G.D. Burrows, T.R. Norman & B. Davies. Amsterdam: Elsevier, pp. 129–147.

Zametkin, A., Rapoport, J.L., Murphy, D.L., Linnoila, M. & Iamond, D. (1985), Treatment of hyperactive children with monoamine oxidase inhibitors. *Arch. Gen. Psychiatry,* 42:962–966.

Zametkin, A.J. & Borcherding, B.G., (1989), The neuropharmacology of attention deficit hyperactivity disorder. *Ann. Rev. Med.,* 40:447–451.

Methylphenidate in the Clinical Office Practice of Child Psychiatry

LAURENCE L. GREENHILL, M.D.

INTRODUCTION

Over 30 years of clinical experience has shown that Ritalin (methylphenidate) is a safe and effective medication for the treatment of attention deficit hyperactivity disorder (ADHD). Success regularly occurs with Ritalin; in multiple controlled studies, as many as 75% of ADHD children respond with a moderate to marked degree of improvement (Barkley, 1982). Methylphenidate, prescribed as Ritalin (Ciba Geigy) or the generic drug (MD Pharmaceuticals) is heavily utilized by family practitioners, pediatricians, pediatric neurologists, and child psychiatrists. One study of annual school nurse records reported that 7% of all Baltimore County third-grade school children were treated with psychoactive drugs in 1987 (Safer and Krager, 1988), and 99% of these children were taking Ritalin. Based on these data, it was estimated that over 750,000 children in the United States are treated with Ritalin. Drug Enforcement Administration production quotas for Ritalin have risen dramatically, jumping from 1221 kilograms per year in 1983 to over 2400 kilograms in 1988 (Cowart, 1988).

Although Ritalin's use may be due to its quick efficacy and low incidence of side effects, the medication has been the most studied and published psychoactive drug for children. Ritalin has surpassed all other agents in sheer publication count; the current Medlars II off-line bibliographic service cites 247 articles between 1966 and 1980, 295 between 1980 and 1989, and 70 for 1990 alone. Ritalin has also been the subject of considerable controversy, with concern raised about its possible overuse to deal with any child who does not conform to standards of classroom behavior (Kohn, 1989; The Medical Letter, 1988).

Although Safer's data suggest that Ritalin use may be doubling every 5 years, standards of practice and monitoring have not always kept step with the medication's popularity. Solomons reported that only 55% of Ritalin-treated children received as much as 2 contacts between physician and family within a 6-month period (Solomons, 1973). Sherman's more recent 1988 survey (see Sherman, pp. 187–193) in Suffolk County used New York State's mandatory reporting triplicate prescription program to more accurately identify all Ritalin scripts written for children within a defined geographical area for a period of time. She found that over 52% of physicians wrote just a single one-month prescription for the 3986 children treated. This may be due, in part, to the relative scarcity of long-term follow-up studies of Ritalin treatment. Most published Ritalin studies are short trials of 6 to 8 weeks, not the longer periods found in clinical practice. Maintenance of behavioral control requires the implementation of an office-based multimodal treatment plan (Abikoff, pp. 147–154; Satterfield et al., 1979a, 1980), defined periods of treatment with medication, and regular monitoring. This chapter will focus on the child psychiatrist as the coordinator of a multimodal treatment plan for a child with ADHD.

Ritalin's prominence as a mainstay treatment for behavior disorders in American medicine may explain its controversial history in the latter half of the 1980s. The Citizen's Commission on Human Rights, a subsidiary of the Church of Scientology, attacked both the medication and the physicians prescribing it (Cowart, 1988). Using television and radio media, the CCHR tried to sway public opinion against Ritalin

---

Columbia College of Physicians and Surgeons, and New York State Psychiatric Institute, New York, New York

treatment by presenting cases of children who became depressed and suicidal during Ritalin therapy (DuPaul and Barkley, 1990). Ritalin is only one of a series of psychoactive medications that can help children with attention deficit hyperactivity disorder, and these other drugs, such as d-amphetamine or magnesium pemoline, were not attacked by name.

Dupaul and Barkley (DuPaul and Barkley, 1990) conceptualize Ritalin as a key but only part component of a comprehensive treatment plan. Its role can be to reduce the most socially disturbing components of ADHD—the calling out, off-task behavior, the disruptiveness to other children, and the impulsivity—so the affected child can benefit more effectively from the rest of the multimodal treatment plan. At its best, the multimodal approach (see Abikoff, pp. 147–154) brings to bear the expertise of several professionals to support and enhance the efforts of the parents, the teacher, and the child himself.

History of Ritalin's use in the treatment of children with behavior disorders

Pediatric psychopharmacology can be traced back to Bradley's serendipitous 1937 treatment of residential children with benzedrine, the racemic form of amphetamine (Bradley, 1937). Soon after taking this medication, these children displayed dramatic increases in compliance, decreases in activity, and performed better in the classroom. Bradley continued to gather cases and publish them during the 1940s, but wider interest in this unusual type of medication response did not occur until the late 1950s and early 1960s, following the investigations of Laufer et al. (1957), Eisenberg et al. (1961), and Conners et al. (1967). These investigators respectively found that psychostimulants increase the seizure threshold to photometrizol, decrease oppositional behavior of boys with conduct disorder in a residential school, and produce improvement on standardized rating forms.

Ritalin, or methylphenidate, was first synthesized by Panzion in 1944 as a cyclized derivative of amphetamine (Perel and Dayton, 1976). Mier replicated this synthesis in 1954, and the medication was marketed by Ciba Geigy in the early 1960s as a geriatric medication. Its similarity to d-amphetamine chemically suggested its use in the treatment of children with behavior disorders. An epidemic of recreational use in Sweden in 1971 led the Food and Drug Administration to reclassify it as a Schedule II compound, thus placing it in the category of substances of abuse.

Several key aspects of Ritalin made it gather popularity as a clinical tool. Though chemically similar to the amphetamines, most clinicians consider it a nonamphetamine. The national concern about adolescents, the young adult drug culture, and the well-publicized practices of diet doctors made d-amphetamine appear dangerous and a less suitable treatment agent than Ritalin for impulsive children.

Second, Ritalin became an important research medication, and its multiple citations in clinical, basic science journals gave it a ubiquitous presence in academic medicine and training. Its quick onset of action, the high likelihood of drug response, and its low incidence of serious side effects made it the ideal tool for psychopharmacological research. Ritalin had an impact on a variety of fields of child research, including psychostimulant growth effects (Gittelman-Klein et al., 1987; Greenhill, 1981, 1984; Greenhill et al., 1981; Hechtman et al., 1978; Safer and Allen, 1973; Safer et al., 1972; Satterfield et al., 1979b); the dissociation of cognitive and social effects of stimulant medications (Sprague and Sleator, 1977); drug-dependent learning (Gan and Cantwell, 1982; Swanson and Kinsbourne, 1976); dose (by weight)-response relationships (Rapport et al., 1989); drug effects at different levels of effortful processing (Brown et al., 1982; Swanson et al., 1991a, 1991b). For adult patients, methylphenidate became an important treatment tool for AIDS dementia (see Fernandez, pp. 177–185) and as a probe in schizophrenia research (see Robinson et al., pp. 307–318).

Even with the explosive growth of Ritalin-based research, the majority of clinical studies are short-term, rarely lasting more than two months; long-term efficacy has yet to be proven. Those follow-up articles covering periods of 6 months have debated whether changes in response to the medication over time reveal that tolerance to Ritalin can develop (Fried et al., 1987; Winsberg et al., 1987). Current research into the feasibility and efficacy of multimodal treatment (see Abikoff, pp. 147–154) may show conclusively the stability of long-term Ritalin treatment.

A third factor was the drug's continued viability as a product. The original Ciba Geigy patent on the medication ran out in the mid 1980s. The company developed and marketed a Sustained-Release Tablet,

Ritalin-SR, in 1984, that essentially maintained Ciba-Geigy's strong market position in the treatment of ADHD children (Whitehouse et al., 1980, 1984, 1988). This meant that at least one psychoactive stimulant medication for ADHD children had marketing support from a major pharmaceutical house, with the resultant advertising and drug representative direct contact with the prescribing physician.

Clinical pharmacology

Ritalin is a cyclized derivative of amphetamine. Like amphetamines, Ritalin bears some structural resemblance to the central nervous system catecholamines, particularly norepinephrine and dopamine. As a psychostimulant, Ritalin improves CNS alertness and, in high doses, increases certain repetitive behaviors (stereotypies) that are associated with high levels of dopamine agonists (Hauger et al., 1990; Weizman et al., 1990). The ability of Ritalin and other psychostimulants to raise dopamine levels in animals has led to the suggestion that the ADHD condition may be due to a relative insufficiency in dopamine. Based on this principal, Shaywitz et al. 1978,1976) attempted to develop an animal model of ADHD. Destruction of dopamine neurons in young rats by intercisternal administration of the dopamine neuron neurotoxin 6-OH dopamine produced hypermotility; d-amphetamine reduced this excess motor behavior. Current research with both animal and human populations has dismissed the single neurotransmitter etiology of ADHD (Zametkin and Rapoport, 1987).

Methylphenidate (MPH) is rapidly absorbed but enters the plasma in concentrations of the parent compound as low as 7 to 10 ng/ml—similar to the range for pituitary hormones (Gualtieri et al., 1982, 1984). These minute amounts are highly effective, because methylphenidate's low plasma binding (15%) makes it highly available to cross the blood-brain barrier (Perel and Dayton, 1976). The drug's main site of action is the central nervous system. The D-enantiometer appears to be more active than the L-enantiomer (Srinivas et al., 1987). The parent compound is reduced by esterases to ritalinic acid in the gastrointestinal tract, than is oxidized (to p-hydroxy methylphenidate) and conjugated in the liver.

Controlled treatment studies consistently have shown methylphenidate effective for the treatment of ADHD children (Abikoff and Gittelman, 1985; Gittelman-Klein, 1980; Pelham et al., 1985). Double-blind ratings by parents, teachers, and professionals report over three-fourths of the children improve while treated with methylphenidate for at least four weeks. Even so, the reports of various observers do not often correlate highly with each other, perhaps because MPH given in the morning may show improvement from the teacher, but not from the parent, who sees the child after the drug has worn off. Approximately 75% of MPH-treated children are moderate to marked responders, showing a reduction in motor activity, an increase in time remaining seated, and much longer time on-task. These changes can be seen as early as 30 minutes after the child's very first dose of methylphenidate. The placebo response rate, on the other hand, is a meager 18% (Ullmann and Sleator, 1986). School-age children increasingly are treated with this drug, as shown in recent epidemiological surveys (Schmidt, 1988).

Response to methylphenidate is not age specific. Adolescents respond just as well as school-age children do (Varley, 1983). Favorable reports have been given for methylphenidate treatment of adults with attentional problems (Wolkenberg, 1987).

It is best to initiate drug treatment with the lowest possible dose of methylphenidate, such as 5 mg once in the morning. Then advance to 5 mg twice a day (one pill each at 8:00 A.M. and at noon). Further increases are accomplished by raising the dose 5 mg per dose every three days. The final recommended maintenance doses may vary, from a total daily dose of 10 mg to 60 mg, and does not seem to be weight dependent (Rapport et al., 1989). If a favorable response occurs, it does so within the first 10 days of treatment. Plasma levels have not proven useful in clinical practice (Gualtieri et al., 1982) due to large interindividual variation, although other investigators have found that MPH levels correlate with some experimental measures (Sebrechts et al., 1986).

Currently, methylphenidate is dispensed in 5 and 10 mg tablets; a liquid formulation has not been available. However, 20 mg sustained-release (SR) methylphenidate (MPH-SR) tablets, which peak at 4.7 hours and show a disappearance half-life of 8 hours, are now available (The Medical Letter, 1984; Birmaher, 1989; Pelham et al., 1987). This formulation avoids involvement of school personnel in medication administration, a prescribing pattern that is ideal for maintenance. Unfortunately, there is evidence that

MPH-SR may not be as effective as standard methylphenidate, when used over 45-day treatment periods (Fried et al., 1987; PDR, 1990; Pelham et al., 1989). This may be due to pharmacodynamic tolerance.

Methylphenidate's side effects include insomnia, anorexia, minor increases in systolic blood pressure, headaches, and stomach aches. There have been rare reports of hallucinosis, particularly in children with a past history of atypical psychosis. A past history of involuntary muscle movements (tics) or a family history of Tourette's disorder is a contraindication to the use of methylphenidate as it may "unmask" or exacerbate Tourette's syndrome (Denckla et al., 1976; El-Defrawi and Greenhill, 1984; Golden, 1974, 1977; Lowe et al., 1982). Growth slow-down can be seen with prolonged use of methylphenidate, although adults formerly treated with the drug do not differ in height from controls (Gittelman-Klein and Mannuzza, 1987). Tolerance to methylphenidate may develop if treatment extends much past one year (Fried et al., 1987; Winsberg et al., 1987). This decrease in response should be treated with a switch to another psychostimulant.

OFFICE PRACTICE

Because other sections of this volume detail standard techniques of Ritalin use, this chapter will focus on its role in child psychiatric practice. Osman's chapter on "Coordinating Care in the Prescription and Use of Methylphenidate with Children" reviews the assessment process and initiation of medication therapy from the point of view of a psychologist and an educational specialist. Fried's chapter on the "Use of Methylphenidate in the Practice of Pediatrics" will touch upon the medical assessment, parents' concerns, drug dose and side effect profile. The section on "Assessment of Hyperactivity in Developmental Evaluation Clinics" shows the special treatment plans called for when administering Ritalin to children with handicapping conditions, including management of drug schedules by impaired parents, families living in the ghetto or with children who are mentally retarded. Abikoff's chapter discusses the "Interaction of Methylphenidate and Multimodal therapy in the Treatment of Attention Deficit-Hyperactive Behavior Disorder." Each of these viewpoints gives the clinician a different perspective, but all list specifics of regular and predictable management using Ritalin.

Where does the child psychiatrist fit in? In essence, the child psychiatrist combines the expertise of a child psychotherapist, family consultant, and pediatric psychopharmacologist. These skills are essential in creating an individual multimodal treatment plan for the ADHD child, including the clinical and diagnostic situations that threaten to derail standard Ritalin management. As a consultant to other clinicians, the child psychiatrist will be referred the most "difficult" cases, involving children who are nonresponders to standard Ritalin titration schedules; those with mixed or "comorbid" diagnoses, or those with a past history of motor tics. Child psychiatrists must also deal with ADHD children who openly refuse to take pills. Some cases may "reverse" the usual clinical picture, displaying the most severe signs of ADHD at home while remaining calm at school. Still other children may be referred when they show only a partial medication response, complicated by severe insomnia or midday anorexia that upsets the parent more than the behavior problems.

The time demands on the child psychiatrist from complicated ADHD cases limits the number that can be realistically carried in any one practice. The child psychiatrist may be able to manage only 10 or 15 such cases at one time, quite different from the large numbers of "average" Ritalin responders that can be carried by pediatricians in a busy office practice. Dosage adjustments may require daily phone contact over the first two weeks of management. Teachers need to be called on a monthly basis, the child and family seen weekly, and two or three different changes of medication may be necessary.

Just a few examples will quickly remind many readers of their time-consuming treatment cases. One such ADHD child may present with a brief episode of transitory tics, or minor muscle movements, two years before the consultation. Although free of the tics now, should the patient be given Ritalin and run the risk of "unmasking" Tourette's disorder? Another type of "unmasking" could occur with a psychotic child. Ritalin clearly exacerbates psychotic symptomatology in adult schizophrenics, as shown in the chapter by Dolber and Liebermann. If the presentation is associated with a nascent psychotic condition, will the psychostimulant "unmask" a full psychotic disorder? Hyperverbal children with ADHD who also have thought disorders will require a full, in-depth psychiatric evaluation to avoid the risk of Ritalin therapy inducing psychotic symptoms.

The child psychiatrist will also be referred preschool and adolescents with ADHD. Should a 14-year-old boy continue taking Ritalin, now that he is pubertal and "should have grown out of ADHD"? What about the boy who presents with anxiety, oppositional behavior, agitation, and an explosive temper at home, but is better controlled at school? He may not meet full criteria for either ADHD or oppositional defiant disorder because of his ability to exert self-control in the classroom, but he meets full criteria at home. Then there is the type of ADHD child with two problems, such as generalized anxiety mixed with ADHD. More and more ADHD children referred to specialists and clinics have multiple axis one psychiatric conditions, and are said to have "comorbid" disorders. The presence of two disorders raises issues of etiology and mechanism: is the disorder that appears first the causal antecedent of the second? Should the treatment be directed at the "primary" condition, referring to the disorder that appeared earliest chronologically, or to the one that is currently causing the most impairment in functioning?

This chapter will trace the progress of a patient through the psychiatric referral process. The protocol presented here is a minimal standard for excellence in the child psychiatric consultation process. If done correctly, the child psychiatric consultation will generate a working multimodal treatment plan.

The consultation question

Carefully defining the consultation question is most helpful to the family and patient. To do this, time must be set aside to call the referring physician. This is particularly true if the parents are unable to clearly state why they have been sent.

What are the reasons for referral? If the referring physician is not a psychiatrist, it will be more difficult for him or her to mount a multimodal plan without help from his colleagues. As described elsewhere in this volume in the chapter by Abikoff, this treatment plan involves medication management, pill counts, and other compliance checks, parental counselling, individual therapy, tutoring for weak academic skills. There may be a need to reassure the patient that his own physician, whether a pediatrician or child neurologist, was correct in prescribing medication for a behavior problem, to allay fears about serious side effects, or to help with a treatment resistant case. If these are the reasons, they can be clarified and restated to the family. A psychologist may need a child psychiatrist to write prescriptions and adjust dosage.

Because a multimodal treatment plan is indicated, it is very important for the child psychiatry consultant to decide immediately if he himself should provide treatment beyond this three-session, limited consultation. This will be determined during the first phone contact with the referring physician. Did the referring physician set up the consultation to work out a transfer? If not, the parents must be informed up front that their appointment will serve only as a consultation. If the psychiatrist sees the case only for three sessions, and the referring physician wants the case transferred, a key part of the consultation will be an effective referral to a colleague who does have treatment time.

In actuality, referrals of ADHD children from one therapist to another are infrequent. Why? Ritalin's record of safety and efficacy has been excellent, and, in most cases, medication management is very simple. For this reason, it is unusual to have the referring physician simply "turn over" the case to the expert for routine care, unless their case loads are too full. Rather, the cases referred all have complexities. Some cases had a previous trial of Ritalin that was inconclusive. Other cases involve preschool children or adolescents with ADHD; age ranges where clinical efficacy has not been as clearly demonstrated in the literature. Complex diagnostic issues, where there is comorbidity of ADHD with generalized anxiety disorder or depression may be sent along. In all these situations, the "expert" is expected to render an opinion and "return" the case.

The most formal, and most professional, manner of handling a consultation referral is to return the patient to the referring physician accompanied by a written report of the proposed treatment plan. Ideally, copies should be sent to the family first, so they can make corrections and rethink the proposed treatment plan before anyone else, even their referring doctor, sees the document. This report should contain a short but accurate restatement of the presenting problem, a brief history, a description of the patient in the form of a mental status, a discussion, a diagnosis, and a recommendation for a treatment plan integrating the use of Ritalin with a behavioral intervention.

Use of Ritalin

Standard indications

Ritalin is most helpful in treating the symptoms of inattention, distractibility, impulsivity, and gross motor hyperactivity found in school-age children with attention deficit hyperactivity disorder (ADHD). This disorder may affect up to 9% of the school-age population (Bird et al., 1988), and produces impairment in academic functioning and peer relationships. Children most often present with classroom difficulties, with complaints of poor compliance with teacher requests, academic underachievement, and poor peer relationships.

The child must be carefully diagnosed, the history of prior psychopharmacological treatments reviewed, and the family and social situation evaluated to determine if Ritalin can be used. Complications can arise if the child is a preschooler (younger than 6 years). Many clinicians still make the diagnosis if the impairment is severe, and obvious signs of distractibility and excessive motor activity are present. Barkley (personal communication) suggests that preschoolers should meet more than the standard 8 out of 14 *DSM-III-R* questions to be considered in ADHD.

The consultation can take place in three visits. The first visit should be devoted to gathering a history from both parents. The presenting problem is carefully reviewed, and the actual list of 14 inquiries in *DSM-III-R* should be read verbatim to the parents. All areas of the patient's current functioning should be screened including the number of friends, existence of peer relationships outside of school, hobbies, sports, relations with siblings, compliance at home, academic progress, and behavior around homework. Then a standard developmental history should be gathered, including information on the presence of ADHD or other psychiatric disorders in first-degree relatives, the history of the pregnancy, delivery, and neonatal period. Some children who later develop ADHD may show signs of the Chess and Thomas "difficult temperament" with high levels of irritability, inability to be soothed, a period of colic during the first 6 months, a reversal of day–night sleep–wake cycle, and difficulty adjusting to transitions. Developmental social, language, and motor milestones should be inquired about, even though most parents do not have an accurate memory of their appearance. It is most important to obtain a medical history, complete with a history of allergies, accidents, surgery, and current medications.

The first step in assessing the child's suitability for psychostimulant medication is making the diagnosis of ADHD. As discussed in the American Psychiatric Association *Diagnostic and Statistical Manual,* Version Three, Revised (American Psychiatric Association, 1987), the clinician arrives at the ADHD diagnosis after collecting the answers to 14 questions (see Table 1) from the parents; if the parent endorses 8 or more of these items, the diagnosis can be made. Additionally, the signs of ADHD must be present for 6 months or more and have started prior to the age of 7. Most clinicians rate impairment, and require that the signs of ADHD cause moderate to severe difficulties in at least two different settings.

Probable indications

Dulcan (Dulcan, 1991) lists probable indications for Ritalin treatment. These include signs of ADHD in preschool children. The greater ratio of liver mass to body mass in this group and resulting higher metabolic rates may explain the greater rate of withdrawal-related adverse treatment-related effects (irritability, "brittle" tearfulness, clinging behavior). Dulcan wisely suggests a more elaborate multimodal plan be applied to preschoolers, including parent training, behavioral modification, and placement in a structured, well-staffed nursery program. Other probable indications include attention deficit disorder, undifferentiated type (known as attention deficit disorder without hyperactivity in *DSM-III*) (American Psychiatric Association, 1980); adolescents and children with mental retardation who exhibit the overactivity, impulsivity, and inattentiveness of ADHD (see Demb, pp. 155–170); and ADDH symptoms in children with fragile X syndrome.

Other more controversial diagnostic conditions may be sent to the child psychiatry consultant to decide the suitability for Ritalin therapy. Overactivity and distractibility by themselves are components of a number of

TABLE 1. DIAGNOSTIC CRITERIA FOR 314.01 ATTENTION-DEFICIT HYPERACTIVITY DISORDER[a]

A. A disturbance of at least six months during which at least eight of the following are present:[b]
  (1) often fidgets with hands of feet or squirms in seat (in adolescents, may be limited to subjective feelings of restlessness)
  (2) has difficulty remaining seated when required to do so
  (3) is easily distracted by extraneous stimuli
  (4) has difficulty awaiting turn in games or group situations
  (5) often blurts out answers to questions before they have been completed
  (6) has difficulty following through on instructions from others (not due to oppositional behavior or failure of comprehension), e.g., fails to finish chores
  (7) has difficulty sustaining attention is tasks or play activities
  (8) often shifts from one uncompleted activity to another
  (9) has difficulty playing quietly
  (10) often talks excessively
  (11) often interrupts or intrudes on others, e.g., butts into other children's games
  (12) often does not seem to listen to what is being said to him or her
  (13) often loses things necessary for tasks or activities at school or at home (e.g., toys, pencils, books, assignments)
  (14) often engages in physically dangerous activities without considering possible consequences (not for the purpose of thrill seeking), e.g., runs into street without looking.
B. Onset Before the age of seven
C. Does not meet the criteria for a pervasive developmental disorder

Criteria for severity of Attention Deficit-Hyperactivity Disorder:
  Mild: Few, if any, symptoms in excess of those required to make the diagnosis *and* only minimal or no impairment in school and social functioning
  Moderate: Symptoms or functional impairment intermediate between "mild" and "severe"
  Severe: Many symptoms in excess of those required to make the diagnosis *and* significant and pervasive impairment in functioning at home and school and with peers

[a] Note: Consider a criterion met only if the behavior is considerably more frequent than that of people of the same mental age.
[b] Note: These items are listed in descending order of discriminating power based on data from a national field trial of the *DSM-III-R* criteria for Disruptive Behavior Disorders.

diagnoses, not just ADHD. Only a careful use of the *DSM-III-R* manual will allow the consultant to decide whether a child's restlessness and distractibility are mere "problems," not the elements of a full-blown ADHD "case." For example, a child with major depressive disorder will often be totally unable to concentrate on schoolwork and may be agitated as well. These signs do not constitute ADHD. Only a careful interview will elicit the signs of depression, namely, the anhedonia and pervasive dysphoria. Although Ritalin has been used to treat adult depression (Chiarello and Cole, 1987), it has not achieved wide use for this indication. Similarly, schizophrenia in childhood may present with severe restlessness, overactivity, distractibility, and inattentiveness. Ritalin therapy could exacerbate the thought disorder, hallucinations, or delusional thinking, and is contraindicated for this reason.

Other disorders have been treated with Ritalin but remain controversial. A number of workers have cautioned against Ritalin treatment of ADHD when the child also has Tourette's disorder (Cohen and Leckman, 1989; Denckla et al., 1976; Lowe et al., 1982). More recent work (Sverd et al., 1989) suggests that Ritalin ameliorates the signs of ADHD without exacerbating the motor tics found in these cases. One could argue that the clinician's top priority is to avoid unmasking Tourette's in a child with chronic motor tics but no evidence of vocal tics. On the other hand, if the child already has Tourette's, the only risk is to temporarily worsen the frequency of the motor symptoms. In any case, the use of Ritalin in these cases remains controversial (Cohen and Leckman, 1989).

Children with early infantile autism (EIA) may demonstrate very high levels of motor drivenness and impulsivity, and may be highly disruptive to both other children and adults. Although psychostimulant effects on motor activity have been shown to be independent of diagnosis (Rapoport et al., 1980), concern that Ritalin might increase the already high rate of perseveration and motor stereotypies in EIA prevented its use in this disorder. Anecdotal reports (Birmaher et al., 1988; Geller et al., 1981) suggest that hyperactive children with EIA do show reductions in motor drivenness without increased stereotypies. One placebo-controlled, intensive study design showed that Ritalin benefitted a 6-year-old autistic male (Strayhorn et al., 1988), without any increase in stereotypy. One author further stated that EIA children with FS IQs less than 48 may worsen during Ritalin therapy (Aman, 1988). Children with schizophrenia, however, should not be treated with Ritalin; such treatment may exacerbate their thought disorder, intensify their hallucinations, depress their activity of daily living skills, and make them more aggressive (Perlmutter, 1989).

Factors in making the decision to treat with Ritalin

Teacher's Reports: Teachers are in an optimal position to observe the nature of and severity of ADHD. The classroom is the most intense cognitive and social demand that is placed upon the ADHD child. Most important will be an actual discussion with the teacher, which allows the child psychiatrist to assess the nature of the child's problem in tackling academic work in a classroom setting. If possible, a visit to the school may provide a direct observation of the ADHD child's inattentiveness, off-task behavior, oversolic-itiveness of the teacher, and the spontaneous fidgeting and noisemaking (Abikoff and Gittelman, 1985).

In lieu of a visit, the use of teacher rating forms can serve to gather information. These forms have been used extensively in research, but also can be used in clinical practice, but should not be used as the only basis for making clinical decisions (Barkley, 1988). In particular, these rating scales cannot be used as diagnostic instruments; they often do not contain items that would directly answer the probes in *DSM-III-R*. They may be useful as symptom inventories, helping the clinician monitor treatment. Many forms have been used in studying and monitoring children with ADHD, including Werry–Weiss–Peters Activity Rating Scale, the Eyeberg Child Behavior Inventory, the Achenbach Child Behavior Check List, and the Louisville Behavior Checklist (Barkley, 1988). Rating scales also exist for teachers, including the Teacher version of the CBCL, the ADD-H Comprehensive Teacher Rating Scale (ACTeRS), the SNAP checklist, and the Conners Teacher Questionnaire (CTQ).

The Conners Teacher Rating Scale (TRS), a 39-item inventory of child behaviors, has been used in countless pediatric studies of Ritalin, because it is sensitive to Ritalin's medication effects (Conners and Barkley, 1985; Goyette et al., 1979). An abbreviated version of this scale, the Conners Abbreviated Rating Scale (ARS), consists of 10 items, and can be used to monitor the child on a weekly basis while the medication is being adjusted. Satin et al. (1985) note, "A mean hyperactivity factor score of 1.5 or above (when the questions are scored on a 0 to 3 scale) has traditionally been used for determining eligibility for pharmacologic studies because this score delineated the highest scoring 2.5% of a sample of "super-normal" boys and girls tested in one of the original studies." Norms for screening have been established for school-age children (Satin et al., 1985; Trites, 1979; Werry and Cohen, 1975), correctly identifying 91% of hyperactives (sensitivity) and 73% of nonhyperactives (specificity). Satin found that the ARS cut score of 1.5 generated fewer false positives than Factor IV of the Conners Teacher Rating Scale. Sensitivity and specificity of the ARS did not change when Satin used only the 5 items (this particular scale Satin named the ARSCOM5) that were common to the ARS and the TRS, and a cut-score of 0.7. The ARSCOM5 is shown in Table 2.

Clinicians can analyze this questionnaire to compare a particular child to those reported in the literature. This may be helpful when combined with the outcome of the *DSM-III-R* interview. The ARS is a scale, so each item or question is answered along a 4-point continuum. Each point can be assigned a multiplier, depending on the scale score. Thus, an answer of "Not at All" is assigned a value of 0; "Just a Little" is assigned a value of 1; "Pretty Much" is assigned a value of 2; and "Very Much" is assigned a 3. One simply adds up these weights for each answer to obtain a summary score. Most reports report an average item score rather than the summary.

The CRS Factor IV (Hyperactivity) consists of 6 CRS questions. If the teacher scored "Very Much" for each of the 6 questions, the summary score for this factor would be 18 ($6 \times 3 = 18$) and an average item score of 3 ($6 \times 3 = 18$; $18/6 = 3.0$). The questions included in Factor IV are: 1 ("Constantly Fidgeting"), 2 ("Hums and makes other odd noises"), 5 ("restless or impulsive"), 6 ("Excitable, impulsive"), 14 ("Disturbs other children"), and 29 ("Teases other children or interferes with their activities"). The clinician simply adds up the values from these 6 questions and divides by 6. Various studies have determined that an average item score of 1.5 or greater is more than 2 standard deviations above the norm (Goyette et al., 1979). Many researchers and clinicians use 1.8 average item score on Factor IV as a "threshold" or "cut score" as an inclusion criterion for ADHD "caseness".

Parents Reports: One scale, and Conners Parent Questionnaire (CPQ), consists of 93 items, and is administered to parents. It can be useful during history gathering for assessing the severity of and variety of a particular patient's symptomatology. Repeated use of this course of treatment becomes impractical due to this rating scale's length.

As mentioned above, the Abbreviated Rating Scale (ARS) includes 10 items that are common to both the CRS (items 1, 3, 5, 6, 7, 8, 13, 14, 16, and 21) and the Conners Parent Questionnaire (Conners and Barkley, 1985). Besides its use as a screening tool, the ARS has been used by Conners and others as a repeated, weekly measure in treatment studies. It has proven to be quite sensitive to treatment effects when used by parents, teachers, and ward personnel. It can be filled out quickly and scored. Dividing the sum by 10 to obtain the average yields a number comparable to the CRS Factor IV. The ARS probably should be used with parents on a weekly basis during dose-adjustment periods, then trimonthly during maintenance. The ARS is shown in Table 3.

The Food and Drug Administration controls the manufacture, distribution, and advertising of Ritalin, as with other controlled medications. The child psychiatrist should be knowledgeable about these guidelines. Ritalin is indicated only for the treatment of narcolepsy and for the treatment of ADHD in childhood. The FDA recommends that children 6 years and older receive the medication in a dose range of between 5 and 60 mg. Relative (not absolute) contraindications for its use include a known sensitivity to Ritalin, excessive anxiety, agitation or "marked tension," personal or family history of Tourette's Disorder, or glaucoma.

TABLE 2. SCREENING FOR ADHD: THE ABBREVIATED RATING SCALES—FULL ABBREVIATED RATING SCALE (ARS)

ARS Hyperactivity Screen Items and Codes

Instructions: For each of the statements below, circle the one number which best describes how often the child showed the behavior during the past week.

	Not at All	Just a Little	Quite Often	Very Much
5. Restless or inactive	0	1	2	3
6. Excitable, impulsive	0	1	2	3
14. Disturbs other children	0	1	2	3
8. Fails to finish things he starts—short attention span	0	1	2	3
1. Constantly fidgeting	0	1	2	3
7. Inattentive, easily distracted	0	1	2	3
3. Demands must be met immediately—easily frustrated	0	1	2	3
13. Cries often and easily	0	1	2	3
16. Mood changes quickly and drastically	0	1	2	3
21. Temper outbursts, explosive and unpredictable behavior	0	1	2	3

Cut Score: Mean score of 1.5 or greater. Item numbers are taken from CRS; items are included in order of discriminating power, so are out of order.

TABLE 3. SCREENING FOR ADHD: THE SATIN ARSCOM5 ABBREVIATED RATING SCALE—SATIN (1985) ABBREVIATED RATING SCALE (ARSCOM5)

ARSCOM5 Hyperactivity Screen Items and Codes

Instructions: For each of the statements below, circle the one number which best describes how often the child showed the behavior during the past week.

	Not at All	Just a Little	Quite Often	Very Much
5. Restless or inactive	0	1	2	3
6. Excitable, impulsive	0	1	2	3
14. Disturbs other children	0	1	2	3
7. Inattentive, easily distracted	0	1	2	3
21. Temper outbursts, explosive and unpredictable behavior	0	1	2	3

Cut Score: Mean score of 0.7 or greater. Item numbers are taken from CRS; items are included in order of discriminating power, so are out of order.

What findings would suggest the clinician not use Ritalin?

Preliminary evaluations before initiating Ritalin therapy involve a good medical history, a history of current medication status, a complete physical with indices of height, weight, blood pressure, and pulse taken. It is also helpful to draw blood for tests of liver function (the main site of Ritalin's metabolism) and a complete blood count, including an absolute neutrophil count. These can all be carried out by the child's pediatrician. The consultant can screen the results of these tests to ward off potential trouble and advise against the use of Ritalin.

Medical Conditions: Other medical conditions provide a frequent reason to be concerned about the use of Ritalin. Children with asthma who are treated with systemic drugs, such as theophylline, may have difficulty with higher doses of Ritalin, feeling agitated, dizzy, or nauseous. It is most helpful to work with the respiratory specialist to have the child's drug regimen switched to topical or inhalation medications for treatment of the asthma condition. Another complicated condition is hypertension in children; Ritalin can dramatically elevate blood pressure in the child already suffering from hypertension.

Rarely, Ritalin can cause a gradual depression of bone marrow function with a resulting drop in neutrophil count. What about seizure disorder? The early anecdotal literature of the 1960s indicated increased seizure activity during treatment with Ritalin. Current practice suggests that Ritalin can be used in conjunction with standard anticonvulsants to help ADHD children who have convulsive disorders without changing the seizure activity. Ritalin and Dilantin (phenytoin) are metabolized by the same P-250 oxidative hepatic enzymes, so the concomitant use of both drugs yields higher plasma levels. The main concern when both medications are used is the appearance of phenytoin toxicity as competitive inhibition of metabolism raises plasma levels of the anticonvulsant.

Parents Say No to Ritalin: Parents living in urban settings may have strong fears about dangers of psychostimulants, and see them as possible "gateway" drugs leading to addiction and recreational drug involvement. Additionally, there actually may be a drug-abusing family member in the household, which may preclude use of the medication. The concern is that the family member may himself take the medication or attempt to sell it on the street.

The Child May Be Too Young for Ritalin: As indicated above, the preschool child may not be the optimal candidate for Ritalin. The medication's short half-life of 3.3 hours (Birmaher, 1989), and the preschooler's higher rate of metabolism will exacerbate the "rebound" withdrawal effects and other adverse treatment emergent symptoms. The clinician should evaluate the entire clinical situation before rushing to medicate; a simple intervention in parent counseling and the use of simple behavioral management techniques may alleviate some of the problem.

The Family May Be Crisis-Oriented, and Not Appropriate for a Long-Term Follow-up Plan: The essence of a multimodal plan described below is the ability to monitor and fine-tune a long-term treatment effort involving regular attendance at appointments, consistent behavioral tracking, medication maintenance, and a willingness to call the physician as soon as trouble erupts. The child psychiatrist will be in a good position to determine this capacity, as his evaluation process involves a number of consecutive visits. Should the family prove unable to attend at least three visits in a row without failing, they probably are poor candidates for a Ritalin medication maintenance program.

The Child May Have Conditions That Make Ritalin Use Inadvisable: A past family history of Tourette's syndrome, or a history of chronic multiple tics should rule out the use of Ritalin. A diagnosis of childhood schizophrenia, or a past history of auditory hallucinations or delusions should also negate the use of psychostimulants, including Ritalin, as a useful behavior-modifying medications.

The Child May Refuse to Take Medications: Many children resist taking medications in school because of a realistic fear they may be ridiculed. Peers associate medications like Ritalin with children who are peculiar, weird, or otherwise socially undesirable. In any case, patients may complain that they cannot swallow pills, or covertly cheek the medications and throw them away. Only prolonged therapeutic contact with the child psychiatrist will allow for this information to emerge.

The treatment plan: a multimodal regimen

Ideally, the child psychiatrist will be ready to recommend multimodal treatment plan following the history-taking, interview and mental status evaluation of the child, and the discussion of a possible plan involving medication. If both parent and child agree to begin a medication trial with Ritalin, then the other elements of the multimodal plan can be brought into play.

At this point, the child psychiatry consultant will have assembled reports from the school and any colleagues whose expertise seems necessary to make an accurate determination of the ADHD child's strength and weaknesses. Psychological assessments, including standard tests of intelligence such as the Wechsler Intelligence Test for Children, Revised (Wechsler, 1974) should be carried out. Additional tests of academic attainment, such as the Peabody Individual Attainment Test (Peabody, 1980) and the Gilmore Reading Test (Gilmore, 1970) may also be given. Hearing tests, as well as speech and language evaluations should also be performed whenever problems in these areas are suspected. The child's academic underachievement may lead to an evaluation by a psychoeducational specialist. This can prove very helpful in planning any needed curriculum changes. The physical examination can be carried out by the child's pediatrician, with special instructions to collect height and weight measures, examine thyroid status (to rule out hyperthyroidism as a possible cause for the impulsivity and overactivity), and a lead level.

The multimodal plan will involve a number of areas. Medication monitoring should involve pill counts on the part of parents. Pill dispensers may improve the family's ability to deliver the medications regularly and to keep track of their usage. An attempt should be made to help the family self-monitor the level of pills remaining. This will avoid the last-minute, rushed call to the physician when the pills run out.

The combination of teacher reports, psychological batteries and the report of the psychoeducational specialist will often provide the impetus for the parents to set up a meeting at the school to plan for the child's education. If the child psychiatrist has decided to act as primary caregiver in this ADHD child's case, he or she can attend this meeting, and establish his or her role as the central planning agent for the child. This meeting, often in the context of the school's Committee on Special Education (CSE), should be interactive. It can establish the relationship between the child psychiatrist and teachers as a collegial sharing of information, and allow the multimodal treatment plan to take shape among the major players (parents, teachers, child psychiatrist). This may result in an application to have the child classified in order to obtain special services, resource room, or even a transfer to a smaller class. Also, teachers will be informed if the child is to receive outside tutoring.

The final element of the multimodal plan involves counseling and therapy, both for the child and for the parents. Bringing together medication and behavioral therapy has been shown to be superior to either therapy alone (Gittelman-Klein, 1980, 1987). The same may be true for individual supportive psychotherapy, but no controlled studies have been carried out. The child himself will enter into regular therapeutic contact with the child psychiatrist. Initially, this can be once a week for a 2-to-3-month period, and then may taper off to once per month. The presence of intense psychological issues (demoralization, severe peer conflict, intense oppositionalism) may make it necessary to prolong this higher rate of regular contact. Additionally, the parents should enter into parental counseling, where principles of behavior management can be explained and put into practice. This may take the form of a short-term intensive course on parenting skills (DuPaul and Barkley, 1990).

Plan of Action: Management of Dosing: Drug management can be divided into two phases: initial titration and long-term monitoring. These two approaches take into account some individual adjustments, not only accounting for interindividual differences between children but also the tendency for each child to become "adjusted" to the medication during the first two weeks of administration.

The titration phase presented here emerged during an NIMH-sponsored, double-blind crossover dose equivalency and efficacy study of 42 school-age males comparing standard Ritalin with Ritalin-SR (Birmaher et al., 1987). During a prestudy phase, each child was started on 5 mg of Ritalin, and increased in a stepwise fashion with 5 mg increases every 5 days until a total daily dose of 20 mg was achieved. This level was continued throughout the next 6 weeks. Comparing side effect data, there was no significant difference between placebo and active Ritalin except for a few side effects (anorexia, weight loss, insomnia). This approach has been continued in our Columbia–Presbyterian Medical Center Disruptive Behavior Disorders Outpatient Clinic. We have had fewer than 5% of children report side effects.

Ritalin is available from Ciba-Geigy Corporation in a number of formulations: 5 mg round yellow unscored tablets; 10 mg round green scored tablets; and 20 mg pale yellow scored tablets (1991). Ciba Geigy has a long-acting, sustained release nonscored white tablet formulation.

The medication trial starts with a baseline assessment. After collecting standard Conners Parent Questionnaires and a single Conners Teacher Questionnaire (39-item), the child is started on 5 mg of standard Ritalin at 8 A.M. Three days later, a second dose is added at noon, after the teacher has been contacted, and appropriate notes written to the school nurse. Three days later, the third 5 mg pill is added to the 8 A.M. dose (for a total of 15 mg). The final step involves the addition of the fourth 5 mg pill at noon, to reach a 20 mg total. Then the first of the regular assessments can be taken.

Parents should initiate the medication trial on a weekend, so the onset of action and the duration of action can be observed all day by the parent. Then, as dosing increments occur, the timing of that crucial early morning dose can be worked optimally to cover the toughest times (getting dressed, getting on the bus, or getting down to work at school). It is probably wise to give the first, and any additional doses, immediately after a meal, to minimize the medication's anorectic action.

Ritalin's wear-off at day's end may produce untoward and unexpected effects. As a rapidly metabolized medication, Ritalin displays a half-life of 3 hours, and lead to a withdrawal-intensified worsening of symptoms. This is sometimes referred to as "Ritalin rebound." It can occur either on arising in the morning or during the late afternoon, and is characterized by an increase in irritability or hyperactivity. In some instances, the child can be terribly grouchy in the morning, go to school where he is well behaved, and return home in "rebound," terrorizing his household. In this instance, the teacher will report improvement while the parent sees only mayhem. This can be managed by giving an additional small dose on arising or when the child first comes home. Ritalin SR may avoid rebound because of its prolonged action.

Tolerance to psychostimulants has been suspected to be a common phenomenon. This may happen, although two carefully controlled trials found no evidence of this effect (Kupietz et al., 1980; Safer and Allen, 1989; Winsberg et al., 1987). If tolerance does develop, the child repeats a pattern of initial responsivity to the medication, followed within 2 to 6 weeks by a return of ADHD signs and symptoms. Each new increase in dose works, then later fails. The problem may suddenly appear after a long stable period of drug response. In most case, tolerance can be handled by switching to another psychostimulant.

The Chart: An Essential Part of Practice: Record keeping is critical during this initial dose adjustment phase, as it is during long-term maintenance. Not only does it help to track and record each adjustment, but it shows the family a professional level of concern that the particulars of their child's history can be recalled quickly. Nothing is easier in psychiatric practice than to forget each child's medication dose, time of dosing, past ineffective drug trials and the reasons the child's Ritalin was lowered last August. Several methods can be used by the psychiatrist to retain these data. Of all the methods, the physician's memory by itself is not adequate for this task. Although each patient may start along the identical treatment path, individual differences will make each case stand alone. It also should be recalled that the child psychiatrist will be referred the most difficult cases, so that he or she must be able to recall past medication complications, even before his first consultation contact with the patient was made.

Charting methods will differ, according to each child psychiatrist's style. The "chart" must contain a basic information section, including the child's date of birth, parents' names, home address, school name, phone numbers of home, work, and school, and the name, address, and phone number of the child's pharmacy. It also must have the written treatment plan (dated) as well as a clear record of each medication change, number of pills dispensed, and reasons for medication changes in the form of proper notes. Most therapists probably will use the standard written chart and make copious notes.

The standard handwritten chart suffers from illegible notes, occasional misfiling, and inaccessibility when the physician must advise his patient when he is away from his office and files. Some child psychiatrists will be fortunate enough to be able to dictate their notes to an always-available typist. For the majority, it is more likely that the physician will be keeping his own records. In these instances, some child psychiatrists carry a packet of 3" by 5" index cards with a compressed version of the basic information as well as one-line, dated entries for each medication change. These memory aids can be very helpful away from the office, but the small cards become quickly filled up.

Other child psychiatrists utilize the personal computer. Using a standard word processor, each patient can be assigned their own file names. Each file can be updated, with the psychiatrist taking notes during phone contacts. Many physicians find the personal computer intrusive during a regular interview, but some have employed laptop computers during clinical interviews. Systems such as the D-TREE DSM-III diagnostic system (First et al., 1989) are too limited, and the child psychiatry module remains to be developed.

Record tracking and reports can be handled with an off-the-shelf database management software program. This level of tracking becomes crucial for clinic-based medication records involving a schedule II drug such as Ritalin. This medical–legal issue highlights the need to focus on monitoring. In theory, medication therapy, with its rich history of detailed research, should be accessible and highly accountable, more than any other area of child psychiatry practice. Yet medication may be continued at a given dose with no complaints from parent, teacher, child, or clinician, even though the drug has become less and less effective. Expectations are that the medication provides a protective blanket that often minimizes the anxiety when the child's report card is not optimal or there is more hyperactivity in the classroom than the teacher usually allows. An active monitoring program will issue regular but infrequent probes in the form of calls and rating scales, but these sheets require analysis, review, and storage. Patterns from a number of these monitoring episodes make sense if they are kept together and displayed in some readily interpretable manner.

How is this information gathered? Individual clinicians keep "logsheets" of all scheduled appointments, which include the date, the clinician's name, the identify of informant accompanying the child (mother, father, grandparent, foster parent), the appointment behavior (on time, late, cancel, fail), the Global Clinical Impressions Score (Conners and Barkley, 1985), the Child-Global Assessment Score (C-GAS), a measure of impairment (Shaffer et al., 1983), and a side effects measure (DuPaul and Barkley, 1990). The log sheet provides for requests or entry of the date of the next appointment, the medication type, and number of pills dispensed. This information can be entered into a standard, off-the-shelf database management system (DBMS), such as PARADOX (Kahn, 1991), and monthly reports can be generated. These reports list the number of appointments, the numbers of patients using medication by type, and the dose ranges. Occurrences and side effects are also given in the reports.

Individual clinicians develop their own method of data management. The child psychiatrist consultant can recommend a monitoring schedule and may even suggest methods for tracking, DBMS management, and report generation. What matters most is that the information is gathered, interpreted, and stored, so that reports can be written when needed. And, make no mistake, reports on these ADHD children will be required as school officials and future therapists plan for these children as they grow and develop.

Therapeutic Drug Monitoring with Ritalin: The style of managing Ritalin that will be outlined here is reminiscent of a drug protocol. Ritalin does lend itself to highly complex, placebo-controlled, counterbalanced medication study designs, but this level of control is too complex, costly, time consuming, and unwieldy in outpatient office practice. Yet Ritalin's quickly apparent effects and patients' response patterns make it appropriate to a more limited type of monitoring possible in a busy office practice of child psychiatry. Documentation, tracking, and follow-through with Ritalin has been mandated by law in 9 states because it has been classified as a schedule II drug (one that can be addictive or misused for "recreational" purposes) by the U.S. Drug Enforcement Administration (DEA). Nine states (New York, California, Hawaii, Rhode Island, Illinois, Idaho, Washington, Michigan, and Indiana) now require the use of triplicate prescription pads for the dispensing of such drugs, and pharmacies in those states report all writing of Ritalin script to a central state agency.

Even though Ritalin can be started the same way for most patients, each case must be treated individually with regard to the selection of the key symptoms and signs to be tracked, time of dosage, use of short-acting or sustained-release preparations, whether the child receives medication during the weekend, and the contact with the school. The careful elegant work of Gualtieri and his colleagues (Brown et al., 1979) and Mark Rapport (Rapport et al., 1989) has shown that identical doses of Ritalin produce very different plasma levels in different children. Plasma levels may also differ day-to-day in the same child! Furthermore, as shown by Pelham elsewhere in this book, each child has a number of domains of medication response: motor activity, ability to attend to tasks, social interactions with peers, individual academic tasks, and compliance with adults' demands. Each ADHD child has a highly individual pattern of responses, showing significant improvements in some areas while hardly changing in others. Just asking the global question, "Is he better?" is not the optimal inquiry. Good tracking involves regularly tapping a number of areas, and this is aided by the use of structured rating forms.

This more elaborate tracking can be implemented without a drastic increase in time required, but it must be present from the very beginning of the consultation. A treatment plan including Ritalin has to be presented to the child and the family, their questions answered, treatment effects and treatment emergent symptoms (or side effects) described, and the guidelines for duration of treatment, type of dosage adjustment, and details of monitoring presented. Monitoring involves the scheduling of appointments for routine follow up, the types of measures used to track the maintenance of behavioral improvement, and regular evaluations for the presence of side effects.

Importance of Parents for Compliance: Parents carry out the medication plan. Once the physician completes and signs the triplicate prescription form, the parents must be down to work. They purchase the medication, and may have to go to more than one pharmacy if Ritalin is not readily available (some pharmacists may keep only a small supply on stock). They, more than the school-age child, have to show self-discipline in remembering to give the pills regularly, twice a day. ADHD children can make this job much harder. Oppositional behavior can be the response to most parental requests, and taking medicine is treated no differently. As a result, the parents may have to insist that the medication be taken, and afterward, ask their child to open his or her mouth to make certain the pill went down the esophagus. Younger patients who complain about swallowing pills can be "trained" to swallow the small, yellow 5 mg Ritalin tablets whole. These various tasks make the parent's daily routine more complicated, and regular supportive phone calls can do much to help the Ritalin treatment become more routine.

Of course, parents beset with worries about Ritalin will have more trouble carrying out the initial dose titration. Parents worry about a variety of matters. They are fearful that the child will become dependent on Ritalin, either using "psychosocially" to excuse bad behavior ("Oh, I forgot to take my medication, that's why I didn't show up") or chemically addicted. Once their child is on the drug, they worry that it can't be stopped and it will be a lifetime prescription. Many parents have heard about growth delays associated with long-term psychostimulant use, and this raises concerns as soon as appetite falls off as an inevitable part of starting treatment with psychostimulants. Other worries include the trade-off involving a loss of spontaneity for a compliant child. This is a reflection of the popular press concept that medication treatment prevents a child from developing an independent sense of moral responsibility and social judgement (Schrag, 1975).

Direct answers, not vague generalizations are most helpful to parents. It is wise to be confident, stating that the ratio of benefit (75% of treated ADHD children improve) to risk (10% show side effects to Ritalin) is good for methylphenidate (DuPaul and Barkley, 1990). Still, pediatric psychopharmacology remains an empirical exercise not an exacting science, and there remains a measure of uncertainty concerning an individual child's response to medication. The prescription of a long-term treatment plan may reduce parental anxiety to some extent.

Children's Worries About Medications: A wide variety of issues can effect child compliance. Some of the younger children have difficulty swallowing pills. They have always taken liquid antibiotics, so the Ritalin tablet may meet with some resistance. Generally, parents can be given a "pep" talk to be patient and encouraging with the child, give the pill with ice cream to "practice" swallowing a pill. Other children's concerns involve the peer ridicule mentioned above. Discarding the noontime dose during the initial titration phase and switching quickly to the Ritalin Sustained-Release pill offers an alternative for the child concerned with peer disfavor.

Despite a concern that ADHD children develop negative attributions about their medicine ("I'm basically no good, only the pill makes me behave") this has not been shown by research. Pelham (see Pelham and Milich, pp. 203–221) has shown that Ritalin-treated children readily take the credit for any accomplishments during the time the medication is active. This attitude can be implemented from the beginning with a straightforward comment that the child, not the pill, is the one who gets the "good grade."

The routine monitoring check: planned follow up

The follow-up package to be described here consists of a monitoring battery of checks employed either by the child psychiatrist or by the physician who referred the child for consultation. It consists of a check for drug efficacy, a check for impairment, and a check for side effects. The measure of drug efficacy, as suggested by Barkley (DuPaul and Barkley, 1990) should involve the use of measures across sources using a limited number of rating scales.

The first month of treatment often requires some fine tuning of drug response. This is best done if the psychiatrist and parents identify a handful of target problems directly observable by the parents in the home. Even if the problems are mostly school-based ones, homework time may bring out high levels of noncompliance, interrupted effort, distractibility and switching from task to task by the ADHD child. These behaviors can be monitored. Parents can contract the child psychiatrist for a brief, scheduled phone contact twice per week. During this time, the psychiatrist can inquire about side effects, improvement in target symptoms, and reports from the school.

Therapeutic drug monitoring of many medications involves measures of the plasma levels. Although sensitive and specific gas-chromatographic, mass spectrometry methods have been developed for Ritalin assays (Hungund, 1979), the meaning of these plasma levels in clinical practice is unclear. A number of studies have both inter- and intraindividual variability (Gualtieri et al., 1982), so that the measures are hard to interpret across individuals and even within the same individuals across different days. Significant correlations between teacher ratings and plasma levels of the parent compound (Sebrechts et al., 1986) have been reported. Significant correlations between methylphenidate plasma levels and a decrease in error rate during a test of motor steadiness has been observed (Greenhill, 1983). Yet these measures are not widely available in clinical practice. Saliva level monitoring can be carried out in practice, but the concentration of Ritalin in saliva is dependent of the saliva flow rate, so its correlation with plasma levels is a suboptimal $r = .49$ (Greenhill et al., 1987). Therefore, the saliva monitoring only informs the clinician that Ritalin has been taken that day, but cannot give reliable indications of plasma or brain concentrations of Ritalin.

Drug Vacations: Drug vacations can serve useful purposes. Off medication, it should be possible to determine the child's current level of ADHD symptoms. If rating scales are filled out just before drug discontinuation, the effects of the current action of Ritalin can be contrasted. A subgroup of hyperkinetic children have been shown to be sensitive to the growth-inhibiting effect of stimulants, particularly D-amphetamine. Children whose weight has fallen during stimulant therapy can recover any height and weight losses that may have occurred. Withdrawal should involve decreasing doses over one week's time to avoid the rebound from a 1-day discontinuation.

On the other hand, these drug-free periods must be carefully planned. A Ritalin-free period at the very end of school could have a major negative impact on the final examination performance of the patient. Although summer vacations involve time away from school, many children are enrolled in summer camp, programs vulnerable to the same types of disruptive ADHD behaviors as school. The child psychiatrist must work closely with the parents to time the off-drug period so it doesn't occur during transition periods and impact negatively on the child's academic school functioning or social life in camp. Children can be withdrawn from psychostimulants at least one time during the year, preferably during the summer.

Before reinstituting medication in the fall semester, it is advisable to wait a 3-week period to ascertain whether or not the child still demonstrates enough behavior problems in the new class to merit continuation

Name _____ Date _____
Person Completing This Form _____

Instructions: Please rate each behavior form 0 (absent) to 9 (serious). Circle only one number beside each item. A zero means that you have not seen the behavior in this child during the past week, and a 9 means that you have noticed it and believe it to be either very serious or to occur very frequently.

Behavior	Absent								Serious	
Insomnia or trouble sleeping	0	1	2	3	4	5	6	7	8	9
Nightmares	0	1	2	3	4	5	6	7	8	9
Stares a lot, daydreams	0	1	2	3	4	5	6	7	8	9
Talks less with others	0	1	2	3	4	5	6	7	8	9
Uninterested in others	0	1	2	3	4	5	6	7	8	9
Decreased appetite	0	1	2	3	4	5	6	7	8	9
Irritable	0	1	2	3	4	5	6	7	8	9
Stomachaches	0	1	2	3	4	5	6	7	8	9
Headaches	0	1	2	3	4	5	6	7	8	9
Drowsiness	0	1	2	3	4	5	6	7	8	9
Sad/unhappy	0	1	2	3	4	5	6	7	8	9
Prone to crying	0	1	2	3	4	5	6	7	8	9
Anxious	0	1	2	3	4	5	6	7	8	9
Bites fingernails	0	1	2	3	4	5	6	7	8	9
Euphoric/unusually happy	0	1	2	3	4	5	6	7	8	9
Dizziness	0	1	2	3	4	5	6	7	8	9
Tics or nervous movements	0	1	2	3	4	5	6	7	8	9

FIG. 1. The Stimulant Drug Side Effects Scale, used to monitor side effects associated with the use of stimulant medication. From *Hyperactive Children: A Handbook for Diagnosis and Treatment*, by Russell A. Barkley, 1990, New York: Guilford Press, Copyright 1990 by The Guilford Press. Reprinted by permission of the author.

of drug therapy. Follow up should occur even if the child does not currently meet criteria for medication, since the need for continued support and guidance will go on throughout the school year.

General Rules for Successful Management: A few guidelines are useful in long-term management of ADHD children on medication. The lowest possible doses of Ritalin should be used, rather than the highest tolerated dose. Target behaviors should serve as a focus, with the objective of decreasing them to a manageable level, not total elimination. Calls from parents concerning the sudden, total loss of medication effects can be met with a careful, conservative response. Often a close review of the home and school situation will reveal a change in the social environment, perhaps not important to the adults, but very important to the child. Always introduce a delay and resist the temptation to suddenly alter the dose, unless the observed change is a clear-cut side effect, such as the appearance of facial grimacing or a body rash. Deterioration in behavior may not be a result of tolerance to the medication but may be caused by environmental stress.

Two cases illustrate this point. One 6-year-old child abruptly became more agitated and began looking around the classroom constantly, paying much less attention to the teacher; reviewing the child's set of friends, the parents realized that the boy's best friend in school had been moved to another class. Three days later, with no change in medication, the boy calmed down. A second child, age 7, became more hyperactive, oppositional, and developed insomnia 3 months after stabilizing on a 30 mg total daily dose of Ritalin. The therapist realized that the parents had gone away for the weekend, leaving him with a sitter he hadn't seen in 6 months; the regular live-in sitter had been fired that week. The change in supervisory personnel at home caused a strong reaction on the child's part, with increased hyperactivity. Again, waiting for several days saw a return of "medication action."

Another issue deals with the parents and dose regulation. Parents should always consult with the physician before modifying the medication dose. If the parents adjust the dose as needed, and use the medication as one uses aspirin, they may inadvertently train themselves to administer it when they believe the child is "bad." Negative attributions for the medication can result. In other families, parental control of medication can lead to high doses being administered, for the parents may regard its actions as totally related to dose level, with higher doses bringing "quicker" relief.

CONCLUSIONS

Children with ADHD comprise a heterogeneous group. The core problems of inattention, impulsivity and overactivity are often complicated with comorbid conditions, including anxiety, depression, conduct disorder and Tourette's disorder. The combined disorder impairs functioning in school, home, and with the peer group. An otherwise bright child proves to be nonproductive in school, an outcast from his peer group, and a disturbing presence to adults and other children. Over the years, ADHD's description, taxonomy, and name have changed, with different components attaining prominence as its "core" deficit, such as "hyperactivity" or "attention deficit disorder." The lack of diagnostic certainty on the one hand, with an effective but nondiagnostically-specific medication treatment on the other, has led to controversy (The Medical Letter, 1988). Some groups fear that professionals may be suppressing childhood spontaneity with medication treatments instead of addressing problems in the educational system. Other professionals worry that children who are not put on medication by parents worried about long-term side effects are being denied a specific remedy. Until the etiology of the disorder is uncovered, ADD will always remain a curious, unexplained disorder of childhood that responds, albeit temporarily, to a medication intervention.

REFERENCES

Abikoff, H. & Gittelman, R. (1985). Hyperactive children treated with stimulants. *Arch. Gen. Psychiat* 42:953–961.

Aman, M. (1988). The use of methylphenidate in autism. *J. Am. Acad. Child Adolesc. Psychiatry,* 27(6):821–822.

American Psychiatric Association. (1980). *Diagnostic and Statistical Manual of Mental Disorders,* Third Edition. Washington, D.C.: APA Press.

———— (1987). *Diagnostic and Statistical Manual of Mental Disorders* Washington, DC: American Psychiatric Association.

Barkley, R. (1988). Child behavior rating scales and checklists. In: *Assessment and Diagnosis in Child Psychopathology,* eds. M. Rutter, H. Tuma, & I. Lann. New York: Guilford Press, pp. 113–155.

Barkley, R.A. (1982). *Hyperactive Children: A Handbook for Diagnosis and Treatment.* New York: Guilford Press.

Bird, H.R., Canino, G., Rubio-Stipec, M., Gould, M.S., Ribera, J., Sesman, M., Woodbury, M., Heurtas-Goldman, S., Pagan, A., Sanchez-Lacay, A., & Moscoso, M. (1988). Estimates of the prevalence of childhood maladjustment in a community sample in Puerto Rico. *Arch. Gen. Psychiatry,* 45:1120–1126.

Birmaher, B., Greenhill, L.L., Cooper, T.S., Fried, J., & Maminski, B. (1987). Sustained-release methylphenidate: pharmacokinetic studies in ADDH males. AACAP Scientific Proceedings of the Ann Meet., October, 1987. Washington, D.C., 3:47.

———— Quintana, H., & Greenhill, L.L. (1988). Methylphenidate treatment of hyperactive autistic children. *J. Am. Acad. Child Adolesc. Psychiatry,* 27(2):248–251.

———— Greenhill, L.L., Cooper, M.A., Fried, J., & Maminski, B. (1989). Sustained release methylphenidate: Pharmacokinetic studies in ADDH males. *J. Am. Acad. Child Adolesc. Psychiatry,* 28(5):768–772.

Bradley, C. (1937). The behavior of children receiving benzedrine. *Am. J Psychiatry,* 94:577–585.

Brown, G.L., Ebert, M.H., Goyer, P.F., Jimerson, D.C., Klein, W.J., Bunney, W.E., & Goodwin, F.K. (1982). Aggression, suicide and serotonin: relationships to CSF amine metabolites. *Am. J. Psychiatry,* 139:741–746.

———— Hunt, R.D., Ebert, M.H., Bunney, W.E., Jr., & Kopin, I.J. (1979). Biological Psychiatry Branch, NIMH Bethesda, Maryland: Plasma levels of D-amphetamine in hyperactive children: Serial behavior and motor responses. *Psychopharmacology (Berlin),* 62:133–140.

Chiarello, R.J. & Cole, J.O. (1987). The use of psychostimulants in general psychiatry. A reconsideration. *Arch. Gen. Psychiatry,* 44(3):286–295.

Cohen, D.J. & Leckman, J.F. (1989). Commentary. *J. Am. Acad. Child Adolesc. Psychiatry,* 28(4):580–583.

Conners, C.K. & Barkley, R. (1985). Rating scales and checklists for child psychopharmacology. *Psychopharmacol. Bull.,* 21(4):816–832.

———— Eisenberg, L., & Barcai, A. (1967). Effect of dextroamphetamine on children: Studies on subjects with learning disabilities and school behavior problems. *Arch. Gen. Psychiatry,* 17:478–485; *Arch. Gen. Psychiatry,* 17:478–485.

Cowart, V.S. (1988). The ritalin controversy: What's made this drug's opponents hyperactive? *JAMA* 259(17):S–W.

Denckla, M.B., Bemporad, J.R., & MacKay, M.C. (1976). Tics following methylphenidate administration: A report of 20 cases. *JAMA,* 235(13):1349–1350.

Dulcan, M. (1991). Using psychostimulants to treat behavior disorders of children and adolescents. *J. Child Adolesc. Psychopharmacol.,* 1:7–20.

DuPaul, G.J. & Barkley, R.A. (1990). Medication therapy. In: *Attention Deficit Hyperactivity Disorder: A Handbook for Diagnosis and Treatment,* ed. R.A. Barkley. New York: Guilford Press, pp. 573–612.

Eisenberg, L., Lachman, R., Molling, P., Lockner, A., Mizelle, J., & Conners, C. (1961). A psychopharmacologic experiment in a training school for deliquent boys: methods, problems and findings. *Am. J. Orthopsychiatry,* 33:431–447.

El-Defrawi, M.H. & Greenhill, L. (1984). Substituting stimulants in treating behavior disorders. *Am. J. Psychiatry,* 141(4):610.

First, M., Williams, J., & Spitzer, R. (1989). *D-TREE Automated DSM-III-R Diagnostic Software Program.* Washington, D.C.: American Psychiatric Press, Inc.

Fried, J., Greenhill, L.L., Torres, D., Martin, J., & Solomon, M. (1987). Sustained-release methylpheni-date: long-term clinical efficacy in ADDH males. *Am. Acad. Child Adoles. Psychiatry (Sci. Proc. Annual Meeting)*, 3:47.

Gan, J. & Cantwell, D. (1982). Dosage effects of methylphenidate on paired associates learning: positive/negative placebo responders. *J. Am. Acad. Child Adolesc. Psychiatry,* 21:237–242.

Geller, B., Guttmacher, L., & Bleeg, M. (1981). Coexistence of childhood onset pervasive developmental disorder and attention deficit disorder with hyperactivity. *Am. J. Psychiatry,* 138:388–389.

Gilmore, A. (1970). *Gilmore Oral Reading Test.* New York: The Psychological Corporation.

Gittelman-Klein, R. (1980). Diagnosis and drug treatment of childhood disorders: attention deficit disorder with hyperactivity. In: *Diagnosis and Drug Treatment of Psychiatric Disorders: Adults and Children,* eds. D.F. Klein, R. Gittelman-Klein, F. Quitkin, & A. Rifkin. Baltimore: Williams and Wilkins.

—— (1987). Pharmacotherapy of childhood hyperactivity: an update. In: *Psychopharmacology: The Third Generation of Progress,* ed. H.Y. Meltzer. New York: Raven Press.

—— & Mannuzza, S. (1987). Hyperactive boys almost grown up, III: methylphenidate effects on ultimate height. *Arch. Gen. Psychiatry,* 45:1131–1134.

—— Landa, B., Mattes, J.A., & Klein, D.F. (1987). Methylphenidate and growth in hyperactive children. *Arch. Gen. Psychiatry,* 45:1127–1130.

Golden, G.S. (1974). Gilles de la Tourette's syndrome following methylphenidate administration. *Dev. Med. Child Neurol.,* 16:76–78.

—— (1977). The effect of central nervous system stimulants on Tourette's syndrome. *Analysis Neurol.,* 2:69–70.

Goyette, C.H., Conners, C.K., & Ulrich, R.F. (1979). Normative data on revised Conners parent and teacher rating scales. *J. Consult. Clin. Psychol.,* 47:1020–1029.

Greenhill, L.L. (1981). Stimulant-relation growth inhibition in children: A review. In: *Strategic Interventions for Hyperactive Children,* ed. M. Gittelman. Armonk, NY: M.E. Sharpe, Incorporated, pp. 39–63.

—— (1984). Stimulant related growth inhibition in children: A review. In: *The Psychobiology of Childhood.* eds. B. Greenhill, & L. Shopsin. New York: SP Medical & Scientific Books, pp. 135–157.

—— Puig-Antich, J., Chambers, W., Rubinstein, B., Halpern, F., & Sachar, E.J. (1981). Growth hormone, prolactin, and growth responses in hyperkinetic males treated with D-amphetamine. *J. Am. Acad. Child Adolesc Psychiatry,* 20:84–103.

—— Perel, J., Curran, S. & Gardner, R. (1983). Attentional measures and plasma level correlations in methylphenidate treated males (Unpublished).

—— Cooper, T., Solomon, M., Fried, J., and Cornblatt, B. (1987). Methylphenidate salivary levels in children. *Psychopharmacol. Bull.,* 23(1):115–119.

Gualtieri, C.T., Hicks, R.E., Patrick, K., Schroeder, S.R., & Breese, G.R. (1984). *Clinical Correlates of Methylphenidate Blood Levels.* New York: Raven Press.

Gualtieri, C.T., Wargin, W., Kanoy, R., Patrick, K., Shen, C.D., Youngblood, W., Mueller, R.A., & Breese, G.R. (1982). Clinical studies of methylphenidate serum levels in children and adults. *J. Am. Acad. Child Psychiatry,* 21:19–26.

Hauger, R.L., Angel, L.I., Janowsky, A., Berger, P., & Hulihan-Gibin, B. (1990). Brain recognition sites for methylphenidate and amphetamines. In: *Application of Basic Neuroscience to Child Psychiatry,* eds. S. Deutsch, A. Weizman, & R. Weizman, New York: Plenum Medical Book Company, pp. 77–100.

Hechtman, L., Weiss, G., & Perlman, T. (1978). Growth and cardiovascular measures in hyperactive individuals as young adults and in matched normals controls. *Can. Med. Assoc. J.,* 118:1247–1250.

Hungund, B.L., Perel, J.M., Hurwic, M.J., Sverd, J. & Winsberg, B.G. (1979). Pharmacokinetics of methylphenidate in hyperactive children. *Br. J. Clin Pharm.,* 8:571–576.

Kahn, P. (1991). Paradox relational database, version 3.5. Users Guide. Scotts Valley, CA: Borland International.

Kohn, A. (1989). Suffer the restless children. *Atlantic Monthly,* 264:90–100.

Kupietz, S.S., Richardson, E., Gadow, K.D., & Winsberg, B.G. (1980). Effects of methylphenidate on learning a 'beginning reading vocabulary' by normal adults. *Psychopharm. J.,* 69:69–72.

Laufer, M.W., Denhoff, E., & Solomon, G. (1957). Hyperkinetic impulsive disorder in children's behavior problems. *Psychosom. Med.,* 19:38–49.

Lowe, T.L., Cohen, D.J., Detlor, J., Kremenitzer, M.W., & Shaywitz, B.A. (1982). Stimulant medications precipitate Tourette's syndrome. *JAMA,* 26:1729–1731.

Peabody, B. (1980). The Peabody Individual Achievement Test (Grades, Kindergarten to 12th Grade). Circle Pines, MN: American Guidance Service.

Pelham, W.E., Bender, M.E., Cadell, J., Booth, S., & Moorer, S. (1985). The dose-response effects of methylphenidate on classroom academic and social behavior in children with attention deficit disorder. Archives of General Psychiatry, 42:948–952, 1985. *Arch. Gen. Psychiatry,* 42:948–952.

———— Sturges, J., Hoza, J., Schmidt, C., Bijlsma, J. & Moorer, S. (1987). Sustained release and standard methylphenidate effects on cognitive and social behavior in children with attention deficit disorder. *Pediatrics,* 80:491–501, 1987.

———— Greenslade, K.E., Vodde-Hamilton, M., Murphy, D.A., Greenstein, J.J., & Gnagy, E.M. (1989). Relative efficacy of long-acting stimulants on ADHD children: A comparison of standard methylpheni-date, Ritalin SR-20, Dexedrine spansule, and pemoline. *Pediatrics,* 80:491–501.

Perel, J.W. & Dayton, P.G. (1976). Methylphenidate. In: *Psychotherapeutic Drugs,* Part II, eds. E. Usdin & I. Forrest. New York: Marcel Dekker.

Perlmutter, I.R., Greenhill, L.L., Chambers, W., & Kestenbaum, C.J. (1989). Childhood schizophrenia: Theoretical and treatment issues. *J. Am. Acad. Child Adolesc. Psychiatry,* 28(6):956–962.

Physicians' Desk Reference, (1991). Oradell, NJ: Medical Economics Data.

Rapoport, J.L., Buchsbaum, M.S., Weingartner, H., Zahn, P., Ludlow, C., & Mikkelsen, E.J. (1980). Dextroamphetamine: Cognitive and behavioral effects in normal and hyperactive boys and normal men. *Arch. Gen. Psychiatry,* 37:933–943, 1980.

Rapport, M.D., DuPaul, G.J., & Kelly, K.L. (1989). Attention deficit hyperactivity disorder and methylphenidate: the relationship between gross body weight and drug response in children. *Psychophar-macol. Bull.,* 25(2):285–290.

Safer, D.J., & Allen, R.P. (1989). Absence of tolerance to the behavioral effects of methylphenidate and inattentive children. *J. Pediatr.,* 115:1003–1008.

———— ———— (1973). Factors influencing the suppressant effects of two stimulant drugs on the growth of hyperactive children. *Pediatrics,* 51:660–667.

———— and Krager, J.M. (1988). A survey of medication treatment for hyperactive/inattentive students. *JAMA,* 260(15):2256–2258.

———— Allen, R., & Barr, E. (1975). Growth rebound after termination of stimulant drugs. *J. Pediatr.,* 86:113–116.

———— ———— ———— (1972). Depression of growth in hyperactive children on stimulant drugs. *N. Engl. J. Med.,* 287:217–220.

Satin, M., Winsberg, B., Monetti, C., Sverd, J., & Ross, D. (1985). A general population screen for attention deficit disorder with hyperactivity. *J. Am. Acad. Child Adolesc. Psychiatry,* 24:756–764.

Satterfield, J.H., Cantwell, D.P., & Satterfield, B.T. (1979a). Multimodality treatment: A one-year follow-up of 84 hyperactive boys. *Arch. Gen. Psychiatry,* 36(8):965–974.

———— ———— Schell, A., & Blaschke, T. (1979b). Growth of hyperactive children with methylphenidate. *Arch. Gen. Psychiatry,* 36:212–217.

———— Satterfield, B.T., & Cantwell, D.P. (1980). Multimodality treatment: A two-year evaluation of 61 hyperactive boys. *Arch. Gen. Psychiatry,* 37(8):915–919.

Schmidt, W.E. (1988). Sales of drug are soaring for treatment of hyperactivity. *The New York Times* C2, 5/12/88.

Schrag, P., & Divoky, D. (1975). *The Myth of the Hyperactive Child*. New York: Pantheon Books.

Sebrechts, M.M., Shaywitz, S.E., Shaywitz, B.A., Jatlow, P., Anderson, G.M., & Cohen, D.J. (1986). Components of attention, methylphenidate dosage, and blood levels in children with attention deficit disorder. *J. Pediatr.*, 77(2):222–228.

Shaffer, D., Gould, M.S., Brasic, J., Ambrosini, P., Fisher, P., Bird, H., & Aluwahlia, S. (1983). A children's global assessment scale (CGAS). *Arch. Gen. Psychiatry*, 40:1228–1231.

Shaywitz, B.A., Klopper, J.H., & Gordon, J.W. (1978). Methylphenidate in 6-hydroxydopamine treated developing rat pups. *Arch. Neurol.*, 35:463–465.

———— Yager, R.D., & Klopper, J.H. (1976). Selective brain dopamine depletion in developing rats: An experimental model of minimal brain dysfunction. *Science*, 191(4224):305–308.

Solomons, G. (1973). Drug therapy: Initiation and follow-up. *Ann. N.Y. Acad. Sci.*, 205:335–344.

Sprague, R.L. & Sleator, E.K. (1977). Methylphenidate in hyperkinetic children: differences in dose effects on learning and social behavior. *Science*, 198:1274–1276.

Srinivas, N.R., Quinn, D., Hybbard, J.W., & Midha, K.K. (1987). Stereoselective disposition of methylphenidate in children with attention-deficit disorder. *J. Pharmacol. Exp. Ther.*, 241:300–306.

Strayhorn, J.M., Rapp, N., Donina, W., & Strain, P.S. (1988). Randomized trial of methylphenidate for an autistic child. *J. Am. Acad. Child Adolesc. Psychiatry*, 27:244–247.

Sverd, J., Gadow, K.D., & Paolicelli, L.M. (1989). Case study: Methylphenidate treatment of attention-deficit hyperactivity disorder in boys with Tourette's disorder. *J. Am. Acad. Child Adolesc. Psychiatry*, 28(4):574–579.

Swanson, J. & Kinsbourne, M. (1976). Stimulant-related state-dependent learning in hyperactive children. *Science*, 192(4246):1354–1357.

———— Posner, M., Potkin, S., Bonforte, S., Youpa, D., Fiore, C., Cantwell, D., & Crinella, F. (1991a). Activating tasks for the study of visual-spatial attention in ADHD children: A cognitive anatomical approach (Unpublished).

Swanson, J.M. Cantwell, D., Lerner, M., McBurnett, K., & Hanna, G. (1991b). Effects of stimulant medication on learning in children with ADHD (unpublished).

The Medical Letter. (1984). Sustained-release methylphenidate. 26(673):97–98.

The Medical Letter. (1988). Methylphenidate (Ritalin) revisited. 30(675):51.

Trites, R.L. (1979). *Hyperactivity in Children*. Baltimore: University Park Press.

Ullmann, R.K. & Sleator, E.K. (1986). Responders, nonresponders, and placebo responders among others during a treatment evaluation. *Clin. Pediatr.*, 25:594–599.

Varley, C.K. (1983). Effects of methylphenidate in adolescents with attention deficit disorder. *J. Am. Acad. Child Adoles. Psychiatry*, 22:351–354.

Wechsler, J. (1974). *Wechsler Intelligence Scale for Children-Revised, 1974*. New York: The Psychological Corporation.

Weizman, R., Weizman, A., & Deutsch, S. (1990). Biological studies of attention-deficit disorder. In: *Application of Basic Neuroscience to Child Psychiatry*, eds. S. Deutsch, A. Weizman, & R. Weiszman, New York: Plenum Publishers, pp. 231–236.

Werry, J.S. & Cohen, M.N. (1975). Conners' Teacher Rating Scale for use in drug studies with children. *J. Abnorm. Child Psychiatry*, 3:217–229.

Whitehouse, D., Shah, U., & Palmer, F.B. (1980). Comparison of sustained-release and standard methylphenidate in the treatment of minimal brain dysfunction. *J. Clin. Psychiatry*, 41(8):282–285.

Winsberg, B.G., Matinsky, S., Strauss, J., Levine, J.D., & Goldstein, M.G. (1987). Is there dose-dependent tolerance associated with chronic methylphenidate therapy in hyperactive children: oral dose and plasma concentrations. *Psychopharmacol. Bull.*, 23:107–110.

Wolkenberg, F. (1987). Out of a darkness. *The New York Times Magazine* 62–83.

Zametkin, A.J., & Rapoport, J.L. (1987). Neurobiology of attention deficit disorder with hyperactivity: where have we come in 50 years? *J. Am. Acad. Child Adolesc. Psychiatry*, 26:676–686.

Coordinating Care in the Prescription and Use of Methylphenidate with Children

BETTY B. OSMAN

INTRODUCTION

Methylphenidate—or Ritalin—has been used for therapeutic maintenance in children with attention deficit disorders (ADD) for well over 30 years. Despite the controversy that still surrounds its use, evidence for its efficacy has been well documented in the literature as well as in clinical practice (Barkley, 1977, 1981; Gittelman-Klein et al., 1980). Ritalin, today, is frequently the first-line of treatment for children 5 years of age and older with moderate to severe attentional problems, impulsivity, and hyperactivity. In 1987, the American Academy of Pediatrics (AAP) endorsed the use of methylphenidate in the treatment of attention deficit disorders, with the stipulation that evaluation, monitoring, and follow up must be included in the regimen (Divoky, 1989). Although not always common practice today, an integrated interdisciplinary program is critical to the success of the treatment, as few physicians have either the knowledge or the resources to oversee all aspects of pharmacotherapy. Additionally, the needs of youngsters with attention deficits and their families are wide-ranging and generally cannot be provided by a single individual or profession. Psychologists, social workers, school nurses, educators, speech and language therapists, church and recreation leaders, may all be called upon to become involved in the therapy for children for whom methylphenidate is prescribed. Forness and Kavale (1988) claim that as medical practitioners expand their knowledge and use of psychopharmacology, educators and clinicians must have access to more information about the drug, its side effects, and effects on learning and behavior.

This chapter reviews the process of coordinating care for children with attention deficits and discusses the role of each professional—from assessment to termination of treatment. While physicians (pediatricians, psychiatrists, neurologists, and family practitioners) obviously play the most significant role in drug therapy, (Herskowitz, et al., 1982) other professionals can also be key in helping to determine if the child is a candidate for medication as well as assuming responsibility for implementing the referral, assessment, and treatment phases of the therapy.

Since the diagnostic criteria for ADHD are covered elsewhere in this volume (see Greenhill, pp. 97–117; Shaywitz & Shaywitz, pp. 45–67; Wender et al., pp. 25–33) they will not be reviewed here. It must be recognized, however, that the behaviors associated with ADHD may reflect a heterogenous group of etiologies. For some youngsters, the determinants are organic, while for others, the cause may be psychogenic, e.g.; a defense against anxiety or depression (Werry, 1972). Mentally retarded, conduct disordered, and learning disabled children may also appear hyperactive or demonstrate deficits in attention. An interdisciplinary perspective must therefore be maintained (Reeves et al., 1987).

The development of an intersystem collaboration (medical/psychological, educational, family) is not easily achieved. The boundaries and diverse goals of each system frequently are constraints to interactive communication. The medical model typically focuses on cure, while the goal of education is the child's academic achievement and socialization. The family, on the other hand, is likely to be most concerned with issues of acceptance and self-esteem. To effectively collaborate, reciprocal role expectations must be established, and perspectives as well as information, must be shared.

White Plains Hospital Medical Center, Child and Adolescent Service, White Plains, New York

REFERRAL

Although the importance of clinic and school involvement in pharmacotherapy is supported in theory, a disparity exists between what is considered adequate standards for care and service delivery. Although exemplary programs based on a body of research do exist, they are not the norm. It is noteworthy that while nonmedical clinicians and educators are called upon to monitor children on medication, the amount of knowledge and training they receive in pharmacotherapy is likely to be negligible or even nonexistent. Personal experience, such as reading, working with children, and television are the typical sources of their information (Gadow, 1984) (and misinformation). It is not uncommon for skepticism and misconceptions to result, based, at least in part, on sensational reporting in the media (Gadow, 1984). Also, ongoing contacts between educator, physician, clinician, and parents are unfortunately the exception rather than the rule, thereby compromising the efficacy of the treatment. The importance of communication and coordination of care during every phase of treatment cannot be overemphasized in the effort to maximize the therapeutic effects of methylphenidate.

The majority of youngsters with attention deficit hypertension disorder (ADHD) come to the attention of the physician or mental health professional primarily because of multiple difficulties in school and/or at home. Our experience at this hospital has been that the reasons most commonly presented for referral include inappropriate or disruptive behavior, poor academic performance, and unsatisfactory social relationships with family, peers, and authority figures. Although there are accounts of children who are hyperactive at home but not in school ("situational hyperactivity"), most demonstrate the problem across situations.

Parents frequently suspect that something is amiss early in the child's life—even as early as infancy. Some precursors of ADHD observed in the first year of life may be irritability, excessive activity, poor sleeping, eating and regulatory functions, and an aversion to being held or cuddled. By three years of age, more than half of all diagnosed ADHD children begin to manifest behavioral problems, particularly overactivity, short attention span, and noncompliance. If the child attends a day care or preschool program, the staff are likely to complain of inattention, restlessness, and oppositional behavior. Typically, in the case of school-age children, it is teachers who initiate the referral process by alerting parents to the child's lack of achievement and behavior problems in school, with the recommendation to seek further diagnosis and/or medical advice.

At that point parents should, and generally do, turn to their pediatricians for guidance. Some physicians, knowledgeable about ADHD and the use of methylphenidate, feel comfortable in assessing the situation in cooperation with the parents. Others, reluctant to get involved because of personal conviction or lack of experience with the drug, refer the family to their specialist colleagues in the areas of neurology or psychiatry.

ASSESSMENT

The decision to initiate pharmacotherapy rarely is a simple one, but rather the outcome of a complex process of diagnostic assessment and evaluation based on a number of factors; the physician's clinical judgment and his or her understanding of the child, the family, and the school environment. The assessment and evaluation phase is perhaps the most important part of the treatment, and generally follows numerous failed attempts to correct the problem by informal means. Without a comprehensive diagnosis and examination of the child's entire situation, there can be no prescription for therapy. And because of the different problems an ADHD child is likely to experience—academic, behavioral, and social, it is most expedient for a team of professionals to coordinate their efforts, relying on data gathered from informants across a variety of settings.

The first step in the process is a thorough physical examination to affirm that the child is healthy and without problems or family history that would contraindicate drug therapy. A referral for psychiatric evaluation would also be warranted if the youngster's behavior or mood deviates sufficiently from established norms. In addition to the physician, professionals in the mental health field can contribute significantly to the diagnostic team. Social workers and psychologists are likely to have knowledge of the child and the dynamics of the family system, whereas the physician may have encountered only the mother/child dyad.

Since academic and behavioral problems are generally most apparent during the school day, school psychologists and educators have an obvious and critical role in helping to define the nature and extent of a child's problems. They also are likely to be viewed by parents as reliable sources of information and advice where their children are concerned. If speech and language therapists, physical or occupational therapists are or have been involved with the child, they should be contacted to provide any background information, including any records maintained, (with written consent of the parents as mandated by law). Current evaluations should also be obtained if warranted.

Proper assessment of a child's difficulties is time consuming and employs multiple instruments and strategies. Parent, child, and teacher interviews, behavior rating scales, direct observation of parents and teachers, as well as the youngster's interaction with peers; psychometric and psychiatric evaluation, self-reports, and laboratory measures should all be part of the clinical protocol where available.

Psychoeducational assessment by a psychologist or team of professionals can appraise a youngster's attention deficits relative to other problems and its impact on cognitive functioning, academic performance, and social adjustment. Identifying the child's strengths and assets is equally important and can be useful in facilitating the treatment.

The next step in the evaluation process is the parent(s) interview conducted by a physician, psychologist, special educator, or social worker. It is advisable that both parents be present, as each may have a different view of the child and his or her difficulties. (Barkley, 1988) In our experience, fathers tend to see their children as less hyperactive than mothers do. This may reflect the amount of time the respective parent spends with the child or a gender difference in tolerance. Barkley (1981, 1988) also found that ADHD boys (and girls) were more negative and noncompliant with their mothers than with fathers. The mothers in turn were more negative and less responsive than fathers to their children's interactions.

Although criticized for its subjectivity and lack of reliability, the parent interview is necessary for diagnosis and serves several purposes. First, it helps to establish a rapport between the parent and the professional that should result in greater cooperation and compliance with the treatment plan. Second, parents are the primary source of descriptive information about their child's behavior and developmental history. Finally, parents' perceptions and views of the child's problem, even if divergent, will help to focus and direct the assessment.

Some of the points that should be covered in the interview include the following:

1. Age and early development of the child
2. Medical history, including other prescribed medications
3. Onset, duration, and severity of the problem
4. History and success of previous diagnostic and treatment efforts
5. Family or personal history of tics or Tourette's syndrome
6. Evidence of depression or excessive anxiety in the child or family
7. Any indication of a thought disorder or psychotic process
8. The quality of the child's social relationships and interactions with parents, siblings, and playmates
9. Parental receptivity and willingness to comply with recommendations for treatment.

Answers in the affirmative to numbers 4–6 (and possibly 7) would, in all probability, militate against the use of Ritalin. For example, it has been found that tics associated with Tourette's syndrome may be exacerbated by methylphenidate. Should the physician choose to prescribe the drug nonetheless, low dosages and very careful monitoring should be planned. If parents or caretakers are unable to provide the information or family history, outside sources such as social service agencies or day care personnel who know the family, may be able to offer some insight and information.

Direct observation of and an interview with the child are always part of the assessment phase. It is important to ascertain whether the child is aware that a problem exists and, if so, how does he or she perceive it? Does the youngster feel "different," unhappy at home or in school? How does he or she view his or her relations within the family, and with teachers and peers? Frequently ADHD children are unaware of the way others perceive them and the chaos they create in their environment. Rather they tend to see others as the source of their problems; being disliked, treated unfairly, or picked on "for no reason."

The role of the teacher and special educator in the diagnostic process is crucial. They may have been the first to recognize a problem based on classroom behavior, and they should be able to provide specific examples of the child's troublesome behaviors in school (Duane, 1988). This can serve to clarify the problem somewhat for parents and physicians, but is nonetheless, subjective. Because individual differences among children are so great and because adults also differ in their perceptions of what is normal, there may be little consistency among raters. Therefore, several opinions should be sought. Standardized and more quantifiable instruments are in the form of behavior rating scales, completed by parents and teachers. The data suggest that if the teacher has guidelines by which to measure a child's impulsivity, distractibility, and inattention prior to medication, he or she will more accurately assess the efficacy of the treatment as well as the presence of side effects once therapy has begun.

The Child Behavior Check List (CBCL) (Achenbach and Edelbrock, 1978, 1983) is a standardized rating scale used to assess common dimensions of childhood pathology. Research has shown that the CBCL significantly discriminates ADHD from normal and other psychiatric illnesses of childhood (Mash and Johnson, 1983). A self-reporting scale, similar to the CBCL has been developed for children 11–18 years of age. Youngsters who are sensitive to how they are feeling may become even more aware of their developmental changes as they occur.

The most commonly used instruments are the Conner's Parent (CPRS) and Teacher Rating Scales (CTRS). Although several versions exist, the CPRS and CTRS-Revised probably provide the best normative data. A number of items on each of the scales are pertinent to the diagnosis of ADHD with norms available for children 3 to 17 years of age. Used in combination, these scales yield information about the child's behavior from the perspective of adults who see the child in a variety of settings (Conners, 1986, 1990).

Some of the items pertaining to classroom behavior (on the CTRS) are:

- Constantly fidgeting
- Hums and makes other odd noises
- Restless or overactive
- Inattentive, easily distracted
- Fails to finish things that are started

Parents are asked to respond to items such as:

- Picks at things (nails, fingers, hair, or clothing).
- Excitable, impulsive
- Restless
- Fails to finish things
- Distractibility

Several other scales are available which can be used for quantitative as well as qualitative measurement. Shaywitz, Shaywitz, et al. (1984, 1986) employ a series of integrated scales (Yale Neuropsychoeducational Assessment Scales, YNPEAS) for systematically recording historical events and clinical observations of a child and family. These parent/physician/school-related instruments provide a framework for establishing a diagnosis and defining an appropriate treatment.

In addition to the physical and neurological examinations encompassed by the YNPEAS, the Yale Children's Inventory (YCI) is central to the diagnosis. This instrument usually is completed by the parents. The YCI transforms clinical data on the child's developmental, social, and educational history and current status into operational statements compatible with *DSM III-R* criteria (Shaywitz et al., 1988). This makes it particularly useful for the pediatrician in making the diagnosis and determining the appropriate course of treatment. The Multigrade Inventory for Teachers (MIT) can yield information about the child's behavior; attention, activity level, academic and language skills, and overall performance in class. After pharmacotherapy is initiated, progress can also be monitored regularly with the aid of these scales used on a regular basis.

Despite the obvious advantages of quantifiable data, no single scale can provide information sufficient to formulate a diagnosis. However, many professionals tend to rely on clinical impression alone, disregarding the variety of standardized assessment tools that are available.

In the past several years, researchers have been exploring whether various laboratory instruments can discriminate ADD-H youngsters from children without hyperactivity. Gordon (1983) developed a computerized device known as the Gordon Diagnostic System (GDS) for assessing children's vigilance and impulse control. Gordon claims the GDS does discriminate between children in the two groups and is sensitive to the efficacy of pharmacologic therapy with ADHD children.

TREATMENT PLAN

Upon completion of the assessment, the findings, diagnosis, and proposed treatment plan must be presented to the parents (if appropriate with the child present). In the process of interpreting the diagnosis, the child's strengths as well as his or her deficits, should be considered. It is also important for parents to understand the etiology of attention deficit disorders and the fact that their child's behaviors are not the result of parental mismanagement, but rather stem from primary difficulties in neurophysiologic control. One theory suggests the influence of abnormal functioning of neurotransmitters in the attention-regulating portion of the brain. Studies have also shown a strong genetic link in the ADHD syndrome.

The child and adolescent also need an explanation of the nature of the disorder and the recommended treatment plan. If medication is proposed, he or she needs to understand why Ritalin is being prescribed and what it can be expected to accomplish. At the same time, the young person must know that the medication will neither solve all his problems, nor take the control of his body and mind out of his hands. Rather the therapy should be an "enhancer" enabling the youngster to be more in charge of his or her actions. Usually a child or adolescent with an attention deficit will acknowledge that there are behaviors he or she would like to change. With Ritalin these youngsters can be helped to assume, rather than relinquish, responsibility for their actions.

For most parents, the idea of putting their child on medication is disturbing and even frightening. It is hard for laypersons to imagine that a drug can alter problem behaviors without being dangerous to a child's health over time. Although there may be transient side effects such as loss of appetite and insomnia, there is no scientific evidence that children treated with appropriate doses suffer any long term effects. Parents may *also* have other concerns that they are reluctant to acknowledge. They need to be reassured that stimulant medication does not sedate children or turn them into "zombies." Nor does it appear to lead to addiction or other health-related problems in adulthood. Parents need to know as well that they can call their physician or other members of the professional team with their questions and concerns (McInerny, 1984). Above all, they must have confidence in the physician and feel comfortable with the way their child's treatment will be monitored. In the early weeks of the medication regimen, frequent contacts with the family should be standard practice. Once an effective and stable dosage has been established, monitoring and follow up can be tapered, except for regularly scheduled check-ups.

For a physician to prescribe Ritalin or any drug and not provide for follow-up is a disservice to parents and children, which borders on malpractice. Yet, an early study (Solomons, 1973) found only slightly more than half the children receiving stimulants were being "adequately" monitored. Two telephone contacts between the family and physician in a six-month period or three times in one year were the criteria. Furthermore, many families in that study and subsequent ones were found to adjust their children's dosage themselves without consulting the physician. We have seen this tendency, as well, in the families who come to the hospital clinic. In Gadow's studies of children in early childhood special education programs (1982), a quarter of the parents felt that the physician did not devote enough time to "discussion of the medication, the child's condition, the therapeutic process, and treatment alternatives." In that study, contacts between parents and teachers were relatively common (63%), while communication between teachers and physicians were reported to be infrequent—only 16%. In the study of trainable mentally retarded children (Gadow,

1986), the percentage was only 9%. Although research with special populations is limited, individuals with mild mental retardation have been found to respond to stimulant medication in much the same way as their nonretarded peers (Birmacher et al., 1988; Gadow, 1985; Varley and Trupin, 1982). For example, Chandler et al. (1988, cited in Demb, pp. 155–170) claim that among the MR population, those who respond well to stimulants are likely to be young and only mildly retarded and to have clear evidence of hyperactivity or attentional problems. More research is needed, though, to support these findings (Briggs et al., 1984).

Despite its widespread use and strict guidelines for administration, Ritalin is still being improperly prescribed and even less appropriately monitored in some instances. In response to irregular practices and medical concerns for children on medication, nine states to date have passed legislation to regulate and restrict the prescribing of Ritalin. As a schedule II drug, only a one-month supply can be given and the prescription must be renewed in writing. While this is cumbersome and time consuming for the physician, it does protect the child and make contacts between physician and parent more likely in the course of therapy.

MONITORING

Once drug therapy is implemented, a coordinated effort to monitor the effects of the drug is crucial, yet this is probably the weakest link in the procedures followed in medicating children. Typically, the initial dosage prescribed is minimum (5 mg given before school), and is gradually increased until the therapeutic level is reached. Close monitoring of the child's behavior by parents and school personnel, including observational measures and parent/teacher ratings, will signal when a child is benefiting from the treatment or appears to be responding adversely. If not titrated correctly, medication can affect behavior to the point of impeding learning (Gadow, 1986; Sleater and Sprague, 1976; Werry, 1988). Sprague and Sleator (1977) found performance on memory tasks to be reduced with higher levels of medications. However, dosage effects may depend on the specific cognitive task presented and the level of attention required. Even when the treatment is successful, the child may not be aware of "feeling different," and parents may not report dramatic behavioral changes observed in the home. Teachers, however, are likely to claim that the child is more organized and "on task," more compliant to commands, and more responsive and sociable with classmates (McBridge, 1988). For those children who do respond dramatically to the drug, significant improvement may be observed within a few hours to a day or two after starting therapy. It is not uncommon for teachers to report changes in attention and social behavior, even without prior notification that Ritalin has been administered.

Janine, a beautiful 7-year-old girl illustrates this point. She attends a private school for children with learning disabilities, having been diagnosed as "dyslexic" and "dysgraphic" in first grade. Hyperactivity or ADHD was never part of the diagnosis, though, as she is a fairly compliant and self-controlled child. As Shaywitz et al. (1984) have found, though, attentional problems, even more than hyperactivity per se, are associated with difficulties in school. Children who cannot concentrate and who tend to "tune out" or daydream in class are likely to have significant academic problems. However, relatively little research has explored the use of Ritalin for children with learning problems who are not hyperactive.

In Janine's case, her teacher complained early in the school year that Janine could not attend to lessons and frequently put her head on the desk, claiming the work was "too hard" and she was "tired." The school recommended a trial of Ritalin. One-on-one, in my office, Janine's difficulties were not obvious, and she did not appear to be a candidate for medication. Her physician and I urged her teacher to use behavioral strategies instead of pharmacologic intervention. Eventually it became clear that Janine was making only minimal progress and was becoming discouraged, unable to keep up with her classmates. After a followup visit and reconsultation with her neurologist, "attention deficit without hyperactivity" was diagnosed, and Ritalin was prescribed. Janine's teacher was made aware of the forthcoming medication trial.

Reports from school after the first day of medication were enthusiastic. Janine stayed alert during the entire reading lesson, she wrote almost a page rather than the usual one sentence, and her handwriting improved. Thereafter, her progress was dramatic, and today she feels "smarter," to quote her.

In addition to benefiting the child, Ritalin sometimes has a secondary gain for teachers and parents (Barkley, 1979). The quality of their interactions with the child is likely to improve as a consequence of the youngster's change in behavior. The child is perceived as being more manageable, more sociable, and less disruptive, which in turn results in greater acceptance and approval of the child. At least one study (Schachar et al., 1981) found evidence of increased mother–child contact and decreased maternal criticism of positive responders to methylphenidate treatment. Although not always the case, we have seen dramatic shifts in family systems following a successful trial of medication. On the other hand, approximately 20% to 30% of the youngsters do not respond positively (Shaywitz and Shaywitz, 1984; Sleator and Sprague, 1976), indicating that the drug should be discontinued and other alternatives considered.

Parent–teacher communication is a mainstay of treatment during this period. In addition to input from the teacher, parents need to be conscientious in informing teachers when medication is not taken or if other stresses and unusual events are occurring at home. Illness or death in the family, divorce, and even vacations can be particularly difficult situations for hyperactive or ADHD children, affecting their responses to the medication. Noncompliance, including irregular administration of medication, is a potential problem for effective medical management. In our experience, this is less likely to occur when there is a sincere effort on the part of parents and professionals to work together in the interest of the child.

Scheduling of the drug and the child's response to medication also needs to be monitored collaboratively. Typically, methylphenidate is given twice a day, at home in the morning before school and at noon, administered by the school nurse. (For some children, a third—usually smaller—dose can be given after school or in the late afternoon to sustain the child through the homework situation or to counter a rebound effect.) Rebound effects, however, can be unpredictable, occurring at different times during the day, even upon awakening. Parents should keep a record or chart of their child's responsiveness in order to monitor indications of increased tolerance or adverse reactions to the medication. Some children resent having to take the medication at school, particularly if it interrupts their lunch period or recess. They may also be concerned about ridicule or rejection by their peers. The understanding and flexibility of the school nurse and the parents may be the key to the success of the therapy. If the child resists the daily visit to the nurse, little will be accomplished and another option should be sought. A possible alternative is the sustained release preparation (SR-20). Although it has the advantage of being given once only per day, in the morning before school, it has generally been found to be less effective than the standard preparation.

The nurse should communicate with the child's physician as well as with the parents and the teacher. A youngster's frequent visits to the nurse with complaints of "not feeling well" could signify an adverse reaction to the medication or, just as likely, emotional stress related to school. It should be determined whether the nurse's office is a haven for an unhappy, frustrated student, or if the medication is causing a problem.

After medication has been taken for a period of time, most clinicians advocate short breaks or "drug holidays" as an important aspect of monitoring the therapy. Among other things, these breaks provide an opportunity for caretakers to assess whether or not the current dosage is still effective and, even more important, to decide whether drug therapy is still needed (Safer & Krager, 1984). Drug-free periods are generally tried during school vacations or in the summer. If all goes well, it may be suggested that the child go back to school without the aid of medication. Parents and the school must maintain close contact, though, in the event that problems develop that indicate a resumption of Ritalin is warranted. Some children, of course, need to continue the medication all through the year with camp directors or day care personnel taking up the monitoring tasks in the summer.

In any case, ongoing, periodic reassessment is necessary to document change or the lack thereof. At the very least, there should be an annual review to evaluate the progress, the value of continuing the drug, and to set goals for the following year. Because disagreement about the efficacy of treatment is a potential source of conflict between home and school, periodic evaluations are also important to determine the degree of agreement. In a study by Gadow (1985), respondents were asked whether improvement was seen as a result of medication. In 61% of cases, there was complete agreement between parents and teachers regarding the efficacy of medication, in contrast to 19% where there was strong disagreement.

Despite its documented efficacy when used appropriately, Ritalin is not a panacea in the treatment of ADHD. Twenty to thirty percent of those for whom the drug is prescribed glean small benefit from it (Shaywitz and Shaywitz, 1984; Ullman and Sleater, 1986), and for some, the medication is clearly contraindicated. While there is agreement about the beneficial effects of Ritalin for the short term, no long-term gains have been found either academically or socially (Dulcan, 1990). It appears evident then, that medication should not be used in isolation but rather as part of an integrated plan of therapeutic services. A study by Weiss and Hechtman (1986) indicated that with stimulant medication alone, a significant percentage of children with ADHD continue to demonstrate poor school performance, low-self-esteem, and poor relationships with peers. However, behavior and social skills training in conjunction with medication are promising (Pelham and Murphy, 1988). Some young people may also need educational therapy, particularly if learning disabilities are involved. Regardless of the child's level of activity, academic skills need to be developed and remediated. Typically, LD/ADHD youngsters work and perform best in a small group or one-on-one. Alternative treatments need to be considered, therefore, for use in conjunction with medication, or, in some instances, in lieu of pharmacotherapy.

A variety of nonmedical therapies have been used successfully for children with attentional problems (Knight and Bakker, 1980). These include behavior therapy and management, cognitive-behavioral therapy (Hinshaw et al., 1984), and multimodal treatment as well as parent management training, counseling, and family therapy. Other alternative treatments remain controversial and without clear evidence of efficacy or substantial research to support their use. These include the use of coffee (caffeine) (Elkins et al., 1981; Rapoport et al., 1984), megavitamins (Cott, 1972), and special diets (Feingold, 1974; Matters, 1983). Most of the studies comparing pharmacotherapy with contingency management strategies have found medication to be more effective (Gittelman-Klein et al., 1976), although a few have found the treatments to be equivalent (O'Leary & O'Leary, 1980).

A relatively large body of research has been conducted using a combination of medical and behavioral intervention (Christenson, 1975; Gadow, 1985; Gittelman-Klein, 1987; Pelham and Murphy, 1985; Satterfield et al., 1981). Although drug therapy has the best documented record of success in treating ADHD children, most studies suggest that a multifaceted approach results in more improved behavioral, social, emotional, and academic functioning than with medication alone (Abikoff, pp. 147–154; Satterfield et al., 1981; Wender, 1987).

TERMINATION

How and when the decision is made to terminate medication has been less than systematically documented in the literature. Clinical reports suggest that therapeutic improvement may not, in fact, be the primary reason for ending drug therapy (Gadow, 1986). Frequently it is the parents, rather than the physician, who decide to terminate the drug. Lack of effectiveness of the medication, concerns about continuing medication, and rebound or side effects are cited as reasons for ceasing therapy. During adolescence, it may be the youngster who stops the medication, refusing to take it any longer. The typical teenager simply does not want to feel "different" (Sleater et al., 1982) or to acknowledge that he or she has a problem that requires medical intervention. Then, too, as indicated earlier, many adolescents express the fear that subjugation to the pill means losing control over their own lives. They need to know that neither the problems they may be experiencing nor the medication they may be taking should allow the adolescent to disavow responsibility for his or her behavior.

On the positive side, most youngsters eventually "outgrow" the need for drug therapy. Although the duration of treatment varies significantly from person to person, there does come a time when it is no longer necessary. As in prescribing the drug initially, the decision to discontinue the therapy should be made by concensus.

CONCLUSION

Children and adolescents with attention deficit disorders (ADHD) represent a diverse group with a broad range of needs. To appropriately serve them, clinical practice and care must be coordinated as well as individualized. Although the efficacy of methylphenidate has been well researched and reported for this group, it is not a panacea for all youngsters (Divoky, 1989). To determine the most appropriate form or forms of intervention, a multidisciplinary evaluation must be made of the child, the family, and the educational setting.

To implement recommendations for treatment, a plan for monitoring and evaluating the therapy or therapies is critical. With the physician in charge of prescription and titration of medical treatment, referral to—and communication with—other professionals are necessary for appropriate coordination of care. The interactions between family, school staff, and physician are actually not different from those for children with other medical problems. The aim is to provide interventions that are realistic as well as beneficial to the child, the family, and the school.

REFERENCES

Achenbach, T.M. & Edelbrock, C. (1983), *Manual for the Child Behavior Checklist and Revised Child Behavior Profile*. Burlington: University of Vermont, Department of Psychiatry.

————— ————— (1978), The classification of child psychopathology: a review and analysis of empirical efforts. *Psychol. Bull.*, 85:1275–1301.

Barkley, R.A. (1979), Using stimulant drugs in the classroom. *School Psychol. Dig.*, 8:412–425.

————— (1981), *Hyperactive Children: A Handbook for Diagnosis and Treatment*. New York: Guilford Press.

————— (1988), Attention deficit disorder with hyperactivity. In: *Behavioral Assessment of Childhood Disorders*, E.J. Mash & L.G. Terdal (Eds). NY: Guilford Press, 69–104.

————— Cunningham, C.E. (1979), The effects of methylphenidate on the mother-child interactions of hyperactive children. *Arch. Gen. Psychiatry*, 36:201–208.

Birmacher, B., Quintana, H. & Greenhill, L. (1988), Methylphenidate treatment of hyperactive autistic children. *J. Am. Acad. Child Adolesc. Psychiatry*, 27:248–251.

Briggs, R., Garrard, S., Hamad, C. & Wells, F. (1984), A model for evaluating psychoactive medication use with MR persons. In *Transition in Mental Retardation*, eds. J.A. Mulich and B.L. Mallory. Norwood, NJ: Able, Vol. 1.

Brutten, M., Richardson, S. & Mangel, C. (1979), *Something's Wrong With My Child*. New York: Harcourt, Brace, Jovanovich.

Chandler, M., Gualtieri, C.T. & Faho, J.S. (1988), Other psychotropic drugs: stimulants, antidepressants, the anxiolytics, and lithium carbonate. In: *Psychopharmacology of the Developmental Disabilities*, (eds.), M.G. Aman & N.N. Singh. New York: Springer-Verlag, pp. 119–145.

Christenson, D.E. (1975), Effects of combining methylphenidate and a classroom token system in modifying hyperactive behavior. *Am. J. Mental Defic.*, 80:266–276.

Conners, C.K. (1990), *Conner's Rating Scales Manual*. North Tonowanda, NY: Multi-Health Systems, Inc.

Conners, C.K. (1986), *Hyperkinetic Children: A Neuropsychosocial Approach*. Los Angeles: Sage Publications, Inc.

Cott, A. (1972), Megavitamins: the orthomolecular approach to behavior disorders and learning disabilities. *Acad. Ther.*, 7:245–258.

Divoky, D. (1989), Ritalin: education's fix-it drug?. *Phi-Delta Kappan*, April:599–605.

Duane, D.D. (1988), The classroom clinician's role in finding the cause of ADD/LD. *Learn. Disabil. Focus*, 4(1):6–8.

Dulcan, M.K. (1990), Using psychostimulants to treat behavioral disorders of children and adolescents. *J. Child Adolesc. Psychopharmacol.*, 1:7–20.

Elkins, R.N., Rapaport, J.L., Zahn, T.P., Buchsbaum, M.S., Weingartner, H., Kopin, I.J., Langer, D. & Johnson, C. (1981), Acute effects of caffeine in normal prepubetal boys. *Am. J. Psychiatry*, 138:178–83.

Feingold, B.F. (1974), *Why Your Child is Hyperactive*. New York: Random House.

Forness, S.R. & Kavale, K.A. (1988), Psychopharmacologic treatments: a note on classroom effects. *J. of Learn. Disabil.*, 21(3):144–147.

Gadow, K.D. (1986), *Children on Medication*, Vol. I. Boston: College Hill Press.

——— (1985), Relative efficacy of pharmacological, behavioral and combination treatments for enhancing academic performance. *Clin. Psychol. Rev.*, 5:513–533.

——— (1984), Educating teachers about pharmacotherapy. *Educ. Train. Mentally Retarded*, 8:69–23.

——— (1982), School involvement in pharmacotherapy for behavior disorders. *J. Spec. Educ.*, 16:385–399.

Gardner, R.A. (1987), *Hyperactivity, The So-Called Attention Deficit Disorder and the Group of MBD Symptoms*. Cresskill, NJ: Creative Therapeutics.

Gittelman-Klein, R. (1987), Pharmacotherapy of childhood hyperactivity: an update. In: *Psychopharmacology: The Third Generation of Progress*. (Ed) H.Y. Meltzer. New York: Raven Press.

——— Klein, D.F., Abikoff, H., Katz, S., Gloisten, A.C. & Kates, W. (1976), Relative efficacy of methylphenidate and behavior modification in hyperkinetic children: an interim report. *J. of Abnormal Child Psychol.*, 4:361–379

——— Abikoff, H., Pollack, E., Klein, D.F., Katz, S. & Mattes, J. (1980), A controlled trial of behavior modification and methylphenidate in hyperactive children. In: *Hyperactive Children: The Social Ecology of Identification and Treatment*, eds. C. Whalen and B. Henker. New York: Academic Press.

Golden, G.S. (1984), Controversial therapist. *Pediatr. Clin. North Amer.*, 31:459–469.

Gordon, M. (1983), *The Gordon Diagnostic System*. Boulder, CO: Clinical Diagnostic Systems.

Gross, M.D., Tofanelli, R.A., Butzirus, S.M. & Snodgrass, E.W. (1987), The effects of diets rich in and free from additives on the behavior of children with hyperkinetic and learning disorders. *J. Am. Acad. Child & Adolescent Psychiatry*, 26(1):53–55.

Henricks, Lorraine (1989), *Kids Who Do/Kids Who Don't: A Parent's Guide to Teens and Drugs*. New York: The PIA Press.

Herskowitz, J. & Rosman, N.P. (1982), Hyperactivity and attentional disorders. In: *Pediatrics, Neurology and Psychiatry—Common Ground*. New York: Macmillan, pp. 403–435.

Hinshaw, S. Henker, B. & Whalten, C. (1984), Self-control in hyperactive boys in anger-inducing situations: effects of cognitive-behavioral training and methylphenidate. *J. Abnorm. Child Psychol.*, 12:55–78.

Hughes, S. (1990), *Ryan: A Mother's Story of Her Hyperactive/Tourette Syndrome Child*. California: Hope Press.

Knight, R. & Bakker, D. (1980), *Treatment of Hyperactive and Learning Disabled Children*. Baltimore: University Park Press.

Levine, M. (1990), *Keep Ahead in School*. Cambridge, MA: Educators Publishing Service.

Lobato, D.J. (1990), *Brothers, Sisters, And Special Needs*. Baltimore, MD: Paul H. Brooker Publishing Co.

Mash, E.J. & Johnson, C. (1983), Parental perceptions of child behavior problems, parenting self esteem and mothers' reported stress in younger and older hyperactive children. *J. Consult. Clin. Psychol.*, 51:68–99.

Matters, J.A. (1983), The Feingold diet: a current reappraisal. *J. Learn. Disabil.*, 16:319–323.

McBridge, M. (1988), Assessing response in children with ADD. *J. Pediatr.*, 113:137–145.

McInerny, T. (1984), Role of the general pediatrician in coordinating care. *Pediatr. Clin. N. Am.*, 31:199–209.

O'Leary, S.G. & O'Leary, K.D. (1980), Behavioral treatment for hyperactive children. In: R.M. Knights & D.J. Bakker (Eds) *Treatment of Hyperactive and Learning Disordered Children: Current Research*. Baltimore: University Park Press, 323–338.

Osman, B.B. (1980), *Learning Disabilities: A Family Affair*. New York: Warner Books.

——— (1982), *No One to Play With: The Social Side of Learning Disabilities*. Novato, CA: Academic Therapy.

Parker, H.C. (1988), *The ADD Hyperactivity Workbook*. Plantation, FL: Impact Publications, Inc.

Pelham, W.E. & Murphy, H.A. (1985), Behavioral and pharmacological treatment of attention deficit and conduct disorders. In: *Pharmacological and Behavioral Treatment: An Integrative Approach,* ed. M. Herson. New York: Wiley.

Powell, T.H. & Ogle, P.A. (1985), *Brothers and Sisters—A Special Part of Exceptional Families.* Baltimore, MD: Paul H. Brookes.

Rapaport, J.L., Berg, C.J., Ismond, D.R., Zahn, T.P. & Neims, A. (1984), Behavioral effects of caffeine in children. *Arch. Gen. Psychiatry,* 41:1073–1079.

Reeves, J.C., Werry, J. & Elkind, G.S. (1987), Attention deficit, conduct, oppositional, and anxiety disorders in children: II. Clinical characteristics. *J. Am. Acad. Child Adolesc. Psychiatry,* 26:133–143.

Safer, D.J. & Krager, J.M. (1984), Trends in medication treatment of hyperactive school children. In: *Advances in Learning and Behavioral Disabilities.* ed. K.D. Gadow. Greenwich, CT: Jax Press, Vol. 3, pp. 125–149.

Satterfield, J.H., Satterfield, B.T. & Cantwell, D.P. (1981), Three year multimodality treatment study of 100 hyperactive boys. *J. Pediatr.,* 98:659–655.

Schachar, R., Rutter, M. & Smith, A. (1981), The characteristics of situationally and pervasively hyperactive children: implications for syndrome definition. *J. Child Psychol. Psychiatry,* 22:375–392.

Shaywitz, S.E., Shaywitz, B.A., Schnell, C. & Towle, Z.R. (1988), Concurrent and predictive validity of the yale children's inventory: an instrument to assess children with attentional deficits and learning disabilities. *Pediatrics,* 81:562–571.

—— Schnell, C., Shaywitz, B.A. & Towle, Z.R. (1986). Yale children's inventory (YCI): an instrument to assess children with attentional deficits and learning disabilities. I scale development and psychometric properties. *J. Abnorm. Child Psychol.,* 14:347–364.

—— Shaywitz, B.A. (1984), Diagnosis and management of attention deficit disorder: a pediatric perspective. *Pediatr. Clin. N. Am.,* 31:429–457.

Silver, L. (1984), *The Misunderstood Child.* New York: McGraw Hill.

Sleater, E.K. & Sprague, R.L. (1976), Pediatric pharmacotherapy. In: *Principles of Psychopharmacology,* eds. W.G. Clark and J. DelGuidice. New York: Academic Press.

—— Ullman, R.K. & Von Neumann, A. (1982), How do hyperactive children feel about taking stimulants and will they tell the doctor? *Clin. Pediatr.,* 21:474, 479.

Smith, S. (1980), *No Easy Answers: The Learning Disabled Child at Home and at School.* NY: Bantam Books.

Sprague, R. & Sleator, E. (1977), Methlyphenidate in hyperkinetic children: differences in effects on learning and social behavior. *Science,* 198:1274–1276.

Solomons, G. (1973), Drug therapy: initiation and follow-up. *Ann. NY Acad. Sci.,* 205:335–344.

Turecki, S. & Tonner, L. (1985), *The Difficult Child.* New York: Bantam Books.

Ullmann, R. & Sleater, E. (1986), Responders, non-responders and placebo responders among children with ADD. *Clin. Pediatr.,* 25:594–599.

Vail, P. (1987), *Smart Kids with School Problems.* New York: I.P. Dutton.

Varley, C.K. & Trupin, E.W. (1982), Double-blind administration of methylphenidate to mentally retarded children with attention deficit disorders: a preliminary study. *Am. J. Mental Defic.,* 86:560–566.

Weiss, G. & Hechtman, L.T. (1986), *Hyperactive Children Grow Up.* New York: Guilford Press.

Wender, P.H. (1987), *The Hyperactive Child, Adolescent and Adult.* New York: Oxford University Press.

Werry, J. (1972), Organic factors in childhood psychopathology. In: H. Quay & J. Werry (Eds.) *Psychopathological Disorders of Childhood.* New York: Wiley, pp. 83–121.

Use of Ritalin in the Practice of Pediatrics

JANE E. FRIED

Problems of attention are among the most common behavioral issues brought to the pediatrician's office. However, the majority of general pediatricians are reluctant to diagnose and treat attention deficit hyperactivity disorder (ADHD) independent of subspecialty consultation. This reluctance is attributable to a number of factors: lack of training and experience in behavioral disorders and psychopharmacology; concern with litigation and reimbursement; and time constraints. In contrast to child psychiatrists and pediatric neurologists, a busy pediatrician may see as many as four to six patients in an hour; scheduling must be adjusted to accommodate more complex problems. Further, although knowledge of age-appropriate behaviors and developmental milestones is at the heart of a pediatrician's function, and assessment of attentional problems is well within the general pediatrician's scope, it may be impractical to assume a task which requires allotting significant time to not only the child and family, but to school personnel and consultants as well.

However, in the past decade, with the decline in the frequency of acute and infectious diseases, the prevalence of children with chronic diseases in the average pediatric practice has increased (Gortmaker and Sappenfield, 1984). The falling birth rate, the abundance of graduating pediatricians, the development of behavioral pediatrics as a subspecialty, and the increasing use of physician's assistants and nurse practitioners, all have contributed to the changing contour of pediatric practice (McInerny, 1984). The care of children with ADHD, and the management of their stimulant therapy, can provide the pediatrician in practice with challenges and rewards not seen with other more devastating chronic illnesses.

The purpose of this chapter is to outline the assessment and care of children with ADHD, with particular emphasis on pharmacotherapy with methylphenidate, from the perspective of the general pediatrician, within the context of a normal practice setting.

DIFFERENTIAL DIAGNOSIS

The criteria for judging a child's behavior as hyperactive vary widely for different age groups. In toddlers and younger children, the attention span is short, and overactive and intrusive behaviors are, in most cases, due to expectations which are not age- or situation-appropriate. Symptoms of ADHD are most commonly noted when a child begins school or, during his elementary school experience, when he or she is required to become more organized and abstract in his or her thinking. Complaints from teachers and guidance counsellors alert the parent to the problem, often with the recommendation to seek psychological assessment, counselling, or medical help.

The causes of inattention and disruptive or unsocialized behavior in a school-aged child are legion: lack of adequate sleep; emotional disturbances in the home, such as a death or illness in the family; major changes at home, such as a new sibling, moving, divorce, parental job change, or even redecoration of the child's bedroom; dietary indiscretions, like caffeine in soft drinks or tea; abuse, both physical and sexual, and neglect; overstimulation from excessive or inappropriate television programs or movies, especially unmonitored access to home movie channels; unrecognized social or academic problems in the classroom, including conflicts between the child and the teacher over issues of style and personality; learning disabilities; perceptual deficits, particularly unrecognized hearing impairment; mental retardation; seizure

Columbia University College of Physicians and Surgeons and New York State Psychiatric Institute, New York, New York

disorders; ADHD; and other psychiatric illnesses. Additionally, medical conditions such as thyroid disorders, hypoglycemia, lead poisoning, allergies and chronic decongestant use, and even pinworm infestation must be ruled out.

ASSESSMENTS

A careful developmental, medical and family history, and a thorough physical and neurological examination, are essential. This interview, although time-consuming, provides factual information, and allows the pediatrician to observe the child at length. How does he (since the vast majority of children with ADHD are male, we shall use "he" for the sake of simplicity) get and maintain attention, either the parent's or the doctor's? Can he sit still, follow instructions, amuse himself? How does he respond to limit-setting? Is he notably immature, depressed, undisciplined, distractable, or impulsive? Frequently, even the most hyperactive child will be calm and attentive in a one-to-one setting where he is the center of attention; it is when he is asked to sit quietly, while the doctor asks the parent some questions, that his symptoms may become manifest. On the other hand, some children who are not truly hyperactive deal with the anxiety of the doctor's office by becoming undisciplined and intrusive. The diagnostic criteria for ADHD, based on *DSM-III-R* (American Psychiatric Association, 1987), are easily incorporated into the pediatrician's interview, and focus on the three core areas of symptomatology: inattention, impulsivity, and hyperactivity (Fig. 1).

In addition to the history from the parent, and the observation of the child, the pediatrician must get corroborative data from the child's school. Reports from the classroom teacher, as well as guidance counselor, principal, special-subject teacher, and anyone else who spends time with the child in school, are essential. There are many standardized questionnaires to choose from; the Connors Abbreviated Symptom Questionnaire (CASQ) (Guy, 1976) is short, easy to fill out, applicable to parental as well as school staff observations, and has proved sensitive to treatment (Sprague et al., 1974). It is thus a useful tool not only for initial assessment, but for longitudinal followup as well.

If the child is in good general health, and the physical examination is normal, there is no indication for extensive neurological evaluation. "Soft signs" are commonly elicited in children with ADHD and other behavioral and learning disorders (Peters et al., 1975), but are not pathognomonic of any particular neurologic or psychiatric disorder. Rather, they are "risk indicators" of neuropsychiatric or developmental dysfunction (Rubenstein and Shaffer, 1985). The neuromaturational assessment, including tests of rapid alternating movements, graphesthesia (ability to identify or reproduce letters or shapes drawn on the child's palm), stereognosis (ability to identify objects such as a key, a ring, a coin, a paper clip, placed in the child's hand when his eyes are closed), and thumb-finger opposition provide not only specific neurologic data, but also the opportunity to observe the child's approach to problem solving (Shaywitz and Shaywitz, 1984).

There is an increased incidence of minor physical anomalies (MPA) in children with ADHD. These features include hypertelorism, abnormally shaped or placed ears, widened space between the first and second toes, and single palmar creases. These anomalies in children with ADHD are, in the vast majority, so minor as to have been unnoticed by all but trained observers, and are of no cosmetic or clinical significance. However, it has been suggested that there may be a common underlying genetic factor linking MPAs and ADHD, and influencing the transmission of both traits (Deutsch et al., 1990).

Electroencephalographic abnormalities are more common in children with ADHD than in unaffected children, but, like soft signs and minor physical anomalies, they are nonspecific and serve no diagnostic purpose in an otherwise normal child. Computerized tomography has likewise been unrewarding. These, and other laboratory tests, should be performed only when clinically indicated; however, routine chemical and hematologic screening can be useful in reassuring the family and providing baseline data for long-term followup.

Individual psychometric testing to assess intelligence, achievement, and the presence of any learning disabilities, is an integral part of the evaluation of a child with ADHD. An experienced psychologist or learning specialist is an indispensable resource for the general pediatrician, not only in administering and interpreting test batteries, but also in recommending educational placement, remedial intervention, and specific learning strategies.

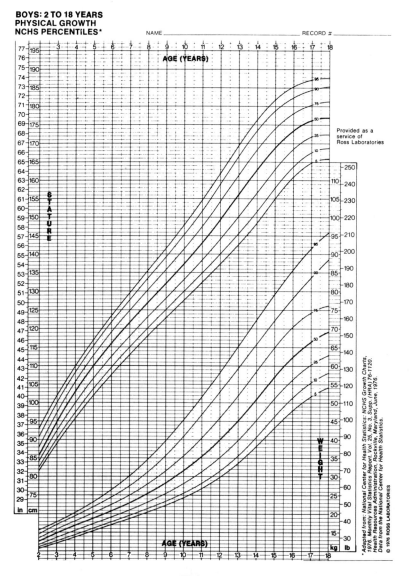

**BOYS: 2 TO 18 YEARS
PHYSICAL GROWTH
NCHS PERCENTILES***

FIG. 1.

Thus, the assessment of a child with the complaints of hyperactivity, impulsivity, and poor academic and social performance is complex, and must include careful investigation of a wide variety of diagnoses. However, with careful history taking and trained observation, the general pediatrician will readily identify most children with ADHD.

PARENTAL CONCERNS

Once the diagnosis of ADHD has been made, the pediatrician, the parent, and the child must make a decision about therapy. The treatment of choice in most cases is a combination of counseling and medication, and the drug of choice is methylphenidate (MPH), or Ritalin. A thorough discussion of treatment options, rates of success, medication side effects, addiction potential, and prognosis is crucial. It is often advisable to give the parents information sheets to read at home, and to defer initiation of pharmacotherapy until they have had time to think about it.

TABLE 1. DIAGNOSTIC INTERVIEW FOR ADHD

*1. Does he find it hard to sit through something he is supposed to do?
*2. Does he often fidget with his hands or feet, or squirm a lot when sitting down?
2a. Is he so hyperactive that he seems to be driven by a motor?
2b. Is he more active than his siblings (or other children) were at his age?
*3. Does he find it difficult to play quietly?
*4. Does he talk much more than you think he should?
*5. Does he often leave something unfinished and start doing something else?
*6. When he is working on a task, does he have difficulty concentrating?
6a. Does he have difficulty concentrating when he is playing?
*7. When you tell him to do something, does he often fail to do it?
7a. Is that because he doesn't understand what you said?
7b. Is that because he doesn't want to do it?
7c. Do you think he just forgets what you said?
*8. When he is concentrating on something, is it easy for a noise or someone moving about or anything else that is distracting to break his concentration?
*9. Does he often interrupt other people when they are talking?
*10. When he is playing games with other kids, does he have trouble waiting his turn?
*11. Does he often do things that might be dangerous without thinking about what might happen, but not for the purpose of thrill-seeking, like running into the street?
11a. On the other hand, do you think he does that because he gets a thrill out of the danger?
*12. Does he often lose pencils, books or assignments?
*13. Does he blurt out answers or answer a question before you have finished asking it?
*14. Does he often not seem to be listening to what is being said to him?

Are eight of the fourteen starred (*) questions positive?
Has he had these problems for at least six months?

An overriding concern for the majority of parents, in our experience, is the issue of drug abuse. Because of this concern, many parents reject pharmacotherapy altogether. There is to date, however, no clear evidence that stimulant therapy in childhood or early adolescence leads to substance abuse in teenagers or young adults (Hechtman, 1985).

Parents frequently express the fear that their child will appear "drugged," or too subdued. Many stress that they like the child just the way he is at home, and want him to do well in school, but without a change in his personality. Some express the concern that the child's creativity may be blunted or stifled by medication. It is important to reassure them that MPH is not a "chemical straight jacket" (Cantwell, 1980), and that most children are not aware of any changes in themselves when taking the medication, other than having less trouble in school. The decision to treat a child with stimulants is not undertaken lightly; but the negative social, academic, and psychological consequences of ADHD generally far outweigh any adverse effects of carefully monitored MPH therapy. Furthermore, in the majority of cases, if the diagnosis is correct, and if the child shows improvement on medication, problems of untoward reactions such as emotional blunting, tearfulness, or overactivity can often be solved by careful adjustment of dosage and timing. Additionally, other medications, such as dextroamphetamine, pemoline, and tricyclic antidepressants provide alternative choices in those cases where MPH is not tolerated.

MULTIMODAL THERAPY

Since children with ADHD are an etiologically and clinically heterogeneous group, it is not surprising that a combination of medication and psychotherapy is more effective than either one alone. A review of the literature (Hechtman, 1985; Weiss and Hechtman, 1986) indicates that with stimulant treatment alone, a significant percentage of children with ADHD continue in adolescence to have symptoms of ADHD, poor peer relationships, and low self-esteem, as well as an increased incidence of antisocial behaviors and deficient academic performance. However, the results of behavior therapy and social skills training in conjunction with stimulant therapy are promising (Pelham et al., 1988, Satterfield et al., 1980a). Additionally, family therapy can be most helpful in reestablishing healthy family function.

Although pediatricians make extensive use of behavior modification techniques and counseling in general practice, they rarely are able to provide these services to the extent they are needed in treating children with ADHD. The development of a treatment plan for each child will simplify the approach to care and follow-up. It is incumbent upon the pediatrician to develop patterns of referral to professionals in the community who can work cooperatively in coordinating care. The pediatrician provides a critical service in coordinating and scheduling office visits, and providing support to the family, as well as serving as the primary physician.

DOSAGE

The recommended dosage range of MPH is 0.3–0.8 mg/kg/dose, administered twice daily, in the morning before school and at midday. Since short-acting MPH comes in 5 mg and 10 mg tablets, the mg/kg recommendation is only a gross guide. Therapy is generally initiated at a very low dose, both to minimize side effects and to reassure parents; it is helpful to begin the course of therapy on the weekend, in order to allow the parent to observe the onset, effect, and duration of action. We begin at 5 mg/day, for two days, then increase to 5 mg bid. In children weighing more than 25 kg, we increase the dose to 15 mg/day for two days (10 mg after breakfast, 5 mg after lunch), and then to 10 mg bid. If indicated, the dose may be increased up to a maximum of 60 mg/day.

It is important to notify the school of the medication plan, since most children will need help in remembering to take their midday dose. Many schools do not have an on-site full-time nurse, and other personnel may be reluctant to take responsibility for medication. With close cooperation and open communication between pediatrician and school, however, a solution can be found; frequently, the classroom teacher or guidance counselor will be willing to remind the child to take his midday dose. The issue of midday dosage must be handled with sensitivity, for many children feel stigmatized by the need to go to the nurse's office every day. The cooperation of the family, the child, and the school personnel must be enlisted in order to ensure compliance.

A return appointment is scheduled for 10–14 days following initiation of medication, in order to assess response and side effects. Any improvement in behavior will have occurred by this time, and since most children do well initially on 10 mg bid, every attempt should be made to achieve this dose before labeling a child a nonresponder. Close followup is essential; parents and child may have to be reassured frequently that the side effects are transient and not of a serious nature.

SIDE EFFECTS

An exhaustive discussion of side effects is presented elsewhere in this volume. Problems such as tics and Tourette's syndrome will rarely be managed primarily by the general pediatrician; if a family history of either is elicited during the evaluation of a child with ADHD, referral to a neurologist or child psychiatrist is appropriate. However, issues relating to problems of eating, sleeping, and growth are common in pediatric practice, and the pediatrician can bring considerable expertise to bear in addressing them.

The most common side effect we see in our clinic is loss of appetite, almost exclusively at lunchtime. Since eating patterns are a very common source of parental, particularly maternal, concern, it is wise to spend extra time reviewing this issue. We advise parents to administer the morning dose of medication after breakfast, and to offer a substantial after-school snack. Further, we encourage administration of any midday dose after lunch, rather than before. Studies have demonstrated no impairment in absorption or behavioral effects of MPH when it is administered with meals rather than before (Chan et al., 1983; Swanson et al., 1983). The problem of anorexia is avoided and compliance is improved if medication is given with or immediately after meals. We counsel school personnel about this side effect, encouraging them to not make an issue of it, and to be sensitive to the potential need, particularly in younger children, for a snack during school time.

Another frequently encountered side effect is insomnia. It can be difficult to assess this symptom, since many children have television sets in their bedrooms and habitually stay up late watching TV. It is important to obtain a baseline assessment of potential side effects before embarking on a course of therapy. Even when a child stays up later than he is accustomed to, he will rarely complain of daytime sleepiness, but may instead be more irritable. The midday dose can then be temporarily decreased. Because of the potential of insomnia, we do not give afternoon doses of MPH initially. However, this side effect is transient, and after two to three weeks on medication, it generally disappears. Afternoon doses then become an option in adjusting day-long coverage. This is particularly common in older children who have more homework, and more structured commitments after regular school hours, such as religious education and competitive sports.

Much less commonly, children may complain of headaches or stomachaches. These symptoms are rarely severe enough to cause a visit to the school nurse or a call to the parent. In our experience, stomachaches have always responded to adjustment of eating and medication times; a well-timed snack can be diagnostic as well as therapeutic. Again, a temporary decrease in dosage may be indicated, to avoid further discomfort and loss of compliance.

An important area of concern for the pediatrician is the effect of stimulants on growth. The effects of chronic MPH administration on height and weight have been estensively studied. The data are conflicting, and the many reported investigations suffer from a variety of methodological flaws (Greenhill, 1984). Recent studies (Gittelman-Klein and Manuzza, 1988; Gittelman-Klein et al., 1988) indicate that, although there is some reduction in growth velocity during treatment, compensatory rebound growth occurs when stimulant therapy is discontinued, resulting in normal predicted height and weight. Drug holidays on weekends and school vacations provide the opportunity for catch-up growth.

Anecdotally, we have reviewed the growth charts of 60 MPH-treated patients followed in our clinic over the past three years, and have noted no decline in either the height or weight percentiles. Most but not all of these children were taking less than 40 mg/day, and most had drug holidays on weekends and school vacations.

Careful long-term followup, with regular assessments of height and weight, is vital; as with most other common growth-related concerns in pediatrics, the use of standardized growth charts is invaluable both for recordkeeping and as a visual aid for parent and child (Fig. 1).

SUSTAINED-RELEASE MPH (MPH-SR)

The brief half-life of standard short-acting MPH makes it necessary to administer the drug twice or three times during an average school day in order to achieve maximal benefit. The need to take a midday dose has plagued some children with ADHD, exposing them to peer ridicule and, on occasion, negative reactions from school personnel. Additionally, problems of rebound hyperactivity, which can occur as the medication wears off, have subjected some children to a roller-coaster effect, which can be exhausting not only for the children, but for parents and teachers as well. A sustained-release preparation of MPH has been developed to avoid the problems of frequent dosing. Reports of its efficacy are conflicting, although its adverse effects have been no different from those of the short-acting preparation (Birmaher et al., 1989; Fried et al., 1987; Pelham et al., 1987; Whitehouse et al., 1980).

For some children, a single 20 mg MPH-SR tablet before school is sufficient. However, in our clinical experience, tolerance frequently develops within several weeks, and initial improvement is followed by deterioration in behavior. It is our practice to initiate therapy with short-acting MPH as outlined in the Dosage section. Once a child has shown sustained improvement for several weeks on 15–20 mg/day, with no significant side effect complaints, the sustained-release medication is substituted. If the improved behavior is not maintained, a second sustained-release tablet may be added in the morning.

An alternative strategy, particularly when problem behaviors occur primarily in the afternoon, is to give the second MPH-SR at midday, if school-time dosing is not a problem. This regimen provides a longer sustained medication effect. Another approach which we have found to be effective is to combine short-acting MPH with the sustained-release form (Fried, 1987). In some cases, 20 mg MPH-SR plus 10 mg short-acting MPH in the morning enables the child to get ready for school and negotiate a school bus ride, while providing medication effect throughout the school day. For some children, MPH-SR, administered either once or twice during the school day, is adequate for school hours, but an additional 5 or 10 mg short-acting tablet after school may be necessary for afternoon or evening coverage. The combination offers rapid onset of action and sustained effect. The addition of short-acting medication during the day, following initial dosing with MPH-SR, may provide something of a "booster rocket" effect, offering prolonged medication action analogous to that of combined insulin therapy in diabetes mellitus.

Each child must be treated individually, with medication dosage and scheduling tailored to his specific needs across the day. In assessing treatment efficacy, information from the classroom teacher is important, both for changes in targeted behaviors, and for the timing of these changes as well. There is a wide margin of safety in juggling the doses we recommend, and since the effectiveness of any particular regimen can be assessed in a matter of days, fine-tuning is not difficult to achieve in the majority of cases.

DRUG INTERACTIONS

Little has been published concerning the interactions of MPH with other drugs. Most of the data concern psychotropic drug interactions (i.e. methylphenidate and imipramine, diazepam, haldol, and lithium) (Fann, 1973; Fjalland and Moller-Nielson, 1974). These problems have little relevance in general pediatric practice.

However, there is some concern for the pediatrician about anticonvulsants and asthma medications in the child with ADHD on MPH. The evidence is convincing that plasma levels of commonly used anticonvulsants are unaffected by concomitant MPH administration (Kupferberg et al., 1972). However, there is to date no published data on MPH–theophylline interaction. Since both drugs have sympathomimetic effects on the cardiovascular system, and since their side effects are similar, it is wise to proceed cautiously, with close clinical surveillance, during periods of dosage adjustment of either medication. Additionally, theophylline can cause irritability and restlessness at therapeutic levels, and the resultant behavior can be confused with ADHD. It would be prudent, then, to monitor plasma levels of both anticonvulsants and brochodilators in those children on multiple drugs.

FOLLOW-UP CARE

Evaluation of the child with ADHD, and initiation of appropriate therapy, are unquestionably time-consuming processes. There is no formula for the timing and frequency of visits, since each family may have different needs for support, information, reassurance, and direction. More frequent visits in the early months of pharmacotherapy will insure fewer problems, and better compliance, later on. In our clinic, we see patients biweekly during medication titration, then monthly. Height, weight, blood pressure, pulse, and side effect assessment are obtained at each visit. Contact with the school is maintained by phone or by mail every two to four months, unless there is a problem requiring more timely communication. The children continue to receive annual health maintenance assessments, with routine blood chemistry and hematology screening. Parents will be reassured by the reports that in children on MPH, there is no evidence of any disturbance in the clinical laboratory values commonly assessed (Satterfield et al., 1980b). Serum levels of MPH are not necessary, since they are currently of no clinical value in assessing response, side effects or tolerance (Gualtieri et al., 1988). However, saliva levels of MPH offer a potentially useful measure of compliance (Greenhill et al., 1987); further investigation of this noninvasive tool is needed.

In most cases, MPH is administered only on school days, with drug vacations on weekends, holidays, and school vacations. However, for many families, medication at home is as necessary as at school. If a child's hyperactive and impulsive behavior is destructive to family function, drug vacations become detrimental. Parents are quite reliable in reporting the need for medication. Each case must be assessed individually.

How long should medication be continued? Unlike the more common physical illnesses in pediatric practice, such as ear infections and pneumonias, there is no clear end-point signaling successful, and therefore completed, treatment. Targeted behaviors, such as ability to stay seated, completion of assignments, and control of physical or verbal outbursts, are monitored in the assessments of therapeutic progress. But school performance and social appropriateness are fluid concepts which change as the child grows and develops. The only means to assess the need for continuing pharmacotherapy is to discontinue medication and observe the child.

A helpful tool is the placebo trial, whereby the teacher can rate a child's classroom behavior while blind to whether the child has medication or not (McBride, 1988). It has also been suggested that a placebo trial may be useful when initiating pharmacotherapy, in order not to subject to long-term treatment that small percentage of children who are placebo responders (Ullmann and Sleator, 1986). It must be noted here that MPH–placebo currently is not available from the manufacturer of Ritalin; special arrangements would have to be made with the Ciba-Geigy Company or with a pharmacist to have placebo tablets manufactured.

Pediatricians treat infants and children, with the upper age limit extending for many patients well into young adulthood. The interests of the pediatrician will determine to a large extent how long a child will be followed before "graduating" to an internist. The role of the pediatrician is to promote the maximal achievement of physical, psychological, social, and academic potential for each child. In caring for children and adolescents with ADHD, initiating and monitoring their pharmacotherapy, coordinating their subspecialty interventions, and ushering them into adulthood, the pediatrician will have fulfilled this role admirably.

REFERENCES

American Psychiatric Association. (1987), *Diagnostic and Statistical Manual of Mental Disorders,* 4th Ed. Washington, DC: American Psychiatric Association.

Birmaher, B., Greenhill, L., Cooper, T., Fried, J. & Maminski, B. (1989), Sustained release methylphenidate: pharmacokinetic studies in ADDH males. *J. Am. Acad. Child Adolesc. Psychiatry,* 5:768–772.

Cantwell, D. (1980), A clinician's guide to the use of stimulant medication for the psychiatric disorders of children. *J. Dev. Behav. Pediatr.,* 1:133–140.

Chan, Y-P., Swanson, J., Soldin, S., Thiessen, J., Macleod, S. & Logan, W. (1983), Methylphenidate hydrochloride given with or before breakfast: Effects on plasma concentration of methylphenidate and ritalinic acid. *Pediatrics,* 72:56–59.

Deutsch, C., Matthysse, S., Swanson, J. & Farkas, L. (1990), Genetic latent structure analysis of dysmorphology in attention deficit disorder. *J. Am. Acad. Child Adolesc. Psychiatry,* 29:189–194.

Fann, W. (1973), Some clinically important interactions of psychotropic drugs. *South Med. J.,* 66:661–665.

Fjalland, B. & Moller-Nielsen I. (1974), Methylphenidate antagonism of haloperidol, interaction with cholinergic and anticholinergic drugs. *Psychopharmacologia,* 34:111–118.

Fried, J., Greenhill, L., Torres, D., Martin, J. & Solomon, M. (1987), Presented at the 34th annual meeting of the American Academy of Child and Adolescent Psychiatry, October 17, Washington, DC.

Gittelman-Klein, R. & Manuzza, S. (1988), Hyperactive boys almost grown up. *Arch. Gen. Psych.,* 45:1131–1134.

———— Landa, B., Mattes, J. & Klein, D. (1988), Methylphenidate and growth in hyperactive children. *Arch. Gen. Psych.,* 45:1127–1130.

Gortmaker, S. & Sappenfield, W. (1984), Chronic childhood disorders: prevalence and impact. *Pediatr. Clin. North Am.,* 31:199–209.

Greenhill, L. (1984), Stimulant-related growth inhibition: a review. In: *The Psychobiology of Childhood,* ed. L. Greenhill & B. Shopsin. New York: SP Medical and Scientific Books, pp. 135–157.

———— Cooper, T., Solomon, M., Fried, J. & Cornblatt, B. (1987), Methylphenidate salivary levels in children. *Psychopharm. Bull.,* 23:115–119.

Gualtieri, C.T., Hicks, R., Evans, R. & Patrick, K. (1988), The clinical importance of methylphenidate blood level determinations. In: *Attention Deficit Disorder,* vol. 3, ed. L. Bloomingdale. Oxford: Pergamon Press, pp. 81–100.

Guy, W. (1976), *ECDEU Assessment Manual for Psychopharmacology,* rev. ed. DHEW Pub. No. (ADM) 76-338. Washington, DC: U.S. Department of Health, Education and Welfare.

Hechtman, L. (1985), Adolescent outcome of hyperactive children treated with stimulants in childhood: a review. *Psychopharm. Bull.,* 21:178–191.

Kupferberg, J., Jeffery, W. & Hunninghake, D. (1972), Effect of methylphenidate on plasma anticonvulsant levels. *Clin. Pharmacol. Ther.,* 13:201–204.

McBride, M. (1988), An individual double-blind crossover trial for assessing methylphenidate response in children with attention deficit disorder. *J. Pediatrics* 113:137–145.

McInerny, T. (1984), Role of the general pediatrician in coordinating care. *Pediatr. Clin. North Am.* 31:199–209.

Pelham, W., Schnedler, R., Bender, M., Nilsson, D., Miller, J., Budrow, M., Ronnei, M., Paluchowski, C. & Marks, D. (1988), The combination of behavior therapy and methylphenidate in the treatment of attention deficit disorders: a therapy outcome study. In: *Attention Deficit Disorder,* vol. 3, ed. L. Bloomingdale. Oxford: Pergamon Press, pp. 29–48.

——— Sturges, J., Hora, J., Schmidt, C., Bjilsma, J., Milich, R. & Moorer, S. (1987), Sustained-release and standard methylphenidate effects on cognitive and social behavior in children with attention deficit disorder. *Pediatrics,* 80:491–501.

Peters, J., Romine, J. & Dykman, R. (1975), A special neurological examination of children with learning disabilities. *Dev. Med. Child Neurol.,* 17:63–78.

Rubenstein, B. & Shaffer, D. (1985), Organicity in child psychiatry. *Psych. Clin. North Am.,* 8:755–777.

Satterfield, J., Satterfield, B. & Cantwell, D. (1980a), Multimodal treatment: a two-year evaluation of 61 hyperactive boys. *Arch. Gen. Psych.,* 37:915–919.

——— Schell, A. & Barb, S. (1980b), Potential risk of prolonged administration of stimulant medication for hyperactive children. *J. Dev. Behav. Pediatr.,* 1:102–107.

Shaywitz, S. & Shaywitz, B. (1984), Diagnosis and management of attention deficit disorder: a pediatric perspective. *Pediatr. Clin. North Am.,* 31:429–457.

Sprague, R., Christensen, D. & Werry, J. (1974), Experimental psychology and stimulant drugs. In: *Clinical Use of Stimulant Drugs in Children,* ed. C. K. Connors. Amsterdam: Excerpta Medica, pp. 141–164.

Swanson, J., Sandman, C., Deutsch, C. & Baren, M. (1983), Methylphenidate hydrochloride given with or before breakfast: I. Behavioral, cognitive, and electrophysiologic effects. *Pediatrics,* 72:49–55.

Ullmann, R. & Sleator, E. (1986), Responders, non-responders, and placebo responders among children with attention deficit disorder. *Clin. Pediatr.,* 25:594–599.

Weiss, G. & Hechtman, L. (1986), *Hyperactive Children Grown Up.* New York: Guilford Press.

Whitehouse, D, Shah, U. & Palmer, F. (1980), Comparison of sustained-release and standard methylphenidate in the treatment of minimal brain damage. *J. Clin. Psych.,* 41:282–285.

Assessment of Hyperactivity in Developmental Evaluation Clinics

SUSAN WALTON GREENHILL

INTRODUCTION

The following is a description of some of the children seen in a multidisciplinary developmental evaluation clinic who present with conditions related to or concurrent with attention deficit hyperactive disorder (ADHD). These observations come from the experience and perspective of a pediatric nurse practitioner working at the Children's Evaluation and Rehabilitation Center (CERC), a program affiliated with the Albert Einstein College of Medicine in the Bronx.[1] A Pediatric Nurse Practitioner/Associate (PNP/A) is a registered nurse who has received advanced clinical training in primary child health care. PNP/A's provide a broad range of health care services, including physical and developmental assessment, coordination of care of chronic problems in children, and provision of assistance to families in meeting their health needs. Thus, PNP/As are well suited to manage children with ADHD. As of January 1991, nurse practitioners in 35 states had some degree of prescriptive authority (Pearson, 1991), and therefore could prescribe medications for children with ADHD, if necessary.

Some special concerns regarding ADHD which are relevant to children seen in developmental clinics are due to the unique nature of the problems of the patients. Special efforts are required regarding identification of concurrent conditions. Monitoring and follow-up procedures also must be tailored to the needs of the patient. Hyperactive children in such a clinic setting present with diverse pediatric and psychological symptoms.

Hyperactive children are brought to developmental clinics with complaints of hyperactivity, short attention span, difficulty in paying attention, and other behaviors characteristic of ADHD. After evaluation, many of these children are found to meet the criteria for ADHD. In addition to ADHD, these children may also be learning disabled (school-age children), mentally retarded, autistic or more generally, have pervasive developmental disorder (PDD), a genetic syndrome or a chronic disease necessitating chronic medication. Therefore, before making the diagnosis of ADHD, it is important to consider other aspects of the child's environment—including the presence of other medical conditions, chronic or intermittent medications used, appropriateness of class placement, home environment and related psychosocial issues, and caregivers[2] feelings about medication.

Monitoring the condition and progress of children taking medication for the treatment of hyperactivity requires attention and compliance from caregivers[2] and teachers. In this population, obtaining accurate reports, maintaining behavior rating scales, and regulating drug dosages can be problematic. An important

Rose F. Kennedy Center, Children's Evaluation and Rehabilitation Center, Albert Einstein College of Medicine, Bronx, New York

[1]The Children's Evaluation and Rehabilitation Clinic of the Albert Einstein College of Medicine is located in an urban area where the patients demonstrate a wide range of environmental problems compounding their medical ones. Insofar as this population is typical of children with developmental problems around the country, the conditions described are generalizable.

[2]The term "caregivers" is used in place of "parent" because many of the patients live with grandparents, foster parents, and other nonparental guardians.

consideration, especially in the urban population, is the prevailing attitude of the caregiver toward the taking of drugs which may alter behavior; hence information about the patients can be colored by reporters' attitudes.

HYPERACTIVITY IN THE DEVELOPMENTALLY DISABLED CHILD

In hyperactive children seen at a developmental center, other possible etiologic factors must be considered. Some of the problems confounding the diagnosis of ADHD are attributable to concurrent medical conditions, the nature of the child's developmental disability, and environmental factors. It is often difficult to sort out these factors.

For example, hyperactivity can occur as part of the spectrum of some genetic syndromes: fragile X syndrome or fetal alcohol syndrome. Children who present with stigmata, particularly facial dysmorphia, or family history of developmental problems, should be referred for genetic evaluation. Diagnosis of a genetic disorder is not necessarily a contraindication to treatment of hyperactivity.

Medications for chronic conditions such as seizures, asthma, and chronic otitis media with effusion may produce the side effect of hyperactivity. Although newer drugs with fewer behavioral side effects are available, phenobarbital and primidone continue to be used for seizure management in children. Phenobarbital causes hyperactivity in many children, particularly those with a history of behavior problems. Theophylline, another drug that may reduce the attention span of some children, although no longer the drug of choice for asthma, continues to be prescribed for children who cognitively are unable to be taught to use inhalers (*Medical Letter,* 1991). Children with chronic otitis media with effusion may be medicated with decongestants, such as pseudoephedrine hydrochloride. Decongestants have also been associated with altered behavior and increased activity levels. Children may have been on chronic medications for long periods, making it difficult for the caregiver to date the onset of hyperactivity. Whenever possible, one should use alternate forms of treatment or drugs with fewer cognitive and behavioral side effects for hyperactive children with chronic medical problems.

Children who are environmentally disadvantaged are at risk for concurrent developmental problems. Poverty, inadequate housing, overcrowded living conditions, neighborhood violence, multiple changes of caretakers, can all impact on children's behavior. Lead poisoning is one of the most prevalent public health problems across the United States, particularly in the inner cities. It is estimated that 33 to 75 percent of children in New York City between the ages of 5 months and 6 years have elevated lead levels (Mahaffey et al., 1982, 1986). Furthermore, retarded children, with their more frequent hand to mouth behavior, may be at greater risk of lead ingestion. Since elevated lead levels in children have been associated with hyperactivity and learning difficulties, every child with these problems should be screened for elevated blood lead levels.

Inappropriate classroom placement may confuse identification of hyperactive children with those who are reacting to a confusing, overwhelming school environment. Mentally retarded, learning-disabled, or language-impaired children in regular classes of 35 to 40 children with one teacher may present initially with the complaint of hyperactivity, especially in the classroom. Since these children may be reacting to problematic school environments and not have ADHD, they may need a need developmental evaluation and class placement appropriate for their developmental diagnosis before treatment of their hyperactivity can commence. Some children with ADHD continue to be hyperactive, even after an appropriate class placement. These children may then benefit from treatment with medication.

The following clinical example demonstrates the value of appropriate class placement.

> R. is a 6 and a half year old boy who was referred to the clinic by his school for evaluation of hyperactivity. Because R had been in a series of foster homes, he had been assigned to several schools. R was one of 33 children in a regular first grade class. His teacher described him as hyperactive, in a world of his own, inattentive, fidgety and sometimes aggressive. Of greatest concern was that he often ran out of the classroom. His foster mother described him as uncooperative and inattentive. Upon developmental evaluation, R attained a test composite of 61 on the Stanford Binet, fourth edition, placing his cognitive ability within the range of mild

mental retardation. He was placed in a class for mildly mentally retarded children with one teacher, one assistant and nine children. The foster mother was counseled about the diagnosis and parenting techniques. R is now described by his teacher as similar to other children in his class, learning at his own pace and mixing in the group. The foster mother continues to have some behavior management problems, but these are reported to be less frequent and less intense.

The procedures for evaluation, treatment and followup/monitoring for the developmentally deviant children parallel approaches employed in child mental health clinics. The usual global rating forms used with ADDH children—the Teacher and Parent Conners Questionnaires (Conners, 1969, 1990; Conners and Barkley, 1985) and the Achenbach Child Behavior List (CBCL) (Achenbach and Edelbrock, 1979)—can be used to assess the numbers and severity of problems in the mentally retarded population. On the other hand, these forms should not be used to make diagnoses or as a basis for deciding about the use of medication. Two concerns impact on the use of these rating forms: an exclusion criterion for the diagnosis of ADDH and the mental age of the child.

The current definition of attention deficit hyperactivity disorder excludes children with the diagnosis of Pervasive Developmental Disorder (PDD) or with Mental Retardation (American Psychiatric Association, 1987). Yet signs of disruptiveness, inattention, gross motor hyperactivity, and impulsivity occur at high rates in these populations. Furthermore, children with PDD and mental retardation respond to medication as do the children in mental health clinics, with a significant decrease in motor activity, lessened impulsivity, decreased aggressivity, increased compliance, and an increase in attention span (see Demb, this volume). In actuality, many of these children resemble the pervasively hyperactive children reported by the Maudsley group (Sandberg et al., 1978), who had cross-situational hyperactivity, and also had lower full-scale IQs as well as positive findings on neurodevelopmental examination. The decision to medicate can be made after a careful assessment of the child's functioning at school and at home, a review of the rating forms, and a direct examination of the child in the PNP/A's office.

Developmentally delayed children exhibit mental ages below their chronological ages. Scoring Conners Teacher Rating Scale (TRS), for example, the examiner may not find the published norms for factor scores helpful in titrating dose or long-term monitoring. The norms published for these rating scales were based on children without developmental deviancy (Barkley, 1988; Goyette et al., 1979), so the use of a "cut-score" or threshold score for making the diagnosis of ADHD (i.e., 1.8 on Factor IV of the Conners Teacher Questionnaire) would be inappropriate for a child with mild mental retardation. The appropriate mental age of the patient must be kept in mind when reviewing the ratings. For example, a 6-year-old with an IQ of 50 and a mental age of 3, may appear quite hyperactive compared with other 6 year olds, but not so when compared to 3 year olds. Additionally, the rating scales use behaviors that may be appropriate for a higher mental age than the observed child has attained. The Conners has only one item that requires a higher cognitive level—"teasing." Similarly, the CBCL has items that would be expected to be scored for a child with developmental disabilities, such as "acts too young for his/her age." Consequently, the monitoring of retarded children must rely on descriptive reports by caregivers and teachers (who compare them with their classmates), and clinical observations, in addition to the rating scales.

Caregivers from inner city areas where drug addiction is prevalent often have strong opinions about medication. Some express great concern about addiction and may refuse treatment with medication despite the severity of the child's behavior. Others view medication as curative, punitive, or may have unrealistic expectations as to its efficacy. There is a growing population of children born addicted to cocaine or crack who are now entering school. They have "state control" or autonomic nervous system problems as babies and many appear to be hyperactive as preschool and school-age children. The treatment of children who are exposed to potentially damaging illicit or illegal drugs raises questions of appropriate treatment modalities to be used.

It is important to explore caregivers' feelings about the use of psychotropic medication and their prior experience with them in order to assess exactly what they think the medication is going to do for their child and to clarify misconceptions. The child should also be approached and talked to at an appropriate level for his cognitive ability, and similarly, have his expectations clarified.

K. is a 7 year old boy with ADHD and a perceptually based learning ability. He was told by his mother that Ritalin would help him sit still in class. When asked what his perception of what Ritalin would do, K told us he thought he would have to sit in school with a large rock on his lap. K. thought that "Ritalin" was the rock's name, and it's weight would pin him to the seat.

MONITORING CONCERNS

After careful medical and developmental evaluation, those children who are treated with medication have to be followed in a regular and systematic way. Close follow up of children with ADHD and coordination of treatment modalities is critical to successful management of hyperactivity. Many children respond well to treatment with medication. However, there are social and environmental problems that raise questions to be considered as ADHD treatment progresses.

Hyperactive children living in a chaotic environment, where there are multiple stimuli, overcrowding, unpredictable bedtimes, lack of routine, and other psychosocial stressors, may continue to exhibit behavior problems while on treatment. The importance of these environmental stimuli is clear when we look at P.

P. is a 7 year old boy who lived with his family in a small, inadequate apartment in the Bronx. He was particularly sensitive to loud noise and would be distracted and hyperactive every time he heard a fire engine, ambulance, firecrackers, or gunshots, frequent occurrences in this neighborhood. He was treated with Ritalin 10 mg three times a day with some decrease in his level of hyperactivity. His family moved to a quiet rural area of New York where he was able to run and play on several acres after school. He was placed in a smaller class where the subjects demanding the most attention are taught in the morning and other classes, such as gym, are the afternoon. Since moving, his behavior has been reported to be significantly less hyperactive, both in school and at home. He is now managed with Ritalin 10 mg in the morning on school days only.

In other cases, medication regimens must be re-evaluated regularly to avoid attributing a treatment emergent symptom (side effect) to the wrong agent. When this happens, removal of the wrong medication can greatly complicate matters.

J. is a 14 year old severely retarded, non-verbal boy with Fetal Alcohol Syndrome, seizure disorder and ADHD who attends an appropriate special class for severely retarded adolescent children. J has been treated with Depakene, 500 mg. three times a day to control seizures and Ritalin 10 mg twice daily, with significant reduction in activity level, according to his foster mother. Because of a recent significant weight loss, Ritalin was discontinued by the primary care provider. A questionnaire completed while he was off drug therapy revealed an increase in hyperactivity. The teacher wrote, "Although J. has been taken off Ritalin for a short time, there is a major difference in his behavior. He is rocking a great deal more, is less attentive and more difficult to work with. I believe J. is noticing this change too, but is unable to control or limit his actions on his own. Perhaps a medication reevaluation would be useful."

At this point, J.'s medication regimen was re-examined. The primary care taker decided that the weight loss was probably associated with the Depakene. This medication was readjusted and Ritalin was restarted with a concomitant decrease in hyperactivity and no further weight loss.

Caregivers' ability to participate in a medication treatment program must be assessed. The problem of how to treat a child with ADHD on medication is troubling when the parent is thought to be using illegal drugs at the same time. In this situation, if the school is agreeable, medication is kept at the school and administered in that environment. One must always keep in mind that controlled substances have abuse potential. Therefore, careful monitoring of prescription renewals should be performed to insure that the child is receiving medication as prescribed. Pill boxes with dated and time-stamped compartments are helpful for parents who have difficulty remembering medication schedules. Counseling about how to administer medication, where to keep medication bottles safe from children, how to renew medication, and the necessity of keeping follow-up appointments is important.

Intellectually limited parents, who frequently report more behavior management problems, need special monitoring when their children are treated with medication. They need more frequent visits, closer telephone monitoring, and continuity of care with the same provider, if possible. Visiting Nurse Service can be helpful in assessing the home environment and the child's behavior in the home, and assuring that medication is being given as prescribed and stored in a safe place. The school should be part of the management of the treatment of the child's behavior.

Proper telephone management can reduce the number of unnecessary office visits. It has been estimated that about one-fifth of contacts in the pediatric health care system are by phone (Katz, 1982). Telephone management can be used to provide education and support for caregivers as well as to gather information. The following data should be collected: date, name and relationship of caller, symptoms, duration of the problem, associated problems, interventions initiated by the caregiver and their results, and level of caregiver's anxiety. After the problem is identified, assessed and discussed with the caregiver, the information should be properly documented in the patient's chart. This provides continuity of care when the next phone call is handled by a different professional (Thayer, 1984).

Often, the families of the developmentally delayed child are involved with multiple social, medical, and or educational agencies, and management of the child's medical treatment can get very complicated. Unless there is frequent communication and coordination of effort, each agency will come up with its own agenda and priorities for treatment, with conflicting appointment times and treatment goals. This can sometimes complicate management of children's medical treatment. It is helpful if one individual can be appointed as case manager.

CONCLUSIONS

Researchers and clinicians should remember that ADHD can occur in association with a variety of developmental problems. Treatment should be targeted both to the mental age and environmental circumstances of the child. Many children with hyperactivity and a developmental disability respond well to treatment with medication such as Ritalin; however, treatment is most effective when multimodal intervention is utilized. Close supervision by a health professional, such as a pediatrician, pediatric nurse practitioner, child psychiatrist, or neurologist is critical during all stages of assessment and treatment, in order to assure proper monitoring of the medication effects and side effects, changes in family, school and environmental circumstances and to assess continuity of care.

REFERENCES

Achenbach, T.M. & Edelbrock, C.S. (1979). The Child Behavior Profile. II. Boys aged 12 to 16 and girls aged 6 to 11 and 12 to 16. *J. Counsult. Clin. Psychol.*, 47:223–233.

Achenbach, T.M. & Edelbrock, C.S. (1983). *Manual for the Child Behavior Checklist and Revised Child Behavior Profile*. Burlington, VT: Thomas A. Achenbach.

American Psychiatric Association. (1987). *Diagnostic and Statistical Manual of Mental Disorders*. Washington, DC: American Psychiatric Association.

Barkley, R. (1988). Child behavior rating scales and checklists. In: *Assessment and Diagnosis in Child Psychopathology*. eds. (M. Rutter, H. Tuma, & I. Lann. New York: Guilford Press, pp. 113–155.

Conners, C.K. (1969). A teacher rating scale for use in drug studies with children. *Am. J. Psychiatry*, 126:152–156.

————(1990). Methodological and assessment issues in pediatric psychopharmacology. In: ed. Wiener, J.M. *Diagnosis and Psychopharmacology of Childhood and Adolescent Disorders* New York: John Wiley and Sons.

———— Barkley, R. (1985). Rating scales and checklists for child psychopharmacology. *Psychopharmacol. Bull.*, 21(4):816–832.

Goyette, C.H., Conners, C.K., & Ulrich, R.F. (1979). Normative data on revised Conners parent and teacher rating scales. *J. Consult. Clin. Psychol.*, 47:1020–1029.

Katz, H.P. (1982). *Telephone Manual of Pediatric Care*. John Wiley and Sons, New York, 1982.

Mahaffey, K., Annest, J., Roberts, J., & Murphy, R. (1982). National estimate of blood lead levels: United States, 1976–1980. *N. Engl. J. Med.*, 307(10):573–579.

————Gartside, P., & Glueck, C. (1986). Blood lead levels and dietary calcium intake in 1- to 11-year old children: The second National Health and Nutrition Examination Survey, 1976 to 1980. *Pediatrics*, 78(2):257–261.

Medical Letter. (1991). Drugs for ambulatory asthma. 33(837):9–12.

Pearson, L.J. (1991). Update: How each state stands on legislative issues affecting advanced nursing practice. *Nurse Practitioner*, 16(1):11.

Sandberg, S.T., Rutter, M., & Taylor, E. (1978). Hyperkinetic disorder in psychiatric clinic attenders. *Dev. Med Child Neurol.*, 20:279–299.

Thayer, M.B. (1984). Telephone management. *Pediatr. Nurs.*, 10:121–154.

Interaction of Ritalin and Multimodal Therapy in the Treatment of Attention Deficit Hyperactive Behavior Disorder

HOWARD ABIKOFF

INTRODUCTION

Attention deficit hyperactivity disorder (ADHD) is one of the most common psychiatric disorders of childhood, with an estimated prevalence rate of 3–5% in school-aged children (Barkley, 1981). The majority of ADHD youngsters come to the attention of mental health professionals because of multiple difficulties in school and/or at home. The most common presenting problems include poor academic performance, faulty peer relationships, and low self-esteem.

Numerous treatment strategies have been used with ADHD children. The interventions investigated most thoroughly have been stimulant treatment, behavior therapy, and cognitive behavior therapy. Limitations associated with each of these approaches are reviewed below, followed by a description of an ongoing, integrative multimodal treatment study with ADHD youngsters.

TREATMENT STRATEGIES

Stimulant medication

Treatment of ADHD youngsters with methylphenidate (Ritalin), and to a lesser extent with dextroamphetamine (Dexedrine) and magnesium pemoline (Cylert), remains the most widely used therapeutic intervention. The short-term clinical effectiveness of Ritalin has been extensively documented (see Klein et al., 1980). With medication, the majority of ADHD youngsters demonstrate substantial improvements in the primary symptoms of the disorder. The children become more attentive, less impulsive and disruptive, and less overactive in situations where activity needs to be modulated (Abikoff and Gittelman, 1985). The productivity and accuracy of their academic work improves (Douglas et al., 1986; Pelham, 1986), as does the nature of the child-directed behaviors of teachers (Whalen et al., 1980) and parents (Barkley and Cunningham, 1979). (See Whalen and Henker, 1991) for a review of the social impact of stimulant treatment). In some cases, the improvements with medication are so dramatic that the youngsters are able to be maintained in regular classes, obviating the need for special class placement.

Notwithstanding its substantial beneficial effects, Ritalin is not a panacea in the treatment of the disorder. First, it is estimated that perhaps 20 to 30% of children treated with Ritalin demonstrate little or no benefit. Moreover, medication alone does not ameliorate unmastered social and academic skills, nor does it appear to improve academic achievement. Further, because of the typical twice daily dosing regimen and Ritalin's short half-life, its effects have invariably worn off by the time the child arrives home from school; consequently, child management problems often continue at home. Finally, and perhaps most important

Albert Einstein College of Medicine, Bronx, New York and Schneider Children's Hospital, Long Island Jewish Medical Center, New Hyde Park, New York

with regard to treatment strategies, are the limitations regarding the sustained and long-term effects of Ritalin. Specifically, the positive changes associated with treatment are frequently not maintained following termination of medication (Gittelman-Klein et al., 1976), and there is little evidence that long-term treatment substantially alters the eventual outcome of the disorder.

Behavioral and cognitive-behavioral interventions

In both clinical research and practice, behavioral and cognitive behavioral interventions are often used with ADHD children. In some cases, the goal has been to determine if these treatments are effective alternatives to medication. In other instances, concern over the limitations of stimulant treatment has led to the use of behavioral and/or cognitive behavioral procedures in combination with medication. There have been a number of reviews of the efficacy of these approaches (e.g., Abikoff, 1987; Hinshaw and Erhardt, 1991; Pelham and Murphy, 1986; Sprague, 1983; Whalen et al., 1985). Therefore, only an overview of the major conclusions will be presented here.

Although there are some reports of the efficacy of behavioral interventions in ADHD children, especially the use of parent management training (e.g., Dubey et al., 1983), the majority of controlled studies provides limited evidence for the effectiveness of behavior therapy as a singular intervention with these youngsters, (e.g., Abikoff and Gittelman, 1984; Gittelman et al., 1980). Additionally, generalization of gains outside the treatment setting is problematic, as are maintenance effects following cessation of behavioral treatment. There is some support for the efficacy of behavior therapy in conjunction with Ritalin, as this combination is more useful than either treatment alone in normalizing ADHD children's classroom behavior (Gittelman et al., 1980). However, the overall clinical utility of this treatment combination is limited because of the absence of maintenance effects following treatment termination, and the fact that it fails to address the academic, social, and emotional difficulties common to the disorder.

Cognitive behavioral therapy (CBT) has an inherent appeal to those working with ADHD children. The approach focuses on teaching youngsters reflective problem-solving skills as a means of self-regulation, with the expectation that they will attain more self-control over their impulsive response style. A variety of procedures are employed, including modeling, self-instruction, self-monitoring, self-reinforcement, attention scanning, and training in cognitive strategies and interpersonal problem solving. It has been suggested that CBT, unlike more traditional behavioral approaches, results in internalized, "portable" metacognitive skills that should enhance the transfer and maintenance of treatment effects across time and settings, especially when generalization "aids" or procedures are programmed into the CBT regimen.

The face validity of CBT as a treatment strategy with ADHD children is obvious. The few positive findings with self-evaluation and anger control procedures suggest that further evaluations of these CBT components may be worthwhile (Hinshaw and Erhardt, 1991). Overall, however, empirical support of its efficacy in these youngsters is extremely limited (see Abikoff, 1987; Hinshaw and Erhardt, in press). To date, not only is there little, if any, evidence from controlled studies for the clinical utility of this treatment approach, but the addition of CBT to medication has not produced incremental improvements in cognitive functioning, academic performance, or behavior.

As this brief overview has indicated, no single treatment has had a satisfactorily broad therapeutic impact with ADHD children. Related to these disheartening results is the fact that most intervention studies have been quite short, with treatment duration ranging from as brief as one or two sessions, to, in a few instances, three or four months. It is quite clear, therefore, that other treatment strategies are warranted. Given the multiplicity of social, emotional, and academic problems experienced by these children, approaches that are broader both in scope and time are needed.

Multimodal therapy

Some support for the utility of broad-based interventions comes from the reports of Satterfield and his colleagues regarding the clinical efficacy of multimodal therapy with hyperactive children (Satterfield et al.,

1979, 1980, 1981). These investigators reported on a treatment regimen with 6- to 12-year-old hyperactive children that consisted of Ritalin, individual psychotherapy, group therapy, educational therapy, individual parent counseling, group counseling for parents, and family therapy. Children and their families received any combination and any number of these treatments, depending on the needs and disabilities of the youngsters and their parents. When compared with other outcome studies, the investigators felt that the outcome of this comprehensively treated group was unusually good; the children showed improvement in home and school behavior and academic achievement, and reductions in antisocial behavior as well. Moreover, improvements in the latter two domains were reportedly related to length of treatment, as children who received three years of treatment had better outcomes than did those with less than a year of treatment.

MULTIMODAL TREATMENT: OVERVIEW OF ONGOING STUDY

The findings from the Satterfield et al. studies are the most promising reports yet of a meaningful clinical intervention with ADHD youngsters. However, the report of treatment efficacy needs to be tempered, because the multimodal therapy received by the children was not provided within the context of a controlled, random assignment treatment study. Such a treatment study is currently supported by the National Institute of Mental Health, under the direction of myself and Dr. Rachel Klein at Schneider Children's Hospital in New York, and at Montreal Children's Hospital under the direction of Dr. Lily Hechtman and Dr. Gabrielle Weiss.

The joint efforts in New York and Montreal reflect the conclusions of an NIMH conference in 1980 that collaborative studies are the best vehicles for implementing long-term investigations of the efficacy of multimodal interventions. A multisite study is able to address both practical and scientific issues that are difficult to manage in a single treatment setting. For example, to carry out long-term treatment studies (treatment in this case lasts for two years), it is necessary to recruit large numbers of children in a relatively short period of time. A single site would find it difficult, if not impossible, to meet these recruitment demands in the time period required. Additionally, the use of multiple sites allows for greater control over factors that impact on the generalizability of results, a critical issue in treatment studies. Specifically, differences or ambiguity in findings across studies can be and often are attributed to differences in sample characteristics and/or treatment interventions.

Procedures implemented in the study sites in New York and Montreal are directed at these concerns. Thus, in both settings, identical diagnostic measures and research diagnostic entry criteria are used. Further, consensus diagnoses, based on review of tapes of diagnostic interviews, must be obtained from the staff at both sites for all study participants. Finally, to minimize treatment differences, detailed treatment manuals and systematic process notes are used, and session tapes in both sites are monitored and compared for treatment fidelity.

The study's treatment strategies and protocol reflect the major aims of the investigation, namely, to determine (1) whether the provision of multimodal treatment (MMT) to ADHD children receiving stimulant medication (Ritalin) results in better social, behavioral, emotional, and academic functioning than that associated with Ritalin alone; and (2) whether exposure to an MMT regimen enables ADHD children to be maintained and to function adequately without medication.

The MMT interventions in the study are intended to address the major deficits associated with ADHD. Thus, the treatment regimen consists of medication, academic study skills training, individualized remedial tutoring, and individual psychotherapy. Additionally, there is social skills training, parent management training and family counseling, and a home-based reinforcement program for school behavior, all of which are integrated into a behavioral systems approach as part of the mutimodal treatment regimen.

The treatment components are provided once a week for a year, and then once a month, in the form of "booster" sessions, for a second year. During the first year, the various treatment sessions are held during two after-school clinic visits a week. The treatment arrangement is viewed best within the context of a partial day treatment program, wherein professional staff provides all the necessary interventions at one site, and can readily share relevant treatment issues with each other.

Children who participate in the study are randomly assigned to either multimodal treatment or to one of two control groups. One group is comprised of youngsters who receive Ritalin alone and crisis intervention if needed. This group serves as a "community control" and to a large extent parallels the manner in which ADHD youngsters are typically treated with stimulants. Likewise, youngsters assigned to an "attention control" group are treated with Ritalin; however, they and their parents also receive professional attention and time equal to that provided to the multimodal group. The professional contacts are clinically viable and parallel closely the multimodal treatments, but do not provide the latter's presumed "active" treatment components. Thus, the children participate in a peer activity group, receive help with homework, and spend weekly individual time with an adult. The parents participate in a psychodeducational/support group and also have weekly supportive meetings with a member of the professional staff.

MULTIMODAL INTERVENTIONS

Because of space limitations, only brief descriptions of the key features of the MMT interventions are provided below.

Stimulant treatment

Ritalin is titrated to the most effective clinical dosage, up to a maximum of 50 mg/day. Weekly feedback from parents, teachers, and the children are used to make dosage adjustments. Included in this feedback are global ratings of improvement, specific behavioral ratings, narrative descriptions of the child's functioning, and assessments of side effects. Also, arithmetic tests are given at baseline, when the children are not on medication, and during titration. The test scores serve as an index of cognitive functioning with stimulant treatment. If there are any deleterious changes in arithmetic performance relative to baseline, then there is a return to the most clinically effective dosage not associated with cognitive impairment. Medication is prescribed on a tid basis, with the smallest dosage (usually 5 or 10 mg) given at approximately 3:30 PM. This regimen is designed to maximize attention and cooperation during the after school treatment sessions. (Difficulties regarding delayed sleep onset are monitored as part of the side effects assessment. To date, untoward sleep problems have not been reported.)

Social skills training

A common complaint of parents and teachers is that the ADHD child does not get along well with his agemates. School observations indicate that the hyperactive child is similar to other children with regard to the occurrence of neutral and positive peer interactions (Abikoff and Gittelman, 1982). What distinguishes ADHD youngsters from their peers is the higher frequency of negative social contacts, characterized by aversive behaviors such as bossiness, intrusiveness, and aggressiveness. Their awkward interpersonal exchanges with peers stem from a seeming lack of sensitivity to social cues, nuances, and demands, and suggest a "social learning disability" (Whalen and Henker, 1991).

The social skills training component focuses on the development and enhancement of age-appropriate interpersonal skills. To this end, a year-long curriculum addresses different social skills each week (e.g., joining a conversation, giving and receiving positive feedback, waiting for one's turn in games, cooperating in a group activity, etc.). In-session training components include the use of modeling, role playing, and children's viewing of previously videotaped training sessions. Homework assignments are employed to increase skills mastery and to aid in generalization outside the treatment setting.

Throughout the social skills training, a behavior modification system is implemented that initially uses concrete rewards to reinforce appropriate behavior in the session. Subsequently, the children self-evaluate their social behavior during the session (see Hinshaw et al. 1984; Turkewitz et al., 1975), and the corresponding points earned or lost by the children are incorporated into the parent management program at home (described below).

Parent training and family counseling

ADHD children have difficulties adhering to the structured demands of the classroom and complying with adult rules and limit setting. The resulting child management problems faced by parents and teachers are a common reason these children are referred to mental health professionals. Accordingly, interventions that emphasize behavior management strategies for use at home and at school are included in the multimodal treatment program.

During the first year, the parents are seen weekly in a group format for the first three months, and then in weekly individual sessions. The group sessions are based in part on Russell Barkley's behavior management training program for parents of defiant and hyperactive children (Barkley, 1987). The parents are taught how to use contingent praise and attention, time out and response cost, and how to set up and implement a token economy system at home. The latter consists of a comprehensive point system whereby daily privileges (e.g., TV, Nintendo) and special activities and rewards are made contingent on points earned by the child in the social skills sessions in the clinic, in school (based on the use of a daily report card format described below), and at home. Included in the behaviors targeted for increase at home are doing daily chores and compliance with parental requests. Points are earned or lost contingent on whether or not the child engages in these positive behaviors. Similarly, there is a list of negative behaviors, individualized for each child, that are targeted for decrease (e.g., noncompliance, tantrums, fighting). A loss of points, and in some instances time out, results when these inappropriate behaviors occur. Additionally, points are earned when the child does *not* show these negative behaviors at home.

Following the group sessions, the parents are seen individually for nine months of once-weekly sessions, of which every fourth session includes the child as well. (During the second year, treatment is comprised of once-monthly sessions.) The individual work with the parents serves to reinforce, support, and clarify parental efforts to apply the behavior management techniques taught in the parent groups. The sessions also focus on any marital discord related to raising and managing an ADHD child, and marital counseling regarding these difficulties is provided if necessary. Family systems approaches are used as well to enhance communication between family members and to examine and help handle such issues as parent–child alliances and scapegoating.

Daily report card

The report card system is a cost-effective procedure that is used to monitor, reinforce, set goals, and modify the child's school behavior, while minimizing the amount of direct teacher and therapist involvement (see Atkeson and Forehand, 1979; Barkley, 1981; Lahey et al., 1977). Each child's report card contains a list of several behavioral items deemed important by the youngster's teacher (e.g., raising hand, staying seated). The teachers rate the children on each item and then initial the card. The children are required to bring the card home every day from school. The daily ratings are associated with a number of points earned or lost. The point totals are incorporated into the home-based reinforcement program managed by the parents, and result in the gain or loss of privileges, activities, or other reinforcers at home.

Academic skills training and remediation

The academic problems of the ADHD child are characterized typically by low or failing grades, grade retention, lower than expected achievement test scores, and resource room or special class placement. These negative outcomes are the consequence of the interaction of a variety of possible factors, including specific academic skills deficits, a concurrent learning disability, inattention during classroom lessons, and poor organizational and study skills.

The goal of the first 12 weeks of the academic treatment component is to improve organizational skills and strategies relevant to successful academic performance. To this end, within a group format, the children are exposed to a variety of tasks and activities, most of them academic in nature, that focus on following written and oral directions, getting ready to work, checking one's work, efficient use of time, and so on. During the subsequent nine months the children receive weekly prescriptive, individual, remedial tutoring that focuses on their specific skill deficits in reading, math, and language.

Psychotherapy

Given their multiple problems, it is not surprising that ADHD youngsters frequently suffer from low self-esteem. The common experience of being shunned by other children, being yelled at by parents and teachers, poor scholastic performance, and a lack of success in ameliorating these problems on their own, leads to feelings of demoralization, low self-worth, and a poor self-image. Accordingly, the multimodal treatment program includes an individual psychotherapy component that attempts to facilitate the child's self-image and feelings of competence.

The psychotherapy manual, developed by Dr. Gabrielle Weiss, describes the theoretical framework and content of therapy, including the various target areas to which psychotherapy is addressed (e.g., problems of low self-esteem, feelings of rejection, coping strategies, etc.). The manual also provides a description of the intervention techniques and strategies that comprise the eclectic therapeutic approach, and the manner in which the individual psychotherapy interfaces with the other multimodal treatment components.

ASSESSMENT OF TREATMENT OUTCOME

Multimodal studies require multiple assessment procedures and measures to evaluate treatment efficacy. In our ongoing study, information regarding functioning in various domains is collected prior to treatment assignment, when the child is on and off medication, and subsequently at six-month intervals, from parents, teachers, and children.

The children's school behavior is evaluated via standardized teacher rating scales and observation procedures. At home, the children's behavior is assessed via parent rating scales. Changes in perceptions of parental self-efficacy, child management strategies, and knowledge of behavioral principles are assessed as well. Rating scales are also completed by the children and serve as change measures of self-concept, social skills, and depression. Finally, testing procedures are used to assess changes in academic achievement and performance, and information-processing skills. Table 1 lists the specific outcome measures used in the study.

Discontinuation of medication

As noted previously, the positive effects of stimulant treatment are often not maintained when medication is discontinued, resulting in remedication for most children. Even when stimulants are combined with other interventions, such as cognitive training, over 85% of ADHD children resume medication within one month of cessation of stimulant treatment (Abikoff and Gittelman, 1985). A major aim of the current study is to determine if exposure to long-term multimodal treatment enables youngsters with ADHD to be maintained off medication. To this end, a blind placebo challenge is implemented after a year of multimodal treatment. Of special interest during the placebo challenge are comparisons between the multimodal and control groups with regard to the percentage of children who can be maintained off medication; and for those children who need to be remediated, the length of time before reinstitution of Ritalin and the dosage levels required.

CLOSING NOTE

Because the four-year multimodal study detailed above is ongoing, it will be some time before the clinical efficacy of this particular integrative approach is known. It is also likely that other long-term multimodal

TABLE 1. STUDY OUTCOME MEASURES

Child Measures	*Teacher Measures*
Self-Rating Scales:	Rating Scales:
Perception of Parent Behavior	Conners Teacher Questionnaire
Social Skills Questionnaire: Student Form	School Situations Questionnaire
Piers-Harris Self-Concept Scale	Taxonomy of Problem Situations
Children's Depression Inventory	Global Improvement Scale
Academic:	*Psychiatrist Measures*
Stanford Achievement Test	Rating Scales:
Arithmetic Test	*DSM-III-R* Symptom Checklist
School Grades	Global Assessment Scale
Cognitive:	Global Improvement Scale
Memory Scan Test	*Observer Measures*
Parent Measures	Behavioral Observations:
Rating Scales:	Revised Stony Brook Classroom Observation
Knowledge of Behavioral Principles	Code
Being A Parent	Social Interaction Code
Parent Practices Questionnaire	Rating Scales:
Home Situations Questionnaire	Hillside Behavior Rating Scale
Conners Parent Questionnaire	Abbreviated Conners Teacher Rating Scale
Homework Problems Checklist	
Social Skills Questionnaire: Parent Form	
Global Improvement Scale	

treatment studies will begin in the near future (see Hinshaw and Erhardt, 1991, for a description of several planned multimodal programs). The results of these efforts, once available, will add to our knowledge of the treatment of the hyperactive child. If multimodal treatment is found to be clinically effective, then subsequent work needs to be conducted to clarify which particular treatment components and combinations are necessary to maximize and maintain treatment gains.

REFERENCES

Abikoff, H. (1987), An evaluation of cognitive-behavior therapy for hyperactive children. In: *Advances in Clinical Child Psychology,* vol. 10, eds. B.B. Lahey & A.E. Kazdin. New York: Plenum, pp. 171–216.

———— Gittelman, R. (1982), The social interactions of hyperactive and normal boys in unstructured school settings. Unpublished data.

———— ———— (1984), Does behavior therapy normalize the classroom behavior of hyperactive children? *Arch. Gen. Psychiatry,* 41:449–454.

———— ———— (1985), The normalizing effects of methylphenidate on the classroom behavior of hyperactive children. *J. Abnorm. Child Psychol.,* 13:33–44.

Atkeson, B.M. & Forehand, R. (1979), Home-based reinforcement programs to modify classroom behavior: A review and methodological evaluation. *Psychol. Bull.,* 86:1298–1308.

Barkley, R.A. (1981), *Hyperactive Children: A Handbook for Diagnosis and Treatment.* New York: Guilford Press.

———— (1987), *Defiant Children: A Clinician's Manual for Parent Training.* New York: Guilford Press.

———— Cunningham, C.E. (1979), The effects of Ritalin on the mother–child interactions of hyperactive children. *Arch. Gen. Psychiatry,* 36:201–208.

Douglas, V.I., Barr, R.G., O'Neill, M.E. & Britton, B.G. (1986), Short-term effects of methylphenidate on the cognitive, learning and academic performance of children with attention deficit disorder in the laboratory and the classroom. *J. Child Psychol. Psychiatry,* 27:191–211.

Dubey, D.R., O'Leary, S.G. & Kaufman, K.F. (1983), Training parents of hyperactive children in child management: A comparative outcome study. *J. Abnorm. Child Psychol.,* 11:229–246.

Gittelman, R., Abikoff, H., Pollack, E., Klein, D.F., Katz, S. & Mattes, J. (1980), A controlled trial of behavior modification and methylphenidate in hyperactive children. In: *Hyperactive Children: The Social Ecology of Identification and Treatment,* eds. C. Whalen & B. Henker New York: Academic Press, pp. 221–243.

Gittelman-Klein, R., Klein, D.F., Katz, S., Saraf, K. & Pollack, E. (1976), Comparative effects of methylphenidate and thioridazine in hyperkinetic children: I. Clinical results. *Arch. Gen. Psychiatry,* 33:1217–1231.

Hinshaw, S.P. & Erhardt, D. (1991), Attention deficit-hyperactivity disorder. In: *Child and Adolescent Therapy: Cognitive-Behavioral Procedures,* ed. P.C. Kendall. New York: Guilford Press, pp. 98–128.

——— Henker, B. & Whalen, C.K. (1984), Cognitive-behavioral and pharmacologic interventions for hyperactive boys: Comparative and combined effects. *J. Consult. Clin. Psychol.,* 52:739–749.

Klein, D.F., Gittelman, R., Quitkin, F. & Rifkin, A. (1980), *Diagnosis and Drug Treatment of Psychiatric Disorders: Adults and Children,* 2nd Ed. Baltimore: Williams and Wilkins.

Lahey, B.B., Gendrich, J.G., Gendrich, S.I., Schnelle, J.F., Gant, D.S. & McNees, M.P. (1977), An evaluation of daily report cards with minimal teacher and parent contacts as an efficient method of classroom intervention. *Behav. Modif.,* 1:381–394.

Pelham, W.E., Jr. (1986), The effects of psychostimulant drugs on learning and academic achievement in children with attention-deficit disorders and learning disabilities. In: *Psychological and Educational Perspectives on Learning Disabilities,* eds. J.K. Torgesen & B.Y.L. Wong. New York: Academic Press, pp. 259–295.

——— Murphy, H.A. (1986), Attention deficit and conduct disorders. In: *Pharmacological and Behavioral Treatment: An Integrative Approach,* ed. M. Hersen New York: John Wiley, pp. 108–148.

Satterfield, J.H., Cantwell, D.P. & Satterfield, B.T. (1979), Multimodality treatment: A one year follow-up of 84 hyperactive boys. *Arch. Gen. Psychiatry,* 36:965–974.

——— Satterfield, B.T. & Cantwell, D.P. (1980), Multimodality treatment: A two year evaluation of 61 hyperactive boys. *Arch. Gen. Psychiatry,* 37:915–919.

——— ——— ——— (1981), Three year multimodality treatment study of 100 hyperactive boys. *J. Pediatr.,* 98:650–655.

Sprague, R.L. (1983), Behavior modification and educational techniques. In: *Developmental Neuropsychiatry,* ed. M. Rutter. New York: Guilford Press, pp. 404–421.

Turkewitz, H., O'Leary, K.D. & Ironsmith, M. (1975), Generalization and maintenance of appropriate behavior through self-control. *J. Consult. Clin. Psychology,* 43:577–583.

Whalen, C.K. & Henker, B. (1991), The social impact of stimulant treatment for hyperactive children. *J. Learn. Disabil.,* 24:231–241.

——— ——— Dotemoto, S. (1980), Methylphenidate and hyperactivity: Effects on teacher behaviors. *Science,* 208:1280–1282.

——— ——— Hinshaw, S.P. (1985), Cognitive-behavioral therapies for hyperactive children: Premises, problems, and prospects. *J. Abnorm. Child Psychol.,* 13:391–410.

Use of Ritalin in the Treatment of Children with Mental Retardation

HOWARD B. DEMB

INTRODUCTION

Sparked by a report that benzedrine improved the intelligence test scores of adult patients in a mental hospital (Sargent and Blackburn, 1936), stimulants have been used to treat behavior disorders in children with a wide spectrum of cognitive abilities for more than 50 years. At this point, while stimulants are reported to be "unquestionably the most commonly prescribed psychotropic drugs for mentally retarded children and youth" (Gadow, 1985, p. 291), the results of research on the effectiveness of stimulants in individuals with mental retardation has been interpreted in somewhat different ways. Emphasizing the positive aspects of the results Gadow (1985), who focused on the upper range of mental retardation, concludes that "what limited data are available suggest that they are highly effective in the treatment of hyperactivity in mildly to moderately retarded individuals" (p. 291). Looking at the data from the point of view of the severely to profoundly retarded, Aman and Singh (1982) concluded "there is simply is no compelling evidence thus far that the stimulants have consistent effects, either beneficial or adverse, on the behavior of severely mentally retarded persons" (p. 355). One year later Aman (1983), in addressing the long-sought-after-use of a medication to treat mental retardation, states "there is currently no compelling proof that the stimulants have a major role to play in treatment of the mentally retarded" (pp. 485–486).

Such differences may be due in part to the fact that mental retardation was an exclusion criterion in drug studies with hyperactivity (Gadow, 1986), to large individual differences in response, and to the fact that research on the use of stimulants with individuals with mental retardation tends to cover a wide range of: ages; IQs; types of pathology; environmental settings; dosages; experimental designs; measures of improvement; statistical measures used; and dependent variables measured. Taken as a whole, the body of research on the use of stimulants with individuals with mental retardation is currently being interpreted as indicating that "retarded people who respond well to stimulants are likelier to be: (a) young; (b) only mildly to moderately retarded; (c) without previous evidence of stereotypy or of perseverative behavior; and (d) affected by straight forward behavioral symptoms, like hyperactivity, inattention, or distractibility" (Chandler et al., 1988, p. 122; Aman, 1989, p. 93). Nevertheless they appear to support the hypothesis put forth by Robbins and Sahakrian (1979), that stimulants produce a focusing of attention in both animals and humans and that stimulants induce stereotypy in children with mental retardation and/or autism by exacerbating the narrow or overfocused attention of at least some children with mental retardation or autism by further severely constricting or focusing their attention (Aman, 1982).

What research findings lead to these conclusions? How are stimulants currently used to treat behavior disorders of children with mental retardation?

Albert Einstein College of Medicine, Bronx, New York

EARLY USE OF STIMULANTS

Early research on the use of stimulants involved institutionalized children who were delinquent and had neurological and behavior disorders (Bradley, 1937; Molitich and Eccles, 1937; Molitich and Sullivan, 1937). Only two of the early studies using benzedrine sulfate included placebo controls. None employed statistical tests of significance to measure treatment effects. Bradley reported "spectacular" changes in behavior including "remarkably improved school performance" (p. 582). Molitich and Eccles, who used a placebo, found improvements in scores on motor, psychomotor, and verbal intelligence tests in both the drug and placebo groups. Although statistical tests of significance were not employed, the results were interpreted as indicating that children tested after taking benzedrine exhibited "a greater improvement than those taking placebo" (p. 590). There is no indication that the groups were matched for IQ nor whether there was an interaction between drug effects and IQ. Molitich and Sullivan reported gains or losses in scores on the New Stanford Achievement Test (Kelly et al., 1929), in children getting benzedrine sulfate and in children getting placebo. Here again, there was no attempt to determine the statistical significance of the drug/placebo differences in the mentally subnormal groups. In discussing the effects of dextroamphetamine or benzedrine in children with mental retardation and the "hyperkinetic impulse disorder," Laufer and Denhoff (1957) report that "it often improves their functioning by removing the handicaps of the hyperkinetic syndrome thus allowing them to focus their intelligence more efficiently." They found these medications helpful to children above and below the age of 6 years even though "it will not confer upon the children any more intelligence than they already have" (p. 472).

There have been a number of studies in which stimulants other than Ritalin have been reported to be ineffective or only marginally effective. One early study (Cutler et al., 1940) was designed to determine the effect of medication on adolescents with mental retardation, described as "moron and borderline defective children" p. 59), of chronic administration of "a small daily dose" (between 5 and 7.5 mg for up to 6 months) of amphetamine sulfate on a number of psychometric tests. No differences were found between the treated and control groups. However, in a study of the acute effect of 5 mg of Benzedrine twice a day, the active medication was felt to favorably effect the outcome of 8 of 14 psychometric tests measuring fine-motor, perceptual motor, and academic skills.

Later well-controlled studies with statistical tests of significance suggested that stimulants were ineffective in the treatment of the mentally retarded. In a placebo-controlled study (Morris et al., 1955), escalating daily doses of up to 15 mg of amphetamine were given to hospitalized individuals ranging in age from 15.5 to 32 years and with IQs from 60 to 74, who were given tests of intelligence, verbal and nonverbal learning, attention, memory, and level of aspiration, no statistically significant improvements were noted on any of the measures. McConnell et al. (1964) used a triple-blind placebo-controlled design to study the effect of Dexedrine on the activity level of 57 children with mental retardation. Age range was from a 6.2 to 15.1 years and mental retardation was mild to profound. No significant drug-placebo differences were found in ballistograph and rating scale measures of hyperactivity. In a double-blind placebo-controlled study of the effect of thioridazine and amphetamine on 14 behavior and academic variables demonstrated by 21 children, aged 7–12 years and with IQs of 55–85, Alexandris and Lundell (1968) found amphetamine in dosages of 7.5 to 75 mg/day to be effective on only two of the academic measures (comprehension and work interest). Lobb's (1968) double-blind placebo-controlled design found that 0.2 mg/kg of DL-amphetamine sulfate was detrimental to institutionalized "mentally retarded" individuals 18 to 30 years of age in a classical conditioning paradigm measuring the galvanic skin response.

In 1969 Anton and Greer studied the effects of acute and chronic 10 mg doses of dextroamphetamine sulfate on urinary levels of catecholamines and their metabolites, and on the behavior of 6 nonverbal and nonambulatory boys (6–9 years old, estimated IQ below 30). At baseline the boys were described as being in a state "characterized by a poverty of behavioral responsiveness" (p. 250). In two of the children there was an increased awareness of stimuli, a persistence in their attitude toward objects confronting them, a lessening of random activity, and an increase in vocalization" (p. 230) during the 3-week chronic drug phase. With continued drug administration these improvements were later replaced by anorexia, restlessness, insomnia, and fretfulness. These behavioral changes were accompanied by a minimal effect on catecholamine metabolism.

Are stimulants good for treatment of mentally retarded individuals?

Besides what some researchers feel is an absence of proof of effectiveness, there is also a fear that stimulants may cause a worsening of symptoms. Campbell et al. (1972) studied the effects of dexedrine on 16 children in a psychiatric inpatient service. Ten of the children were schizophrenic, 2 were autistic, and the rest were not psychotic. The children ranged in age from 3 to 6 years and had IQs and DQs ranging from 20 to 102. Approximately half of the children had mental retardation. The dose of dextroamphetamine was titrated for each child. "Optimal" doses of dextroamphetamine ranged from 1.25 to 10 mg per day. Psychotic children were said to tolerate lower doses of dextroamphetamine (M = 4 mg/day) than the nonpsychotic children (M = 7.5 mg/day). Slight global improvement was reported in 3 of the schizophrenic children (two of whom were of normal intelligence) and in one autistic child with mental retardation. The authors felt that dextroamphetamine had a generally disorganizing and deteriorating effect on the psychotic and nonpsychotic children. Of note was a worsening in irritability, withdrawal, and stereotypy in approximately half of the children taking dextroamphetamine, but there was no information about how symptom deterioration correlated with IQ. In 1975, Campbell reviewed the literature on pharmacotherapy in early infantile autism and concluded that "The psychotic child who shows some overall improvement on dextroamphetamine with decrease in hyperactivity and increase in attention span, may at the same time become more withdrawn and less verbal" (p. 124). The review did not take into consideration the cognitive abilities of the psychotic children being discussed except to state that most autistic children were "severely deviant and retarded" (p. 411).

METHYLPHENIDATE (RITALIN)

Behavior problems associated with mental retardation

One of the early reports of the use of methylphenidate (MPH) with children and adults with severe behavior disorders involved reserpine as the comparison drug (Zimmerman and Burgemeister, 1958). Subjects were private patients ranging in age from 4 years to 33 years, and "several of the patients were mentally retarded." Target symptoms or behaviors were anxiety, hyperactivity, aggression, withdrawal, depression, and irritability. The behavior problems of the patients with mental retardation were said to "differ little from the others except in degree," at "any intellectual level" (p. 323). Based on ratings by a neuropsychiatrist (better, same, worse), the drugs were found to have overlapping effects, but MPH appeared to be more effective for symptoms of fatigue, listlessness, poor self-motivation, or lack of energy. There was no mention of a differential effect based on either intellectual level or age. Blue et al. (1962) used a placebo-controlled design to measure the effects of MPH on intellectually handicapped children with measured IQs between 48 and 78. The results were suggestive of an improved performance on some areas of tests of achievement, and mental maturity, and a teacher rating scale.

Connors and Eisenberg (1963) used a double-blind placebo-controlled strategy to study the effect of up to 30 mg of MPH twice a day on behavioral and emotional symptoms, paired-associate learning, and Porteus maze (Porteus, 1959) performance of 81 institutionalized children in children 7 to 15 years with IQs between 65 and 135. The experimental and control groups were matched for IQ. The results showed large individual differences in response to the drug, with a total weighted symptom score showing a significant improvement in the treated group. Of note was the finding that, while the drug group had significantly higher scores on both the paired-associate learning task and the mazes, the children with IQs between 65 and 79, and between 80 and 91, showed significantly greater gains from the MPH in the maze test than did children with IQs between 94 and 135.

A double-blind placebo-controlled crossover design, with each child acting as his own control, was used to study the effect of a fixed dose of 10 mg of MPH twice a day on academic functioning and behavior in three classes of children with mental retardation (Blacklidge and Ekblad, 1971). The class IQs ranged from 66 to 73. Teacher ratings of classroom behavior showed statistically significant improvement when the drug was administered. There were no significant improvements in standardized tests of reading or arithmetic.

Davis (1971) studied the effects of a stimulant (MPH) versus a "depressant" (thioridazine) on operant learning of 10 institutionalized males with mental retardation. Five of the subjects had IQs below 30 and the rest were described as moderately retarded with IQs above 30. The severely retarded group ranged in age from 15-1 to 21-7 years. The moderately retarded group ranged in age from 12-9 to 16-9 years. MPH was given in a dose of 0.5 mg/kg two hours before the experimental session began, and placebos were used. Dependent variables were response rate, pause time between the start of a session and the correct response (either rocking or bar pressing), and total number of reinforcements obtained. MPH resulted in significantly improved response rate for most subjects and an improvement in the pause time measure for some subjects. MPH also produced a deterioration in pause time for those subjects whose baseline measures were poor. The author did not speculate about whether the results might be due to a drug-induced increase in stereotypic behavior (rocking) or rather represented a drug-related enhancement of learning, but she did conclude that there are significant individual differences in response to drug administration which could be due to biological factors, for example, drug absorption rates, neurophysiological differences, or environmental-organismic interactions.

A double-blind placebo-controlled crossover design was used on 10 children ranging in age from 4.6 to 15 years, with IQs ranging from 49 to 77, who were living with their families or in stable foster homes, and who were attending special education programs in public schools (Varley and Trupin, 1982). The children were diagnosed as having an attention deficit disorder and were treated with MPH 5–120 mg/day in two divided doses. Measures of "hyperkinesis" were scores on the Conners Parent and Teachers Questionnaire (Conners, 1973). Half of the children received significantly improved mean ratings on the drug as compared to the placebo condition. The high-dose condition (0.6 mg/kg/day) showed significantly more improvement than the low-dose condition (0.3 mg/kg/day). Measures of cognition or learning were not obtained.

Using a within-subject, double-blind placebo-controlled design, Christensen (1975) compared the effect of a token reinforcement program with and without MPH on 10 behavioral and academic measures on 16 hyperactive institutionalized children (age range 9–15.8 years) with mental retardation. Fourteen subjects were in the mild to moderately retarded range while one each was classified as borderline or severely retarded. MPH was given 1.5 h before class in a dose of 0.3 mg/kg and time-sampled observations of deviant and attending or work-oriented behavior were recorded. The classroom management program was found to be very effective in reducing deviant behavior and there was only a weak enhancement of behavioral treatment effect on two measures (deviant behaviors and inappropriate vocalizations) when MPH was substituted for placebo.

Aman and Singh (1982) studied the effects of two doses of MPH (0.3 mg/kg and 0.6 mg/kg given once daily at breakfast) on the behavior of 28 institutionalized adolescents and adults with severe to profound mental retardation (X IQ 11.96). The design was double-blind, placebo-controlled, crossover. The high dose resulted in some subjects showing significant improvement in social behavior, posturing during meals, and rating scale measures of Aggression/Disruption and Emotionality/Crying. Because the evidence for consistent beneficial effects of stimulants on the behavior of persons with severe mental retardation was not compelling, the authors recommend that further investigations of these drugs in people with severe mental retardation be discouraged.

More recently, Aman et al. (1990) reported data to support the earlier idea that the response of children with mental retardation to MPH varies with the intelligence of the child. In a group of 30 hyperactive children ages 4.1 to 16.5 years, with IQs between 25 and 90 and mental ages (MA) between 2.0 and 9.9 years, they measured the effect of MPH (0.4 mg/kg/day given once a day in the morning) and thioridazine (1.75 mg/kg/day in two doses) on teacher and parent reports of behavior, as well as on a variety of laboratory tests. They found improvement, especially with MPH, on a global teacher rating and on teacher ratings of conduct, inattention, and hyperactivity. This improvement was significantly greater in the children with MAs equal to or greater than 5 years than in children with MAs below 5 years. In general, only the higher MA children (57% of the group) could perform the laboratory tests, but there was a significant enhancement of functioning, especially with MPH, on tests of: matching to a sample (measures of accuracy and the longest delay recorded); tremor on a test of fine motor coordination; and, continuous performance (measuring errors of omission and seat activity). Ten of the seventeen children with IQs above 45 were recommended to continue with MPH, while only 1 of the 13 children with IQs below 45 were recommended for continuation of MPH at the conclusion of the study.

Looking at specifically defined hyperactive behaviors in three boys with mild retardation in a psychiatric inpatient program, Payton et al. (1989) used double-blind placebo-controlled single case strategies to study the effect of MPH on excessive movement, on-task responses, and ratings of a 15-item modification of the Conners Teacher Rating Scale (Conners, 1969) in two of the boys. The boys were diagnosed as having an attention deficit disorder with hyperactivity (ADHD) (APA, 1980, pp. 41–44), and were referred for hospitalization because of physical intrusiveness, noncompliance, aggression, and/or self-abusive behavior. The study was carried out while the boys were part of a comprehensive behavior management program. One child was studied on 10 mg (0.40 mg/kg/dose), 15 mg (0.60 mg/kg/dose), or 20 mg (0.80 mg/kg/dose) of MPH twice a day, while the other was given 5 mg (0.28 mg/kg/dose), 10 mg (0.55 mg/kg/dose), 15 mg (0.83 mg/kg/dose), or 20 mg (1.10 mg/kg/dose) of MPH twice a day. Observations of classroom behavior were made 90 minutes after the morning dose. There was a greater reduction in percentage of intervals with excessive movement and improvement of percentage of intervals with on-task behavior, as well as a significant reduction of the Conners scores, during the MPH phase compared with baseline and placebo phases. For one child the effects of the 15 and 20 mg doses were indistinguishable, while for the other, 5 mg was ineffective and the data did not clearly distinguish between the magnitude of the beneficial effects of the 10, 15, or 20 mg doses. For this child, dyskinetic movements of the mouth, head, and shoulders were noted during the administration of the 15 and 20 mg doses, but not following administration of 10 mg bid either during the study and with continued administration after the study. The authors note that the improvement in the children's functioning was gradual rather than immediate, suggesting, among other things, an interaction between the behavioral and medication components of the treatment and/or a learning effect.

Pervasive developmental disorders

Until recently, most textbooks and articles dealing with pharmacotherapy of children with pervasive developmental disorders indicated that stimulants had a limited role in the treatment of autism because, on balance, negative side effects (e.g., worsening of pre-existing stereotypies, stereotypies de novo, withdrawal, irritability, aggressiveness, psychosis, and oversedation) far outweigh the positive effects (e.g., decreased hyperactivity and increased attention span) (Campbell, 1975, 1978; Campbell et al., 1972, 1985; Klein et al., 1981). The current report of the Task Force on Treatment of Psychiatric Disorders of the American Psychiatric Association (Aman, 1989) concludes that "at this time, the use of stimulants in autism must be regarded as contentious at best" (p. 92). In a new text, a discussion of the use of stimulants in the treatment of autistic children (Holm and Varley, 1989) concludes that "Consideration for their use might be entertained in a high-functioning autistic child in whom short attention span, distractibility, and excitability are significant symptoms" (p. 388).

Nevertheless, there have been some more enthusiastic single case reports of children with mental retardation and pervasive developmental disorders (Geller et al., 1981; Strayhorn et al., 1988; Vitriol and Farber, 1981) as well as reports of groups of children with mental retardation and pervasive developmental disorders (Birmaher et al., 1988; Hoshino et al., 1977) who on balance, appeared to improve on dextroamphetamine or MPH.

Hoshino et al. reported treating autistic children with MPH in doses of 0.3–1.0 mg/kg per day, given before breakfast. A 4-point global estimate of clinical improvement was used based on clinical observations and 2 rating scales. Sixty percent of the children were rated as "much improved" or "very much improved," with symptoms such as "hyperactivity," "impulsiveness," and "extreme aloneness" showing improvement in more than 50% of the cases. Self-mutilative or aggressive behavior was seen as a side effect in 4 children, but this responded to dosage reduction. There were not enough data to show how many of these autistic children also had mental retardation, however, one of the two case reports in the article stated that a 3-year-old male showed "retardation of intelligence" (p. 611).

In the Birmaher et al. study there were 9 children between the ages of 4 and 16 years whose measured intelligence ranged from severe mental retardation to borderline intellectual functioning. This was an open trial, with the dose of MPH ranging from 10 to 50 mg/day. The children showed significant improvement in both the Conners Parent Questionnaire and Conners Teacher Questionnaire (Conners, 1969, 1973). There was no significant worsening of, or de novo, stereotypic movements. The authors felt that the discrepancy between their results and results reported by others could either represent the fact that different diagnostic entities (e.g., childhood schizophrenia vs. autism) were studied or that amphetamines are more potent inducers of stereotypic movements than MPH.

Strayhorn et al. (1988) conducted a single case experiment with an open trial of MPH, up to 10 mg (0.5 mg/kg) twice a day, in a 6-year-old boy with mild to moderate mental retardation. Drug and placebo days were assigned randomly. Both teacher and parent ratings were used. According to parent ratings, MPH significantly helped to improve concentration and to reduce hyperactivity. There were also significant improvements on destructiveness (of own and others property), disobedience, and stereotyped movements. There were significant deteriorations in ratings of sadness and temper tantrums. Teachers reported significantly fewer stereotyped movements and the boy had significantly higher ratings of obedience. "Blinded" research associates reported significantly more appropriate verbal behavior on drug days.

Both Birmaher et al.(1988) and Strayhorn et al. (1988) feel that their results warrant further investigation of the use of MPH with mentally retarded autistic children.

For drug-induced drowsiness

There have been reports of the use of MPH to counteract drug-induced drowsiness or over sedation. Carter (1956), citing reports of MPH being found to be useful in reducing reserpine-induced lethargy and depression, gave 5 to 10 mg of MPH 2 or 3 times a day to institutionalized patients with mental retardation or epilepsy who were felt to be lethargic, dull, or oversedated as a result of being treated with reserpine for hypertension and/or behavior problems, and/or anticonvulsants for seizure disorders. The patients ranged in age from 3 to 58 years with IQs ranging from 19 to 68. Although no tests of significance were used, ratings by staff members indicated that the reserpine–MPH combination was useful in improving learning, behavior, and sociability, and was free of side effects of appetite, sleep, or degree of nervousness. MPH was also felt to reduce the lethargy and dullness of epileptics who were on high doses of anticonvulsants, and to increase the functional level of these individuals.

One year later there was a report of a double-blind, placebo-controlled study of the effects of MPH on 61 institutionalized patients who were receiving reserpine or chlorpromazine for "antisocial behavior" (assaultiveness, self-mutilation, persistent noiseness, etc.) and/or phenobarbital or Dilantin for seizures (Levy et al., 1957). Patients' IQ range was 20–80 and the youngest was 11 years of age. Drowsiness ratings were slight to severe. MPH was given in doses of 10 mg, tid, and 20 mg, tid. The patients were rated by ward aides as being significantly more alert when taking 20 mg tid dose and there was no significant deterioration in antisocial behaviors, numbers of seizures, or sleep patterns.

Stereotypy

Randrup and Munkvad (1967) used the word "stereotype" to describe "a form of behavior with little variation" (p. 300) which is felt to be purposeless or compulsive and which dominates the behavior of a human or an animal. Such behavior had been used to describe abnormal behavior of animals after amphetamine administration, and Randrup and Munkvad described a number of experiments in which animals ranging from birds to primates developed stereotypies when injected with amphetamines in doses of 1 to 20 mg/kg. They also reviewed the literature on the production of psychosis in humans following the administration of higher than therapeutic doses. They noted that a prominent features of amphetamine psychosis is stereotyped activity.

Since stereotypies are often a prominent symptom of individuals with mental retardation (Baumeister and Forehand, 1973) and autism, (Freeman et al., 1981), Davis et al. (1969) studied the effect of what they felt to be therapeutic doses of MPH (0.44 mg/kg) and thioridazine (Mellaril) (1.3 mg/kg) on the behavior of 9 institutionalized males, from 11.10 to 20.5 years. IQ range was 4–24. Each subject was his own control and placebo doses were used. The experimenters used a checklist to measure whole body, head, face, and arm movements as well as self-abuse and environmental manipulation. They also used a telemetric motion transducer to record movements. They found large inter- and intraindividual variations in measured behaviors, but MPH neither increased nor decreased stereotypies over the 4 days of the study. Campbell et al. (1972) reported an increase in stereotypies in psychotic children given dextroamphetamine, but this study included children with a wide range of cognitive abilities and it was not clear whether worsening of stereotypies was in any way related to IQ. Aman and Singh (1982), studying the effects of MPH on a variety of problem behaviors, including stereotypic behavior of adolescents and adults with severe to profound mental retardation, found no difference on the stereotypy dimension of the AAMD Adaptive Behavior Scale (Nihira et al., 1974).

RECENT USE OF RITALIN IN THE COMMUNITY

Children with mental retardation living in the community are more likely to be administered stimulant drugs than those living in institutions (Gadow, 1985).

In 1981, Gadow and Kalachnick reported on the results of a questionnaire mailed to teachers of trainable mentally retarded (TMR) students in public schools. They received an 87% response rate, and found that 4.9% of the TMR students were receiving medication for behavior disorders (e.g., hyperactivity, aggression, attention deficits, and psychotic behaviors). MPH was prescribed for 2.7% of the TMR students and for 42% of all the students treated for behavior disorders. In this group, psychotropic drugs were prescribed most often to students between 9 and 14 years of age and MPH was prescribed in daily doses of between 5 and 80 mg. The median daily dose of MPH was 48 mg, and the duration of treatment with medication ranged from 4 to 156 months.

Gadow (1982, 1983) used a teacher questionnaire and parent interview to determine the prescribing practices and the frequency and type of parent and teacher involvement when children in early childhood special education programs (ECSE) and in classrooms for TMR were placed on medication for behavior disorders. He found that hyperactivity was the most common reason for prescribing medication in both groups and that MPH was the most commonly prescribed drug in both groups. The 52 children in the ECSE sample were between 4 and 6 years old and the 48 students in the TMR sample were between 8 and 22 years. School personnel (26%) and physicians (14%) were cited as most often suggesting that the child receive a medical evaluation. In the TMR group, pediatricians (40%), general practice physicians (19%), neurologists (12%), and psychiatrists (12%) were the types of physicians who most often decided to prescribe medication. Up to 61% of the TMR students were monitored by three or more office visits per year while 43% of the ECSE students were seen at this rate. About a fourth of the parents felt that the doctors did not allow them enough time to inquire about medication, their child's condition, therapeutic progress, and treatment alternatives. Teachers and physician interaction was reported to be uncommon. In 61% of the cases there was complete agreement between parents and teachers regarding the efficacy of drug treatment, and in 19% there was complete disagreement. Teachers reported side effects in 42% of the ECSE students treated with stimulants. Such symptoms as blank or zombie-like stare, spaced-out look, unusual stillness, withdrawal from social interaction, stereotyped behavior, and drowsiness and/or lethargy are felt to represent an overfocusing of attention. Over a third of the parents claimed they were allowed to adjust the dosage of medication if the parent believed that the amount of medication should be increased for special situations. The studies showed that while the teachers participated in the treatment process in over three-fourths of the cases, behavior rating scales were rarely used to monitor and document the medication effects, two-thirds of the teachers were not informed of the side effects associated with the prescribed medication, and a third to half of the teachers participated in the decision to terminate treatment. Teachers in both types of classes felt that MPH was an effective treatment for hyperactivity and there was disagreement about drug effectiveness between teacher and parent in only a small percentage of cases.

Some recommendations for outpatient monitoring of Ritalin

Gadow (1983) makes a number of recommendations which he feels would enhance the efficacy and utility of outpatient pharmacotherapy. He feels that standardized procedures should be used to evaluate both the positive and negative effects of medication. He urges that lines of communication be kept open with the school and that medication should be reduced and possibly discontinued periodically to see if it is still needed. He points out that while carrying out dosage reduction one must wait long enough for rebound effects to wear off before deciding on a future course of action. There also should be some way to try to monitor child and parent compliance; however, this is not as easy to do with stimulants as it is with neuroleptics, tricyclic antidepressants, anticonvulsants, or lithium. Finally, he urges that the effects of the medication on the acquisition of new skills be assessed.

THE CHILDREN'S EVALUATION AND REHABILITATION CENTER (CERC)

The Children's Evaluation and Rehabilitation Center (CERC) of the Albert Einstein College of Medicine is a University-based outpatient diagnostic and treatment center, in an urban setting, serving developmentally disabled children and adolescents from birth to the age of 21 years. One of the treatment components of CERC is a multidisciplinary Medication Clinic. The Medication Clinic was designed so that both pediatricians and psychiatrists could evaluate the behavior and medication requirements of children referred to the clinic by other CERC units. Since this clinic provides training to pediatricians rotating through CERC the prescribing physicians could be pediatric residents, board-certified or eligible pediatric fellows in developmental pediatrics or board-certified or board-eligible child psychiatrists. The clinical director is a child psychiatrist, while many administrative as well as clinical details are handled by a pediatric nurse practitioner. The parent(s) and child are seen at least once during the initial evaluation of the child and on an as-needed basis by a certified social worker. All children referred to the clinic from other CERC units have been seen by a pediatrician with neurodevelopmental training and almost all have had a psychological evaluation. Many have had psychoeducational evaluations and/or speech and language evaluations, and many parents have been seen by a social worker for a psychosocial evaluation prior to being referred to the Medication Clinic. Some children are receiving other treatment services (occupational therapy, physiotherapy, speech and/or language therapy, educational remediation, nutritional counseling, or psychotherapy) in conjunction with pharmacotherapy.

The intake process of the Medication Clinic entails a pediatrician reviewing the reports of the evaluations the child has had at CERC or other agencies. This is followed by a history from the parent(s) and child (if appropriate) of the past and present behavioral problems for which the child has been referred to the Medication Clinic. An appropriate treatment plan is then discussed with a child psychiatrist. The treatment options are discussed with the parent(s) and child (if appropriate). If medication is agreed upon as a part of the treatment plan the parent(s) and child (if appropriate) are told about possible beneficial medication effects and possible adverse effects of the medication. The parent(s) and child (if appropriate) then sign a written consent for Medication (see Appendix 1) to document that they have been informed of the potential benefits and side effects of the medication the child is to receive. Appropriate baseline laboratory tests are performed or ordered and a medical screening (height, weight, blood pressure, pulse rate, osculation of the heart and lungs) is done.

Methylphenidate

When hyperactivity or impulsivity or a short attention span are target symptoms we feel that MPH is the drug to be tried first in children as young as 3 years of age. Although hyperactivity is associated with many diagnoses (Fish, 1971) (i.e., attention deficit hyperactivity disorder, mental retardation, pervasive developmental disorders, depression, anxiety, childhood schizophrenia) we feel that, except for childhood schizophrenia and anxiety disorders, MPH has the lowest risk/benefit ratio of most alternative medications (e.g., neuroleptics, tricyclics, antidepressants). The latter have much more serious short- and long-term side effects (e.g., cardiac conduction defects, tardive dyskinesia), than does MPH.

The short version of the Conners Teacher Rating Scale is sent to the child's teacher to get a baseline measure of the child's behavior. If the child is not yet in school, parents are asked to rate those items.

The hospital pharmacy used by CERC only stocks the 10 mg standard MPH tablet and the 20 mg sustained release preparation. Because of this, all children are started with 5 mg or 10 mg of Ritalin once or twice a day.

The parent is asked to split the 10 mg tablet in half to get the 5 mg dose. The dosage is adjusted at subsequent clinic visits.

Children are seen at the clinic between once every 2 weeks and once every 3 months. More frequent visits are necessary at the beginning of treatment to monitor side effects and adjust dosage or dosage schedule. Measures of height, weight, blood pressure, and pulse rate are taken each visit. The parent(s) and child (if appropriate) are asked about side effects and main effects of MPH. The clinician rates the degree of change in target symptoms on a 5-point scale ("much worse," "worse," "same," "improved," "much improved"). If necessary, there is an adjustment of dose or schedule of administration.

The clinician should investigate further when the teacher is dissatisfied with the results of the pharmacotherapy. One can start by asking the teacher to complete another Conners Teachers Rating Form and/or contact her by telephone. Teachers usually are aware of who is prescribing the medication and on occasion, will telephone the clinic to speak to the clinic physician. Even when classroom behavior is improved, teachers are most often concerned about the apparent lack of effectiveness of medication as evidenced by impulsive, aggressive, or hyperactive behavior on the school bus, in the cafeteria, or in the playground. Such problems often require some environmental manipulation (e.g., an additional bus monitor, a paraprofessional to help the child in the cafeteria) and/or an adjustment in dosage or schedule of administration of the drug.

The children: response to MPH in the CERC population

There are 37 children with mental retardation currently active in CERC who are or have been treated with Ritalin. This population consists of 34 males and 3 females. Seventeen children with mental retardation are currently receiving the drug. The average age of the children at the time they began treatment was 7 years with a range of 3 to 15 years. There was no difference between the currently active and discontinued groups with respect to gender, or age at which they began treatment. The average length of time on medication for the entire sample was 29.8 months (range, 1–86 months). The children/adolescents who discontinued treatment did so at an average age of 9 years 4 months (range, 4–21 years), while the group that continues to receive MPH has an average age of 10 years 4 months (range, 4–21 years).

Sixteen of the children had mild retardation (Table 1), while 7 had moderate retardation and 10 had severe to profound mental retardation. In 4 children the degree of retardation was not specified. In addition to the diagnosis of mental retardation, 17 children had an attention deficit hyperactivity disorder (ADHD) (APA, 1987, pp. 50–53), 10 had an autistic disorder (AD) (APA, 1987, pp. 38–39), and 8 had a pervasive developmental disorder not otherwise specified (PDDNOS) (APA, 1987, p. 39). Additionally, 4 children had developmental language disorders, 2 had an oppositional defiant disorder (APA, 1987, pp. 56–58), and 1 had functional enuresis. The children also had other medical disorders such as a seizure disorder (5 children), cerebral palsy (2 children), and one child each had one of the following: fetal alcohol syndrome; psoriasis; profound hearing loss; Laurence-Moon-Biedl syndrome; and the Cornelia de Lange syndrome.

The symptoms

The presenting problems (Table 2) of the children with mental retardation who were treated with MPH ran the gamut of internalizing and externalizing symptomatology. Hyperactivity was present in all of the children. Seventy percent of the children had impulsivity and 57% were aggressive. Sleep disturbance and/or negativism were present in slightly more than a third of the children. Autistic symptomatology, for example, mannerisms or rocking, were occasionally among the presenting symptoms (8%), but these were not the primary target symptoms when MPH was used. Symptoms of depression were present in only two children.

Dosage

The children were started off at mean of 0.24 mg/kg/dose (range, 0.1–0.5 mg/kg/dose). There was no significant difference between the children whose MPH had been discontinued and those who continue to

TABLE 1. DIAGNOSES OF 37 CHILDREN TREATED WITH MPH

Diagnosis	Number of Children
Mental Retardation	
Mild	16
Moderate	7
Severe/Profound	10
Unspecified	4
ADHD/ADDH	17
AD/IA	10
PDDNOS/APDD	8
ODD	2
Functional enuresis	1
Developmental language disorder	4
Profound hearing loss	1
Seizure disorder	5
Cerebral palsy	2
Fetal alcohol syndrome	1
Laurence-Moon-Biedl syndrome	1
Cornelia de Lange syndrome	1
Psoriasis	1

Abbreviations: Attention deficit hyperactivity disorder/Attention deficit disorder with hyperactivity; Autistic disorder/Infantile autism; Pervasive developmental disorder not otherwise specified/Atypical pervasive developmental disorder; Oppositional defiant disorder.

receive it at: the currently prescribed mg/kg/dose; the highest total daily dose of MPH; or, the highest mg/kg/dose. For the entire sample, the mean mg/kg/dose is 0.47 (range, 0.1–1.2). The mean highest mg/kg/dose is 0.52 (range, 0.1–1.3), and the mean highest daily dose is 30.1 mg. (range, 10–90).

Although 60 mg of Ritalin is the suggested maximum dose (*PDR*, 1990), some patients with mental retardation require more. The individual currently receiving 90 mg of MPH is 21 years old and is taking 0.7 mg/kg/dose three times a day. He has an autistic disorder and has been receiving MPH for 7 years. He is also receiving 125 mg of Thorazine at bedtime and 350 mg of Benadryl throughout the course of the day to relieve itching caused by psoriasis. He lives at home and his mother feels that smaller doses of MPH result in a deterioration of her son's behavior. A nine-year-old boy, with an autistic disorder and profound mental retardation, had been taking 80 mg of MPH per day, when it was discontinued after 6 years because of a lack of effectiveness. At the time of discontinuation he was taking 1.2 mg/kg per dose as well as 25 mg of Mellaril twice a day and 64 mg of phenobarbitol at bedtime. He is currently on 200 mg Mellaril twice a day, 0.1 mg clonidine twice a day, as well as 200 mg Tegretol twice a day, and 32 mg phenobarbital twice a day.

Results

Children with mild and severe/profound mental retardation are as likely to remain on MPH as to be discontinued for reasons of adverse side effects or ineffectiveness (Table 2). There is a trend for children with moderate retardation to be overrepresented in the discontinued group, but this is not statistically significant. Children with ADD and ADHD are also as likely to benefit from MPH over a continued period of time as to be discontinued because of side effects or lack of effect. Children with PDDNOS, however, are more likely to be discontinued ($p = 0.05$) from MPH treatment than to continue on treatment. Most of these children were discontinued because of reported side effects, but it is the authors' impression that children who present with hyperactivity as a symptom of PDDNOS are unlikely to have a significant reduction in this symptom

TABLE 2. CONTINUATION OF TREATMENT ACCORDING TO DIAGNOSIS AND
COMMON SYMPTOMS

Diagnosis	Number of Ritalin Continued (%)	Number with MPH Discontinued (%)	
Mental Retardation			
Mild	8 (47)	8 (40)	NS
Moderate	1 (6)	6 (30)	NS
Severe/Profound	5 (29)	5 (25)	NS
Unspecified	3 (18)	1 (5)	NS
ADHD/ADDH	10 (59)	7 (35)	NS
cAD/IA	4 (24)	6 (30)	NS
PDDNOS/APDD	1 (6)	7 (35)	$p = 0.05$
Symptoms			
Hyperactivity	17 (100)	20 (100)	NS
Impulsivity	11 (65)	15 (75)	NS
Aggression	10 (59)	11 (55)	NS
Negativism	6 (35)	7 (35)	NS
Sleep disturbance	7 (41)	7 (35)	NS
Anxiety	1 (6)	7 (35)	$p = 0.05$
Depression	1 (6)	1 (5)	NS

Abbreviations: See Table 1.

from pharmacotherapy in general and MPH in particular. One other difference between the children who remained on MPH and those who did not occurred around the presence or absence of anxiety as a presenting symptom. Children who presented with anxiety in their symptom picture were more likely to have discontinued ($p = 0.05$) than to remain on this drug.

There were two children in this study who did not have a psychiatric diagnosis other than mental retardation. Both of these children are currently receiving MPH with good results. One child is 12 years 10 months, has an unspecified degree of mental retardation, and has been taking MPH for 28 months. The other child is 4 years 2 months, has severe retardation, and has been on MPH for 3 months.

Side effects

Seventeen children developed significant side effects which fell into 11 different categories (Table 3). Sleep disturbance, appetite changes, and mood changes were the most common side effects reported. MPH had to be discontinued in 12 children (32%) because of side effects, but in 3 of these cases the dosage level had been raised to 0.8 mg/kg/dose or above before the side effects became a problem. This suggests that, in these three cases the drug was simply ineffective for these children.

Of the 10 children with severe to profound mental retardation, all had reported side effects and 3 (30%) had side effects (anxiety, depression, possible psychosis) severe enough to require discontinuation. A 14-year-old boy with severe mental retardation and a PDDNOS had his MPH dose raised from 30/mg per day (0.3 mg/kg/dose) to 40 mg per day (0.4 mg/kg/dose). He then became increasingly agitated and violent. Of the 7 children with moderate mental retardation, 3 (43%) had side effects (elevated pulse and blood pressure, irritability and crying, loss of appetite) severe enough to warrant discontinuation. Six of the 16 (38%) children with mild retardation had side effects significant enough to require discontinuation. Of these, 2 had sleep disturbance, 1 had an appetite disturbance with weight loss, 1 was tearful and irritable, 1 complained that his teeth hurt, and 1 child had an elevation in his anticonvulsant (carbamazepine) blood level to a toxic range. In all cases the side effects disappeared when the MPH was discontinued.

TABLE 3. SIDE EFFECTS REPORTED IN 17 CHILDREN

Types of Side Effects	Number of Children
Sleep disturbances	6
Poor appetite/weight loss	4
Mood changes: crying, irritable, depressed	3
Cardiovascular: rapid pulse, elevated blood pressure	1
Anxiety with increased activity level	1
Amphetamine like psychosis	1
Stereotyped behavior/tics	1
Sore teeth/gums	1
Sedation	1
Enuresis	1
Increased anticonvulsant level (carbamazepine)	1

CONCLUSION

Common behavioral problems associated with varying degrees of mental retardation include a variety of internalizing and externalizing symptoms. One recurring finding in research on the use of stimulants (e.g., MPH) with children with mental retardation has been a lack of consistency or predictability with regard to just which patient characteristics (i.e., age, IQ, associated diagnosis, type of symptoms) are associated with positive treatment effects with minimal side effects. There has been some agreement that children in the upper range of mental retardation, with associated symptoms of hyperactivity and impulsivity, are more likely to benefit from stimulant medication. Nevertheless, there are some children with moderate to severe mental retardation and/or with symptoms of a pervasive developmental disorder who do have symptoms of hyperactivity or impulsivity which are ameliorated by stimulants. This study indicates that a trial of MPH seems warranted when a child with mental retardation has symptoms of hyperactivity or impulsivity. Neither IQ alone nor psychiatric diagnosis alone (with the possible exception of PDDNOS) were found to be useful in predicting which particular child will not benefit from MPH. The drug is a particularly safe medication compared with other medications (e.g., neuroleptics, tricyclic antidepressants) used to treat children with mental retardation and other psychiatric disorders.

Our clinic employs a broad range of therapeutic dosages. The average mg/kg/dose required for clinical improvement in children who continue to take MPH (0.41) is well within the range which is reported to be effective in children without cognitive limitations. Relatively high doses (greater than 1.0 mg/kg/dose; more than 50 mg/day) have been employed with good clinical results and, for the most part, minimal side effects.

The incidence of side effects leading to discontinuation of MPH in children with mental retardation is at least as high, or perhaps higher than the general population of children receiving MPH. However, with the exception of 2 cases, 1 in which the drug resulted in an elevation of the blood level of carbamazepine to a toxic range, and the other in which there were symptoms suggestive of an amphetamine psychosis, the side effects were unpleasant but not excessively distressing to the child. In all cases the children recovered rapidly after the MPH was discontinued. The major complaints from teachers are of irritability or loss of appetite. There have been no complaints about a decrement in the ability to learn. MPH was more likely to be discontinued when parents or children complained of side effects. The reporting of side effects approached significance as a marker of a poor prognosis for continued MPH use in children with mental retardation living in an urban community.

Although there do not appear to be any absolute contraindications for the use of MPH in children with mental retardation this author does not use it as first-line medication when associated diagnoses are either childhood schizophrenia (especially when hallucinations are present) or any diagnosable anxiety disorder. The presence of tics in the child, or a family history of tics, is also a relative contraindication for its use. This study also suggests the lack of effectiveness of MPH in those atypical children with mental retardation who are hyperactive but have too few symptoms of a pervasive developmental disorder to be classified as having an autistic disorder. The results of the present study also indicate that even when there is no diagnosable anxiety disorder, MPH probably will not be useful in children with mental retardation if anxiety exists as a prominent presenting symptom along with hyperactivity or impulsivity.

APPENDIX 1

ROSE F. KENNEDY CENTER
CHILDREN'S EVALUATION AND REHABILITATION CENTER
CONSENT FOR MEDICATION
STIMULANTS

I know that medications are a necessary elements of my child's treatment program. I have been informed of the type of medication, dose, treated symptoms, side effects, and toxic effects of the medication my child is taking. I know that this medication is being given to treat my child's _____ ..

If my child is taking a stimulant drug (Ritalin, Dexedrine, or Cylert), I understand that this may result in a loss of appetite, and a slowing down of the rate of growth and rate of weight gain. There may also be the appearance of facial tics or the onset of stomach aches or headaches. Depression or sudden unexplained episodes of crying may also be present. There may be a sleep disturbance, or a rise in blood pressure.

There may be a lowering of the seizure threshold or the appearance of stereotypic behaviors. A transient toxic psychosis may occur.

I understand that side effects will be monitored during my child's visits to the CERC Medication Clinic. If I have any questions about side effects between visits I will call the telephone number on my clinic appointment card. If I am unable to reach a doctor or nurse I will stop the medication until I am able to do so.

I have been informed of other methods used to treat these symptoms and I have had my questions about this form of treatment answered. I have received no guarantee regarding results that may be obtained from the use of these medications.

MINOR'S ASSENT:_____

DATE:_____

SIGNATURE: _____   RELATIONSHIP:_____

WITNESS: _____   CHILD'S NAME:_____

CONSENT OBTAINED BY: _____

REFERENCES

Alexandris, A. & Lundell, F.W. (1968), Effect of thioridazine, amphetamine, and placebo on the hyperkinetic syndrome and cognitive area in mentally deficit children. Can. Med. Assoc. J., 98:92–96.

Aman, M.G. (1982), Stimulant drug effects in developmental disorders and hyperactivity—Toward a resolution of disparate findings. J. Aut. Devel. Dis., 12:385–398.

——— (1983), Psychoactive drugs in mental retardation. In: Treatment Issues and Innovations in Mental Retardation, eds. J.L. Matson & F. Andrasik. New York: Plenum Press, pp. 453–513.

———— (1989), Psychostimulant drugs. In: *Treatment of Psychiatric Disorders: A Task Force Report of the American Psychiatric Association*, Vol. 1. Washington, DC: American Psychiatric Association, pp. 91–93.

———— Singh, N.N. (1982), Methylphenidate in severely retarded residents and the clinical significance of stereotypic behavior. *Appl. Res. Mental Retard.*, 3:345–358.

———— Marks, R.E., Turbott, S.H., Wilsher, C.P. & Merry, S.N. (1991), Clinical effects of methylphenidate and thioridazine in intellectually subaverage children. *Adolsc. Psychiatry*, 30:246–256.

American Psychiatric Association (1980), *Diagnostic and Statistical Manual of Mental Disorders*, 3rd Ed. Washington, DC: American Psychiatric Association.

———— (1987), Diagnostic and Statistical Manual of Mental Disorders, 3rd Ed., rev. Washington, DC: American Psychiatric Association.

Anton, A.H. & Greer, M. (1969), Dextroamphetamine catecholamines and behavior. Arch. Neurol., 21:248–252.

Baumeister, A.A. & Forehand, R. (1973), Stereotyped acts. In: *International Review of Research in Mental Retardation*, Vol. 6, ed. N.R. Ellis. New York: Academic Press, pp. 55–96.

Birmaher, B., Quintana, H., & Greenhill, L.L. (1988), Methylphenidate treatment of hyperactive autistic children. *J. Am. Acad. Child Adolesc. Psychiatry*, 27:248–251.

Blacklidge, V. & Ekblad, R. (1971), The effectiveness of methylphenidate hydrochloride (Ritalin) on learning and behavior in public school educable mentally retarded children. *Pediatrics*, 47:923–926.

Blue, A.W., Lytton, G.J., & Miller, D.W. (1960), The effect of methylphenidate on intellectually handicapped children (Abstr). *Am. Psychologist*, 15:393.

Bradley, C. (1937), The behavior of children receiving Benzedrine. *Am. J. Psychiatry*, 94:577–585.

Campbell, M. (1975), Pharmacotherapy in early infantile autism. Biol. *Psychiatry*, 10:399–423.

———— (1978), Pharmacotherapy. In: *Autism: A Reappraisal of Concepts and Treatment*, eds. M. Rutter & E. Schopler. New York: Plenum Press, pp. 337–355.

————Green, W.H., & Deutsch, S.I. (1985), Stimulants. In: *Child and Adolescent Psychopharmacology*. Beverly Hills, CA: Sage Publications, pp. 71–91.

————Fish, B., David, R., Shapiro, T., Collins, P. & Koh, C. (1972), Response to triiodothyronine and dextroamphetamine: A study of preschool schizophrenic children. *J. Autism Child. Schizophrenia*, 2:343–358.

Carter, C.H. (1956), The effects of reserpine and methylphenidate (Ritalin) in mental defectives, spastics and epileptics. *Psychiatric Res. Rep.*, 4:44–48.

Chandler, M., Gualtieri, C.T., & Faho, J.J. (1988), Other psychotropic drugs: Stimulants, antidepressants, the anxiolytics, and lithium carbonate. In: *Psychopharmacology of the Developmental Disabilities*, eds. M.G. Aman & N.N. Singh. New York: Springer-Verlag, pp. 119–145.

Christensen, D.E. (1975), Effects of combining methylphenidate and a classroom token system in modifying hyperactive behavior. *Am. J. Mental Defic.*, 80:266–276.

Conners, C.K. (1969), A teacher rating scale for use in drug studies with children. *Am. J. Psychiatry*, 126:884.

Conners, C.K. (1973), Rating scales for use in drug studies with children. *Psychopharmacol. Bull* (Special Issue: Pharmacotherapy of children): 24–84.

————& Eisenberg, L. (1963), The effects of methylphenidate on symptomatology and learning in disturbed children. *Am. J. Psychiatry*, 120:458–464.

Cutler, M., Little, J.W. & Strauss, A.A. (1940), The effects of Benzedrine on mentally deficient children. *Am. J. Mental Defic.*, 45, 59–65.

Davis, K.V., (1971), The effects of drugs on stereotyped and nonstereotyped operant behavior in retardates. *Psychopharmacologia*, 22:199–213.

————Sprague, R.L. & Werry, J.S. (1969), Stereotyped behavior and activity level in severe retardates: The effect of drugs. *Am. J. Mental Defic.*, 73:721–727.

Fish, B. (1971), The "one child, one drug" myth of stimulants in hyperkinesis. *Arch. Gen. Psychiatry*, 25:193–203.

Freeman, B.F., Ritvo, E.R., Schroth, P.C., Tonick, I., Guthrie, D. & Wake, L. (1981). Behavioral characteristics of high- and low-IQ autistic children. *Am. J. Psychiatry*, 138:25–29.

Gadow, K.D. (1982), School involvement in pharmacotherapy for behavior disorders. *J. Spec. Educ.*, 16:385–399.

———— (1983), Pharmacotherapy for behavior disorders: Typical treatment practices. *Clin. Pediatr.*, 22:48–53.

———— (1985), Prevalence and efficacy of stimulant drug use with mentally retarded children and youth. *Psychopharmcol. Bull.*, 21:291–303.

———— (1986), *Children on Medication*, Vol. I; *Hyperactivity, Learning Disabilities, and Mental Retardation*. San Diego, CA: College-Hill Press.

———— Kalachnick, J. (1981), Prevalence and pattern of drug treatment for behavior and seizure disorders of TMR students. *Am. J. Mental Defic.*, 85:588–595.

Geller, B., Guttmacher, L. & Bleeg, M. (1981), Coexistence of childhood onset pervasive developmental disorder and attention deficit disorder with hyperactivity. *Am. J. Psychiatry*, 138:338–389.

Holm, V.A. & Varley, C.K. (1989), Pharmacological treatment of autistic children. In: *Autism: Nature, Diagnosis, and Treatment*, ed. G. Dawson. New York: Guilford, pp. 386–404.

Hoshino, Y., Kumashiro, H., Kaneko, M. & Takahashi, Y. (1977), The effects of methylphenidate on early infantile autism and its relation to serotonin levels. *Folia Psychiatr. Neurol. Jpn.*, 31:605–614.

Kelly, T.L., Ruch, G.M. & Terman, L.M. (1929), *The New Stanford Achievement Test*, New York: World Book Company.

Klein, D., Gittelman, R., Quitkin, F. & Quitkin, A. (1981), Diagnosis and drug treatment of childhood disorders. In: *Diagnosis and Drug Treatment of Psychiatric Disorders: Adults and Children*. Baltimore: Williams & Wilkins, pp. 590–775.

Laufer, M.W. & Denhoff, E. (1957), Hyperactive behavior syndrome in children. *J. Pediatr.*, 50:463–474.

Levy, J.M., Jones, B.E. & Croley, H.T. (1957), Effects of methylphenidate (Ritalin) on drug-induced drowsiness in mentally retarded patients. *Am. J. Mental Defic.*, 62:284–287.

Lobb, H. (1968), Trace GSR conditioning in mentally defective and normal adults. *Am. J. Mental Defic.*, 73:239–246.

McConnell, T.R., Cromwell, R.L., Bialer, I. & Son, C.D. (1964), Studies in activity level: VII. Effects of amphetamine drug administration on the activity level of retarded children. *Am. J. Mental Defic.*, 68:647–651.

Molitch, M. & Eccles, J.P. (1937), Effects of benzedrine sulfate on the intelligence scores of children. *Am. J. Psychiatry*, 94:587–590.

Molitch, M. & Sullivan, J.P. (1937), Effects of benzedrine sulfate on children taking the New Stanford Achievement Test. *J. Orthopsychiatry*, 7:519–522.

Morris, J.V., MacGillvrary, R.C. & Mathieson, C.M. (1955), The results of the experimental administration of amphetamine sulphate in oligophrenia. *J. Mental Sci.*, 101:131–140.

Nihira, K., Foster, R., Shellhaas, M. & Leland, H. (1974), *AAMD Adaptive Behavior Scale*, 1974 revision. Washington, DC: American Association on Mental Deficiency.

Payton, J.B., Burkhart, J.E., Hersen, M. & Helsel, W.J. (1989), Treatment of ADDH in Mentally retarded children: A preliminary study. *J. Am. Acad. Child Adolesc. Psychiatry*, 28:761–767.

Porteus, S.D. (1959), *The Maze Test and Clinical Psychology*. Palo Alto, CA: Pacific Books.

Randrup, A. & Munkvad, I. (1967), Stereotyped activities produced by amphetamine in several animal species and man. *Psychopharmacologia*, 11:300–310.

Robbins, T.W. & Sahakian, B.J. (1979), "Paradoxical" effects of psychomotor stimulant drugs in hyperactive children from the standpoint of behavioral pharmacology. *Neuropharmacology,* 18:931–950.

Sargant, W. & Blackburn, J.M. (1936), The effect of benzedrine on intelligence scores. *Lancet,* 11:1385.

Strayhorn, J.M., Rapp, N., Donina, W. & Strain, P.S. (1988), Randomized trial of methylphanidate for an autistic child. *J. Am. Acad. Child Adolesc. Psychiatry,* 27:244–247.

Varley, C.K. & Trupin, E.W. (1982), Double-blind administration of methylphenidate to mentally retarded children with attention deficit disorder: A preliminary study. *Am. J. Mental Defic.,* 86:560–566.

Vitrol, C. & Faber, B. (1981), Stimulant medication in certain childhood disorders. *Am. J. Psychiatry,* 138:1517–1518.

Zimmerman, F.T. & Burgemeister, B.B. (1958), Action of methylphenidylacetate (Ritalin) and reserpine in behavior disorders in children and adults. *Am. J. Psychiatry,* 115:323–328.

Psychostimulants in Traumatic Brain Injury

C. THOMAS GUALTIERI

INTRODUCTION

It was the neuropharmacology of stimulants in hyperactive children, in fact, that began our interest in patients with traumatic brain injury (TBI). The Neuropsychiatry Research Program had completed a series of experiments in attention deficit hyperactive (ADH) children (Evans et al., 1986) to suggest that methylphenidate (MPH) exercised an effect on the consolidation of long-term memory that was dissociated from the drug effect on attention (Evans et al., 1986, 1987). The stimulant effect on memory had long been appreciated in the preclinical literature, but it had never received attention, to speak of, in the clinical literature.

We felt that it was necessary to extend the line of research into other groups of memory-impaired patients. TBI patients were a large group, growing in numbers, and sorely in need of intelligent psychiatric attention. It was a natural fit.

EFFECTS OF METHYLPHENIDATE ON CLINICAL STATUS OF TBI PATIENTS

There were, of course, other reasons to believe that dopamine agonist drugs like MPH might improve the clinical state of TBI patients. For example, stimulants are known to improve symptoms of inattention, distractibility, disorganization, hyperactivity, impulsiveness, and emotional lability in children and adults with attention deficit hyperactivity disorder (ADHD). Many TBI patients have similar symptoms and respond well to low or moderate doses of stimulant drugs. This was suggested by anecdotal reports in the psychiatric literature and our own clinical experience.

Stimulants are known to improve symptoms of hypersomnia, apathy, anergia, and hypoarousal in narcoleptic patients, in patients with the Kleine-Levin syndrome (Orlosky, 1982) and in "senile apathy." TBI patients who are afflicted with similar symptoms may respond favorably to low-to-moderate doses of stimulant drugs.

Stimulants are known to improve perceptual–motor function in ADHD children (Golinko et al., 1981), to improve fine motor speed, accuracy, and steadiness (Gualtieri et al., 1986) and (in normals) to alleviate the perception of fatigue that accompanies strenuous exercise (Novick, 1973). Some of these effects have also been reported in TBI patients (Gualtieri and Evans, 1988).

It has been suggested that stimulant drugs exercise a therapeutic effect by modulating or by enhancing dopaminergic neurotransmission to rostral brain structures, especially in the frontal neocortex (Gualtieri and Hicks, 1985). They may be particularly useful for TBI patients whose deficits are attributable to frontal lobe damage; these deficits include diminished flexibility, inability to execute complex behavioral programs, poor planning, lack of initiative, and poor impulse control, in addition to the "hyperactive" and the "anergic" elements described above.

Profound deficits in monoaminergic neurotransmission are seen in TBI patients presumably as a consequence of shear damage to axial brain structures, where the cell bodies of neurons that synthesize monoamines are concentrated. The administration of monoaminergic drugs such as stimulants is, in this

---

North Carolina Neuropsychiatry and REBOUND, Inc., Chapel Hill, North Carolina

context, "rational pharmacotherapy"; that is, drug therapy intended to correct an underlying neurochemical deficit.

EXPERIMENTAL APPLICATIONS

There followed, then, a series of experiments with TBI patients who had persistent problems with attention and memory, and other residual symptoms as well, but who were in a relative stable "plateau," one to five years after TBI (Evans et al., 1987; Gualtieri and Evans, 1988). None were actively engaged in rehab, because it was the opinion of their therapists that they had achieved all that they were likely to achieve. The conclusions of this line of research can be summarized:

1. MPH improves neuropsychological deficits in attention and memory in TBI patients.
2. MPH also leads to improvement in symptoms of hyperactivity, impulsivity, excitability, poor judgment; and, conversely, symptoms of abulia and anergia.
3. Medication treatment is only necessary for a few months, after which the patients seemed to maintain their improvement without further drug treatment.
4. TBI patients who were "high-level," that is, ambulatory, communicative, and intellectually intact (more or less), did very well on MPH, while TBI patients who were more substantially impaired did not do very well at all. In fact, they tended to show signs of stimulant toxicity.
5. There was the suggestion, from the data, and from clinical observations of the patients' status, that stimulant treatment led to a "reactivation" or to an "acceleration" of the cortical recovery process. That is, the general state of the patients appeared to advance over their previous "plateau."

Stimulants have become, then, standard treatment for a certain class of TBI patients at the Neuropsychiatry Clinic in Chapel Hill.

Stimulants like MPH have proved to be comparatively easy to use in TBI patients, and positive effects, when they occur, are apparent within days, or even hours, after an optimal dose is achieved. Methylphenidate (MPH) and dextroamphetamine (DEA) are the stimulants most frequently prescribed for ADHD, narcolepsy, Kleine-Levin syndrome, and senile apathy, and also for TBI. Pemoline (PEM) is a third alternative, but not a terribly good one.

SIDE EFFECTS

The side effects of stimulants are not hard to monitor in TBI patients. Anorexia and insomnia are amenable to dosage or dose schedule adjustments; headache and dysphoria, irritability, "on-off," and "rebound" reactions usually respond to minor changes in prescription. The stimulant side effect profile is, in fact, a model of clarity: Acute toxic effects are clear and apparent, and they resolve quickly as soon as the drugs are withdrawn. Once the hurdle of initial sensitivity is past there is no long-term toxicity, no hidden effect that will surface after months or years of treatment. Stimulants have the enormous advantage of being "yes–no" drugs; they either work or they do not; when they do work, positive effects are readily apparent.

This is not to suggest that stimulants can be administered freely, or that they can be prescribed by inexperienced physicians. Stimulant therapy is perfectly safe in the hands of a knowledgeable and responsible practitioner; but stimulants are complex drugs, and acute toxicity is not an insignificant manner. Adults, for example, seem to be very sensitive to stimulants, and very low doses (0.1–0.2 mg/kg/dose) may be sufficient for a 70 kg male (Gualtieri et al., 1982). Higher doses may cause cognitive overfixation, stereotyped thinking, perseveration, or palilalia. High doses may actually impair memory and clear thinking (Wetzel et al., 1981). A patient who is sensitive to stimulants may become anxious or disorganized, fearful, agitated, paranoid, or frankly psychotic. Somatosensory hallucinations may occur. Patients can develop increased spasticity, choreic and athetoid dyskinesias, or motor and phonic tics. Patients may become intensely dysphoric, irritable, and prone to range attacks. Although stimulants may alleviate the symptoms of posttraumatic headache, or enhance the effect of analgesic agents, they may also cause headache or precipitate migraine. This is not a trivial list by any means, and it addresses the need for careful monitoring.

Patients have raised the question of long-term side effects of stimulant therapy, and we took the occasion to address this question, on the basis of a clinical survey involving 47 adults, ages 18 to 38 who met diagnostic criteria for attention deficit disorder ("residual type"), and of 31 adults who had neurobehavioral sequelae of TBI, and who also had problems with attention, memory, and impulsive, temperamental behavior. The first group of patients (ADD adults) included a series of 22 who were described in a report by Gualtieri et al. (1985). The second group of 31 (TBI adults) included a series of 15 who were described by Gualtieri and Evans (1988). It was the policy of the Neuropsychiatry Clinic to follow these patients very closely, on a monthly basis, over the years, and we have reviewed their long-term followup status (Gualtieri, 1990).

Of a total N of 78, where stimulants were prescribed, there were no cases of stimulant abuse, in any traditional sense. No patient ever evidenced inappropriate drug-seeking behavior, or expressed the need for increasing doses as time went by. There were no cases of social disruption, disorganization, or toxic psychosis. There was no one who progressed to other drugs of abuse (e.g., cocaine). In fact, the large majority of cases discontinued treatment after 6–18 months, mainly because the drug had seemed to exercise its maximum benefit, and further treatment was no longer necessary.

Of the 78, four patients were compelled to discontinue stimulant treatment by virtue of psychological difficulties. One man took an overdose of methylphenidate during an argument with his wife. Three women developed mild depressive disorders, in two of the cases, related to severe family problems, and were hospitalized because of suicidal ideation. In one case, there was severe depression and a suicide attempt. All of these patients had attention deficit disorder; there were no such problems with TBI patients.

It has become our policy to monitor adults on stimulants very carefully for the development of depressive disorders. It is not surprising that some people with a lifelong history of academic and occupational failure might develop depression at some time during their adult lives, but the prevalence of depression in this sample really is no higher than in the general population (e.g., Blazer et al., 1988). However, there is always the risk that chronic stimulant therapy may lead to a depressive state, and patients should be monitored accordingly.

Although stimulant treatment can be stopped abruptly in ADHD patients, even after years of treatment, with no withdrawal symptoms at all, TBI patients seem to have a different tendency. In TBI patients, abrupt TBI discontinuation may lead to a severe withdrawal reaction, with symptoms of depression, anergia, or agitation. Thus a clinical trial should never be undertaken lightly in a TBI patient, since the medication cannot be withdrawn suddenly without risking the additional problem of rebound depression. No TBI patient should be treated with stimulants unless there is a physician experienced in the use of the drugs in close attendance, and unless the patient and his family fully understand the attendant risks.

Research has not advanced to a point where it is possible to predict *which* TBI patients should be treated with stimulant drugs. It is the authors' clinical impression, however, that the best response occurs in relatively high-level, mild to moderately impaired patients, with relatively circumscribed deficits in attention, memory, organization, or initiative. More severely impaired subjects, especially those with severe motor impairment, seem less likely to respond, and they also seem to be more prone to acute toxic effects and to withdrawal reactions. Such patients are more likely to respond to dopamine agonist therapy with such direct agonists as amantadine or bromocriptine (Gualtieri et al., 1989).

This parallels the clinical experience of child psychiatrists and developmental physicians: ADHD children are less likely to respond to stimulants if they have associated emotional, behavioral, or cognitive problems; mild to moderately retarded children are more likely to respond to stimulants than the severe to profoundly retarded. For the mentally retarded patient with hyperactivity, a postsynaptic agonist such as amantadine is more likely to work well than a presynaptic agonist such as MPH (Chandler and Gualtieri, 1990).

There is evidence from animal experiments that stimulants may influence the cortical recovery process in some way, conceivably by correcting the monoaminergic deficits that accompany TBI. There is a new preclinical literature concerned with pharmacological effects on the growth and recovery of nervous tissue: compounds reported to be beneficial, in addition to the stimulants, include naloxone and thyrotropin-releasing hormone (TRH) (Faden, 1984). This is an incipient literature, however, and none of the animal research has yet proved useful for human beings with brain or spinal cord injury. Nor is it even clear how clinical studies should be designed to demonstrate the utility of a compound on cortical recovery, and this point is not likely to be resolved soon.

DISCUSSION

Stimulants are currently indicated for TBI patients who have prominent symptoms of: (1) attention deficit/hyperactivity; (2) anergia/apathy or abulia; and (3) disinhibition.

The functional neuroanatomy of stimulant effects in TBI is presumed to be this: dopamine agonists may work to correct deficits in dopaminergic neurotransmission from brain-stem nuclei to striatum and to the frontal lobes. We have come to consider the dopamine agonists as prototypic frontal lobe drugs.

Stimulants may also be used in some patients with symptoms of emotional incontinence ("catastrophic reactions"), emotional lability, or rage outbursts, although the usual treatment for this syndrome is a serotonergic antidepressant or carbamazepine. They may someday be indicated as a kind of "tonic" to improve the pace of cortical recovery after TBI, although this is, at present, only speculation, and the routine use of stimulants for asymptomatic TBI patients, in hopes of improving the rate of recovery, cannot be recommended.

There is no absolute contraindication to stimulant therapy, except perhaps in the case of patients with a prior history of drug abuse or addiction. Stimulants have very few untoward interactions with other drugs. They are likely to raise, not lower, the seizure threshold in epileptic patients, PDR to the contrary (Feldman et al., 1989); although it is true that very high doses may be epileptogenic (Alldredge et al., 1989). In low doses, the cardiovascular effects of psychostimulants are minimal.

Side effects of stimulants may include agitation, disorientation, emotional lability, cognitive perseveration, increased spasticity, tremor, and dyskinesia, especially in patients with severe motor sequelae of TBI.

Abrupt stimulant withdrawal in TBI patients may lead to severe symptoms of depression, agitation, or suicidal ideation. For this reason the prescription must never be allowed to lapse; the fact that methylphenidate and amphetaimine are Schedule II drugs, that prescriptions can only be written for a month at a time, and that prescriptions cannot be refilled by phone, mean that a greater degree of vigilance is required in followup.

The contention that psychostimulants may exercise some benefit against symptoms of inattention, abulia, and anergia is hardly controversial; one would be surprised if such were not the case. The idea that stimulants are treatment of choice for many of the depressive syndromes that accompany TBI requires a small degree of imagination, but it is not a staggering inferential leap. There is, however, a third area of speculation, and this does require the most critical scrutiny, because it speaks to the effect of stimulant drugs upon the very process of cortical recovery.

There is, as we have mentioned, at least suggestive evidence from the preclinical literature that stimulant treatment may advance the recovery of brain-injured animals (e.g., Feeny et al., 1982). There is the clinical evidence from experience with ADHD children on stimulants, who require treatment limited to a couple of years, on the average, because they appear to mature, and to acquire more stable patterns of relating to their environment after a course of treatment with stimulants. Finally, there is evidence from controlled studies of TBI patients on stimulants, that the drugs may exercise lasting effects, even after they have been discontinued (Gualtieri and Evans, 1988). The issue is whether this particular pharmacologic intervention is capable of actually accelerating the recovery process, whether it restores a lasting balance to neuromodulatory monoamine systems that have been upset by traumatic injury.

The issue probably will not be settled for a long time, but it carries sufficient weight at this point to lend impetus to clinical trials in appropriate patients.

REFERENCES

Alldredge, B.K., Lowenstein, D.H. & Simon, R.P. (1989), Seizures associated with recreational drug abuse. *Neurology*, 39:1037–1039.

Balzer, D., Swartz, M., Woodbury, M., Manton, K.G., Hughes, D. & George, L.K. (1988), Depressive syndromes and depressive diagnoses in a community population. *Arch. Gen Psychiatry*, 45:1078–1084.

Chandler, M.C. & Gualtieri, C.T. (1990), Amantadine: A medical, neuropsychological & psychiatric profile. In: *Mental Retardation: Developing Pharmacotherapies,* ed. J.J. Ratey. Washington, DC: American Psychiatric Press.

Evans, R.W., Gualtieri, C.T., & Amara, I. (1986), Methylphenidate and memory: dissociated effects in hyperactive children. *Psychopharmacology,* 90:211–216.

————— ————— Patterson, D.R. (1987), Treatment of chronic closed head injury with psychostimulant drugs: a controlled case study and an appropriate evaluation procedure. *J. Nerv. Mental Dis.,* 175:106–110.

Faden, A.I. (1984), Opiate antagonists and thyrotropin-releasing hormone. II. Potential role in the treatment of central nervous system injury. *J. Am. Med. Assoc.,* 252:1452–1454.

Feeney, D.M., Gonzalez, A. & Law, W.A. (1982), Amphetamine, haloperidol and experience interact to affect rate of recovery after motor cortex surgery. *Science,* 217:855–857.

Feldman, H., Crumrine, P., Handen, B.L., Alvin, R. & Teodori, J. (1989), Methylphenidate in children with seizures and attention-deficit disorder. *Am. J. Dis. Child.,* 143:1081–1086.

Golinko, B.E., Rennick, P.M. & Lewis, R.F. (1981), Predicting stimulant effectiveness in hyperactive children with a repeatable neuropsychological battery. *Prog. Neuropsychopharmacol.,* 5:65–68.

Gualtieri, C.T. (1990), *Neuropsychiatry and Behavioral Pharmacology.* Berlin: Springer-Verlag.

————— Chandler, M., Coons, T. & Brown, L. (1989), Amantadine: a new clinical profile for traumatic brain injury. *Clin. Neuropharm.,* 12:258–270.

————— Evans, R.W. (1988), Stimulant treatment for the neurobehavioral sequelae of traumatic brain injury. *Brain Injury,* 2:273–290.

————— Hicks, R.E. (1985), The neuropharmacology of methylphenidate and a neural substrate of childhood hyperactivity. *Psychiatr. Clin. North Am.,* 8:875–892.

————— ————— Levitt, J., Conley, R. & Schroeder, S.R. (1986), Methylphenidate & exercise: Additive effects on motor performance, variable effects on the neuroendocrine response. *Neuropsychobiology,* 15:84–88.

————— Ondrusek, M.G. & Finley, C. (1985), Attention deficit disorder in adults. *Clin. Neuropharmacol.,* 8:343–356.

————— Wargin, W., Kanoy, R., Shen, C., Patrick, K., Youngblood, W., Mueller, R. & Breese, G. (1982), Clinical studies of methylphenidate serum levels in children and adults. *J. Am. Acad. Child Psychiatry,* 21:19–26.

Novick, N.M. (1973), Drug abuse and drugs in sports. *NY J. Med.,* 73:2597–2600.

Orlosky, M.J. (1982), The Kleine-Levin syndrome: A review. *Psychosomatics,* 23:609–617.

Wetzel, C.D., Squire, L.R. & Janowsky, D.S. (1981), Methylphenidate impairs learning and memory in normal adults. *Behav. Neural. Biol.,* 31:413–424.

Ritalin in HIV Dementia

FRANCISCO FERNANDEZ

INTRODUCTION

The human immunodeficiency virus (HIV) may manifest various symptomatology, ranging from uncomplicated seropositivity to the immunological ravages of the fully developed acquired immunodeficiency syndrome (AIDS) (Fauci et al., 1985). By means of past studies, we now know that HIV adversely affects the immune system through a direct attack on the CD4 subset of T cells (helper) which may ultimately lead to a total suppression of the patient's cell-mediated immune function. At this point, the patient would be openly vulnerable to overwhelming opportunistic infections or unusual cancers such as *Pneumocystis carinii* pneumonia and Kaposi's sarcoma, respectively.

Studies are now addressing suspected neurotropic effects of HIV infection (Price et al., 1988). When compared with other known neurodegenerative pathogens, such as syphilis, the prospects of dangerous and debilitating disabilities loom quite ominously in the minds of the infected individuals and in those of scientists and clinicians who hope one day to conquer the intricacies of this perplexing disease (Felgenhauer, 1987). We are aware that HIV may attack the central nervous system (CNS) at any point in the progression of the disease, but the precise mode of action upon the brain and how it induces dementia is still unclear. It has been proposed that HIV enters the brain by way of the endothelial gaps in the capillary vascular bed (Gyorkey et al., 1987). From there, it may bind to glial and perhaps neural cells containing the T-helper, CD-4 receptor whereby it is able to enter the cells and replicate (Funke et al., 1987; Vazeux et al., 1987; Wiley et al., 1986). Changes in the white matter of the CNS in HIV-infected individuals are consistent with the proposition that these suspected actions of HIV result in a cellular reaction causing inflammation and degeneration of myelin. Thus, any person who is HIV-infected could theoretically also have HIV–CNS involvement at any stage of disease.

The range of psychological and psychiatric symptomatology for seropositive HIV-infected individuals encompasses a spectrum from stress–distress-related manifestations to organic mental disorders (Fernandez, 1987). In this chapter, we look at the most common organic mental disorders associated with HIV infection which is the progressive dementia known as AIDS dementia complex (Price et al., 1988). Current methods of managing these disturbances with the psychostimulant methylphenidate (Ritalin) as an adjuvant pharmacotherapeutic strategy will be discussed.

HIV DEMENTIA

General issues

Progressive dementia in HIV infection occurs in a significant proportion of fully developed AIDS cases (Beckett, 1990). It is considered to be the most common CNS complication of HIV disease (Levy and

---

Baylor College of Medicine, Houston, Texas.

Bredesen, 1988). Symptoms of cognitive or neuropsychiatric impairment may even precede the manifestations of immune compromise (Navia and Price, 1987). Among those patients with pre-AIDS conditions, such as progressive lymphadenopathy syndrome (PGL) and AIDS-related complex (ARC), and even in those in the asymptomatic state, the incidence of cognitive impairment has only begun to be quantified (Grant et al., 1987; McArthur et al., 1989). Nonetheless, cognitive and neuropsychiatric disturbances among all HIV-infected individuals must be regarded seriously in view of objective clinical findings and subjective complaints among this patient population. Any psychiatric symptom occurring in conjunction with HIV infection should first be considered as having an organic etiology until ruled out or proved otherwise. As the number of AIDS patients continues to increase, the evidence of significant CNS involvement also becomes more clear. It is therefore important for clinicians to have a working knowledge of HIV-related organic mental disorders (Perry, 1990) in order to provide judicious assessment and beneficial intervention for each individual.

Dementia resulting from HIV has multiple manifestations. AIDS patients have been known to present with cognitive impairment, language disorders, mood disturbances, and/or delirium which may overlap or further compound the symptomatology associated with dementia. Therefore, a systematic and methodical mental status evaluation (Levy, 1990) is most useful in the accurate assessment of the possible neuropsychiatric basis for any psychological disturbance associated with HIV-related disease. Obviously, the differential diagnosis of cognitive impairment in HIV infection is quite varied, and affective medical intervention cannot be undertaken unless an adequate diagnosis has been formulated.

Neurobehavioral assessment in HIV infection

Although most cognitively impaired HIV-infected individuals may be grossly diagnosed using the criteria set forth in the *Diagnostic and Statistical Manual of Mental Disorders,* Third Edition-Revised (*DSM-III-R*) (American Psychiatric Association, 1987), the complexity of HIV-related dementia requires that more sensitive and precise discriminators of observable cognitive function be made when attempting to determine degrees of cognitive impairment for particular patients. In our own studies (Fernandez et al., 1987a, 1988), the Mini Mental State Examination (Folstein et al., 1975) did not appear to have the ability to quantify degrees of cognitive impairment among HIV-infected patients who were immunologically asymptomatic, versus those with either PGL or ARC, versus those with AIDS. In a separate investigation, we used Reisburg's Global Deterioration Scale (GDS) (Reisberg et al., 1982) for primary degenerative primary dementia of the Alzheimer's type to distinguish the finer differences in observable clinical (i.e., cognitive) function in HIV-infected patients (Fernandez et al., 1987a). Applying criteria from this observational scale, interpretation of our results indicates that the most severe impairment tends to occur in patients with ARC or AIDS. Although this correlation might appear to be an obvious one, it is important to note that the levels of cognitive functioning for the PGL patients varied significantly from all the other groups. This finding leads us to believe that serious cognitive impairment is likely to be present as soon as the systemic effects of HIV become clinically apparent, even in the absence of obvious opportunistic infection. From this observation, we also concluded that HIV appears to be neurologically opportunistic in and of itself. Although our studies showed 21% of PGL patients as having some early confusional or early dementia characteristics, other studies have assessed the incidence to be up to 40% of the PGL sample (Janssen et al., 1988). It is imperative, therefore, that clinicians be alert to even subtly progressive changes appearing to arise acutely or progress temporally among HIV-asymptomatic seropositive individuals because it is suspected that HIV-CNS involvement may remain as a latent infection with subacute degenerative CNS changes having an indolent demyelinating course (Diederich et al., 1988; Navia et al., 1986). Thus, early in the course of HIV spectrum disorders, subtle changes in cognitive function may only become apparent with careful neuropsychological assessment.

An accurate assessment of a given patient's ability to comprehend and comply with his or her regimen is obviously vital to any effective clinical management plan (Fernandez and Levy, 1990). A suggested battery of sensitive neuropsychological testing is listed in Table 1 (Fernandez, 1989):

TABLE 1. HIV NEUROPSYCHOLOGICAL SCREENING BATTERY[a,b]

General
    Mini-Mental State Examination (Folstein et al., 1975)

Memory
    Verbal Selective Reminding Test (Levin, 1986)
    Benton Visual Retention Test (Bonton, 1974)
    Rey-Osterrieth Complex Figure (Lezak, 1983)

Language/Speech
    Controlled Oral Word Association (from Benton Multilingual Aphasia Examination) (Beton and des
        Hamsher, 1983)
    Visual Naming Test (from Benton Multilingual Aphasia Examination) (Benton and des Hamsher,
        1983)

Orientation
    Benton Temporal Orientation Test (Benton et al., 1983)

Visuospatial
    Bender-Gestalt Test (Lacks, 1984)
    Raven Progressive Matrices (Raven et al., 1983)

Intellectual/Executive/Psychomotor
    Digit Span, Arithmetic, Digit Symbol from the WAIS or WAIS-R (Golden, 1981)
    Trail Making Test, Parts A and B (Golden et al., 1981)
    Wisconsin Card Sorting (Benton and des Hamsher, 1983)
    Finger Oscillation Test (Golden et al., 1981)
    Grooved Pegboard (Benton and des Hamsher, 1983)
    Reaction Time—Simple Auditory, Simple Visual, and Four-choice Visual (Pirozzolo et al., 1981)
    Shipley Institute of Living Scale (Zacharay, 1987)
    Stroop Color Word Test (Golden, 1978)

[a]Suggested battery for evaluating the CNS effects of HIV infection and neurotoxic effects from antivirals and chemotherapeutic agents.
[b]Adapted from Fernandez, 1989.

The type of cognitive disturbance originally associated with HIV-CNS infection was characterized as a "subcortical" (Whitehouse, 1986) dementing process (Navia et al., 1986). For this reason, it is imperative that appropriate neuropsychological evaluation include an assessment of memory (registration, storage, and retrieval), psychomotor speed, and rate of information processing (Van Gorp et al., 1989). Accordingly, verbal memory problems and psychomotor slowing are early and persistent features of HIV-related cognitive disorder (Levy et al., 1988). As with all medically ill patients, the assessment regimen must be guided by the patient's stamina and responsiveness. At the end stage of AIDS, when both the stamina and responsiveness of the patient may be negligible, neurocognitive assessment will likely be restricted to purely behavioral observations. For individuals who are infected by the AIDS dementia complex, this battery, although comprehensive, may be too cumbersome and time consuming. Nevertheless, elements can be adapted for the assessment of grossly developed demented or critically ill patients (Levy and Fernandez, 1989). Thus, neuropsychological testing can help assess a number of important factors including competency, progression of cognitive decline, and organic versus functional issues. Finally, we find that these tests are also helpful in determining the type of clinical management and selection of pharmacotherapy for HIV-infected patients.

Methylphenidate treatment of HIV-related organic mental disorders

At the present time, zidovudine (AZT) is the only agent reliably known to ameliorate various components of the AIDS dementia complex (Pizzo et al., 1988; Portiegies et al., 1989; Schmitt et al., 1988). However, it has been proposed that psychopharmacological strategies could also be formulated to achieve qualitative and quantitative improvement in cognition for those patients with the AIDS dementia complex (Fernandez, 1987; Fernandez et al., 1988). Some physicians are reluctant to initiate such medical interventions for psychological symptoms, or may avoid psychotropic medications due to their various adverse side effects in this population. However, we feel that such conservativism is unjustified in view of the established role of stimulants in general medical practice and their potential benefit to the individual patient. Adjuvant psychopharmacotherapy for HIV-related cognitive impairment and dementia should not remain underutilized as it presently is (Fernandez, 1987).

Although stimulants have been used in general medical practice for over 50 years, the therapeutic role of amphetamines in psychiatry has, with few exceptions, never been firmly established, (Tesar, 1982). During the early 1960s, increasing illicit use of amphetamines and indiscriminate prescription of amphetamines for various conditions led some states to impose severe restrictions or prohibitions on the use of these potentially addictive agents. More recently, however, clinical and investigative experience with the psychostimulants has demonstrated them to be both safe and beneficial when prescribed and used appropriately in medically ill, depressed, and cognitively impaired populations. Although current FDA approval is limited to narcolepsy, attention deficit disorder with hyperactivity, and obesity, clinical reports have found that stimulants may be of benefit for nocturnal enuresis, postencephalitic parkinsonism, analgesic adjuvants, neurasthenia fatigue syndromes, hiccups, and some forms of seizures (Levy and Fernandez, 1989). The psychostimulants may also be effective in treating apathetic and withdrawn states due to major "secondary" depressive syndromes in the medically ill and in the elderly (Fernandez et al., 1987b; Jenicke, 1988; Woods et al., 1986). Clinical response is highlighted by a quick remission of depression and cognitive inefficiencies without treatment-related side effects. Therefore, psychostimulant therapy should not be overlooked when treating HIV-infected patients with or without cognitive impairment (Fernandez et al., 1988). The optimal care of patients who suffer from HIV infection and secondary neuropsychiatric disturbances should include the judicious use of psychostimulants in order to provide improved functioning for the patients.

In a report pertaining to HIV and psychosis (Maccario and Scharre, 1987), the authors, from their clinical observations, speculated that HIV has a tendency to affect the CNS by way of dopaminergic systems. For example, they reported that HIV-related psychosis was noted in patients without previous histories of thought disorders who were HIV infected. Further evidence that HIV affects the dopaminergic system is drawn from the occurrence of serious cases of extrapyramidal reactions. In some cases, when the extrapyramidal reactions were treated with anticholinergics, these symptoms resolved, but the psychosis was exacerbated. In other cases, the development of motor dysfunction occurred while patients were taking antiemetics or metoclopramide, further suggesting an instability of the dopaminergic systems in HIV-infected patients. Cases of extrapyramidal syndromes occurring de novo implicating basal ganglia involvement in HIV disease have also been reported (Neith et al., 1987). Anatomically, support for these hypotheses comes from Price and colleagues (1989), who have found HIV viral protein in white matter and basal ganglia of patients with neurological manifestations of the AIDS dementia complex (Pumarola-Sune et al., 1986). Moreover, other investigators have demonstrated a localization of the CD4 antigen/HIV receptor in primate limbic regions (Hill et al., 1986). Damage to these areas could explain the impairments in neuropsychological functioning as well as the psychotic symptomatology found in individuals with HIV-CNS infection. The findings of cognitive slowing and verbal forgetfulness, along with complaints of fatigue and dysphoria, in the presence of intact higher level abstract reasoning suggest a subcortical disturbance. Several investigators have reported improvement in these symptoms following treatment with the stimulant methylphenidate (Fernandez et al., 1988a, 1988b; Holmes et al., 1989). In our own studies both AIDS-related complex (ARC) and AIDS patients showed statistically significant improvement in speed of cognitive tracking and long-term verbal memory function after methylphenidate treatment. Of these patients who had simultaneous affective or other psychiatric complaints, clinical improvement was also demonstrated when treated with methylphenidate.

We have reviewed our psychiatric consultations (Fernandez, 1990) at an outpatient care facility where the consulting psychiatrists had recommended methylphenidate as treatment for secondary depression of varying etiologies. "Secondary depression" represents any depressive syndrome with onset after or coincident with the HIV infection. We found an excellent response to methylphenidate (see Table 2).

The medical record, notes from the consulting psychiatrist, primary physicians, other consultants, and the nursing staff were used to rate each patient's response to methylphenidate on the Clinical Global Improvement Scale. Using this scale, "markedly improved" referred to complete or near complete remission of the depressive symptomatology. "Moderately improved" indicated there was evidence for decided improvement in several symptom areas but without complete remission of the depressive symptomatology. "Minimal improvement" referred to cases where minor increases in mood or energy were noted without any other improvements. Any side effects attributable to methylphenidate were also recorded.

Methylphenidate was prescribed over the course of one year for 97 patients with symptomatic HIV infection (PGL = 24; ARC = 36; and, AIDS = 37). The average daily dose of methylphenidate was 20 mg a day (range, 5 to 50 mg/day). Of the 97 patients, 88 patients (91%) experienced at least mild improvement as a result of treatment with methylphenidate. Of these, 70 patients (72%) were rated as "markedly" or "moderately" improved. Of the 27 patients with major depression, 25 patients (92%) had at least "mild" improvement, while 23 patients (85%) experienced a marked to moderate response to treatment. Of 52 patients with varying organic mental disorders, including dementia, 46 (88%) had at least "mild" improvement. Thirty-five patients (67%) were rated as "markedly" or "moderately" improved with methylphenidate treatment.

Nine patients (9%) who showed no clinical response to methylphenidate were crossed over to dextroamphetamine (Dexedrine). Some improvement occurred in 5 (55%) of those 9 patients. Therefore, it can be assumed that both methylphenidate and dextroamphetamine can be used in patients with the AIDS dementia complex, organic personality disorders, amnestic syndromes, and organic mood disturbances. Marked improvements may occur for symptoms of affective and cognitive impairment (Fernandez, 1990; Fernandez et al., 1988a, 1988b; Holmes et al., 1989). Even in cases of severely impaired or demented patients, when cognitive function may not improve, patients will be more spontaneous and exhibit a more positive appreciation of life. These improvements are maintained with negligible side effects, including the precipitation of a psychosis or anorexia. A subgroup of patients with AIDS dementia complex developed abnormal involuntary dyskinetic movements on the psychostimulant dextroamphetamine when 15–20 mg/day were exceeded (Fernandez et al., 1988b). No such adverse effects have been reported to date for methylphenidate doses of up to 90 mg, even for seriously neurologically impaired HIV patients. Thus, we recommend that if dextroamphetamine is to be used, it should be prescribed cautiously and at lower doses. This will avoid precipitating a dyskinesia which may not be reversible even with drug discontinuation.

CONCLUSIONS

Human immunodeficiency virus infection is an insidious process, and is virulent to both the immune system and the central nervous system. There is a large degree of variance among the systemic manifestations as well as the neuropathological manifestations of HIV infection. These systemic and neuropathological manifestations do not necessarily correlate reciprocally with the severity of infection, as some neurodegenerative symptoms may even precede definitive evidence of immunological compromise.

Mental disorders associated with HIV infection can significantly affect both the quality of life and extent of survivability for a particular patient. An optimal treatment plan will allow for sensitive and accurate diagnosis and for rapid and effective relief of these symptoms. Many studies have noted the benefits of the psychostimulants, specifically methylphenidate, in achieving both qualitative and quantitative improvement in higher cortical functions, self-esteem, affective state, and self-sufficiency for patients infected with HIV who have concurrent organic mental disorders, including dementia. The minimal adverse side effects of methylphenidate, when judiciously prescribed, do not outweigh their benefit to a suffering patient with HIV disease whose quality of life may have been undermined by HIV-CNS involvement.

TABLE 2. METHYLPHENIDATE TRIALS AND RESPONSE

	Major Depression[a] (N = 27)	Adjustment Disorder with Depressed Mood[a] (N = 18)	Dementia + Depressed Mood (N = 26)	Dementia (N = 12)	Organic Affective (N = 3)	Organic Personality (N = 9)	Amnestic Syndrome (N = 2)	Total (%) (N = 97)
Marked	15	7	16	1		1		40
Moderate	8	5	6	4	1	6		30
Minimal	2	5	2	6		2	1	18
None	2	1	2	1	2		1	9

[a]Diffuse cognitive deficits were present and were greater than those expected from the primary psychiatric diagnosis alone.

REFERENCES

American Psychiatric Association. (1987), *Diagnostic and Statistical Manual of Mental Disorders,* 3rd Ed., rev. Washington, DC: American Psychiatric Press.

Beckett, A. (1990), The neurobiology of human immunodeficiency virus infection. In: *Review of Psychiatry,* eds. A. Tasman, S.M. Goldfinger, & C.A. Kaufman. Washington, DC: American Psychiatric Press, pp. 543–613.

Benton, A.L. (1974), *Revised Visual Retention Test,* 4th Ed. New York: The Psychological Corporation.

Benton, A.L. & des Hamsher, K. (1983), *Multilingual Aphasia Examination.* Iowa City: The University of Iowa.

Benton, A.L., des Hamsher, K., Varney, N.R. & Spreen, O. (1983), *Contributions to Neuropsychological Assessment: A Clinical Manual.* New York: Oxford University Press.

Diederich, N., Ackermann, R., Jurgens, R. et al. (1988), Early involvement of the nervous system by human immune deficiency virus (HIV). *Eur. Neurol.,* 28:93–103.

Fauci, A.S., Masur, H., Gelmann, E.P. et al. (1985), The acquired immunodeficiency syndrome: An update. *Ann. Intern. Med.,* 102:800–813.

Felgenhauer, K. (1987), Another venereal disease with frequent nervous system involvement: neuro-AIDS. *J. Neurol.,* 234:65–66.

Fernandez, F. (1987), Psychiatric complications in HIV-related illnesses. in: *American Psychiatric Association's AIDS Primer.* Washington, DC: American Psychiatric Association.

Fernandez, F. (1989). Anxiety and the neuropsychiatry of AIDS. *J. Clin. Psychiatry* 50(11,Suppl):9–14.

Fernandez, F. (1990), Addressing the psychiatric needs of the ambulatory AIDS patients. Workshop #48, American Psychiatric Association, 143rd Annual Meeting, New York, May 15, 1990.

Fernandez, F. & Levy, J.K. (1990), Diagnosis and management of HIV primary dementia. In: *Behavioral Aspects of AIDS,* ed. D.G. Ostrow. New York: Plenum Publishing Corporation, pp. 235–246.

Fernandez, F., Levy, J.K. & Salmeron, G. (1987a), The incidence of dementia and other organic mental disorders associated with human immunodeficiency virus infection. *Psycho-Oncology III,* p. 389.

Fernandez, F., Adams, F., Holmes, V.F. et al. (1987b), Methylphenidate for depressive disorders in cancer patients. *Psychosomatics,* 28:455–461.

Fernandez, F., Adams, F., Levy, J.K. et al. (1988a), Cognitive impairment due to AIDS-related complex and its response to psychostimulants. *Psychosomatics,* 29:38–46.

Fernandez, F., Levy, J.K. & Galizzi, H. (1988b), Response to HIV-related depression to psychostimulants: Case reports. *Hosp. Comm. Psychiatry,* 39:628–631.

Folstein, M.F., Folstein, S.E. & McHugh, P.R. (1975), "Mini-Mental State": a practical method for grading the cognitive state of patients for the clinician. *J. Psychiatric Res.,* 12:189–198.

Funke, I., Hahn, A., Rieber, E.P. et al. (1987), The cellular receptor (CF4) of the human immunodeficiency virus is expressed on neurons and glial cells in the human brain. *J. Exp. Med.,* 165:1230–1235.

Golden, C.J. (1978). *Stroop Color and Word Test: A Manual for Clinical and Experimental Uses.* Chicago: Stoelting Company.

Golden, C.J. (1981), *WAIS-R Manual.* New York: The Psychological Corporation.

Golden, C.J., Osmon, D.C., Moses, J.A., Jr. et al. (1981), *Interpretation of the Halstead-Reitan Neuropsychological Test Battery: A Case Book Approach.* New York: Grune & Stratton.

Grant, I., Atkinson, H., Hesselink, J.R. et al. (1987), Evidence for early central nervous system involvement in the acquired immunodeficiency syndrome (AIDS) and other human immunodeficiency virus (HIV) infections: Studies with neuropsychological testing and magnetic resonance imaging. *Ann. Intern. Med.,* 107:828–836.

Gyorkey, F., Melnick, J.L. & Gyorkey, P. (1987), Human immunodeficiency virus in brain biopsies of patients with AIDS and progressive encephalopathy. *J. Infect. Dis.,* 155:870–876.

Hill, J.M., Farrar, W.I. & Pert, C.B. (1986), Localization of the T4 antigen/AIDS virus receptor in monkey and rat brains: prominence in cortical regions. *Psychopharm. Bull.*, 22:689–694.

Holmes, V.F., Fernandez, F. & Levy, J.K. (1989), Psychostimulant response in ARC/AIDS patients. *J. Clin. Psychiatry*, 50:5–8.

Janssen, R.S., Saykin, A.J., Kaplan, J.E. et al. (1988), Neurological complications of human immunodeficiency virus infection in patients with lymphadenopathy syndrome. *Ann. Neurol.*, 23:49–55.

Jenicke, M.A. (1988), Assessment and treatment of affective illness in the elderly. *J. Geriatr. Psychiatry Neurol.*, 1(2):91–107.

Lacks, P. (1989). *Bender Gestalt Screening for Brain Dysfunction.* New York: John Wiley-Interscience.

Levin, H.S. (1986), Learning and memory. In: *Experimental Techniques in Human Neuropsychology*, ed. H.J. Hannay. New York: Oxford University Press.

Levy, J.K. (1990), Mental status examination pivotal in diagnosing HIV encephalopathy. *AIDS Med. Rep.*, 3(7):71–76.

Levy, J.A. & Bredesen, D.E. (1988), Central nervous system dysfunction in acquired immunodeficiency syndrome. *J. AIDS*, 1:41–64.

Levy, J.K. & Fernandez, F. (1989), Neuropsychiatric care for critically ill AIDS patients. *J. Crit. Illness*, 4:33–42.

Levy, J.K., Fernandez, F. & Pirozzolo, F.J. (1988), Patterns of cognitive impairment in HIV infection: A preliminary report. *J. Clin. Exp. Neuropsychol.*, 10:77.

Lezak, M.D. (1983), *Neuropsychological Assessment*, 2nd Ed. New York: Oxford University Press.

McArthur, J.C., Cohen, B.A., Selnes, O.A. et al. (1989), Low prevalence of neurological and neuropsychological abnormalities in otherwise healthy HIV-1 infected individuals: Results from the multicenter AIDS cohorts study. *Ann. Neurol.*, 26:601–611.

Maccario, M. & Scharre, D.W. (1987), HIV and acute onset of psychosis. *Lancet* 2:342.

Nath, A., Jankovic, J. & Pettigrew, L.C. (1987), Movement disorders and AIDS. *Neurology*, 37:37–41.

Navia, B.A. & Price, R.W. (1987), The acquired immunodeficiency syndrome dementia complex as the presenting or sole manifestation of human immunodeficiency virus infection. *Arch. Neurol.*, 44:65–69.

Navia, B.A., Cho, E-S., Petito, C.K. et al. (1986), The AIDS dementia complex: II. Neuropathology. *Ann. Neurol.*, 19:525–535.

Perry, S.W. (1990), Organic mental disorders caused by HIV: Update on early diagnosis and treatment. *Am. J. Psychiatry*, 147(6):696–710.

Pirozzolo, F.J., Christensen, K.J., Ogle, K.M. et al. (1981), Simple and choice reaction time in dementia: clinical implications. *Neurobiol. Aging*, 2:113.

Pizzo, P.A., Eddy, J., Falloon, J. et al. (1988), Effect of continuous intravenous infusion of zidovudine (AZT) in children with symptomatic HIV infection. *N. Engl. J. Med.*, 319:899–896.

Portegies, P., de Gans, J., Lange, J.M.A. et al. (1989), Declining incidence of AIDS dementia complex after introduction of zidovudine treatment. *Br. Med. J.*, 299:819–821.

Price, R.W., Brew, B., Sidtis, J. et al. (1988), The brain in AIDS: Central nervous system HIV-1 infection and AIDS dementia complex. *Science* 239:586–592.

Price, R.W., Koch, M.A., Sidtis, J.J. et al. (1989), Zidovudine (AZT) treatment of the AIDS dementia complex (ADC): Results of a placebo-controlled multicenter therapeutic trial. Abstracts of the V International Conference on AIDS. Montreal, Canada.

Pumarola-Sune, T., Navia, B.A., Cordon-Cardo, C. et al. (1986), HIV antigen in the brains of patients with the AIDS dementia complex. *Ann. Neurol.*, 21:490–496.

Raven, J.C., Court, J.H. & Raven, J. (1983), *Manual for Raven's Progressive Matrices and Vocabulary Scales: Section 3: Standard Progressive Matrices.* London: H.K. Lewis & Co., Ltd.

Reisberg, B., Ferris, S.H., de Leon, M.J. et al. (1982), The global deterioration scale (GDS): an instrument for the assessment of primary degenerative dementia (PDD). *Am. J. Psychiatry*, 139:1136–1139.

Schmitt, F.A., Bogley, J.W., McKinnis, R. et al. (1988), Neuropsychological outcome of zidovudine (AZT) treatment of patients with AIDS and AIDS-related complex. *N. Engl. J. Med.*, 319:1573–1578.

Tesar, G.E. (1982), The role of stimulants in general medicine. *Drug Therapy* July:186–196.

Van Gorp, W.G., Staz, P., Hinkin, C. et al. (1989), The neuropsychological aspects of HIV-1 spectrum disease. *Psychiatr. Med.*, 7:59–78.

Vazeux, R., Brousse, N., Jarry, A. et al. (1987), AIDS subacute encephalitis: Identification of HIV-infected cells. *Am. J. Pathol.* 126:403–410.

Whitehouse, P. (1986), The concept of subcortical and cortical dementia: another look. *Ann. Neurol.*, 19:1–7.

Wiley, C.A., Schrier, R.D., Nelson, J.A. et al. (1986), Cellular localization of human immunodeficiency virus infection within the brains of acquired immunodeficiency syndrome patients. *Proc. Natl. Acad. Sci.*, 83:7089–7093.

Woods, S.W., Tesar, G.E., Murray, G.B. et al. (1986), Psychostimulant treatment for depressive disorders secondary to medical illness. *J. Clin. Psychiatry*, 47:12–15.

Zachary, R.A. (1987), *Shipley Institute of Living Scale Revised Manual.* Los Angeles: Western Psychological Services.

Prescribing Practices of Ritalin:
The Suffolk County, New York Study

MIRIAM SHERMAN and MARGARET E. HERTZIG

INTRODUCTION

For more than 50 years stimulant medications have been the major psychotropic agents employed in the management of childhood behavior problems. Despite much concern in the lay press regarding prescribing practices for the most widely used stimulant—methylphenidate—Ritalin (*New York Times,* 1987), very few surveys have addressed the issue of prescribing practices. Safer and Krager (1988) have conducted nine biannual surveys of school nurses in Baltimore County, Maryland, since 1971, regarding medication treatment for hyperactive school children. The rate of medication treatment has grown steadily over this time period, doubling every 5 to 7 years. These workers predicted, that were present trends to continue, more than one million children would be receiving stimulant medication by the early 1990s in the United States. The 1987 data from Baltimore County indicated that a total of 3.4% of school-age children were receiving stimulant medication, 93% of which was methylphenidate. The majority of the prescriptions written were for elementary school-age children (age 7–11 years). The male:female ratio of medicated children was 5:1. The average duration of medication use was two years for children in public elementary schools, while in middle schools the duration averaged four years, and in senior high schools it averaged seven years. Medication was prescribed by private practitioners, most commonly pediatricians.

The Baltimore County school surveys clearly document a steady increase in the prevalence of medication treatment for hyperactivity/inattentiveness among school children over the past two decades, findings that are consistent with national trends as estimated by the Drug Enforcement Administration's aggregate production quotas for methylphenidate (*Federal Register,* 1987) and the Food and Drug Administration estimate of medical need for methylphenidate (Drug Enforcement Administration, 1986; *Federal Register,* 1987). Nevertheless, the rate of stimulant medication use in Baltimore County may well be relatively higher than elsewhere. Children in advantaged suburban areas such as this generally receive more medical care and more prescriptions for stimulants. Furthermore, the impact on prescribing practices of Baltimore county's state-funded clinics for hyperkinetic children is unknown, yet may be related to increased medication use (Safer and Krager, 1983, 1988).

For these reasons we sought to examine systematically prescribing practices for methylphenidate in another geographic area, New York State's Suffolk County. Suffolk County occupies the Eastern two-thirds of Long Island. It is 30 miles from the New York City border. Suffolk is 86 miles long, 20 miles wide, and covers 900 square miles. The total population of this suburban community is approximately 1,300,000 of which 100,000 are nonwhite. The majority of the resident population works locally or in adjacent Nassau County, although a relatively small number of residents commute to Manhattan. The county is connected to New York City by several expressways and the Long Island Railroad system. It is a popular tourist and vacation area. The county is home to several institutions of higher education, the largest being the State University of New York at Stony Brook, which includes a medical school. Additionally, the county is the site of three large state mental institutions, including a state-run acute care psychiatric facility for children. The

SUNY Stony Brook, Stony Brook, New York; Cornell University Medical College, New York, New York population is primarily middle and upper-middle class with some poverty pockets. Annual income below the poverty line has been estimated for 6.8% of the population (Suffolk County Planning Department, 1983).

This study utilized data derived from triplicate prescription forms for controlled substances to determine:

1. The number and characteristics of methylphenidate prescriptions written during one year, 1986, in Suffolk County.
2. Prescribing practices of physicians with regard to number of children receiving prescriptions, dosage prescribed, age of children receiving the drug, number of prescriptions written during the year, gender associations.
3. The types of medical specialists who wrote these prescriptions.

METHODS

Methylphenidate is a "controlled" Schedule II drug in all 50 states of the United States. It has been a controlled drug in New York State since 1972. In New York State, no prescription for a Schedule II drug may exceed a one month supply. Triplicate prescription forms are required in New York State and in five other states. Therefore, the New York State Bureau of Controlled Substances of the New York State Department of Health maintains records based on copies of the triplicate prescription forms. Each of these forms contains one copy to be retained by the physician, one copy to be retained by the pharmacy, and one copy to be sent to the Bureau. Data on these forms include the usual information on any "noncontrolled" prescription form. Additional information includes the practitioner's Drug Enforcement Administration (DEA) number, and if the prescription originates from an institution, the facility DEA number as well.

The study involved analysis of the computerized data for a one-year period beginning January 1986. These data were made available in anonymous form to the investigators. Each individual for whom methylphenidate was prescribed was identified by number, enabling the number of prescriptions received by each child to be ascertained. Each physician was identified by medical specialty.

RESULTS

A total of 3,893 prescriptions were written for methylphenidate (Ritalin) by physicians practicing in Suffolk County in 1986. Prescriptions were written throughout the year, with the greatest number being written in October ($N = 408$; 10.5%), followed by April ($N = 377$; 9.7%). The fewest prescriptions were written during the summer months of July and August (Table 1).

A total daily dose of 20 mg was the dose most commonly prescribed (approximately 36% of all prescriptions), followed by 30 mg and 10 mg per day. These three dosage levels account for over 70% of all the prescriptions written during the year. A daily dosage level above 60 mg was found on only 89 prescriptions (2.3%). The highest dose level, 150 mg/day, was found on three prescriptions (Table 2).

The greatest number of prescriptions were written for school age children age 8–11 years (mean age: 9.3). The youngest child receiving the drug was 3 years old (Fig. 1). There were 3,351 prescriptions written for boys (85.4%) and 575 prescriptions written for girls (14.6%). Thus the gender distribution was approximately 6:1, male:female. A total of 1,635 children from age 3 to 17 years received methylphenidate in 1986. In that year 386,309 children in this age group lived in Suffolk County, thus 0.4% (1 of every 250) of the child population received at least one prescription for the drug. Table 3 shows the age distribution of the children. The vast majority ($N = 1463$; 98%) of children who received one or more prescriptions were between age 6 and 13 years. Both mean and modal ages for children receiving the drug was age 9; 14.7% of all children receiving the drug were this age.

Figure 2 shows the number of prescriptions written for each child. Over half the prescriptions were written only *once* for a given child ($N = 883$; 52.2%). Between two and five prescriptions were written for 1,535 children (90.7%).

TABLE 1. NUMBER OF RITALIN PRESCRIPTIONS
WRITTEN IN 1986, BY MONTH

Month	Frequency/ Number of Prescriptions	Percent
January	330	8.5
February	299	7.7
March	361	9.3
April	377	9.7
May	366	9.4
June	285	7.3
July	179	4.6
August	249	6.4
September	372	9.6
October	408	10.5
November	355	9.1
December	312	8.0

Table 4 shows the number of children of each age receiving various total daily doses of methylphenidate. The great majority received a total daily dose of 40 mg/day or less (1,480 children; 90.6%). The most common dose was 20 mg/day (578 children; 35.4%). For children over five years of age, the relationship between dosage prescribed and the children's ages was not significant.

We examined the medical specialties of the prescribing physicians. Table 5 shows these specialties, the number of children treated by the physicians of each specialty, and the mean ages of the children. Pediatricians treated the greatest number of children ($N = 905$; 54.4%). Child neurologists ($N = 187$; 11.4%) and child psychiatrists ($N = 170$; 10.4%) ranked next in numbers of children they treated. We were able to statistically analyze the mean ages of children treated by different specialists. (Surgery and ophthalmology were excluded from this analysis because each of those specialists treated only one child.) The mean age of children treated by adult psychiatrists was 10.4 years (SD = 3.6). This mean age was significantly higher than the mean age treated by other specialists.

TABLE 2. NUMBER OF RITALIN PRESCRIPTIONS WRITTEN IN 1986, BY TOTAL
DAILY DOSE

Daily Dose (mg)	Frequency/ Number of Prescriptions	Percent
5	13	0.3
10	787	19.9
15	63	1.6
20	1,421	35.9
25	38	1.0
30	852	21.5
35	35	8.9
40	377	9.5
45	12	0.3
50	112	2.8
55	18	0.5
60	143	3.6
over 60	89	2.3

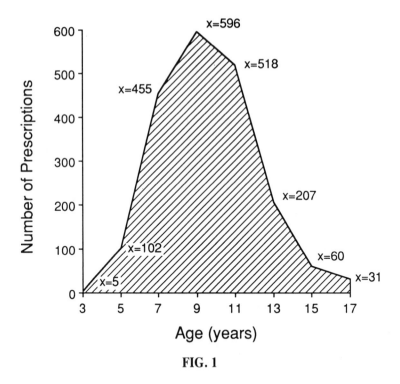

FIG. 1

DISCUSSION

Guidelines for the prescription of methylphenidate have been promulgated by both the American Academy of Pediatrics (Brown et al., 1987) and the American Academy of Child and Adolescent Psychiatry. (Facts for Families, 1990). These professional bodies have underscored the fact that stimulant medication can be an important component of the treatment of children who manifest signs of attention deficit hyperactivity

TABLE 3. NUMBER OF CHILDREN OF EACH AGE
RECEIVING PRESCRIPTIONS FOR RITALIN

Age	Number of Children	Percent
3	2	0.1
4	18	1.1
5	53	3.2
6	165	10.1
7	203	12.4
8	218	13.3
9	240	14.7
10	222	13.6
11	199	12.2
12	114	7.0
13	102	6.2
14	47	2.9
15	22	1.3
16	17	1.0
17	13	0.8

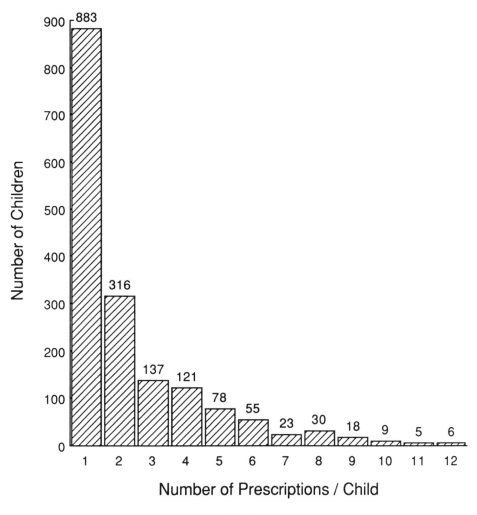

FIG. 2.

disorder (ADHD), such as short attention span, easy distractibility, impulsive behavior, motor restlessness, and overactivity which interfere with an ability to learn in the classroom, socialize with peers, and participate appropriately in family life. However, it is also emphasized that medication for children with attention deficit hyperactivity disorder should be prescribed only after a complete diagnostic assessment of behavioral as well as learning problems has been made. Medication should never be used as an isolated treatment, but should be integrated into a comprehensive plan based on a consideration of individual psychotherapy, family therapy, behavior modification, and remediation of academic deficiencies. Once a decision to medicate is decided upon, it is recommended that the initial dose usually be given twice daily (Popper, 1988).

Concerns in the lay press have focused on the number of school-age children receiving stimulant medication and the apparent casualness with which it is prescribed (*New York Times,* 1987). The American Academy of Pediatrics has also noted the frequency with which requests to prescribe medication are made by parents, school principals, teachers, special educators, and school nurses, and have urged that pediatricians be cautious of becoming surrogate prescribers of medications (American Academy of Pediatrics, 1987).

What do the data of the Suffolk County survey tell us about the concerns of both professional organizations and the lay press regarding the prescription of methylphenidate? In this county, 0.4% of the preschool and school-age child population (ages 3–17 years) had received at least one prescription for methylphenidate during the 1986 calendar year. The most recently available comparative data from Baltimore County in 1987

TABLE 4. NUMBER OF CHILDREN AT EACH AGE RECEIVING VARIOUS DAILY DOSES OF RITALIN

Total Daily Dose (mg)	Age of Children (years)															Total Receiving Each Dose
	3	4	5	6	7	8	9	10	11	12	13	14	15	16	17	
5		1							1							2
10		3	11	36	34	44	40	47	23	24	18	12	2	4	3	301
15		2	2	2	3	2	3	3	1	3		1				22
20		3	19	55	83	80	85	80	68	39	29	15	12	5	5	578
25			1	1	5	1		1	2	4	2			1		18
30		8	12	46	52	51	61	53	46	30	17	4	4	4	1	392
35			1	1	1				1		2	1	1			8
40	2	2	2	12	16	25	25	19	26	8	12	5	1	2	2	159
>40	0	0	5	11	10	13	27	19	22	8	19	7	1	2	1	162

has indicated that 3.4% of school-age children were receiving stimulant medication. Suffolk County data included all children between the ages of 3 and 17, while in Baltimore County only school-age children were included. It has been estimated that approximately 10% of all children meet diagnostic criteria for ADHD (Popper, 1988) and that approximately 70% of these are responsive to medication. Given these estimates, it appears that physicians are surely not overmedicating in Suffolk County.

The doses prescribed for children appear to conform to usual and accepted prescribing practices. The data confirm other studies that report primary care physicians are the specialists who wrote the majority of prescriptions.

Prescribing practices, based on these data, *do* seem to be cause for concern. The fact that more than half (52%) of children who received prescriptions for methylphenidate received only *one* prescription in the year 1986, leads one to wonder about the appropriateness of the Academy of Pediatrics' caution regarding pediatricians who provide a "rubber stamp" for drug treatment. While the "single prescription phenomenon" may in part reflect patient noncompliance, this phenomenon may also reflect the fact that pediatricians may be responding to pressures put upon them by school personnel. If this were indeed the case, then one could wonder about the adequacy of the initial evaluation and the integration of pharmacotherapy into a total treatment plan.

TABLE 5. SPECIALTIES OF PHYSICIANS PRESCRIBING RITALIN AND NUMBER OF CHILDREN TREATED

Specialty of Prescribing Physicians	Number of Children	Mean Age of Child
Pediatrics	905	9.3
Family practice	138	9.5
Psychiatry	110	10.4
Child psychiatry	170	9.3
Neurology (child neurology)	187	8.6
Internal medicine	59	9.6
Surgery	1	6.0
Ophthalmology	1	16.0
Unknown specialty	63	8.6
Pediatricians treated the greatest number of children (N = 905; 54.4%)		

Although data from this study provide no information about other treatment modalities offered, one wonders again about the nature and adequacy of the followup care of these children.

REFERENCES

Brown, R.T., Borden, K.A., Wynne, M.E., Spunt, A.L. & Clingerman, S.R. (1987), Compliance with pharmacological and cognitive treatments for attention deficit disorder. *Am. Acad. Child Adolesc. Psychiatry,* 26:521–525.

Facts for Families (1990), Children who can't pay attention. *Am. Acad. Child Adolesc. Psychiatry.*

Drug Enforcement Agency (1987), DEA-Controlled Substances: Establishment of the 1987 aggregate production quota for methylphenidate. *Fed. Reg.,* 52:20650–20651.

Drug Enforcement Administration (1987), *Quarterly Per Capita Consumption of Drugs by State: Fourth Quarter 1986.* Author.

Editorial Committee on Children with Disabilities, Committee on Drugs (1987), Medication for children with an attention deficit disorder, *Pediatrics,* 80(5):758–759.

Popper, C.W. (1988), Disorders usually first evident in infancy, childhood and adolescence. In: *Textbook of Psychiatry,* eds. J.A. Talbott, R.E. Hales, & S.E. Yudofsky. Washington, DC: American Psychiatric Press, pp. 651–664.

Safer, D.J. & Krager, J.M. (1983), Trends in medication treatment of hyperactive school children. *Clin. Pediatr.,* 23:500–504.

———— ———— (1988), A survey of medication treatment for hyperactive/inattentive students. *J. Am. Med. Assoc.,* 260(15):2256–2258.

Schmidt, W.E. (1987), Sales of drugs are soaring for treatment of hyperactivity. *New York Times,* May 5, 1987, p. C3.

Suffolk County Planning Department (1983), *Suffolk County: A Place to Live,* Hauppauge, NY: Author.

Effects of Ritalin on Arithmetic Tasks

CARYN L. CARLSON and MARCUS L. THOMEER

INTRODUCTION

While the efficacy of stimulant medication in decreasing the problem behaviors of children with attention deficit hyperactivity disorder (ADHD) has long been recognized, the utility of methylphenidate (MPH) in enhancing the academic productivity of these children remains a topic of debate. The central issue in this debate involves the distinction between acute improvements on academic tasks brought about following the administration of MPH and "long-term" improvements in academic achievement following a course of stimulant treatment. The purpose of this chapter is to review and critique the research addressing both of these outcome measures as they relate to effects of MPH on arithmetic performance. Additionally, speculations about the possible mechanisms underlying stimulant enhancement of arithmetic performance and suggestions for future research on this area will be offered. Finally, guidelines for conducting assessments of stimulant effects on arithmetic performance of individual children will be offered.

STUDIES OF LONG-TERM EFFECTS OF MPH

Rie et al. (1976a) sought to determine the effects of MPH on the Iowa Test of Basic Skills for 28 "underachieving" primary grade children using a double-blind, counterbalanced design. Of the 28 children, 13 were regarded as "hyperactive" by the teacher and or parent report although no formal diagnoses of ADHD were made. Each treatment condition (MPH and placebo) lasted 12 weeks, with assessments occuring prior to treatment, at 12 weeks, and again at the end of the study. Dosage was determined on an individual basis based on "weekly phone calls and a review of side effects," with a mean dose of 21.07 mg/day. Seven of the children received more than 1 mg/kg/day, 15 received .5 to 1.0 mg/kg/day, and 6 received less than .5 mg/kg/day. No significant difference arose between groups on either math subtest of the Iowa Test of Basic Skills.

In a replication of their study, Rie et al. (1976b) report similar results, with no drug effect found on measures of math. In this study, 10 of the 18 subjects were rated as hyperactive by either teacher or parent. A crossover design was again used, with each treatment condition (MPH or placebo) lasting 15 weeks. The mean dose in this second study was 23.06 mg/day, with 6 of the children receiving more than 1 mg/kg/day, 10 receiving .5 to 1.0 mg/kg/day, and 2 receiving less than .5 mg/kg/day.

In an evaluation of 57 children, Charles and Schain (1981) examined the effects of varying durations of MPH therapy (with one subject on pemoline) on the Wide Range Achievement Test (WRAT) and the Peabody Individual Achievement Test (PIAT). There were five groups compared, based on the duration of stimulant therapy (Group 1: 0–6 months; Group 2: 6 months to 2 years; Group 3: 2–3 years; Group 4: 3–4 years with discontinuation at least one month prior to followup examination; Group 5: still taking stimulants). Results indicated that most of the children were functioning well below the norms for children their age. On the WRAT, Groups 1–4 were at least two grades below grade level and Group 5 was one grade below grade level in their math performance. On the PIAT, Groups 1 and 2 were more than a year behind their expected achievement for their age, while Groups 3–5 were within their age group and expected

The University of Texas at Austin, Austin, Texas

achievement in math. While analyses comparing the five groups revealed no significant effect of time on MPH on the overall pattern of academic performance, the authors note that there was a nonsignificant tendency for the groups on MPH longest (Groups 4 and 5) to be performing closer to expected achievement level than those on MPH for shorter durations (Groups 1 and 2). An examination of the means presented in the tables in this study appear to indicate that this trend was particularly strong for PIAT arithmetic measures, with children in Groups 4 and 5 averaging one month ahead on this measure and children in Groups 1 and 2 averaging 18 months behind in achievement. However, the overall *t*-test conducted across groups for this measure was evidently not significant.

Gittelman et al. (1983) examined the effects of MPH and reading remediation on children's academic and behavioral performance. Children were referred to the study by teachers because of poor academic performance. Although subjects were rated as more deviant on the inattention factor of the Conners Teacher Rating Scale (Conners, 1969), they were required to obtain ratings below the mean of 1.5 on the CTRS Hyperactivity factor, and none of the children were perceived by teachers as disruptive. All children received an 18-week program of reading remediation; additionally, half were randomly assigned to receive MPH (*n* = 31) and half to receive placebo (*n* = 30). For subjects who received MPH, dosage was determined contingent upon the absence of side effects after a 4-week period of receiving 60 mg/day MPH. The average dose received was 44.19 mg/day (1.19 mg/kg) MPH, with the range of daily doses being from 10 to 60 mg/day. Children were evaluated prior to and following the 18-week remediation program, and two months and six months after treatment. Posttreatment, no differences were found between the MPH group and the placebo group on the arithmetic test of the WRAT. However, on the Stanford Achievement Test, the MPH group had significantly higher scores than the placebo group on three of the four arithmetic measures. Although no significant differences between groups on math measures were found at 2- or 6-month followup, it should be noted that MPH was discontinued at the end of the 18-week treatment.

In a two-year followup of 72 "hyperactive" boys, Riddle and Rapoport (1976) examined the effects of continued medication treatment on children's academic performance as measured by the WRAT. Sixty-five percent of the sample (*n* = 47) were still on medication at the time of followup (40 on stimulants and 7 on imipramine), although medication was discontinued for at least three weeks prior to the evaluation. Comparisons were made between the entire sample and 20 children who had been initially randomly assigned to MPH conditions and who the authors judged to have been initially good responders and consistent in taking medication. The total group performed significantly more poorly on WRAT reading and arithmetic than a control group of children, and the subgroup of 20 consistently MPH-treated children obtained scores nearly identical to those of the hyperactive sample as a whole.

In a five-year followup study, Blouin et al. (1978) investigated the effects of MPH on academic achievement of 42 children who had been formally diagnosed as ADHD (based on neuropsychological test results, detailed history, school record information, and physician referal letters). Of the 42 subjects, 27 were MPH-treated and 15 were not medicated. Interestingly, a subject was considered treated with MPH if at any time during the five years foliowup, MPH had been administered. Knowledge on dosages was only available for 15 of the subjects (X = 20 mg/day) and knowledge on duration was only known for 25 subjects (X = 1.88 years). No differences were found between the MPH-treated group and the nontreated group in terms of academic achievement at initial assessment or at five-year followup.

STUDIES OF SHORT-TERM EFFECTS OF MPH

All the studies reviewed below examined immediate effects of MPH on arithmetic performance. Although an attempt was made to review all relevant studies, some studies are not included because placebo procedures were not employed or because arithmetic performance was evaluated as part of a test battery, but arithmetic results were not reported separately.

Douglas and colleagues (1986) examined the short-term effects of MPH on the arithmetic performance of 16 ADHD children in both laboratory and classroom settings. The experimental task consisted of sets of addition, subtraction, and, when appropriate, multiplication problems, with difficulty level adjusted during screening. Within both laboratory and classroom settings, children receiving .3 mg/kg MPH attempted and solved more problems correctly on MPH than on placebo. Additionally, MPH resulted in higher ratios of correctly completed problems ("accuracy" score) and higher rates of items completed for each minute spent on task "efficiency" score) than placebo. Interestingly, children on MPH did not differ significantly from those on placebo in time spent on the task in the laboratory, and, in the classroom, these children spent significantly less time on the task than those on placebo. A final dependent measure related to arithmetic performance was a self-correction task, in which children were allowed time at the end of experimental sessions to correct their own work. Compared with placebo, children on MPH spent more time on self-correction and were rated by examiners as expending more effort; additionally, they corrected a greater proportion of their total errors after receiving MPH (X = 20%) than after receiving placebo (X = 7%). Based on this pattern of findings, Douglas et al. (1986) concluded that ADHD children on MPH work harder than those not receiving MPH. They noted that the beneficial effects of MPH cannot be attributed to either "slowing children down" or to simply increasing output; rather, children are more accurate and efficient in their academic performance with MPH than with placebo.

In a study designed to examine dose effects on academic performance, Douglas et al. (1988) examined the effects of .15 mg/kg, .3 mg/kg, and .6 mg/kg MPH on the arithmetic performance of 19 children diagnosed as ADHD. Trend analyses revealed a significant beneficial effect of MPH on number of problems attempted, number of problems correct, "efficiency" score, and examiner's effort ratings; there was a trend (p < .06) toward greater "accuracy" scores. The pattern of results comparing dosage effects across the dependent variables was complex and not crucial to the current discussion; however, for all variables the .6 mg/kg dosage optimized performance.

Several studies examining MPH effects on arithmetic performance have been conducted in the ADHD Summer Treatment Program (STP) directed since 1980 by William Pelham, initially at Florida State University and currently at Western Psychiatric Institute and Clinic. A detailed description of the procedures used in conducting medication assessments in the STP is contained in Pelham and Hoza (1987); briefly, arithmetic evaluations are conducted in a classroom type setting using double-blind, placebo-controlled procedures, with each child typically completing multiple evaluations on each dose over the course of the summer.

Pelham et al. (1985a) examined dose effects of MPH on the academic and social behavior of 29 ADHD children participating in the STP. Children received, in random order, three dosages of MPH (.15, .3, and .6 mg/kg) for one week each and two weeks of placebo. Among the academic measures, subjects completed daily arithmetic worksheets matched to their independent level through pretesting and in which only one problem type (addition, subtraction, multiplication, or division) was presented each day. Trend analyses revealed a significant linear effect of MPH on arithmetic measures, with children on MPH attempting and completing more problems correctly than those on placebo. Although peak improvement for arithmetic measures was found for the .3 mg/kg dosage, the curvilinear trend was not significant. The proportion of problems correctly completed was not affected by MPH; the authors suggest that the initially high levels of accuracy (approximately 85%) may have resulted in a ceiling effect. They also point out that results of their study indicate that a .3 mg/kg dosage of MPH might be expected to result in a 30% increase in the number of arithmetic problems practiced by ADHD children, with no loss in accuracy.

In a study conducted to compare sustained-release and standard methylphenidate, Pelham et al. (1985b) compared the effects of Ritalin SR-20 to twice-daily doses of Ritalin 10 mg on the academic and social behavior of 13 ADHD boys in the STP. Among other measures, each subject completed two-minute timed arithmetic drills using materials appropriate to his instructional level. Comparisons between the average performance across the two MPH dosages and placebo revealed that children on MPH attempted significantly more problems and were significantly more accurate than those on placebo, with no significant differences found in these measures between the sustained and standard MPH formulae.

Carlson, Pelham, Milich, and Dixon (1990) examined the single and combined effects of methylphenidate and behavior therapy on the classroom behavior and academic performance of 27 5–12-year-old ADHD boys participating in the STP. Subjects received placebo, .3 and .6 mg/kg MPH in a randomly determined order on the Tuesday, Wednesday, and Thursday of each of 6 weeks. Among other classroom measures, the same two-minute timed arithmetic task used by Pelham et al. (1987) was completed by each subject daily. In comparisons of behavior modification to regular classroom settings, results collapsed across classroom conditions revealed significant effects of MPH on number of problems attempted, with children attempting more problems on .6 mg/kg (X = 19.5) and .3 mg/kg (X = 20.3) than on placebo (X = 15.2). No significant medication effects were found for ratio of correct problems.

STUDIES EXAMINING PROCESSES UNDERLYING MPH EFFECTS ON ARITHMETIC

While the studies cited thus far consistently found that stimulants improve arithmetic productivity in ADHD children, they do not provide information regarding the processes that might underlie these improvements. In the only study that has addressed processes mediating stimulant-induced improvements in arithmetic, Carlson et al. (in press) used a divided attention paradigm to examine effects of Ritalin on the arithmetic performance of 13 ADHD boys enrolled in the STP. Using a counterbalanced design, subjects completed the experimental task on two consecutive days, after receiving either .3 mg/kg methylphenidate or a placebo. Boys were required to complete 80 single-digit addition problems (with answers greater than 9) presented on a computer screen. On half the trials, they were also required to respond to a tone that was presented either before (single-task conditions) or after (dual-task conditions) problem presentation; the trials on which the tone occurred after problem presentation represented the dual-task condition. For the purposes of this study, results under both single- and dual-task conditions are of interest. Methylphenidate had a significant effect on accuracy and speed of arithmetic performance: boys solved more problems correctly when receiving MPH (X = 90%) than when receiving placebo (X = 79.6%) and answered problems faster on medication (X = 4912 ms) than on placebo (X = 5432 ms). Interestingly, medication also decreased latencies between problems, with children pressing the spacebar to receive the next problem significantly more quickly after receiving MPH (X = 871 ms) than placebo (X = 1178 ms). Thus, it appears that at least part of children's improved performance on arithmetic tasks with stimulant treatment is related to nonspecific increases in efficiency (i.e., less "down time" between problems). Finally, the pattern of results in single- versus dual-task conditions was examined to explore the cognitive processes underlying stimulant-related improvements in arithmetic. Since medication decreased reaction time to the tone during single-task conditions, but not during dual-task conditions, it was suggested that methylphenidate resulted in reallocation of existing cognitive capacity from the secondary reaction time task to the primary arithmetic task.

CONCLUSIONS

Consistent findings emerge from the studies examining short-term effects of MPH, with every study reviewed documenting that the drug enhances arithmetic productivity and most also finding that it improves arithmetic accuracy. Importantly, these studies each employed excellent experimental procedures, including adequate diagnostic techniques using a variety of measures, double-blind, placebo-controlled medication procedures, standardized medication dosages, and appropriate and relevant dependent measures. The robustness of the findings across six well-designed and implemented studies (total n = 117) lends strong support to the conclusion that MPH leads to short-term enhancements in the arithmetic productivity of ADHD children.

Given that MPH improves the arithmetic performance of ADHD children, what dosage might be expected to optimally enhance this performance? The issue of dosage effects is one of great concern clinically, particularly since the report of Sprague and Sleator (1977) that, while lower dosages of MPH appear to improve cognitive functioning, higher dosages may impair it. The three studies reviewed that addressed dosage effects (Carlson et al., 1990; Douglas et al., 1988; Pelham et al., 1985) obtained somewhat different findings. While Douglas et al. reported that .6 mg/kg optimized performance on all measures, Carlson et al. (1990) and Pelham et al. (1985) found no significant differences between .3 and .6 mg/kg MPH, with both significantly improving arithmetic performance compared with placebo. Indeed, in these latter two studies, performance on .3 mg/kg was slightly but nonsignificantly better than on .6 mg/kg. It should be noted that none of these results are necessarily inconsistent with those of Sprague and Sleator (1977), who reported decrements in cognitive performance only at a higher dosage (1.00 mg/kg) of MPH than used by Carlson et al. (1990), Douglas et al. (1988), or Pelham et al. (1985). Based on available evidence, then, it is not clear what dosage of MPH optimizes arithmetic performance for the "average" ADHD child. As other authors have suggested, however (Douglas et al., 1986; Pelham, 1983; Pelham and Hoza, 1987), the large range of individual patterns of response to MPH dosage suggests the importance of individual medication trials with both behavioral and cognitive measures for all children for whom MPH is prescribed.

A major issue related to MPH effects on academic achievement involves whether its beneficial effects are limited to short-term improvements following a single dosage, or whether a treatment regimen of MPH might bring about improved long-term academic functioning. It has been suggested that no evidence exists that MPH enhances academic performance, and that the immediate benefits of MPH on academic performance occur too quickly to reflect actual achievement gains, and may merely reflect improved ability to perform in the test setting (Jacobvitz et al., in press). It is our opinion, however, that this conclusion is premature, and we will advance three arguments to support this position. First, the results of at least two of the studies reviewed (Carlson et al., in press; Douglas et al., 1986) suggest that MPH effects cannot be attributed entirely to increased productivity. Second, the studies of MPH effects on long-term academic functioning yield findings that are virtually uninterpretable, and, third, even if these effects are found to be limited to increased productivity, this effect might be expected to result in long-term gains.

Douglas et al. (1986) showed that, in addition to completing more problems, children on MPH were more efficient (completing more problems per minute) and accurate (completing a greater ratio of correct problems) in their arithmetic performance. Carlson et al. (in press) found that medication resulted in a significant decrease in children's latencies between problems, suggesting that at least some of the increased productivity brought about by stimulant treatment is related to "nonspecific" enhancement of efficiency. It was not the case, however, that improved performance could be attributed entirely to decreased time between problems, since answer time for each problem independent of latency between problems was also significantly decreased following methylphenidate. Again, it appears that MPH allows children to make better use of their time—actually increases their efficiency—when solving arithmetic problems.

As stated previously, the results of the studies reviewed provide consistent evidence that MPH enhances arithmetic performance following a single dose administration. Every study reviewed found increases in productivity, and the majority also reported improved accuracy with MPH. On the other hand, no study examining long-term effects of MPH treatment have found improvements in global outcome measures, such as achievement tests. However, as other authors have concluded (Douglas et al., 1986; Pelham, 1983), these studies are so conceptually and/or methodologically flawed that they provide little useful information about the therapeutic effects of MPH on academic achievement. For example, studies vary widely in adequacy of outcome measures, dosages administered, procedures used to assign children to treatment groups, length of time on medication, and procedures used to determine adherence to medication regimens. Most of these issues have been examined elsewhere (Douglas et al., 1986; Pelham, 1983), although the former three will be mentioned here due to their importance to this topic.

Most of the studies examining long-term effects used achievement tests as the sole measure of academic outcome. Although this may be appropriate for a study spanning at least a year, such tests may not be sensitive to changes occurring after shorter treatment periods. Of the six studies reviewed above, three (Gittelman et al., 1983; Rie et al., 1976a, 1976b) examined performance after 18 weeks or less of MPH treatment. The WRAT, in particular, has been criticized for its poor psychometric properties and few items at each grade level (e.g., Witt, 1986).

Given the widely accepted finding that some higher dosages of MPH that optimize behavioral improvements may actually have a deleterious effect on cognitive functioning (e.g., Sprague and Sleator, 1977), the method used in these studies to determine dosage is particularly crucial. None of the studies reviewed appeared to evaluate MPH effects on cognitive functioning as part of the procedures for determining dosage. It seems reasonable to expect that long-term academic benefits will be more likely to occur when dosage determinations are made using cognitive as opposed to behavioral criteria.

Random assignment to treatment and control groups was employed only in three studies (Gittelman et al., 1983; Rie et al., 1976a, 1976b). While there clearly are ethical constraints on this practice, the conclusions that can be drawn based on studies not using this design are severely limited. Clearly, differences between groups other than treatment condition can account for negative findings; for example, children in the nonstimulant-treated group may be less severely disabled, or the parents of children who decide, for whatever reason, not to pursue stimulant treatment may be more likely to pursue other treatment methods than the parents of children in the stimulant-treated group. Interestingly, the Gittelman et al. (1983) study, which employed random assignment, did find significantly better arithmetic performance for children receiving MPH than for those receiving placebo immediately following the 18-week treatment program, although it should be noted that the subjects used did not have ADHD.

The optimal experimental study to address this issue would be one in which children are randomly assigned to treatment and placebo groups, treated with a dosage determined based on optimal academic enhancement, and evaluated on a variety of outcome measures following a long-term, carefully monitored treatment regimen. Given the ethical objections to such a design, it is unlikely that such a study will ever be conducted. In lieu of such evidence, however, it seems more prudent to conclude that we know little about long-term effects of MPH than to base conclusions about the lack of its efficacy in enhancing academic achievement on studies with serious methodological flaws.

Even if the positive effects of MPH on arithmetic productivity are found to be limited to general enhancement of efficiency rather than some central processing improvement, this finding should not be taken as evidence that stimulants cannot improve long-term academic functioning. Pelham et al. (1985) address this issue by citing the importance of drill and practice in gaining arithmetical computation skills (Resnick and Ford, 1981; Yoshida, 1980) and suggesting that MPH may therefore be expected to result in long-term gains in arithmetic skill provided effective teaching is offered and adverse effects do not occur. Thus, regardless of the mechanism underlying the increased productivity, the increased opportunity to practice brought about through MPH treatment may enhance long-term achievement.

DIRECTIONS FOR FUTURE RESEARCH

It is clear from the above discussion that further examination of long-term effects of MPH on arithmetic functioning is the most crucial area in need of further research. In addition, a question of more theoretical than practical interest involves further exploration of the possible mechanisms underlying the MPH-induced enhancements of arithmetic productivity. Of central interest is the question of whether MPH improvements result from an actual enhancement of children's arithmetic strategies or whether medication simply allows children to execute their current strategies more efficiently.

Siegler (1987) has discussed the use of solution-time patterns and self-report in determining strategies children use in solving addition problems. He found that individual children often use diverse problem-solving strategies, with most children using at least three. Examining the effects of MPH on the strategies children use to solve addition problems might broaden our understanding of whether improvements seen with MPH treatment are more quantitative or qualitative in nature.

ARITHMETIC MEASURES IN CLINICAL PRACTICE: INDIVIDUAL MEDICATION ASSESSMENTS

In our lab and others (W. E. Pelham, personal communication; J. M. Swanson, personal communication), evaluations of stimulant effects on arithmetic performance are often conducted as part of a comprehensive medication assessment for individual children. Pelham and Hoza (1987) emphasize several general points related to conducting individual medication trials with ADHD children, including the importance of varying dosage levels across days and obtaining several evaluations on each dosage. In addition to these general suggestions, the following brief guidelines may be useful to clinicians who wish to incorporate arithmetic performance in medication assessment batteries.

Materials used in arithmetic assessments can be obtained from a variety of sources. We have often used arithmetic problems obtained from the *Mad Minute* (Addison-Wesley, 1981) workbook series, which contains arithmetic problems at various difficulty levels. When possible, children are evaluated in the laboratory by completing as many problems as possible in a standardized time period (e.g., 5 or 10 minutes). If frequent laboratory visits are not practical, we have also successfully recruited teachers to participate in the assessment procedure by administering the task at school each day of the medication trial. Measures of both number of problems completed and accuracy are obtained, and we have found this information to be useful to physicians in making decisions regarding dosage levels.

REFERENCES

Addison-Wesley. (1981), *The Mad Minute*. Reading, MA: Author.

Blouin, A.G., Bornstein, R.A. & Trites R.L. (1978), Teenage alcohol use among hyperactive children: A five year follow-up study. *J. Pediatr. Psychol.*, 3:188–194.

Carlson, C.L., Pelham, W.E., Swanson, J.M. & Wagner, J.L. (in press), A divided attention analysis of the effects of methylphenidate on the arithmetic performance of children with attention deficit hyperactivity disorder. To appear in *J. Child Psychol. Psychiatry*.

—— —— Milich, R. & Dixon, J. (1990), *Single and Combined Effects of Methylphenidate and Behavior Therapy on the Classroom Behavior, Academic Performance and Self-Evaluations of Children with Attention Deficit Hyperactivity Disorder*. Paper presented at Society for Research in Child & Adolescent Psychopathology Annual Meeting, Costa Mesa, CA.

Charles L. & Schain, R. (1981), A four-year follow-up study of the effects of methylphenidate on the behavior and academic achievement of hyperactive children. *J. Abnorm. Child Psychol.*, 9(4):495–505.

Conners, C.K. (1969), A teacher rating scale for use in drug studies with children. *Am. J. Psychiatry*, 126:884–888.

Douglas, V.I., Barr, R.G., O'Neill, M.E. & Britton B.G. (1986), Short term effects of methylphenidate on the cognitive, learning, and academic performance of children with attention deficit disorder in the laboratory and classroom. *J. Child Psychol. Psychiatry*, 27:191–211.

—— —— Amin, K., O'Neill, M.E. & Britton, B.G. (1988), Dosage effects and individual responsivity to methylphenidate in attention deficit disorder. *J. Child Psychol. Psychiatry*, 29(4):453–475.

Gittelman, R., Klein, D.F. & Feingold, I. (1983), Children with reading disorders-II. Effects of methylphenidate in combination with reading remediation. *J. Child Psychol. Psychiatry*, 24:193–212.

Jacobvitz, D., Sroufe, L.A., Stewart, M. & Leffert N. (in press). Treating problem children with stimulant drugs: A fifteen year update. To appear in *J. Am. Acad. Child Psychiatry*.

Pelham, W.E. (1983), The effects of psychostimulants on academic achievement in hyperactive and learning-disabled children. *Thalamus*, 3:1–47.

—— & Hoza, J. (1985), Behavioral assessment of psychostimulant effects on ADD children in a summer day treatment program. In *Advances in Behavioral Assessment of Children and Families*, ed. R. Prinz. Greenwich, CT: JAI Press Inc.

—— Bender, M.E., Caddell, J., Booth, S. & Moorer, S.A. (1985a), Methylphenidate and children with attention deficit disorder. Dose effects on classroom academic and social behavior. *Arch. Gen. Psychiatry*, 42:948–952.

—— Sturges, J., Hoza, J., Schmidt, C., Bijlsma, J.J., Milich, R. & Moorer, S.A. (1985b), Sustained release and standard methylphenidate effects on cognitive and social behavior in children with attention deficit disorder. *Pediatrics*, 80(4):491–501.

Resnick, L.B. & Ford, W.W. (1981), *The Psychology of Mathematics for Instruction*. Hillsdale, NJ: Lawrence Earlbaum Associates Inc.

Riddle, K.D. & Rapoport, J.L. (1976), A 2-year follow-up of 72 hyperactive boys: Classroom behavior and peer acceptance. *J. Nerv. Mental Dis.*, 162:126–132.

Rie, H.E., Rie, E.D., Stewart, S. & Ambuel J.P. (1976a), Effects of methylphenidate on underachieving children. *J. Consult. Clin. Psychol.*, 44:250–260.

—— —— —— —— (1976b), Effects of ritalin on underachieving children: A replication. *Am. J. Orthopsychiatry*, 46(2):313–322.

Siegler, R.S. (1987), The perils of averaging data over strategies: An example from children's addition. *J. Exper. Psychol.: Gen.,* 116(3):250–264.

Sprague, R.L. & Sleator, E.K. (1977), Methylphenidate in hyperkinetic children: Differences in dose effects on learning and social behavior. *Science,* 198:1274–1276.

Witt, J.C. (1986), Review of the Wide Range Achievement Test-Revised. *J. Psychoeduc. Assess.,* 4:87–90.

Yoshida, H. (1980), Effects of drill practice on aptitude in learning of arithmetic. *J. Educ. Psychol.,* 72:706–715.

Individual Differences in Response to Ritalin in Classwork and Social Behavior

WILLIAM E. PELHAM and RICHARD MILICH

The key question facing most practitioners working with a patient with attention deficit hyperactivity disorder (ADHD) is how to decide whether a psychostimulant should be included as a component of the child's treatment. Attempts to answer the question have varied, with three types of response predominating. First, many professionals simply prescribe medication following traditional guidelines (e.g., start with a low dose and work upward), employ minimal or no standard monitoring procedures, and hope that the child improves. They assume that the 70% positive response rate that has been reported in the literature is sufficiently high and that potential adverse effects will be so easily detected that they will be correct more often than not in their decision to prescribe. However, it is becoming increasingly clear that ADHD children's response to psychostimulants is far more complex than previously thought, and that this traditional approach to medication results in many children receiving medication that is unnecessary, at an incorrect dosage, or harmful.

A second approach to deciding whether medication is useful has taken place in research settings and has involved attempting to find base-state measures from which response to medication can be reliably predicted. This approach assumes that a static measure made in the office or laboratory can pinpoint children who will be responders to medication. Indeed, early reviews suggested that ADHD children's response to stimulant medication could be predicted from base state information such as severity of the child's attention deficit (e.g., Hastings and Barkley, 1978). Further, clinical lore has long held that putative indices of organicity such as soft neurological signs could be used to determine whether a child would respond to a stimulant. However, systematic research has failed to support this belief. No physiological, neurological, or psychological measures of functioning have been identified that are reliable predictors of response to psychostimulants (for review see Solanto, 1984, and Zametkin & Rapoport, 1987). It is the case that some child characteristics (e.g., age) *are* correlated with response to medication, but the correlations are not large enough to facilitate clinical prediction (e.g., Taylor et al., 1987). Thus, there is becoming general agreement that the response of ADHD children to stimulant medication cannot be predicted with accuracy from any baseline measure or child characteristic.

A third approach to deciding whether to medicate an ADHD child has become widely advocated in recent years. This approach involves conducting a brief, controlled trial to measure a child's acute response to medication, and making a decision regarding a long-term regimen based on the results of the initial trial. The advantages of this tactic are obvious: systematic and controlled information regarding an individual child's response is exactly what the clinician needs to decide whether or prescribe medication. However, this approach itself raises a series of questions. What procedures should be used to conduct such an assessment? What variables should be measured to evaluate a child's response? This latter question is a basic one that involves logic similar to that which underlies the attempt to find base-state predictors of response; specifically, is there a single or are there a limited combination of measures of response to medication that can adequately predict a child's response on all important domains of functioning? This is an important question with both theoretical and practical implications.

Western Psychiatric Institute and Clinic, University of Pittsburgh, Pittsburgh, Pennsylvania;
Department of Psychology, University of Kentucky, Lexington, Kentucky

With respect to the practical implications, we have for some time, advocated employing comprehensive measures of stimulant effects in children as part of a lengthy but essential initial assessment of treatment effectiveness (e.g., Pelham, 1982, 1986; Pelham and Hoza, 1987). Our approach has involved measuring medication response on a large number of ecologically relevant variables on children in a summer treatment program. While clearly the most comprehensive approach that has been proposed to measure response, it is also one of the least practical, requiring a specialized setting and staff. Other more practical approaches have involved outpatient-based evaluations. For example, some authors have suggested that a single measure of learning administered in the doctor's office is the best way to assess drug effects (e.g., Swanson et al., 1978; et al., 1983). Still others have suggested that one or two measures taken in the doctor's office and/or a parent or teacher rating provide an adequate assessment (e.g., Barkley et al., 1988; Rapport et al., 1985; Sleator, 1986). Obviously, protocols that involve only a single or a few measures would be more cost effective and practical than drug evaluation protocols that require measurement of a broad number of aspects of children's behavior in the natural environment. However, those few measures must reliably predict drug response in the natural environment in order for the limited-measure assessment to have external validity.

Regarding the theoretical implications of the response–prediction question, a very large number of studies have been conducted that compare drug-responder and drug-nonresponder groups of ADHD children on biochemical or electrophysiological measures with the dual goals of discovering the underlying biological basis for response to stimulants, as well as drawing subsequent inferences about the biological nature of ADHD (for review see Zametkin and Rapoport, 1987). However, most of these studies have defined response to medication on a single measure, such as a learning task (e.g., Swanson et al., 1983) or a teacher rating scale (e.g., Shekim et al., 1982). If these single measures do not reflect a comprehensive response to medication on a full range of appropriate variables and therefore do not reflect the intended underlying neurobiological variables, then the validity of results from such studies may be seriously compromised.

Both practical and theoretical implications of the question of predicting drug response from single measures assume that dose–response curves are comparable for different dependent measures or domains of functioning. For many years, the most prevalent belief regarding stimulant response was that children's responsiveness was similar across most dependent measures and domains of functioning. Although some researchers (e.g., Sprague and Sleator, 1977; Swanson et al., 1978) have argued that the cognitive and social domains respond to different doses of stimulants, most professionals have ignored these putative differences in considering the degree of children's response to medication. Teacher rating scales are far more widely used in measuring drug response in clinical settings than are tests of learning. More recently, based on analyses of dose-response curves for group data, investigators have argued that dose-response curves for cognitive and social behaviors do not differ (e.g., Pelham et al., 1985; Rapport et al., 1985). If response to stimulant medication is not consistent across dependent measures, then it may not be possible to accurately predict comprehensive responsiveness from single measures.

This chapter presents data from a group study and from individual case examples that address the question we have raised. In the experimental study, we examine whether single measures of drug response that are commonly employed in both clinical and research settings reliably predict response on a wide range of variables that reflect ecologically valid measures of functioning for ADHD boys. In the case examples, we address the same question from an individual difference perspective.

EXPERIMENT 1

The measures that we selected as predictors in this study are the following, all of which have been most commonly advocated and used in both clinical and research settings (e.g., Barkley et al., 1988; Swanson et al., 1983): (1) a continuous performance task (CPT); (2) a laboratory learning task; and (3) the Abbreviated Conners Teacher Rating Scale (ACTRS; Conners, 1973).

CPTs have been perhaps the most frequently used laboratory task to measure medication effects in ADHD children, and they have proved highly sensitive to medication effects (for review, see Pelham, 1986). Many of those recommending instruments for outpatient medication assessments have recommended using a CPT to measure drug response (e.g., Barkley et al., 1988). The subjects in the present study were included in a separate study in which the CPT was employed as a dependent measure, and they showed significant effects of .3 mg/kg methylphenidate on the task (Rodgers, 1988).

Laboratory learning tasks have been advocated as more conservative measures of medication effects than CPTs (Swanson and Kinsbourne, 1979). The learning task that has been most often employed is a paired-associate learning (PAL) task (e.g., Swanson et al., 1978, 1983). The task employed herein is a nonsense spelling task that provides information regarding medication effects that is comparable to that obtained with the PAL (e.g., Stephens et al., 1984). The subjects in the present study were included in a separate study in which the spelling task served as a dependent measure, and in which significant effects of .3 mg/kg methylphenidate were obtained (Pelham et al., 1986).

The ACTRS has been by far the most widely used measure of medication effects in ADHD children. It was originally developed to include items sensitive to drug effects, and it has proved highly sensitive to the effects of stimulant medication (for review see Gittelman and Kanner, 1986). Further, the ACTRS is almost universally included when outpatient medication assessment protocols have been proposed. The children in this study were part of a larger sample of children who showed significant effects of .3 mg/kg methylphenidate on the ACTRS (Hoza, 1989).

The purpose of this study was thus to determine whether the three selected measures, alone or in combination, could reliably predict drug response across other areas of functioning in a very comprehensive assessment that tapped a number of important domains of ADHD children's behavior and academic performance.

Subjects

Twenty-six ADHD boys who enrolled in the 1985 summer day treatment program at the Florida State University underwent a double-blind, placebo-controlled assessment of the effects of .3 mg/kg methylphenidate twice a day. Based on a structured interview, parent and teacher ratings scales, and observational data gathered during the summer program, the 26 subjects were diagnosed by the first author as meeting *DSM III-R* criteria for an attention deficit disorder. Additionally, 22 were diagnosed as having an oppositional/defiant disorder, 5 were diagnosed as having a conduct disorder, and 12 had a specific learning disability. Twenty-five of the boys met criteria for an ADHD diagnosis based on teacher ratings on the SNAP Rating Scale (Atkins et al., 1985), and 13 of the boys exceeded cutoff on the Aggression factor of the IOWA Conners Rating Scale (Pelham et al., 1989). None of the subjects was mentally retarded or had gross neurological disorders. The mean IQ (WISC-R) for the group was 98.8 (SD = 14.6), and the mean reading achievement score (Woodcock–Johnson) was 85.9 (SD = 22.2). The mean age of the sample in months was 97.9 (SD = 17.7). The mean ACTRS score was 19.3 (4.26).

Procedure

The study was conducted in the context of a summer day treatment program conducted at the Florida State University in 1985. A broad-spectrum behavioral intervention was implemented in the program; treatment included a point system, social skills training, time out, parent training, and numerous other components. Children were assigned to groups based on age, with the 10 children in each group supervised by four or five counselors. A typical day for a group of children in the program was divided into the following activities: two academic classroom periods, each staffed by a special education teacher and an aide, an art class, swimming, three supervised outdoor recreational activities (e.g., kickball), and lunch. The first two weeks of the program served as a period of adaptation for children and staff, following which the clinical medication assessments that produced the data for this study were conducted.

The clinical medication assessment procedure has been described in detail elsewhere (Pelham and Hoza, 1987). It was a double-blind, placebo-controlled evaluation in which each child received, in random order with condition varied daily, placebo (bid), 3 mg/kg methylphenidate (bid), and other stimulant doses. Only the data from placebo and .3 mg/kg days were used in the present report. Active medication and placebo were disguised in gelatin capsules and prepackaged in individual, dated envelopes. Medication was dispensed by parents with breakfast and by the program staff just before lunch. Five to nine days of data were gathered per medication condition, with the exact number depending on children's attendance, the number of medication conditions being evaluated, and other factors.

Dependent measures

The nonlaboratory-dependent variables that were gathered in the clinical medication assessments are described in detail in Pelham and Hoza (1987). The measures, which are described briefly below, have acceptable reliability (Hoza, 1989; Pelham et al., 1985; Pelham and Hoza, 1987).

Daily frequencies

As part of a behavior modification point system in effect in all settings except the academic classrooms, counselors recorded the frequencies with which numerous appropriate and inappropriate behaviors occurred daily. The following five categories were derived: (a) following rules; (b) positive peer behaviors (e.g., good sportsmanship); (c) noncompliance; (d) conduct problems (e.g., aggression); and (e) negative verbalizations (e.g., name-calling/teasing).

Classroom measures

Teacher-recorded rates of on-task behavior and rule-following behavior were derived from a response-cost procedure. Children lost points immediately upon the occurrence of a classroom-rule violation and for being off task during random teacher checks made five times per class period. The percentages of points that each child kept were measures of medication effects on classroom on-task and rule-following behavior.

Each boy completed a 2-min, timed, arithmetic drill and a 10-min, timed, reading task, using materials selected as appropriate to his instructional level. The number of arithmetic problems and reading questions attempted and the percentage completed correctly within the allotted time served as the dependent measures. Other daily academic tasks were also individualized according to each child's needs (e.g., language, spelling, additional reading, and arithmetic). Accuracy (percentage correct) and productivity (percentage of assigned seatwork completed) in these tasks were recorded daily.

Rating scales

Teacher ratings on the ACTRS were obtained for each child from 1 to 3 times in each medication condition. Counselor ratings were gathered 1 to 3 times per condition using a modification of the Revised Behavior Problem Checklist (Quay and Peterson, 1983) that included 35 items characteristic of ADHD and conduct disorders rated on a 7-point scale.

Daily report card

Three to five of each child's individual behavioral and academic goals were selected to be included on daily report cards. Positive daily report cards were rewarded at home and monitored through weekly parent-training sessions. The percentage of days the child reached his daily report criterion was used as an individualized measure of drug response.

Observed peer interaction

Direct observations were made daily while children were in supervised recreational periods. The percentages of time that individual children were engaged in positive, negative, or no interactions with their peers were recorded using a modification of the RECESS code (Walker et al., 1978). Approximately 5 min of time-sampled observations were gathered per child per day.

Continuous performance task (CPT)

A CPT consisting of 600 shape and color stimuli was presented with a 500 msec stimulus presentation and 1200 msec ISI (Lindgren and Lyons, 1985). The task was modified from the standard to produce a target rate of 50%. The child's task was to respond with a button press when he saw the target stimulus and withhold pressing otherwise. Errors of omission (failure to press when the target occurred) and commission (pressing when the target was absent) were recorded. The CPT was performed in individual sessions once per drug condition, with medication order randomized across subjects.

Nonsense spelling task

A learning task in which children were required to learn how to spell a list of nonsense words was also administered once per condition (see Pelham et al., 1986 for a complete description). The task, which is directly analogous to a type of learning required of children in classroom settings, involved the subjects' learning to spell lists of 10 nonsense words (e.g., ki, bot, tein, orscht). Based on the child's performance during pretesting, an optimal level of difficulty (i.e., number of letters in the word) was determined for each child. The children were then tested in small groups on two successive days, one medication and one placebo, with order counterbalanced across children. In each session, testers presented a new list of words, one at a time. As in a spelling test in school, children were required to write the correct spelling after each word was presented. As in a paired-associates format, the tester gave feedback following each word. After a list was presented once, the words were randomized and presented again, and this procedure continued until children learned the list or until 10 trials had elapsed. The total number of errors a child made before criterion (two consecutive correct spellings of the list or after the tenth trial without two correct spellings) was the dependent measure.

RESULTS AND DISCUSSION

In order to determine whether single measures predicted drug response, correlations were computed between drug effects (placebo score minus drug score) on (1) the classroom teacher's ACTRS scores, (2) errors on the nonsense spelling task, and (3) errors of omission and commission on the CPT—and drug effects (placebo score minus drug score) on the 17 other dependent measures gathered in the day treatment program. In addition to bivariate correlations, partial correlations were computed with the effects of age and IQ controlled.

The resulting correlations are presented in Tables 1 and 2. As the tables show, the bivariate correlations were generally quite low, accounting occasionally for as much as 30% of the variance but usually no more than 10%. Further, after controlling for the effects of age and IQ, only nine of 68 partial correlations were significantly different from zero at the .05 level, with an additional eight showing a trend ($p < .10$) toward significance. Many of the remaining 50 correlations (as well as some of the significant ones) were not even in the expected direction [the r should be positive for variables when a decrease reflects improvement (e.g., noncompliance) and negative for variables on which an increase reflects improvement (e.g., positive peer interactions)]. For example, the highest correlation, the partial r of $-.59$ between commission errors and conduct problems, is quite difficult to interpret, as it suggests that large drug effects on the CPT are

TABLE 1. BIVARIATE AND PARTIAL[a] CORRELATIONS BETWEEN MEDICATION EFFECTS ON THE CPT ERRORS, NONSENSE SPELLING ERRORS, THE ACTRS SCORES, AND THE OTHER MEASURES OF STIMULANT RESPONSE

Dependent Measure	Omission Errors		Commission Errors		ACTRS		Nonsense Spelling	
	r	Partial r	r	Partial r	r	Partial r	r	Partial r
Recreational Settings:								
Daily frequencies								
Following rules	-.32[b]	-.35[c]	-.01	.07	-.41[c]	-.27	-.06	.13
Noncompliance	.37[c]	.35[c]	-.01	-.02	.47[d]	.35[b]	.34[b]	.27
Positive peer behaviors	-.37[c]	-.30[b]	.04	-.01	-.55[c]	-.35[b]	-.34[b]	-.24
Conduct problems	.26	.23	-.50[d]	-.59[d]	.30[b]	.12	.34[b]	.19
Negative verbalizations	.22	.19	.46[d]	.49[d]	.33[b]	.21	.00	-.15
Counselor rating	.07	.03	.16	.12	.38[c]	.20	.25	.09
Observed interactions								
Positive peer	-.11	-.17	-.12	-.05	-.08	-.06	.10	.15
Negative peer	.01	.11	.31	.22	.09	.11	-.11	-.14
No interactions	.10	.12	.00	-.03	.00	-.01	-.09	-.13
Classroom Setting:								
On task (%)	-.32[b]	-.25	.12	.01	-.43[c]	-.44[c]	-.40[c]	-.43[c]
Following rules (%)	-.40[c]	-.40[c]	-.27[b]	-.31[c]	-.51[d]	-.31[b]	-.57[c]	-.48[c]
Timed Math								
Number attempted	.02	-.03	.08	.08	.20	.06	-.06	-.20
Percentage correct	-.35[b]	-.32[b]	.06	.03	-.54[d]	-.53[c]	-.29[b]	-.23
Timed Reading								
Number attempted	.06	.00	.21	.25	.29	.09	.14	.04
Percentage correct	-.17	-.30[b]	-.18	-.13	-.17	-.57[c]	.15	.01
Seatwork								
Completion (%)	-.30[b]	-.25	-.14	-.17	-.41[c]	-.30	-.35[b]	-.25
Correct (%)	-.02	.00	.30[b]	.30[b]	.05	.13	-.31[b]	-.31[b]

Note. The medication effect for each variable was computed by subtracting the score on .3 mg/kg methylphenidate from the score on placebo for that variable. The *ns* for these correlations range from 22 to 26, depending on missing values.
[a]Effects of Age and IQ controlled.
[b]$p < .10$.
[c]$p < .05$.
[d]$p < .01$

TABLE 2. MULTIPLE REGRESSIONS OF THE COMBINATION OF MEDICATION EFFECTS ON THE
NONSENSE SPELLING TASK, THE CPT, AND THE ACTRS ON THE 17 OTHER MEASURES
OF STIMULANT RESPONSE

Dependent Measure	N	R^2 (total)	R^2 (cov.)	R^2 (change)	F (change)
Recreational Settings:					
Daily frequencies					
Following rules	22	.41	.14	.27	1.69
Noncompliance	22	.32	.07	.25	1.34
Positive peer behaviors	22	.44	.24	.20	1.30
Conduct problems	22	.59	.31	.28	2.59
Negative verbalizations	22	.48	.17	.31	2.23
Counselor Rating	21	.32	.26	.06	<1
Observed interactions					
Positive peer	22	.26	.14	.12	<1
Negative peer	22	.44	.27	.17	1.16
No interactions	22	.10	.04	.06	<1
Classroom Setting:					
On task (%)	22	.41	.24	.17	1.10
Following rules (%)	22	.51	.05	.46	3.62[a]
Timed Math					
Number attempted	21	.15	.09	.06	<1
Percentage correct	21	.31	.06	.25	1.30
Timed Reading					
Number attempted	21	.30	.21	.09	<1
Percentage correct	21	.40	.13	.27	1.74
Seatwork					
Completion (%)	22	.26	.07	.19	<1
Correct (%)	22	.25	.01	.24	1.22

Note. Medication effects were computed by subtracting the score on .3 mg/kg methylphenidate from the score for placebo for that variable. Age and IQ were entered first in a heirarchical regression. R^2 (total) reflects the variance accounted for by Age, IQ, and the three predictor variables. R^2 (cov.) reflects the effects of Age and IQ alone, and R^2 (change) reflects the effects of the three predictor variables *beyond* the effects of Age and IQ. F (change) reflects the significance of the R^2 (change).
[a]$p < .05$.

associated with small effects on conduct problems—a counterintuitive relationship. Even when the partial correlations are significant and in interpretable directions, none of them accounts for as much as 25% of the variance in the predicted measures.

The differential pattern of change with the partial correlations is noteworthy. There was very little or no reduction in the bivariate correlations involving the nonsense spelling and CPT. However, the reduction in the rs was dramatic for the ACTRS, with many significant correlations losing significance when the covariates were partialled out. We know from other research (Hoza, 1989) that it is the age covariate rather than the IQ that is accounting for this relationship. Younger ADHD boys tend to perform/behave worse than older ADHD boys in both the laboratory and in school settings. When a sample includes a wide age range of children, an apparently large correlation between effects on two measures in which younger children perform more poorly is often a function of age rather than the drug effect per se. The differences between the bivariate and partial correlations between the ACTRS and the Daily Frequencies are very clear examples of such an effect.

It is interesting that prediction was no better for correlations within domains than for correlations across behavioral domains. For example, the nonsense spelling task was as equally correlated with measures of social behavior such as noncompliance and following rules in the classroom as with academic measures such as seatwork completed and correct. The ACTRS showed a similar pattern, being equally correlated with measures of disruptive behavior and academic performance. This is quite a surprising outcome. Swanson and colleagues have argued that tests of learning should be used to guard against adverse *cognitive* effects of stimulants. They have argued that laboratory tasks that tap learning are more highly correlated with academic classroom measures such as seatwork than with overt classroom behavior. We clearly did not obtain that outcome.

Clearly none of the three single measures of drug response was sufficient in itself to predict clinical response to medication on the 17 dependent measures. In order to determine whether the nonsense spelling task, the ACTRS, and the CPT could be *combined* to improve prediction of the other dependent variables, multiple regressions were conducted for each criterion measure. Age and IQ were entered first, and the amount of additional variance (R^2 change) accounted for by the three predictor variables was measured. As Table 3 shows, in only one of the 17 multiple regressions (following rules in the classroom) did the predictors account for a significant R^2 beyond the variance accounted for by age and IQ. Thus, combining the three variables failed to improve prediction of drug response across all of the dependent measures.

In summary, a child's drug response on the ACTRS, a learning task, and a CPT task did not either singly or together reliably predict that child's response on 17 dependent measures of key behaviors gathered in a somewhat naturalistic setting across both classroom and recreational settings. These data show quite clearly that these three commonly recommended and used single measures cannot either alone or in combination be used to determine a child's responsivity to psychostimulant medication. Current recommendations for the use of these measures as the sole mechanisms of assessing stimulant response in short-term drug trials therefore lack credibility. Similarly, studies that employ only these or similar measures to dichotomize children as responders or nonresponders to medication in order to examine underlying neurophysiology of medication response or ADHD are unlikely to provide useful information because response on one measure does not reflect response, and presumably underlying physiology, on others.

These data might appear to leave the clinician in a quandary. If such commonly used measures do not predict to a child's response across important academic and social domains, how should drug response be measured in a short-term trial? It is our firm belief that the only adequate procedure for analyzing an ADHD child's response to psychostimulant medication for either clinical or research purposes is to conduct a comprehensive assessment that includes (a) the presenting symptoms (i.e., problems in daily life functioning) on which a change is desired in the patient, and (b) other domains in which a change with medication is unwanted (i.e., side effects). Further, such an assessment should be conducted in as naturalistic a setting as possible so as to maximize the generalizability of the results to the child's natural setting.

The following case examples from assessments conducted in our summer treatment program illustrate how comprehensive assessments can be conducted and interpreted. They also illustrate the clear individual differences in children's responsiveness to stimulants—both across children within domains and within children across domains. As such, the examples provide further indications of the limited utility of some of the single measures of response discussed above.

CASE EXAMPLES

Case 1: Darryl

Darryl, an 11-year-old boy, was brought to the clinic by his mother with complaints of academic difficulties, problems in peer relationships, and oppositional behavior. Darryl had long-standing diagnoses of ADHD and learning disabilities (LD), and exhibited his problems in the school setting, even though his mother rated him as exhibiting more extreme symptoms of ADHD than did his teachers. A psychological report from his school stated that Darryl had a short attention span, was easily distracted, demonstrated inconsistent work, and had few interactions with peers. Darryl had been taking SR-20 Ritalin, prescribed by his pediatrician, for approximately three years prior to clinic contact, but he continued to exhibit the problems for which he was referred. During the 1988 Summer Treatment Program, Darryl underwent a clinical medication assessment

TABLE 3. RESULTS OF THE CLINICAL MEDICATION ASSESSMENT FOR CASE EXAMPLE 1: DARRYL[a]

Variable Measured	Placebo bid 7 days	10 mg Methylphenidate bid 5 days	SR-20 Ritalin qam 4 days	56.25 mg Pemoline qam 5 days	10 mg Dexedrine Spansule qam 4 days
Recreational Settings:					
Daily frequencies					
Following rules (%)	86 ± 3	83 ± 6	85 ± 7	83 ± 4	87 ± 2
Noncompliance	1.9 ± 1.7	0.9 ± 1.3	1.6 ± 1.7	1.2 ± 2.7	1.1 ± 0.8
Positive peer interaction	70.3 ± 13.7	41.8 ± 20.4	52.4 ± 12.8	53.4 ± 25.0	58.2 ± 26.3
Conduct problems	0.0 ± 0.0	0.0 ± 0.0	0.0 ± 0.0	0.0 ± 0.0	0.0 ± 0.0
Negative verbalizations	0.7 ± 0.5	0.8 ± 1.0	0.5 ± 0.6	0.8 ± 0.8	0.5 ± 1.0
Counselor rating (ACTRS)	1.7 ± 0.6	1.7 ± 0.6	1.7 ± 0.6	1.7 ± 0.6	1.0 ± 0.0
Positive daily report card					
Days received (%)	71 ± 49	20 ± 45	50 ± 58	40 ± 55	75 ± 50
Classroom Setting:					
Following rules (%)	99 ± 4	100 ± 0	100 ± 0	98 ± 4	98 ± 5
Seatwork completion (%)	90 ± 16	88 ± 26	81 ± 39	75 ± 24	75 ± 22
Seatwork correct (%)	96 ± 4	75 ± 8	89 ± 14	96 ± 4	85 ± 22
Teacher rating (ACTRS)	1.7 ± 2.9	0.0 ± 0.0	0.0 ± 0.0	0.3 ± 0.6	0.7 ± 1.2

[a] All values are ± SD.

in the context of a protocol in which he received placebo bid, 10 mg methylphenidate bid, SR-20 Ritalin qam, 56.25 mg pemoline qam, and 10 mg Dexedrine Spansule q.a.m. (see Pelham et al., 1990a for a complete description of the protocol). On days on which he received long-acting forms of medication (the latter three), a noontime placebo was also administered. The dependent measures involved in Darryl's assessment were in most respects identical to those described above, with the few changes noted below.

The results of Darryl's medication assessment are presented in Table 4 and Figure 1. As indicated in the table, Darryl showed no response to medication on most dependent measures. For example, Darryl demonstrated very high rates of rule following on placebo days, and these rates did not change with medication. He also had very low rates of negative behavior such as noncompliance, conduct problems, and negative verbalizations, and medication could not improve his behavior further. As might be expected given Darryl's low rates of negative behaviors, his counselors rated him very positively on placebo, and this rating did not change with medication. On one important measure of social functioning, positive peer interactions, Darryl showed a dramatic adverse effect of medication. He had a relatively low rate of positive peer interactions on placebo days, and this rate decreased markedly on medication days and was accompanied by concurrent increases in variability. As the summary table indicates, Darryl was also considerably less likely to meet his daily report criteria on medication compared with placebo days, with the percentage of days that he received a positive report decreasing from 71% on placebo to between 25% and 50% on active medication days. The criteria established for a positive daily report specifically targeted Darryl's primary presenting problems.

On measures of academic performance gathered in the classrooms, Darryl again showed either no response to medication or an adverse response. On placebo days, Darryl performed exceptionally well in seatwork completion and percentage of seatwork correct. In contrast, on each of the four medication conditions he showed significant decreases in seatwork accuracy and/or completion. For example, his accuracy on 10 mg Ritalin days decreased by 5 standard deviations from his placebo level. Similarly, on days on which he received SR-20 Ritalin, he showed decreases of .5 and 1.5 standard deviations for seatwork completion and accuracy, respectively. Clearly, all four active medications had substantial adverse effects on either productivity, accuracy, or both in Darryl's seatwork performances in the classroom.

Darryl performed a CPT four times daily (60, 120, 240, 369, and 540 min following pill ingestion) on one day each of the five medication conditions. The results are shown in Figure 1, which shows that his performance in all four active drug conditions was superior to placebo. He demonstrated an overall decrease in the number of errors of omission made during the Continuous Performance Task, and the effects of medication maintained across times of the day. It is worth noting that the results of the CPT appear to be confounded with a practice effect, with his performance improving somewhat independent of medication each time he took the task.

The numerous measures of side effects gathered during the summer program reveal that Darryl was rated by counselors and teachers as consistently showing withdrawal and irritable behavior across all medications relative to placebo. Additionally, he had difficulty falling asleep on nights that he received Cylert or Dexedrine. Finally, Darryl showed a moderately adverse behavioral rebound in the evenings of days on which he had received 10 mg methylphenidate bid. That is, his mother's ratings of his unmedicated evening behavior were worse on evenings when he had received 10 mg methylphenidate during the day than on evenings when he had received a placebo during the day.

In summary, Darryl demonstrated a mixed response to the four stimulants evaluated. All medications appeared to improve his CPT performance, but on most measures of functioning in the STP, stimulants had little effect. Further and most important, he became withdrawn and had profound decreases in positive social interactions and measures of academic performance on all four medications. Given that social interactions and academic performance are the two domains for which Darryl was referred for treatment, these are the dependent measures on which stimulant response has the greatest ecological validity.

Thus, medication results on CPT omission errors did not reflect medication response on the social and academic symptoms for which Darryl was referred. Because of the adverse medication response on those measures and despite the beneficial response on the CPT, continued stimulant medication was *not* recommended as a component of Darryl's treatment plan. It is important to note that Darryl had been receiving Ritalin SR-20 for three years prior to this assessment. As in most cases in clinical practice, that administration was initiated and continued without any systematic evaluation of the medication's effects.

TABLE 4. RESULTS OF THE CLINICAL MEDICATION ASSESSMENT FOR CASE EXAMPLE 2: JERRY[a]

Variable Measured	Placebo bid 6 days	7.5 mg Ritalin bid[b] 6 days	15 mg Ritalin bid[c] 7 days	22.5 mg Ritalin bid[d] 6 days
Recreational Settings:				
Daily frequencies				
Following rules (%)	35.0 ± 7.0	47 ± 7	65 ± 5	68 ± 8
Noncompliance	25.6 ± 7.0	18.3 ± 6.7	7.8 ± 6.3	8.9 ± 6.1
Interrupting	0.4 ± 0.1	0.5 ± 0.1	0.7 ± 0.0	0.7 ± 0.1
Positive peer interaction	39.6 ± 12.4	41.8 ± 12.3	36.6 ± 13.9	38.3 ± 12.5
Conduct problems	4.2 ± 3.6	1.3 ± 1.2	0.6 ± 0.5	1.8 ± 3.5
Negative verbalizations	34.8 ± 6.4	12.2 ± 6.4	7.0 ± 4.3	10.0 ± 13.8
Attention check correct (%)	55.0 ± 17.3	68.6 ± 18.5	59.3 ± 13.9	70.1 ± 11.3
Counselor rating (ACTRS)	18.2 ± 3.6	10.4 ± 4.4	8.8 ± 1.8	7.6 ± 2.4
Positive daily report card				
Days received (%)	0 ± 0	40 ± 55	60 ± 55	60 ± 55
Classroom Setting:				
Following rules (%)	2 ± 4	5 ± 12	30 ± 41	36 ± 50
On task behavior (%)	54 ± 17	39 ± 27	67 ± 11	76 ± 5
Disruptive behavior (%)	74 ± 41	61 ± 25	26 ± 29	18 ± 9
Seatwork completion (%)	67 ± 34	75 ± 27	58 ± 21	61 ± 20
Seatwork correct (%)	90 ± 13	89 ± 9	79 ± 15	93 ± 6
Teacher rating (ACTRS)	25.0 ± 3.5	20.8 ± 7.6	15.6 ± 9.6	11.7 ± 4.9

[a]Values are ± SD.
[b].3 mg/kg.
[c].6 mg/kg.
[d].9 mg/kg.

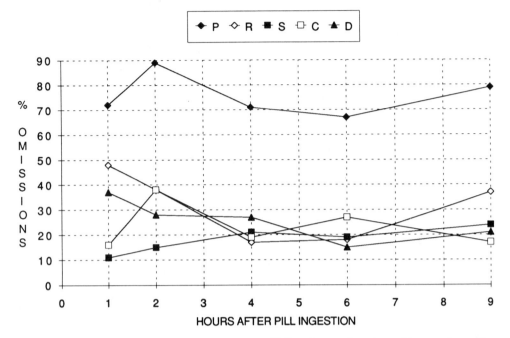

FIG. 1. Percentage errors of omission on the CPT task as a function of hours after pill ingestion. *P* = Placebo bid; R = 10 mg methylphenidate bid; S = Ritalin SR-20 qam; C = 56.25 mg pemoline qam; D = 10 mg Dexedrine Spansule qam.

Darryl's case certainly *both* highlights the importance of using an assessment procedure when prescribing a stimulant *and* illustrates the importance of employing multiple measures that reflect as closely as possible the child's presenting symptoms and are gathered in as naturalistic a setting as possible.

Case 2: Jerry

Jerry was an 8-year-old male with a long history of severe behavior and learning problems. He showed a mixture of symptoms consistent with diagnoses of ADHD, ODD, and severe learning disabilities. Additionally, he exhibited some behaviors suggestive of a residual pervasive developmental disorder, but did not clearly fit that diagnostic category. His main presenting problems were reported by both mother and teachers to be off-task and disruptive behavior at school, argumentativeness with adults, and fighting with and teasing his peers. Teacher ratings in particular reflected severe levels of these symptoms, particularly the disruptive and oppositional behaviors. He had been receiving special education for several years (full-time LD placement) and .9 mg/kg methylphenidate tid for two years prior to treatment in the Summer Treatment Program.

Jerry was evaluated during the 1989 STP on a protocol that included 7.5 mg Ritalin (.3 mg/kg) bid for 6 days, 15 mg Ritalin (.6 mg/kg) bid for 7 days, 22.5 mg Ritalin (.9 mg/kg) bid for 6 days, and placebo bid for 6 days. Medication was administered in the morning and at noon in a random order with medication varying over days. The dependent measures employed in Jerry's assessment were similar to those described in Experiment 1, with several additions: (1) A measure of on-task behavior in recreational settings (attention check) was implemented; (2) interrupting others was added as a point category; (3) independent observers coded on-task and disruptive behavior in the classroom setting; and (4) counselor ratings were gathered using the ACTRS. As with our other assessments, Jerry's medication assessment was conducted in the context of the behavioral treatment program that operated in all settings of the STP.

In general, Table 5 shows that Jerry continued to exhibit very high rates of inappropriate behavior on placebo days in the behavioral treatment program. There was therefore clear room for improvement with

TABLE 5. RESULTS OF THE CLINICAL MEDICATION ASSESSMENT FOR CASE EXAMPLE 3: ANDY[a]

Variable Measured	Placebo bid 10 days	8.75 mg Ritalin bid[b] 9 days	17.5 mg Ritalin bid[c] 9 days
Recreational Settings:			
Daily frequencies			
Following rules (%)	48.0 ± 14	67 ± 8	70 ± 18
Noncompliance	11.9 ± 6.5	3.9 ± 2.5	1.3 ± 1.1
Interrupting	16.1 ± 8.3	5.0 ± 2.5	2.3 ± 2.1
Positive peer interaction	55.1 ± 19.1	62.0 ± 31.6	51.3 ± 29.2
Conduct problems	2.1 ± 1.5	0.9 ± 1.1	0.1 ± 0.4
Negative verbalizations	17.6 ± 6.0	6.4 ± 2.9	3.0 ± 2.6
Attention check correct (%)	67.8 ± 13.3	78.6 ± 6.4	82.9 ± 9.1
Counselor rating (ACTRS)	9.1 ± 2.1	6.1 ± 2.3	5.4 ± 3.4
Positive daily report card			
Days received (%)	38 ± 52	86 ± 38	100 ± 0
Classroom Setting:			
Following rules (%)	50 ± 42	80 ± 22	84 ± 13
On-task behavior (%)	60 ± 14	79 ± 8	79 ± 10
Disruptive behavior (%)	14 ± 12	4 ± 3	6 ± 3
Seatwork completion (%)	45 ± 30	68 ± 31	70 ± 24
Seatwork correct (%)	91 ± 7	95 ± 6	98 ± 3
Teacher rating (ACTRS)	22.2 ± 5.2	12.2 ± 7.4	11.9 ± 8.8

[a] All values are ± SD.
[b] .3 mg/kg.
[c] .6 mg/kg.

medication, and beneficial MPH effects are apparent on numerous measures. For example, on measures of social behavior from the daily point system, Jerry showed considerable improvement with medication, with most of the improvement occurring on the 15 mg dose of Ritalin. His rule-following increased from 35% to 65% on this dose of medication, and his negative verbalizations decreased from 35 per day to 7 per day. Similar changes were obtained on measures of noncompliance and conduct problems, on which peak improvement was obtained at the 15 mg dose. Further, Jerry's performance on his daily report card, which reflected his individualized target symptoms, was dramatically improved with medication (from zero placebo days to 60% of 15 mg days), and the effect peaked at 15 mg. In contrast, Jerry showed no medication effect on his positive peer interactions or the frequency with which he interrupted others' activities. Jerry's counselor ratings revealed a large effect of the lowest dose of methylphenidate, with small incremental improvement with increasing dosage beyond that level.

Turning to the classroom setting, measures of classroom rule-following and observed disruptive behaviors improved dramatically with medication. These improvements were maximized with the 15 mg dose of MPH despite the fact that Jerry continued to disrupt his classroom even on the highest dose. Despite these improvements in disruptive behavior, Jerry showed high variability and little consistent effect of MPH on his seatwork completion and correctness in the classroom. As might be expected given his improvements in observed disruption, Jerry's teacher's rating on the ACTRS also improved across all medication conditions, with a linear decrease of 4 or 5 points obtained with the addition of each .3 mg/kg MPH. The best rating with the concomitant lowest variability was obtained on the highest dose of MPH.

On measures of side effects taken during the Summer Treatment Program, Jerry was observed to show some facial grimaces and tongue/lip movements, which were most apparent at 22.5 mg Ritalin and less apparent on 15 mg and lower doses. The reports were made primarily by the counselors who worked with Jerry throughout the day; his teachers did not report facial or mouth movements, and his mother reported them only to a slight degree. These movements dissipated when medication wore off, and the frequency and intensity of the tics decreased over the course of the summer with continued low dosages of medication, although they continued to occur at a high rate at the .9 mg/kg dose. No other side effects of medication were noted by teachers, counselors, or Jerry's mother.

Finally, on a CPT, valid data could not be obtained on placebo days due to Jerry's uncooperative behavior. On medication days, he showed consistent medication-related improvement, with omission rates of 50%, 44%, and 21%, and commission rates of 8, 36, and 15, on .3, .6 and .9 mg/kg MPH, respectively. As on his teacher's rating, Jerry clearly showed the greatest improvement on this task with the highest dose of medication.

In summary, as might have been expected given pretreatment reports from his regular school setting, Jerry's behavior on placebo days during the STP, in which an intensive behavioral intervention was in effect, was sufficiently problematic that additional treatment was clearly necessary. The assessment showed that MPH had clear incremental effectiveness as an adjunctive treatment, but different dependent measures provided different information regarding which dose was best. As indicated by the daily frequency counts, the counselor ratings, observations in the classroom, and the daily report card, the .6 mg/kg dose (15 mg bid) appeared to maximize response on most of the dependent measures. Additionally, the facial tics were not nearly as pronounced on this dose as the higher dose. However, both the ACTRS and the CPT documented clear additional improvement at the highest, .9 mg/kg dose. Had these two measures been relied upon in an outpatient medication assessment, then the highest dose of medication would have been recommended *even though it did not produce incremental improvement on most measures* and even though it caused the greatest exacerbation of Jerry's facial tics, which were not noted by his teacher. It is important to note that prior to contact with our clinic Jerry *had* undergone a "controlled" medication assessment at a local clinic prior to receiving MPH. However, that assessment used *only* the ACTRS and a laboratory learning task to determine response to medication, with the result that Jerry had been receiving .9 mg/kg MPH tid for the two years prior to this assessment.

Case example 3: Andy

Andy, a 9-year-old, fourth grader, was referred to the summer treatment program with extreme and long-standing symptoms of ADHD, ODD/CD. Parent and teacher ratings on standardized scales were consistent in describing Andy as having extreme symptoms of inattention, impulsivity, hyperactivity, disruptiveness, oppositional behavior, and severe difficulties getting along with other children. His parents reported that Andy exhibited these problems from an early age. In the school setting, they were first noticed in his kindergarten year, and midway through the first grade year he was placed in a special education class and MPH was prescribed by his pediatrician. Despite these interventions, Andy's problems persisted. At the time of intake, he was receiving 10 mg bid on school days only. Andy was evaluated on a protocol that included 8.75 mg MPH (.3 mg/kg) bid, 17.5 mg MPH (.6 mg/kg) bid, and placebo bid. Medication was administered twice daily in a random order with medication varying over days with 9 or 10 days per condition. The dependent measures employed in Andy's assessment were the same as described above for Case Example 2. The results of Andy's assessment are shown in Table 5.

As the table illustrates, Andy exhibited the symptoms for which he was referred in the STP setting, having relatively high rates of inappropriate and low rates of appropriate behavior on placebo days. On days when he received MPH, he was substantially improved in both his behavior and his academic performance. Of particular interest for our purposes are the somewhat discrepant dose effects apparent in the recreational and classroom settings. On every measure in the classroom, Andy's improvement maximized at the .3 mg/kg dose, affording no further improvement when the dosage was increased to .6 mg/kg. This was true for the ACTRS, as well as the objective observational and product measures. The same pattern was obtained on comparable dependent variables obtained in recreational settings (e.g., following rules and attention checks). However, on measures that reflected oppositional behavior directed toward his counselors (noncompliance and the "back talk" component of negative verbalizations), and particularly on behaviors that involved negative interactions with peers, Andy showed incremental improvement with the higher dose of MPH. For example, most of Andy's interrupting, conduct problems (e.g., aggression), and negative verbalizations (e.g., name-calling and teasing peers) were peer directed, with the unsurprising result that he was one of the most disliked members of his group. The magnitude of this additional improvement can best be illustrated by totalling all of the negative behaviors included in the daily frequency counts. Andy exhibited 47.7 inappropriate behaviors per day on placebo days, 16.2 on .3 mg/kg days, and 6.7 on .6 mg/kg days. Thus, although the bulk of the MPH effects on Andy's inappropriate behaviors in recreational settings came at the .3 mg/kg dose, the higher dose of MPH eliminated an additional 10 highly salient negative behaviors per day from Andy's interactions with peers and counselors.

In addition to the measures from the clinical medication assessment, Andy was tested individually on a CPT task six times—twice per medication condition—during the STP. He showed no clear pattern of MPH response, averaging 53% omission errors on placebo and .3 days and 61% on days when he received .6 mg/kg. The overlap between his performance across testing days was great, with medication and placebo error rates virtually identical.

In Andy's case, he had been receiving MPH for three years, prescribed by his pediatrician at his school's request, and he had never had an evaluation of the medication's effectiveness. His physician had prescribed only .3 mg/kg despite the fact that Andy continued to exhibit sufficiently severe behavior problems to have been maintained in a special education classroom. It is noteworthy that many of his continued problems occurred in unstructured settings when he was out of his special class placement and many of them involved oppositional behavior and negative peer interactions. Our assessment revealed that a .6 mg/kg dose would likely provide incremental benefit for Andy in these important domains, even though it would not result in improvement on the ACTRS. Finally, the CPT did not reveal a beneficial medication effect for Andy.

HOW TO DO A COMPREHENSIVE AND PRACTICAL OUTPATIENT MEDICATION ASSESSMENT

This study and these case examples illustrate the complexities involved in assessing medication effects in ADHD children for whom MPH or another stimulant is being considered as a component of a multimodal intervention. They show that widely used measures such as the ACTRS, CPT, and laboratory learning tasks do not necessarily provide the information for which they are intended, and that the individual differences in responsiveness are considerable. Where does this leave the practitioner? The question facing every clinician with an ADHD patient is how to decide whether a stimulant should be used and what the correct dose should be. The kinds of assessments that we conduct in the STP are clearly too complicated to be implemented in practice in outpatient and/or school settings. However, the principles involved—assessing a wide range of ecologically valid measures of functioning in a natural setting and emphasizing individual differences in response—can be followed in medication assessments that can be designed and conducted in less structured settings. What follows are guidelines for conducting outpatient medication assessments.

First, researchers, professional organizations, and pharmaceutical manufacturers are virtually unanimous in their agreement (1) *that stimulants should be used with ADHD children only after appropriate psychosocial and psychoeducational interventions have been conducted and are insufficient, and (2) that stimulants should be used only in conjunction with these other interventions.* It has been clearly established that the appropriate psychosocial intervention for ADHD is a behavioral intervention, and that behavioral and psychostimulant interventions often have beneficial combined effects (Pelham, 1989; Pelham and Murphy, 1986). For that reason, the first step in determining whether to use medication with an ADHD child is to establish a behavioral intervention first. After a sufficient period of parent training (e.g., Barkley, 1987) and classroom intervention (e.g., Pfiffner and Barkley, 1990), if the child has not shown maximal improvement, then the clinician should proceed with a medication assessment.

The behavioral intervention should include components that can serve as dependent measures in the medication assessment. For example, in the classroom, a daily report card or task sheet that includes the child's individual target behaviors, both academic and social, should be used. The targets on the report card or task sheet must be operationalized and monitored closely. For example, the number of assignments completed and accuracy on them should be a target for a child for whom "finishing work" was a presenting complaint. The number of times a child is "benched" on a recess timeout bench should be tracked by playground aides if peer difficulties at recess are a target area.

If the primary clinician is not a physician, he or she obviously must discuss the assessment with the child's or clinic's physician and elicit his or her cooperation. The child should have a physical examination to rule out conditions that preclude an assessment with stimulants. The clinician and cooperating physician should select the type and doses of medication to be employed. Our standard protocol includes placebo, .3 mg/kg methylphenidate bid, and .6 mg/kg methylphenidate bid (reduced to .15 and .3 mg/kg for low and high doses, respectively, for overweight children, for older and therefore heavier children, and for children who do not have behavior problems). Other preparations could be employed for a variety of reasons. For example, a child may need a long-acting preparation because the school will not administer a midday dose (see Pelham et al., 1990a). If D-amphetamine is used, the dose recommended for MPH should be halved. If pemoline is used, the dose should be six times a single methylphenidate dose with A.M. administration only (Pelham et al., 1990a; Stephens et al., 1984). All pills should be encapsulized to disguise the active medication and placebo. Most local pharmacists are able to perform this function.

When determining the medication schedule, the clinician should ensure that times of the day during which the child exhibits his target symptoms will overlap with peak medication times (for methylphenidate, between 60 and 180 minutes after ingestion). For example, if problems with peers in neighborhood recreational activities are a problem, then an after-school dose should be administered (Pelham et al., 1990b). Similarly, if a child works on his most difficult academic assignment immediately upon arrival at school, he must receive his morning dose sufficiently early to affect performance on that task (i.e., at least 60 minutes beforehand).

Although the most common recommendation is to vary medication condition on a weekly basis, we have found a great deal of difficulty interpreting data for individuals when employing such schedules. The major problem is that events at school or home become confounded with medication condition, making it difficult to separate medication effects from other variables that influence the child's behavior at home and in school. Because of their brief half lives, stimulants can be varied on a daily basis. A daily manipulation of condition affords many alternations between drug and placebo conditions and distributes error associated with other events across drug conditions, therefore clarifying interpretation of medication effects for the individual.

Thus, a random schedule should be established in which medication condition changes daily, but the randomization should be limited to ensure that each dose is given at least once per week (e.g., Wk 1: P, .3, P, .6, .3). Each dose should be administered between 5 and 10 times *or* until stable data have been obtained and a pattern or lack thereof is clear. Thus the entire assessment may take from three to six school weeks. The pharmacist should package the medication in dated, individual envelopes according to the random order, and these should be given to the parents one week at a time.

The therapist should make certain that all adults involved with the child, as well as the child, know that the assessment is occurring. At the same time, everyone who will provide any information regarding the child's response should be kept blind to condition.

As discussed above, the dependent measures should include the daily report targets and other objective information from the school regarding child's major behavioral and academic problems. Additionally, the IOWA Conners TRS should be completed daily by the teacher (Pelham et al., 1989), and teacher and parents should complete standard side effects rating scales daily. If a late afternoon or evening dose of medication is used, parents' ratings and records of objective behavior problems should be employed (e.g., records of point charts for the ongoing behavioral interventions).

After the assessment is completed, the clinician should break the blind, collate all of the information gathered, and compute means and standard deviations for dependent measures within each condition. Then, *giving most weight to the child's major problem areas*, the clinician should determine whether the *incremental* (*beyond* the ongoing behavioral intervention) improvement obtained with medication outweighs any side effects observed, and if so, the minimal dose that produces the desired change. Unfortunately, there are no clearcut guidelines for deciding how much of an effect is sufficient to recommend medication. We generally consider the salience of the child's problematic behaviors and where in regards to a "normal" range of functioning he or she falls with medication. For example, given that disturbed peer relations are a hallmark of ADHD and one of the best predictors of long-range maladjustment (Milich and Landau, 1989; Pelham and Bender, 1982), it might be prudent to give improvement in peer interactions more weight than a teacher rating of inattention in deciding which dose to recommend for a particular child (see Case Example 3 above).

CONCLUSION

It has become increasingly accepted in recent years that ADHD is a chronic condition that most often requires long-term treatment. Unfortunately, it has become equally well accepted that long-term pharmacotherapy with a stimulant, as the medications have been prescribed over the past several decades, is not an adequate long-term intervention (Weiss and Hechtman, 1986). Although the kinds of medication assessments that have been suggested herein might appear at first glance to be unnecessarily complex, they would appear essential to making an accurate determination of a child's stimulant responsiveness. It is certainly reasonable to speculate that the failure of previous studies to demonstrate long-term beneficial effects of stimulants may stem from their failure to employ adequate procedures for determining the dose and effects of the medications in the treated children. Widespread utilization of the medication assessments we have discussed should yield a better outcome for long-term stimulant regimens. Given that most medicated ADHD children will continue their medication and other components of treatment for many years, the initial short-term investment of time and effort expended to evaluate medication response should have clear long-term benefits.

REFERENCES

Atkins, M.S., Pelham, W.E. & Light, M. (1985), A comparison of objective classroom measures and teacher ratings of attention deficit disorder. *J. Abnorm. Child Psychol.*, 13:155–167.

Barkley, R.A. (1987), *Defiant Children: A Clinician's Manual for Parent Training*. New York: Guilford Press.

———— Fischer, M., Newby, R.F. & Breen, M.J. (1988), Development of a multimethod clinical protocol for assessing stimulant drug response in ADD children. *J. Clin. Child Psychol.*, 17:14–24.

Conners, C.K. (1973), Conners parent and teacher questionnaire. *Psychopharmacology Bulletin Special Issue: Pharmacotherapy of Children* (Publication No. HSM 73-9002). Washington, DC: NIMH.

Gittelman, R. & Kanner, A. (1986), Psychopharmacotherapy. In: *Psychopathological Disorders of Childhood edition* eds. H. Quay and J. Werry. New York: John Wiley and Sons, pp. 455–495.

Hastings, J.E. & Barkley, R.A. (1978), A review of psychophysiological research with hyperactive children. *J. Abnorm. Child Psychol.*, 6:413–448.

Hoza, J. (1989), *Response to Stimulant Medication Among Children with Attention Deficit Hyperactivity Disorder*. Unpublished doctoral dissertation. Florida State University.

Lindgren, S. & Lyons, D. (1985), *Pediatric Assessment of Cognitive Efficiency*. Iowa City, IA: University of Iowa, Department of Pediatrics.

Milich, R. & Landau, S. (1989), The role of social status variables in differentiating subgroups of hyperactive children. In: *Attention Deficit Disorders IV: Current Concepts and Emerging Trends in Attentional and Behavioral Disorders of Childhood*, London: Pergamon, pp. 1–16.

Pelham, W.E. (1982), Childhood hyperactivity: Diagnosis, etiology, nature and treatment. In: *Behavioral Medicine and Clinical Psychology: Overlapping Disciplines,* eds. R. Getchel, A. Baum, & J. Singer. Hillsdale, NJ: Lawrence Erlbaum Associates.

———— (1986), The effects of stimulant drugs on learning and achievement in hyperactive and learning-disabled children. In: *Psychological and Educational Perspectives on Learning Disabilities,* eds. J.K. Torgesen & B. Wong. New York: Academic Press, pp. 259–295.

———— (1989), Behavior therapy, behavioral assessment, and psychostimulant medication in treatment of attention deficit disorders: An interactive approach. In: *Attention Deficit Disorders IV: Current Concepts and Emerging Trends in Attentional and Behavioral Disorders of Childhood,* eds. J. Swanson & L. Bloomingdale. London: Pergamon, pp. 169–195.

———— Bender, M.E. (1982), Peer relationships in hyperactive children: Description and treatment. In: *Advances in Learning and Behavioral Disabilities,* Vol. 1, eds. K. Gadow & I. Bialer. Greenwich, CT: JAI Press, pp. 366–436.

—— Hoza, J. (1987), Behavioral assessment of psychostimulant effects on ADD children in a Summer Day Treatment Program. In: *Advances in Behavioral Assessment of Children and Families,* Vol. 3, ed. R. Prinz. Greenwich, CT: JAI Press, pp. 3–33.

—— Murphy, H.A. (1986), Behavioral and pharmacological treatment of attention deficit and conduct disorders. In: *Pharmacological and Behavioral Treatment: An Integrative Approach,* ed. M. Hersen. New York: John Wiley and Sons, pp. 108–148.

—— Bender, M.E., Caddell, J., Booth, S. & Moorer, S. (1985), The dose-response effects of methylphenidate on classroom academic and social behavior in children with attention deficit disorder. *Arch. Gen. Psychiatry,* 42:948–952.

—— Milich, R. & Walker, J. (1986), The effects on continuous and partial reinforcement and methylphenidate on learning in children with attention deficit disorder. *J. Abnorm. Psychol,* 95:319–325.

—— Milich, R., Murphy, D.A. & Murphy, H.A. (1989), Normative data on the IOWA Conners teacher rating scale. *J. Clin. Child Psychol.,* 18:259–262.

—— Greenslade, K.E., Vodde-Hamilton, M.A., Murphy, D.A., Greenstein, J.J., Gnagy, E.M. & Dahl, R.E. (1990a), Relative efficacy of long-acting CNS stimulants on children with attention deficit-hyperactivity disorder: A comparison of standard methylphenidate, sustained-release methylphenidate, sustained-release dextroamphetamine, and pemoline. *Pediatrics,* 86:226–237.

—— McBurnett, K., Harper, G., Milich, R., Clinton, J., Thiele, C. & Murphy, D.A. (1990b), Methylphenidate and baseball playing in ADD children: Who's on first? *J. Consult. Clin. Psychol.,* 58:130–133.

Pfiffner, L.J. & Barkley, R. (1990), Educational placement and classroom management. In: *Attention Deficit Hyperactivity Disorders: A Handbook for Diagnosis and Treatment,* ed. R.A. Barkley. Guildford Press.

Quay, H.C. & Peterson, D.R. (1983), Interim manual for the *Revised Behavior Problem Checklist.* Box 248074, University of Miami, Coral Gables, FL 33124.

Rapport, M.D., Stoner, G., DuPaul, G.J., Birmingham, B.K. & Tucker, S. (1985), Methylphenidate in hyperactive children: Differential effects of dose on academic, learning, and social behavior. *J. Abnorm. Child Psychol.,* 13:227–244.

Rodgers, P.A. (1988), *Sustained Attention and Impulsivity in ADHD: Comparison with Normal Children and Methylphenidate Effects.* Unpublished Master's thesis. Florida State University.

Shekim, W.O., Dekirmenjian, H., Javaid, J., Bulund, D.B. and Davis, J.M. (1982), Dopamine-norepinephrine interaction in hyperactive boys treated with d-amphetamine. *J. Pediatr.,* 100(5):830–834.

Sleator, E.K. (1986), Diagnosis. In: *Dialogues in Pediatric Management:* (Vol. 1), *Attention Deficit Disorder,* eds. E. Sleator and W. Pelham. Norwalk, CT: Appleton-Century-Crofts, pp. 11–43.

Solanto, M.V. (1984), Neuropharmacological basis of stimulant drug action in attention deficit with hyperactivity: A review and synthesis. *Psychol. Bull.,* 95:387–409.

Sprague, R.L. & Sleator, E. (1977), Methylphenidate in hyperkinetic children: Differences in dose effects on learning and social behavior. *Science,* 198:1274–1276.

Stephens, R., Pelham, W.E. & Skinner, R. (1984), The state-dependent and main effects of pemoline and methylphenidate on paired-associated learning and spelling in hyperactive children. *J. Consult. Clin. Psychol.,* 52:104–113.

Swanson, J. & Kinsbourne, M. (1979), The cognitive effects of stimulant drugs on hyperactive (inattentive) children. In: *Attention and the Development of Cognitive Skills,* eds. G. Hale & M. Lewis. New York: Plenum Press, pp. 249–274.

—— Roberts, W. & Zucker, K. (1978), Time-response analysis of the effect of stimulant medication on the learning ability of children referred for hyperactivity. *Pediatrics,* 61:21–29.

—— Sandman, E., Deutsch, C. & Baren, M. (1983), Methylphenidate (Ritalin) given with or before breakfast: Part I. Behavioral, cognitive & electrophysiological effects. *Pediatrics,* 72:49–55.

Taylor, E., Schachar, R., Thorley, G., Wieselberg, H.M., Everitt, B. & Rutter, M. (1987), Which boys respond to stimulant medication? A controlled trial of methylphenidate in boys with disruptive behavior. *Psychol. Med.,* 17:121–143.

Walker, H.M., Street, A., Garrett, B., Crossen, J., Hops, H. & Greenwood, C.R. (1978), *RECESS: Reprogramming Environmental Contingencies for Effective Social Skills.* Eugene, OR: Center at Oregon for Research in the Behavioral Education of the Handicapped.

Weiss, G. & Hechtman, L. (1986), *Hyperactive Children Grown Up.* New York: Guilford Press.

Zametkin, A.J. & Rapoport, J.L. (1987), Neurobiology of attention deficit disorder with hyperactivity: Where have we come in 50 years? *J. Am. Acad. Child Adolesc. Psychiatry,* 26:6:676–686.

Methylphenidate: Effects on Sustained Attention

ANDREA BERGMAN, Ph.D.,[1] LYNN WINTERS, Ph.D.,[2]
and BARBARA CORNBLATT, Ph.D.[1]

Attention deficit hyperactivity disorder (ADHD), as defined by *DSM-III-R* (American Psychiatric Association, 1987), is most prominently characterized by disturbances in attention and motor functioning. While excessive motor activity is perhaps the most disruptive symptom exhibited by ADHD children, problems in concentrating may have the most serious long-term consequences, especially with respect to academic achievement (McGee and Share, 1988). However, it now appears that stimulants can improve both types of symptoms (e.g., Kupietz et al. 1988; Pelham, 1986), although the mechanisms of drug action are still not clearly understood.

For clinical purposes, while it is not crucial to determine how stimulants work, it is important to know how *well* they work. For example, it is critical to measure such things as patient responsiveness, optimal drug dose, and presence of side effects. In order to meet these needs, a variety of techniques have been used such as the Revised Conners Teacher Rating Scale (Goyette et al., 1978) to measure improvement in school and the Subject Treatment Emergent Symptoms Scale (Guy, 1976) to detect side effects. In terms of research, the cognitive effects of stimulants are frequently assessed by measuring improvement in attention on laboratory tasks. Of these measures, one of the most popular is a computer-generated test of sustained attention, known as the Continuous Performance Test (CPT).

DESCRIPTION OF THE CPT

Sustained attention refers to the ability to concentrate on a source of information over an extended period of time. In experimental research, such as human factors studies for the military, this type of attention is referred to as "vigilance." Operating a sonar device on a submarine is an example of a "real world" vigilance task. This involves continually monitoring a sonar screen for a blip that would indicate a ship on the surface. The CPT is a similar task that requires a subject to sit in front of a video screen and continually watch for particular target stimuli embedded in a long series of similar stimuli. This procedure provides a way of quantifying, in the laboratory or office, the concentration problems characteristic of ADHD children.

Although there are many different versions of the CPT, all share some common features. They all involve the very rapid presentation of a series of stimuli over a considerable period of time (which can vary from 15 minutes to over 1 hour). For example, 500 letters might be presented one after another, with each letter shown on the screen for only a few milliseconds (the most common stimulus exposure times fall in the range of 50 to 100 msec). In this case, the subject might be told to respond only when the letter "X" appears on the screen (Rosvold et al., 1956). Usually the letter "X" makes up approximately 20 to 30% of the total number of letters shown, which can include all the letters of the alphabet or might be restricted to only a few. In recent studies, responses are most often measured when the subject pushes a button on a reaction time key as soon as he or she sees the target stimulus (e.g., the "X"). Each response and response time is then recorded on the computer.

[1]Elmhurst Hospital Center, Elmhurst, New York and Mount Sinai School of Medicine, New York, New York
[2]State University of New York at Purchase, Purchase, New York and New York State Psychiatric Institute, New York, New York

This procedure does not have to involve letters. Other stimuli that have been used are series of numbers, where the target might be a "5" (Nuechterlein, 1983) or an "8" (Friedman et al., 1981, 1986) or, for very young children, pictures of animals, where the subject is told to respond only when a rabbit appears (Weissberg et al., 1990).

Thus, the CPT is more accurately viewed as a family of measures. Various versions have been used widely in psychopathology research, especially in the areas of schizophrenia and ADHD. A number of CPT modifications have been introduced in both fields in order to make the task sufficiently difficult for use with normal or only moderately disturbed subjects across a wide age range. This was necessary because some of the easier tasks, while effective in demonstrating deficits in affected patients, resulted in ceiling effects when given to normals and subjects with subclinical symptoms. An early modification of the CPT "X" design, made the task slightly more difficult by requiring subjects to respond to the letter "X" only when it directly follows the letter "A." This variant is known as the AX CPT (e.g., Kornetsky and Mirsky, 1966).

Another version for younger children (approximately ages 7–10) is the "playing card" CPT that involved images of standard playing cards, including the 2–10 of clubs and the 2–10 of spades (Rutschmann et al., 1977). In this task, subjects are instructed to respond whenever there are two cards in a row that were exactly the same (e.g., the six of spades following a six of spades). This task is more difficult than the AX task because it requires the children to store each stimulus in memory to match with the next one to establish identity. In the AX task, by comparison, the child only has to look for the "A," which can be considered a type of warning signal, and then remember to respond if an "X" follows it. Only the two target letters, the "A" and the "X" have to be kept in memory during the task. The Playing Card CPT is also somewhat more difficult because for every target pair there are an equal number of "catch" pairs, which are two cards in sequence that are almost but not quite identical—e.g., a six of spades following a six of clubs.

Other ways of making the task more difficult have been to degrade the stimuli (i.e., by blurring them on the screen and superimposing visual noise; Nuechterlein, 1983), or to make presentation speed dependent on subject performance. The latter task is referred to as the "dynamic" CPT (Buchsbaum and Sostek, 1980; Rapoport et al., 1980). In the dynamic version, the better the subject performs, the harder the task becomes. A block of correct responses will cause the task to speed up; errors will slow it down. Thus, task difficulty is regulated by the subject's own performance.

In all of these measures, responding to the designated target (e.g., the "X," the "X" following an "A," the two identical playing cards, or degraded stimulus) are called correct responses or hits. Responses to any other stimuli or combinations are errors, frequently referred to as commission errors or false alarms. A number of investigators also use reaction times as an additional response measure, that is how fast (in milliseconds) it takes a subject to make a response. ADHD children have been found to have generally slower reaction times than normal controls (Rapoport, 1983). Stimulants appear to normalize reaction times in ADHD subjects, speeding up response times and improving accuracy (Coons et al., 1987).

ADVANTAGES/DISADVANTAGES OF THE CPT

There are many advantages to using the CPT as a measure of treatment effectiveness in research. First of all, as indicated above, the CPT has excellent face validity. That is, it seems to be measuring an aspect of cognitive functioning that is highly impaired in ADHD children, namely, the ability to concentrate on a single task for an extended period of time. This is notably a problem in school, and the CPT is therefore a fairly good analogue of the kind of situations encountered in school. Second, the CPT represents an objective way of quantifying improvement or decompensation in attention as a result of treatment. Third, the test is relatively inexpensive and easy to administer and score.

A major disadvantage of using the CPT results from the considerable differences that exist among the versions. To interpret changes in patients on one version based on research with a different CPT can lead to a variety of difficulties. This is especially true when using a very easy CPT in clinical practice and comparing the results with a much more difficult research procedure. Similarly, samples have to be matched on variables that are likely to affect CPT performance. Inferences about improvement/decompensation of patients cannot be based on research using samples that differ from the patients in terms of potentially confounding variables such as intelligence, ethnicity or social class.

However, a more basic difficulty is involved in attempting to use any version of the CPT for diagnostic or clinical reasons. This correlates with the fact that the CPT is essentially a research instrument that has been developed to look at differences between *groups* of subjects as a result of pharmacological manipulations, genetic variations, environmental differences, etc. On an individual level (e.g., to assess how much a particular patient improves in response to medication), the CPT, like other similar research procedures, is inaccurate and can lead to a multitude of interpretive errors. Nevertheless, while it will be several years before any CPT task is perfected enough to be used by clinicians with confidence (especially for diagnostic purposes), as research tools, nearly all versions of the CPT can provide critical information about ADHD and how to deal with the disorder.

WHAT RESEARCH CAN TELL US

A major question of critical interest to both clinicians and researchers is how well stimulants improve attention—both immediately, as measured in the laboratory and the classroom, and in the long run, as reflected in improved school achievement. In general, most of the evidence indicates that stimulants— primarily methylphenidate or amphetamines—have quite good short-term effects in terms of improvement on the CPT and immediate changes in classroom behavior (Kupietz and Balka, 1976; Pelham et al., 1990; Rapoport et al., 1980; Whalen and Henker, 1976). Long-term academic gains, on the other hand, have been far more disappointing (Barkley and Cunningham, 1978; Charles and Schain, 1981; Rie et al., 1976). A number of explanations have been offered to account for this discrepancy.

One possibility is that medication primarily treats the motor symptoms of the disorder and that ADHD children are more attentive simply because they are sitting still. Questions have been raised as to whether improved attention is due to decreased motor hyperactivity or whether stimulants affect attention directly (Gittelman-Klein and Klein, 1975, 1976). However, many researchers believe that methylphenidate and other stimulants actually do improve cognitive functioning independent of beneficial motor effects. There is evidence that reports of behavioral improvements and changes in sustained attention due to drug treatment are not associated, rather that these effects are independent of one another (Conners and Taylor, 1980; Taylor, 1983). If we assume that improvements in attention are indepedent of behavior change, the question then becomes: What aspect of attention is improved and how can this account for short-term but not long-term treatment gains?

Some studies have already addressed this issue. For example, Adams (1982) conducted a study using a simple reaction time task and a more complex choice reaction time task. The simple task was viewed as consisting of two components, attention and response time. The choice reaction time task added a decision making component. Through the use of this paradigm, the "attentional" and "thinking" phases of related cognitive processes were separated. Adams found that methylphenidate improved performance on the simple task but not the complex task. He therefore proposed that stimulants affect attentional processes but may not affect the more complex cognitive processes that are essential for long-term academic gains.

In support of the above hypothesis, Weingartner et al. (1980) utilized a paradigm whereby children processed some words based on meaning and others based on acoustic properties (i.e., rhyming). They hypothesized that while rhyming requires only a weak processing strategy, processing of meaning is far more complex, elaborate, and relevant to classroom learning. Normal and hyperactive children were tested following placebo and amphetamine treatment. The results indicated that, for hyperactive children, the cognitive component affected most by stimulants involved acoustic rather than semantic processing. These findings, along with those of Adams (1982), suggest that stimulants primarily improve simple cognitive functions rather than the level of processing most involved in acquiring academic skills.

Alternate explanations attribute the lack of long-term academic gains in treated ADHD children to improper dosage and/or the short half-life of stimulants. Some studies have indicated that the dosage of stimulant medication that is effective in treating hyperactive behavior may not be optimal for improving cognitive performance (e.g., Peeke et al., 1984; Sprague and Sleator, 1977), although Kupietz et al. (1988) compared three dosages of methylphenidate (0.3, 0.5, and 0.7 mg/kg) and found that both hyperactive behavior and cognitive performance showed the most improvement at the highest dose. Alternately, Pelham et al. (1990) point out that due to the rapid onset and brief half-life of methylphenidate, an ADHD child on a standard (twice daily) dosage will be maximally affected for only part of the school day. Therefore, according to these authors, one reason for the lack of long-term academic improvement may be that methylphenidate has a narrow window of effect on cognitive functioning that does not overlap with academic tasks in school. In other words, the time when the medication is actually the most effective for cognitive functioning may be during periods of the school day which are not academically focused (e.g., recess or free-play periods). One proposed solution to this problem is the use of a longer acting stimulant, such as the recently developed sustained-release preparation of methylphenidate.

A third factor possibly confounding studies of long-term treatment gain may be the presence of disorders that are co-morbid with ADHD. ADHD children frequently display other syndromes, including reading disabilities, conduct disorders, anxiety and depression (Biederman et al., 1990; McClellan et al., 1990; McGee et al., 1990). There is some question as to the specificity of attentional deficits to ADHD as opposed to a general association with many of the frequently co-occuring childhood disorders. In particular, there appears to be an overlap in deficits between ADHD and learning disabilities. For example, in their review, Aylward and Whitehouse (1988) report that deficits in sustained attention appear to be as characteristic of subjects with ADHD plus reading disabilities as of children with ADHD alone. The question remains as to whether treatment will affect children with "pure" ADHD differently than those with comorbid diagnoses.

In order to test these competing hypotheses (i.e., type of cognition vs. type of medication vs. comorbidity) for factors possibly accounting for the lack of long-term improvement, we adapted a complex version of the CPT for a double-blind cross-over study comparing short-acting versus sustained-release methylphenidate in ADHD boys. Type of attention and presence/absence of reading disabilities were also manipulated in this study.

The version of the CPT used was the CPT-IP (Identical Pairs version of the CPT; Cornblatt et al., 1988), that has been standardized across a number of psychiatric and normal populations. This task, which evolved from the much easier "playing card" CPT described above, taps a variety of information processing abilities, including distractibility, speed of processing, ability to discriminate between highly similar stimuli, and right versus left hemisphere processing skills. The latter are measured by comparing performance on verbal versus spatial conditions, assumed to tap abilities in the left and right hemispheres, respectively. The verbal stimuli are 4-digit numbers and the spatial stimuli consist of nonsense shapes. (See Cornblatt et al., 1988 for more details.)

As was the case in the earlier playing card task, subjects are told to respond when they detect two identical stimuli in a row (thus the name, "Identical Pairs"). For the CPT-IP, however, the stimuli are much more complicated than in the playing card version or in most standard CPTs. Thus, the requirement that each target be maintained in short term memory and matched against the next stimulus in the series constitutes a task that is particularly demanding on working memory.

Study design

In an attempt to investigate the efficacy of sustained-release methylphenidate versus regular methylphenidate, subjects were tested on the CPT-IP in three phases: during the first phase they were on placebo; in two additional phases subjects received either short-acting methylphenidate or sustained-release methylphenidate, in counterbalanced order. Therefore, over the course of the study, subjects were tested six times, on the morning and afternoon of three test days. Of the three days, the first was always the placebo condition and served to establish the drug-free baseline response levels. On the two additional test days, the subjects either received a single morning dose of 20 mg of sustained-release methylphenidate or separate morning and afternoon doses of 10 mg of short-acting (regular) methylphenidate in a randomized double-blind cross-over design.

Subjects

Forty-two boys between the ages of 6 and 12 with a primary *DSM-III* (APA, 1980) diagnosis of attention deficit disorder with hyperactivity (ADDH) were included in the study (for simplicity, these subjects will be referred to as ADHD so as to be consistent with the most recent diagnostic terminology). In order to address the question of comorbidity, the sample was subdivided into children with and without reading disabilities. The resulting sample consisted of 11 subjects who met criteria for reading disability (ADHD/RD) and 31 ADHD subjects (Cornblatt et al., in preparation). Assessment of reading disability was based on a "Reading Quotient" index which was calculated by dividing the Wide Range Achievement Test–Revised (WRAT-R; Jastek and Wilkinson, 1984) Reading test score by the Wechsler Intelligence Scale for Children-Revised (WISC-R; Wechsler, 1974) full scale IQ score. If the resulting RQ score was less than .85, indicating a discrepancy of more than one standard deviation between reading and IQ scores, the subject was categorized as reading disabled (ADHD/RD).

Furthermore, while no normal control group was included in this study, in order to obtain some idea of the performance of the ADHD subjects relative to other children of their age, comparisons were made with a sample of normal children independently tested as part of the New York High-Risk Project (Cornblatt et al., 1989; Erlenmeyer-Kimling and Cornblatt, 1987). For purposes of comparison, 29 children between the ages of 6 and 12 years were selected from the High-Risk Project normal control group.

Study results

The major findings of this study have been summarized in Table 1. In general, when compared with the independently tested normal controls, the ADHD boys were more distractible and performed worse on both the verbal and spatial conditions of the CPT-IP. The generally lower performance level is consistent with a large body of previous research (e.g., Douglas, 1983; Michael et al., 1981; Rapoport et al., 1980; Sykes et al., 1973). However, the distraction finding contradicts earlier reports by Douglas and Peters (1979) suggesting that ADHD subjects are not more distractible than controls. Interestingly, in the current study, although impaired in overall performance, the ADHD subjects were similar to the normal controls in pattern of processing skills. More specifically, ADHD boys were much better on shapes than numbers. This is consistent with previous findings which have shown that children and adolescents invariably perform better on the spatial conditions of the CPT (which are equal to the verbal conditions in difficulty level for adults) and, in fact, substantially outperform adults on these conditions (Cornblatt et al., 1988).

Medication effects

The results of the double-blind cross-over study indicated that the ADHD subjects improved on all conditions for both types of methylphenidate, but that the sustained-release form did not significantly differ from short-acting methylphenidate on any of the conditions. There was a trend, however, for sustained-released

TABLE 1. SUMMARY OF STUDY RESULTS

- OVERALL CPT performance: ADHD versus Normal Controls
  √ADHD worse than Normals—Verbal and Spatial
  √ADHD more DISTRACTIBLE than Normals
  √ADHD = Normals in PATTERN of performance:
      Spatial > Verbal
- MEDICATION EFFECTS FOR ADHD BOYS
  √Improved Verbal and Spatial
  √Greater improvement for Spatial
  √Did NOT improve distractibility
- Comorbidity: ADHD and Reading Disability
  √Pure ADHD worse than Normals—Verbal and Spatial
  √ADHD/RD worse than Normals—Verbal ONLY

---

methylphenidate to be less effective in the afternoon sessions, suggesting that a higher dose of sustained-release might be needed to be equivalent to the short-acting form.

Interestingly, neither form of medication had any effect on distraction. That is, even though there was an improvement in overall performance, subjects were just as distractible when medicated as when tested off medication. These findings may help to account for those of Pelham et al. (in press) who found that sustained-release methylphenidate improved behavior and CPT performance, but not reading or seatwork accuracy.

Comorbidity

Comparisons between those subjects with (ADHD/RD) and without (ADHD) reading disabilities generated some of the most interesting findings of this study. When compared with independently tested normal control subjects, the ADHD boys were impaired across the board (i.e., both verbally and spatially), whereas ADHD/RD subjects were deficient only verbally. This suggests that the ADHD/RD deficit is more specific and more closely resembles the cognitive difficulties characterizing subjects with pure reading disabilities. It also indicates that hyperactivity may be secondary to the reading problems in this group of subjects. In a recent review, McGee and Share (1988) arrived at a similar conclusion; that ADHD, particularly in the classroom, may be a consequence of learning difficulties. They also reported findings comparing four groups of boys (ADD, ADD and reading disability, reading disability alone, and normal) on a battery of neuropsychological measures which indicated that reading disability (with or without ADD) was associated with poorer verbal learning and verbal skills. These results are in contrast to other research suggesting that there is little or no basis to distinguish between ADHD children with and without reading disabilities (Halperin et al., 1984).

Type of attention

As mentioned above, both ADHD and ADHD/RD children show a significant spatial advantage. That is, both groups do markedly better on the spatial as compared with verbal conditions. The difference between these groups, however, is that the ADHD/RD subjects perform as well as normal controls spatially, whereas the pure ADHD boys are deficient in both spatial and verbal abilities. Interestingly, methylphenidate differentially improves spatial processing. That is, while verbal processing does improve, spatial processes undergo a more significant positive change. Therefore, for both groups of subjects, medication primarily affects those areas of processing that need it least, and, in terms of the reading disabled group, the area that is not even deficient. In both cases, the processing dimension that is most impaired—namely verbal skills—is least helped by stimulant treatment.

The fact that the primary area of improvement concerns the simpler of the two tasks supports the findings by Weingartner et al. (1980) and by Adams (1982) that suggest that cognitively, methylphenidate only elevates the most simple of cognitive skills. Thus, it can be concluded that for ADHD subjects, stimulants do not improve the area of cognition that is most impaired, namely verbal abilities.

Considered overall, these findings suggest that amphetamines do not improve a specific cognitive deficit, but appear to have a nonspecific effect on performance in general. This is supported by the findings of a number of investigators that amphetamines improve attention and decrease motor restlessness in normal adults and children as well as in ADHD subjects (Rapoport et al., 1980; Weingartner et al., 1980). Since stimulant treatment does not affect the cognitive problems specifically related to ADHD, it is not surprising that there is no improvement in long-term learning or achievement levels. However, short-term gains should not be minimized because of this. Stimulant treatment clearly keeps ADHD children in school and out of trouble. In themselves these are extremely important benefits that can help to change the downward spiral of these children and may enhance other treatment strategies.

OVERVIEW AND CONCLUSIONS

1. Subjects with primary ADHD appear to have a different pattern of attentional problems than subjects with ADHD combined with reading disabilities. ADHD subjects show a global impairment whereas those who also have reading disabilities appear specifically impaired in their verbal skills.

2. Stimulant treatment appears to have a similar effect on both groups. It does not reduce distractibility and has a significantly positive effect on both verbal and spatial attention, with greater improvement for spatial processing. Stimulants, therefore, appear to have the greatest impact on the areas that are least impaired to begin with. This suggests that in terms of long-term cognitive gains, treatment, at best, will be moderately effective for pure ADHD children and only minimally helpful for those with reading disabilities.

3. There is no clear difference in effectiveness between sustained release and short-acting methylphenidate.

In conclusion, measures such as the CPT have considerable potential to assist in evaluating treatment efficacy of various types of medication. They can also provide information about the similarities of diagnostically overlapping groups. However, these measures cannot yet be used as cognitive "blood tests." They are not adequate as diagnostic instruments on an individual patient level. In particular, to develop the CPT for diagnostic or screening assessments, a number of problems must be solved such as establishing norms across different versions and demonstrating specificity of performance patterns in ADHD children.

ACKNOWLEDGMENTS

Funding for this research was provided in part by NIMH Grant MH 38838-05 to Dr. Laurence Greenhill and NIMH Grant MH 30906-09 to the Psychiatric Institute Computer Center.

REFERENCES

Adams, W. (1982). Effect of methylphenidate on thought processing time in children. *Dev. Behav. Pediatr.*, 3(3):133–135.

American Psychiatric Association. (1980). *Diagnostic and Statistical Manual of Mental Disorders*, 3rd Ed. Washington, DC: American Psychiatric Association.

——(1987). *Diagnostic and Statistical Manual of Mental Disorders*, 3rd Ed. revised. Washington, DC: American Psychiatric Association.

Aylward, E.H. & Whitehouse, D. (1988). Learning disability with and without attention deficit disorder. In: *Advances in Clinical Child Psychology* (vol. 11), eds. B.B. Lahey & A.E. Kazolin. New York: Plenum Press, pp. 321–341.

Barkley, R.A. & Cunningham, C.E. (1978). Do stimulant drugs improve the academic performance of hyperkinetic children? *Clin. Pediatr.*, 17:85–92.

Biederman, J., Farone, S.V., Keenan, K., Knee, D., & Tsuang, M.T. (1990). Family-genetic and psychosocial risk factors in DSM-III Attention Deficit Disorder. *J. Am. Acad. Child Adolesc. Psychiatry*, 29:526–533.

Buchsbaum, M.S. & Sostek, A.J. (1980). An adaptive-rate continuous performance test: Vigilance characteristics and reliability for 400 male students. *Percept. Motor Skills*, 51:707.

Charles, L. & Schain, R. (1981). A four-year follow-up study of the effects of methylphenidate on the behavior and academic achievement of hyperactive children. *J. Abnorm. Child Psychol.*, 9:495–505.

Conners, C.K. & Taylor, E. (1980). Pemoline, methylphenidate and placebo in children with minimal brain dysfunction. *Arch. Gen. Psychiatry*, 37:922–930.

Coons, H., Klorman, R., & Borgstedt, A. (1987). Effects of methylphenidate on adolescents with a childhood history of attention deficit disorder: II. Information processing. *J. Am. Acad. Child Adolesc. Psychiatry*, 26(5):368–374.

Cornblatt, B., Risch, N., Faris, G., Friedman, D., & Erlenmeyer-Kimling, L. (1988). The Continuous Performance Test, Identical Pairs Version (CPT-IP): I. New findings about sustained attention in normal families. *Psychiatry Res.*, 26:233–238.

———— Winters, L., & Erlenmeyer-Kimling, L. (1989). Attentional markers of schizophrenia: Evidence from the New York High-Risk Study. In: *Schizophrenia: Scientific Progress*, eds. S. Schultz and C. Tamminga. New York: Oxford University Press, pp. 83–92.

———— ———— Maminski, B., & Greenhill, L. (in preparation). Attentional performance in hyperactive children: Stimulant effects on the CPT-IP.

Douglas, V. (1983). Attentional and cognitive problems. In: *Developmental Neuropsychiatry*, ed. M. Rutter. New York: Guilford, pp. 280–329.

———— Peters, K. (1979). Toward a clearer definition of the attentional deficit of hyperactive children. In: *Attention and the Development of Cognitive Skills*, eds. G.A. Hale & M. Lewis. New York: Plenum Press, pp. 173–247.

Erlenmeyer-Kimling, L. & Cornblatt, B. (1987). The New York High-Risk Project: A follow-up report. *Schizophrenia Bull.*, 13:411–424.

Friedman, D., Cornblatt, B., Vaughan, H., & Erlenmeyer-Kimling, L. (1986). Event-related potentials in children at risk for schizophrenia during two versions of the continuous performance test. *Psychiatry Res.*, 18:161–177.

———— Vaughan, H., & Erlenmeyer-Kimling, L. (1981). Multiple late positive potentials in two visual discrimination tasks. *Psychophysiology*, 18:635–649.

Gittelman-Klein, R. & Klein, D.F. (1975). Are behavioral and psychometric changes related in methylphenidate-treated, hyperactive children? *Int. J. Mental Health*, 4:189–198.

———— ———— (1976). Methylphenidate effects in learning disabilities: 1. Psychometric changes. *Arch. Gen. Psychiatry*, 33:655–664.

Goyette, C.H., Conners, C.K., & Ulrich, R.F. (1978). Normative data on revised Conners parent and teacher rating scales. *J. Abnorm. Child Psychol.*, 10:33–60.

Guy, W. (ed.). (1976). Subject treatment emergent symptoms scale. In: *ECDEU Assessment Manual for Psychopharmacology*. Rockville, MD: National Institute of Mental Health.

Halperin, J., Gittelman, R., Klein, D., & Rudel, R. (1984). Reading-disabled hyperactive children: A distinct subgroup of attention deficit disorder with hyperactivity? *J. Abnorm. Child Psychol.*, 12(1):1–14.

Jastek, S. & Wilkenson, G. (1984). *Wide Range Achievement Test-Revised*. Wilmington, DL: Jastak Associates, Inc.

Kornetsky, C. & Mirsky, A. (1966). On certain pharmacological and physiological differences between schizophrenics and normal persons. *Psychopharmacologia*, 8:309–318.

Kupietz, S. & Balka, E. (1976). Alterations in the vigilance performance of children receiving amitriptyline and methylphenidate pharmacotherapy. *Psychopharmacology*, 50:29–33.

———— Winsberg, B., Richardson, E., Maitinsky, S., and Mendell, N. (1988). Effects of methylphenidate dosage in hyperactive reading-disabled children: I. Behavior and cognitive performance effects. *J. Am. Acad. Child Adolesc. Psychiatry*, 27 (1):70–77.

McClellan, J.M., Rubert, M.P., Reichler, R., & Sylvester, C.C. (1990). Attention deficit disorder in children at risk for anxiety and depression. *J. Am. Acad. Child Adolesc. Psychiatry*, 29:534–539.

McGee, R. & Share, D.L. (1988). Attention deficit disorder-hyperactivity and academic failure: Which comes first and what should be treated? *J. Am. Acad. Child Adolesc. Psychiatry*, 27 (3):318–325.

———— Feehan, M., Williams, S., Partridge, F., Silva, P., & Kelly, J. (1990), DSM-III disorders in a large sample of adolescents. *J. Am. Acad. Child Adolesc. Psychiatry*, 29:611–619.

Michael, R.L., Klorman, R., Salzman, L.F., Borgstedt, A.D., & Dainer, K.B. (1981). Normalizing effects of methylphenidate on hyperactive children's vigilance performance and evoked potentials. *Psychophysiology*, 18:665–677.

Nuechterlein, K.H. (1983). Signal detection in vigilance tasks and behavioral attributes among offspring of shizophrenic mothers and among hyperactive children. *J. Abnorm. Psychol.*, 92:4–28.

Peeke, S., Halliday, R., Callaway, E., Prael, R., & Reus, V. (1984). Effects of two doses of methylphenidate on verbal information processing in hyperactive children. *J. Clin. Psychopharmacol.*, 4:82–88.

Pelham, W. (1986). The effects of psychostimulant drugs on learning and academic achievement in children with Attention-Deficit Disorders and Learning Disabilities. In: *Psychological and Educational Perspectives in Learning Disabilities,* eds. J. Torgeson & Y. Wong. New York: Academic Press, pp 259–295.

———— Greenslade, K.E., Vodde-Hamilton, M., Muphy, D.A., Greenstein, J.J., Griagy, E.M., Guthrie, K.J., Hoover, M.D., & Dahl, R.E. (1990). Relative efficacy of long-acting stimulants on children with attention deficit-hyperactivity disorder: A comparison of standard methylphenidate sustained-release methylphenidate, sustained-release dextroamphetamine, and pemoline. *Pediatrics,* 86:226–237.

Rapoport, J.L. (1983). The use of drugs: Trends in research. In: *Developmental Neuropsychiatry,* ed. M. Rutter. New York: Guilford, pp. 385–403.

———— Buchsbaum, M.S., Weingartner, H., Zahn, T.P. Ludlow, C., & Mikkelsen, E.J. (1980). Dextroamphetamine. Its cognitive and behavioral effects in normal and hyperactive boys and normal men. *Arch. Gen. Psychiatry,* 37:933–943.

Rie, H.E., Rie, E.D., & Steward, S. (1976). Effects of methylphenidate on underachieving children. *J. Consult. Clin. Psychol.,* 44:250–260.

Rosvold, H.E., Mirsky, A., Sarason, M., Bransome, E.D., Jr., & Beck, L.H. (1956). A Continuous Performance Test of brain damage. *J. Consult. Psychol.,* 20:343.

Rutschmann, J., Cornblatt, B., & Erlenmeyer-Kimling, L. (1977). Sustained attention in children at risk for schizophrenia. *Arch. Gen. Psychiatry,* 34:571–575.

Sprague, R.L. & Sleator, E.K. (1977). Methylphenidate in hyperkinetic children: differences in dose effects on learning and social behavior. *Science,* 198:1274–1276.

Sykes, D.H., Douglas, V.I., & Morgenstern, G. (1973). Sustained attention in hyperactive children. *J. Child Psychol. Psychiatry,* 14:213–220.

Taylor, E. (1983). Drug response and diagnostic validation. In: *Developmental Neuropsychiatry,* ed. M. Rutter. New York: Guilford Press, pp. 348–369.

Wechsler, D. (1974). *Wechsler Intelligence Scale for Children—Revised.* New York: Psychological Corporation.

Weingartner, H., Rapoport, J.L., Buchsbaum, M.S., Bunney, W.E., Ebert, M.H., Mikkelson, E.J. & Caine, E.D. (1980). Cognitive processes in normal and hyperactive children and their response to amphetamine treatment. *J. Abnorm. Psychol.*, 89:(1)25–37.

Weissberg, R., Ruff, H.A. & Lawson, K.R. (1990). The usefulness of reaction time tasks in studying attention and organization of behavior in young children. *J. Dev. Behav. Pediatr.,* 11:(2)59–64.

Whalen, C. & Henker, B. (1976), Psychostimulants and children: A review and analysis. *Psychol. Bull.,* 83:1113–1130.

Dosage Effects of Ritalin on Cognition

MARY V. SOLANTO

There is widespread concern among clinicians that Ritalin, particularly at higher doses, may have adverse effects on cognitive function in children with attention deficit hyperactivity disorder (ADHD). This concern is readily understandable given that the drug is specifically administered so as to be active during the school day and is most often prescribed for several years continuously.

Concern about this issue was heightened by a report by Sprague and Sleator, appearing in *Science* in 1977 (Fig. 1) which revealed a disparity between the Ritalin dosage which maximally improved behavior as rated by teachers (1.0 mg/kg) and that which optimized performance on a short-term memory task (.3 mg/kg). Whereas performance on the memory task was improved by the .3 mg/kg dosage, it was no better than placebo on the higher 1.0 mg/kg dose. The suggestion from these data was that a Ritalin dosage which maximally improved the child's behavior in the classroom might have no effect, or might even have an adverse effect, on ability to learn and retain academic material.

Concern has also been expressed about another potential negative effect of Ritalin. Stimulant drugs exert their beneficial effect by facilitating focusing, disregard of extraneous stimuli, and sustained attention to a task. However, a phenomenon of "overfocusing" or "constriction" has been described clinically following Ritalin such that the child may persist at a task for an abnormally long period of time, may disregard even relevant peripheral stimuli, or may be unable to shift cognitive set to adapt to situational demands (Solanto, 1984). Such effects of Ritalin, if shown reliably to occur at all, might be found to be integral to its therapeutic effects in all children, might occur only at high doses, or might occur only in a subgroup of children with ADHD.

Since the report by Sprague and Sleator, numerous studies have examined the effects of varying dosages of Ritalin on laboratory measures of learning, memory, cognitive style (impulsive versus reflective), and academic performance. In some of these studies, researchers simultaneously examined dosage effects on cognitive tasks and on behavioral measures in order to specifically assess the contention by Sprague and Sleator of different dose–response curves for these two types of variables. Additionally, a few studies have attempted to operationalize the construct of constriction, and have examined the effects of Ritalin on these tasks. It is the purpose of this chapter to review and integrate the results of these studies, to consider their implications for clinical use of the drug, and to indicate directions for future research.

DOSE–RESPONSE RELATIONSHIPS ON COGNITIVE MEASURES

In order to fully appreciate the results of studies of the effects of Ritalin on cognitive function, it is necessary to have an understanding of dose–response relationships. A dose-response *curve* is obtained when dose of drug is plotted on the *x* axis and the magnitude of a particular response (e.g., activity level) at that dose is plotted on the *y* axis. Dose-response curves may assume various shapes which can be described mathematically. When the dose-response curve assumes the form of a straight line, the slope is a constant number, and the curve is described as *linear* (Fig. 2). In this instance, an increase in dosage will yield a stronger response. Curves which assume a form other than a straight line are described as *curvilinear*. Among these are the *quadratic* curve in which there is *one* change in direction and, the *cubic* curve in which there are *two* changes in direction of the curve. These are shown in their extreme forms in Figures 3 and 4,

Albert Einstein College of Medicine, Bronx, New York

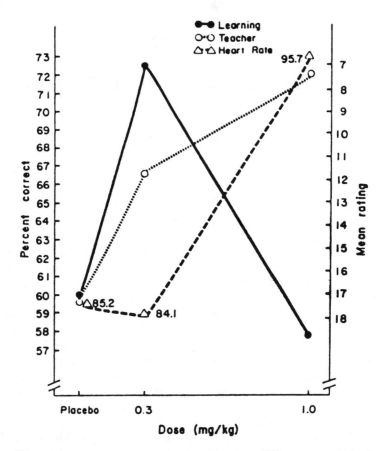

FIG. 1. Three different dose–response curves produced by three different target behaviors. The learning curve is the same as the accuracy curve from matrix 15 of the laboratory learning task. The teacher curve represents social behavior as rated by the teacher, who used a scale on which the numbers become smaller as the child improves. The heart rate curve indicates the number of beats per minute. From Sprague and Sleator (1977).

respectively. In the instance of the quadratic curve, there is an optimal dosage; above *and* below that dosage clinical response falls off. In the cubic curve there may be more than one optimal dosage.

When statistical analysis of group data yields a significant effect of dosage, the data can be further probed via a *trend analysis* to determine the shape of the curve. The finding of a significant *linear* component means that at least part of the curve assumes the form of a straight line. If there is, in addition, a significant *quadratic* component and/or *cubic* component, then the curve will have a form which resembles at least in part that shown in Figures 3 or 4, respectively. If *only* the linear component is significant, the curve will most closely resemble a straight line.

It is important to note that although the averaged data for the *group* in any study may yield curves such as those described above, this does *not* indicate that the response of any individual child will be predicted by the same curve. As will be discussed more fully, research in the field of stimulant drug response has revealed great variability between subjects in dosage effects on cognition and behavior.

COGNITIVE IMPULSIVITY

Children with ADHD display impulsivity in the cognitive sphere as well as in the behavioral realm; in other words, they are prone to choose an answer or jump to a conclusion without sufficient consideration of alternatives.

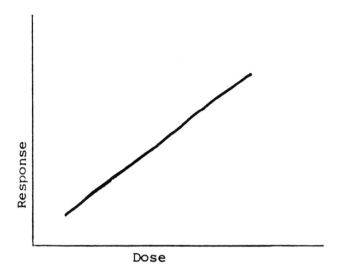

FIG. 2. Linear dose-response curve.

The Matching Familiar Figures Test (MFFT) was developed to assess the impulsive-reflective dimension of cognitive style. On each item of this test, the child is presented with a stimulus picture of a familiar object (e.g., a house) and then must choose, from among six very similar response pictures, the one item which is identical to the stimulus figure in every detail. The most successful strategy involves systematically comparing each response figure with the stimulus figure. Both the number of correct responses and the mean latency to response are recorded.

Despite concerns about the reliability and validity of the MFFT (Block et al., 1974), this test has been employed in several Ritalin dose-response studies. Rapport and colleagues (1985a) reported a *linear* relationship between reduction in errors on this task and increasing Ritalin dosage (5, 10, and 15 mg, corresponding to a range of approximately .17–.75 mg/kg). Post hoc tests revealed that the 15 mg dose was significantly more effective than either the 5 or 10 mg doses in reducing error scores. These results were replicated in a subsequent study by Rapport et al. (1988), who expanded the dosage range to 20 mg (Fig. 5).

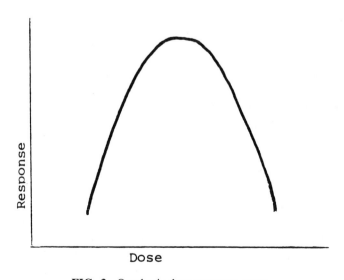

FIG. 3. Quadratic dose-response curve.

235

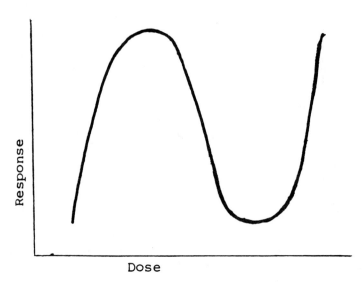

FIG. 4. Cubic dose-response curve.

Post hoc analysis revealed that the 20 mg condition was significantly more effective than the 5 mg condition in reducing errors. Latency was significantly increased by the 15 and 20 mg doses, compared with the 5 mg dose. Furthermore, the linear curve for improvement in performance on the MFFT paralleled the curves for on-task behavior, teacher ratings of self-control (TSCRS), and percentage of academic assignments completed correctly (AES).

Despite significant group effects, both of these studies presented data illustrating striking intersubject variability. Individual children varied greatly in dose-response curves on a given task or behavioral measure, with some children showing their best performance at the highest dosage and others performing best at lower dosages. Furthermore, *intra*subject variability was apparent across measures; that is, an individual child might exhibit different dose-response curves on different measures.

Douglas et al. (1988) examined the effects of Ritalin dosages of .15, .3, and .6 mg/kg on a variety of academic and laboratory measures of cognition. As did Rapport et al. (1988), Douglas and her colleagues reported that both errors and latency on the MFFT improved as a linear function of increasing dosage. Post hoc tests revealed that the .60 mg/kg dosage was more effective than either .15 or .30 both in reducing errors and increasing latency.

Only two studies have examined the effect of a high Ritalin dosage of 1.0 mg/kg on the MFFT, with conflicting results. Brown and Sleator (1979) reported that performance was a *quadratic* function of dosage such that while .3 mg/kg reduced errors on the task, the 1.0 mg/kg dosage was no more effective than placebo. Tannock and her colleagues observed no effect of Ritalin on errors, but reported that both .3 and 1.0 mg/kg were equally effective in increasing latency on the task (Tannock et al., 1989a). These authors also examined effects of Ritalin on a "stopping task" which appeared to be a more sensitive measure of inhibitory control than was the MFFT and did show the expected linear improvement with increase in dosage.

LEARNING AND MEMORY

As a laboratory measure of new learning, tasks such as the paired-associated learning test may have relevance for a child's ability to learn new material in school. On paired-associate learning tests, the individual is required to learn to associate each of a list of words, numbers, pictures, or symbols ("the stimulus") with another word, number, picture, or symbol ("the response"). Research by Swanson and his colleagues (Swanson et al., 1978) suggested that a paired-associate learning test may be useful in distinguishing favorable from adverse responders to Ritalin. These authors used a version of the task,

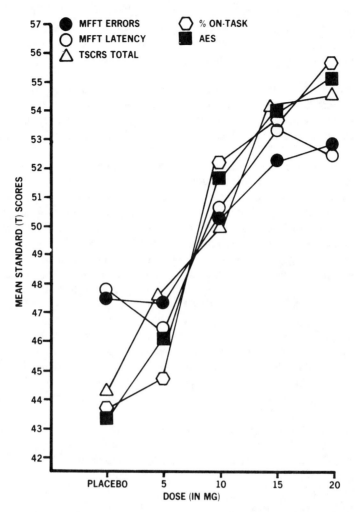

FIG. 5. The mean group response frequencies expressed as standard (T) scores for each dependent variable (MFFT error and latency, % on-task, AES, and TSCRS total score) are plotted as five distinct dose-response curves. Scores were derived based on the performance of the present sample ($N = 22$) aggregated across all conditions (excluding baseline). MFFT errors were inverted such that improvement on all dependent variables is indicated by upward movement on the vertical axis. From Rapport et al., (1988).

henceforth referred to as the PALT, in which the child was told to associate a given animal picture with a particular "zoo" (North, South, East, West). Ritalin dosage was begun at 5 mg and incremented by 5 mg until the child exhibited either a 25% reduction in errors (a "favorable" response) or a 25% increase in errors (an "adverse" response). Using this method, the researchers were able to classify 69.8% of their 53 subjects as favorable responders and the remainder as adverse responders.

Subsequent research has not validated the PALT as an index of Ritalin responsiveness on behavioral or other cognitive measures. Furthermore, studies have been inconsistent with respect to both overall drug effects and dosage effects of Ritalin on this task.

Gan and Cantwell (1982) examined the effects of three dosages of Ritalin (.3, .5, and 1.0 mg/kg) in 20 ADDH boys and reported that only the lowest dose was effective in improving performance on the PALT.

In contrast to these results are those of Wender and Kinsbourne (1985), who subsequently examined the effects of Ritalin dosages of .3, .5, and .75 mg/kg on the same task. They reported that the effect of dosage (beginning with placebo) reached significance only when the analysis was limited to children who were classified as favorable responders on the task (75% of the total sample of 23). When the frequency of the individual favorable, adverse, and nonresponses on the task following each of these three Ritalin doses were examined, however, a chi-square analysis revealed that there were significantly more favorable responses, and a smaller total number of adverse plus nonresponses at the *highest* dose, compared to either of the two lower doses.

Wender and Kinsbourne (1985) also compared performance on the PALT against behavioral response to Ritalin in the home–school setting. The results did not support the predictive validity of the task. Five children who exhibited an adverse response on the PALT improved behaviorally in the field trial, and all three of the children who had an adverse behavioral response exhibited a positive response to Ritalin on the PALT.

Rapport and his colleagues (Rapport et al., 1985b) assessed 12 children using the PALT, observations of on-task behavior, academic seat work (percent complete and percent correct), and teacher behavior ratings at baseline, following placebo, and following fixed Ritalin doses of 5, 10, and 15 mg (corresponding to mean dosages of .22, .43, and .65 mg/kg, respectively). There were significant effects of dosage (beginning with baseline and placebo levels) on all dependent measures *except* the PALT. (This finding held true even when two PALT nonresponders were eliminated from the analysis.) Subsequent trend analyses conducted on the significant variables yielded significant linear but not quadratic or cubic trends.

On the PALT, significant drug effects were obtained only when the *best* of each subject's drug response scores was compared with baseline and placebo performance. An examination of figural results suggested a leveling off of performance on the PALT at the 10 and 15 mg doses, but no post hoc tests were done to compare specific doses.

In their 1988 study, Douglas et al. utilized a paired-associate learning test consisting of arbitrarily associated word pairs, which was administered in three trials (Douglas et al., 1988). Although there were no effects of Ritalin on overall performance, examination of individual trials revealed that on the second and third trials, only the .3 mg/kg dosage was effective in increasing the number of word pairs learned when compared with placebo. The authors suggest that this may be evidence of a negative effect of a higher dose of Ritalin on a complex cognitive task.

Douglas et al. further reported, as had Rapport's group, marked variability in subjects' response. Response to Ritalin on the PALT did not predict response to the drug on other cognitive, academic, or behavioral measures. Not one subject, of 19 tested, was a consistent positive or adverse responder. Furthermore, the dosage of Ritalin (or placebo) which maximized performance varied considerably across measures for any individual child.

Research employing other paired-associate learning tests, also obtained inconsistent results. Kupietz and his colleagues employed a novel paired-associate learning test in which a six-item list of beginning Chinese vocabulary words was paired with their English equivalents. Whereas in a study with nine adults (Kupietz et al., 1980) a dosage of 5 but not 10 mg was effective in reducing errors on this task, there was no significant effect of Ritalin, administered in doses of .3, .5, and .7 mg/kg, in a subsequent study with ADDH children (Kupietz et al., 1988).

Intersubject variability may be a major reason for lack of consistency among studies in effects of Ritalin on PALT performance. Data of subjects who improve on Ritalin may be combined with that of others who respond adversely, resulting in failure to find an effect in the group data. The finding thus far that response to Ritalin on the PALT does not predict an individual's response to Ritalin on behavioral or other cognitive measures may be due to the nature of the measures selected. As a measure of new learning, the PALT may only predict to *new* academic learning; the academic measures used thus far have tapped performance on tasks in areas such as arithmetic in which the child had presumably already acquired skills.

Results of a study employing the Buschke Selective Reminding Test (SRT), suggests another possible basis for failure to find significant effects of Ritalin in studies employing the PALT. On the SRT, the subject is required to learn a list of unrelated words. Whereas both the SRT and PALT are scored for immediate retention (i.e., the total number of items recalled on a given trial), only the SRT is typically scored for "long-term" storage (i.e., items recalled on *two* consecutive trials), and "long-term" retrieval (i.e., recall, on a given trial, of items in long-term storage). Evans and his colleagues (Evans et al., 1986) reported that there were no significant effects of Ritalin (in dosages of .2, .4, and .6 mg/kg) on immediate recall, when scored either as the number of words recalled on the first trial, the total number of words recalled across trials, or the *slope* (rate of learning) of words recalled across trials. By contrast, there *were* significant linear dose–response effects for the long-term storage and retrieval variables. The authors interpret these findings as indicating an effect on memory storage and retrieval which was *not* mediated by immediate effects on attention or arousal. Since the PALT generally is scored only for immediate retention, these effects on long-term storage and retrieval would not have been observed.

Finally, conflicting results have been obtained in studies of the effects of stimulant drug dosage on verbal learning tasks in which subjects encode words semantically or acoustically. Peeke and her colleagues (Peeke et al., 1984) reported that a Ritalin dosage of 10 mg (.25–.30 mg/kg) but not one of 21 mg (.5–.6 mg/kg) improved recognition and delayed recall scores in a study of nine ADD children. On the other hand, Weingartner et al. (1980) reported that a dosage of Dexedrine (dextroamphetamine) of .5 mg/kg, which is approximately equivalent to a Ritalin dosage of 1.0 mg/kg, and thus significantly higher than the highest dosage used by Peeke et al., *did* improve free and cued recall performance on a similar task in 15 hyperactive children. Differences between the tasks, as well as in the drug administered, may have contributed to differences in results.

ACADEMIC TASKS

Acute effects of various doses of Ritalin on academic tasks administered in the laboratory have been assessed in a number of studies. Pelham et al. (1985) assessed the effects of Ritalin dosages of .15, .3, and .6 mg/kg on arithmetic and reading tasks. The linear effect of dosage on both number of arithmetic problems completed and number correct was significant, and the quadratic component approached marginal significance with a *p* value less than .11. An examination of the figure suggested that these results were due to increases in performance from placebo to the .3 dosage with a leveling off in performance at the .6 mg/kg dosage (Fig. 3). The significant effect of Ritalin appears to have been on productivity, in that accuracy (percent correct) remained constant. Simultaneous classroom observations yielded a linear increase in on-task behavior with increasing dosage.

Douglas et al. (1988) administered 60 arithmetic items to their subjects in order to avoid ceiling effects. Perhaps because of this precaution, these authors reported a *linear* increase in output and number correct which extended to the .6 mg/kg dosage; post hoc tests showed that the .6 mg/kg dosage was significantly more effective than either the .15 or .3 mg/kg dosages when the task was administered in the classroom.

A recent study by Tannock and colleagues (1989b) is the only one to have assessed the effect of a dosage of 1.0 mg/kg on an academic type of task. The "arithmetic" task used comprised three levels of complexity: checking as many digits as possible, checking as many odd (or even) digits as possible, and lastly (the only task which involved an actual arithmetic operation), solving a simple addition or subtraction problem in memory and then checking if the result was odd (or even). Assignment to the odd or even condition was constant for any given subject within and across test sessions.

Results of the analysis of variance (ANOVA) revealed main effects of dosage and task level but no interaction between dosage and levels. Post hoc tests showed that the 1.0 mg/kg dosage was as effective as the .3 mg/kg dosage in reducing total errors (summed across task levels) on the task. It is possible, however, that an intermediate dosage of Ritalin would have been more effective than either the .3 or the 1.0 mg/kg dosages, thereby yielding a quadratic effect of dosage.

Acute dosage effects of Ritalin have been examined on other types of academic tasks as well. Pelham et al. reported in their 1985 study that Ritalin dosages between .15 and .6 mg/kg produced a linear increase in the proportion of reading problems completed correctly (Fig. 6). Rapport and his colleagues reported conflicting results in their two studies of the effects of fixed Ritalin dosages of 5, 10, and 15 mg on "academic seat work in language arts or arithmetic." In the first study (Rapport et al., 1985b), which incorporated a baseline condition, there was a linear and not a quadratic effect of dosage on percent completed and percent correct. In the second study (Rapport et al., 1986), the curves for percent correct and percent complete were curvilinear (although the quadratic effect was significant only for percent complete) with no further improvement generated by the highest dose. Ceiling effects may account for the asymptote found in the 1986 study, since the subjects were performing in the 70–80% range at placebo, compared with 60–70% in the 1985 study.

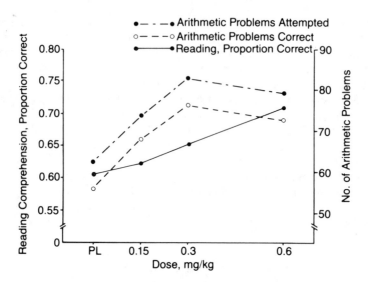

FIG. 6. Average number of arithmetic problems attempted and completed correctly during 15-minute period as function of drug dosage. Proportion of reading problems completed correctly during 15-minute period as function of drug dosage. PL indicates placebo. From Pelham et al. (1985).

While further research is necessary to resolve the inconsistencies between studies, the evidence so far suggests that even at dosages as high as 1.0 mg/kg there is no *adverse* effect of Ritalin on performance on academic tasks in the laboratory; that is, no worsening compared with performance on placebo. Dosages up to .6 mg/kg may produce a predominantly linear increase in performance or there may be a leveling off in performance between .3 and .6 mg/kg, as a function of task and measurement variables yet to be clearly delineated.

COGNITIVE CONSTRICTION

Cognitive constriction may be conceptualized as a narrowing of attentional focus, such that stimuli which are "peripheral" in space, time, or meaning to the subject are relatively ignored. As a result, cognitive performance on certain types of tasks may be impaired either because the subject disregards relevent cues or becomes unable to *shift* perceptual set or strategy in order to meet changing situational demands (reductions in cognitive flexibility). Constriction may be manifested in overt behavior as obsessive preoccupation with one activity, withdrawal from social activity, or repetitiveness in verbal or nonverbal (e.g., artistic) expression.

Research with adult subjects has suggested that an increase in *arousal*, whether induced via anxiety, noise, introduction of monetary incentive, or threat of shock, has the effect of narrowing attentional focus (for review see Wachtel, 1967). Similar effects were claimed for stimulant drugs, which, of course, also increase physiological arousal (Callaway, 1959). Careful review of these early drug studies, however, indicated that the empirical findings were not statistically robust, or admitted of other explanations.

Pharmacological research with animals has suggested a basis in the central nervous system for the postulated constrictive effects of stimulants in humans. It is well known that both Dexedrine and Ritalin can produce stereotypic behaviors in animals, which are defined as repetitive, nongoal-oriented motor behaviors, such as gnawing, rearing, spitting, or biting, with a concomitant narrowing in the range of behaviors exhibited. Such effects have been observed to occur at doses of 5–10 mg/kg of Dexedrine and 8–16 mg/kg of Ritalin. Similar effects have been observed to occur in the perceptual domain. Campbell and Raskin (1981), for example, report that Dexedrine produced a decrease in the range of surrogate stimuli which elicited huddling behavior in rat pups; the effect was described as a steepening of the stimulus generalization gradient.

Few experiments with human subjects have attempted to directly assess constrictive effects of stimulants, which is partly due to a difficulty in identifying or devising tasks which are valid measures of this construct and which can also be administered on a repeated basis as is required when dosage is manipulated within subjects. Instrument selection is also constrained by the fact that there are few tests which would *not* be sensitive to positive Ritalin effects on attention, memory, or motivation, thereby militating against the emergence of negative constrictive effects on testing.

The Wisconsin Card Sorting Test (WCST) is perhaps the best validated measure of cognitive flexibility. Performance on this task has been shown to be sensitive to lesions involving the frontal lobe (Robinson et al., 1980), the area of the brain concerned with executive planning and judgment and which is also implicated as the site of central dysfunction in ADHD children. A methodological problem in using the WCST, however, is that only one form of the test is available, making it arguably unsuitable for repeated testing. Nonetheless, Dyme and his colleagues (1982) employed the task in a repeated measures design and reported that Dexedrine, administered in a high dose of 1.0 mg/kg, produced an increase in perseverative errors on the WCST in three of five ADD children in a pilot sample. Although the order of placebo and Ritalin was randomized among subjects, we are not told the order received by the three "perseverative" subjects in this very small sample; thus, order and drug effects may have been confounded.

Other measures of cognitive flexibility emerged from J.P. Guilford's analysis of the structure of intellect (Guilford, 1956, 1967). On the basis of his factor analysis of intellectual abilities, Guilford differentiated two types of intellectual function; *convergent* thinking in which there is only one predesignated correct answer, exemplified by traditional tests of intelligence, and *divergent* thinking in which there are multiple correct answers, exemplified by tests of creativity. "Spontaneous flexibility" was one factor which emerged within the category of divergent thinking. Tests of this ability require the subject to generate, according to given specifications, *multiple* responses representing different conceptual classes. Wallach and Kogan (1965) modified Guilford's tests of spontaneous flexibility and included them in their creativity test battery. After piloting these five tests, we choose two for use in our dose-response study (Solanto and Wender, 1989): The Alternate Uses Test requires the subject to name as many uses as possible for each of a list of eight common objects (e.g., brick, button, newspaper, knife). Responses were scored on five dimensions: (1) the total number of responses; (2) the number of responses in which a functional use was clearly specified; (3) the number of conceptual classes or categories of use represented among the functional items; (4) the number of unintended uses for the object; (5) the number of classes represented among the unintended uses. On the Instances Test, the subject was asked to generate as many exemplars as possible of verbally specified class concepts (e.g., "Name all the *round* things you can think of"). The score was simply the total number of appropriate responses given to the test item.

Nineteen ADDH children were each tested following three doses of placebo and three different Ritalin dosages (.3, .6, and 1.0 mg/kg), administered in random order. A significant interaction between drug vs. placebo status and dose indicated that rather than constricting or inhibiting output on the Alternate Uses Test, Ritalin significantly *increased* the total and functional number of responses (Fig. 7), as well as the number of classes of response, with a trend for an increase in the number of unintended uses. Ritalin appeared to just compensate for a decrease in output over successive placebo days that may have been a function of loss of interest or loss of motivation with repeated testing. A similar result, approaching statistical significance was obtained on the Instances test.

Although the group data did not reveal a constrictive effect of Ritalin, it was possible to identify a subgroup of eight ADDH children who did appear to manifest a form of cognitive perseveration. These children had significantly more total and functional responses following drug, without a commensurate increase in the number of classes represented among the responses; thus, they appeared to perseverate within a response class. This subgroup of children showed little decline in output across placebo days and showed a steeper increase in output with increasing Ritalin dosage than did the other children. On Ritalin, the responsiveness of these children took on a compulsive quality; they appeared to be unable to stop responding after a reasonable interval. Furthermore, there was a decrease in lucidity of some individual responses as well as a decrease in the cohesion of the spontaneous speech produced by some of the children during the free play period. These observations were made following the .6 mg/kg dosage as well as the 1.0 mg/kg dosage.

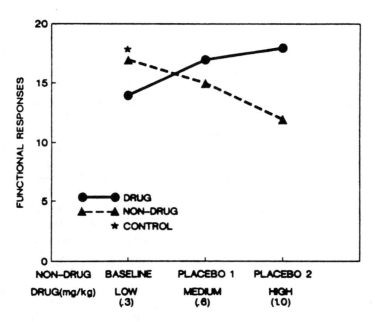

FIG. 7. Functional responses on Alternate Uses Test. (Placebo but *not* drug days are in order of administration.) From Solanto and Wender (1989).

When the subgroup was compared with the remaining 11 children within the sample, no differences emerged in age, absolute dose of drug administered, IQ on the Peabody Picture Vocabulary Test, frequency or type of additional diagnosis, or presence or absence of a learning disability. The subgroup of children did differ from the remaining group of children in having better baseline scores on the PALT and the Children's Checking Test (a measure of vigilance), as well as a greater percentage improvement on the drug day of optimal dosage. Although there was no difference between groups in baseline Conners Parent or Teacher Hyperkinesis Index scores, the subgroup had a significantly larger *discrepancy* between these scores, as well as lower scores on the hyperactivity and inattentiveness factors of the Teacher Child Behavior Checklist and a lower internalizing score on this measure. Finally, interestingly, the subgroup had a significantly better mean arithmetic score (103.5 vs. 95.8) on the Wide Range Achievement Test. One may speculate that the subgroup represents an atypical, less conventionally hyperactive subgroup of children, with better baseline cognitive performance, who became overaroused on Ritalin.

The effects of Ritalin have been assessed on other tasks which may be sensitive to cognitive constriction or narrowing of attentional focus, with generally negative results for constriction. Douglas et al. (1988) employed a word discovery task in which children were required to construct as many new words as possible from stimulus words containing 10 letters. Consistent with Solanto and Wender (1989), the results revealed a significant linear effect of Ritalin dosage in *increasing* output and efficiency on this test. Post hoc tests revealed that the .3 and .6 mg/kg dosages were not significantly different in their effects on this task and were each more effective than the .15 mg/kg dosage.

Malone and her colleagues predicted, but did not find, a negative effect of Ritalin on a word processing test requiring semantic matching (Malone et al., 1988). Fiedler and Ullmann (1983) assessed effects of Ritalin on curiosity and found that the drug reduced scores on only one of five tests assessing conceptual, manipulative, and perceptual curiosity; on that test, scores were reduced only to the level of the normal controls.

Finally, Thurston and her colleagues (Thurston et al., 1979) tested the effect of individually titrated optimal doses of Ritalin on performance in the central-incidental learning paradigm (Hagan, 1967). As might be predicted by a "constriction hypothesis," they reported that Ritalin enhanced recall of the central (task–relevant) stimuli but impaired recall of the incidental (task–irrelevant) stimuli. This study awaits replication.

CONCLUSIONS AND IMPLICATIONS

Laboratory and observational measures of behavioral inhibition and control have generally revealed significant linear effects of increasing Ritalin dosage. Results of studies of the effects of Ritalin on laboratory measures of learning and memory have been notably inconsistent. Studies of the impact of Ritalin dosage on paired-associate and other verbal learning tests have generally *not* yielded quadratic dose–response curves in which higher dosages were less effective than lower ones. Results do reveal considerable sample-to-sample heterogeneity, with some studies reporting no drug effect on the tasks at all and others reporting significant dosage effects for only a subgroup of "responders." In only two studies did the group data indicate that a higher dose was *less* effective than a lower dose, and one of these studies was not replicated with Dexedrine. In both of these reports there was *no* effect, rather than an adverse effect, of the higher dosages, which ranged from .5 to 1.0 mg/kg.

With the exception of one study documenting a decrease in performance on an incidental learning task following Ritalin, research has not validated a "constrictive" effect of the drug for group data; results suggestive of constriction were reported for a significant subgroup in one study.

Assessment of effects of Ritalin on academic tasks is clearly still in its early stages. Results thus appear to vary according to the subject area assessed (e.g., math vs. reading), (Pelham et al., 1985), the maximal dose used, and whether or not ceiling effects were avoided. Perhaps the most compelling single study was that by Douglas et al. (1988), which explicitly took steps to avoid ceiling effects and clearly showed linear improvement in arithmetic with dosages from .15 to .6 mg/kg. Other studies have variably shown a linear increase or an asymptote in academic performance with doses up to 1.0 mg/kg. *No* study has shown an actual decline in performance with an increase in dose. Studies that have simultaneously assessed effects of Ritalin on cognitive performance and classroom behavior have generally shown no differences in dose-response curves for cognition and behavior.

In contrast to these group results were the results for individual subjects, which revealed broad intersubject variability in dose-response curves on any given measure, including cases in which higher doses produced a decline in performance. Also shown were *intra*subject differences in dose-response curves across different cognitive and behavioral measures.

Clinical and research implications

These findings have a number of important implications for clinical work and research. The first is that the effect of any given dosage on a child's behavior and cognitive function can only be ascertained during a clinical trial in which the child's performance in different domains is closely monitored. Second, the dosage which, for any particular child, maximizes performance on one measure of academic functioning—reading, for example—may not be the same as that which maximizes performance on a different measure—for example, arithmetic, or percentage of on-task behavior. The clinician must, therefore, first *prioritize* the goals to be achieved via stimulant drug treatment and then titrate the dosage so as to maximize performance in the target area(s) while minimizing negative effects in other domains.

The results of dose-response studies thus far clearly reveal that we have yet to identify a laboratory task which can be used to assess responsiveness to Ritalin in a way which would predict the child's response to the medication in the home or at school, behaviorally or academically. The long-term challenge for researchers, of course, is to identify individual subject variables which predict individual dose-response patterns. The elusiveness of such variables so far suggest they may come to light only in large-scale studies employing multiple regression analyses of promising indices.

REFERENCES

Block, J., Block, J.H. & Harrington, D.M. (1974), Some misgivings about the Matching Familiar Figures Test as a measure of reflection-impulsivity. *Dev. Psychol.*, 10:611–632.

Brown, R.T. & Sleator, E.K. (1979), Methylphenidate in hyperkinetic children: differences in dose effects on impulsive behavior. *Pediatrics,* 64:408–411.

Callaway, E. (1959), The influence of amobarbital (amylobarbitone) and methamphetamine on the focus of attention. *J. Mental Sci.,* 105:382–392.

Campbell, B.A. & Raskin, L.A. (1981), Canalization of arousel in the preweanling rat: effects of amphetamine on aggregation with surrogate stimuli. *Dev. Psychobiol.,* 14:127–137.

Douglas, V.I., Barr, R.G., Amin, K., O'Neill, M.E. & Britton, B.G. (1988), Dosage effects and individual responsivity to methylphenidate in attention deficit disorder. *J. Child Psychol. Child Psychiatry,* 29:453–475.

Dyme, I.Z., Sahakian, B.J., Golinko, B.E. & Rabe, E.F. (1982), Perseveration induced by methylphenidate in children: Preliminary findings. *Prog. Neuropsychopharmacol. Biol. Psychiatry,* 6:269–273.

Evans, R.W., Gualtieri, C.T. & Amara, I. (1986), Methylphenidate and memory: Dissociated effects in hyperactive children. *Psychopharmacology,* 90:211–216.

Fiedler, N. & Ullman, D.G. (1983), The effects of stimulant drugs on curiosity behaviors of hyperactive boys. *J. Abnorm. Child Psychol.,* 11:193–206.

Gan, J., & Cantwell, D.P. (1982), Dosage effects of methylphenidate on paired associate learning: Positive/negative placebo responders. *J. Am. Acad. Child Psychiatry,* 21:237–242.

Guilford, J.P. (1956), The structure of intellect. *Psychol. Bull.,* 53:267–293.

———— (1967), Some theoretical views of creativity. In: *Contemporary Approaches to Psychology,* ed. H. Nelson & W. Bevan. Princeton: Van Nostrand.

Hagan, J.W. (1967), The effect of distraction on selective attention. *Child Dev.,* 38:685–694.

Kupietz, S.S., Richardson, E., Gadow, K.D. & Winsberg, B.G., (1980), Effects of methylphenidate on learning a "beginning reading vocabulary" by normal adults. *Psychopharmacology,* 69:69–72.

———— Winsberg, B.G., Richardson, E., Maitinsky, S. & Mendell, N. (1988), Effects of methylphenidate dosage in hyperactive reading-disabled children: I. Behavior and cognitive performance effects. *J. Am. Acad. Child Adolesc. Psychiatry,* 27:70–77.

Malone, M.A., Kershner, J.R. & Siegel, L. (1988), The effects of methylphenidate on levels of processing and laterality in children with attention deficit disorder. *J. Abnorm. Child Psychol.,* 16:379–395.

Peeke, S., Halliday, R., Callaway, E., Prael, R. & Reus, V. (1984), Effects of two doses of methylphenidate on verbal information processing in hyperactive children. *J. Clin. Psychopharmacol.,* 4:82–88.

Pelham, W.E., Bender, M.E., Caddell, J., Booth, S. & Moorer, S.H. (1985), Methylphenidate and children with attention deficit disorder. *Arch. Gen. Psychiatry,* 42:948–952.

Rapport, M.D., DePaul, G.J., Stoner, G., Birmingham, B.K., & Masse, G. (1985a), Attention deficit disorder with hyperactivity: Differential effects of methylphenidate on impulsivity. *Pediatrics,* 76:938–943.

———— Stoner, G., DuPaul, G.J., Birmingham, B.K. & Tucker, S. (1985b), Methylphenidate in hyperactive children: Differential effects of dose on academic, learning, and social behavior. *J. Abnorm. Child Psychol.,* 13:227–244.

———— DuPaul, G.J., Stoner, G., Jones, J.T. (1986), Comparing classroom and clinic measures of attention deficit disorder: Differential, idiosyncratic, and dose-response effects of methylphenidate. *J. Consult. Clin. Psychol.,* 54:334–341.

———— Stoner, G., DuPaul, G.J. Kelly, K.L., Tucker, S.B. & Schoeler, T. (1988), Attention deficit disorder and methylphenidate: A multilevel analysis of dose response effects on children's impulsivity across settings. *J. Am. Acad. Child Adolesc. Psychiatry,* 27:60–69.

Robinson, A.L., Heaton, R.K., Lehman, R.A.W. & Stilson, D.W. (1980), The utility of the Wisconsin card sorting test in detecting and localizing frontal lobe lesions. *J. Consult. Clin. Psychol.,* 48:605–614.

Solanto, M.V. (1984), Neuropharmacological basis of stimulant drug action in attention deficit disorder with hyperactivity: A review and synthesis. *Psychol. Bull.*, 95, 387–409.

———— Wender, E.H. (1989), Does methylphenidate constrict cognitive functioning? *J. Am. Acad. Child Adolesc. Psychiatry*, 28:897–902.

Sprague, R.L. & Sleator, E.K. (1977), Methylphenidate in hyperkinetic children: differences in dose effects on learning and social behavior. *Science*, 198:1274–1276.

Swanson, J.M., Kinsbourne, M., Roberts, W., & Zucker, K. (1978), Time-response analysis of the effect of stimulant medication on the learning ability of children referred for hyperactivity. *Pediatrics*, 61:21–29.

Tannock, R., Schachar, R.J., Carr, R.P., Chajczyk, D. & Logan, G.D. (1989a), Effects of methylphenidate on inhibitory control in hyperactive children. *J. Abnorm. Child Psychol.*, 17:473–491.

———— ———— ———— & Logan, G.D. (1989b), Dose response effects of methylphenidate on academic performance, and overt behavior in hyperactive children. *Pediatrics*, 84:648–657.

Thurston, C.M., Sobol, M.P., Swanson, J. & Kinsbourne, M. (1979), Effects of methylphenidate (Ritalin) on selective attention in hyperactive children. *J. Abnorm. Child Psychol.*, 7:471–481.

Wachtel, P.L. (1967), Conceptions of broad and narrow attention. *Psychol Bull.*, 68:417–429.

Wallach, M.A. & Kogan, N. (1965), *Modes of Thinking in Young Children*. New York: Holt, Rinehart, & Winston.

Weingartner, H., Rapoport, J.L., Buchsbaum, M.S., Bunney, W.E. Jr., Ebert, M.H., Mikkelsen, E.J. & Caine, E.D. (1980), Cognitive processes in normal and hyperactive children and their response to amphetamine treatment. *J. Abnorm. Psychology*, 89:25–37.

Wender, E.H. & Kinsbourne, M. (1985), Validation of the paired associates task as a measure of stimulant medication response in attention deficit disorder. Paper presented at the Annual Meeting of the Ambulatory Pediatric Association, Washington, DC.

Ritalin Blood Levels and Their Correlations with Measures of Learning

SAMUEL S. KUPIETZ

There has been relatively little investigation of the relationship of methylphenidate (MPH) blood levels and learning performance. Apart from a better understanding of its effects, study of plasma concentration of MPH is important from the standpoint of its possible inclusion in the clinical management of hyperactivity. The Division of Child Psychiatry's research program at the Nathan Kline Institute has been studying the effects of methylphenidate on behavioral and learning outcome in hyperactive and learning-disabled children. The development in our laboratory of a sensitive and accurate procedure for determining the concentration of methylphenidate in human plasma (Hungund et al., 1978) led us to initiate a study of MPH plasma concentration and its relationship to measures of behavioral response and learning outcome. Given the moderately large dose–response variability, we and others have observed in hyperactive children, we were interested in determining whether a biological measure of drug concentration would allow us to explain the variance in drug response and improve our understanding of MPH's cognitive and behavioral effects.

METHYLPHENIDATE EFFECTS ON LEARNING-RELATED TASKS

The usefulness of methylphenidate in the treatment of hyperactivity is well established. So too are its effects in improving performance on learning-related tasks such as sustained attention (Conners and Rothschild, 1968; Kupietz and Balka, 1976; Sykes et al., 1971, 1973) paired-associates learning (Conners et al., 1964; Kupietz et al., 1982; Swanson et al., 1978) and short-term memory (Sprague and Sleator, 1977; Sprague et al., 1970). Other studies have shown MPH to increase speed and accuracy on academic tasks (Douglas et al., 1986; Pelham et al., 1985). Nevertheless, despite the consistency with which MPH has facilitated performance on learning-related tasks, the expectation that stimulant therapy should result in improved academic learning has not been consistently supported by research findings (Barkley and Cunningham, 1978; Gadow and Swanson, 1985; Rie et al., 1976; Weiss et al., 1975). Moreover, there is evidence to suggest that Ritalin dose effects on learning may be nonlinear, with higher doses resulting in learning performance that is no better or possibly worse than would occur without treatment (Brown and Sleator, 1979; Kupietz et al., 1980; Sprague and Sleator, 1977). Because many hyperactive children have concomitant academic difficulties, we have considered the question of the effect of MPH on learning ability to merit serious research attention.

In addition to several methodological issues relevant to the question of the drug's inconsistent effects on school achievement (see Richardson, 1988 for a review of these issues) a major variable in assessing drug effects on learning is individual differences in behavioral response to MPH. In a study of its effects on the reading achievement of reading-disordered hyperactive children, only limited evidence was obtained for any direct facilitation of reading achievement among children receiving MPH doses of placebo, 0.3, 0.5, or 0.7 mg/kg for six months while participating in a reading therapy program (Richardson et al., 1988). However, when in a post–hoc analysis the children's response to MPH was taken into consideration, a clear relationship between drug response and reading achievement emerged. This work is discussed in more detail below.

New York University Medical Center, New York, New York

MPH PLASMA CONCENTRATION AND MEASURES OF
BEHAVIORAL RESPONSE

Prior to discussing the relationship of plasma concentration to learning outcome, it is useful to consider the general findings with regard to measures of behavioral response. Winsberg et al. (1982) administered successive one-week treatments of 0.25, 0.50, and 1.0 mg/kg MPH to hyperactive children and found that information regarding a child's MPH plasma concentration was comparable to oral dose in predicting behavioral outcome as measured by the Conners Teacher Rating Questionaire, and that the combination of the two drug measures did not enhance predictability of outcome beyond that of each measure independently. Shaywitz and her collegues (1982) found a significant correlation between peak plasma concentration (obtained 2 hours following oral dose) and percent of improvement on the Conner's Abbreviated Parent-Teacher Rating Scale ($r = .77$) after one month of treatment. Using a reaction time measure of impulsive response style, Sebrechts et al. (1986) reported a linear relationship between MPH plasma concentration in children with attention deficit disorder (ADD) and their reaction time in a Matching Familiar Figures Test. However, for most of the other tasks they used, variance in task performance could be accounted for by dose.

Gualtieri's group (1982, 1984) reported a series of studies of MPH serum levels and clinical response and, in contrast to other investigations, found no significant associations between blood levels and clinical response in behavioral measures or laboratory tests of attention or activity. In one study they report, of a total of 91 correlations arising out of two dosage levels and a large array of dependent measures, MPH plasma was a significant correlate in only four comparisons, a number expected on the basis of chance alone. They point out, and correctly so, that even where studies have shown a relationship between MPH plasma concentration and clinical outcome the important question is not whether blood level correlates with response, but whether it provides better prediction about a patient's clinical response than does dose. Thus far, the evidence from a limited number of studies indicates that it does not.

Our group has conducted a long-term study of MPH dose effects on behavior and learning outcome (Kupietz et al., 1988; Richardson et al., 1988). Four groups of reading-disabled children with attention deficit disorder were given MPH twice a day in doses of 0.3, 0.5, or 0.7, mg/kg or placebo, and provided with six-months of reading therapy. Behavioral and cognitive measures were obtained at pretreatment, 2, 14, and 27 weeks. Results regarding the relationship of MPH plasma to learning outcome is described later; here our interest is primarily in the behavioral findings. Children receiving the highest MPH dose were rated both by teachers and parents as significantly less symptomatic than children receiving placebo. MPH plasma concentration derived by gas chromatography of blood samples obtained at the second and 27th test week was found to be significantly different in the four groups with higher doses yielding higher mean plasma concentrations. As indicated above, the question is whether plasma concentration provides us with more information about clinical response than does oral dose. Regression analysis was used to compare plasma concentration (transformed into natural logarithms and averaged across the two samples obtained for each child) and oral dose as predictors of behavior change with treatment. Using the Conners Teacher Rating Questionaire as the measure of change in hyperactive behaviors, our analysis indicated that the two measures were both significant and did not differ in their ability to predict the behavior ratings at each of the test weeks. Thus, plasma concentration provided no more information in predicting behavior change than did knowing the oral dose.

MPH PLASMA CONCENTRATION AND LEARNING MEASURES

To date, the investigation of methylphenidate's effect on learning through measurement of its presence in blood has been undertaken in only a handful of studies. Although measures of plasma concentration were not obtained in their study, Swanson et al. (1978) obtained findings indicative of a relation between learning performance and plasma concentration. These investigators found that among hyperactive children classified as "favorable" or "adverse" responders to MPH (based upon whether learning errors decreased or increased relative to baseline and placebo performance) errors made on a paired-associate learning task followed approximately the same time course as methylphenidate's effect on their social behavior. Maximum effect on learning performance occurred within 2 hours after oral administration of the MPH dose (e.g., "favorable" responders showed a maximum reduction in learning errors within 2 hours). This finding is very consistent with the results of pharmacokinetic studies showing that maximum MPH plasma concentration occurs between 2 to 3 hours following dose administration (Hungund et al., 1979; Iden and Hundgund, 1979; Shaywitz et al., 1982) and strongly suggests that the changes in learning errors obtained by Swanson et al. (1978) were related to MPH blood level.

To investigate whether changes in methylphenidate plasma concentration could affect learning performance, five hyperactive boys, clinically judged to be MPH responders, were given a paired-associate learning (PAL) task prior to receiving their usual MPH dose, and again at at 1, 2, 3, 5, and 7 hours following the dose (Kupietz et al., 1982). The PAL task is a good analogue of many rote-learning academic tasks in which a response must be learned in rote fashion to be correctly associated with a given stimulus term. Our interest in the PAL task was primarily as a simulation of the sight-word learning component of beginning reading in which a child might be shown a word and asked to pronounce it. The PAL task used in the present study was similar to one we had used previously (Kupietz et al., 1980) and was constructed so that previously learned associations to the stimulus materials would be minimal, thereby making the task useful with both children and adults. To accomplish that objective, the stimulus materials were comprised of Chinese characters and the rote responses to be associated with them were their English equivalents.

The children learned a different eight-pair list at each of the six test sessions, at which time a 10 cc sample of blood was also drawn and assayed for MPH plasma concentration. As shown in Figure 1, peak MPH concentration occurred 3 hours following the dose for three children, and a fourth child (S1) showed peak concentration in 2 hours. The fifth child (S5) showed no clear peak in the plasma curve. We could find no basis for explaining the differences in individual plasma curves. However, the fact that four of the five children showed maximum drug absorption between 2 and 3 hours following dose administration is in good agreement with the values reported by others for adults.

Figure 2 compares mean MPH concentration and PAL errors over the course of the 7-hour test period. Keeping in mind that this was a small sample showing individual differences in plasma absorption, there is a marked inverse relation in the group data between the two measures. An increase in plasma concentration was associated with a decrease in PAL errors. Although the group data indicate that a reduction in learning errors occurred prior to maximum drug absorption, this temporal relation was not consistent among individual children. Regression analysis of the data indicated that plasma concentration was a significant source of variation in learning errors. Errors decreased on the average by .22 for every 1 ng/ml increase in MPH concentration. Similarly, a linear relationship between peak MPH concentration and reaction time in an impulsivity test (Matching Familiar Figures Test) was reported by Sebrechts and his associates (Sebrechts et al., 1986) but they did not report any relationship between plasma measures and task errors. Thus, while the nature of the relationship between MPH plasma concentration and learning performance has yet to be specified, it seems clear that plasma can provide predictive information regarding the effect of MPH on learning.

We have also looked at blood levels of a related psychostimulant, dextroamphetamine (Kupietz et al., 1985), an agent we have found to be of comparable clinical efficacy to methylphenidate for the management of hyperactivity (Winsberg et al., 1974). This work was carried out with normal adult volunteers as part of a study which investigated the metabolism and behavioral effects of dextroamphetamine as a function of food intake. Six adults learned a 12-item list of Chinese characters and their English equivalents prior to drug administration and hourly for the next five hours. Dextroamphetamine was administered orally at a dose of 0.25 mg/kg and individual doses ranged from 12.5 to 20 mg. The results, shown in Figure 3, show a striking similarity to the results obtained for children with methylphenidate. Averaged across the sample, PAL errors and dextroamphetamine plasma concentration obtained over the hourly test sessions yielded a correlation of -0.96. The maximum plasma concentration and improvement in learning performance occurred between two and three hours, a finding consistent with that observed for methylphenidate blood levels in children.

Thus far, we have been considering the relationship between stimulant plasma concentration and learning performance within the same individual. Where effects have been found, the evidence suggests that intraindividual changes in plasma drug level may provide us with useful information regarding concurrent (but not necessarily causal) changes in learning performance.

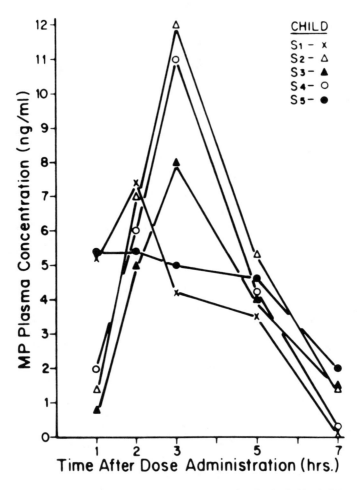

FIG. 1. Methylphenidate plasma concentration for individual children at each test interval.

INTERINDIVIDUAL COMPARISONS

The usefulness of plasma concentration for predicting differences in learning performance among individuals is more problematic. In the previously described study of children receiving a single MPH dose and given the PAL task at 1, 2, 3, 5, and 7 hours, plasma levels were not consistently correlated with learning errors across individual children. That is, high plasma concentrations were not necessarily associated with low errors in individual children, or vice versa. The correlations of MPH plasma concentration and PAL errors for the study sample at each of the five postdrug test sessions showed little consistency (0.33, −0.51, −0.51, 0.14, and −0.22). During the period of peak plasma concentration, however (2–3 hours), there was a modest but nonsignificant inverse relationship between the two measures which might have reached significance had a larger sample size been used.

Since one can reasonably expect to find individual differences among children in how MPH is metabolized and, therefore, in how much of it is present in plasma at any given time, one strategy for assessing the relationship between MPH and learning is to derive a measure of drug response which would take into account the individual differences in drug metabolism. We used such a measurement strategy in a recent long-term study of MPH dose effects in reading-disabled hyperactive children described previously (Kupietz et al., 1988; Richardson et al., 1988). In that investigation, four groups of children were treated with MPH

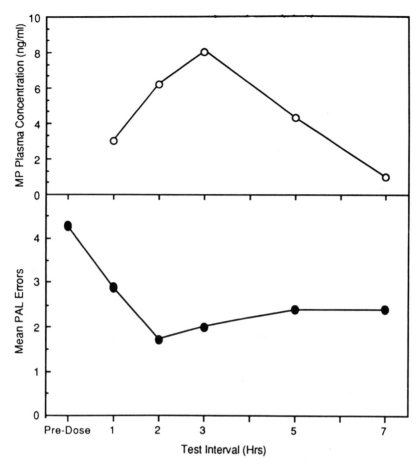

FIG. 2. Paired-associate learning (PAL) errors and methylphenidate plasma concentration in hyperactive boys during the 7-hour test period.

at doses of either 0.3, 0.5, 0.7 mg/kg, or placebo for a six-month period and were also given a concomitant program of structured reading therapy. On a group basis, plasma concentration was found to increase significantly with increases in oral dose. However, for the sample as a whole, little evidence was obtained that MPH plasma concentration was associated with gains in reading achievement. Although, across the groups, we found that mean MPH blood levels increased with increases in oral dose, children receiving the higher doses would not necessarily demonstrate a uniformly better behavioral response than children receiving a lower dose. That is, for some proportion of the children, drug response to the lower doses might be better than that to the higher dose. We therefore sought to use a measure of drug response that could incorporate interindividual differences in dose–respone and plasma concentration and represent "a final common pathway" in the child's response to MPH. We chose as our clinical response measure the reduction in rated symptom severity in the first two weeks of MPH treatment (prior to the initiation of reading therapy) as measured with the Conners Teacher Rating Questionaire, a rating scale commonly used to evaluate children's hyperactivity. The top third of the children who changed most and the bottom third of children who changed least were considered "good" responders and "poor" responders, respectively. When the children's behavioral response to MPH was taken into consideration in this manner, we found that a significant relationship existed between children's response to MPH treatment, in terms of reduction in their

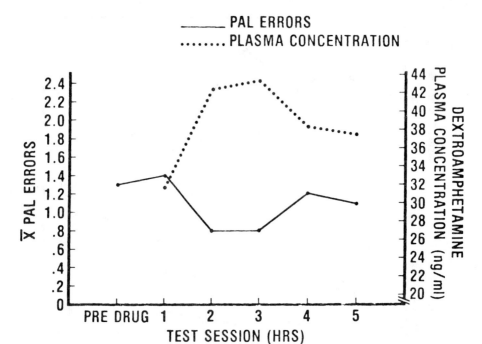

FIG. 3. Paired-associate learning (PAL) errors and dextroamphetamine plasma concentration in normal adults during the 5-hour test period.

hyperactivity, and overall gains in subsequent reading achievement. This relationship can be seen in Figure 4. By Week 14 of the study, the "good" responder group achieved a reading level approximately seven months higher than that of the "poor" responder group and this difference was maintained for the remainder of the study.

CONCLUSIONS

The relationship of MPH plasma concentration to clinical response and learning outcome has not received widespread research attention in pediatric psychopharmacology. In part, the reason for this may have to do with the failure of plasma measures to yield useful information beyond that provided by oral dose and, in general, with the absence of consistent findings establishing plasma concentration as a potentially useful index of drug response. Most promising are the group data showing that intraindividual variations in plasma concentration (following a single dose) appear to be related to corresponding changes in learning performance over time. However, both the intra- and interindividual variability of these measures tends to be large and the findings based upon the group data do not consistently characterize the results obtained for individuals. In the work conducted by our research group, we now have two studies: one with methylphenidate and one with dextroamphetamine—in which the group data are comparable in showing an inverse relationship between plasma concentration and learning errors over time. Although the range of correlations for individual subjects are indicative of the variability inherent in the samples, namely $-.22$ to $-.96$ for the methylphenidate study and $-.20$ to $-.83$ for the dextroamphetamine study—the data are sufficiently intriguing to lend support to the hypothesis that intraindividual changes in plasma concentration can provide a useful index of learning performance once the subject factors and temporal variables associated with the observed variability have been satisfactorily delineated.

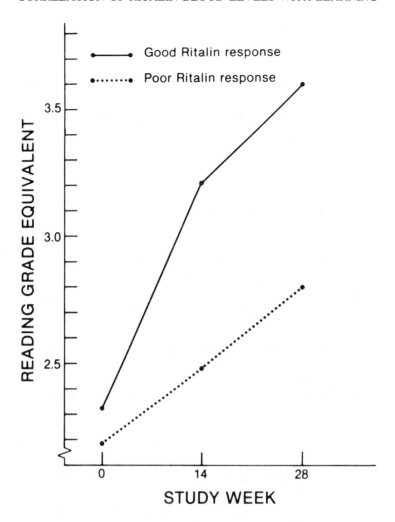

FIG. 4. Children with "good" and "poor" methylphenidate (Ritalin) response (hyperactivity reduction) after two weeks of drug treatment and subsequent reading achievement scores.

REFERENCES

Barkley, R.A. & Cunningham, C.E. (1978), Do stimulant drugs improve the academic performance of hyperkinetic children? *Clin. Pediatr.*, 17:85–92.

Brown, R.T. & Sleator, E.K. (1979), Methylphenidate in hyperactive children: Differences in dose effects on impulsive behavior. *Pediatrics,* 64:408–411.

Conners, C.K. & Rothschild, G.H. (1968), Drugs and learning in children. In: *Learning Disorders,* vol. 3, ed. S. Helmuth. Seattle: Special Child Publications, pp. 193–218.

Conners, C.K., Eisenberg, L. & Sharpe, L. (1964), Effects of methylphenidate (Ritalin) on paired-associate learning and Porteus maze performance in emotionally disturbed children. *J. Consult. Psychol.,* 28:14–22.

Douglas, V.I., Barr, M.E., O'Neill, E. & Britton, B.G. (1986), Short term effects of methylphenidate on the cognitive, learning and academic performance of children with attention deficit disorder in the laboratory and the classroom. *J. Child Psychol. Psychiatry,* 27:191–211.

Gadow, K.D. & Swanson, H.L. (1985), Assessing drug effects on academic performance. *Psychopharmacol. Bull.,* 21:877–886.

Gualtieri, O.T., Wargin, W., Kanoy, R., Patrick, K., Shen, C.D., Youngblood, W., Mueller, R.A. & Breese, G.R. (1982), Clinical studies of methylphenidate serum levels in children and adults. *J. Am. Acad. Child Psychiatry*, 21:19–26.

——— Hicks, R.E., Patrick, K., Schroeder, S.R. & Breese, G.R. (1984), Clinical correlates of methylphenidate blood levels. *Therap. Drug Mon.*, 6:379–392.

Hungund, B.L., Hanna, M. & Winsberg, B.G. (1978), A sensitive gas chromatographic method for the determination of methylphenidate (Ritalin) and its major metabolite alpha-phenyl-2 piperidine acetic acid (ritalinic acid) in human plasma using nitrogen-phosphorous detector. *Comm. Psychopharmacol.*, 2:203–208.

——— Perel, J.M., Hurwic, M.J., Sverd, J. & Winsberg, B.G. (1979), Pharmacokinetics of methylphenidate in hyperactive children. *Br. J. Clin. Pharmacol.*, 8:571–576.

Iden, C. & Hungund, B.L. (1976), A chemical ionization selected ion monitoring assay for methylphenidate and ritalinic acid. *Biomed. Mass Spectrom.*, 6:422.

Kupietz, S.S. & Balka, E. (1976), Alterations in the vigilance performance of children receiving amytriptyline and methylphenidate pharmacotherapy. *Psychopharmacology*, 50:29–33.

——— Richardson, E., Gadow, K.D. & Winsberg, B.G. (1980), Effects of methylphenidate on learning a "a beginning reading vocabulary" by normal adults. *Psychopharmacology*, 69:69–72.

——— Winsberg, B.G. & Sverd, J. (1982). Learning ability and methylphenidate (Ritalin) plasma concentration in hyperactive children. *J. Am. Acad. Child Psychiatry*, 21:27–30.

——— Bartlik, B., Angrist, B. & Winsberg, B.G. (1985), Psychostimulant plasma concentration and learning performance. *J. Clin. Psychopharmacol.*, 5:293–295.

——— Winsberg, B.G., Richardson, E., Maitinsky, S. & Mendell, N. (1988), Effects of methylphenidate dosage in hyperactive reading-disabled children: I. Behavior and cognitive performance effects. *J. Am. Acad. Child and Adoles. Psychiatry*, 27:70–77.

Pelham, W.E., Bender, M.A., Caddell, J., Booth, S. & Moorer, S.H. (1985), Methylphenidate and children with attention deficit disorder. *Arch. Gen. Psychiatry*, 42:948–952.

Richardson, E., Kupietz, S.S., Winsberg, B.G., Maitinsky, S. & Mendell, N. (1988), Effects of methylphenidate dosage in hyperactive reading-disabled children: II. Reading achievement. *J. Am. Acad. Child Adolesc. Psychiatry*, 27:78–87.

Rie, H., Rie, E., Stewart, S. & Ambuel, J. (1976), Effects of methylphenidate on underachieving children. *J. Consult. Psychol.*, 44:250–260.

Sebrechts, M.M., Shaywitz, S.E., Shaywitz, B.A., Jatlow, P., Anderson, G.M. & Cohen, D.J. (1986), Components of attention, methylphenidate dosage, and blood levels in children with attention deficit disorder. *Pediatrics*, 77:222–228.

Shaywitz, S.E., Hunt, R.D., Jatlow, P., Cohen, D.J., Young, J.G., Pierce, R.N., Anderson, G.M. & Shaywitz, B.A. (1982), Psychopharmacology of attention deficit disorder: Pharmacokinetic, neuroendocrine, and behavioral measures following acute and chronic treatment with methylphenidate. *Pediatrics*, 69:688–694.

Sprague, R.L. & Sleator, E.K. (1977), Methylphenidate in hyperactive children: Differences in dose effects on learning and social behavior. *Science*, 198:1274–1276.

Sprague, R.L., Barnes, K.R. & Werry, J.S. (1970), Methylphenidate and thioridazine: Learning, reaction time, activity, and classroom behavior in disturbed children. *Am. J. Orthopsychiatry*, 40:615–628.

Swanson, J., Kinsbourne, M., Roberts, W. & Zucker, K. (1978), Time-response analysis of the effect of stimulant medication on the learning ability of children referred for hyperactivity. *Pediatrics*, 61:21–29.

Sykes, D.H., Douglas, V.I., Weiss, G. & Minde, K.K. (1971), Attention in hyperactive children and the effect of methylphenidate (Ritalin). *J. Child Psychol. Psychiatry*, 12:129–139.

——— ——— Morgenstern, G. (1973), Sustained attention in hyperactive children. *J. Child Psychol. Psychiatry*, 14:213–220.

Weiss, G., Kruger, E., Danielson, U. & Elman, M. (1975), Effects of long-term treatment of hyperactive children with methylphenidate. *Can. Med. Assoc. J.,* 112:150–169.

Winsberg, B.G., Press, M., Bialer, I. & Kupietz, S. (1974), Dextroamphetamine and methylphenidate in the treatment of hyperactive-aggressive children. *Pediatrics,* 53:236–241.

―――― Kupietz, S.S., Sverd, J., Hungund, B.L. & Young, N.L. (1982), Methylphenidate oral dose plasma concentrations and behavioral response in children. *Psychopharmacology,* 76:329–332.

Ritalin Treatment in Attention Deficit Disorder Without Hyperactivity

KEITH McBURNETT,[1] BENJAMIN B. LAHEY,[2] and JAMES M. SWANSON[1]

The topic of Ritalin treatment for children who show problems of inattention and distractability, but not motor hyperactivity, involves a complex set of issues. In this chapter, we briefly address some of these issues, including the following: (a) Is attention deficit disorder (ADD) without hyperactivity (ADD/WO) a valid diagnostic category? (b) Are attention deficit disorders with and without hyperactivity similar disorders, except for the hyperactivity symptoms? (c) Do ADD children with and without hyperactivity have similar cognitive symptoms? (d) Does methylphenidate have different dose–response curves for cognitive versus behavioral symptoms in these variants of ADD? We also review the very small research literature on Ritalin treatment of attention deficit disorder without hyperactivity. In referring to these two subtypes of attention deficit disorders, we use the nomenclature from the third revision of the *Diagnostic and Statistical Manual of Mental Disorders* (*DSM-III;* American Psychiatric Association, 1980). Our use of this convention is in keeping with the evidence that the symptom clusters described by these two labels represent separate disorders that differ on a variety of important indicators of external validity. Also, the available research base that is relevant to methylphenidate response has used children identified as having ADD/WO, rather than the *DSM-III-R* category of Undifferentiated Attention Deficit Disorder (UADD).

IS ADD/WO A VALID DIAGNOSTIC CATEGORY?

There are numerous ways of judging whether ADD is an appropriate and distinct category of child psychiatric disorders. For example, one question that is relevant to the *internal validity* of the ADD/WO category (or its successor) is whether the disorder can be reliably diagnosed by clinicians who make their diagnoses from the same clinical information, but without consulting each other (independent diagnoses). While the answer to this question is not available for UADD (and is unlikely, given its lack of specific criteria), there is evidence supporting the diagnostic reliability of ADD/WO (e.g., Lahey et al., 1987).

Another important consideration is whether children placed in a given ADD category exhibit the same kinds of problems. For example, does the overall category of ADD (or attention deficit hyperactivity disorder [ADHD]) show sufficient *homogeneity,* or does it classify children with quite different kinds of symptoms (and who thereby might respond differently to stimulant treatment) under the same rubric? The narrow question addressed here is whether ADD symptoms in individual children tend to occur in distinct patterns—patterns that justify a categorical distinction based on the presence of hyperactivity. Recent studies have examined how the various inattentive, impulsive, and hyperactive *symptoms* of ADD tend to be associated with each other. Using the statistical technique of factor analysis, which yields the loadings (strength of relationship) of items to underlying factors or "latent traits," these studies have shown that most items describing ADD symptoms fall into two primary factors (e.g., Hart et al., 1989; Lahey et al., 1988). One factor represents the hyperactivity and impulsive behavior symptoms, and the other factor represents the inattention and disorganization symptoms. When items representing such symptoms as forgetfulness and

[1]Child Development Center, University of California, Irvine, and California State Developmental Research Institutes, Costa Mesa, California
[2]University of Miami School of Medicine, Miami, Florida

sluggishness have been included, these have emerged as a third factor which has been termed "sluggish tempo" (Lahey et al., 1988).

The two studies cited above subjected the derived factors to the statistical technique of cluster analysis. This procedure examines how the symptom factors tend to occur in individual children. These studies show that three profiles of factor elevations emerge. On one profile, both the hyperactive/impulsive and the inattentive/disorganized factors are low. These profiles are associated with children who do not have ADD. On a second profile, both factors are high. This profile is associated with children diagnosed with ADD with hyperactivity (ADD/H). On the third profile, the hyperactive/impulsive factor is low, but the inattentive/disorganized factor is high. When the "sluggish tempo" factor is included in the cluster analysis (as in Lahey et al., 1988), this factor is also high on the third type of profile. This profile is associated with children diagnosed with ADD/WO. The statistical procedures used to obtain symptom cluster profiles were completely independent from the diagnostic procedures used to determine clinical diagnoses (except for sharing sources of information about the presence of symptoms). Both studies found very high agreement between the cluster profiles and the clinical diagnoses that individual children received.

Thus, factor and cluster analytic studies of ADD symptoms suggest that ADD is not a unidimensional disorder. The cluster profiles of symptom factors indicate that a bipartite division, such as ADD with and without hyperactivity, is supported by the available taxometric evidence.

ARE ADD/H AND ADD/WO SIMILAR, EXCEPT FOR THE HYPERACTIVITY SYMPTOMS?

This question actually touches on two separate issues, both of which are germaine to the choice of treatment. The first issue is whether ADD/H and ADD/WO have the same behavioral, emotional, diagnostic, and prognostic correlates. Finding that ADD/H and ADD/WO have different correlates supports the *external validity* of the with/without distinction. For purposes of this discussion, we focus on how certain differences in correlates may have relevance for treatment response. The second issue, discussed later, is whether the cognitive and attention symptoms associated with the two disorders are the same.

Studies that have contrasted the correlates of ADD/H and ADD/WO have used two basic approaches to define these diagnostic groups. In one approach, behavior rating scales have been used. These studies have assigned children rated high on factors related to inattention *and* hyperactivity to the ADD/H group, and children rated high on factors related to inattention but *not* hyperactivity to the ADD/WO group (e.g., Barkley et al., 1990a; King and Young, 1982; Lahey et al., 1984, 1985; Pelham et al., 1981). These studies have found that ADD/H children are rated higher by their teachers than ADD/WO children on dimensions related to conduct problems and aggression, whereas ADD/WO children are often rated higher on dimensions of anxiety/withdrawal and sluggishness/apathy. ADD/H children defined in this way also have been found to have a greater prevalence of oppositional disorder and conduct disorder (Barkley et al., 1990a). The other approach has been to constitute ADD/H and ADD/WO groups on the basis of clinical diagnosis. These comparisons (e.g., Berry et al., 1985; Lahey, 1988; Lahey et al., 1987) have tended to corroborate the findings with ratings-defined groups. That is, children diagnosed with ADD/H tend to be rated higher on dimensions related to aggression and other antisocial behavior than those with ADD/WO, and children diagnosed with ADD/WO tended to be rated as more shy, withdrawn, and anxious. Additionally, children diagnosed with ADHD are more likely to receive a codiagnosis of conduct disorder, whereas children diagnosed with ADD/WO are more likely to have a coexisting anxiety disorder. When only ADD children who have a comorbid conduct disorder are examined, ADD/H children are found to exhibit greater severity of conduct disorder (Lahey et al., 1987).

These studies of the behavioral and emotional correlates of ADD subtypes, while differing in methodology and specific findings, present a fairly consistent picture with regard to coexisting diagnoses and other psychosocial disturbances for ADD/H children: they are more likely to show comorbid problems from the *externalizing* dimension of psychopathology. ADD/WO children may be more likely to show problems from the *internalizing* dimension, but this finding is less robust and is not as consistently identified. Two reviews of this literature, (Carlson 1986; Lahey and Carlson, 1989) question whether these two diagnoses belong together as subtypes of ADD. Perhaps ADD/WO may not even belong in the grouping of disruptive behavior disorders, but rather in some grouping of internalizing disorders.

The differences in behavioral and emotional correlates have implications for choice of treatment. The aggressive and oppositional problems that are more commonly associated with ADD/H often respond to methylphenidate (e.g., Barkley et al., 1989; Hinshaw et al., 1989; Miczek, 1987; Pelham et al., 1985, 1987). However, stimulants theoretically should exacerbate some aspects of anxiety. Overarousal or overreactivity of the sympathetic branch of the autonomic nervous system has long been recognized as a feature of anxiety in adults. There has been little investigation of the physiological correlates of child anxiety disorders (Quay and La Greca, 1986); on purely theoretical grounds, however, the effects of a sympatho-mimetic such as methylphenidate should be antitherapeutic for anxiety symptoms. Similar reasoning suggests caution in using methylphenidate with children who are socially withdrawn. Because (a) social withdrawal is sometimes observed as a side effect or as an overdosage effect of the drug (Cantwell and Carlson, 1978; Swanson et al., 1978, Whalen and Henker, 1984), and (b) social withdrawal is more prevalent in ADD/WO, it is logical to hypothesize that methylphenidate (especially at high dosages) may cause more adverse effects on social interaction in ADD/WO children than in ADD/H children. Careful monitoring of social approach and peer interactions and of anxiety symptoms would be advisable in clinical treatment of ADD/WO with methylphenidate.

Pliszka (1989) examined the differential response to methylphenidate in children diagnosed with ADD/H with and without a comorbid anxiety disorder. Children with elevated teacher ratings of inattention/overactivity were referred for clinical diagnostic interviews. Thirteen children who were diagnosed as having ADHD and overanxious disorder (OA) were compared with 30 children who received diagnoses of ADHD, but not OA. A four-week, placebo-controlled, within-subjects (crossover) dose–response study of methylphenidate was conducted. The dependent measures were teacher ratings of inattention and aggression and laboratory observations of various off-task behaviors during academic seatwork. Methylphenidate failed to produce a significant effect on *any* of these measures for the ADHD with OA group. The ADHD without OA group responded positively only to the high dose (0.45–0.70 mg/kg) of methylphenidate on teacher-rated aggression. This same group responded positively to the low dose (0.25–0.40 mg/kg), with no further improvement at the high dose, on teacher-rated inattention/overactivity and on laboratory-coded off-task behaviors. When the response of individual cases was evaluated (using teacher-rated inattention/overactivity as the criterion), 31% of the ADHD with OA group (4 children) were determined to be positive drug responders. In the ADHD without OA group, 87% (26) of the children were positive responders. Thus, a major finding of this study is that the presence of an anxiety disorder along with ADHD is associated with poorer response to methylphenidate, although a substantial percentage of these children (over 30% in this study) do show a positive response. This finding is consistent with other studies that have shown an inverse relationship between internalizing symptoms and response to stimulants (Taylor et al., 1987; Zahn et al., 1975). Because ADD/WO is more frequently associated with an anxiety disorder than ADHD, it would be reasonable to expect a lower percentage of positive responders to stimulants among ADD/WO children.

DO ADD CHILDREN WITH AND WITHOUT HYPERACTIVITY HAVE SIMILAR COGNITIVE SYMPTOMS?

Since ADD/WO children by definition are not hyperactive, the targets of drug treatment are the cognitive symptoms for which they were referred—inattention, distractability, academic performance, etc. There is evidence that children diagnosed with ADD/WO differ in cognitive symptoms from children with ADD/H. However, these findings are inconsistent and provide no implications for drug treatment distinctions between the two disorders. As described above, ADD/WO children tend to be rated higher on items related to sluggishness, apathy, daydreaming, and what in common parlance is called "spaciness." A recent comparison of psychometric performance found that the only difference between ADD/H and ADD/WO children on measures from the Wechsler Intelligence Scale for Children–Revised was on Coding (Barkley et al., 1990a). The lower score for ADD/WO on Coding, a timed clerical performance task, is consistent with a hypothesis of slower processing or psychomotor performance in ADD/WO. However, when tested in a structured, one-on-one simple and choice reaction time paradigm, ADD/WO children were found not to differ from other clinic-referred children on reaction speed, processing speed, or variability in reaction times

(Hynd et al., 1990). In the Hynd et al. (1990) study, the ADD/H group became slower and more variable in choice reaction time as the choice task was made more difficult. Other comparisons using laboratory or neuropsychological measures sometimes have found differences between ADD/H and ADD/WO groups (Conte et al., 1986; Frank and Ben-Nun, 1988) and sometimes have found few or no differences (Carlson et al., 1986; Neeper, 1985; Schaughency et al., 1988). Studies which have examined academic performance also present an inconclusive picture. In one study, over two-thirds of ADD/WO children had been retained (failed) in at least one grade, while only 17% of ADD/H children had been retained (Edelbrock et al., 1984). However, some studies using achievement testing have found no differences between ADD children with and without hyperactivity in academic achievement or in the prevalence of learning disabilities as indexed by IQ achievement discrepancies (Barkley et al., 1990b); Carlson et al., 1986; Lahey, 1988).

Barkley et al. (1990a,b) reported that ADD/H children made nonsignificantly more errors of omission and commission on a continuous performance task than ADD/WO children, whereas ADD/WO children were less able to consistently recall memorized words across repeated trials of a verbal learning test. They suggested that the attentional deficits in ADD with hyperactivity occur as deficits in vigilance or *sustained* attention, and that qualitatively different attentional deficits in ADD/WO present as impairment in *focused* attention or processing speed. However, other investigators have argued convincingly that ADHD children do not show specific or differential deficits in sustained attention on laboratory measures (e.g., Van der Meere and Sergeant, 1988). The hypothesis of qualitatively different attentional deficits in ADD with and without hyperactivity awaits further evaluation, but there is little to suggest that the attentional symptoms in ADD/WO may respond differently to methylphenidate than attentional symptoms in ADD/H. Thus, while there is a fairly consistent pattern of differential inattentive and cognitive symptoms between ADD/H and ADD/WO when rating scales are used, the available database using laboratory measures is inconsistent. In any case, investigations of differential cognitive symptoms have not provided a basis for guiding treatment choice or predicting response to stimulants.

DOES METHYLPHENIDATE HAVE DIFFERENT DOSE–RESPONSE CURVES FOR COGNITIVE VERSUS BEHAVIORAL SYMPTOMS OF ADD?

An influential study by Sprague and Sleator (1977) reported that the dose-related effects of methylphenidate varied according to the aspect of behavior being studied. Dosages of 0.3 and 1 mg/kg, and placebo were given to hyperactive children. Their social behavior was evaluated with a rating scale. Their cognitive performance was evaluated using a visual recognition task (Sternberg-type memory scanning paradigm). The complexity of the cognitive task was varied so that greater effort was required to perform the more difficult versions of the task. Methylphenidate improved disruptive social behavior in a linear fashion—the behavior ratings improved at the low dose and even more at the high dose. Accuracy on the cognitive task was not affected by methylphenidate in the easiest version. In the most difficult version of the cognitive task, accuracy improved at the low dose but then deteriorated at the high dose, back to the placebo accuracy level. These findings have been interpreted as evidence of *cognitive toxicity*, a phenomenon in which high doses of a stimulant result in worse performance on a task requiring effortful learning or mental processing than low doses of the same stimulant. When difficult cognitive tasks have been used to evaluate stimulant dose effects, and the dose range has included high dosages, two different dose-response curve shapes have been obtained (Pelham et al., 1980; Swanson and Cantwell, 1989; Swanson and Kinsbourne, 1978). Hyperactivity and disruptive social behavior, and many cognitive and performance tasks, show a linear or curvilinear dose-response curve. Tasks requiring effortful mental processing show a quadratic inverted "U" shape dose-response curve. Optimal benefits on these tasks are seen at low to moderate doses, with lesser or no benefits at high doses (Swanson et al., 1990).

It is precisely these kinds of tasks that are required of children in school seatwork and homework. The findings of an inverted-U dose-response function for effortful learning have implications for methylphenidate treatment of ADD/WO. Low to moderate doses are more likely to produce optimal benefits on learning and cognitive symptoms. Moderate to high doses are more likely to produce "cognitive toxicity," with no real benefits in academic work (and possible adverse effects) over placebo or no treatment.

Another implication of these findings concerns the criteria for determining whether an individual child with ADD will have a positive response to methylphenidate and what the optimal dose for improving the cognitive symptoms might be. Teacher reports or behavior ratings are used frequently in clinical practice as indications of stimulant response. However, the differences in effortful learning associated with different doses of methylphenidate are unlikely to be observed or to show up on behavior rating scales. When academic and cognitive problems are of paramount concern, it may be especially important to objectively evaluate methylphenidate response with a double-blind assessment procedure that includes a measure of effortful learning (Swanson, 1988; Swanson et al., 1990).

EMPIRICAL FINDINGS OF METHYLPHENIDATE RESPONSE IN CHILDREN WITH ADD/WO

Only a handful of studies have been conducted to evaluate the response of children with ADD/WO to methylphenidate. In one of these studies, ADD/WO children were grouped together with ADD/H children (Ullman and Sleator, 1985). Methylphenidate improved teacher ratings of inattention and hyperactivity for the group. The ADD/WO children made up 18% of the subject group, but because their results were pooled with the entire group and not reported separately, no conclusions regarding ADD response can be drawn.

Famularo and Fenton (1987) conducted a multiple baseline study of methylphenidate response in six girls and four boys, ages 7 to 12 years, who met DSM-III criteria for ADD/WO but not for any other disorder. This study is particularly interesting because it used academic grades as the dependent variable. Dosages were individually determined by balancing clinical response with adverse effects. The doses reported ranged from 0.4 to 1.2 mg/kg/day in two doses, so apparently the highest single dose was 0.6 mg/kg. The children's grades in each of five subjects (science, reading, spelling, mathematics, and social studies) were obtained for three consecutive grading periods in the same school year. During the middle grading period, the children received the twice-daily methylphenidate treatment. The children's grade average for the pretreatment grading period was 2.02. This increased to 2.84 during treatment and fell to 2.30 following discontinuation of methylphenidate. The treatment grade average was found to be significantly higher than the pre- and posttreatment grade averages. When grades were examined for individual children, eight of the ten children showed grade improvement in at least three of the five subjects during treatment, compared with pretreatment baseline. Though not specifically reported, the data in this study show that five of the children showed a grade decline in at least three of the subjects upon discontinuation of treatment. (Not included in the subject group were an additional three children whose parents requested continuation of methylphenidate following grade improvement during the treatment period.) This study has numerous design and method-ological limitations, such as the absence of a placebo condition and the fact that neither teachers nor parents were blind to treatment conditions. Nonetheless, the study does suggest that methylphenidate may be beneficial for some ADD/WO children, and that these benefits may be reflected in school grades.

The best-designed study of methylphenidate in ADD/WO children to date was reported by Barkley's group (1990c). The study evaluated 23 ADHD and 17 ADD/WO children between the ages of 6 and 11 in a triple-blind, placebo-controlled crossover (within-subject) design for response to twice-daily doses of 5, 10, and 15 mg methylphenidate. The dependent measures included parent and teacher behavior ratings, psychological tests, and behavioral observations during an arithmetic task. For both the teacher and parent ratings of behavior, there were no significant drug condition by group interactions, indicating that the dose-related effects of methylphenidate on behavior ratings were the same for ADD with and without hyperactivity. Likewise, there were no significant drug condition by group interaction for any of the psychological measures or behavior observations, again suggesting equivalent response of the clinical groups to methylphenidate.

Separate analyses of variance were not reported for the ADD/WO group alone. This would have been helpful, because the absence of any drug condition by group interactions for measures related to hyperactivity is puzzling. (It is reasonable to expect hyperactive children to show greater decreases than ADD/WO children in response to methylphenidate on rated or observed hyperactivity.) There were main effects for methylphenidate for all of the behavior rating subscales, substantiating the beneficial effect of methylphenidate on behavior ratings for the combined group of ADD subtypes. There were no main effects of methylphenidate on most of the psychological measures. Methylphenidate did improve math accuracy, but not the total number of problems worked. The drug also reduced omission (but not commission) errors on a continuous performance task. On most of the behavioral observation measures, methylphenidate produced a significant improvement. There were no significant drug effects on ratings of the number of severity of side effects.

At the conclusion of the study, a psychologist and a pediatrician reviewed each individual case and made a clinical judgment regarding the optimal dosage, based on summaries of the dependent measures. Clear differences in the recommended dosage for clinical management resulted between the ADD/H and ADD/WO groups. In the ADD/WO group, 24% were judged to have no response, 35% were recommended for the low dose (5 mg bid), 29% were recommended for the moderate dose (10 mg bid), and 12% were recommended for the high dose (15 mg bid). In the ADD/H group, only 5% were determined to have no response, 24% were recommended for the low dose, 52% were recommended for the moderate dose, and 19% were recommended for the high dose. It was not reported whether the two clinicians were blind to group status, whether they made the clinical response decisions independently, or whether any tests of reliability were conducted for the decision process. However, these differences in recommended clinical management doses suggest that more ADD/WO children respond optimally to methylphenidate at low to moderate doses, whereas in comparison more ADD/H children respond optimally to moderate to high doses. Additionally, it appears that a greater percentage of ADD/WO children do not show a positive response to any dose of methylphenidate.

SUMMARY AND CONCLUSIONS

Although more empirical investigations of stimulant treatment of attention deficit disorders are needed, some tentative conclusions can be offered. The disorder that we have referred to as ADD/WO in this chapter appears to be a syndrome that is distinct from ADHD and ADD/H, not only because of the absence of clinical hyperactivity, but because of other markers of internal and external validity. The inattention and other cognitive symptoms of ADD/WO appear to differ in some respects from those seen in ADD/H. In particular, ADD/WO children tend to appear more sluggish, drowsy, daydreamy, and/or apathetic. However, their cognitive and attentional response to methylphenidate does not appear to differ, in any qualitative way, from that seen with ADD/H children. There is preliminary evidence that the percentage of nonresponders to methylphenidate is higher in ADD than in ADD/H. There is also preliminary evidence that the methylphenidate dosage that is optimal for clinical management tends to be lower in ADD/WO than in ADD/H. Specifically, this optimal dosage appears to be in the low to moderate range for most ADD/WO children, although a percentage (12% in one study) of these children may respond best to a high dosage.

ADD/WO may be more likely than ADD/H to be accompanied by anxiety and by social inhibition. When present in ADD/H, anxiety has been associated with a poorer response to methylphenidate. Social withdrawal is sometimes a side effect or an overdosage effect of methylphenidate. Therefore, it would be wise to evaluate anxiety symptoms and peer interactions when considering a child with ADD/WO for treatment with methylphenidate, and to monitor these areas for adverse effects if treatment is recommended. If possible, medication response and proper dosage should be guided by a double-blind medication assessment in which one measure of response is a test of effortful learning or mental processing. If this is not possible, careful monitoring of academic productivity is essential. In the absence of an objective medication assessment, dosage should probably be kept low for a child with ADD/WO. Extrapolating from the available data, an ADD/WO child who fails to respond to a low to moderate dose is highly likely (88%) to be a nonresponder or an adverse responder to methylphenidate. Finally, as with ADHD, methylphenidate should never be used as the sole treatment modality in ADD/WO, but should be one component in a comprehensive management plan.

REFERENCES

American Psychiatric Association. (1980), *Diagnostic and Statistical Manual of Mental Disorders* 3rd Ed. Washington, DC: Author.

Barkley, R.A., McMurray, M.B., Edelbrock, C.S. & Robbins, K. (1989), The response of aggressive and nonaggressive ADHD children to two doses of methylphenidate. *J. Am. Acad. Child Adolesc. Psychiatry,* 28:873–881.

———— DuPaul, G.J. & McMurray, M.B. (1990a), Comprehensive evaluation of attention deficit disorder with and without hyperactivity as defined by research criteria. *J. Consult. Clin. Psychology,* 58:775–789.

———— ———— ———— (1990b), Attention deficit disorder with and without hyperactivity: Clinical response to three dose levels of methylphenidate. *Pediatrics,* in press.

Berry, C.A., Shaywitz, S.E. & Shaywitz, B.A. (1985), Girls with attention deficit disorder: A silent minority? A report on behavioral and cognitive characteristics. *Pediatrics,* 76:801–809.

Cantwell, D.P. & Carlson, G.A. (1978), Stimulants. In: *Pediatric Psychopharmacology: The Use of Behavior Modifying Drugs in Children,* ed. J.S. Werry. New York: Brunner/Mazel, pp. 171–207.

Carlson, C.L. (1986), Attention deficit disorder without hyperactivity: A review of preliminary experimental evidence. In: *Advances in Clinical Child Psychology,* Vol. 9 eds. B.B. Lahey & A.E. Kazdin. New York: Plenum Press, pp. 153–175.

———— Lahey, B.B. & Neeper, R. (1986), Direct assessment of the cognitive correlates of attention deficit disorders with and without hyperactivity. *J. Behav. Assess. Psychopathol.,* 8:69–86.

Conte, R., Kinsbourne, M., Swanson, J., Zirk, H. & Samuels, M. (1986), Presentation rate effects on paired associate learning by attention deficit disordered children. *Child Devel.,* 57:681–687.

Edelbrock, C., Costello, A.J. & Kessler, M.D. (1984), Empirical corroboration of the attention deficit disorder. *J. Am. Acad. Child Adolesc. Psychiatry,* 23:285–290.

Famularo, R. & Fenton, T. (1987), The effect of methylphenidate on school grades in children with attention deficit disorder without hyperactivity: A preliminary report. *J. Clin. Psychiatry,* 48:112–114.

Frank, Y. & Ben-Nun, Y. (1988), Toward a clinical subgrouping of hyperactive and nonhyperactive attention deficit disorder: Results of a comprehensive neurological and neuropsychological assessment. *J. Dis. Child.,* 142:153–155.

Hart, E.A., Lahey, B.B., Hern, K., Hynd, G.W., Frick, P.J. & Hanson, K. (1989), *Dimensions and types of ADD:* Two replications. Manuscript under review.

Hinshaw, S.P., Hencker, B., Whalen, C.K., Erhardt, D. & Dunnington, R.E., Jr. (1989), Aggressive, prosocial, and nonsocial behavior in hyperactive boys: Dose effects of methylphenidate in naturalistic settings. *J Consult. Clin. Psychology,* 57:636–643.

Hynd, G.W., Nieves, N., Conner, R.T., Stone, P., Town, P. & Becker, M.G. (1990), Speed of neurocognitive processing in children with attention deficit disorder with and without hyperactivity. *J. Learn. Disabil.,* in press.

King, C. & Young, R.D. (1982), Attentional deficits with and without hyperactivity: Teacher and peer perceptions. *J. Abnorm. Child Psychol.,* 10:483–495.

Lahey, B.B. (1988), *Attention Deficit Disorder Without Hyperactivity: Issues of Validity.* Paper presented to the annual meeting of the Bloomingdale/High Point Hospital Conference on Attention Deficit Disorder, Seattle, WA.

———— Carlson, C.L. (1989), Validity of a diagnostic category of Attention Deficit Disorder without Hyperactivity: A literature review for the Committee on Disruptive Behavior Disorders of the Task Force for DSM-IV. Unpublished manuscript.

———— Pelham, W.E., Schaughency, E.A., Atkins, M.S., Murphy, H.A., Hynd, G.W., Russo, M., Hartdagen, S. & Lorys-Vernon, A. (1988), Dimensions and types of attention deficit disorder. *J. Am. Acad. Child Adolesc. Psychiatry* 27:330–335.

———— ———— Hynd, G.W., Carlson, C.L. & Nieves, N. (1987), Attention deficit disorder with and without hyperactivity: comparison of behavioral characteristics of clinic-referred children. *J. Am. Acad. Child Adolesc. Psychiatry*, 26:718–723.

———— ———— Frame, C.L. & Strauss, C.C. (1985), Teacher ratings of attention problems in children experimentally classified as exhibiting attention deficit disorders with and without hyperactivity. *J. Am. Acad. Child Adolesc. Psychiatry*, 26:613–616.

———— ———— Strauss, C.C. & Frame, C.L. (1984), Are attention deficit disorders with and without hyperactivity similar or dissimilar disorders? *J. Am. Acad. Child Psychiatry*, 23:302–309.

Miczek, K.A. (1987), The psychopharmacology of aggression. In L. L. Iverson *Handbook of Psychopharmacology: New Directions in Behavioral Pharmacology* Vol. 19, eds. S. D. Iverson, & S. H. Snyder. New York: Plenum.

Neeper, R. (1985), *Toward the empircial delineation of learning disability subtypes*. Unpublished doctoral dissertation, University of Goergia.

Pelham, W.E., Bender, M., Wilson, J. & Swanson, J. (1980), *Dose-response effects of pemoline on learning and social behavior*. Paper presented at the annual meeting of the American Psychological Association, Montreal.

———— Atkins, M.S. & Murphy, H.A. (1981), *Attention Deficit Disorder with and without Hyperactivity: Definitional issues and correlates*. Presented at the annual meeting of the American Psychological Association, Los Angeles.

———— Bender, M.E., Caddell, J., Booth, S. & Moorer, S.A. (1985), Methylphenidate and children with attention deficit disorder: dose effects on classroom academic and social behavior. *Arch. Gen. Psychiatry*, 42:948–952.

Pelham, W.E., Jr., Sturges, J., Hoza, J., Schmidt, C., Bijlsma, J.J., Milich, R. & Moorer, S. (1987), Sustained release and standard methylphenidate effects on cognitive and social behavior in children with attention deficit disorder. *Pediatrics*, 80:491–501.

Pliszka, S.R. (1989), Effect of anxiety on cognition, behavior, and stimulant response in ADHD. *J. Am. Acad. Child Adolesc. Psychiatry*, 28:882–887.

Quay, H.C. & La Greca, A.M. (1986), Disorders of anxiety, withdrawal, and dysphoria. In: *Psychopathological Disorders of Childhood*, 3rd Ed, eds. H. C. Quay & J. S. Werry. New York: Wiley, pp. 73–110.

Schaughency, E.A., Lahey, B.B., Hynd, G.W., Stone, P.A., Piacentini, J.C. & Frick, P.J. (1988), Neuropsychological test performance and the attention deficit disorders: Clinical utility of the Luria-Nebraska Neuropsychological Battery—Children's Revision. *J. Consult. Clin. Psychology*, 57:112–116.

Sprague, R.L. & Sleator, E.K. (1977), Methylphenidate in hyperkinetic children: Differences in dose effects on learning and social behavior. *Science*, 198:1274–1276.

Swanson, J.M. (1988), Measurement of serum concentrations and behavioral response in ADDH children to acute doses of methylphenidate. In: *Attention Deficit Disorder*, Vol. 3, *New Directions in Attention, Treatment, and Psychopharmacology*, ed. L. M. Bloomingdale. Oxford, UK: Pergamon Press, (pp. 107–126).

———— Cantwell, D. (1989), *Cognitive toxicity of methylphenidate: Evidence from reaction time studies of memory scanning*. Presented at the annual meeting of the American Academy of Child and Adolescent Psychiatry, New York.

———— Kinsbourne, M. (1978), Should you use stimulants to treat the hyperactive child? *Mod. Med.*, 46:71–80.

———— Cantwell, D., Lerner, M., McBurnett, K. & Hanna, G. (1991), Effects of stimulant medication on learning in children with ADHD. *J. of Learning Disabilities*, 24:219–230.

———— Kinsbourne, M., Roberts, W. & Zucker, M.A. (1978), Time-response analysis of the effect of stimulant medication on the learning ability of children referred for hyperactivity. *Pediatrics*, 61:21–29.

Taylor, E., Schachar, R., Thorley, G., Wieselberg, H.M., Everitt, B. & Rutter, M. (1987), Which boys respond to stimulant medication? A controlled trial of methylphenidate in boys with disruptive behaviour. *Psychol. Med.,* 17:121–143.

Ullman, R.K. & Sleator, E.K. (1985), Attention deficit disorder children with or without hyperactivity: Which behaviors are helped by stimulants? *Clin. Pediatr.,* 24:547–551.

Van der Meere, J.J. & Sergeant, J.A. (1988), Controlled processing and vigilance in hyperactivity: Time will tell. *J. Abnorm. Child Psychol.,* 16:641–655.

Whalen, C.K. & Henker, B. (1984), Hyperactivity and the attention deficit disorders: Expanding frontiers. *Pediatr. Clin. North Am.,* 31:397–427.

Zahn, T.P., Abate, F., Little, B.C. & Wender, P.H. (1975), Minimal brain dysfunction, stimulant drugs, and autonomic nervous system activity. *Arch. Gen. Psychiatry,* 32:381–387.

Neurobiological Theories of ADHD and Ritalin

ROBERT D. HUNT, LEE MANDL, SERENA LAU, and MARK HUGHES

PROCESSING THEORIES

Early theories of attention recognized that filtering and selection operate in narrowing the perceptual field and sustaining cognitive focus. Emerging theories of information processing attempt to explain the role of attention in relation to specific structures in the multistore model of sequential organization of information.

In the earliest theory, Broadbent's "Filter theory," material stored in the sensory register is subject to preattentive analysis which rapidly processes incoming sensory input by identifying physical characteristics such as tone and intensity (Neisser, 1967). The selective filter then chooses which material will continue on to the channel for further analysis or will be discarded. Since only a limited amount of information can be more intensively transmitted and processed, there appears to be a limited "channel capacity" from the initial sensory register into short-term memory where conscious processing occurs. A series of filters must operate at levels of increasing discrimination to determine the significance of competing data. Since the resources of this channel must divide its capacity between information, some information will be lost. Information that is not given significance in the sensory register will not be filtered through to short-term memory.

The "attenuation model" developed by Treisman (1960), suggests that attention is graduated and dimensional, rather than categorical. Treisman places more importance on preattentive (preconscious) analysis, considering it to discriminate not only the physical properties of stimuli, but their linguistic and semantic dimensions as well. Thus, a great deal of "meaningful" discrimination occurs before stimuli are selected for conscious analysis. This model emphasizes selective components of attention; in order to focus on one item, it is necessary to tune out surrounding distractions.

The "late selection model" is a less sequentially oriented theory articulated by Deutsch and Deutsch (1963). Incoming stimuli are transmitted through parallel "simultaneous processes" into short-term memory where the importance of the information is decided. All stimuli that are considered important are evaluated in a later stage of cognition. Thus, multiple stimuli may be held in consciousness or memory for simultaneous analysis and integrated processing.

"Capacity models" shift the focus of memory from structures to processes. In Kahneman's model (1973), attention constitutes a pool of cognitive resources that are affected by the individual's state of arousal. The allocation of attention is affected by enduring dispositions (or intrinsic characteristics) of the stimuli—such as intensity (brightness of light or loudness of noise)—and by momentary dispositions, competing situations, or events that also demand attention. Interference in memory may be due to lack of cognitive resources that may be allocated to any specific incoming stimuli. Since this allocation is flexible, performance on one task will decline if an attempt is made to perform a second task—especially if the total demands of the tasks overload available processing capacity. Thus, attention is affected by the characteristics of the signal, the complexity of the tasks, and intensity of other competing performance demands. Attention is also altered by momentary biological variables such as the degree of arousal and anxiety that may affect cognitive competence or functional capacity.

Vanderbilt University Medical School, Nashville, Tennessee

Shiffrin and Schneider's "automatic versus controlled" model of attention and memory (1977) considers controlled processes as being capacity limited and serial in nature. Controlled processes are often slow and are subject to interference by other processes. Automatic processes, on the other hand, occur in response to familiar input and can be activated without the conscious control of the individual. This is similar to the concept of behavioral engrams or response patterns that can be accessed as large units of rather autonomous interactions. For example, an experienced driver can drive a car with limited conscious attention while thinking of something else. A good typist can attend to the words rather than the location of the keys. Since these automatic processes are not capacity limited, they are minimally affected by competing stimuli and pose less interference with other tasks that demand greater conscious attention.

Hasher and Zacks (1979) modified Schneider's model of cognition to emphasize "effortful versus automatic" components of attention. They view attentional processes along a continuum of effort and automatic functioning. Hasher and Zacks emphasize that environmental and organismic (biological) states affect processing capacity, thereby altering effortful processing. These issues are relevant to attention deficit hyperactivity disorder (ADHD) children who may have greater difficulty encoding automatic behavioral engrams and appropriately selecting among them. Additionally, the cognitive functioning of ADHD children often reflects a skewing of biological state emphasized by Hasher and Zacks. Their attentional capacity is impaired by either excessive or labile arousal, or by inadequate inhibitory processes.

A clinically useful framework proposed by Tariot and Weingartner (1986) differentiates cognitive processes from noncognitive processes. The *cognitive processes* include: (1) episodic learning and memory, (2) knowledge memory, (3) effort-demanding processes, and (4) automatic processes. Episodic learning and memory is likened to memory for recent events, for example, where and when something occurred, and what preceded and followed that event. Knowledge memory is likened to long-term memory. It is responsible for use of language, meaning, logic, relationships between events, procedures, and skills. It is necessary for perceiving, appreciating, and encoding ongoing experiences. Effort-demanding processes are responsible for the learning, storing, and remembering of an experience. Finally, automatic processes are responsible for remembering surrounding, incidental information. *Noncognitive* processes are able to modulate the cognitive processes. They include: (1) sensitivity to reinforcement, (2) degree of activation (arousal), (3) sensorimotor function, and (4) mood.

Different subgroups of ADHD children may have distinct origins for their diminished cognitive processing capacities. A variety of explanations exist, including (1) improper allocation of a normal amount of processing capacity, (2) the processing reservoir is overly devoted to irrelevant external or internal stimuli, (3) effortful processing is required to complete processes that are normally automatic, and (4) the total pool of cognitive processing capacity may be reduced.

Information processing models may assist in understanding the attentional deficits of ADHD children. The filtering component of attention reflects the process of perceptual screening identification and selection, frequently impaired in ADHD. The limited capacity for sequential or simultaneous processing of attention is relevant to the cognitive limitations evident in sustained attention in ADHD children on performance of tasks such as the continuous performance task (CPT). The networking components of attention are involved in accessing *memory, ego functions* of analytic assessment and judgment, and *response selection* and execution.

The effect of other brain regulatory systems on attention is emphasized in Kahneman's consideration of variable capacity for attention that may be reflected in changes in arousal, an important consideration for very energetic ADHD children. Hasher and Zacks' focus on the continuum of effort in attentional processes includes the demands of the task, the burden on attention of learning difficulties, and the stress of noncognitive processes relevant to ADHD including low frustration tolerance, high anxiety, and responsiveness to reward. Tariot and Weingartner's elaboration of cognitive and noncognitive processes is consonant with our model that derives from and emphasis on neurobiological rather than information processing systems. We recognize the importance of reinforcement and arousal processes, but add consideration of inhibitory processes in ADHD. Mood appears a less central issue in our population, but can profoundly alter cognitive capacity in depressed adolescents and adults.

Earlier models of attention can account for the cognitive limitations of many ADHD children in performing very concrete tasks unencumbered by external distractions or not requiring complex, effortful analysis or abstraction. These models may define performance of stimulus processing tasks that sample selective attention (Matching Familiar Figures Test), vigilance (continuous performance task), or measures of encoding and retrieval of discrete information from memory (paired-associate learning task). They may be adequate to explain the effects of Ritalin on increasing the valence of stimuli in perception and the zoom-lens effect of Ritalin on the breadth of attention.

However, these models do not sufficiently explain processes related to contemplative or inwardly directed attention essential to problem solving and value formation. The attentional mediation of concepts and fantasy abstraction required for reasoning, negotiation and social processing may not be adequately explained by a model of sequential processing of discrete bits of information. Consequently, the concrete tasks that measure cognition and the effects of Ritalin may not adequately capture the breadth of attentional impairment in ADHD children who have broad impairments in behavioral regulation, social relations, learning and task completion (Whalen et al., 1987, 1989). More comprehensive models of the intersection of brain function and cognition may be required (Edelman, 1987). The preoccupation with the stimulus processing component in ADHD as measured by tasks that are enhanced by Ritalin may miss important, valid effects of other medications that improve cognitive and noncognitive environment though indirect effects on arousal and inhibitory processes. More sophisticated cognitive tasks are needed that place a larger burden on abstraction and frustration tolerance in order to capture the effects of other medications on complex reflective attentional processes (Rapport and Kelly, in press).

COGNITIVE MEASURES OF ATTENTION IN ADHD

The primary method of measuring attention in ADHD consists of using a battery of stimulus-dependent tasks that recruit increasing complex cognitive processes. Several tasks have been widely applied in studies of ADHD that are usually found to be responsive to stimulant medications. These tasks have varied in complexity from studies of simple reaction time, to include measures of sustained attention that include an index of inhibition (CPT), to more complex measures of visual selection and scanning (MFFT, Stroop), and to tasks that assess the encoding and recall of learned matches in memory (PAL). Most tasks can be scored to reflect a combination of speed and accuracy (errors of omission and commission) that can be integrated to measure caution, oppositionality, or impulsivity.

More specifically, the continuous performance task (CPT) provides a measure of reaction time (latency), impulsivity (errors of commission), and sustained attention (Nuechterlein, 1983; Sykes et al., 1971, 1973). The Matching Familiar Figures Test (MFFT), a type of Matching to Sample task, assesses selective attention, distractibility and impulsivity (Kagan et al., 1964; Sargent et al., 1979). The paired-associate learning task (PAL) measures the rate and accuracy of learning an arbitrarily assigned match of unrelated stimuli, and assesses "effortful" learning and memory (Douglas et al., 1986; Swanson and Kinsbourne, 1976; Swanson et al., 1983).

All of these tasks are useful in ADHD because they address attentional deficits commonly found in this disorder and are sensitive to treatment effects of Ritalin. Most of these tasks have been studied with and without reward to monitor the effect of reinforcement. However, they do not sample deficits in contemplative attention—attention directed to problem solving and deductive logic in which stimuli may primarily serve as distractions. We are currently piloting a task that appears sensitive to these issues.

BRAIN SYSTEMS AND ATTENTION

While the information processing model coupled with cognitive tasks assists in describing the phenomenology of inattention, it does not define the neurophysiology of ADHD. Numerous brain structures and systems are involved in components of information processing, attention, abstraction, memory and action. An understanding of brain function in ADHD must include knowing where and how information is processed in specific brain regions. Fortunately, techniques in neurophysiology, neuroanatomy, and brain imaging in animals and humans are enhancing the study of brain function.

In one of the earliest and most influential models of neuropsychology, Luria suggested that all behavior involves the dynamic interaction of three functional units: *Unit 1* located in the brain stem reticular-activating system regulates arousal and alertness. *Unit 2*, localized in the postcentral cerebral regions, is essential to two fundamental cognitive processes: (1) perception, comprehension, and (2) interpretation processes of reception, analysis, storage, and integration of input. *Unit 3*, located in precentral cerebral regions, mediates (1) planning, execution, and evaluation of output, (2) overall regulation of voluntary action, and (3) delay and inhibition of behavior. Our model of ADHD dysfunction distinguishes subgroups based on a very similar system of classification that emerged phenomenologically from patient observation.

Processing of external stimuli begins with perception through sense organs, such as the eye. Thereafter, multiple neurofunctional systems are nearly simultaneously involved in identification, assessment of change, risk and significance. Much of this occurs prior to conscious processing of stimuli that are accorded importance. The anatomy of this processing is essential to understanding brain mechanisms of attention.

Visual images are focused on the retina and the stimuli are transmitted to the lateral geniculate bodies. Here, a synaptic connection links visual and auditory systems for aggregation of stimulus characteristics into perception of an event. Signals are then transmitted to the occipital cortex through the optical radiations that contain direct projections from rods and cones enabling feature detection. This series of events produces immediate imagery (memory) in a "sensory register" consisting of patterns, shapes, and features that can be further analyzed by aggregation for feature detection and recognition. The parietal lobe is engaged in monitoring the location of the stimulus in space and tracking its movement. Concurrently the stimulus is being transmitted to the hippocampus for analysis of change utilizing a rapid (<300 millisecond) recycling loop for comparison of novelty. Images detected at this level are transmitted forward and laterally toward the temporal lobes where most memory is stored. Generated patterns can be compared with those stored in memory, allowing the possibility of pattern recognition. Here, earliest memories are stored medially, while recent memories are more laterally.

Memory retrieval begins as a complex process of approximations that include pattern recognition, and associations encoded by concept, event, sequence, and affect. In associative cortical areas the visual, auditory, tactile, and olfactory components of the stimulus are interlinked in order to coordinate multisensory construction of an event. The limbic lobes become engaged in attribution of affective components to the experience. This may occur partially by the addition of emotion color to retrieval from long-term memory in the sensory register.

As the preattentional (often preconscious) characterization of a new stimulus event proceeds in immediate memory, a judgment is made regarding significance (opportunity and danger) in relation to the importance of the current thought or focus. A new stimulus may partially or completely interrupt overt processing of a prior idea, or may be minimally assessed and discarded. Much of the early formulation of this "shift/stay" judgment occurs in the nucleus accumbens which receives efferent stimuli from the prefrontal cortex and imputs the preoptical areas and the amygdala (Margulies, 1985).

More diffuse connections within the cortex are essential for contemplation and abstraction. Such complex processes require additional accessing of long-term memory and creative or novel restructuring essential for problem solving (Oades, 1987). This process of conscious direction of thinking and cognitive effort occurs on several levels of brain functioning.

As events are integrated that require further conscious processing (in short-term memory) the prefrontal cortex becomes engaged in judgments regarding meaning, prioritization, and response preparation. The prefrontal cortex performs much of the functions commonly attributed to executive ego functioning. It is engaged in determining what additional information might be needed in order to enhance analysis or clarify opportunity or risk. Similarly the prefrontal cortex is essential to the determination of judgement about the execution of response. For example, in the face of danger, the prefrontal cortex may assess that negotiation is a better strategy than running or fighting. Issues of competing values and commitments, empathy, and social learning must all be compared in making such a judgment. The prefrontal cortex executes volitional processing essential to self-directed or goal-directed behavior. This center is essential to decision making, value acquisition, and strategy formation. Lesions or damage to the prefrontal cortex are frequently associated with the inability to plan and direct willful, goal-oriented behavior, and utilize appropriate social judgment. The frontal (motor) cortex houses memories of learned response routines involving speech and movement. Well-rehearsed behaviors, memorized engrams or patterns of movement or thought can be accessed with minimal effort. New learning, or execution of a motor response when limited by peripheral muscle or orthopedia injury, requires greater cognitive effort and volitional attention.

Relevance to ADHD

Errors in information processing can occur anywhere along this cognitive sequence. Some cognitively impaired ADHD children have such breadth of attention that they cannot ignore any intense incoming stimuli. Deficits in filtering may burden attention by increasing the processing load. The capacity to sustain attention may be impaired at the level of the hippocampus (familiar things are inaccurately considered novel), or at the level of the nucleus accumbens which inadequately buffers against interruption of ongoing thought.

Perceptual misrepresentations, such as word reversals, or errors in feature detection, may reflect a deficit in the occipital cortex or the associative interface between occipital/temporal lobes, and may further burden attention. Some ADHD children with learning disabilities (LD) have modality-specific deficits in perceptual processing that impairs integration of visual, auditory, tactile, or proprioceptive stimuli. A deficit in one area may lead to excessive reliance on another modality. Many ADHD children may have recruitment and associative deficits; that is they seem unable to accurately link cross-modality stimuli.

Some children make inappropriate cognitive or amnestic associations; they are inconsistent in use and "localization" of encoding and retrieval strategies form long-term memory. Others have difficulty efficiently accessing encoded motor, language, and social routines. They "know" better than they can "do."

ADHD has been considered a disorder of prefrontal cortical functioning. The executive functions of planning, analysis, and judgment essential to deliberative organization of action are impaired in impulsive children. Their capacity for patience and delay, perquisite to reflection is compromised. While these deficits clearly exist, and are nearly pathogonomonic for ADHD, the impairment of executive functioning may reflect generalized dysregulation arousal or inhibitory processes or primary failures in cognitive integration. The cognitive deficits do not account for all of the problems of ADHD. The hyperactivity and inattention are clinically differentiable components of ADHD (Henker and Whalen, 1989). Similarly, the deficits in impulse control may have distinct phenomenology and neuropathology (Shapiro and Garfinkel, 1986; Gray et al. 1983).

NEUROCHEMISTRY OF ATTENTION

Neurochemical components of information processing

The major thesis here is that disturbance in the cardinal behaviors of ADHD may be due to distinct underlying mechanisms predominantly altered in different subtypes of ADHD. These behavioral pattern subtypes are not likely to be discovered by an epidemiological approach to diagnosis. Most clinical surveys employ contemporary scientific philosophy by applying *DSM-III-R* descriptive criteria for diagnosis of ADHD, LD, and other disorders. However, this level of descriptive analysis may be simultaneously too broad and too narrow to identify underlying neurobiological processes. The biological etiology may not be apparent at the level of diagnosis, whether or not there is a learning disability, conduct disorder (CD), or hyperactivity. Any of several distinct neuropathological deficits or etiologies may underlie any of these diagnoses. Hence, these neurobiological systems may be submerged at the level of descriptive, diagnostic psychiatry that summates the behavioral effect of genetic predisposition and life events. A detailed assessment of patients who have common characteristics that cross individual diagnoses may be the wave that reflects the underlying homogeneous current of neurobiological dysfunction.

These underlying patterns may emerge from a more "surgical" consideration of where along the cognitive sequence, from perception to behavior, a failure of integration or modulation occurs. Is there a difference between the neurobiology of perceptual filtering and the neurobiology of reflection? Are problems with long-term memory storage and retrieval distinct from difficulties in language expression? These specific components of cognition may all be subjugated to more general alterations in neurobiological processes that encompass mood, activity level, aggression, and thought; processes that reflect global influences, such as basal brain arousal and cortical inhibition. In developmental psychopathology, these general modulatory processes may be extraordinarily significant in that they alter attention and behavior and mature at different rates.

The connection between neurons occurs across synapses that communicate through release and response to selected neurotransmitters. Specific receptors located at structures within the brain are variably sensitive to specific neurotransmitters. Preattentional processing in immediate memory may be affected by changes in catecholamines such as dopamine that affects breadth of attention and norepinephrine that affects basal brain arousal. Norepinephrine (NE) is involved in hippocampal recognition of change. Dopamine (DA) is essential in modulating cortical breadth of attention and gating shift/stay functions in the nucleus accumbens—functions that are augmented by dopamine agonists such as Ritalin. Short-term memory is highly vulnerable to changes in acetylcholine and can be impaired by anticholinergic agents (Drachman and Leavitt, 1974). Long-term memory consolidation and some components of reinforcement may be augmented by norepinephrine.

Many other neurotransmitters indirectly affect attention. The capacity for behavioral inhibition is substantially mediated by brain serotonin from the central raphe nucleus. Processing of attachment and reward may involve endorphins. Modulation of anxiety may reflect action of gamma-aminobutyric acid (GABA) and sensitivity of benzodiazepine receptors. Thus, multiple neurotransmitter systems may be involved in integrated cognitive/behavioral functioning of normal and ADHD children. The relative balance of these neurotransmitters and these neurofunctional systems determines the modulation of behavior. The absolute levels of any neurotransmitter are unlikely to correlate with any pattern of complex behavior. It is not surprising that there is no singular neuropathology for the complex behavioral patterns of ADHD.

A major problem in neurobiological studies of ADHD has been the assumption that this is a unitary disorder that derives from a singular etiology. This simplistic presumption assumes that all symptoms must be due to deficient dopamine, because it clearly has a role in mediating the breadth of attention, the coordination of moments, and is affected by Ritalin. Alternatively, ADHD has been globally attributed to dysfunction in the prefrontal cortex because of impairments in impulsivity and judgment evidenced by these patients.

A more sophisticated formulation is that the behavior of ADHD may reflect the ratio of dopamine to norepinephrine. Since these neurotransmitter systems are functionally interrelated, compensatory balances between these systems must be considered. However, the levels of these neurotransmitters are site specific rather than global, and developmentally variable, and partially symptom specific. Changes in DA and NE may not produce a global increase or decrease in all of the 14 behaviors deemed diagnostic to ADHD. The behaviors that characterize ADHD may cluster into patterns organized along a spectrum of arousal and activity, inhibition and impulsivity, and attention and distractability. However, they may affect specific patterns of behavior and the effectiveness of cognitive operations; collectively the amines mediate overall level of activity and alter the capacity to restrain behavior and reflect. This formation has greater power since these neurotransmitter systems are functionally interrelated and compensatory relationships or balance between them alter cognition and behavior.

Dopamine

The DA hypothesis has been the major theory in ADHD since the pioneer work by Wender et al. (1971). Several lines of evidence suggest the possible significance of DA in this disorder: (1) Stimulant medications act via promoting the release of DA; (2) DA systems are clearly involved in the control of movement; (3) DA depletion in rat pups following administration of 6 hydroxydopamine produces a transient state of hyperactivity and impaired learning. Dopamine appears to play an important role in disorders of movement and thought, specifically Parkinson's disease (retarded movement) and Huntington's chorea (excessive movement). Norepinephrine plays a major role in disorders of energy and mood such as major depression and manic-depressive disorders.

Role of DA in attention

Dopamine acts on the nucleus accumbens and provides a barrier for preventing distraction. High levels of dopamine tend to close the gate of information processing from the hippocampus up to the prefrontal cortex, thereby enhancing the ability of the brain to continue attending to an ongoing subject.

While many neurotransmitter systems are involved in mediating the complex cognitive circuits involved in attention, dopamine clearly plays a substantial role in regulating breadth of attention and processes of cognitive selection. Medications that deplete dopamine (reserpine) or block dopamine receptors (haloperidol) can blunt attention (Campbell, 1982; Levy and Hobbes, 1988). Dopamine agonists, such as psychostimulants, narrow the attentional field, enhance the focus on and the salience of a stimulus, and diminish the power of distractions (Pelham et al., 1985; Sebrechts et al., 1986). Dopamine augmentation may act predominantly by increasing the focus of attention on an object, but have less effect on enhancing sustained processing of ongoing (stimulus-free) thoughts—which requires rejecting or ignoring intrusive stimuli (Zametkin & Rapoport, 1987).

Animal models of DA in attention

An animal model of ADHD was developed by destruction of presynaptic dopamine (DA) cells following 6-OHDA administration in neonatal rat pups producing hyperactivity and impaired T-maze learning (Shaywitz et al., 1976). These animals demonstrated normalization of activity and learning in response to treatment with D-amphetamine and MPH (Shaywitz et al., 1978; Sorenson et al., 1977). A strain of hyperactive rats (Fischer 344) has been identified that exhibits increased density of [^{3}H]sulpiride D-2 receptors in the caudate putamen (Kerr et al., 1988).

Effect of psychostimulants on DA and hormones

Methylphenidate acts primarily by releasing reserpine-sensitive presynaptic stores of DA and NE (Clemens and Fuller, 1979) but may alter the disposition of dopamine primarily by reducing catecholamine uptake (Ross et al., 1976). [^{3}H]methylphenidate binds with relatively high affinity to a site in the brain that is associated with the dopamine transport complex (Janowsky et al., 1985; Schweri et al., 1985). Amphetamine, however, has greater direct postsynaptic stimulating effect and inhibits monoamine oxidase (MAO) activity (Ferris et al., 1972).

Therapeutic response

Human studies of DA in ADHD have been less convincing of the possible relationship between DA and ADHD. Treatment of ADHD with the pure DA agonist piribedil did not produce clinical improvement (Brown et al., personal communication). The dopaminergic agent Sinemet (L-dopa and carbidopa) was only mildly effective in improving inattention and classroom restlessness during a three-week placebo-controlled trial in 8 ADHD boys. Urinary 3-hydroxy-4-methoxyphenethyl glycol (MHPG) and vanillmandelic acid (VMA) secretion increased with treatment but did not correlate with changes in individual clinical improvement (Langer et al., 1981). Similarly, only mild improvement with Sinemet was noted in adults with residual ADHD. Separate response patterns may occur from specific pharmacological agents depending on their mechanism of action. Dopamine agonists may not improve "ADHD" as globally measured by Conners ratings, but may narrow the breadth of attention in highly distractible individuals.

Direct measures of DA in ADHD

Despite the implications from pharmacological studies that DA affects breadth and persistence of attention, studies in children with ADHD have failed to demonstrate a DA deficit in ADHD (Rogeness et al., 1989).

Cerebrospinal fluid studies of catecholamine levels performed without (Shetty and Chase, 1976) and following probenecid administration (Shaywitz et al., 1977) did not show widely abnormal levels of homovanillic acid (HVA), a metabolite of DA, in relation to controls, although the ratio of HVA/probenecid was significantly decreased (Shaywitz et al., 1977). Urinary HVA levels have not been found to be abnormal in subjects with ADHD (Wender et al., 1971). Urinary HVA is not altered by treatment with D-amphetamine (Shaywitz et al., 1982). Norepinephrine may modulate the sensitivity of receptors to other neurotransmitters including DA (Cooper et al., 1986).

There are several possible explanations for the failure to find a postulated DA deficit in ADHD. These may reflect variability in localization and generalization of dopamine deficits and diversity in the neurobiological origins of ADHD subtypes.

Localization and specificity: Within the brain, DA is organized in specific tracts that serve functionally defined purposes. Nigrostriatal tracts are involved in control of movement while mesolimbic tracts affect neuroendocrine functioning. Several groups of DA receptors existing in the brain respond selectively to differential agonists or antagonists. D1 receptors stimulate adenylate cyclase and respond to SKF 38393, D2 receptors function as brain autoreceptors that inhibit adenylate cyclase and respond to agonists such as quinperole and antagonists such as sulpiride (Cooper et al., 1986). Thus, even CSF measures may reflect such a large aggregate of DA functioning that a selective deficit relevant to attention may be obscured. Most peripheral (plasma and urinary) measures of DA or its metabolites (HVA, DOPAC) will reflect autonomic rather than central functioning.

Clinical subtypes: Some attention deficits may be due to alternations in basal brain arousal or cortical inhibition systems that primarily reflect the effect of other neurotransmitters, and thereby dilute the salience of a dopamine deficit that might predominate in those ADHD children with a primary attentional filtering deficit.

Norepinephrine

Role of NE in arousal, attention, and habituation

In general, norepinephrine in concert with dopamine, serotonin, and glucocorticoids constitute general modulating neurotransmitters that affect processes of arousal. The locus coeruleus fires during transition states requiring arousal, such as awakening; continuous firing produces a state of vigilant arousal. Excessive NE firing may erroneously label routine stimuli as significant, thereby, increasing the amount of information requiring active processing and diminishing selective attention (Carli et al., 1983; Hunt et al., 1988). In children with immature behavioral inhibition systems, this increase in unbalanced arousal systems may result in excessive, poorly directed activity. The diffuse neuroanatomical distribution of NE suggests it functions as a neuromodulator of many integrative cortical processes, rather than as a discrete neurotransmitter for highly specific actions. The connection between arousal processes, anxiety, and impulsivity has physiological as well as psychological basis (Gray et al., 1983).

Animal models of NE in attention

Recently, Bloom and collaborators studied the spontaneous firing of the locus coeruleus (LC, the site of most NE cell bodies) in unanesthetized, freely moving rats and monkeys (Aston-Jones and Bloom, 1981; Foote and Bloom, 1979; Foote et al., 1980). During the vegetative activities of grooming and feeding, the LC was quiescent. However, when a novel stimulus of light or sound was introduced, the LC abruptly fired. This activation preceded and facilitated the response of other neurons to external stimuli. Pharmacologic or anatomic destruction of the locus coeruleus or its NE projections in the dorsal bundle prior to animals being trained in a continuous reinforcement paradigm inhibits the process of extinction during subsequent nonreward (Mason and Inversen, 1978). NE has a role in facilitating reinforcement at the level of cellular physiology. Intracellular pulsatile infusion of NE can alter and entrain cell firing rates (Stein et al., 1974). The mechanism for this dorsal bundle extinction effect (DBEE) reflects an increasing distractibility during the learning task, producing a state analogous to intermittent reward which has a longer extinction phase. Such distractibility is, perhaps, clinically similar to the inattention of ADHD children, whose symptoms may reflect a noradrenergic imbalance (Hunt et al., 1988).

Model of NE effects in attention

A role for NE in animal models of attention is suggested by the effects of neurotoxin DSP-4, which selectively destroys NE projections from the locus coeruleus. This decreased NE reduces avoidance acquisition in rats subjected to distracting stimuli (Archer et al., 1981). One model for the neurophysiology of ADHD suggests that a deficiency of inhibitory noradrenaline in the cortex or an alteration in sensory alpha-$_2$-adrenoreceptor number and affinity enables unmodulated NE firing, thereby, producing a hypervigilant state. Psychostimulants produce an increase in intraneuronal noradrenaline in the brainstem that serves as a substrate for phenylethylamine-N-methyl-transferase, while clonidine directly inhibits locus coeruleus firing. The primary deficit may occur at the locus coeruleus or in the alpha-$_2$ receptor response to adrenaline (Mefford and Potter, 1989).

Effects of psychostimulants on NE

Acute administration of MPH produces a transient rise in NE, epinephrine (EPI), and growth hormone (GH), while chronic administration has little effect on GH release (Greenhill, 1981; Joyce et al., 1984). A single acute dose of Ritalin increases plasma GH in ADHD children (Shaywitz E, 1984). Chronic treatment with psychostimulants has not produced a clear model of catecholamine effects requisite for a clinical response. Despite their clinical similarity, Ritalin and D-amphetamine have contrasting or inconsistent effects on excretion of urinary NE and its metabolites (Brown et al., 1981).

Chronic treatment with MPH increased urinary NE, NMN, and DOPAC in an initial study (Zametkin, 1985a), but results could not be replicated in a second study (Zametkin and Hamburger, 1988). Ritalin did *not* significantly increase urinary MHPG excretion (Zametkin and Hamburger, 1988). In the combined sample, no differences in any catecholamines occurred in 13 responders (>50% lower parent ratings) versus 8 nonresponders to Ritalin (x dose = 0.74 ng/kg) for two weeks (Zametkin and Hamburger, 1988). This contrasted with earlier findings of an increase in NE and NMN, and a decrease in NE turnover, and did not support earlier conclusions that a two-week washout from Ritalin was insufficient for neurochemical stabilization. Another study reported that a large sample of nonresponders had significant decreases in urinary MHPG, but the fluorometric assay used may have lacked sufficient sensitivity to reach this conclusion (Yu-Can and Yu-Feng, 1984). The large baseline differences in this sample, and that of Shekim (1979, 1983) and Brown et al. (1981) make the data on urinary monoamine metabolites difficult to interpret in children with ADHD (Kahn and Dekirmenjian, 1981).

Chronic treatment with MPH may diminish postsynaptic noradrenergic receptor sensitivity, as suggested by reduced GH response following a single oral dose of clonidine given during MPH treatment (Hunt et al., 1984). MPH may also diminish the availability of NE in certain brain regions such as the rat hippocampus via a reduction in the synthesis of Dopa.

Effects of antidepressants on NE

The role of the NE system in ADHD is suggested by the therapeutic efficacy of other noradrenergic agents in ADHD. Imipramine (Rapoport et al., 1974), desipramine (DMI) (Donnelly et al., 1986), and MAO-A inhibitors (Zametkin et al., 1985) may increase NE available in the synapse. Presynaptic autoreceptor-negative feedback inhibition reduce endogenous NE turnover.

Effects of clonidine on NE

Clonidine may downregulate NE release in highly aggressive, overaroused ADHD children (Hunt et al., 1985, 1986, 1987). As an alpha-$_2$-adrenergic agonist, clonidine acts preferentially on the presynaptic noradrenergic receptor (Titeler and Seeman, 1980), causing a negative feedback inhibition of NE release. In low doses, clonidine diminishes endogenous NE production by inhibiting the activity of NE cell bodies concentrated in the LC (Cedarbaum and Aghajanian, 1976; Starke and Altman, 1973) and indirectly decreasing LC firing (Aghajanian and Bunney, 1977; Starke and Altman, 1973). Clonidine inhibits stress-induced (phasic) NE release, thus decreasing plasma NE and MHPG (Charney et al., 1982,; Hunt et al., 1984; Roth et al., 1982). A single challenge dose of clonidine stimulates GH release and reduces plasma NE in ADHD patients (Gil-Ad et al., 1979; Hunt et al., 1984). This contrasts with the physiological effect of yohimbine, an alpha-$_2$-noradrenergic antagonist that releases NE (Charney et al., 1984; Hunt et al, in submission).

Direct measures of NE in ADHD

Studies of NE in ADHD suggest that there may be two groups of ADHD children, one high and the other low in baseline NE turnover.

Urinary Excretion. The NE metabolite 3-methoxy-4-hydroxyphenylglycol (MHPG) is a useful index of NE activity in the brain, since 50–80% of the urinary MHPG is of central origin (Kopin, 1978). Studies of urinary MHPG excretion in children with ADHD have produced contradictory findings. Shekim's studies (1979, 1983) of pretreatment urinary MHPG excretion in ADHD children demonstrated a bimodal distribution, with the majority exhibiting reduced 24-h excretion (Shekim et al., 1982). Most ADHD children demonstrate diminished MHPG excretion compared with controls; a smaller percent excrete increased MHPG. Similarly, Serfontein (1984) found decreased MHPG levels in ADHD. Kahn and Dekirmenjian (1981) reported subjects with predominantly increased urinary MHPG excretion, although their control subjects showed high baseline levels of urinary MHPG. Clinical studies have shown decreased urinary levels of MHPG following treatment with D-amphetamine (Brown et al., 1981; Shekim et al., 1983; Zametkin, et al., 1985b).

Plasma Levels of Enzymes. Dopamine beta hydroxylase (DBH) is a genetically controlled enzyme located on chromosome 9q34, that converts DA to NE in NE terminals (Craig et al., 1988; Kobayashi and Shohmori, 1989). The relationship between peripheral DBH and catecholamine function in the brain is not established. Rogeness et al. (1989) has reported low or absent DBH levels in two groups of conduct-disordered children who tended to be schizoid, sociopathic, and antisocial, but not necessarily aggressive (Rogeness, personal communication). DBH has been reported to be low in ADHD (Rapoport et al., 1974) and to be elevated (23%) by treatment with MPH.

As with DA, peripheral measures of NE may reflect central nervous system (CNS) neurophysiology. However, to the extent that peripheral and central activity correlate, these findings suggest two distinct neurobiological patterns in ADHD. One subtype of ADHD may be high in locus coeruleus–norepinephrine (LC-NE) release and perhaps be overaroused. Another subgroup, with low LC–NE activation, may have decreased cortical processing reflecting diminished DA inhibition. Collectively these neuropharmacological data suggest that ADHD may be improved by medications that affect both NE and DA functioning. DA agents may be more effective in directly modulating selective attention while NE agents may primarily diminish excessive arousal and activity that indirectly affect cognition.

Serotonin

Serotonin functioning may be most relevant to inhibitory and aggressive processes in ADHD. Serotonin has been implicated in obsessionality, aggression, and suicidality. Medications such as chlomipramine reduce obsessional symptoms by altering serotonin levels, primarily by reducing 5-hydroxytryptamine (5-HT) reuptake (Leonard et al., 1989). ADHD children may represent the opposite end of the clinical spectrum of focusing, from obsessionality to distractability and aggression. In analogous neurochemical processes, ADHD children may be underinhibited, possibly reflecting a deficit in cortical sertonin.

Aggression is one of the most prominent and ominous behaviors exhibited by many ADHD children (Hinshaw et al., 1989; Millich et al., 1982). A model of affective, impulsive aggression in humans must incorporate an interaction between arousal systems, partially mediated by NE, and inhibition systems reflective of serotonergic inhibition of action (Burrows et al., 1988; Van Praag et al., 1987). Many models for human aggression derive from extrapolations regarding predatory and affective aggression in some animal species that reflect interaction of acetylcholine, norepinephrine, and serotonergic neuroregulation. The most consistent evidence suggests the importance of serotonergic activity in modulation of aggressive behavior. Diminished CSF levels of the serotonin metabolite 5-hydroxyindolacetic acid (5-HIAA) have been replicated in studies of aggressive adults (Brown et al., 1978), and in the self-directed aggression of suicide attempters. However, aggressive behavior in humans probably reflects the relative balance of multiple neurotransmitter systems, including the degree of arousal (that may be noradrenergically mediated) in relation to the capacity for behavioral inhibition (nonimpulsivity) which may be increased by serotonin. Between these general variables lies affective regulation and the capacity for cognitive analysis of stressful situations.

From phenomenological studies of aggressive conduct disorder in children, Price and Dodge (1987) have postulated the presence of instrumental and impulsive patterns of aggression. Instrumentally aggressive children utilize bullying and intimidation as a means of social persuasion and may lack alternative negotiating strategies. Affective or impulsively aggressive children may fight instantly when they become irritated or angry and be unable to access known alternative strategies of conflict resolution.

Disturbances in serotonin systems have also been implicated by direct measures in ADHD. Wender (1971) studied 14 children diagnosed as having minimal brain dysfunction (MBD) and found no correlation between peripheral serotonin levels and hyperactivity. In three patients, however, diminished serotonin appeared to correlate with excessive hyperactivity. Diminished platelet serotonin levels occurred in approximately 50% of children with MBD. Coleman (1971) determined serotonin concentration in whole blood of 25 hyperactive children. A decreased concentration of platelet 5-hydroxyindole was found in 88% of this group. Two of the more severely affected patients who subsequently demonstrated increased attention span following milieu therapy showed an increase in peripheral 5-HIAA, suggesting an association between diminished serotonin and hyperactivity. Rapoport et al. (1974) found normal blood serotonin levels in hyperactive children. While both MPH and imipramine improved behavior, imipramine alone lowered blood serotonin levels. Other studies in children who were both hyperactive and retarded showed that they had lower blood serotonin levels than controls. Serotonin appeared to increase as behavior following nonpharmacological treatment regimens (Greenberg and Coleman, 1976).

Much of these earlier studies are difficult to interpret due to methodological problems related to localization of serotonin in platelets and fragility of platelet membranes. Whole blood serotonin may be more reliable, but remains of limited value as an index of CNS activity since most peripheral serotonin comes from the gut. Alternative measures of serotonin include [^{3}H]imipramine binding to serotonin receptors in platelets or dynamic measures of serotonin using the fenfluramine challenge. However, these studies may not be revealing in generalized ADHD, but might be relevant to the subgroup of ADHD who are primarily underinhibited.

AROUSAL AND INHIBITION: EFFECT ON ATTENTION AND ACTIVITY

We postulate a reciprocal balance between arousal systems and inhibition systems. Arousal systems increase both the amount of information to be further processed and the amount of activity to be emitted, while inhibition systems inhibit behavior, and thereby allow analysis, judgment, and selection of action. In the cardiovascular system as well as in the brain, NE and 5-HT often have opposing behavioral effects. Pharmacological alteration of norepinephrine affects the levels of serotonin (Leckman et al., 1984; Sugita et al., 1989). One group of ADHD children may become distracted and hyperactive because they are mainly overaroused. This may reflect primarily overactivity in noradrenergic release in the locus coeruleus, that secondarily affects the hippocampus, and increases the information considered novel or significant. Other ADHD children may have predominant difficulties inhibiting their activity, and secondarily become overactive, and poorly focused. They bypass utilization of the analytic capacities and have little opportunity for reflection. A third group have primary impairments in actual cognitive activities, including stimulus filtering and prioritization or gating of conscious attention. This may reflect principally a dopamine deficit operating at the level of the sensory screening (somatosensory cortex) and cognitive gating in the nucleus accumbens. Additionally, motivation and willful direction of attention requires a sense of goals and values—a reason to focus effort. Some children who present with inattention and overactivity may have fundamental impairment in experience of rewards and linking these to behavior.

Concept of arousal

Any concept taken from cellular neurobiology and applied to gross levels of behavior is subject to vagueness and distortion. On a cellular level, arousal implies activation of cell firing. On a behavioral level, arousal implies overall activation of the organisms. Luria (1973) utilized the concepts of arousal to describe generalized CNS activation arising from the basal brain reticular-activating system. However, even that generalization is subject to brain regional differentiation. If the cortex fails to respond to this activation due to immaturity, structural abnormality, or alteration in metabolic pathways (as suggested by Mefford and Potter, 1989), cognition and behavior may become disorganized. Activation at the level of the basal brain may overwhelm cortical processing, evidenced as filtering and dampening of extraneous incoming stimuli, maintaining cognitive set, analysis and selection of appropriate, goal-directed response.

The arousal system has both baseline and response components. One component of response is the recognition of change. A novel event or stimulus requires additional preconscious or conscious analysis. Within the hippocampus rapid memory loops continuously compare current stimuli with previous, familial events to determine change. Stimuli that have changed are identified and transmitted for greater analysis. Baseline levels of arousal affect a threshold for identification of stimuli as novel and for emission of activity (speech, movement, aggression). Additionally, response arousal, reflecting the impact of stress, frustration, fear, excitement, or anticipation can impact cognition and behavior. Some ADHD children function well when calm, but decompensate under the stress of excessive stimulation, emotional excitement, or performance stress.

Anatomy of arousal

In the basal brain, arousal occurs at the level of the reticular formation and the locus coeruleous and is substantially mediated by norepinephrine (Bloom et al., 1985). Regulation of arousal occurs in the reticular activating system and locus coeruleous (LC) where 80% of norepinephrine cell bodies are located. Projections from the LC include dendrites extending into the cerebral cortex, the cerebellum, the hippocampus via the dorsal bundle, and to the neuroendocrine system via the ventral bundle.

Physiology of arousal

Firing of the locus coeruleous induces a state of alert arousal. LC firing occurs in response to novel stimuli and activates secondary analytic processes to facilitate identification, determination of threat or opportunity, and initiate analysis of significance and response. At the level of the cortex, variations in arousal have significant effects on attention and activity. Diminished arousal during fatigue or depression slows cognitive rate, diminishes effort and perceptual and analytic acuity. Moderate increases in arousal in the mature brain can enhance attention by increasing alertness and focus. Moderate stress or heightened reward or interest may enhance receptive and analytic capacity and improve processing efficiency of effortful cognition. Excessive arousal, especially in an immature cortex, can disturb attentional focusing by diminishing the effectiveness of the primary perceptual filters.

Animal models of arousal

As evident from work by Bloom and colleagues (Foote et al., 1980), locus coeruleous stimulation in unanesthetized monkeys induces a state of alert activation and visual scanning. NE stimulation affecting the hippocampus labels stimuli as being "new" or "changed," thereby necessitating further cognitive analysis by cortical processing systems (Gray, 1982; Quay, 1984). Thus, excessive NE release appears to burden and ultimately overload intact information processing systems. In the mature animal, NE stimulation also activates compensatory (cortical) behavioral inhibition systems, producing a state of controlled, prepared vigilance. However, in developing children, this excessive basal brain activation, unbalanced by sufficient prefrontal cortical inhibition may produce a state of hyperactive behavior in which many stimuli are deemed significant and require further processing or generate excessive response. Thus, the high level of basal arousal may impair cortical processing and intensify behavioral activity, including restlessness, fidgeting, and overactivity.

Relevance to ADHD

For an ADHD child in such a hyperaroused state, trivial stimuli become distractions to more pertinent ones and attention is repeatedly shifted from stimuli to stimuli. Frustration that accompanies trying to process too much unselected information may lead to secondary oppositionality as a child attempts to ward off the task demands (such as homework) that have become cognitively overwhelming and emotionally demoralizing. In such a state, an ADHD child would rather fight than work. The fight refocuses attention, redefines identity and purpose, and eventually produces a release of energy that diminishes hyperarousal. After a 2-hour fight the ADHD child frequently completes his assignment in 15 minutes.

The concept of inhibition

Another major neurofunctional system that affects multiple aspects of behavior is the behavioral inhibition system (Gray, 1982). If arousal is the neurophysiological equivalent of acceleration and activation, inhibition is analogous to the neural brake.

Physiology of inhibition

On a cellular level, many neurotransmitters inhibit cellular firing on a behavioral level. Throughout much of the cardiovascular system, NE activates vasoconstriction while serotonin facilitates vasodilation. Similarly, on the gross behavioral level, emission of many forms of behavior are delayed or aborted by the behavioral inhibition system. Behavioral inhibition is essential to the expression and direction of sexual activity, appetite, and motor activity and aggression. Additionally, inhibitory processes affect persistence of thought and complex behavior as evidenced by excessive inhibition in obsessive compulsive disorder.

The site of the altered inhibitory process in obsessive compulsive disorder (OCD) and ADHD may differ. The cingulate gyrus functions as an internal "motivation detector" (prioritizer) for innate impulses; the striatum functions as an external stimulus transmitter (prioritizer) for external cortical signal content. Both structures have inputs on the globus pallidus that have inhibitory effects on the thalamus. In OCD, excessive firing of the cingulate gyrus decreases the inhibitory action of the globus pallidus (GP), thereby liberating the thalamic transmission of basal brain impulses (grooming and territorial protection) to the cortex. Activation of the GP via serotonin diminishes obsessionality; diminished GP output could increase obsessionality. Serotonergic medications (chlomipramine) ultimately reduce serotonergic receptors (reduces inhibitory control) in the GP thereby facilitating GP inhibition of thalamic impulses that can repetitively dominate thought (Archer et al., 1981). Similar behavioral inhibition processes in ADHD may occur at the level of the striatum and involve prefrontal cortical systems (Rapoport et al., 1988).

Attention also requires inhibition to appropriately delay activity to allow reflection and consideration of response options. An active, albeit inhibitory, process is also involved in letting go of a thought or cognitive focus in order to shift attention to a new subject (Posner, 1986).

This component of the behavioral inhibition system may occur at several levels of brain function. Caudate-based inhibitory processes act to control movements. The major site of cortical inhibition is the prefrontal cortex that is involved in judgment, information searching, prioritization, and inhibiting behavior pending adequate consideration.

Neurochemistry of inhibition

Much of the behavioral inhibition system appears to be serotonergically mediated. If NE is the principal behavioral activating neurotransmitter, serotonin is the predominant central behavioral inhibiting neurotransmitter. While an increase in serotonin may be associated with obsessional thinking, a decrease in serotonin is associated with impulsive action, aggression, and perhaps fragmented or inadequately persistent thought processes. A primary deficit in serotonergically mediated inhibition systems may constitute an alternative route to ADHD. Other neurotransmitters also have profound effects on behavioral inhibition, including GABA systems, which appear to be functionally related to the experience of anxiety.

Relevance to ADHD

Many children with symptoms of ADHD, especially those characterized by impulsivity without high levels of arousal, may have a deficit in response inhibition. They act and speak without thinking. Frequently their fist or words hit their opponent before their thoughts can reach their hand. They are almost surprised at their reflexive aggressive actions. They cannot override the expression of their needs, affects, or drives. Sometimes this is expressed as excessive emotional need for support and attention—frequently labeled as "immaturity." Other times the lack of inhibition is behaviorally evident as an inability to cease behaviors such as talking, playing with a pencil, or eating. In the face of inadequate inhibition, their needs or impulses are tyrannical. They blurt out inappropriate thoughts, tease and "unintentionally" insult peers, and require the vigilance of teachers. They require continual external monitoring to maintain focus and avoid danger to themselves and others. Their uninhibited behavior is evidenced in their lack of direction of activity. While they do not exhibit the excessive energy of the highly aroused ADHD patients, who do not have a primary cognitive deficit in information processing, they qualify as ADHD by their impulsivity, fidgetiness, and inattention.

Concept of reward

The reward system is another important component of attention and information system (Haenlein and Caul, 1987). This system is involved in attribution of emotional significance relevant to motivation and short- and long-term goals. These rewards may be external (such as praise, smiles, nickels, or ice cream) of internal, as defined by one's sense of identity or values. While initially connected to a sense of pleasure and gratification, values that direct subjective attention ultimately comprise a sense of personal identity and long-term ambition. Reinforcement initially reflects emotional processes of attachment that during development shift from preoccupation with parental approval to investment in curiosity, intimacy, and task performance. The ability to willfully direct attention requires a sense of identity, goals, and rewards that constitutes a framework for prioritization of effort. This competence requires input from limbic as well as cognitive systems.

An inability to experience reward occurs at two different levels. Cognitive impairment may reduce the ability to integrate values and social awareness into thought processes. Thus, it may be difficult to assign meaning to rewards, resulting in no sense of fulfillment or pleasure. In some children, however, the reward system itself may be intact, with meaning assigned to specific events and emotions attached to specific behavioral responses, yet the child remains unable to access the system.

Neurochemical interactions

Thus, an appreciation of brain function and attention requires consideration of events at the level of the synapse of neurotransmitters and neuropeptides that bridge the action of nerve cells and must be considered in the context of brain functional systems, especially those involved in perception, arousal, cognitive processing, inhibition, and reward. Alterations in specific neurotransmitter systems such as norepinephrine, dopamine, serotonin, and others, may variably affect attention through effects on brain processes of arousal, cognition, or inhibition. Similarly, anatomical or developmental disturbances in specific brain regions or brain functional systems may also alter attention competence. This model of brain function suggests that there may be multiple ways in which children come to exhibit similar behavioral symptoms of overactivity, inattention, distractibility, and impulsivity. However, it also suggests that these very sites of brain dysfunction may optimally respond to different medications; medications directed toward decreasing noradrenergic activation (clonidine), increasing dopaminergic functioning in cognition (Ritalin or amphetamine), or perhaps, eventually, medications that increase serotonergic functioning or enhance the experience of reward.

Relevance to ADHD

Severe deficits in reward processing occur in pervasive psychiatric disorders such as autism and in atypical personality development. Some ADHD children demonstrate deficits in processes of consequence or significance. Even when unstressed and relaxed they are relatively unresponsive to consequences of praise or punishment. They seem indifferent to the emotional significance of their actions. Unless they are threatened with immediate punishment or pain, their actions have little meaningful direction. They may become obsessively preoccupied with a redundant task such as a puzzle and protest violently if interrupted. But their thoughts and behavior appear disorganized due to a lack of emotional rather than cognitive integration.

CONCLUSION

Attention deficit hyperactivity disorder has several cardinal components: high levels of activity, impaired attention, and impulsivity. These related disturbances may have somewhat distinctive neurochemical mediation. The diversity of underlying neurochemical processes may explain the failure to find a singular deficit in any one catecholamine system or a unique pharmacological treatment in the multiplex syndrome of ADHD. Primary cognitive deficits may occur at the level of perceptual filtering, or of networking essential to cross-modality integration, encoding and decoding from memory, analysis, judgment, and response selection. Information processing models may assist in defining the temporal sequences involved in cognition. The standard stimulant-sensitive tasks assess the response to specific stimuli and some components of literal recall, but do not monitor attention contributions to processes of contemplation, abstraction, and problem solving. Cognitive impairments in ADHD patients who are primarily distractible may reflect a dopaminergic deficit that affects breadth of perception (selective attention) and attentional gating (sustained attention). Psychostimulants facilitate attentional focusing and increase the "strength" or valence of a perceived stimulus.

Disturbances in noncognitive dimensions of brain functioning may indirectly affect attention and activity. High levels of basal brain arousal may lead to frenetic activity and impair information processing by overloading the amount and intensity of stimuli that are deemed novel or important. In this subgroup, impulsive and aggressive actions may be secondary to overburdened processing, low frustration tolerance, and high levels of emitted behavior. Excessive arousal may reflect primarily exaggerated noradrenergic activity in the locus coeruleus projected to basal and cortical brain regions. This hyperarousal appears clinically responsive to clonidine in doses that reduce noradrenergic turnover.

Impairment in the behavioral inhibition system may constitute the primary pathology in another subgroup of ADHD patients. Diminished inhibition may also lead to fidgety, unfocused activity, inability to sustain attention, and impulsive, unconsidered activity. Much of behavioral inhibition may be mediated by serotonin, a neurotransmitter implicated in disorders of aggression and obsessionality. Medications that act principally on serotonin systems may be helpful in this subgroup.

Other general brain processes, such as the capacity to process reward, affect, control anxiety, and experience meaning also affect attention and behavior in ADHD. The relative functioning of multiple neurotransmitters must be simultaneously considered in understanding this complex disorder. Clinical research, neurochemical studies, response to acute pharmacological challenge, and chronic treatment may help illuminate brain processes in ADHD. Molecular genetics may assist in defining transmission and ontogeny. Brain imaging techniques may clarify localization of neurofunctional processes in this spectrum disorder. However, these research techniques may not be productive in a heterogeneous population of ADHD with undifferentiated underlying pathophysiology. Hopefully this or related models of ADHD will provide a clinical foundation for seeking neurobiological correlates.

ACKNOWLEDGMENTS

Funding for this reseach and paper was provided through the March of Dimes.

We extend appreciation to Brad Anderson, M.D., Andrew Ragland, and Jeff Ryu for contributions to this article.

REFERENCES

Aghajanian, G.K., Bunney, B.S. (1977), Dopamine "autoreceptors": pharmacological characterization by microintophoretic single cell recording studies. *Nauwyn-Schmiedberg's Arch Pharmacol*, 297:1–7.

Archer, T., Ogren, S.O. & Johanssen, C. (1981), The acute effects of *p*-chloroamphetamine on the retention of fear conditioning in the rat: evidence for a role of serotonin in memory consolidation. *Neurosci. Lett.*, 25(1):75–81.

Aston-Jones, G. & Bloom, F.E. (1981), Norepinephrine-containing locus coeruleus neurons in behaving rats exhibit pronounced responses to non-noxious environmental stimuli. *J. Neurosci.*, 1(8):887–900.

Bloom, F.E. (1978), Central noradrenergic systems: physiology and pharmacology. In: *Psychopharmacology: A 20-Year Progress Report*, eds. M.E. Lipton, K.C. Killam, & A. DiMascio. New York: Raven Press, pp. 131–142.

—————— Battenberg, E., Ferron, A., Mancillas, J.R., Milner, R.J., Siggins, G. & Sutcliffe, J.G. (1985), Neuropeptides: interactions and diversities. *Recent Prog. Horm. Res.*, 41:339–367.

Brown, G.L., Ebert, M.H., Hunt, R.D. & Rapoport, J.L. (1981), Urinary 3-methoxy-4-hydroxyphenyl-glycol and homovanillic acid response to D-amphetamine in hyperactive children. *Biol. Psychiatry*, 16:779–787.

—————— Goodwin, F.K., Ballenger, J.C., Goyer, P.F., & Major, L.F. (1978), CSF amine metabolites in human aggression. *Scientific Proceedings of the American Psychiatric Association*, 131:88.

Brown, R.T., Borden, K.A., Wynne, M.E., Spunt, A.L. & Clingerman, S.R. (1987), Compliance with pharmacological and cognitive treatments for attention deficit disorder. *J. Am. Acad. Child Adolesc. Psychiatry*, 26(4):521–526.

Burrows, G.D., McIntyre, I.M., Judd, F.K. & Norman, T.R. (1988), Clinical effects of serotonin reuptake inhibitors in the treatment of depressive illness. *J. Clin. Psychiatry*, 49(suppl):18–22.

Campbell, S.B. (1982), A multidimensional assessment of parent-identified behavior problem toddlers. *J. Abnorm. Child Psychol.*, 10:569–591.

Carli, M., Robbins, T.W., Evenden J.L. & Everitt, B.J. (1983), Effects of lesions to ascending noradrenergic neurones on performance of a 5 choice serial reaction task in rats: Implication for theories of dorsal noradrenergic bundle function based on selective attention and arousal. *Behav. Brain Res.* 9(3):361–380.

Cedarbaum, J.M. & Aghajanian, G.K. (1976), Noradrenergic neurons of the locus coeruleus: inhibition by epinephrine and activation by the alpha-antagonist piperoxan. *Brain Res.*, 1112:412–419.

Charney, D.S., Heninger, G.R., Breier, A.: *Noradrenergic Function in Panic Anxiety: Effects of Yohimbine in Healthy Subjects and Patients with Agoraphobia and Panic Disorder*. Arch. Gen. Psychiatry, 41:751–763, 1984.

—— —— Sternberg, D.E., Hafstad, K.M., Giddings, S. & Landis, D.H. (1982), Adrenergic receptor sensitivity in depression: Effects of clonidine in depressed patients and healthy subjects. *Arch. Gen. Psychiatry,* 39(3):290–294.

Coleman, M. (1971), Serotonin levels in whole blood of hyperactive children. *J. Pediatr.,* 78:985–990.

Cooper, J.R., Bloom, F.E. & Roth, R.H. (1986), The Biological Basis of Neuropharmacology, 5th Ed. New York: Oxford University Press, pp. 86–105.

Craig, S.P., Buckle, V.J., Lamouroux, A., Mallet, D.J. & Craig, I.W. (1988), Localization of the human dopamine beta hydroxylase (DBH) gene to chromosome 9q34. *Cytogen. Cell Genetics,* 48(1):48–50.

Donnelly, M., Zametkin, A.J, Rapoport, J.L., Ismond, H.R., Weingartner, H., Lane, E., Oliver, J., Linnoila M. & Potter, W.Z. (1986), Treatment of childhood hyperactivity with desipramine: Plasma drug concentration, cardiovascular effects, plasma and urinary catecholamine levels, and clinical response. *Clin. Pharmacol. Ther.,* 39:72–81.

Douglas, V.I., Barr, R.G., O'Niel, M.E. et al. (1986), Short term effects of methylphenidate on the cognitive, learning and academic performance of children with attention deficit disorder in the laboratory and in the classroom. *J. Child Psychol. Psychiatry,* 27:191–212.

Drachman, D.A. & Leavitt, J. (1974), Human memory and the cholinergic system: A relationship to aging? *Arch. Neurol.,* 30:113–121.

Edelman, G.M. (1987), *Neural Darwinism: The Theory of Neuronal Group Selection*. New York: Basic Books.

Ferris R., Tang F. & Maxwell R. (1972), A comparison of the capacities of isomers of amphetamine, deoxypiradol, and methylphenidate to inhibit the uptake of tritiated catecholamines into rat, cerebral cortex slices, synaptosomal preparations of rat nerves, and rabbit aorta. *J. Pharmacol. Exp. Therap.,* 181:407–416.

Foote, S. & Bloom, F.E. (1979). Activity of norepinephrine-containing locus coeruleus neurons in the unanesthetized squirrel monkey. In: *Catecholamines: Basic and Clinical Frontiers,* eds. E. Usdin, I. Kopin, & J. Barchas. New York: Pergamon Press, pp. 625–627.

—— Aston-Jones, G. & Bloom, F.E. (1980), Impulse activity of locus coeruleus neurons in awake rats and squirrel monkeys is a function of sensory stimulation and arousal. *Proc. Natl. Acad. Sci. U.S.A.,* 77:3033–3037.

Gil-Ad, I., Topper, E. & Laron, Z. (1979), Oral clonidine as a growth hormone stimulation test. *Lancet,* 2:278–279.

Gray, J.A. (1982), The Neuropsychology of Anxiety: An Enquiry into the Functions of the Septal-Hippocampal System. New York: Oxford Press.

—— Owen, S., Davis, N. & Tsaltas, E. (1983), Psychological and physiological relations between anxiety and impulsivity. In: *Biological Bases of Sensation Seeking, Impulsivity, and Anxiety,* ed. M. Zuckerman. Hillside, NJ: Erlbaum Associates Publishers, pp. 181–217.

Greenberg, A. & Coleman, M. (1976), Depressed 5-hydroxyindole levels associated with hyperactive and aggressive behavior: Relationship to drug response. *Arch. Gen. Psychiatry,* 33:331–338.

Greenhill, L.L. et al. (1981), Growth hormone, prolactin, and growth responses in hyperkinetic males treated with D-amphetamine. *J. Am. Acad. Child Psychiatry,* 20:135–147.

Haenlein, M. & Caul, W.F. (1987), Attention deficit disorder with hyperactivity: A specific hypothesis of reward dysfunction. *J Am. Acad. Child Adolesc. Psychiatry,* 26(3):356–362.

Hasher, L. & Zacks, R.T. (1979), Automatic and effortful processes in memory. *J. Exp. Abnorm. Psychology,* 88:217–233.

Hectman, L. et al. (1985), Hyperactives as young adults: Various clinical outcomes. *Adolesc. Psychiatry,* 9:295–306.

Henker, B. & Whalen, C.K. (1989), Hyperactivity and attention deficits. *Am. Psychologist,* 44(2):216–223.

Hinshaw, S.P., Henker, B., Whalen, C.K., Erhardt, D. & Dunnington, R.E., Jr. (1989), Aggressive, prosocial and nonsocial behavior in hyperactive boys: dose effects of methylphenidate in naturalistic settings. *J. Consult. Clin. Psychol., 57*(5):636–43.

Hunt, R.D. (1987), Treatment effects of oral and transdermal clonidine in relation to methylphenidate—an open pilot study in ADDH. *Psychopharmacol. Bull.,* 23(1):111–114.

——— (1988), Attention deficit disorder: Diagnosis, assessment and treatment. In: *Clinical Assessment of Children and Adolescents—A Biopsychosocial Approach,* eds. E. Kestenbaum & D. Williams. New York: New York University Press, pp. 519–551.

——— (Submitted), Strategies for integrating the study of cognition and neurochemistry of attention deficit disorder.

——— Cohen, D.J. & Anderson, G. (1984), Possible change in noradrenergic receptor sensitivity following methylphenidate treatment: Growth hormone and MHPG response to clonidine challenge in children with attention deficit disorder and hyperactivity. *Life Sci.,* 35(8):885–897.

——— Minderaa, R.B. & Cohen, D.J. (1985), Clonidine benefits children with attention deficit disorder and hyperactivity: report of a double-blind placebo-controlled crossover study. *J. Am. Acad. Child Psychiatry,* 24(5):617–629.

——— ——— ——— (1986), The therapeutic effect of clonidine in attention deficit disorder with hyperactivity: A comparison with placebo and methylphenidate. *Psychopharmacol. Bull.,* 22(1):229–236.

——— Brunstetter, R. & Silver, L. (1987), Attention deficit disorder: Diagnosis, etiology and neurochemistry. In: *Basic Handbook of Child Psychiatry,* ed. J. Noshpitz ed. New York: Basic Books, pp. 337–354, 483–494.

——— Anderson, G.A. & Cohen, D.J. (1988), Noradrenergic mechanisms inattention deficit disorder. In: *Attention Deficit Disorder and Hyperactivity,* Vol. 3, *New Research in Attention Treatment and Psychopharmacology,* ed. L. Bloomingdale. New York: Pergamon Press, pp. 129–148.

Janowsky, A., Schweri, M.M., Berger, P., Long, R., Skolnick, P. & Paul, S.M. (1985), The effects of surgical and chemical lesions on striatal (^{3}H)threo-(+/−)-methylphenidate binding: Correlation with (^{3}H)dopamine uptake. *Eur. J. Pharmacol.,* 108(2):187–191.

Joyce, P.R., Nicholls, M.G. & Donald, R.A. (1984), Methylphenidate increases heart rate, blood pressure and plasma epinephrine in normal subjects. *Life Sci.,* 34(18):1707–1711.

Kagan, J., Rosman, B.L., Day, D., Albert, J. & Phillips, W. (1964), Information processing in the child: significance of analytic and reflective attitudes. *Psychol. Monogr.,* 78(578):4.

Kahn, A.U. & Dekirmenjian, H. (1981), Urinary excretion of catecholamine metabolites in hyperkinetic child syndrome. *Am. J. Psychiatry,* 138:108–109.

Kahneman, D. (1973), *Attention and Effort.* Englewood Cliffs, NJ: Prentice-Hall, Inc.

Kerr, L.M., Unis, A.S. & Wamsley, J.K. (1988), Comparison of the density and distribution of brain D-1 and D-2 dopamine receptors in Buffalo vs. Fischer 344 rats. *Pharmacol. Biochem. Behav.,* 30(2):325–330.

Kobayashi, K. & Shohmori, T. (1989), Comparative study of sulpiride and haloperidol on dopamine turnover in the rat brain. *Neurochem. Res.,* 14(5):459–464.

Kopin, I. (1978), Measurement of neurotransmitter turnover. In: *Psychopharmacology: Generation of Progress.* New York: Raven Press, pp. 933–942.

Langer, D.H., Rapoport, J.L., Brown, G.L., Ebert, M.H. & Bunney, W.E., Jr. (1981), Questioning a dopaminergic hypothesis (letter). *Am. J. Psychiatry,* 138(4):537–538.

Leckman, J.F., Anderson, G.M., Cohen, D.J., Ort, S., Harcherik, D.F., Hoder, E.L. & Shaywitz, B.A. (1984), Whole blood serotonin and tryptophan levels in Tourette's disorder: Effects of acute and chronic clonidine treatment. *Life Sci.,* 35(25):2497–2503.

Levy, F. & Hobbes, G. (1988), The action of stimulant medication in attention deficit disorder with hyperactivity: Dopaminergic, noradrenergic, or both? *J. Am. Acad. Child Adolesc. Psychiatry*, 27(6):802–805.

Luria, A.R. (1973), *The Working Brain: An Introduction to Neuropsychology*. Middlesex: Penguin Press.

Margulies, D.M. (1985), Selective attention and the brain: A hypothesis concerning the hippocampal-ventral striatal axis, the mediation of selective attention, and the pathogenesis of attentional disorders. *Med. Hypo.*, 18:221–264.

Mason S.T. & Iversen, S.D. (1978), Reward, attention and the dorsal noradrenergic bundle. *Brain Res.*, 150:135–148.

Mefford, I.N., & Potter, W.Z. (1989), A neuroanatomical and biochemical basis for attention deficit disorder with hyperactivity in children: a defect in tonic adrenaline mediated inhibition of locus coeruleus stimulation. *Medical Hypothese*, 29:33–42.

Milich, R., Loney, J. & Landau, S. (1982), Independent dimensions of hyperactivity and aggression: A validation with playroom observation data. *J. Abnorm. Psychol.*, 91:183–198.

Neisser, U. (1967), *Cognitive Psychology*. New York: Appleton-Century-Crofts.

Neuchterlein, K.H. (1983), Signal detection in vigilance tasks and behavioral attributes among offspring of schizophrenic mothers and among hyperactive children. *J. Abnorm. Psychol.*, 93:4–83.

Oades, R.D. (1987), Attention deficit disorder with hyperactivity (ADDH): The contribution of catecholaminergic activity. *Progr. Neurobiol.*, 26:165–391.

Pelham, W.E., Bencher, M.E., Caddell, J., Booth, S. & Mower, S.H. (1985), Methylphenidate and children with attention deficit disorder. *Arch. Gen. Psychiatry*, 42:948–952.

Posner, M.I. (1986), A framework for relating cognitive to neural systems. In: *Cerebral Psychophysiology: Studies in Event-Related Potentials* [EEG Suppl 38], ed. W.C. McCallum, R. Zappoli & F. Denoth. New York: Elsevier Science Publishers.

Quay, H. (1984), The behavioral reward and inhibition system in childhood behavior disorder. In: *Attention Deficit Disorder*, ed. L.M. Bloomingdale. New York: Spectrum Press.

Rapoport, J.L. (1986), Childhood obsessive compulsive disorder. *J. Child Psychol. Psychiatry*, 27(3):289–95.

———— Quinn, P.O. & Lamprecht, P. (1974), Minor physical anomalies and plasma dopamine beta hydroxylase activity in hyperactive boys. *Am. J. Psychiatry*, 131:386–392.

Rapport, M.D. & Kelly, K.L. (in press) Psychostimulant effects on learning and cognitive function: Findings and implications for children with attention deficit hyperactivity disorder. *Clin. Psychol. Rev.*

Rogeness, G.A., Maas, J.W., Javors, M.A., Macedo, C.A., Fischer, C., & Harris, W.R. (1989), Attention deficit disorder symptoms and urine catecholamines. *Psychiatry Res.*, 27:241–251.

Ross, C.A., Trulson, M.E. & Jacobs, B.L. (1976), Depletion of brain serotonin following intraventricular 5,7-dihydroxytryptamine fails to disrupt sleep in the rat. *Brain Res.*, 114(3):517–523.

Roth, R.H., Elsworth, J.D. & Redmond, D.E., Jr. (1982), Clonidine suppression of noradrenergic hyperactivity during morphine withdrawal by clonidine: Biochemical studies in rodents and primates. *J. Clin. Psychiatry*, 43(6 Pt 2):42–46.

Sargent, J.A., van Velthoven, R. & Virginia, A. (1979), Hyperactivity, impulsivity and reflectivity and examination of their relationship and implications for clinical child psychology. *J. Child Psychol. Psychiatr.*, 20:47–60.

Schweri, M.M., Skolnick, P., Rafferty, M.F., Rice, K.C., Janowsky, A.J. & Paul, S.M. (1985), [^{3}H]Threo-($+/-$)-methylphenidate binding to 3,4-dihydroxyphenylethylamine uptake sites in corpus striatum: correlation with the stimulant properties of ritalinic acid esters. *J. Neurochem.*, 45(4):1062–1070.

Sebrechts, M.M., Shaywitz, S.E., Shaywitz, B.A. et al. (1986), Components of attention, methylphenidate dosage, and blood levels in children with attention deficit disorder. *Pediatrics*, 77:222–228.

Serfontein, G.I., Earl, J.W., & Johnston, L.J. (1984), *Attention Deficit Disorder and Hyperactivity*, Vol. 3, ed. L. Bloomingdale. New York: Spectrum Publications.

Shapiro, S.K. & Garfinkel, B.D. (1986), The occurrence of behavior disorders in children: The interdependence of attention deficit disorder and conduct disorder. *Am. Acad. Child Psychiatry*, 25(6):809–819.

Shaywitz, B.A., Cohen, D.J. & Bowers, M.B. Jr. (1977), CSF monoamine metabolites in children with minimal brain dysfunction: evidence for alteration of brain dopamine. *J. Pediatr.*, 90:67–71.

———— Klooper, J.H. & Gordon, J.W. (1978), Methylphenidate in 6-hydroxydopamine treated developing rat pups. *Child Neurol.*, 35:463–469.

———— ———— Yager, R.D. & Gordon, J.W. (1976), Paradoxical response to amphetamine in developing rats treated with 6-hydroxydopamine. Nature, 261:153–155.

———— Hunt, R.D., Jatlow, P., Cohen, D.J., Young, J., Pierce, R.N., Anderson, G.M. & Shaywitz, B.A. (1982), Psychopharmacology of attention deficit disorder: Pharmacokinetic, neuroendocrine, and behavioral measures following acute and chronic treatment with methylphenidate. *Pediatrics*, 69(6):688–694.

———— Teichner, M.H., Cohen, D.J., Anderson, G.M., Young, J.G. & Levitt, P. (1984), Dopaminergic but not noradrenergic mediation of hyperactivity and performance deficits in the developing rat pup. *Psychopharmacology (Berlin)*, 82(1–2):73–77.

Shekim, W.O., Dekirmenjian, H. & Chapel, J.L. (1979), Urinary catecholamine metabolites in hyperactive children treated with D-amphetamine. *Am. J. Psychiatry*, 134:1276–1279.

———— Javaid, J., Davis, J.M. & Bylund, D.B. (1983), Urinary MHPG and HVA excretion in boys with attention deficit disorder and hyperactivity treated with D-amphetamine. *Biol. Psychiatry*, 18:707–714.

Shetty, T. & Chase, T.N. (1976), Central monoamines and hyperkinesis of childhood. *Neurology*, 26:1000–1006.

Shiffrin, R.M. & Schneider, W. (1977), Controlled and automatic human information processing. II: Perceptual learning, automatic attending, and a general theory. *Psychol. Rev.*, 84:127–190.

Sorenson, C.A., Vayer, J.S. & Goldberg, C.S. (1977), Amphetamine reduction of motor activity in rats after neonatal administration of 6-Hydroxydopamine. *Bio. Psychiatry*, 12(1):133–137.

———— George, S.A. & Friedman, A.J. (1978), The effect of D-amphetamine on gamma efferent activity in the acute decerebrate rat. *Brain Res.*, 143(2):387–391.

Starke, K. & Altmann, K.P. (1973), Inhibition of adrenergic neurotransmission by clonidine: An action on prejunctional receptors. *Neuropharmacology*, 12:339–347.

Stein, L., Belluzzi, J.D., Ritter, S. & Wise, C.D. (1974), Self-stimulation reward pathways: Norepinephrine vs. dopamine. *J. Psychiatr. Res.*, 11:115–24.

Sugita, S., Kobayashi, A., Suzuki, S., Yoshida, T. & Nakazawa, K. (1989), Correlative changes of serotonin and catecholamines with pharmacokinetic alterations of imipramine in rat brain. *Eur. J. Pharmacol.*, 165(2–3):191–198.

Swanson, J. & Kinsbourne, M. (1976), Stimulant related state-dependent learning in hyperactive children. *Science*, 192:1354–1356.

———— Sandman, C., Durtisch, C. & Baren, M. (1983), Methylphenidate hydrochloride given with or before breakfast: Behavioral, cognitive, and electrophysiologic effects. *Pediatrics*, 72(1):49–59.

Sykes, D.H., Douglas, V.I., Weiss, G. & Minde, K. (1971), Attention in hyperactive children and the effect of methylphenidate (Ritalin). *J. Child Psychol. Psychiatry*, 12:129–139.

———— Morgenstern, G. (1973), Sustained attention in hyperactive children. *J. Child Psychol. Psychiatry*, 44:267–273.

Tariot, P.N. & Weingartner, H. (1986), A psychobiologic analysis of cognitive failures. Structure and mechanisms. *Arch. Gen. Psych.*, 43(12):1183–8.

Titeler, M. & Seeman, P. (1980), Presynaptically acting catecholamines bind to alpha-2 adrenoreceptors labeled by ^{3}H-clonidine. *Eur. J. Pharmacol.*, 67(2–3):187–192.

Treisman, A.M. (1960), Contextual cues in selective listening. *Quar. J. of Experimental Psychol.*, 12:242–248.

Van Praag, H.M., Kahn, R.S., Asnis, G.M., Wetzler, S., Brown, S.L., Bleich, A. & Korn, M.L. (1987), Denosoligization of biological psychiatry or the specificity of 5-HT disturbances in psychiatric disorders. *J. Affect. Disord.*, 13(1):1–8.

Wender, P.H., Epstein, R.S., Kopin, I.J. & Gordon, E.K. (1971), Urinary monoamine metabolites in children with minimal brain dysfunction. *Am. J. Psychiatry*, 127:1411–1415.

Whalen, C.K., Henker, B., Swanson, J.M., Granger, D., Kliewer, W. & Spencer, J. (1987), Natural social behaviors in hyperactive children: Dose effects of methylphenidate. *J. Consult. Clin. Psychol.*, 55(2):187–193.

———— Buhrmester, D., Hinshaw, S.P., Huber, A. & Laski, K. (1989), Does stimulant medication improve the peer status of hyperactive children? *J. Consult. Clin. Psychol.*, 57(4):545–549.

Yu-Cun, A. & Yu-Feng, W. (1984), Urinary 3-methoxy-4-hydroxyphenylglycol sulfate excretion in seventy-three school children with minimal brain dysfunction syndrome. *Biol. Psychiatry*, 19:861–870.

Zametkin, A.J. & Hamburger, S.D. (1988), The effect of methylphenidate on urinary catecholamine excretion in hyperactivity: A partial replication. *Biol. Psychiatry*, 23(4):350–356.

———— Rapoport, J. (1987), Neurobiology of attention deficit disorder with hyperactivity. *J. Am. Acad. Child Adolesc. Psychiatry*, 26:676–686.

———— Karoum, F., Linnoila, M. et al. (1985a), Stimulants, urinary catecholamines and indoleamines in hyperactivity: A comparison of methylphenidate and dextroamphetamine. *Arch. Gen. Psychiatry*, 42:251–255.

———— Rapoport, A.J.L., Murphy, D.L., et al. (1985b), Treatment of hyperactive children with monoamine oxidase inhibitors: II Plasma and urinary monoamine findings after treatment. *Arch. Gen. Psychiatry*, 42:969–973.

Neuroendocrine and Growth Regulation:
The Role of Sympathomimetic Medication

ELIZABETH REEVE and BARRY GARFINKEL

INTRODUCTION

The term neuroendocrine generally refers to one of several systems involving a hypothalamic–pituitary–end organ pathway. Typically the hypothalamic–pituitary connection composes the "neuro" pathway and the end organ is responsible for the endocrine portion of the response. In general, all neuroendocrine pathways are characterized by the transmission of a releasing factor or an inhibitory factor from the hypothalamus, which in turn stimulates the pituitary gland to secrete the appropriate hormonal peptide. This peptide eventually acts on the end organ for the final response (Brown et al., 1978). In attention deficit hyperactivity disorder (ADHD), the neuroendocrine pathway studied most often has been the hypothalamic–pituitary–growth hormone axis. A few studies have investigated thryoid and adrenal pathways (Khan, 1987; Puig-Antich et al., 1978; Weizman et al., 1987).

In the case of growth hormone, growth hormone-releasing factor (GHRF) is produced in the medial region of the hypothalamus, and transported to the anterior pituitary where it stimulates the release of growth hormone (Brown et al., 1978). Secretion of growth hormone-releasing factor is facilitated by alpha-adrenergic, serotonergic, and dopaminergic input into the hypothalamus, and is inhibited by beta-adrenergic stimulation (Schaff-Blass et al., 1984). These neurotransmitters are affected by exogenous conditions such as stress, exercise, sleep, or medications. Multiple neurotransmitters have been identified which may also stimulate growth hormone release including: GABA, alpha-$_2$ adrenergic agonists (clonidine), dopaminergic agonists (apomorphine), L-dopa (levodopa), bromocriptine, and serotonergic agonists (tryptophan, 5-hydroxytrypltamine; 5HT) (Jensen and Garfinkel, 1988). Proteins such as arginine, prostaglandin E$_2$, vasopressin, insulin, and glucagon will also stimulate growth hormone release. Somatostatin, originating from the preoptic and paraventricular areas of the hypothalamus has an inhibitory effect on the release of growth hormone (Fig. 1). The release of other hormones such as cortisol, thyroid hormone, and prolactin are controlled by mechanisms similar to that of growth hormone. The hypothalamus produces a releasing factor or inhibiting factor which in turn affects anterior pituitary hormonal release. The pituitary release of adrenal corticotropin hormone (ACTH) is controlled by hypothalamic corticotropin-releasing factor. Likewise, thyroid-stimulating hormone is controlled by thyrotropin-releasing hormone. Prolactin secretion from the pituitary is under the control of prolactin-inhibiting factor, which is now recognized to be dopamine. Release of dopamine causes an inhibition of prolactin secretion.

In psychiatric disorders such as ADHD, attempts have been made to identify abnormalities in neuroendocrine pathways and neurotransmitters. Several different neurotransmitters have been identified as possibly playing a causal role in the development of ADHD. Neurotransmitters, norepinephrine, dopamine, and serotonin can each effect neuroendocrine pathways (Zametkin and Rapoport, 1987). By measuring quantitative changes in the end products of these pathways, for example, serum growth hormone levels in response to a norepinephrine stimulus, it is hoped that specific relationships between neuroendocrine pathways and neurotransmitters will be identified. Specific neurotransmitters theories have been formulated

University of Minnesota Medical School, Minneapolis, Minnesota

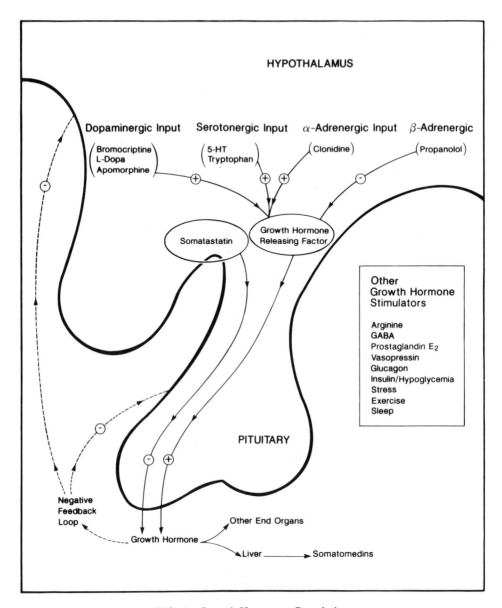

FIG. 1. Growth Horomone Regulation.

on the basis of the clinical and neuroendocrine responses of children with ADHD treated with sympathomimetic agents. For example, D-amphetamine, a potent dopamine agonist, markedly improves behavior in some ADHD children. From this response, it has been hypothesized that ADHD children may suffer from a decreased dopamine turnover. Because dopamine also inhibits prolactin release, comparison of the clinical response to D-amphetamine to changes in serum prolactin level may facilitate our understanding of any abnormalities in the underlying dopaminergic system. Unfortunately, most pharmacologic agents activate more than one neurotransmitter and a variety of neurotransmitters can effect a single neuroendocrine pathway. A one-to-one correspondence between ADHD, neuroendocrine response, and neurotransmitters has yet to be identified.

NEUROENDOCRINE MARKERS IN ADHD

The lack of a one-to-one relationship between neurotransmitters and neuroendocrine response has not slowed the effort to identify a neuroendocrine pattern which is unique to the ADHD patient. Provocative endocrine testing has looked most extensively at the response of growth hormone, prolactin, and cortisol to sympathomimetic agents. Other endocrine systems have been studied to a much lesser degree. Neuroendocrine testing for this disorder is divided into two major areas; studies establishing that sympathomimetics are activators of known neuroendocrine pathways and studies which look at the integrity and changes of these pathways before and after treatment with sympathomimetics. Methylphenidate, because of its high frequency of use in children with ADHD, has been the pharmacologic agent studied most often (Table 1).

Aarskog et al. (1977) established that D-amphetamine and methylphenidate are growth hormone agonists in children with ADHD. The growth hormone agonist effect of D-amphetamine had previously been studied in adult males (Besser et al., 1969). Aarskog et al. (1977) found that 15 mg of D-amphetamine and 20 mg of methylphenidate stimulated growth hormone response in children with ADHD (adequate growth hormone response was arbitrarily chosen as greater than 5 mg/ml). No significant difference in growth hormone response to L-dopa, methylphenidate, or D-amphetamine was observed. This study also evaluated growth hormone response to L-dopa and D-amphetamine after six to eight months of treatment with methylphenidate. A trend toward elevated base-line growth hormone levels was found, suggesting a possible long-term effect on growth hormone regulation by methylphenidate. Shaywitz et al. (1982) expanded the examination of methylphenidate effects on neuroendocrine systems to include both growth hormone response and acute changes in prolactin. Not only was a significant growth hormone-stimulating effect secondary to methylphenidate observed, but a significant decrease in serum prolactin levels after an acute dose of methylphenidate was also noted. These findings suggests that methylphenidate acts primarily through dopaminergic pathways. In a study examining neuroendocrine and cognitive responses to D-amphetamine, a significant increase in growth hormone in both ADHD subjects and normal controls was found, with no significant effect of D-amphetamine on prolactin secretion (Garfinkel et al., 1986). Of specific interest in this study is the finding that the growth hormone (GH) response to D-amphetamine in ADHD subjects was significantly more robust and occurred at a specific time (between 120 and 140 minutes) when compared with a control group. The time of elevated GH response corresponds to what has previously been observed as the peak absorption of D-amphetamine (Brown et al., 1978).

Further studies specifically sought to determine whether or not changes in neuroendocrine pathways occur with chronic sympathomimetic treatment. As previously mentioned, Aarskog et al., (1977) repeated growth hormone testing six to eight months after treatment with methylphenidate and found a trend toward elevated baseline growth hormone levels. Greenhill et al. (1981) found that after six months of treatment with D-amphetamine, there were no effects on growth hormone secretion, but prolactin secretion fell significantly. Subsequently, Greenhill et al. (1984) studied methylphenidate, finding no change in prolactin secretion with chronic use, but mildly increased sleep-related growth hormone secretion. Schultz et al. (1982) studied the growth hormone response of ADHD children after treatment with D-amphetamine for one year. No significant differences in growth hormone response (as measured by insulin tolerance test and serum peak levels during slow wave sleep) were found when comparing children treated with D-amphetamine and an ADHD control group treated with phenothiazines. This study also noted that cortisol levels were unaffected by D-amphetamine treatment whereas prolactin response showed a significant drop from baseline levels. This prolactin change suggested possible dopamine release occurring as a result of chronic D-amphetamine treatment resulting in prolactin suppression.

Two studies have measured multiple serum hormone and neurotransmitter levels before, during, and after treatment with methylphenidate (Hunt et al., 1984; Weizman et al., 1987). Hunt et al. (1984) used clonidine to stimulate growth hormone release after Ritalin treatment for 12 weeks. Prior to methylphenidate treatment, clonidine was found to be an adequate stimulator of growth hormone release. During treatment with methylphenidate, minimum of 0.3 mg/kg per day, the growth hormone response to clonidine stimulation fell significantly, returning to pretreatment levels as soon as one day after discontinuation of methylphenidate. Responses of 3-methoxy-4-hydroxy-phenylglycol (MPHG), epinephrine, and norepinephrine to a clonidine-challenge test were not affected by treatment with Ritalin. Pretreatment growth

TABLE 1. NEUROENDOCRINE CHALLENGE TESTS IN CHILDREN WITH ADHD

Investigators	Number of Subjects	Control Group	Pharmacologic Agent	Acute Response vs. Chronic Response	Significant Findings
Aarskog et al., 1977	20	No	L-dopa		Increased GH
		—	MPH	Acute	Increased GH
			MPH	Chronic	Increased baseline GH (trend only)
			D-Amphetamine		Increased GH
Puig-Antich et al., 1978	7	Yes	D-Amphetamine	Chronic	No change in GH
		—	D-Amphetamine	Chronic	Decreased Prolactin
Greenhill et al., 1981	13	No	D-Amphetamine	Chronic	Decreased PRL
					No change GH
Schultz et al., 1982	9	No	MPH	Acute	Increased GH
Shaywitz et al., 1982	14	No	MPH	Acute	Increased GH
					Decreased PRL
Greenhill et al., 1984	8	No	MPH	Chronic	PRL unchanged
					Increased GH sleep secreted (trend only)
Hunt et al., 1984	8	No	MPH	Chronic	Decreased GH to clonidine challenge
					No change NE, EPI, MHPG
Garfinkel et al., 1986	44	Yes	D-Amphetamine	Acute	Increased GH
					No change PRL
Weizman et al., 1987	16	Yes	MPH	Acute	Increased B-endorpin
					Increased cortisol
			MPH	Chronic	Decreased PRL
					Decreased basal PRL

hormone response was significantly greater than the response found in two groups previously studied, Tourette's syndrome, and children with short stature. This suggests the possibility that ADHD children have increased noradrenergic sensitivity. Weizman et al. (1987) evaluated growth hormone, cortisol, prolactin, and beta-endorphin response in 16 ADHD children before and after 4 weeks of methylphenidate treatment. Basal levels of growth hormone, cortisol, prolactin, and beta-endorphin were similar in ADHD subjects and normal controls before treatment. A significant decrease in basal prolactin levels occurred in ADHD subjects after treatment. Prior to chronic methylphenidate treatment, ADHD subjects responded to a challenge test of 5 mg oral methylphenidate with significantly increased beta-endorphin and cortisol release, and a significant decrease in prolactin. There was a trend toward increased growth hormone release in response to methylphenidate stimulation. Four weeks after treatment, repeat stimulation with methylphenidate produced a significant rise in beta-endorphin and growth hormone, but not in cortisol. No decrease was noted in serum prolactin levels. The authors conclude the beta-endorphins were not affected by long-term methylphenidate use, and that cortisol and prolactin responses may have been unchanged because of a decrease in sensitivity to the dopamine effect of methylphenidate.

Two other endocrine responses have been indirectly studied in ADHD children. In a study of the thyroid stimulation test in depressed adolescents Khan (1987) included seven ADHD subjects as a control group. All seven subjects showed normal, that is nonblunted, responses to thyroid-releasing hormone, suggestive of an intact hypothalamic–pituitary–thyroid pathway. Hoshino et al. (1984) studied the dexamethasone suppression test in autistic subjects and used five control subjects with a diagnosis of minimal brain dysfunction. Although not specifically diagnosed as ADHD, subjects with minimal brain dysfunction may exhibit a similar symptom pattern. All five subjects showed appropriate suppression with dexamethasone, implying no dysfunction of the hypothalamic–pituitary–adrenal axis.

Neuroendocrine studies in children with ADHD therefore have been infrequent and have reached inconsistent conclusions. With the exception of one study, most investigators have clearly demonstrated the growth hormone-stimulating effect of both D-amphetamine and methylphenidate when given as acute challenge doses (Weizman et al., 1987). The response of prolactin to acute stimulant administration has been variable. Studies by Shaywitz et al. (1982) and Weizman et al. (1987) found decreased prolactin levels acutely. Two other studies found no change in serum prolactin levels (Garfinkel et al., 1986; Schultz et al., 1982). Furthermore, prolactin levels after chronic stimulant use have been shown to be decreased in some studies and unchanged in others (Greenhill et al., 1981; Puig-Antich et al., 1978; Weizman et al., 1987). The cortisol response to acute methylphenidate administration was measured in only one study, and was found to be increased (Weizman et al., 1987). Chronic D-amphetamine administration produced no change in cortisol levels (Puig-Antich et al., 1978).

Unfortunately, a neuroendocrine pattern unique to ADHD cannot be formulated from these studies. In interpreting these findings, it is necessary to consider the potential methodological errors of each study. These studies show marked variability in the number of subjects used, the age of subjects, the definition of such terms as "chronic treatment," the doses of stimulant medication administered both during treatment and for provocative testing, as well as in methods for endocrine testing. The results of each of these studies needs to be reviewed carefully with consideration given to potential methodological flaws.

Of significance in all but three of the above studies is the lack of control groups. Weizman et al. (1987) used aged-matched volunteer controls. Garfinkel et al. (1986) recruited controls from local schools, and Puig-Antich et al. (1978) used controls of ADHD children who were being treated with phenothiazines. Unfortunately, the remainder of the studies reviewed did not include control groups. Of the control groups utilized, only two population types were represented; normal children and ADHD subjects treated with nonstimulant medications. There were no studies with control groups of children diagnosed with other endocrinologic or psychiatric disorders. Ideally, one would hope for an endocrinologic control group such as short-statured children as well as a psychiatric control. This would help establish that any response abnormalities within the ADHD subjects were unique to that group, and not commonly found in other psychiatric or endocrine populations.

Further methodologic difficulties are manifest by the lack of careful definitions of such terms as "acute response" and "chronic treatment." First, as commonly understood, the term "acute" refers to "immediate" and is generally used in these studies to refer to the immediate response of the neuroendocrine system to a provocative stimulus. Unfortunately, there are differences between these studies in the methods in which these provocative tests were completed. This raises the question whether or not the acute response in one study is comparable to that of another. For instance, studies vary significantly in the amount of time allowed to lapse between the last dose of prescribed sympathomimetic medication and the onset of provocative testing. They also differ significantly in the chronicity of treatment prior to provocative testing. For example, is the growth hormone response to 20 mg of methylphenidate the same after a one week discontinuation of all previous sympathomimetics, as it is if medication has been discontinued for two weeks? Variations also exist in the length of time allowed to lapse between consecutive provocative tests. Furthermore, the term "chronic treatment" as used in these studies refers to the length of sympathomimetic treatment between baseline provocative testing and followup testing. This varied between four weeks and nine months (Greenhill et al., 1981; Weizman et al., 1987). These differences make comparisons between studies very difficult and conclusions which are made based on the results of multiple studies then become questionable.

The possible neuroendocrine response resulting from physiologic changes such as sleep or activity level needs to be considered when assessing these studies. Although authors universally reported that their subjects were fasting at the time of the neuroendocrine studies, no study commented on the level of activity maintained by the subject during the testing period. These issues are important because it has been established that growth hormone response is easily affected by physiologic states such as anxiety, stress, exercise, sleep, and blood glucose level.

Differences also exist between the pharmacologic properties of the stimulant medications. One must employ caution when extrapolating from responses of individual agents to the class of all sympathomimetics. Each of the most widely prescribed sympathomimetics, pemoline, D-amphetamine, and methylphenidate has a different half-life and differing sites of pharmacologic action. Methylphenidate increases stored catecholamine release from reserpine-sensitive granules and D-amphetamine releases newly synthesized amines from reserpine-resistant granules (Zametkin and Rapoport, 1987). Subjects who do not respond to one medication may respond to another, further emphasizing the possible neurochemical and neurotransmitter differences between these agents.

Finally, one should not overlook the small sample size of most of these studies. Some studies evaluated as few as 7 subjects and the maximum number used was only 44 subjects (Garfinkel et al., 1986; Puig-Antich et al., 1978). Despite these small samples sizes, significant differences were found, suggesting that actual differences were being evaluated and further aggressive research in this area is warranted. Although numerous methodologic flaws have been mentioned in these previous studies, the problems are not insurmountable. Firm ground has already been laid in this area and with careful planning, the "definitive study" may one day be completed.

LONG-TERM GROWTH EFFECTS OF SYMPATHOMIMETIC MEDICATION

The possible adverse effects of sympathomimetic medication on the growth of children is a significant clinical concern; and has increased based on findings of neuroendocrine studies with alluded to possible long-term medication-induced changes in the growth hormone neuroendocrine pathway (Aarskog et al., 1977). In the same year that Besser et al., (1969) published studies showing the growth hormone stimulatory effect of D-amphetamine in adult men, a study showing an initial period of weight loss in children being treated with sympathomimetic medication was completed (Knights and Viets, 1975). Since the early 1970s, pediatricians and child psychiatrists have struggled with the question of whether or not sympathomimetics can inhibit growth, and if so, whether the effect is temporary or permanent. Literature in this area is extensive. Unfortunately, like the neuroendocrine studies, most growth suppression studies are fraught with methodologic problems.

Studies that examine the growth of children on sympathomimetic medication are of two basic types: those that assess the effects of sympathomimetics on height and weight during treatment and in followup and those that look at related phenomena such as the effects of medication holidays, dose-related growth changes, and rebound growth. Although the vast majority of studies have investigated the growth effects of methylphenidate, there are a few studies involving D-amphetamine and pemoline (Table 2).

The first study to examine the issue of growth on ADHD children treated with sympathomimetic medication was done by Safer et al. (1972). This study involved an initial group of 20 ADHD children being

TABLE 2. HEIGHT AND WEIGHT CHANGES IN ADHD TREATED CHILDREN

Investigator	Subject	Followup	Medication	Results
Safer et al., 1972	29	2 years	MPH	Decreased Wt
	—		D-Amphetamine	Decreased Ht & Wt
Safer and Allen, 1973	63	2+ years	MPH	Decreased Ht
			D-Amphetamine	Decreased Ht & Wt
Knights and Viets, 1975	30	18 mo.	Pemoline	No Ht/Wt effect
Beck et al., 1975	30	6 mo.	MPH	No Ht/Wt effect
Gross, 1976	100	2+ years	MPH	No Ht/Wt effect
			D-Amphetamine	No Ht/Wt effect
			Trichloroacetic acid	No Ht/Wt effect
Hechtman et al., 1978	65	10 years	None	No Ht/Wt change
			Phenothiazines	Increased Ht
McNutt et al., 1979	26	1 year	MPH	No Ht/Wt effect
Dickinson et al., 1979		26 mos.	Pemoline	Decreased Ht
Satterfield et al., 1979	72	1 year	MPH	Decreased Ht & Wt
		2 years	MPH	Increased Ht velocity rate
Werry et al., 1979	30	4 wks.	MPH	No Ht effect
Friedman et al., 1981	22	18 mo.	Pemoline	Decreased Ht & Wt
		4 years	Pemoline	No Ht/Wt effect
Greenhill et al., 1981	13	1 year	D-Amphetamine	Decreased Ht & Wt
Kalachnik et al., 1982	26	1 year	MPH	No Ht/Wt effect
		2 years	MPH	No Ht/Wt effect
Mattes and Gittelman, 1983	86	1 year	MPH	Decreased Ht
		2 yrs–4 yrs	MPH	Decreased Ht & Wt
Hechtman et al., 1984	25	10+ years	MPH	No Ht/Wt effect
Greenhill et al., 1984	10	1 year	MPH	Decreased Wt
				No Ht effect
Gittleman-Klein et al., 1988	103	5+ years	MPH	No Ht effect

treated with either methylphenidate or D-amphetamine. Height and weight measurements were obtained on these subjects "in the standard manner" for a period of one year. Thirteen of the participating children did not take medication during the summer. Safer found that the children given summer "drug holidays" gained significantly more weight during the summer than children who continued on their medication year round. This statistically significant finding was accountable by those children being treated with D-amphetamine. Weight gain was unaffected by methylphenidate unless a dose greater than 30–40 mg was administered. Children had a rebound weight gain of 130% of their expected weight gain if they were taken off medications during the summer months (Safer et al., 1975). Children who were treated for longer than a two-year period showed a significant decline in their weight percentiles. Changes in height, when compared with baseline height were not significant. Safer concluded that weight was affected by both acute and chronic administration of sympathomimetic medication. D-Amphetamine caused more weight loss than low-dose methylphenidate. Height was affected, but in a variable way that did not allow for significant findings. One year after this study, a second study was published replicating the findings with D-amphetamine and also showing that higher doses of methylphenidate affected weight gain (Safer and Allen, 1973). Height was similarly affected. Both duration of treatment and frequency of medication given were identified as significant factors affecting loss of height and weight in children treated with D-amphetamine. The use of drug holidays during the summer months was significantly related to the presence or absence of height loss while on Ritalin, but not while on D-amphetamine. Weight loss did not appear to be affected by drug holidays.

Numerous investigations followed, in an attempt to replicate and clarify these original observations. Of particular significance is a study which established that untreated children with ADHD did not have a decrease in their expected adult stature (Hechtman et al., 1978). This is of importance as it implies that it is not an intrinsic growth abnormality in children with ADHD that accounts for any reduction in adult height or weight. Sixty-five hyperactive individuals who had obtained adult stature and who had not taken sympathomimetic medication during childhood were evaluated. No significant differences in height or weight were found between the subjects and the control group of nonhyperactive individuals.

A series of studies followed Safer's work. Knight and Viets (1975), Beck et al. (1975), Gross (1976), and McNutt et al. (1977) all concluded that stimulant medications did not have an effect on height or weight. These studies had a range of followup times between six months to two years and included the drugs pemoline, Ritalin, D-amphetamine, and tricyclic antidepressants. The next series of studies followed subjects for longer periods of time, between one and four years. Studies by Dickinson et al. (1979), Greenhill et al. (1981), and Mattes and Gittelman (1983) concluded that sympathomimetics did have long-term growth effects. Dickinson et al. (1979) studied the effects of pemoline prospectively on 24 children with ADHD. After 12 months of continuous pemoline therapy, growth height velocity had decreased significantly. During the second year, nearly all the subjects showed an increase in their growth velocity. This occurred regardless of whether or not they had discontinued medications during the summer months. In two separate studies Greenhill et al. (1981, 1984) followed ADHD children treated with D-amphetamine or methylphenidate for up to 21 months. In response to D-amphetamine a significant decrease in both height and weight percentile was found, with children who were larger before treatment was started suffering the greatest losses. Ritalin-treated children showed a significant decrease in weight velocity, but not in height velocity. In the last of this series, Mattes and Gittelman (1983) followed methylphenidate-treated children for four years and found significant decreases in height and weight. This study makes several other important conclusions including: weight decreases significantly before height decreases; larger children have increased vulnerability to growth suppression, and the effect of methylphenidate is relatively weak after controlling for children's age and pretreatment height and weight.

Although some early studies already mentioned addressed the issues of drug holidays, growth rebound, or dose-dependent drug effects, these secondary questions were examined more specifically in later studies (Gittelman-Klein and Mannuzza, 1988; Kalachnik et al., 1982; Satterfield et al., 1979). Satterfield et al. (1979) took a comprehensive look at these secondary issues, studying 72 ADHD children for up to two years. Results indicated significant decreases in height and weight after one year of methylphenidate treatment, but not after two years. Subjects followed for two years demonstrated significant growth rebound during their second year. Height changes were not a result of total drug administration or continuation of drug therapy during the summer months. Weight loss, however, was greater in subjects who continued methylphenidate all year round. Kalachnik et al. (1982) studied 26 ADHD subjects for up to three years and compared them with unmedicated ADHD children and normal controls. Subjects were further divided according to the dose of medication they received, and whether or not they continued the drug for more or less than eight months of the year. No significant differences were found on height after one, two, or three years of followup. Growth suppression did occur with methylphenidate dose ranges up to 0.8 mg/kg per day. Drug holidays had no effect on height changes.

Two studies by Gittelman-Klein et al. (1988) examined the issues of growth rebound and drug holidays. One of these studies also assessed the possible effect of methylphenidate on final adult height (Gittelman-Klein and Mannuzza, 1988). Sixty-one ADHD children treated with methylphenidate for up to five years did not differ in final adult stature when compared with a normal control group. Careful assessment was also made of the phenomenon of rebound growth. The population studied had shown height reduction during childhood while being treated with methylphenidate, yet reached their expected adult height. The achievement of expected adult height necessitates a period of compensatory growth at some time in order to "catch up." Drug holidays increased height velocity only after a period of two consecutive summers off stimulant medication.

What, if any, conclusions can be made from these studies? More than twn years ago, Roche et al. (1979) reviewed the subject of sympathomimetic-related growth inhibition. At that time, he concluded that "reasonable evidence" had been presented suggesting that stimulant medications suppress weight with some minor suppression of height. Periods of "catch up" growth occur whereby growth suppression does not affect final adult height. Even with many additional further studies, these conclusions have not changed. Most researchers have shown no effect on expected weight or height in long-term followup studies. Initially, sympathomimetics may cause decreases in expected weight gain, especially with higher doses of D-amphetamine (Greenhill et al., 1984). Transient decreases in height velocity may also occur. In reviewing studies that followed subjects for longer than a two-year period, all but one study found no long-term effect on height or weight (Mattes and Gittelman, 1983). Initial growth suppression appears to be corrected by rebound growth at a later date. The use of drug holidays may enhance weight gain (Satterfield et al., 1979). Accelerated height growth may also occur if summer drug holidays occur for more than one summer (Gittelman-Klein et al., 1988). One may conclude that sympathomimetic-induced growth suppression appears to be a transient phenomena that is self-correcting. It is not an indication for discontinuation of stimulant treatment in a child with ADHD who has had a significant positive clinical response. Although these studies provide clinicians with a favorable growth prognosis for their patients, there still are questions to be answered. What mechanism can account for the transitory growth-suppressive effect of stimulants? Are these studies methodologically sound, and therefore suitable for use when making decisions about individual patient care?

Several mechanisms have been proposed to explain the temporary growth suppression of sympathomimetic medications. The most simplistic of these is suppressed growth secondary to decreased food intake caused by the anorectic side effect of sympathomimetic medication. It has been generally believed that this anorectic effect is not significant in growth reduction because it is relatively short term, resolving early in the course of treatment (Dickinson et al., 1979). Possible growth hormone suppression has also been a suggested mechanism, but this has been well refuted by studies which demonstrate the growth hormone stimulatory effects of stimulants and establish that ADHD children respond normally to growth hormone provocative testing. Greenhill suggested that a decrease in sleep-related prolactin secretion is correlated with growth retardation (Greenhill et al., 1981). Other studies have found no change in prolactin secretion while on stimulant medications. It is possible that sympathomimetic medication may inhibit growth via a direct effect on growing cartilage and bone. Although this is one possible hypothesis, the lack of long-term growth effects would imply the development of tolerance to any acute effect that stimulant medication would have on bone or cartilage growth. No studies have specifically addressed this hypothesis.

Furthermore, the question of methodologic issues needs to be discussed. Most growth studies suffer from the lack of established medication compliance. Only one study reviewed provided an objective measure of compliance with medication (Satterfield et al., 1979). This was a monthly urinalysis for ritalinic acid. Two other studies attempted to monitor compliance by less stringent methods, such as pill counts and school reports or prescription renewal dates (Greenhill et al., 1984; Mattes and Gittelman, 1983). Without establishing medication compliance all results of chronic administration studies need to be reviewed as speculative. A second prominently noted inconsistency in these studies was in the reporting of drug dosage used. Most studies separated subjects into treatment groups based on the average mg/day of drug consumed. A few studies were more specific and reported drug dosage in mg/kg. per day (Greenhill et al., 1981; Kalachnik et al., 1982; McNutt et al., 1977; Satterfield et al., 1977). Only one study reviewed discussed medications in relation to total cumulative dose. Knowledge of total dose may be particularly useful when trying to study long-term effects. No study reviewed addressed the issue of how variations in an individual's diet could potentially impact growth outcome. Although dietary intake is clearly difficult to control, this potential complicating factor should be studied. Of concern also was the variety of diagnoses used in subject groups. Although this inconsistency can generally be attributed to changes in accepted psychiatric nosology, it is not entirely clear that children who are labeled as attention deficit hyperactivity disorder in the 1980s or 1990s are the same group of children who were labeled as hyperkinetic syndrome in the 1970s. Other diagnostic groups included were minimal brain dysfunction, hyperactive children, hyperkinetic reaction of childhood, and hyperkinetic syndrome. These studies showed marked differences in the methods in which they reported their findings, further compounding the difficulty in comparing one with another. Some studies reported actual inches or centimeters lost, others reported decreases in height percentiles, while others reported all findings as height velocity.

SUMMARY

This chapter provides a review of the neuroendocrine and growth effects of sympathomimetic medications. To date, preliminary neuroendocrine studies have been scarce, have utilized small sample sizes, and have had numerous methodologic flaws. Despite these problems, there are several findings worth recognizing. Early studies have clearly established the acute growth hormone-stimulating effect of D-amphetamine and methylphenidate in both adults and children. Preliminary investigations suggest that this acute affect may also be responsible for changes in prolactin, cortisol, and beta-endorphins. Chronically administered sympathomimetics do not appear to cause long-term effects on the hypothalamic–pituitary–growth hormone axis.

It appears that early growth inhibitory effects may develop with sympathomimetic treatment, but these effects are well tolerated and do not have long-term effects on adult stature. Initial losses in height gain may occur, but a normally developing child should then progress at his expected growth rate along a slightly lower growth percentile curve. This shift in the growth curve should be alarming only if persistent loss of height velocity occurs, or if height plateaus and does not follow the path of the newly established growth curve. A more thorough endocrinologic investigation including thyroid function tests, growth hormone, and bone age may then be warranted.

Unlike height, which may or may not show initial changes when sympathomimetic treatment is initiated, weight can be expected to change in nearly every patient treated. The studies reviewed universally found initial weight loss in their subjects. Knowledge of this expected effect before beginning treatment with a sympathomimetic may alleviate anxieties for the physician and the family. Most studies suggest an initial weight loss of 0.5 to 0.9 kg below expected weight gain after a period of initial treatment (Gross, 1976; Safer et al., 1972). This weight loss may not be regained as long as treatment continues, but progressive weight loss should not occur. The identification of progressive weight loss would require complete medical evaluation and should be considered a significant clinical abnormality.

There are practical methods available to minimize these growth changes. Drug holidays may be beneficial in some children to allow for a period of growth rebound, especially if treatment is to be long term. A 4-week summer-time drug holiday likely will be easily tolerated by the patient and his family and may also decrease any possible risk for developing drug tolerance. The use of methylphenidate in place of D-amphetamine when possible, and the use of the lowest therapeutic dose will decrease growth effects. Parents should be told that larger children may show a greater weight loss than smaller children. Standard height and weight charts should be maintained by the prescribing physician. Although medical practitioners and families may focus on growth changes as a potentially serious side effect of sympathomimetics, these side effects have generally been reported to be mild. One should keep in mind that more serious side effects such as the development of tics or nightly insomnia may cause much more stress on both the patient and the family.

In summarizing both the neuroendocrine studies as well as the growth effects of sympathomimetics, it is necessary to briefly address how these two areas may interrelate. Other psychiatric disorders, such as anorexia nervosa, clearly demonstrate an overlap between issues of physical growth and development and neuroendocrine systems. Anorexia nervosa has been associated with multiple endocrine abnormalities including hypocortisolemia, hypothyroidism, hyperprolactinemia, and elevated growth hormone secretion. These patients may develop symptoms of impulsivity, irritability, and motor hyperactivity not unlike symptoms found in ADHD children. It is intriguing to speculate how sympathomimetics, which may induce anorexia, work to alleviate symptoms of motoric hyperactivity in ADHD children. This seemingly paradoxical effect of sympathomimetic treatment has been well recognized from a neurotransmitter standpoint, but has not been explored from a neuroendocrine perspective.

How can these past research experiences be used to better study neuroendocrine and growth phenomena in the future? One must carefully construct research protocols taking into consideration the need for better control groups, medication compliance, subject diagnosis, definitions of treatment, and methods of data collection. Careful control of the research environment must be maintained as we now know how sensitive hormonal measures are to outside influences such as sleep, food intake, and psychological stressors. Issues that may be beyond our control such as long-term manipulation of diet, need to be recognized and addressed. Further research in this area is needed, and will continue to add to an expanding database. Hopefully, neuroendocrine testing may one day help establish diagnostic and treatment recommendations for ADHD children.

REFERENCES

Aarskog, D., Fevang, F.O., Klove, H., Stoa, K.F. & Thorsen, T. (1977), The effects of the stimulant drugs, dextroamphetamine and methylphenidate, on secretion of growth hormone in hyperactive children. *J. Pediatr.*, 90:136–139.

Beck, L., Langford, W.S., Mackay, M., & Sum, G. (1975), Childhood chemotherapy and later drug abuse and growth curve: A follow-up study of 30 adolescents. *Am. J. Psychiatry*, 132:436–438.

Besser, B.M., Butler, B.W.P., Landon, J. & Rees, L. (1969), Influence of amphetamines on plasma corticosteroid and growth hormone levels in man, *Br. Med. J.*, 2:258.

Brown, G.M., Seggie, J.A., Chambers, J.W. & Ettigi, P.G. (1978), Psychoendocrinology and growth hormone: A review. *Psychoneuroendocrinology*, 3:131–153.

Dickinson, L.C., Lee, J., Ringdahl, I.R., Schedewie, H.K., Kilgore, B.S. & Elders, M.J. (1979), Impaired growth in hyperkinetic children receiving pemoline. *J. Pediatr.*, 94:538–541.

Friedmann, N., Thomas, J., Carr, R., Elders, J., Ringdahl, I., & Roche, A. (1981), Effect on growth in pemoline-treated children with attention deficit disorder. *Am. J. Dis. Child.*, 135:329–332.

Garfinkel, B.D., Brown, W.A., Klee, S.H., Braden, W., Beauchesne, H. & Shapiro, S.K. (1986), Neuroendocrine and cognitive responses to amphetamine in adolescents with a history of attention deficit disorder. *J. Am. Acad. Child. Psychiatry*, 25:503–508.

Gittelman-Klein, R. & Mannuzza, S. (1988), Hyperactive boys almost grown up. *Arch. Gen. Psychiatry*, 45:1131–1134.

——— Landa, B., Mattes, J.A. & Klein, D.F. (1988), Methylphenidate and growth in hyperactive children. *Arch. Gen. Psychiatry*, 45:1127–1130.

Greenhill, L.L., Chambers, W., Rubinstein, B., Halpern, F. & Sachar, E.J. (1981), Growth hormone, prolactin, and growth responses in hyperkinetic males treated with d-amphetamine. *J. Am. Acad. Child Psychiatry*, 20:84–103.

———, Novacenko, H., Solomon, M., Anghern, C., Florea, J., Goetz, R., Fiscina, B. & Sachar, E.J. (1984), Prolactin, growth hormone and growth responses in boys with attention deficit disorder and hyperactivity treated with methylphenidate. *J. Am. Acad. Child Psychiatry*, 23:58–67.

Gross, M.D. (1976), Growth of hyperkinetic children taking methylphenidate, dextroamphetamine, or imipramine/desipramine. *Pediatrics*, 58:423–431.

Hechtman, L., Weiss, G., & Perlman, T. (1978), Growth and cardiovascular measures in hyperactive individuals as young adults and in match normal controls. *CMA J.*, 118:1247–1250.

——— (1984), Young adult outcome of hyperactive children who receive long-term stimulant treatment. *J. Am. Acad. Child Psychiatry*, 23:261–269.

Hoshino, Y., Ohno, Y., Murata, S., Yokoyama, F., Kaneko, M. & Kumashiro, H. (1984), Dexamethasone suppression test in autistic children. *Folia Psychiatr. Neurol. Jpn.*, 38:445–449.

Hunt, R.D., Cohen, D.J., Anderson, G. & Clark, L. (1984), Possible chance in noradrenergic receptor sensitivity following methylphenidate treatment growth hormone and MHPG response to clonidine challenge in children with attention deficit and hyperactivity. *Life Sciences*, 35:885–897.

Jensen, J.B. & Garfinkel, B.D. (1988), Neuroendocrine aspects of attention deficit hyperactivity disorder. *Endocrinol. Metabol. Clin. North Am.*, 17:111–129.

Kalachnik, J.E., Sprague, R.L., Sleator, E.K., Cohen, M.N., & Ullmann, R.K. (1982), Effect of methylphenidate hydrochloride on stature of hyperactive children. *Devel. Med. Child Neurol.*, 24:586–595.

Khan, A.U. (1987), Sensitivity and specificity of the stimulation test in depressed and nondepressed adolescents. *Psychiatry Res.*, 25:11–17.

Knights, R.M. & Viets, C.A. (1975), Effects of pemoline on hyperactive boys. *Pharmacol. Biochem. Behav.*, 3:1107–1114.

Mattes, J.A. & Gittelman, R. (1983), Growth of hyperactive children on maintenance regimen of methylphenidate. *Arch. Gen. Psychiatry*, 40:317–321.

McNutt, B.A., Boileau, R.A. & Cohen, M.N. (1977), The effects of long-term stimulant medication on the growth and body composition of hyperactive children. *Psychopharmacol Bull.*, 13:36–38.

Puig-Antich, J., Greenhill, L.L., Sassin, J. & Sachar, E.J. (1978), Growth hormone, prolactin and cortisol responses and growth patterns in hyperkinetic children treated with dextroamphetamine. *Am. Acad. Child Psychiatry*, 17:457–475.

Roche, A.F., Lipman, R.S., Overall, J.E. & Hung, W. (1979), The effects of stimulant medication on the growth of hyperkinetic children. *Pediatrics*, 63:847–850.

Safer, D. and Allen, R. (1973), Factors influencing the suppressant effects of two stimulant drugs on the growth of hyperactive children. *Pediatrics*, 51:660–666.

Safer, D., Allen, R. & Barr, E. (1972), Depression of growth in hyperactive children on stimulant drugs. *N. Engl. J. Med.*, 287:217–220.

————— ————— (1975), Growth rebound after termination of stimulant drugs. *J Pediatr*, 86:113–116.

Satterfield, J.H., Cantwell, D.P., Schell, A. & Blaschke, T. (1979), Growth of hyperactive children treated with methylphenidate. *Arch. Gen. Psychiatry*, 36:212–217.

Schaff-Blass, E., Burstein, S., & Rosenfield, R.L. (1984), Advances in diagnosis and treatment of short stature, with special reference to the role of growth hormone. *J. Pediatr.* 104:801–813.

Schultz, F.R., Hayford, J.T., Wolraich, M.L., Hintz, R.L. & Thompson, R.G. (1982), Methylphenidate treatment of hyperactive children: Effects on the hypothalamic-pituitary-somatomedin axis. *Pediatrics*, 70:987–992.

Shaywitz, S.E., Hunt, R.D., Jatlow, P., Cohen, D.J., Young, J.G., Pierce, R.N., Anderson, G.M. & Shaywitz, B.A. (1982), Psychopharmacology of attention deficit disorder: Pharmacokinetic, neuroendocrine, and behavioral measures following acute and chronic treatment with methylphenidate. *Pediatrics*, 69:688–694.

Weizman, R., Dick, J., Gil-Ad, I., Weitz, R., Tyano, S. & Laron, Z. (1987), Effects of acute and chronic methylphenidate administration on b-endorphin, growth hormone, prolactin and cortisol in children with attention deficit disorder with hyperactivity. *Life Sci*, 40:2247–2252.

Werry, J.S., Aman, M.G. & Diamond, E. (1979), Imipramine and methylphenidate in hyperactive children. *J. Child Psychol. Psychiatry*, 21:27–35.

Zametkin, A.J. & Rapoport, J.L. (1987), Neurobiology of attention deficit disorder with hyperactivity: Where have we come in 50 years? *J. Am. Acad. Child Psychiatry*, 26:676–686.

Ritalin and Brain Metabolism

CHRISTINE A. REDMAN and ALAN J. ZAMETKIN

INTRODUCTION

Methylphenidate (Ritalin) has complex effects on human brain metabolism and function. To understand these actions, the methodology involved in measuring brain metabolism must be appreciated. This chapter traces the development of studies that have allowed human research on brain metabolism to proceed in adults with attention deficit hyperactivity disorder (ADHD). These studies have permitted localization of the metabolic effects of stimulants in general and Ritalin in particular. We will first review basic studies of stimulant effects on brain metabolism using animal models. This will illuminate the pathway leading to later human studies and reinforce the difficulty in interpreting human brain metabolism research. Clinical ramifications of this work will also be briefly discussed.

BACKGROUND

Before medications could be used to study human brain metabolism, years of preliminary laboratory studies were carried out. Pivotal to the field was the development of the deoxyglucose method by Louis Sokoloff and collaborators in the Laboratory of Cerebral Metabolism at the National Institute of Mental Health (Sokoloff et al., 1977). The groundwork for today's human studies utilizing positron emission tomography (PET) and fluorodeoxyglucose (FDG) were initially carried out on rats using the quantitative autoradiographic deoxyglucose method of brain imaging. Autoradiographic technique requires application of brain slices to radiosensitive slides allowing for detection of glucose uptake (specifically deoxyglucose) that has been tagged or labeled with carbon-14 (^{14}C). These early studies led to today's PET studies utilizing tomographic scanners which detect similar glucose tracers such as fluorine-18- (^{18}F) labeled deoxyglucose to measure glucose uptake and utilization without invasive brain sectioning.

The quantitative autoradiographic deoxyglucose method of brain imaging has been very useful for showing how methylphenidate (MPH) alters local cerebral glucose utilization (LCGU) in the brains of rats. Several studies (Porrino et al., 1984; Sokoloff et al., 1977) have used this method as an indicator of how LCGU is altered by different dosage levels of various stimulant medications. An early study by Porrino et al. (1984) set precedence by using autoradiography to measure LCGU in conscious rats following acute administration of dextroamphetamine. Measurement of rates of LCGU was made on 24 rats in accordance with procedures described by Sokoloff et al. (1977). Behavioral observations were made with timed blood sampling during uptake in order to assess the behavioral manifestations associated with measurable glucose utilization.

The results of Porrino's research show three separate patterns of change occurring in LCGU in specific regions of the rat brain after dextroamphetamine treatment. Acute administration (0.2–5.0 mg/kg) was shown to produce dose-dependent alterations. The effects at the lowest doses employed (0.2 and 0.5 mg/kg) were clearly selective to the nucleus accumbens. With increasing doses (1.0 mg/kg), alterations in LCGU rates involved components of the nigrostriatal, mesolimbic, and mesocortical dopaminergic systems, as well as the neocortical and allocortical areas. The third observed pattern was characterized by activity in the nigrostriatal extrapyramidal system at the highest dose of 5.0 mg/kg. Porrino et al. suggested that the

Laboratory of Cerebral Metabolism, National Institute of Mental Health, Bethesda, Maryland dopaminergic structures share a heterogeneous responsiveness to dextroamphetamine but have at least three different sensitivity thresholds (see Fig. 1). Porrino et al. also suggested that special attention should be paid to the nucleus accumbens because of evidence which supports a role for it in the mediation of locomotor behavior.

Dose-dependent changes produced by stimulant medication were also observed in the behavior of the animals under the partial restraint that was required for this study. At the lowest level of administration (1.25 mg/kg), increased arousal was shown by sniffing and heightened reaction to environmental stimuli. At the 2.5 and 5.0 mg/kg doses, the behavioral response was characterized by increased head and limb movement, head bobbing, reaching, and arching of the body, in addition to the behaviors seen at the lowest dose. Chewing behavior was displayed in some of the animals at the 5.0 mg/kg dose. Stereotypy and focused behavior were seen at the highest dose (15 mg/kg), the predominant behaviors being licking, chewing, intense reaching of the forelimbs, and arching of the body.

Bell et al. (1983) and Porrino et al. (1984) have used the autoradiographic technique to assess the changes in LCGU with respect to MPH. Bell et al. reported that Ritalin decreased metabolism in the motor cortex. They postulated that the difficulty that hyperactive patients face lies in a problem with sensory–motor integration, specifically the role of dopaminergic pathways.

Because Bell's study used only one dosage level (15 mg/kg), well above the known therapeutic range for humans, the results are not readily applicable to clinical populations. Their work led Porrino's group to further studies that clarified behavioral and physiological response to a wider variety of dose ranges.

Porrino's (1984) study extended the previous work in two ways. First, the effects of MPH were shown to be dose dependent. Second, LCGU changes were observed to be more widespread than was seen in previous studies (see Fig. 2).

When the rates and distribution of LCGU alterations in 31 cerebral structures were examined, it was observed that different areas were affected by different amounts of MPH. At the lowest of administration (1.25 mg/kg), significant increases in glucose metabolism were seen only in the nucleus accumbens, the olfactory tubercle, mediodorsal nucleus of the thalamus, the substantia nigra pars reticulata, and lateral frontal granular cortex.

At the 2.5 mg/kg dose, the extrapyramidal system, specifically the globus pallidus, entopendoncular nucleus, and the subthalamic nucleus were significantly affected as well in the compacta and reticulata portions of the substantia nigra. No significant increases, however, were seen in the caudate nucleus. In the limbic forebrain, the nucleus accumbens and the olfactory tubercle showed significant alterations.

The pattern of LCGU changes that resulted from administration of the 5.0 mg/kg were very similar to that of the 2.5 mg/kg dose.

The third observed pattern of metabolic change occurred at the 15 mg/kg dose level. While no overall increase or decrease in the average LCGU was observed in the caudate nucleus, visual inspection showed two dark bands of intense glucose use in the most lateral portion of the caudate. This is further evidence for the heterogeneity of function in the striatum in relation to methylphenidate metabolism.

A variety of imaging techniques have been used to study the effects of Ritalin and other stimulants on brain physiology. This section will review those human studies.

HUMAN STUDIES: BLOOD FLOW STUDIES

There are several methods available for the study of the effects of methylphenidate on human brain physiology. Hans Lou and colleagues chose the Xenon-133 inhalation method and computed emission tomography (Lou et al., 1984). This technique gives a three-dimensional image of the regional cerebral blood flow (rCBF). Lou's subjects were children divided into three groups: (1) children with pure ADHD, (2) children with ADD plus dyslexia, and (3) normal children. Six of the ADD subjects were restudied with Ritalin treatment.

The six children receiving Ritalin (10–30 mg) were examined immediately prior to receiving medication and 30 and 60 minutes after medication. The rCBF pattern before medication was subtracted from the rCBF after medication in each patient to determine which regions of neuronal activity were affected.

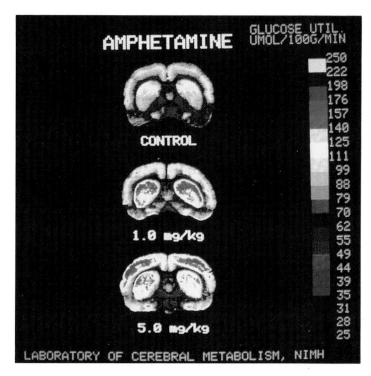

FIG. 1. The effect of two doses of D-amphetamine on glucose utilization in the rat. Warm colors denote higher glucose uptake (printed with permission of Linda Porrino.)

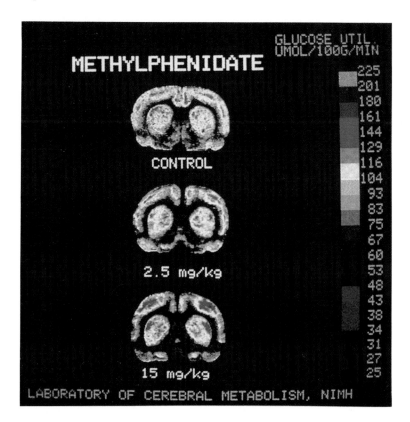

FIG. 2. The effect of two doses of methylphenidate on glucose utilization in the rat. Warm colors denote higher glucose uptake (printed with permission of Linda Porrino).

The results of Lou et al. show hypoperfusion in blood flow activity in the anterior medial frontal lobes in all patients with ADD. Seven of the subjects with ADD showed hypoperfusion in the caudate nuclei region. After methylphenidate treatment, all six children showed increased flow in the mesencephalon and the basal ganglia.

A followup study by Lou et al. (1989) extended the previous work by expanding the number of patients. The population consisted of six patients with pure ADHD and 13 patients with ADHD in combination with other neurologic symptoms. Again the Xenon-133 inhalation and emission tomography method was used.

This study argued that the caudate region may have hypoperfused blood flow and that the head of the caudate is dysfunctional in ADHD. This dysfunction may be partially reversed with Ritalin. However, both studies used children who were atypical because of multiple neurological insults and there was inadequate age matching in controls.

BRAIN METABOLISM AND PET

Positron emission tomography (PET) is one of the most important advances in helping us understand the living brain. It is uniquely suited to neuropsychiatric research in that it allows us to see the living, functioning brain, in fine resolution. PET enables one to visualize tracers with extreme sensitivity and high spatial resolution with uniform quantification that can be obtained only with a PET scanner. These studies result from the use of positron-emitting radionuclides such as [^{18}F]fluorodeoxyglucose (FDG).

A positron-emitting radionuclide decays by emitting a positron from a proton that changes to a neutron. As the FDG is taken up by brain tissue, it emits a positron that travels a few millimeters before it meets its antiparticle, the electron. This results in annihilation of both particles and production of two 511 keV photons that travel at an 180° angle. By creating a scanner that makes use of simultaneous detection of photons in a specific geometrical arrangement, one achieves the quantitative imaging power possible only with PET.

The four most commonly used radionuclides and their half-lives are: ^{15}O (2 min), ^{13}N (10 min), ^{11}C (20 min), and ^{18}F (110 min). All of these are very effective in allowing for reasonable resolution with acceptable radiation exposure to the patient. The most commonly used PET tracer for cerebral metabolic studies is [^{18}F]2,fluoro-2-deoxy-D-glucose (FDG).

PET AND ATTENTION DEFICIT HYPERACTIVITY DISORDER (ADHD)

Although the syndromal validity of attention deficit hyperactive disorder is not clear and remains controversial, family and longitudinal studies have clearly demonstrated a genetic component to this disorder. Furthermore, followup studies (Weiss et al., 1985) have demonstrated that at least 50% of "grown-up" hyperactive children continue to complain of at least one disabling symptom of ADHD.

Only the dramatic and well-documented response to stimulant medication and family studies of inheritance of ADHD support a biological basis for this disorder. No consistent biological/biochemical differences have been found to differentiate normal from hyperactive children.

Serious methodological difficulties exist in early CT and blood flow studies of this disorder. Given our laboratory's interest in selective attention and its effects on cerebral glucose metabolism in normals and neuropsychiatric disorders, we set out to determine the rates of glucose metabolism in adults with ADHD. Because of the ethical restraints on research in children involving ionizing radiation, we chose to study adult parents of children currently diagnosed with attention deficit disorder with hyperactivity (ADDH) who were themselves hyperactive in childhood and who continue to be symptomatic as adults.

Patients were included if they: (1) met the Wender Utah Criteria for ADD Residual Type, (2) had clear-cut childhood history of ADHD, (3) were a parent of currently diagnosed child with attention deficit disorder with hyperactivity and, (4) free of all axis I, *Diagnostic and Statistical Manual III* diagnoses except specified developmental disorders (i.e., reading, arithmetic). No subject was studied who had ever met criteria for any substance abuse disorder. Assessment of patients included structured psychiatric interview (SADS), and neuropsychological testing including academic achievement assessment. Self and spouse behavioral ratings were obtained. Retrospective childhood ratings by parents of the adult subjects were obtained when available. Because widespread cerebral metabolic decrements in cerebral glucose metabolism had been established in prefrontal, premotor, and superior parietal regions of adults with ADDH (Zametkin et al., 1990) our group became interested in studying the effects of stimulants in these adults. A subgroup of these adults was chosen for participation in a second PET study preceded by a single dose of methylphenidate.

The patient group consisted of 6 males and 1 female, mean age 38.3. None of the subjects scanned had been previously treated with stimulant medication. A battery of life adjustment questions was also used to assess global functioning, social adjustment, and quantification of alcohol use as well as contact with the judicial system.

Cerebral metabolic rates are very sensitive to the behavioral state during the PET scan procedure. To control for this phenomena, both controls and patients performed an auditory attention task during the scan. This task activates medial frontal areas in normals (Cohen et al., 1987).

Scans were performed with eyes patched. Subjects performed the auditory attention task during the injection of 4–5 mCi of [^{18}F]2-fluoro-2-deoxyglucose (FDG) and for 30 minutes during uptake of the tracer. Tracer input curve was calculated from blood samples obtained from the right radial artery.

Twenty eight slices were obtained from each subject starting at 5 mm above the plane parallel to the canthomeatal line (CM). The interslice interval was approximately 3.5 mm, each parallel to the CM line. Scans were performed with a Scanditronix scanner with a 5-6 mm full-width half-maximum (FWHM) in-plane resolution and used a transmission scan for calculation of attenuation. The subjects' heads were stabilized throughout the scan procedure by a hexalite plastic mask.

For the extraction of regional glucose metabolic rate, 60 regions of interest were measured in five standard planes by two independent raters unaware of the identity and diagnosis of the individual they were evaluating (see Fig. 3). This technique is similar to the analysis of Clark et al. (1985). Raw pixel values were converted to glucose metabolic rates.

Global glucose rates refer to the estimates of the average value for glucose metabolism obtained for all the gray matter-rich areas of the brain sampled. Regional metabolic rates presented here are the average of normalized glucose metabolic data obtained from the region of interest. The normalization procedure is designed to minimize the effects of individual variation in global glucose metabolism. Normalization is accomplished by dividing an individual's glucose metabolic rate in the region of interest by his or her global (gray) glucose metabolic rate (region/global). This procedure is similar in principle to the "reference ratio" or "landscape method" of Phelps et al. (1981).

Given differences between controls and adults with ADHD (Zametkin et al., 1990), we wondered whether stimulant medications, clearly effective in 75% of children treated, would alter brain metabolism. To answer this question, 7 hyperactive adults returned for a second PET scan. Each individual received a single oral dose of methylphenidate .35 mg/kg 90 minutes prior to isotope injection. To control for order effects, several subjects were first scanned on medication and later rescanned off medication. Statistical analysis was by paired t-test between patients on and off medications.

RESULTS

Figure 3 graphically illustrates the effect of a single oral dose of MPH in 7 individuals with attention deficit disorder in adulthood. No effects were noted on global metabolism. Of 60 regions of interest, 2 showed significant increases in brain metabolism following medication administration. These areas are confined to the B plane approximately 81 mm above the canthomeatal line. Bilaterally, the left and right anterior frontal areas showed a trend for increased metabolism. Similarly the left rolandic and left parietal regions were metabolically activated over baseline. Interestingly, in the "E" plane, the left temporal region metabolism was depressed. When subcortical regions were examined most regions showed reductions in metabolism (see Table 1).

Several notes of caution are necessary in interpreting these preliminary findings from our laboratory. First and foremost is the incomplete nature of our ongoing study. A sample size of approximately 12 pairs of scans will be necessary to reach enough statistical power to draw firm conclusions. Of interest however, even at this preliminary stage, are the increases in metabolism not previously seen in other human PET studies with

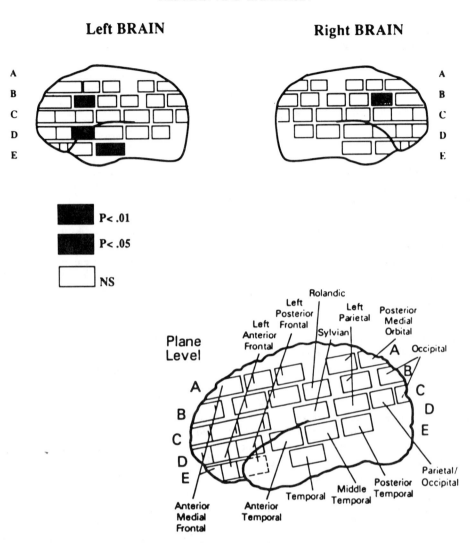

FIG. 3. The effects of a single oral dose (.35 mg/kg) of methylphenidate on metabolism in human brain. Rates increased in B plane and decreased in D and E planes. Figure shows statistical difference of on-drug vs. off-drug in seven subjects.

dextroamphetamine. For example, Wolkin et al. (1987) have reported global and widespread reductions in cerebral metabolism following treatment with 0.25 mg/kg of dextroamphetamine in both normals and schizophrenic patients. The limited metabolic increases here are consistent with animal studies (Porrino et al., 1984) reviewed earlier. There are several major differences with the animal studies that likely will make comparisons difficult at best. The most obvious difference is the exceedingly high doses used in the animal work as compared with the human studies. Furthermore, animal studies involved intravenous administration of drug and glucose uptake periods were 15 minutes after drug administration. The human study reported here involved administration by mouth and glucose uptake period was 90 minutes after medication administration.

Will different stimulants have different metabolic patterns? Clearly, dose will be an important variable. Given known potency differences between stimulants, only imaging studies at a variety of doses will allow comparisons between stimulants. Differential clinical response to stimulants in hyperactive children, at least at the lower dose ranges, has been reported (Elias, personal communication), and earlier biochemical studies have shown differential effects of a variety of stimulants upon the excretion of urinary catecholamines

TABLE 1. STIMULANT EFFECTS ON SUBCORTICAL
GLUCOSE METABOLISM (PERCENT CHANGE
FROM BASELINE)

	Ritalin (N = 7)
Left thalamus	+6.0
Right thalamus	−1.0
Left caudate	−6.0
Right caudate	−4.0
Left anterior putamen	−9.0
Right anterior putamen	−8.0
Left anterior basal ganglia	−7.0 (.04)
Right anterior basal ganglia	−6.0
Left basal ganglia	−4.0
Right basal ganglia	−5.0

(Zametkin et al., 1989). Therefore, differential effects on brain metabolism of a variety of stimulants might be expected.

The future of the field of brain imaging and medication effects holds promise. At some point metabolic patterns in unmedicated states might allow better medication selection. Studies of treatment response in relation to metabolic change produced by medications such as Ritalin are already underway.

REFERENCES

Bell, R., Guillermo, A.M. & Schwartzman, R.J. (1983), Methylphenidate decreases local glucose metabolism in the motor cortex. *Pharmacol. Biochem. Behav.*, 18:1–5.

Clark, C., Carson, R., Kessler, R. et al. (1985), Alternative statistical models for the examination of clinical positron emission tomography/fluorodeoxyglucose data. *J. Cerebral Blood Flow Metab.*, 5:142–150.

Cohen, R.M., Semple, W.E., Gross, M., Nordahl, T.E. et al. (1987), Dysfunction in a prefrontal substrate of sustained attention in schizophrenia. *Life Sci.*, 40:2031–2034.

Lou, H.C., Henrikson, L., Bruhn, P., Psych, C. (1984), Focal cerebral hypoperfusion in children with dysphasia and/or attention deficit disorder. *Arch. Neurol.*, 41:825–829.

——— ——— ——— Broker, H. & Nelson, J.B. (1989), Striatal dysfunction in attention deficit and hyperkinetic disorder. *Arch. Neurol.*, 46:48–52.

Phelps, M.E., Mazziotta, J.C., Kuhl, D.E. et al. (1981), Tomographic mapping of human cerebral metabolism visual stimulation and deprivation. *Neurology*, 31:517–529.

Porrino, L.J., Lucignani, G., Dow-Edwards, D. & Sokoloff, L. (1984), Correlation of dose-dependent effects of acute amphetamine administration on behavior and local cerebral metabolism in rats. *Brain Res.*, 307:311–320.

Sokoloff, L., Reivich, M., Kennedy, C., Dies Razors, M.H., Potluck, C.S., Pettigrew, K.D., Sakurada, O. & Shanohara, M. (1977), The [^{14}C]deoxyglucose method for the measurement of local cerebral glucose utilization: Theory, procedure and normal values in the conscious and anesthetized albino rat. *J. Neurochem.*, 28:897–916.

Weiss, G., Hechtman, L., Milray, T. & Perlman, T. (1985), Psychiatric status of hyperactives as adults: A controlled perspective 15-year follow-up of 63 hyperactive children. *J Am. Acad. Child Adolesc. Psychiatry*, 24:211–220.

Wolkin, A., Angrist, B., Wolf, A. et al. (1987), Effects of amphetamine on local cerebral metabolism in normal and schizophrenic subjects as determined by positron emission tomography. *Psychopharmacology*, 92:241–246.

Zametkin, A. & Rapoport, J.L. (1987), Neurobiology of attention deficit disorder with hyperactivity: Where have we come in 50 years? *Am. Acad. Child Adolesc. Psychiatry*, 26:676–686.

—— Nordahl, T., Gross, M., King, A.C., Semple, W., Rumsey, J., Hamburger, S. & Cohen, R. (1990), Brain metabolism in hyperactive adults with childhood onset. *N. Engl. J. Med.*, 323:1361–1366.

Provocative Tests with Methylphenidate in Schizophrenia and Schizophrenia Spectrum Disorders

DELBERT ROBINSON, M.D.,[1] DARLENE JODY, M.D.[2] and
JEFFREY A. LIEBERMAN, M.D.[1]

INTRODUCTION

Research psychiatrists have reason to envy their medical colleagues in hematology and dermatology who routinely obtain tissue specimens for evaluation of pathologic changes. Except under very rare circumstances, psychiatrists do not have direct access to the brain to study pathophysiologic correlates of psychiatric diseases. Instead, psychiatrists are forced to use indirect methods to study neurochemical factors in psychiatric illnesses. A common method used in these endeavors is the use of pharmacologic probes. In these paradigms, subjects are given a pharmacologic agent and their behavior is then monitored. Behavioral changes following administration of the agent are assumed to be secondary to the agent given. If the agent used as a probe has known effects on neurotransmitter systems, one can make hypotheses about the role of these particular neurotransmitter systems in the behaviors observed.

This chapter discusses the use of methylphenidate challenges in the study of schizophrenia. Since a large body of work has been done using other psychostimulants, primarily amphetamine, as pharmacologic probes in schizophrenia, studies with other psychostimulants will also be reviewed to provide a context for the methylphenidate studies. Challenge studies with psychostimulants have been important in our understanding of the neurochemistry of schizophrenia. They also have potential clinical utility in areas such as predicting propensity to relapse in patients withdrawn from neuroleptics. At the end of the chapter, psychostimulant challenges in disorders related to schizophrenia are discussed.

BACKGROUND: WHY USE PSYCHOSTIMULANT CHALLENGES TO STUDY SCHIZOPHRENIA?

Three years after the first reported use of amphetamine in a medical context (Prinzmetal and Bloomberg, 1935), Young and Scoville (1938) described the first case of amphetamine-induced psychosis. Since then, chronic use of psychostimulants has been shown to produce psychotic episodes, closely resembling paranoid schizophrenia in some individuals (Angrist and Gershon, 1970; Bell, 1973; Connell, 1958; Griffith et al., 1972). Further, repeated high doses of amphetamine have been demonstrated to have psychotogenic effects in normal control subjects who do not have a history of previous drug usage or psychotic symptoms (Angrist et al., 1974; Griffith et al., 1968). Thus, psychostimulant administration, either chronically or in high doses acutely, can produce psychotic symptoms resembling schizophrenia. Assuming that psycho-stimulant-induced psychotic symptoms are a valid model for schizophrenic symptoms, then psychostimulants could be useful in studying the biology of schizophrenia (Angrist and vanKammen 1984). This chapter will focus on the psychostimulant challenge paradigm as one method to study schizophrenia. This strategy is distinguished from other strategies, such as the chronic amphetamine studies described above, in that schizophrenic subjects are hypothesized to have an increased vulnerability to the psychotogenic effects of psychostimulants. As such, doses of psychostimulants used in challenge paradigms are subpsychotogenic;

---

[1]Hillside Hospital, Glen Oaks, New York; [2]Sandoz Research Institute, East Hanover, New Jersey

i.e. low enough so as not to provoke psychotic symptoms in nonschizoprenic subjects, in order to obtain a differential behavioral response between schizophrenic and nonschizoprenic subjects. Additionally, challenge paradigms involve acute, usually one time, administration of psychostimulants.

NEUROTRANSMITTER EFFECTS

In order to assess the results of psychostimulant challenges in schizophrenia, a knowledge of the neurotransmitter effects of psychostimulants is helpful. Methylphenidate and other psychostimulants exert agonistic effects on catecholamine neurotransmission (Ferris et al., 1972; Groves and Rebec, 1976; Moore 1978; Scheel-Krüger, 1971). Psychostimulants predominantly act by releasing biogenic amines from storage sites in presynaptic nerve terminals and blocking their reuptake. Within the class of psychostimulants, differences in biochemical effects exist. Although psychostimulant drugs exert agonistic effects on several neurotransmitter systems including dopamine, norepinephrine, and to a lesser extent serotonin, methylphenidate preferentially inhibits the neuronal reuptake of dopamine (Ferris et al., 1972, Nielsen et al., 1983; Scheel-Krüger, 1971). Amphetamine releases dopamine from a small newly synthesized extravesicular pool while methylphenidate releases dopamine from a synthesis independent pool that is reserpine sensitive (McMillen, 1983). While amphetamine stimulates dopamine synthesis in vitro and in vivo, methylphenidate does not alter dopamine biosynthesis in vivo at doses which produce behavioral effects in animals (Fung and Uretsky, 1982). These biochemical differences within the group of psychostimulant drugs may result in differences in their behavioral effects. In particular, psychostimulant drugs may differ in their psychotogenic potency with methylphenidate being more potent in causing psychotic activation than other psychostimulants.

BEHAVIORAL EFFECTS OF PSYCHOSTIMULANTS IN NORMAL AND NONSCHIZOPHRENIC PSYCHIATRICALLY ILL SUBJECTS

Psychostimulant challenge paradigms are concerned with the differential effects of psychostimulants in schizophrenics compared with the effects in normal subjects or nonschizoprenic psychiatric patients. In this section, we briefly review the effects of psychostimulants in normal and nonschizophrenic psychiatrically ill subjects before discussing psychostimulant effects in schizophrenic subjects.

In normal subjects, acute psychostimulant challenge with subpsychotogenic doses primarily produces feelings of elation and well being, vigor, and talkativeness, although depression and sedation can occur in some subjects (Brown, 1977; Dommisse et al., 1984; Smith and Davis, 1977). Some of these effects are dose related. Brown (1977) compared the effects of 10 mg of oral methylphenidate, 20 mg of oral methylphenidate, and placebo in 17 normal volunteers. Vigor and surgency (composed of items related to being "carefree, playful and witty") scores did not differ between placebo and 10 mg of methylphenidate but were significantly increased with 20 mg of methylphenidate compared with either placebo or 10 mg of methylphenidate. Elation scores significantly increased between placebo, 10 mg and 20 mg doses of methylphenidate. Normal subjects may also vary in their response to different psychostimulants. Smith and Davis (1977) compared the effects of D-amphetamine, L-amphetamine, and methylphenidate in 16 normal subjects. Euphoric response to one isomer of amphetamine was significantly predictive of response to the other amphetamine isomer but was not correlated with euphoric response to methylphenidate.

In regard to subjects with nonschizophrenic psychiatric disorders, the predominant responses to psychostimulant challenge that have been reported for euthymic bipolar subjects are activation and euphoric mood (Meyendorff et al., 1985; Silberman et al., 1981; Wald et al., 1978). Subjects with major depression have variable mood responses to psychostimulant challenge with responses ranging from elevated mood to no effect to dysphoria reported (Baxter et al., 1988; Brown and Brawley, 1983; Joyce et al., 1986; Sabelli et al., 1983; Silberman et al., 1981). Thus, the response of nonschizophrenic subjects to psychostimulants is heterogeneous. This heterogeneity must be considered in evaluating the response of schizophrenic subjects to psychostimulant challenge.

Limitations of psychostimulant challenges

In evaluating the psychostimulant studies in schizophrenia discussed below, several limitations of the psychostimulant challenge strategy should be kept in mind. First, in trying to relate behavioral response to specific neurotransmitter systems, it is important to remember that psychostimulant challenges are only indirect measures of a specific neurotransmitter system's involvement in a particular behavior. Although the finding that sustained psychostimulant usage could produce a toxic psychosis closely resembling schizophrenia was a significant contribution to the dopamine hypothesis of schizophrenia (Meltzer and Stahl, 1976; Snyder, 1973), psychostimulant challenges cannot provide direct proof of dopamine or any other neurotransmitter system's involvement in schizophrenia. One could argue that the behavioral effects seen following psychostimulant challenge are an epiphenomenon and not related to the neurotransmitter system(s) primarily involved in schizophrenia. The nonselective nature of psychostimulants adds further to the difficulty in attributing the effect to a particular neurotransmitter in schizophrenia. Psychostimulants act on several neurotransmitter systems including dopamine, norepinephrine, and, to a lesser extent, serotonin. Thus, although psychostimulant challenges can provide suggestive evidence that dopamine systems are involved in a particular behavior, definitive proof of dopamine system involvement in a behavior requires the use of more specific methods.

A second limitation of psychostimulant challenges is the physical effects of psychostimulants which restrict the subjects who are eligible for psychostimulant challenge studies. The major limiting factor is the cardiovascular effects of psychostimulants. Lucas et al. (1986, 1987) reported that 2 of 12 medically healthy subjects developed premature ventricular contractions after methylphenidate (0.3 mg/kg IV in one patient and 0.15 mg/kg IV in the other patient). One of the subjects also developed premature ventricular contractions during a placebo infusion. Robinson et al. (1988) reported on 77 patients (72 with schizophrenia and 5 with borderline personality disorder) who underwent a total of 102 infusions with methylphenidate 0.5 mg/kg intravenously. Subjects uniformly had elevations of blood pressure and pulse rate. Peak heart rate averaged 123.5 beats/min (range 94–160). Peak systolic blood pressure averaged 150 mmHg (range 104–182), and peak diastolic blood pressure averaged 88.7/mmHg (range 74–114). These blood pressure and pulse changes are within the limits allowed for young subjects during cardiac stress testing (Ellestad, 1986). All subjects had continuous cardiac monitoring during the infusions. ECG records of the last 26 subjects studied were reviewed. Most developed a sinus tachycardia, two developed a sinus arrhythmia, and one developed a supraventricular tachycardia. None developed premature ventricular contractions. Thus, methylphenidate challenges do not represent a serious risk to young, medically healthy subjects who receive adequate medical monitoring after the challenge. However, these physical effects of psychostimulant do limit the use of the psychostimulant challenges in older subjects or in subjects with preexisting, especially cardiovascular, medical conditions.

OVERVIEW OF PSYCHOSTIMULANT CHALLENGES IN SCHIZOPHRENIA

Lieberman et al. (1987a) reviewed 36 studies measuring psychostimulant response in schizophrenia (Anderson, 1938; Angrist et al., 1980; 1985; Askar et al., 1970; Belart, 1942; Bischoff, 1951; Davidoff and Reifenstein, 1939; Delay, 1949; Flugel, 1938; Gottlieb and Coburn, 1944; Gottlieb et al., 1945; Guile, 1963; Guttman and Sargant, 1937; Hope et al., 1951; Janowsky and Davis, 1976; Janowsky et al., 1973, 1977, 1978; Jonas, 1954; Kiloh et al., 1974; Kornetsky, 1976; Lehmann and Ban, 1964; Levine et al., 1978; Liddell, 1953; Modell and Hussar, 1965; Pennes, 1954; Schube et al., 1937; Simon and Taube, 1946; vanKammen et al., 1977, 1980, 1982a,b,c; Witton, 1960a,b; Woolley, 1938). In eight of these studies (Guile, 1963; Janowsky and Davis, 1976; Janowsky et al., 1973, 1977, 1978; Lehman and Ban, 1964; Witton, 1960a,b), methylphenidate was one of or the only psychostimulant used. Given the varying original goals of the studies and the range of 48 years over which the studies were published, the design and methodology of the studies varied widely. For studies that did not define response explicitly, response was defined as either worse (a clinically significant deterioration in mental condition or behavior), improved (a decrease in mental symptoms or improvement in behavior), or no change (no significant difference in mental condition or behavior from pretreatment). For schizophrenic subjects, worsening required increased

ROBINSON ET AL.

psychotic symptoms. For nonschizophrenic subjects, two categories of worsening were used, worsening and worsening with psychotic symptoms (defined as the development or exacerbation of psychotic symptoms). The 36 studies included 1,218 subjects, approximately half of whom had schizophrenia. However, in eight studies (Davidoff and Reifenstein, 1939; Gottlieb et al., 1945; Janowsky et al., 1978; Kiloh et al., 1974; Lehmann and Ban, 1964; Liddell and Weil-Malherbe, 1953; Modell and Hussar, 1965; Witton, 1960a), individual response rates could not be determined. The remaining 28 studies included 939 subjects of whom 48% had schizophrenia. Nonschizophrenic subjects for these studies were diagnostically heterogeneous with few having a history of psychotic symptoms. Overall, in these 28 studies, 40% of schizophrenic subjects worsened after psychostimulant administration, 19% improved, and 41% showed no change. For the nonschizophrenic subjects, 18% worsened, 2% worsened with psychotic symptoms, 40% improved, and 40% showed no change. These differences in response rates of the schizophrenic and nonschizophrenic groups were significant at the $p = 0.001$ level. In 11 studies (Anderson, 1938; Askar et al., 1970; Flugel, 1938; Guile, 1963; Janowsky et al., 1973, 1977; Jonas, 1954; Kiloh et al., 1974; Schube et al., 1937; Simon and Taube, 1946; Woolley 1938), within study comparisons of response rates of schizophrenic versus nonschizophrenic subjects could be made. In seven of these studies (Askar et al., 1970; Guile, 1963; Janowsky et al., 1973, 1977; Jonas, 1954; Simon and Taube, 1946; Woolley, 1938), rates of worsening were substantially higher in the schizophrenic compared with the nonschizophrenic subjects whereas in four of these studies (Anderson, 1938; Flugel, 1938; Kiloh et al., 1974; Schube et al., 1937) this pattern was not detected. Of note is that three of the four studies which did not have higher rates of worsening in schizophrenic compared with nonschizophrenic subjects were done in the 1930s. In the fourth study by Kiloh et al. (1974), schizophrenic subjects "with florid symptoms and disturbed behavior" were excluded. In all eleven studies, no consistent pattern in improvement or no change responses was detected. For comparison, rates of worsening for the nonschizophrenic subjects varied from 0% to 50% in the different studies. However, worsening with psychotic symptoms was very rare and occurred in only nine subjects in three studies (Janowsky et al., 1973, 1977; Schube et al., 1937).

Several important conclusions can be derived from the Lieberman et al. review. First, psychostimulant challenge in schizophrenic subjects produces a heterogeneous response in terms of activation of psychotic symptoms. A large number of subjects (40% and 41%, respectively) worsen or have no change in psychotic symptoms after psychostimulant challenge with a much smaller number (19%) improving. Second, schizophrenic subjects are significantly more likely to have a psychotogenic response to psychostimulant challenge than nonschizophrenic subjects without a history of psychotic symptoms. Third, given the heterogeneity in the response of schizophrenic subjects to psychostimulant challenge, one or more factors besides diagnosis must affect psychostimulant psychotogenic response. Possible factors modifying psychostimulant response in schizophrenic subjects will be examined next. These include the type of psychostimulant used, the route and dose of psychostimulant administered, the stage of illness, and neuroleptic treatment status.

TYPE OF PSYCHOSTIMULANT ADMINISTERED

In comparison with other psychostimulants, methylphenidate has been shown to be the most potent psychotogen. Janowsky and Davis (1976) gave equimolar (0.11 mmol) intravenous doses of dextroamphetamine, levamfetamine, and methylphenidate in a randomized order on different days to 16 acutely ill schizophrenic subjects. Not all subjects received each drug, but all subjects received at least two different drugs. After infusion, subjects were rated on items of psychosis, conceptual disorganization, unusual thoughts, anger, irritability, interactions, and talkativeness. All three medication conditions caused statistically significant increases over baseline scores on a combined psychosis rating (which included the global psychosis, conceptual disorganization, and unusual thoughts ratings) and on an activation rating (which combined the talkativeness and interaction ratings). At equimolar dosages, methylphenidate was 300% and dextroamphetamine was 207% as effective as levamfetamine in increasing the combined psychosis scores from baseline values. Consistent with the findings of the Janowsky and Davis study are pooled data from the previously described Lieberman et al. (1987a) review of 36 psychostimulant challenge studies. Comparing the rates of improvement, no change and worsening in the five studies (N = 65) using

312

methylphenidate with the nine studies (N = 127) using *d*-ephedrine and the 13 studies (N = 281) using amphetamine, methylphenidate produced the highest worsening rate (74%) and lowest improvement (0%) and no change rates (26%) in schizophrenic subjects of the three agents. Differences in pooled rates of response in the Lieberman et al. review could be influenced by many factors besides drug used. Despite this, the Lieberman et al. review with its large number of subjects and the Janowsky and Davis study with its methodologic rigor but small number of subjects provide strong evidence that psychostimulants differ in their psychotogenic potency, with methylphenidate being the most potent psychotogen.

DOSE AND ROUTE OF ADMINISTRATION

For a given psychostimulant, dose and route of administration affect the amount of psychotic activation elicited. High acute doses of psychostimulants can produce psychotic symptoms in normals (Angrist and Gershon, 1970; Griffith et al., 1968). Since a requirement of psychostimulant challenge paradigms in schizophrenia is to use subpsychotogenic doses (i.e., doses that do not produce psychotic symptoms in nonschizophrenic subjects), dose is obviously an important aspect of study design. Unfortunately for ease in comparing results from studies using different doses of psychostimulants, the dose by psychosis response curve is not linear. Janowsky and Davis (1976) in their study of 0.11 mmol intravenous doses of dextroamphetamine, levamfetamine, and methylphenidate in acutely ill schizophrenics also gave subjects 0.055 mmol doses of dextroamphetamine. Dextroamphetamine doses of 0.11 mmol were 207% as effective as 0.11 mmol of levamfetamine in increasing psychotic activation from baseline levels. However, 0.055 mmol of dextroamphetamine was only 41% as effective as 0.11 mmol of levamfetamine in psychotic activation. Thus, decreasing the dose of dextroamphetamine by half reduced the psychotogenic effectiveness compared to 0.11 mmol of levamfetamine from 207% to 41%.

Besides the dose given, route of administration may also affect psychotogenic potency of psychostimulants. Parenteral administration, especially intravenous, produces a more potent pharmacological effect than oral administration possibly because of differences in bioavailability. Janowsky et al. (1978) compared two doses of methylphenidate, 0.5 mg/kg intravenously and 1.0 mg/kg orally. The intravenous dose was more potent than the oral dose. This may be secondary to a substantial "first-pass" metabolism of orally administered methylphenidate. Parenteral administration also is more potent than oral administration for other psychostimulants. Parenteral amphetamine has been associated with more profound worsening than oral administration (Bischoff, 1951; Davidoff and Reifenstein, 1939; Schube et al., 1937). In pooled data from Lieberman et al. (1987a), parenteral administration was associated with higher rates of worsening (53% vs. 27%) and a lower no change rate (26% vs. 55%) than oral administration. Thus, both the dose of psychostimulant given and the route of administration must be considered when evaluating psychostimulant challenges.

STAGE OF ILLNESS

Psychotogenic response to psychostimulants appear to be state dependent and not trait dependent. Janowsky et al. (1973) administered methylphenidate challenges to 13 schizophrenics both during an acute episode of psychosis and after a therapeutic response to neuroleptics. Subjects who had a psychotic symptom exacerbation while acutely ill did not have psychotic symptom exacerbation when retested after response to neuroleptics. In a similar finding, vanKammen et al. (1982d) give two intravenous amphetamine challenges four months apart to 17 subjects with schizophrenia or schizoaffective disorder. During the four month interval between infusions, clinical status of many patients had improved. Responses to the repeat infusions were heterogeneous. Of eight subjects who worsened on initial infusion, only three worsened on repeat infusion. Thus, schizophrenic subjects do not appear to be equally susceptible to the psychotogenic effects of psychostimulant challenge during all phases of their illness.

The differences in response to repeat psychostimulant challenge noted by Janowsky et al. (1973) and vanKammen et al. (1982d) are not totally explained by the presence or absence of active symptoms. In many studies, pre-existing active symptoms are not always associated with more psychotogenic responses. Pooled data from 36 studies reviewed by Lieberman et al. (1987a) showed little difference (43% vs. 35%) in rates of worsening between subjects with active symptoms (N = 339) compared with subjects without them (N = 69). Subjects with active symptoms had higher rates of improvement (21% vs. 6%) and lower rates of no change (36% versus 59%) to psychostimulant administration than subjects without active symptoms. These pooled data are consistent with the findings of Angrist et al. (1980) who found no relationship between baseline level of psychopathology and change after oral challenge with 0.5 mg/kg of D-amphetamine in hospitalized schizophrenic patients. Further, in the vanKammen et al. (1982d) study, schizophrenic subjects who improved after the initial intravenous challenge with 20 mg of D-amphetamine were significantly more psychotic before the infusion than subjects who did not improve.

The finding that active symptoms do not always predict worsening from psychostimulant challenge suggests that apparent, observable symptoms do not fully reflect patients' underlying conditions. Some patients who are stable by clinical behavioral criteria in this model may have a continuing biochemical abnormality which is sensitive to psychostimulant administration. If this is the case, psychostimulant challenge could then be used to define periods of biochemical abnormality in patients. Presumably, patients in remission from their illness both behaviorally and biochemically as assessed by psychostimulant challenge would have less chance of relapse than subjects who, although clinically stable, have continuing biochemical abnormalities. Given the difficult choices clinicians frequently face between exposing clinically stable schizophrenic subjects to the side effects of continuing neuroleptic treatment versus the risks of psychotic relapse with neuroleptic withdrawal, a way of predicting which patients will relapse off neuroleptics has great potential clinical utility.

To determine if psychostimulant challenge could predict relapse off medication, vanKammen et al. (1982a) gave 20 mg of D-amphetamine intravenously to 13 patients on pimozide prior to the pimozide being discontinued. Six patients had a psychotogenic response to the challenge on pimozide. All six of these subjects had a psychotic relapse within 20 days of stopping pimozide. In a sample of 34 subjects, Lieberman et al. (1987b) gave two challenges, one with 0.5 mg/kg of intravenous methylphenidate and the other with placebo, one week apart, to stable outpatients on neuroleptics in remission for at least six months. Subjects were withdrawn from neuroleptics and were given a second set of infusions, again with methylphenidate and placebo, 20 days (or 42 days if they had been on long-acting injectable neuroleptics) after stopping neuroleptics. Eleven subjects had a positive psychotogenic response to methylphenidate infusion and 23 had a negative response. Subjects were followed for up to 52 weeks (mean ±SD 21.4 ± 16.6 weeks). Subjects classified as positive responders to methylphenidate were significantly more likely to relapse during the follow-up period than negative responders. Of the 11 subjects with a positive psychotogenic response to the infusions, 10 relapsed during the follow-up period compared with 14 of the 23 negative responders who relapsed. Besides psychotogenic response to methylphenidate, tardive dyskinesia response to methylphenidate also predicted relapse rates. Subjects who had greater increases in tardive dyskinesia as measured by a modified version of the Simpson Dyskinesia Scale (Lieberman et al., 1984) relapsed sooner than subjects with lower increases in tardive dyskinesia ratings after methylphenidate. Examining other physical responses to methylphenidate, there was a trend association between greater blink-rate increases after methylphenidate and smaller pulse-rate increases after methylphenidate and shorter time to relapse. Since these physiologic responses have been reported to be mediated by dopaminergic mechanisms, changes in tardive dyskinesia, blink-rate, and pulse-rate from methylphenidate may be another measure of the dopaminergic mechanisms presumably also involved in the psychotic activation response to methylphenidate.

EFFECTS OF NEUROLEPTIC TREATMENT

Since psychostimulants enhance dopamine synaptic activity and neuroleptics block dopamine receptors, one could hypothesize that neuroleptic treatment would antagonize the psychotogenic effects of psychostimulants in schizophrenics. However, in pooled data from a review of 36 studies by Lieberman et al. (1987a), subjects on neuroleptics (N = 52) had higher rates of worsening (62% vs. 41%) than subjects off neuroleptics

(N = 300). Furthermore, subjects on neuroleptics had lower rates of no change from psychostimulants than did subjects off neuroleptics (33% vs. 43%). However, interpretation of these data is difficult because of the confound of differential presence of active symptoms among the groups.

To assess better the effects of neuroleptics on methylphenidate response, a test–retest design using the same subjects is required. In the test–retest studies of Janowsky et al. (1973, 1976, 1977, 1978) and vanKammen et al. (1977, 1980, 1982a,b,c), clinical status rather than neuroleptic status was the most important variable. However, in some of the vanKammen et al. studies (1980, 1982b), a lower proportion of subjects had a psychotogenic response to D-amphetamine when studied while on neuroleptics than when off neuroleptics. In the Janowsky et al. (1973) study, there was a nonsignificant decrease in psychotic symptom change scores for subjects tested while receiving neuroleptics compared with when tested off neuroleptics. Finally, Lieberman et al. (1987b) found a greater increase in psychosis ratings and a smaller increase in tardive dyskinesia and blink-rate responses to methylphenidate in subjects on neuroleptics than in the same subjects off neuroleptics. However, these changes were not statistically significant.

In summary, neuroleptic attenuation of the psychotogenic and physiologic responses of schizophrenic subjects to methylphenidate is present in some studies. However, chronic neuroleptic treatment does not block the pharmacologic effects of methylphenidate. Moreover, the effect of neuroleptics does not appear to be as robust as some of the previously discussed variables which modify methylphenidate response.

PSYCHOSTIMULANT CHALLENGES IN SCHIZOPHRENIA SPECTRUM DISORDERS

Besides their use in schizophrenia research, psychostimulant challenges have also been employed to study schizophrenia spectrum disorders. Schulz et al. (1985, 1988) gave oral amphetamine challenges, under double-blind conditions, to subjects with borderline personality disorder. In their first study, 4 of 8 subjects were rated as having a psychotic response to active amphetamine. No subject had a psychotic response to placebo. In a second sample of 16 subjects (8 with both borderline and schizotypal personality disorders and 8 with personality disorder only), significant increases in mean total scores on the Brief Psychiatric Rating Scale (BPRS) (Overall and Gorham, 1962) and in the activation and thought disturbance factors of the BPRS were found after amphetamine administration. Robinson et al. (1989) performed challenges with intravenous methylphenidate 0.5 mg/kg and nicotinic acid as an active placebo, under double-blind conditions, in 10 medication-free female inpatients (7 with borderline personality disorder, 1 with schizotypal personality disorder, and 2 with both borderline and schizotypal personality disorders). Subjects were assessed with the Schedule for Affective Disorders and Schizophrenia—Change Version (SADS-C) (Spitzer and Endicott, 1978a) and the Schedule for Affective Disorders—Psychosis and Disorganization (SADS-PD) (Spitzer and Endicott, 1978b) scales both before and 80 minutes after the infusions. Greater increases from baseline ratings occurred after methylphenidate than after nicotinic acid infusion in the SADS-C and SADS-PD items of psychic anxiety, agitation, motor hyperactivity, poor appetite, and depersonalization. Ratings of distrustfulness and being more energetic decreased after nicotinic acid but increased after methylphenidate administration. These differences were significant.

In summary, both Schulz et al. (1988) and Robinson et al. (1989) reported an activating response to psychostimulant challenge in their subjects. However, in contrast to the psychotic activation found by Schulz et al. (1985, 1988), Robinson et al. (1989) found significant increases after methylphenidate as compared to nicotinic acid infusion in the SADS-PD items of depersonalization and distrustfulness but not in the SADS-PD items covering hallucinations, delusions, or thought disorder. Thus, the amount of psychotic activation after psychostimulant challenge in subjects with schizophrenia spectrum disorders remains unclear. One possible explanation of the differences between the two studies is sample difference. The lower proportion of subjects with schizotypal personality disorder in the Robinson et al. (1989) study compared to the Schulz et al. (1988) study could possibly account for the differences in psychotogenic response between the studies. However, further larger series are required to determine the variables which affect psychostimulant response in subjects with borderline and schizotypal personality disorders.

CONCLUSIONS

By virtue of their agonistic effects on catecholamine neurotransmission, methylphenidate and other psychostimulants have been used as pharmacologic probes in schizophrenia research. The rationale underlying this strategy is that behavioral changes following psychostimulant administration must be related to the biochemical effects of the psychostimulant. By observing which, if any, behaviors change after psychostimulant administration, one can make hypotheses about the role of catecholamine systems in the behavior(s) elicited.

This chapter focused on one type of psychostimulant probe study in schizophrenia; the psychostimulant challenge paradigm. In these studies, schizophrenic subjects are given doses of psychostimulants which are subpsychotogenic; that is, low enough so as not to provoke psychotic symptoms in nonschizophrenic subjects. In terms of psychotic symptoms, schizophrenic subjects have a heterogeneous response to these doses of psychostimulants. A large number of subjects (40% and 41%, respectively) worsen or have no change after psychostimulant challenge with a much smaller number (19%) improving. Given this heterogeneity of response, one or more variables besides diagnosis or heterogeneity within the diagnostic group must affect psychostimulant response in schizophrenic subjects. Comparison of different psychostimulants shows methylphenidate to be a more potent psychotogen than amphetamine. For a given psychostimulant, parenteral, especially intravenous, administration produces more psychotic responses than oral administration. Phase of illness also affects psychotogenic response to psychostimulants. This finding has led to attempts to use psychostimulant challenge response to define periods of illness remission in schizophrenia. Presumably, subjects in remission as determined by psychostimulant challenge will have a lower likelihood of relapse after neuroleptic discontinuation. Finally, neuroleptic treatment may diminish psychotogenic responses to psychostimulants, however this effect is not found in all studies.

Psychostimulant challenges have provided much information, albeit often indirect, about the neurochemistry of schizophrenia. They also have potential clinical utility as the studies of psychostimulant response in predicting relapse of neuroleptic-free patients demonstrate. These techniques also may increase our knowledge in the future of disorders related to schizophrenia. However, much remains to be learned about the variables which influence schizophrenic subjects' responses to psychostimulants and ways of using this information in the clinical setting.

ACKNOWLEDGMENTS

Jean Mitchell, M.A., provided editorial assistance in the preparation of this manuscript.

This work was supported by NIMH Grants MH38880 and MH41646, a Research Scientist Development Award to Dr. Lieberman (MH00537), and the Hillside Hospital MHCRC for the Study of Schizophrenia (MH41960).

REFERENCES

Anderson, E.W. (1938); Further observations on benzedrine. *Br. Med. J. [Clin. Res.]* 2:60–64.

Angrist, B. & Gershon, S. (1970), The phenomenology of experimentally induced amphetamine psychosis—preliminary observations. *Biol. Psychiatry,* 2:95–107.

———— vanKammen, D.P. (1984), CNS stimulants as tools in the study of schizophrenia. *Trends Neuro Sci.,* 7:388–390.

———— Sathananthan, G., Wilk, S. & Gershon, S. (1974), Amphetamine psychosis: behavioral and biochemical aspects. *J. Psychiatr. Res.,* 11:13–23.

———— Rotrosen, J. & Gershon, S. (1980), Responses to apomorphine, amphetamine, and neuroleptics in schizophrenia subjects. *Psychopharmacology* 67:31–38.

———— Peselow, E., Rubinstein, M., Wolkin, A. & Rotrosen, J. (1985), Amphetamine response and relapse risk after depot neuroleptic discontinuation. *Psychopharmacology,* 85:277–283.

Askar, A.M., Rakhawy, Y.T. & Shaheen, O. (1970), The quantitative assessment of therapeutic effect of methamphetamine on psychiatric patients. *J. Egypt Med. Assoc.*, 53:563–577.

Baxter, L.R., Kelly, R.C., Peter, J.B., Liston, E.H. & Touserkami, S. (1988), Urinary phenylacetate and response to methylphenidate. *J. Psychiatr. Res.*, 22:131–139.

Belart, V.W. (1942), Pathogenetisches und therapeutisches aus Pervitinversuchen bei Schizophrenie. *Schweiz Med. Wochenschr.*, 2:41–43.

Bell, D.S. (1973), The experimental reproduction of amphetamine psychosis. *Arch. Gen. Psychiatry*, 29:35–40.

Bischoff, A. (1951), Uber eine therapeutische Verwendung der sogenannten "week-amine" an der Behandlung schizophrener Erregungszustande. *Monatsschr. Psychiatr. Neurol.*, 121:329–344.

Brown, P. & Brawly, P. (1983), Dexamethasone suppression test and mood response to methylphenidate in primary depression. *Am J Psychiatry*, 140:990–993.

Brown, W.A. (1977), Psychologic and neuroendocrine response to methylphenidate. *Arch. Gen. Psychiatry*, 34:1103–1108.

Connell, P.H. (1958), *Amphetamine Psychosis.* Maudsley Monograph No. 5. London: Chapman Hall.

Davidoff, E. & Reifenstein, E.C. (1939), Treatment of schizophrenia with sympathomimetic drugs: benzedrine sulfate. *Am. J. Psychiatry* 95:127–143.

Delay, J. (1949), Section of psychiatry, pharmacological explorations of the personality: narcoanalysis and methedrine shock. *Proc. R. Soc. Med.*, 62:491–496.

Dommisse, C.S., Schulz, S.C., Narasimhachiar, N., Blackard, W.G. & Hamer, R.M. (1984), The neuroendocrine and behavioral response to dextroamphetamine in normal individuals. *Biol. Psychiatry,* 19:1305–1315.

Ellestad, M.H. (1986), *Stress Testing Principles and Practice.* Philadelphia: F.A. Davis, pp. 172, 359.

Ferris, R., Tang, F. & Maxwell, R. (1972), A comparison of the capacities of isomers of amphetamine, deoxypiradrol and methylphenidate to inhibit the uptake of tritiated catecholamines into rat cerebral cortex slices, synaptosomal preparations of rat cerebral cortex, hypothalamus and striatum and into adrenergic nerves of rabbit aorta. *J. Pharmacol. Exp. Ther.*, 181:407–416.

Flugel, F.E. (1938), Medikamentose Beeinflussung psychischer Hemmengszustacnde. *Klin. Wochenschr.*, 17:1286–1288.

Fung, Y.K. & Uretsky, J. (1982), The differential effects of amphetamine and methylphenidate on the biosynthesis of [^{3}H]dopa from [^{3}H]tyrosine in mouse striata in vivo. *J. Pharm. Pharmacol.* 34:531–532.

Gottlieb, J.S. & Coburn, F.E. (1944), Psychopharmacologic study of schizophrenia and depressions. *Arch. Neurol. Psychiatry,* 51:260–263.

Gottlieb, J.S., Krause, H. & Friedinger, S.W. (1945), Psychopharmacologic study of schizophrenia and depressions. II. Comparison of tolerance to sodium amytal and amphetamine sulfate. *Arch. Neurol. Psychiatry,* 54:372–377.

Griffith, J.D., Cavanaugh, J., Held, J. & Oates, J.A. (1972), Dextroamphetamine: evaluation of psychotomimetic properties in man. *Arch. Gen. Psychiatry,* 26:97–100.

——— Oates, J. & Cavanaugh, J. (1968), Paranoid episodes induced by drugs. *JAMA* 205:39.

Groves, P.M. & Rebec, G.V. (1976), Biochemistry and behavior: some central actions of amphetamine and antipsychotic drugs. *Annu. Rev. Psychol.*, 27:91–127.

Guile, L.A. (1963), Intravenous methylphenidate—a pilot study. *Med. J. Aust.*, 2:93–97.

Guttman, E. & Sargant, W. (1937), Observations on benzedrine. *Br. Med. J.*, 1:1013–1015.

Hope, J.M., Callaway, E., & Sands, S.L. (1951), Intravenous pervitin and the psychopathology of schizophrenia. *Dis. Nerv. Syst.*, 12:67–72.

Janowsky, D.S. & Davis, J.M. (1976), Methylphenidate, dextroamphetamine, and levamphetamine. Effects on schizophrenic symptoms. *Arch. Gen. Psychiatry,* 33:304–308.

———— El-Yousef, M.K., Davis, J., et al. (1973), Provocation of schizophrenic symptoms by intravenous administration of methylphenidate. *Arch. Gen. Psychiatry,* 28:185–191.

———— Huey, L., Storms, L. & Judd, L. (1977), Methylphenidate hydrochloride effects on psychological tests in acute schizophrenic and non-psychotic patients. *Arch. Gen. Psychiatry,* 34:189–194.

———— Leichner, P., Clopton, P., et al. (1978), Comparison of oral and intravenous methylphenidate. *Psychopharmacology,* 59:75–78.

Jonas, A.D. (1954), The adjunctive use of an intravenous amphetamine derivative in psychotherapy. *J. Nerv. Ment. Dis.,* 119:135–147.

Joyce, R.P., Donald, R.A., Nichols, M.G., Livesey, J.H. & Abbott, R.M. (1986), Endocrine and behavioral responses to methylphenidate in depression. *Psychol. Med.,* 16:531–540.

Kiloh, L.G., Neilson, M. & Andrews, G. (1974), Response of depressed patients to methylamphetamine. *Br. J. Psychiatry,* 125:496–499.

Kornetsky, C. (1976), Hyporesponsivity of chronic schizophrenic patients to dextroamphetamine. *Arch. Gen. Psychiatry,* 33:1425–1428.

Lehmann, H.E. & Ban, T.A. (1964), Notes from the log-book of a psychopharmacological research unit II. *Can. Psychiatr. Assoc. J.,* 9:111–113.

Levine, J., Rinkel, M. & Greenblatt, M. (1978), Psychological and physiological effects of intravenous pervitin. *Am. J. Psychiatry,* 105:429–434.

Liddell, D.W. & Weil-Malherbe, H. (1953), The effects of methedrine and of lysergic acid diethylamine on mental processes and on the blood adrenaline level. *J. Neurol. Neurosurg. Psychiatry,* 16:713.

Lieberman, J.A., Kane, J.M., Alvir, J. (1987a), Provocative tests with psychostimulant drugs in schizophrenia. *Psychopharmacology,* 91:415–433.

———— ———— Sarantakos, S., Gadaleta, D., Woerner, M., et al. (1987b), Prediction of relapse in schizophrenia. *Arch. Gen. Psychiatry,* 44:597–603.

———— ———— Woerner, M., Weinhold, P., Basavaraju, N., Kurucz, J. & Bergmann, K. (1984), Prevalence of tardive dyskinesia in elderly samples. *Psychopharmacol. Bull.,* 20:382–386.

Lucas, P.B., Gardner, D.L., Wolkowitz, O.M., et al. (1987), Dysphoria associated with methylphenidate infusion in borderline personality disorder. *Am. J. Psychiatry,* 144:1577–1579.

———— ———— ———— ———— (1986), Methylphenidate-induced cardiac arrythmias (letter). *N. Engl. J. Med.,* 315:1485.

McMillen, B.A. (1983), CNS stimulants: two distinct mechanisms of action for amphetamine-like drugs. *Trends Phar.,* 4:429–432.

Meltzer, H.Y. & Stahl, S.M. (1976), The dopamine hypothesis of schizophrenia: A review. *Schizophr. Bull.,* 2:19–76.

Meyendorff, E., Lerer, B., Moore, N.C., Bow, J. & Gershon, S. (1985), Methylphenidate infusion in euthymic bipolars: effect of carbamazepine pretreatment. *Psychiatry Res.,* 16:303–308.

Modell, W. & Hussar, A.E. (1965), Failure of dextroamphetamine sulfate to influence eating and sleeping patterns in obese schizophrenic patients. *JAMA,* 194:95–98.

Moore, K.E. (1978), The actions of amphetamine on neurotransmitters: a brief review. *Biol. Psychiatry,* 12:451–462.

Nielsen, J.A., Chapin, D.S. & Moore, K.E. (1983), Differential effects *d*-amphetamine, *d*-phenylethyl-amine, cocaine and methylphenidate on the rate of dopamine synthesis in terminals of nigrostriatal and mesolimbic neurons and on the efflux of dopamine metabolites into cerebroventricular perfusates of rats. *Life Sci.,* 33:1899–1907.

Overall, J. & Gorham, D. (1962), The brief psychiatric rating scale. *Psychol. Rep.,* 10:149–165.

Pennes, H.H. (1954), Clinical reactions of schizophrenics to sodium amytal, pervitin hydrochloride, mescaline sulfate, and d-lysergic acid diethylamide (LSD 25). *J. Nerv. Ment. Dis.,* 119:95–111.

Prinzmetal, M. & Bloomberg, W. (1935), The use of benzedrine for the treatment of narcolepsy. *JAMA*, 105:2051–2054.

Robinson, D.R., Bailine, S., Alvir, J., Levy, D., Valentino, C. & Smith, M. (1989), Pharmacological responses to psychostimulants in borderline and schizotypal personality disorders. American College of Neuropsychopharmacology Annual Meeting.

—————— —————— Lieberman, J. (1988), Dysphoria associated with methylphenidate infusions (Letter to Editor). *Am. J. Psychiatry*, 145:1321–1322.

Sabelli, H.C., Fawcett, J., Javaid, J.I. & Bargi, S. (1983), The methylphenidate test for differentiating desipramine-responsive from nortriptyline-responsive depression. *Am. J. Psychiatry*, 140:212–214.

Scheel-Krüger, J. (1971), Comparative studies of various amphetamine analogue demonstrating different interactions with the metabolism of the catecholamines in the brain. *Eur. J. Pharmacol.*, 14:47–59.

Schube, P.G., McManamy, M.C. & Trapp, C.E. (1937), The effect of benzedrine sulphate on certain abnormal mental states. *Am. J. Psychiatry*, 94:27–32.

Schulz, S.C., Cornelius, J., Schulz, P.M., et al. (1988), The amphetamine challenge test in patients with borderline disorder. *Am. J. Psychiatry*, 145:809–814.

—————— Schulz, P.M., Dommisse, C., et al. (1985), Amphetamine response in borderline patients. *Psychiatry Res.*, 15:97–108.

Silberman, E.K., Reus, V.I., Jimerson, D.C., Lynott, A.M. & Post, R.M. (1981), Heterogeneity of amphetamine response in depressed patients. *Am. J. Psychiatry*, 138:1302–1307.

Simon, J.L., Taube, H. (1946), A preliminary study on the use of methedrine on psychiatric diagnosis. *J. Nerv. Ment. Dis.*, 104:593–596.

Smith, R.C. & Davis, J.M. (1977), Comparative effects of d-amphetamine, l-amphetamine and methylphenidate on mood in man. *Psychopharmacology*, 53:1–12.

Snyder, S.H. (1973), Amphetamine psychosis: a "model" schizophrenia mediated by catecholamines. *Am. J. Psychiatry*, 130:61–67.

Spitzer, R.L. & Endicott, J. (1978a), *Schedule for Affective Disorders and Schizophrenia—Change Version*, 3rd ed. New York: New York Biometrics Research Division, New York State Psychiatric Institute.

—————— —————— (1978b), *Schedule for Affective Disorders and Schizophrenia—Psychosis and Disorganization*. New York: Biometrics Division, New York State Psychiatric Institute.

van Kammen, D., Bunney, W., Docherty, J. et al. (1982a), d-Amphetamine induced heterogeneous changes in psychotic behavior in schizophrenia. *Am. J. Psychiatry*, 139:991–997.

—————— —————— —————— —————— (1977), Amphetamine-induced catecholamine activation in schizophrenia and depression. In: *Advances in Biochemical Psychopharmacology*, eds. E. Costa, G.L. Gessa, New York: Raven Press, pp 655–659.

—————— Docherty, J., Marder, S., Schulz, S.C. & Dalton, L. (1982b), Antipsychotic effects of pimozide in schizophrenia. *Arch. Gen. Psychiatry* 39:261–266.

—————— —————— —————— —————— Bunnery, W.E. (1980), Lack of behavioral supersensitivity to d-amphetamine after pimozide withdrawal. *Arch. Gen. Psychiatry*, 37:287–290.

—————— —————— —————— Rayner, J.N. & Bunney, W.E. (1982c), Long-term pimozide pretreatment differentially affects behavioral responses to dextroamphetamine in schizophrenia. *Arch. Gen. Psychiatry*, 39:275–281.

—————— —————— Bunney, W. (1982d), Prediction of early relapse after pimozide discontinuation by response to d-amphetamine during pimozide treatment. *Biol. Psychiatry*, 17:233–242.

Wald, D., Ebstein, R.P. & Belmaker, R.H. (1978), Haloperidol and lithium blocking of the mood response to intravenous methylphenidate. *Psychopharmacology*, 57:83–87.

Witton, K. (1960a), Clinical observations on Ritalin HCl (methylphenidylacetate) injectable multiple dose vial. *Am. J. Psychiatry*, 7:117–156.

Witton, K. (1960b), Directive psychotherapy with parenteral Ritalin in advanced schizophrenia. *Dis. Nerv. Syst,* 21:681–685.

Woolley, L.F. (1938), The clinical effects of benzedrine sulfate in mental patients with retarded activity. *Psychiatry Q.,* 12:66–83.

Young, D. & Scoville, W.B. (1938), Paranoid psychosis in narcolepsy and possible dangers of benzedrine treatment. *Med. Clin. North Am.,* 22:637–643.

ADHD Resources and Support Groups

National

American Academy of Child and Adolescent Psychiatry

3615 Wisconsin Avenue, N.W.
Washington, DC 20016
202/966-7300

Resources: Fact sheets on ADHD, referral service

American Academy of Pediatrics

P.O. Box 927
141 Northwest Point Boulevard
Elk Grove Village, IL 60009-0927
847/981-7935

Resources: Policy statement

American Counseling Association

801 North Fairfax Street, Suite 310
Alexandria, VA 22314
703/683-2722
800/306-4722

Resources: Position statements

American Psychological Association

750 1st Street, N.E.
Washington, DC 20002
202/336-5500

Resources: Information on services in special education, policy issues and qualifications of psychologists

Association of Educational Therapists

14852 Ventura Boulevard, Suite 207
Sherman Oaks, CA 91403
818/788-3850

Resources: Referrals for professionals needing information on ADHD

Children With Attention Deficit Disorders (CH.A.D.D.)

499 Northwest 70th Avenue, Suite 101
Plantation, FL 33317
305/587-3700

Resources: Information and support to parents of children with ADHD; referrals to local chapters and technical assistance in forming chapters

Council for Exceptional Children/Education Resources Information Center (ERIC) on Handicapped and Gifted Children

1920 Association Drive
Reston, VA 22091
703/620-3660

Resources: Information clearinghouse

Learning Disabilities Association of America (L.D.A.)

4156 Library Road
Pittsburgh, PA 15234
412/341-1515

Resources: Provides information on learning disabilities and available services; more than 650 chapters nationwide; newsletter, bimonthly journal, publications

Names, addresses, and phone numbers have been updated in 1996.
Adapted from *Parents Helping Parents: A Directory of Support Groups for Attention-Deficit Hyperactivity Disorder* (1990), CIBA—GEIGY Pharmaceuticals, Summit, NJ. Used by permission.

National Attention Deficit Disorder Association

107 Rosewood, Suite A
Ann Arbor, MI 48104
313/769-6690
E-mail CyberADDA @aol.com
www.azstarnet.com/ ~ sled/

Resources: National Alliance of ADHD Support Groups; provides referrals and information to parents and parent support groups; 40,000 members; annual meeting; newsletter

National Center for Learning Disabilities

381 Park Avenue, Suite 1420
New York, NY 10016
212/545-7510

Resources: Publications, public awareness, grantmaking in the field of learning disabilities and related activities, computerized referral services

National Easter Seal Society

230 West Monroe Street, Suite 1800
Chicago, IL 60606
312/726-6200

Resources: "How-to" information for volunteer/nonprofit groups

Office of Disease Prevention and Health Promotion (O.D.P.H.P.) National Health Information Center

P.O. Box 1133
Washington, DC 20013-1133
800/336-4797
301/565-4167

Resources: ADHD referral agency

Orton Dyslexia Society

Chester Building
Suite 382
8600 LaSalle Road
Baltimore, MD 21286-2044
410/825-2881

Resources: Fact sheet explaining ADHD

Parents Helping Parents: A Directory of Support Groups for Attention Deficit Hyperactivity Disorder

External Communications
Pharmaceuticals Division
CIBA-GEIGY Corporation
Summit, NJ 07901

Self Help Clearing House

St. Claire's Riverside Medical Center
25 Pocono Road
Denville, NJ 07834
800/367-6274 (in NJ)
201/625-9565

Resources: Local and national referral service; computerized database of support groups and referral agencies nationwide

Tourette Syndrome Association, Inc.

42-40 Bell Boulevard, Suite 205
Bayside, NY 11361-2861
718/224-2999

Puerto Rico

L.D.A. of Puerto Rico

76 Kings Court, Apartment 701
Santurce, PR 00911
809/728-5166
Contact: Elisa Blum, President

Parent Organization: Learning Disabilities Association of America

England

Hyperactivity Children's Support Group

c/o Sally Bunday
71 Whyke Lane
Chichester, West Sussex
England, PO 192LD
44/1903725182

Newsletters

CHADDER

Suite 185
499 Northwest 70th Avenue, Suite 100
Plantation, FL 33317
305/587-3700

National biannual publication with articles by experts

The CHADDer Box

Suite 185
499 Northwest 70th Avenue, Suite 100
Plantation, FL 33317
305/587-3700

Information newsletter published eight times a year providing information about CH.A.D.D.

CHALLENGE

P.O. Box 2001
West Newbury, MA 01985
508/462-0495
Editor: Jean Harrison

National bimonthly newsletter for parents and professionals concerned with ADHD; 1,500 subscribers

Subject Index

A

Abulia, stimulant therapy, 172
Abbreviated Reading Scale (ARS), 105
Academic achievement, 19, 52
Academic skills training, 151
Academic tasks, 239–240
Activation, cognitive energetic model, 4
Activity
  inhibition and arousal, 277–281
  stimulant effects, 51–52
  see also Hyperactivity
Addiction, stimulants, 173
Additive factor method (AFM), attention
  deficits, 2–3
Adolescents
  ADHD therapy, 79
  hyperactivity disorders, 6
  mental retardation, 160
  schizophrenia, 88
  stimulant effects, 53–54
  see also Children
Adrenocorticotropic hormone (ACTH), growth
  regulation, 289
Adults
  ADD treatment, 25, 54
  ADHD, 31, 85
  clonidine therapy, 85
  stimulant effects, 54
Age-related prescribing practices, 188–192
Aggression
  rating scales, 19
  serotonin, 276–277
  stimulant effects, 53
Alternate uses test, 242
Alternate therapies, 120–126
  ADHD, 75–76
  amino acid supplementation, 91
  antidepressant drugs, 76–80
  clonidine, 80–87
  dietary intervention, 89–91
  MAO inhibitors, 79
  neuroleptic drugs, 88–89
American Academy of Child and Adolescent
  Psychiatry, 190
American Academy of Pediatrics (AAP), 119,
  190

American Psychiatric Association (APA), 15,
  159
Amino acids
  ADD treatment, 25
  phenylalanine, 91
  supplementation therapy, 91
AIDS (acquired immunodeficiency syndrome)
  Ritalin, 177
  see also HIV dementia
AIDS-related complex (ARC), 178
Aminobutyric acid (GABA), 289, 290
Amphetamines
  administration, 55
  Benzedrine, 69, 98, 156
  carcinogenicity, 41
  dosage, 55
  drug trials, 27, 29
  HIV infections, 180
  mental retardation, 156
  PET studies, 7
  pharmacokinetics, 56–57
  vs. Ritalin, 36
  schizophrenia, 309, 315
  toxicity, 36
  see also Dextroamphetamine
Anemia, 42
Anergia, stimulant therapy, 171
Anger
  control procedures, 148
  see also Aggression
Anorexia, 135, 297
Anticonvulsant drugs, 137
Antidepressants
  ADHD, 76–80
  bupropion, 79–80
  cognitive effects, 80
  norepinephrine effects, 275
  serotonergic, 75
  tricyclic, 76–79
  usage, 80
  see also specific drugs
Antigens, food, 91
Antisocial behavior, reserpine therapy, 160
Anxiety disorders, 259
Apathy, 171
Appetite, stimulants, 57